Management Concepts and Practice

PEARSON

We work with leading authors to develop the strongest
educational materials bringing cutting-edge thinking and best
learning practice to a global market.

Under a range of well-known imprints, including Financial
Times/Prentice Hall, Addison Wesley and Longman, we craft
high quality print and electronic publications which help
readers to understand and apply their content, whether
studying or at work.

Pearson Custom Publishing enables our customers to
access a wide and expanding range of market-leading
content from world-renowned authors and develop their
own tailor-made book. You choose the content that meets
your needs and Pearson Custom Publishing produces a
high-quality printed book.

To find out more about custom publishing, visit
www.pearsoncustom.co.uk

PEARSON CUSTOM PUBLISHING

Management Concepts and Practice

Compiled from:

Management & Organisational Behaviour
Ninth Edition
by Laurie J. Mullins

Management: An Introduction
Fifth Edition
by David Boddy and Steve Paton

Management: Concepts & Practices
Fifth Edition
by Tim Hannagan

Management
Eleventh Edition
by Stephen P. Robbins and Mary Coulter

Fundamentals of Management:
Essential Concepts and Applications
by Stephen P. Robbins, David A. Decenzo
and Mary Coulter

Management: A Focus on Leaders
by Annie McKee

Business Studies
Fourth Edition
by Dave Hall, Rob Jones, Carlo Raffo
and Alain Anderton

ALWAYS LEARNING

PEARSON

Harlow, England • London • New York • Boston • San Francisco • Toronto • Sydney • Auckland • Singapore • Hong Kong
Tokyo • Seoul • Taipei • New Delhi • Cape Town • Sao Paulo • Mexico City • Madrid • Amsterdam • Munich • Paris • Milan

Pearson Education Limited
Edinburgh Gate
Harlow
Essex CM20 2JE

And associated companies throughout the world

Visit us on the World Wide Web at:
www.pearsoned.co.uk

Contents

Introduction ix

SECTION 1: INTRODUCTION TO MANAGEMENT 1

Chapter 1 A Brief History of Management 3

Cases 33
The Story of the Middleman 35
Dell Computers: The World at your Fingertips 36
Review Questions and Tests 39

Chapter 2 The Role of the Manager 43

Cases 81
Ryanair 83
More Than a Good Story 85
A New Way of Working 87
Review Questions and Tests 89

SECTION 2: STRATEGY AND PLANNING 93

Chapter 3 Planning 95

Cases 109
Short-Term & Long-Term Planning in the
UK Construction Industry 111
Test: What Are My Course Performance Goals 113
Review Questions and Tests 115

Chapter 4 Strategic Management Overview 117

Chapter 5 Strategic Management in Detail 135

Cases 161
Gaga Over Gaga 162
Managing the Magic 164
HMV Group 165
Review Questions and Tests 167

SECTION 3: MARKETING, ENVIRONMENT AND ETHICS 171

Chapter 6   Organisation Environment   173

             Cases   209
             Nokia   211
             Watch Out for an Epidemic of Petty Fraud   215
             Review Questions and Tests   *217*

Chapter 7   Marketing Management   219

             Cases   245
             Manchester United FC   247
             The Virgin Group   249
             Review Questions and Tests   *253*

Chapter 8   Social Responsibility and Ethics   255

             Cases   275
             Lessons from Lehman Brothers: Will we Ever Learn? 277
             Green Up on Aisle Two   278
             Trade-offs in the Moral Maze   279
             Review Questions and Tests   *281*

             SECTION 4: ORGANISATION STRUCTURE   283

Chapter 9   Organisation Structure   285

Chapter 10   Structure Advantages and Disadvantages   307

             Cases   315
             A Taxing Merger   316
             A New Kind of Structure   317
             Unconventional Design   318
             StarCars   319
             Review Questions and Tests   *321*

             SECTION 5: ORGANISATION CULTURE   323

Chapter 11   Organisation Culture   325

             Cases   353
             Out of Control   354

SECTION 6: CHANGE MANAGEMENT   **357**

Chapter 12   Change Management   359

Cases   379
Too Big to Change   380
The Port of Rotterdam   381
CLP Power in Hong Kong   382
Review Question and Tests   *383*

SECTION 7: TEAMS   **387**

Chapter 13   Teams   389

Cases   427
Top Gear   428
Cisco Systems   431
Making Order out of Chaos   433
Review Questions and Tests   *435*

SECTION 8: LEADERSHIP   **439**

Chapter 14   Styles of Management   441

Chapter 15   Trait Theories of Leadership   465

Cases   473
Managing the Mood is Crucial   475
Being Apple: Steve Jobs   476
Review Questions and Tests   *479*

SECTION 9: MOTIVATION   **481**

Chapter 16   Motivation Theories and Management   483

Cases   523
Top Marks for the Best Employee Awards   524
Don't Get Mad, Get On-line   525
The Eden Project   528
Review Questions and Tests   *531*

SECTION 10: HUMAN RESOURCE MANAGEMENT   533

Chapter 17   Human Resource Management   535

Chapter 18   Employee Relations   559

Cases   573
Thinking Outside the Box   574
Social Connections   575
HRM in the Hong Kong Police Force   576
Don't get Fooled Again - You're not too Old for the Job   577
Review Questions and Tests   *579*

SECTION 11: OPERATIONS, QUALITY AND PRODUCTION METHODS   581

Chapter 19   What is Operations Management?   583

Cases   601
Zara   602
Review Questions and Tests   *603*

Chapter 20   Quality   605

Cases   641
British Areospace   642
GNY Building Materials   643
Lean Manufacturing in China   644
Review Questions and Tests   *645*

Chapter 21   Production Methods   647

Cases   653
Nacional   654
Review Questions and Tests   *655*

Chapter 22   Just-in-Time Management   657

Cases   665
FTL Company Ltd   666
Review Questions and Tests   *667*

Index   669

INTRODUCTION

Students in Higher Education are expected to extensively use various sources in their studies such as books, articles, case studies, exercises and relevant web-sites. However, students new to Higher Education usually find this process difficult and very time-consuming. We believe that the first year is a transitional period where students need to be initiated to this process and a compiled book composed of materials gathered from various sources and authors provides a practical solution. This unique book, "Management Concepts & Practice" has been compiled from seven books, the benefits of which can be summarised as follows:

- For students the primary advantage of this book is the ease in finding information relevant to their studies.
- It is composed of eleven sections, each of which provides an in-depth review of what is learned in lectures and seminars and should be used in conjunction with other course materials supplied.
- All the topics contained in this book are relevant to the purpose of the module "Management Concepts and Practice" and include all the necessary concepts.
- At the end of each section there are various case studies which are intended to improve understanding by visualising the concepts using real life business applications.
- There are also exercises and mini-tests to assess your understanding and learning.
- This book also provides an acceptable reference for most academic writing (for instance, term papers, essays, etc.).
- One of the main deterrents to reading academic books is the difficulty level of the information provided. Therefore, this book is compiled in such a way that the difficulty level increases gradually, making retention of key points easier.
- Although this book provides the necessary reading required for the module, it is hoped that after reading each section, students will not only understand and enjoy the topics, but will also be motivated to seek more information and knowledge by searching various other sources such as books and articles, which will prepare them for their studies in the coming years.

Dr Şöhret Başaran Howells

SECTION I:
INTRODUCTION TO MANAGEMENT

Chapter 1:

A Brief History of Management

THEORY OF MANAGEMENT

A central part of the study of organisation and management is the development of management thinking and what might be termed management theory. The application of theory brings about change in actual behaviour. Managers reading the work of leading writers on the subject might see in their ideas and conclusions a message about how they should behave. This will influence their attitudes towards management practice.

The study of management theory is important for the following reasons:

- It helps to view the interrelationships between the development of theory, behaviour in organisations and management practice.
- An understanding of the development of management thinking helps in understanding principles underlying the process of management.
- Knowledge of the history helps in understanding the nature of management and organisational behaviour and reasons for the attention given to main topic areas.
- Many of the earlier ideas are of continuing importance to the manager and later ideas on management tend to incorporate earlier ideas and conclusions.
- Management theories are interpretive and evolve in line with changes in the organisational environment.

As *McGregor* puts it:

Every managerial act rests on assumptions, generalizations, and hypotheses – that is to say, on theory. Our assumptions are frequently implicit, sometimes quite unconscious, often conflicting; nevertheless, they determine our predictions that if we do a, b will occur. Theory and practice are inseparable.[1]

Miner makes the point that the more that is known about organisations and their methods of operation, the better the chances of dealing effectively with them. Understanding may be more advanced than prediction, but both provide the opportunity to influence or to manage the future. Theory provides a sound basis for action.[2] However, if action is to be effective, the theory must be adequate and appropriate to the task and to improved organisational performance. It must be a 'good' theory.

DEVELOPMENTS IN MANAGEMENT AND ORGANISATIONAL BEHAVIOUR

It is helpful, therefore, to trace major developments in management and organisational behaviour and what has led to the concentration of attention on such topics as motivation, groups, leadership, structure, and organisation development.[3]

Writing on organisation and management, in some form or another, can be traced back thousands of years.[4] Also, *Shafritz* makes an interesting observation about the contribution of William Shakespeare (1564–1616):

While William Shakespeare's contribution to literature and the development of the English language have long been acknowledged and thoroughly documented, his contribution to the theory of management and administration have been all but ignored. This is a surprising oversight when you consider that many of his plays deal with issues of personnel management and organizational behavior.[5]

However, the systematic development of management thinking is viewed, generally, as dating from the end of the nineteenth century with the emergence of large industrial organisations and the ensuing problems associated with their structure and management.[6] In order to help identify main trends in the development of organisational behaviour and management theory, it is usual to categorise the work of writers into various 'approaches', based on their views of organisations, their structure and management. Although a rather simplistic process, it does provide a framework in which to help direct study and focus attention on the progression of ideas concerned with improving organisational performance.

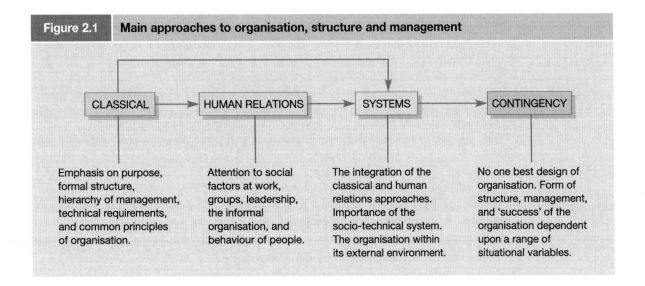

Figure 2.1 Main approaches to organisation, structure and management

CLASSICAL	HUMAN RELATIONS	SYSTEMS	CONTINGENCY
Emphasis on purpose, formal structure, hierarchy of management, technical requirements, and common principles of organisation.	Attention to social factors at work, groups, leadership, the informal organisation, and behaviour of people.	The integration of the classical and human relations approaches. Importance of the socio-technical system. The organisation within its external environment.	No one best design of organisation. Form of structure, management, and 'success' of the organisation dependent upon a range of situational variables.

A framework of analysis

There are, however, many ways of categorising these various approaches. For example, *Skipton* attempts a classification of 11 main schools of management theory.[7] Whatever form of categorisation is adopted, it is possible to identify a number of other approaches, or at least sub-divisions of approaches, and cross-grouping among the various approaches. The choice of a particular categorisation is therefore largely at the discretion of the observer.

The following analysis will revolve around a framework based on four main approaches, shown in Figure 2.1:

- classical – including scientific management and bureaucracy;
- human relations – including neo-human relations;
- systems;
- contingency.

Attention is also drawn to other 'approaches' or ideas, including:

- decision-making;
- social action;
- postmodernism.

See Figure 2.4 on page 63.

THE CLASSICAL APPROACH

The **classical** writers thought of the organisation in terms of its purpose and formal structure. They placed emphasis on the planning of work, the technical requirements of the organisation, principles of management, and the assumption of rational and logical behaviour. The analysis of organisation in this manner is associated with work carried out initially in the early part of the last century, by such writers as Taylor, Fayol, Urwick, Mooney and Reiley, and Brech. Such writers were laying the foundation for a comprehensive theory of management.

A clear understanding of the purpose of an organisation is seen as essential to understanding how the organisation works and how its methods of working can be improved. Identification of general objectives would lead to the clarification of purposes and responsibilities at all levels of the organisation and to the most effective structure. Attention is given to the division of work, the clear definition of duties and responsibilities, and maintaining specialisation and co-ordination. Emphasis is on a hierarchy of management and formal organisational relationships.

Sets of principles

The classical writers (also variously known as the formal or scientific management writers – although scientific management is really only a part of the classical approach) were concerned with improving the organisation structure as a means of increasing efficiency. They emphasised the importance of principles for the design of a logical structure of organisation. Their writings were in a normative style and they saw these principles as a set of 'rules' offering general solutions to common problems of organisation and management.

Most classical writers had their own set of principles but among the most publicised are those of *Fayol* and *Urwick* (*see* Chapters 11 and 14). Fayol recognised there was no limit to the principles of management but in his writing advocated 14.[8] Urwick originally specified eight principles, but these were revised to ten in his later writing.[9]

Mooney and Reiley set out a number of common principles which relate to all types of organisations. They place particular attention on:

■ **the principle of co-ordination** – the need for people to act together with unity of action, the exercise of authority and the need for discipline;
■ **the scalar principle** – the hierarchy of organisation, the grading of duties and the process of delegation; and
■ **the functional principle** – specialisation and the distinction between different kinds of duties.[10]

Brech attempts to provide a practical approach to organisation structure based on tried general principles as opposed to the concentration on specific cases or complex generalisations of little value to the practising manager. He sets out the various functions in the organisation and the definition of formal organisational relationships.[11] Although clearly a strong supporter of the formal approach in some of his views such as, for example, on the principle of span of control, Brech is less definite than other classical writers and recognises a degree of flexibility according to the particular situation.

Brech does place great emphasis, however, on the need for written definition of responsibilities and the value of job descriptions as an aid to effective organisation and delegation. This work builds on the ideas of earlier writers, such as Urwick, and therefore provides a comprehensive view of the classical approach to organisation and management.

Evaluation of the classical approach

The classical writers have been criticised generally for not taking sufficient account of personality factors and for creating an organisation structure in which people can exercise only limited control over their work environment. The idea of sets of principles to guide managerial action has also been subject to much criticism. For example, *Simon* writes:

> *Organisational design is not unlike architectural design. It involves creating large, complex systems having multiple goals. It is illusory to suppose that good designs can be created by using the so-called principles of classical organisation theory.*[12]

Research studies have also expressed doubt about the effectiveness of these principles when applied in practice.[13] However, the classical approach prompted the start of a more systematic view of management and attempted to provide some common principles applicable to all organisations. These principles are still of relevance in that they offer a useful starting point in attempting to analyse the effectiveness of the design of organisation structure. The application of these principles must take full account of:

■ the particular situational variables of each individual organisation; and
■ the psychological and social factors relating to members of the organisation.

Major sub-groupings

Two major 'sub-groupings' of the classical approach are:

1 **scientific management**, and
2 bureaucracy.

SCIENTIFIC MANAGEMENT

Many of the classical writers were concerned with the improvement of management as a means of increasing productivity. At this time emphasis was on the problem of obtaining increased productivity from individual workers through the technical structuring of the work organisation and the provision of monetary incentives as the motivator for higher levels of output. A major contributor to this approach was *F. W. Taylor* (1856–1917), the 'father' of scientific management.[14] Taylor believed that in the same way that there is a best machine for each job, so there is a best working method by which people should undertake their jobs. He considered that all work processes could be analysed into discrete tasks and that by scientific method it was possible to find the 'one best way' to perform each task. Each job was broken down into component parts, each part timed and the parts rearranged into the most efficient method of working.

Principles to guide management

Taylor was a believer in the rational–economic needs concept of motivation. He believed that if management acted on his ideas, work would become more satisfying and profitable for all concerned. Workers would be motivated by obtaining the highest possible wages through working in the most efficient and productive way. Taylor was concerned with finding more efficient methods and procedures for co-ordination and control of work. He set out a number of principles to guide management. These principles are usually summarised as:

- the development of a true science for each person's work;
- the scientific selection, training and development of the workers;
- co-operation with the workers to ensure work is carried out in the prescribed way;
- the division of work and responsibility between management and the workers.

In his famous studies at the Bethlehem Steel Corporation, Taylor, who was appointed as a management consultant, applied his ideas on scientific management to the handling of pig iron. A group of 75 men were loading an average of $12\frac{1}{2}$ tons per man per day. Taylor selected a Dutch labourer, called Schmidt, whom he reported to be a 'high-priced' man with a reputation for placing a high value on money, and a man of limited mental ability. By following detailed instructions on when to pick up the pig iron and walk, and when to sit and rest, and with no back talk, Schmidt increased his output to $47\frac{1}{2}$ tons per day. He maintained this level of output throughout the three years of the study. In return Schmidt received a 60 per cent increase in wages compared with what was paid to the other men.

One by one other men were selected and trained to handle pig iron at the rate of $47\frac{1}{2}$ tons per day and in return they received 60 per cent more wages. Taylor drew attention to the need for the scientific selection of the workers. When the other labourers in the group were trained in the same method, only one in eight was physically capable of the effort of loading $47\frac{1}{2}$ tons per day, although there was a noticeable increase in their level of output.

Reactions against scientific management

There were strong criticisms of, and reaction against, scientific management methods from the workers who found the work boring and requiring little skill. Despite these criticisms Taylor attempted to expand the implementation of his ideas in the Bethlehem Steel Corporation. However, fears of mass redundancies persuaded the management to request Taylor to moderate his activities. Yet Taylor's belief in his methods was so strong that he would not accept management's interference and eventually they dispensed with his services.

Scientific management was applied for a time in other countries with similar criticisms and hostile reactions. The ideas of scientific management were also adopted in the American Watertown Arsenal despite the lingering doubts of the controller. He was not convinced about the benefits of paying bonuses based on methods which reduced time taken to complete a job; also the workers reacted unfavourably to time and motion studies and he was fearful of a strike. The controller eventually gave way, however, and the scientific management approach was adopted – to be followed almost immediately by a strike of moulding workers. The strike at Watertown Arsenal led to an investigation of Taylor's methods by a House of Representatives Committee which reported in 1912.

The conclusion of the committee was that scientific management did provide some useful techniques and offered valuable organisational suggestions, but gave production managers a dangerously high level of uncontrolled power. The studies at Watertown Arsenal were resumed but the unions retained an underlying hostility towards scientific management. A subsequent attitude survey among the workers revealed a broad level of resentment and hostility, by both union and non-union members, to scientific management methods. As a result of this report the Senate banned Taylor's methods of time study in defence establishments.

Taylorism as management control

There has also been considerable interest in 'Taylorism' as representing a system of management control over workers. Taylor placed emphasis on the content of a 'fair day's work' and on optimising the level of workers' productivity. A major obstacle to this objective was 'systematic soldiering' and what Taylor saw as the deliberate attempt by workers to promote their best interests and to keep employers ignorant of how fast work, especially piece-rate work, could be carried out.

According to *Braverman*, scientific management starts from the capitalist point of view and method of production, and the adaptation of labour to the needs of capital. Taylor's work was more concerned with the organisation of labour than with the development of technology. A distinctive feature of Taylor's thought was the concept of management control.[15] Braverman suggests Taylor's conclusion was that workers should be controlled not only by the giving of orders and maintenance of discipline but also by removing from them any decisions about the manner in which their work was to be carried out. By division of labour, and by dictating precise stages and methods for every aspect of work performance, management could gain control of the actual process of work. The rationalisation of production processes and division of labour tends to result in the de-skilling of work and this may be a main strategy of the employer.[16]

Cloke and Goldsmith also suggest that Taylor was the leading promoter of the idea that managers should design and control the work process scientifically in order to guarantee maximum efficiency. He believed in multiple layers of management to supervise the work process and in rigid, detailed control of the workforce.

Taylor's theories justified managerial control over the production process and removed decision making from employees and from owners as well. The increasingly authoritative operational role of management diminished the direct involvement of owners in day-to-day decision making. Managers saw this as an opportunity to solidify their power and adopted Taylor's ideas wholesale. In the process, they affirmed efficiency over collaboration, quantity over quality, and cost controls over customer service.[17]

Critical reflection

'Despite the strong criticisms of scientic management, in the right circumstances the underlying principles still have relevance and much to offer business organisations today. It is just that many commentators appear reluctant to openly admit that this is the case.'

What are your views? Where could scientific management be applied for the best overall effect?

RELEVANCE OF SCIENTIFIC MANAGEMENT

While Taylor's work is often criticised today it should be remembered that he was writing at a time of industrial reorganisation and the emergence of large, complex organisations with new forms of technology. Taylor's main concern was with the efficiency of both workers and management. He believed his methods of scientific management would lead to improved management–labour relations and contribute to improved industrial efficiency and prosperity.

Taylor adopted an instrumental view of human behaviour together with the application of standard procedures of work. Workers were regarded as rational, economic beings motivated directly by monetary incentives linked to the level of work output. Workers were viewed as isolated individuals and more as units of production to be handled almost in the same way as machines. Hence, scientific management is often referred to as a machine theory model.

Taylor's work continues to evoke much comment and extreme points of view. For example, *Rose* suggests:

> It is difficult to discuss the 'contribution' of F. W. Taylor to the systematic study of industrial behaviour in an even-tempered way. The sheer silliness from a modern perspective of many of his ideas, and barbarities they led to when applied in industry, encourage ridicule and denunciation.[18]

The theme of inefficiency

Rose argues that Taylor's diagnosis of the industrial situation was based on the simple theme of inefficiency. Among his criticisms are that Taylor selected the best workers for his experiments and assumed that workers who were not good at one particular task would be best at some other task. There is, however, no certainty of this in practice. Taylor regarded workers from an engineering viewpoint and as machines, but the one best way of performing a task is not always the best method for every worker.

The reduction of physical movement to find the one best way is not always beneficial and some 'wasteful' movements are essential to the overall rhythm of work. Rose also argues that the concept of a fair day's pay for a fair day's work is not purely a technical matter. It is also a notion of social equity and not in keeping with a scientific approach. *Drucker*, however, claims:

> Frederick Winslow Taylor may prove a more useful prophet for our times than we yet recognize . . . Taylor's greatest impact may still be ahead . . . the under-developed and developing countries are now reaching the stage where they need Taylor and 'scientific management' . . . But the need to study Taylor anew and apply him may be the greatest in the developed countries.[19]

According to Drucker, the central theme of Taylor's work was not inefficiency but the need to substitute industrial warfare by industrial harmony. Taylor sought to do this through:

- higher wages from increased output;
- the removal of physical strain from doing work the wrong way;
- development of the workers and the opportunity for them to undertake tasks they were capable of doing; and
- elimination of the 'boss' and the duty of management to help workers.

Drucker also suggests that Taylor's idea of functional foremen can be related to what is now known as matrix organisation (matrix organisation is discussed in Chapter 14). Support for Drucker's views appears to come from *Locke* who asserts that much of the criticism of Taylor is based on a misunderstanding of the precepts and that many of his ideas are accepted by present-day managers.[20]

Impetus to management thinking

Whatever the opinions on scientific management, Taylor and his disciples have left to modern management the legacy of such practices as work study, organisation and methods, payment by results, management by exception and production control. The development of mass assembly line work ('Fordism'), which was invented by Henry Ford in 1913 and which dominated production methods in Western economies, can be seen to have many common links with the ideas of scientific management.[21] The concept of Six Sigma, which is discussed in Chapter 20, can also be related to Taylor's quest for 'systematic management'. For example, in his book on the future of management, *Hamel* makes the following observation:

> *One can imagine Taylor looking down from his well-ordered heaven and smiling fondly at the Six Sigma acolytes who continue to spread his gospel. (His only surprise might be that 21st-century managers are still obsessing over the same problems that occupied his inventive mind a hundred years earlier.)*[22]

The principles of Taylor's scientific approach to management appear still to have relevance today. We can see examples of Taylorism alive and well, and management practices based on the philosophy of his ideas. As an example, Figure 2.2 shows a 'Hanger Insertion

Figure 2.2	Hanger Insertion Programme: an example of scientific management

KEY IDEAS

Hanger Insertion

- The new programme involving the process of hanging merchandise on hangers efficiently and effectively.

The purposes of this new programme:

- To assist the stores in better customer service – by having the merchandise ready to go on the floor, saving space in the stockroom, and creating customer goodwill.
- To increase the units per hour produced.
- To perform the job duties as efficiently and effectively as possible.

TECHNIQUES

- Keep the necessary items needed in your range. All supplies should be within arm's reach. For example, place the trash bin next to you, have your hanger supply near you. You should not need to take any steps.
- For ANY prepack, Unpack merchandise in the prepack or unpack enough of the prepack in the amount to be placed on the trolley, tearing the plastic off of the entire group.
  Lay the merchandise out on the unpack table, and if applies, unfold each piece, removing tissue, etc.
  Insert the hangers and hang the *entire group* of merchandise at once.
- When removing hangers from the merchandise, have the merchandise in a group on the unpack table; remove these hangers working from the front to the back.
- When inserting hangers, as a group, insert working from the back to the front of the group on the unpack table. Hang pieces as a group.
- If merchandise is bulky, Leave merchandise folded, **remove all of the plastic at once**, insert hangers for merchandise unpacked, hang all pieces on the trolley, then remove at the same time all excess plastic, clips, etc.
- When possible, it is more efficient to remove all the plastic at once after the merchandise is hung.
- When hanging pants, skirts, etc., slip the hanger over both sides of the piece of merchandise and push metal clips down at the same time. This will alleviate additional steps.
- When pants are in plastic and hangers have to be removed, hang them first, take pants off hangers, lay on table, throw away plastic, insert hangers.
- When having to button pants, skirts, etc., take the top of the button through the hole first. This makes the process flow easier and more efficient.
- Put your supply of hangers in the cover of a tote and place on the table next to you.

Programme' for a large American department store. Large hotel organisations often make use of standard recipes and performance standard manuals and it is common for housekeeping staff to have a prescribed layout for each room, with training based on detailed procedures and the one best way. Staff may be expected to clean a given number of rooms per shift with financial incentives for additional rooms. The strict routine, uniformity, clearly specified tasks, detailed checklists and close control in fast-food restaurants such as McDonald's also suggest close links with scientific management.

Whatever else Taylor did, at least he gave a major impetus to the development of management thinking and the later development of organisational behaviour. For example, *Crainer and Dearlove* suggest that although Taylor's theories are now largely outdated, they still had a profound impact throughout the world and his mark can be seen on much of the subsequent management literature.[23] And *Stern* goes a stage further:

> The 'scientific management' of Frederick Taylor . . . shaped the first coherent school of thought with application to the industrialised world. He was our first professional guru and Taylorism – with its twin goals of productivity and efficiency – still influences management thinking 100 years on.[24]

It is difficult to argue against the general line of Taylor's principles but they are subject to misuse. What is important is the context and manner in which such principles are put into effect. There is arguably one best way *technically* to perform a job, particularly, for example, with factory assembly line production. However, account needs to be taken of human behaviour. People tend to have their preferred way of working and the need for variety and more interesting or challenging tasks. Provided work is carried out safely and to a satisfactory standard and completed on time, to what extent should management *insist* on the 'one best way'?

It seems that Taylor did not so much ignore (as is often suggested) but was more *unaware* of the complexity of human behaviour in organisations and the importance of the individual's feelings and sentiments, group working, managerial behaviour and the work environment. However, we now have greater knowledge about social effects within the work organisation and about the value of money, incentives, motivation, and job satisfaction and performance.

BUREAUCRACY

A form of structure to be found in many large-scale organisations is **bureaucracy**. Its importance in the development of organisation theory means that it is often regarded as a subdivision under the classical heading and studied as a separate approach to management and the organisation of work. The ideas and principles of the classical writers were derived mainly from practical experience. Writers on bureaucracy, however, tend to take a more theoretical view.

Weber, a German sociologist, showed particular concern for what he called 'bureaucratic structures', although his work in this area came almost as a side issue to his main study on power and authority.[25] He suggested that 'the decisive reason for the advance of bureaucratic organization has always been its purely technical superiority over any other form of organization'. Weber pointed out that the definition of tasks and responsibilities within the structure of management gave rise to a permanent administration and standardisation of work procedures notwithstanding changes in the actual holders of office.

The term 'bureaucracy' has common connotations with criticism of red tape and rigidity, though in the study of organisations and management it is important that the term is seen not necessarily in a deprecative sense but as applying to certain structural features of formal organisations. Weber analysed bureaucracies not empirically but as an 'ideal type' derived from the most characteristic bureaucratic features of all known organisations. He saw the development of bureaucracies as a means of introducing order and rationality into social life.

Main characteristics of bureaucracies

Weber did not actually define bureaucracy but did attempt to identify the main characteristics of this type of organisation. He emphasised the importance of administration based on expertise (rules of experts) and administration based on discipline (rules of officials).

■ The tasks of the organisation are allocated as official duties among the various positions.
■ There is an implied clear-cut division of labour and a high level of specialisation.
■ A hierarchical authority applies to the organisation of offices and positions.
■ Uniformity of decisions and actions is achieved through formally established systems of rules and regulations. Together with a structure of authority, this enables the co-ordination of various activities within the organisation.
■ An impersonal orientation is expected from officials in their dealings with clients and other officials. This is designed to result in rational judgements by officials in the performance of their duties.
■ Employment by the organisation is based on technical qualifications and constitutes a lifelong career for the officials.[26]

The four main features of bureaucracy are summarised by *Stewart* as specialisation, hierarchy of authority, system of rules and impersonality.

■ **Specialisation** applies more to the job than to the person undertaking the job. This makes for continuity because the job usually continues if the present job-holder leaves.
■ **Hierarchy of authority** makes for a sharp distinction between administrators and the administered or between management and workers. Within the management ranks there are clearly defined levels of authority. This detailed and precise stratification is particularly marked in the armed forces and in the civil service.
■ **System of rules** aims to provide for an efficient and impersonal operation. The system of rules is generally stable, although some rules may be changed or modified with time. Knowledge of the rules is a requisite of holding a job in a bureaucracy.
■ **Impersonality** means that allocation of privileges and the exercise of authority should not be arbitrary, but in accordance with the laid-down system of rules. In more highly developed bureaucracies there tend to be carefully defined procedures for appealing against certain types of decisions. Stewart sees the characteristic of impersonality as the feature of bureaucracy which most distinguishes it from other types of organisations. A bureaucracy should not only be impersonal but be seen to be impersonal.[27]

CRITICISMS OF BUREAUCRACY

Weber's concept of bureaucracy has a number of disadvantages and has been subject to severe criticism.

■ The over-emphasis on rules and procedures, record keeping and paperwork may become more important in its own right than as a means to an end.
■ Officials may develop a dependence upon bureaucratic status, symbols and rules.
■ Initiative may be stifled and when a situation is not covered by a complete set of rules or procedures there may be a lack of flexibility or adaptation to changing circumstances.
■ Position and responsibilities in the organisation can lead to officious bureaucratic behaviour. There may also be a tendency to conceal administrative procedures from outsiders.
■ Impersonal relations can lead to stereotyped behaviour and a lack of responsiveness to individual incidents or problems.

Restriction of psychological growth

One of the strongest critics of bureaucratic organisation, and the demands it makes on the worker, is *Argyris*.[28] He claims that bureaucracies restrict the psychological growth of the individual and cause feelings of failure, frustration and conflict. Argyris suggests that the organisational environment should provide a significant degree of individual responsibility and self-control; commitment to the goals of the organisation; productiveness and work; and an opportunity for individuals to apply their full abilities.

When these ideas are related to the main features of bureaucracy discussed above, such as specialisation, hierarchy of authority, system of rules and impersonality, it is perhaps easy to see the basis of Argyris' criticism.

A similar criticism is made by *Caulkin* who refers to the impersonal structure of bureaucracy as constructed round the post rather than the person and the ease with which it can be swung behind unsocial or even pathological ends.

> *The overemphasis on process rather than purpose, fragmented responsibilities and hierarchical control means that it's all too easy for individuals to neglect the larger purposes to which their small effort is being put.*[29]

EVALUATION OF BUREAUCRACY

The growth of bureaucracy has come about through the increasing size and complexity of organisations and the associated demand for effective administration. The work of the classical writers has given emphasis to the careful design and planning of organisation structure and the definition of individual duties and responsibilities. Effective organisation is based on structure and delegation through different layers of the hierarchy. Greater specialisation and the application of expertise and technical knowledge have highlighted the need for laid-down procedures.

Bureaucracy is founded on a formal, clearly defined and hierarchical structure. However, with rapid changes in the external environment, de-layering of organisations, empowerment and greater attention to meeting the needs of customers, there is an increasing need to organise for flexibility. *Peters and Waterman* found that excellent American companies achieved quick action just because their organisations were fluid and had intensive networks of informal and open communications.[30] By contrast, the crisis IBM experienced in the 1980s/1990s over the market for personal computers is explained at least in part by its top-heavy corporate structure, cumbersome organisation and dinosaur-like bureaucracy.[31]

According to *Cloke and Goldsmith*, management and bureaucracy can be thought of as flip sides of the same coin. The elements of bureaucracy generate organisational hierarchy and management, while managers generate a need for bureaucracy.

> *Bureaucracies provide a safe haven where managers can hide from responsibility and avoid being held accountable for errors of judgement or problems they created or failed to solve. In return, managers are able to use bureaucratic rules to stifle self-management and compel employees to follow their direction . . . Yet bureaucratic systems can be broken down and transformed into human-scale interactions. We have seen countless managers recreate themselves as leaders and facilitators, employees reinvent themselves as responsible self-managing team members, and bureaucracies transform into responsive, human-scale organizations. Alternatives to organizational hierarchy are both practical and possible.*[32]

Organisational solutions

As organisations face increasing global competitiveness and complex demands of the information and technological age, the need arises for alternative forms of corporate structure and systems. *Ridderstrale* points out that in the past century the hallmark of a large company was hierarchy, which rests on principles at odds with the new strategic requirements. 'Bureaucracies allowed people with knowledge to control ignorant workers. Now, new structures are needed as knowledge spreads.' Ridderstrale suggests four specific ways in which high-performing organisations have responded to increasingly complex knowledge systems by developing organisational solutions which depart from the traditional bureaucratic model:

- more decentralised and flatter structures in order that quick decisions can be taken near to where the critical knowledge resides. Flatter structures can be achieved by increasing the span of control and reducing layers from the top or removing layers of middle management;
- the use of more than a single structure in order that knowledge may be assembled across the boundaries of a traditional organisation chart. If people have less permanent places in the hierarchy they are more readily able to move across functional and geographical borders;
- converting companies into learning organisations and giving every employee the same level of familiarity with personnel and capabilities. Successful companies develop a detailed inventory of core competencies. In order fully to exploit current knowledge, managers need to know what the company knows;
- the broader sharing of expertise and knowledge, which may be located in the periphery where little formal authority resides. Managers need to share principles to ensure co-ordination and to encourage 'lowest common denominators' and the development of 'tribal' qualities through shared ownership and rewards, common norms, culture and values.[33]

Public sector organisations

In the case of public sector organisations, in particular, there is a demand for uniformity of treatment, regularity of procedures and public accountability for their operations. This leads to adherence to specified rules and procedures and to the keeping of detailed records. In their actual dealings with public sector organisations people often call for what amounts to increased bureaucracy, even though they may not use that term. The demands for equal treatment, for a standard set of regulations that apply to everyone, and that decisions should not be left to the discretion of individual managers are in effect demands for bureaucracy.

Green argues that, although bureaucracies are becoming less and less the first-choice format for organisational shape, there is still a place for bureaucracy in parts of most organisations and especially public sector organisations such as local authorities and universities. The use and implementation of tried and tested rules and procedures help to ensure essential values and ethics, and that necessary functions are run on a consistent and fair basis.[34] New forms of information technology such as electronic transactions processed from home or public access terminals are likely to change processes of government service delivery, administrative workloads and the nature of bureaucracy.[35]

Relevance today

By their very nature, bureaucracies are likely to attract criticism. For example, there appears to be a particular dilemma for management in personal service industries. The underlying characteristics of bureaucracy would seem to restrict personal service delivery which requires a flexible approach, responsiveness to individual requirements and the need for initiative and inventiveness.[36] Much of this criticism is valid, but much also appears unfair.

Stewart suggests that more organisations today contain mainly or a considerable number of professionals. Such organisations will still have bureaucratic features although there is more reliance on professional discretion and self-regulation than on control through rules and regulations.[37] However, despite new forms of organisation which have emerged, many writers suggest that bureaucracy is still relevant today as a major form of organisation structure.[38]

Critical reflection

'Despite the frequent criticisms of bureaucratic structures, it is difficult to envisage how large-scale organisations, especially within the public sector, could function effectively without exhibiting at least some of the features of a bureaucracy. Demands for alternative forms of structure are unrealistic.'

How would you attempt to justify the benefits of bureaucratic structures?

STRUCTURALISM

Sometimes Weber's work is associated with the ideas of writers such as Karl Marx under the sub-heading of the **structuralism** approach, which is a synthesis of the classical (or formal) school and the human relations (or informal) school.[39] A major line of thought was that the earlier approaches were incomplete and lacked adequate theoretical assumptions and background. The structuralism approach provides a radical perspective of social and organisational behaviour.[40] Greater attention should be given to the relationship between the formal and informal aspects of the organisation, and the study of conflict between the needs of the individual and the organisation, and between workers and management. (See also the discussion on conflict in Chapter 3.) Structuralism is sometimes associated as part of a broader human relations approach, which is discussed below.

THE HUMAN RELATIONS APPROACH

The main emphasis of the classical writers was on structure and the formal organisation, but during the 1920s, the years of the Great Depression, greater attention began to be paid to the social factors at work and to the behaviour of employees within an organisation – that is, to **human relations**.

The Hawthorne experiments

The turning point in the development of the human relations movement ('behavioural' and 'informal' are alternative headings sometimes given to this approach) came with the famous experiments at the Hawthorne plant of the Western Electric Company near Chicago, America (1924–32) and the subsequent publication of the research findings.[41] Among the people who wrote about the Hawthorne experiments was Elton Mayo (1880–1949), who is often quoted as having been a leader of the researchers. However, there appears to be some doubt as to the extent to which Mayo was actually involved in conducting the experiments and his exact contribution to the human relations movement.[42]

There were four main phases to the Hawthorne experiments:

■ the illumination experiments;
■ the relay assembly test room;
■ the interviewing programme;
■ the bank wiring observation room.

The illumination experiments

The original investigation was conducted on the lines of the classical approach and was concerned, in typical scientific management style, with the effects of the intensity of lighting upon the workers' productivity. The workers were divided into two groups, an experimental group and a control group. The results of these tests were inconclusive as production in the experimental group varied with no apparent relationship to the level of lighting, but actually increased when conditions were made much worse. Production also increased in the control group although the lighting remained unchanged. The level of production was influenced, clearly, by factors other than changes in physical conditions of work. This prompted a series of other experiments investigating factors of worker productivity.

The relay assembly test room

In the relay assembly test room the work was boring and repetitive. It involved assembling telephone relays by putting together a number of small parts. Six women workers were transferred from their normal departments to a separate area. The researchers selected two assemblers who were friends with each other. They then chose three other assemblers and a layout operator. The experiment was divided into 13 periods during which the workers were subjected to a series of planned and controlled changes to their conditions of work, such as hours of work, rest pauses and provision of refreshments. The general environmental conditions of the test room were similar to those of the normal assembly line.

During the experiment the observer adopted a friendly manner, consulting the workers, listening to their complaints and keeping them informed of the experiment. Following all but one of the changes (when operators complained too many breaks made them lose their work rhythm) there was a continuous increase in the level of production. The researchers formed the conclusion that the extra attention given to the workers, and the apparent interest in them shown by management, were the main reasons for the higher productivity. This has become famous as the 'Hawthorne Effect'.

The interviewing programme

Another significant phase of the experiments was the interviewing programme. The lighting experiment and the relay assembly test room drew attention to the form of supervision as a contributory factor to the workers' level of production. In an attempt to find out more about the workers' feelings towards their supervisors and their general conditions of work, a large interviewing programme was introduced. More than 20,000 interviews were conducted before the work was ended because of the depression.

Initially, the interviewers approached their task with a set of prepared questions, relating mainly to how the workers felt about their jobs. However, this method produced only limited information. The workers regarded a number of the questions as irrelevant; also they wanted to talk about issues other than just supervision and immediate working conditions. As a result, the style of interviewing was changed to become more non-directive and open-ended. There was no set list of questions and the workers were free to talk about any aspect of their work. The interviewers set out to be friendly and sympathetic. They adopted an impartial, non-judgemental approach and concentrated on listening.

Using this approach, the interviewers found out far more about the workers' true feelings and attitudes. They gained information not just about supervision and working conditions but also about the company itself, management, work group relations and matters outside of work such as family life and views on society in general. Many workers appeared to welcome the opportunity to have someone to talk to about their feelings and problems and to be able to 'let off steam' in a friendly atmosphere. The interviewing programme was significant in giving an impetus to present-day human resource management and the use of counselling interviews, and highlighting the need for management to listen to workers' feelings and problems. Being a good listener is arguably even more important for managers in today's work organisations and it is a skill which needs to be encouraged and developed.[43]

The bank wiring observation room

Another experiment involved the observation of a group of 14 men working in the bank wiring room. It was noted that the men formed their own informal organisation with sub-groups or cliques, and with natural leaders emerging with the consent of the members. The group developed its own pattern of informal social relations and 'norms' of what constituted 'proper' behaviour. Despite a financial incentive scheme where the workers could receive more money the more work produced, the group decided on a level of output well below the level they were capable of producing.

Group pressures on individual workers were stronger than financial incentives offered by management. The group believed that if they increased their output, management would raise the standard level of piece rates. The importance of group 'norms' and informal social relations are discussed in Chapter 8.

EVALUATION OF THE HUMAN RELATIONS APPROACH

The human relations approach has been subjected to severe criticism. The Hawthorne experiments have been criticised, for example, on methodology and on failure of the investigators to take sufficient account of environmental factors – although much of this criticism is with the value of hindsight. The human relations writers have been criticised generally for the adoption of a management perspective, their 'unitary frame of reference' and their over-simplified theories.[44]

Other criticisms of the human relations approach are that it is insufficiently scientific and that it takes too narrow a view. It ignores the role of the organisation itself in how society operates.

Sex power differential

There are a number of interpretations of the results of the Hawthorne experiments, including the possible implications of the 'sex power differential' between the two groups. In the relay assembly room where output increased, the group was all female, while in the bank wiring room where output was restricted, the group was all male. The workers in the relay assembly test room were all young unmarried women. All except one were living at home with traditional families of immigrant background. In the work environment of the factory the women had been subjected to frequent contact with male supervisors and therefore 'the sex power hierarchies in the home and in the factory were congruent'. It is suggested, therefore, that it was only to be expected that the women agreed readily to participate with management in the relay assembly test room experiment.[45]

Importance of the Hawthorne experiments

Whatever the interpretation of the results of the Hawthorne experiments, they did generate new ideas concerning the importance of work groups and leadership, communications, output restrictions, motivation and job design. They placed emphasis on the importance of personnel management and gave impetus to the work of the human relations writers. The Hawthorne experiments undoubtedly marked a significant step forward in providing further insight into human behaviour at work and the development of management thinking. The Hawthorne experiments are regarded as one of the most important of all social science investigations and are recognised as probably the single most important foundation of the human relations approach to management and the development of organisational behaviour.

In a review of humane approaches to management, *Crainer* asserts: 'The Hawthorne Studies were important because they showed that views of how managers behaved were a vital aspect of motivation and improved performance. Also, the research revealed the importance of informal work groups.'[46]

Humanisation of the work organisation

Whereas supporters of the classical approach sought to increase production by rationalisation of the work organisation, the human relations movement has led to ideas on increasing production by humanising the work organisation. The classical approach adopted more of a managerial perspective, while the human relations approach strove for a greater under-standing of people's psychological and social needs at work as well as improving the process of management. It is usually regarded as the first major approach to organisation and manage-ment to show concern for industrial sociology.

The human relations approach recognised the importance of the informal organisation which will always be present within the formal structure. This informal organisation will influence the motivation of employees who will view the organisation for which they work through the values and attitudes of their colleagues. Their view of the organisation deter-mines their approach to work and the extent of their motivation to work well or otherwise.

Human relations writers demonstrated that people go to work to satisfy a complexity of needs and not simply for monetary reward. They emphasised the importance of the wider social needs of individuals and gave recognition to the work organisation as a social organ-isation and the importance of the group, and group values and norms, in influencing indi-vidual behaviour at work. It has been commented that the classical school was concerned about 'organisations without people' and the human relations school about 'people without organisations'.

Critical reflection

'The human relations approach to organisations and management makes all the right sounds with an emphasis on humane behaviour, considerate management and recognition of the informal organisation. However, it is more about what people would like to believe and lacks credibility and substance.'

To what extent do the criticisms and shortcomings of the human relations approach detract from its potential benefits?

NEO-HUMAN RELATIONS

Certainly there were shortcomings in the human relations approach and assumptions which evolved from such studies as the Hawthorne experiments were not necessarily supported by empirical evidence. For example, the contention that a satisfied worker is a productive worker was not always found to be valid. However, the results of the Hawthorne experiments and the subsequent attention given to the social organisation and to theories of individual motivation gave rise to the work of those writers in the 1950s and 1960s who adopted a more psychological orientation. New ideas on management theory arose and a major focus of concern was the personal adjustment of the individual within the work organisation and the effects of group relationships and leadership styles. This group of writers is often (and more correctly) categorised separately under the heading of '**neo-human relations**'. The works of these writers are examined in more detail in Chapter 7 and Chapter 12 but are sum-marised broadly here.

The work of Maslow

A major impetus for the neo-human relations approach was the work of *Maslow* who, in 1943, put forward a theoretical framework of individual personality development and moti-vation based on a hierarchy of human needs.[47] The hierarchy ranges through five levels from, at the lowest level, physiological needs, through safety needs, love needs and esteem needs, to the need for self-actualisation at the highest level. Individuals advance up the hierarchy only as each lower-level need is satisfied. Although Maslow did not originally intend this need hierarchy to be applied necessarily to the work situation it has, nevertheless, had a significant impact on management approaches to motivation and the design of work organ-isation to meet individual needs. The work of Maslow provides a link with the earlier human relations approach.

Some leading contributors

Among the best-known contributors to the neo-human relations approach are *Herzberg* and *McGregor*. Herzberg isolated two different sets of factors affecting motivation and satisfaction at work. One set of factors comprises those which, if absent, cause dissatisfaction. These are 'hygiene' or 'maintenance' factors which are concerned basically with job environment. However, to motivate workers to give of their best, proper attention must be given to a different set of factors, the 'motivators' or 'growth' factors. These are concerned with job content.[48]

McGregor argued that the style of management adopted is a function of the manager's attitudes towards human nature and behaviour at work. He put forward two suppositions called Theory X and Theory Y which are based on popular assumptions about work and people.[49]

Other major contributors to the neo-human relations approach are *Likert*, whose work includes research into different systems of management;[50] *McClelland*, with ideas on achievement motivation;[51] and *Argyris*, who considered the effects of the formal organisation on the individual and psychological growth in the process of self-actualisation.[52] Argyris' major contributions include his work on organisational learning and on effective leadership.[53]

The neo-human relations approach has generated a large amount of writing and research not only from original propounders but also from others seeking to establish the validity, or otherwise, of their ideas. This has led to continuing attention being given to such matters as organisation structuring, group dynamics, job satisfaction, communication and participation, leadership styles and motivation. It has also led to greater attention to the importance of interpersonal interactions, the causes of conflict and recognition of 'employee relations' problems.

THE SYSTEMS APPROACH

More recently, attention has been focused on the analysis of organisations as 'systems' with a number of interrelated sub-systems. The classical approach emphasised the technical requirements of the organisation and its needs – 'organisations without people'; the human relations approaches emphasised the psychological and social aspects, and the consideration of human needs – 'people without organisations'.

The **systems approach** attempts to reconcile these two earlier approaches and the work of the formal and the informal writers. Attention is focused on the total work organisation and the interrelationships of structure and behaviour, and the range of variables within the organisation. This approach can be contrasted with a view of the organisation as separate parts. The systems approach encourages managers to view the organisation both as a whole and as part of a larger environment. The idea is that any part of an organisation's activities affects all other parts.

Systems theory

Systems theory is not new and has been used in the natural and physical sciences for a number of years. One of the founders of this approach was the biologist *Ludwig von Bertalanffy* who used the term 'systems theory' in an article published in 1951 and who is generally credited with having developed the outline of General Systems Theory.[54] The systems approach to organisation has arisen, at least in part, therefore, from the work of biologists, and *Miller and Rice* have likened the commercial and industrial organisation to the biological organism.[55]

Using a General Systems Theory (GST) approach, *Boulding* classified nine levels of systems of increasing complexity according to the state of development and knowledge about each level.[56] Organisations are complex social systems and are more open to change than lower-level simple dynamic or cybernetic systems. Boulding felt there were large gaps in both theoretical and empirical knowledge of the human level and the social organisations level of systems, although some progress has now been made with recent theories of organisational behaviour.

The business organisation as an open system

The business organisation is an open system. There is continual interaction with the broader external environment of which it is part. The systems approach views the organisation within its total environment and emphasises the importance of multiple channels of interaction. Criticisms of earlier approaches to organisation are based in part on the attempt to study the activities and problems of the organisation solely in terms of the internal environment. The view of the organisation as an open system is examined in Chapter 3.

The systems approach views the organisation as a whole and involves the study of the organisation in terms of the relationship between technical and social variables within the system. Changes in one part, technical or social, will affect other parts and thus the whole system.

Longwall coal-mining study

The idea of socio-technical systems arose from the work of *Trist* and others, of the Tavistock Institute of Human Relations, in their study of the effects of changing technology in the coal-mining industry in the 1940s.[57] The increasing use of mechanisation and the introduction of coal-cutters and mechanical conveyors enabled coal to be extracted on a 'longwall' method.

Shift working was introduced, with each shift specialising in one stage of the operation – preparation, cutting or loading. However, the new method meant a change in the previous system of working where a small, self-selecting group of miners worked together, as an independent team, on one part of the coalface – the 'single place' or 'shortwall' method.

Technological change had brought about changes in the social groupings of the miners. It disrupted the integration of small groups and the psychological and sociological properties of the old method of working. There was a lack of co-operation between different shifts and within each shift, an increase in absenteeism, scapegoating and signs of greater social stress. The 'longwall' method was socially disruptive and did not prove as economically efficient as it could have been with the new technology.

The researchers saw the need for a socio-technical approach in which an appropriate social system could be developed in keeping with the new technical system. The result was the 'composite longwall' method with more responsibility to the team as a whole and shifts carrying out composite tasks, the reintroduction of multiskilled roles and a reduction in specialisation. The composite method was psychologically and socially more rewarding and economically more efficient than the 'longwall' method.

The socio-technical system

The concept of the organisation as a 'socio-technical' system directs attention to the transformation or conversion process itself, to the series of activities through which the organisation attempts to achieve its objectives. The **socio-technical system** is concerned with the interactions between the psychological and social factors and the needs and demands of the human part of the organisation, and its structural and technological requirements.

Recognition of the socio-technical approach is of particular importance today. People must be considered as at least an equal priority along with investment in technology. For example, *Lane et al.* point out that major technological change has brought about dramatic changes in worker behaviour and requirements. It is people who unlock the benefits and opportunities of information communication technology.[58]

Technology determinism

The concept of socio-technical systems provides a link between the systems approach and a sub-division, sometimes adopted – the **technology approach**. Writers under the technology heading attempt to restrict generalisations about organisations and management and emphasise the effects of varying technologies on organisation structure, work groups and individual performance and job satisfaction. This is in contrast with the socio-technical approach which did not regard technology, *per se*, as a determinant of behaviour.

Under the heading of the technology approach could be included the work of such writers as *Walker and Guest* (effects of the assembly line production method on employee behaviour);[59] *Sayles* (relationship between technology and the nature of work groups);[60] and *Blauner* (problems of 'alienation' in relation to different work technologies).[61] Chapter 16 examines technology and organisations.

THE CONTINGENCY APPROACH

The classical approach suggested one best form of structure and placed emphasis on general sets of principles while the human relations approach gave little attention at all to structure. In contrast the **contingency approach** showed renewed concern with the importance of structure as a significant influence on organisational performance. The contingency approach, which can be seen as an extension of the systems approach, highlights possible means of differentiating among alternative forms of organisation structures and systems of management. There is no one optimum state. For example, the structure of the organisation and its 'success' are dependent, that is contingent upon, the nature of tasks with which it is designed to deal and the nature of environmental influences.

The most appropriate structure and system of management is therefore dependent upon the contingencies of the situation for each particular organisation. The contingency approach implies that organisation theory should not seek to suggest one best way to structure or manage organisations but should provide insights into the situational and contextual factors which influence management decisions. Contingency models of organisation and management are discussed in Chapter 15.

A summary of management theory and some links with other chapters is set out in Figure 2.3.

OTHER APPROACHES TO THE STUDY OF ORGANISATIONS

The four-fold framework of classical, human relations, systems and contingency approaches provides a helpful, although rather simplistic, categorisation. The study of organisations, their structure and management is a broad field of inquiry. Depending on the views and preferences of the writer, other possible main approaches include decision-making and social action.

THE DECISION-MAKING APPROACH

The systems approach involves the isolation of those functions most directly concerned with the achievement of objectives and the identification of main decision areas or sub-systems. Viewing the organisation as a system emphasises the need for good information and channels of communication in order to assist effective decision-making in the organisation. Recognition of the need for decision-making and the attainment of goals draws attention to a sub-division of the systems approach, or a separate category, that of the **decision-making (decision theory) approach**. Here the focus of attention is on managerial decision-making and how organisations process and use information in making decisions.

Successful management lies in responding to internal and external change. This involves the clarification of objectives, the specification of problems and the search for and implementation of solutions. The organisation is seen as an information-processing network with numerous decision points. An understanding of how decisions are made helps in understanding behaviour in the organisation. Decision-making writers seek to explain the mechanisms by which conflict is resolved and choices are made.

Figure 2.3   Concept map of management theory

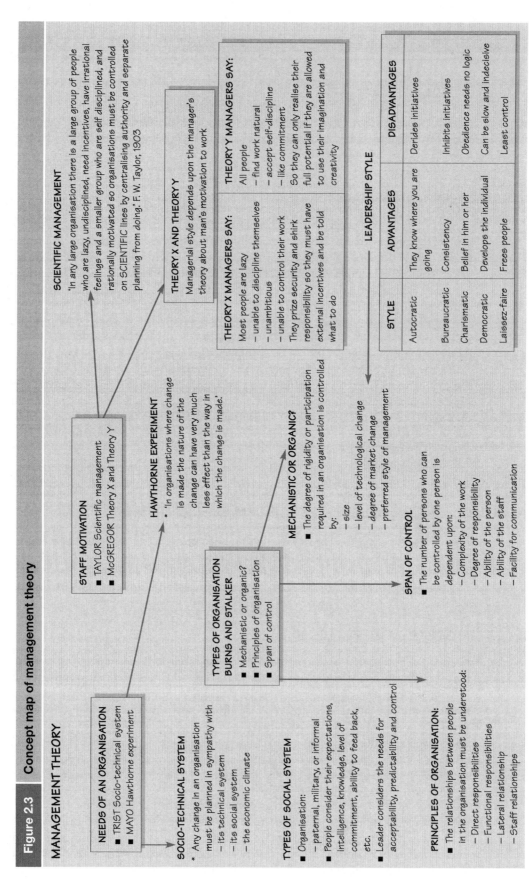

Some leading writers

Leading writers on the decision-making approach include *Barnard, Simon* and *Cyert and March*. The scope of the decision-making approach, however, is wide and it is possible to identify contributions from engineers, mathematicians and operational research specialists in addition to the work of economists, psychologists and writers on management and organisation.

Barnard stressed the need for co-operative action in organisations. He believed that people's ability to communicate, and their commitment and contribution to the achievement of a common purpose, were necessary for the existence of a co-operative system.[62] These ideas were developed further by Simon. He sees management as meaning decision-making and his concern is with how decisions are made and how decision-making can be improved. Simon is critical of the implication of man as completely rational and proposes a model of 'administrative man' who, unlike 'economic man', 'satisfices' rather than maximises. Administrative decision-making is the achievement of satisfactory rather than optimal results in solving problems.[63]

Economic models of decision-making, based on the assumption of rational behaviour in choosing from known alternatives in order to maximise objectives, can be contrasted with behavioural models based not so much on maximisation of objectives as on short-term expediency where a choice is made to avoid conflict and to stay within limiting constraints. Managers are more concerned with avoiding uncertainties than with the prediction of uncertainties.[64]

SOCIAL ACTION

Social action represents a contribution from sociologists to the study of organisations. Social action writers attempt to view the organisation from the standpoint of individual members (actors) who will each have their own goals and interpretation of their work situation in terms of the satisfaction sought and the meaning that work has for them. The goals of the individual, and the means selected and actions taken to achieve these goals, are affected by the individual's perception of the situation. Social action looks to the individual's own definition of the situation as a basis for explaining behaviour. Conflict of interests is seen as normal behaviour and part of organisational life.

According to *Silverman*, 'The action approach . . . does not, in itself, provide a theory of organisations. It is instead best understood as a method of analysing social relations within organisations.'[65]

Criticisms of earlier approaches

A main thrust of social action is the criticism of earlier approaches to organisation and management and of what is claimed to be their failure to provide a satisfactory basis for the explanation or prediction of individual behaviour. For example, criticism is directed at approaches which focused on the goals and needs of the organisation rather than on considerations of the effectiveness of an organisation in meeting the needs of its individual members.

The human relations approaches have been criticised because of their focus on generalised theories of good management, group psychology and the suggestion of needs common to all individuals at work. The technology approach has been criticised for attributing feelings of alienation to the nature of technology and the status of work groups rather than an analysis which focused on concern for the individual's expectations of, and reactions to, work. The systems approach has been criticised for failure to examine the orientation of individual members to the organisation, the different expectations people have of their work or ways in which the environment influences expectations of work.

Unitary or pluralistic view

Important contributors to a social action approach include *Goldthorpe* (industrial attitudes and behaviour patterns of manual workers)[66] and *Fox*. In a research paper written for the

Royal Commission on Trade Unions and Employers' Associations (the Donovan Report), Fox suggests two major ways of perceiving an industrial organisation – a 'unitary' approach and a 'pluralistic' approach.[67]

With the unitary approach the organisation is viewed as a team with a common source of loyalty, one focus of effort and one accepted leader. The pluralistic approach views the organisation as made up of competing sub-groups with their own loyalties, goals and leaders. These competing sub-groups are almost certain to come into conflict. The unitary and pluralistic perspectives of the organisation are also referred to in Chapter 3 and Chapter 13.

Action theory

A theory of human behaviour from an 'action approach' is presented by *Bowey*.[68] She suggests that action theory, systems theory and contingency theory are not necessarily incompatible approaches to the understanding of behaviour in organisations. It would be possible to take the best parts of the different approaches and combine them into a theory that would model empirical behaviour and also facilitate the analysis of large numbers of people in organisations. Bowey goes on to present such a theory as a particular form of an action theory approach. According to Bowey, action theory is not capable of dealing with the analysis of the behaviour of a large number of people in organisations. Her theory is based, therefore, on three essential principles of action theory, augmented by four additional concepts taken from systems theory.

The three essential principles of action theory can be summarised as below:

■ Sociology is concerned not just with behaviour but with 'meaningful action'.
■ Particular meanings persist through reaffirmation in actions.
■ Actions can also lead to changes in meanings.

Bowey suggests that these three principles apply mainly to explanations of individual, or small-scale, behaviour. She gives four additional concepts, taken from systems theory, on which analysis of large-scale behaviour can be based. These concepts are redefined in accordance with an action approach.

■ **Role.** This is needed for the analysis of behaviour in organisations. It explains the similar action of different people in similar situations within the organisation and the expectations held by other people.
■ **Relationships.** This is needed to explain the patterns of interaction among people and the behaviours displayed towards one another.
■ **Structure.** The relationships among members of an organisation give rise to patterns of action which can be identified as a 'transitory social structure'. The social factors, and non-social factors such as payment systems, methods of production and physical layout, together form the behavioural structure.
■ **Process.** Human behaviour can be analysed in terms of processes, defined as 'continuous interdependent sequences of actions'. The concept of process is necessary to account for the manner in which organisations exhibit changes in structure.

The three principles of action theory, together with the four additional concepts from systems theory, provide an action approach to the analysis of behaviour in organisations. Bowey goes on to illustrate her theory with case studies of five different types of organisations, all in the restaurant industry.

A NUMBER OF APPROACHES

We can now see that within the broad four-fold classification of classical, human relations, systems and contingency approaches it is possible to identify a number of other approaches or at least sub-divisions of approaches, although there is no consensus on the categorisation of these different approaches or on the identification of the various contributors to one particular approach. So far we have established a possible nine-fold classification: classical (including scientific management); bureaucracy; human relations; neo-human relations; systems; technology; contingency; decision-making; and social action – and if structuralism is included, we have a ten-fold classification. This classification could be extended still further. For example, another more recent categorisation sometimes identified as a separate approach is management science – with emphasis on quantitative analysis, mathematical models, operational research and computer technology (*see* Figure 2.4).

Figure 2.4	An outline of developments of approaches to organisation and management

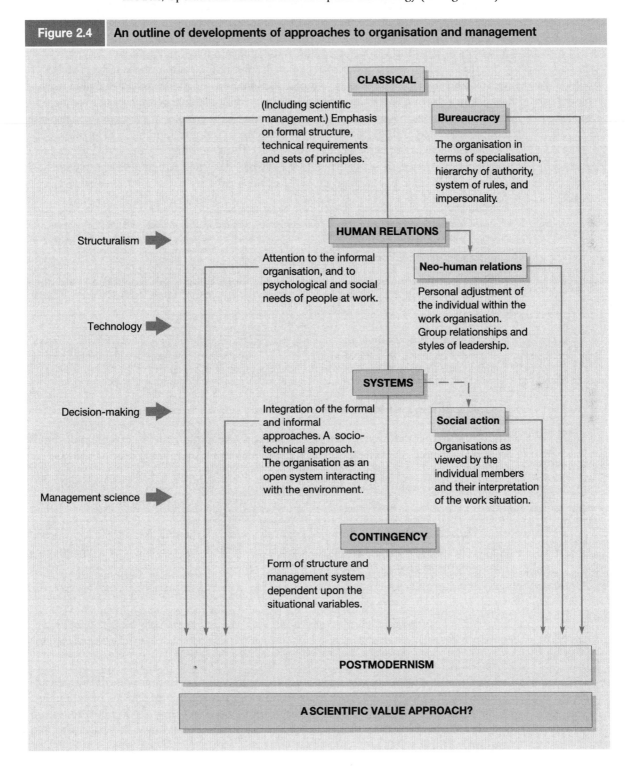

POSTMODERNISM

The work of contemporary writers discussed above together with the achievements of practitioners such as Alfred P. Sloan Jr (1875–1966, Chief Executive and Honorary Chairman of General Motors) gave rise to the so-called 'modern organisation'.[69] With the development of the information and technological age a more recent view of organisations and management is the idea of **postmodernism**. In the 1990s, writers such as *Clegg* described the postmodern organisation in terms of the influence of technological determinism, structural flexibility, premised on niches, multiskilled jobs marked by a lack of demarcation, and more complex employment relationships including subcontracting and networking.[70]

Postmodernism rejects a rational systems approach to our understanding of organisations and management and to accepted explanations of society and behaviour. Highly flexible, free-flowing and fluid structures with the ability to change quickly to meet present demands form the basis of the new organisation. For example, *Watson* suggests that the modernism inherent in the systems-control approach to understanding work organisations and their management is naïve and unrealistic. The possibility of any kind of complete and coherent body of management knowledge has increasingly been brought into question.

> To enable us to move toward a more realistic or pragmatically reasonable way of 'framing' work organisation and its management, a shift has first to be made in our deeper assumptions about the social world. These are the modernist assumptions which inevitably underpin the whole edifice of work organisation and management thinking.[71]

By contrast, postmodernism places greater attention on the use of language and attempts to portray a particular set of assumptions or versions of the 'truth'. Watson defines postmodernism as:

> A way of looking at the world that rejects attempts to build systematic (or 'foundationalist') explanations of history and society and which, instead, concentrates on the ways in which human beings 'invent' their words, especially through the use of language or 'discourse'.[72]

A generalised sociological concept

The idea of postmodernism is, however, not easy to explain fully in clear and simple terms. It is arguably more of a generalised sociological concept rather than a specific approach to organisation and management. There is even some discussion of two connotations, and theories or philosophies of the concept depending on whether the term is hyphenated or not.[73] Perhaps understandably, therefore, the concept of postmodernism appears to have little interest or appeal to the practical manager.

Indeed Watson, for example, questions the value of labelling more flexible forms of bureaucratic structure and culture as postmodern or post-bureaucratic and differentiating these from the modernist bureaucratic organisation.

> There is no postmodern or post-bureaucratic organisational form available to us that is essentially different from the modernist bureaucratic organisation. We are indeed seeing different mixes of direct and indirect management control attempts as the world changes. But the world was always changing. Probably from the very beginning of industrialisation there has been a mixing of direct and indirect controls with emphases in one direction and then the other being made at different times.[74]

Nevertheless, postmodernist organisation can arguably be seen as a healthy challenge to more traditional approaches. It puts forward alternative interpretations of rationality, credibility and ambiguity, and a thoughtful critical perspective on disorders in work organisations, and reminds us of the complexities in our understanding of management and organisational behaviour.

> ### *Critical reflection*
>
> 'The idea of postmodernist organisation can be likened to the "Emperor's new clothes". In reality it is too theoretical and too vague, and lacks any real adaptive value for the practical manager.'
>
> *How would you attempt to challenge this assertion? What is your own opinion of postmodernism?*

RELEVANCE TO MANAGEMENT AND ORGANISATIONAL BEHAVIOUR

The different possible categorisations are not necessarily a bad thing; they illustrate the discursive and complex nature of management. The possible sub-divisions and cross-groupings help illustrate the many factors relevant to the study and practice of management and organisational behaviour. Discussion on the various categorisations of approaches and the identification of individual writers within a particular approach can provide a useful insight into the subject.

Positive advantages

Whatever form of categorisation is adopted, the division of writers on organisation and management into various approaches offers a number of positive advantages.

- It is helpful to students in the arrangement and study of their material.
- It provides a setting in which to view the field of management and to consider the contribution of individual writers.
- It traces the major lines of argument developed by writers seeking to advise practising managers on how they might improve performance.
- It provides a framework in which the principles enunciated can be set and against which comparisons with management practice can be made.
- It helps in organisational analysis and in the identification of problem areas. For example, is the problem one of structure, of human relations or of the socio-technical process?
- It enables the manager to take from the different approaches those ideas which best suit the particular requirements of the job. For example, in dealing with a problem of structure, the ideas of the classical writers or of contingency theory might be adopted. When there is a problem relating to human resource management, ideas from the human relations movement might be of most value. If the problem is one of environmental influence, insights from the systems approach might prove most helpful. For problems of a more quantitative nature, ideas from the decision-making approach or from management science might be applicable.

Caveats to be noted

There are, however, a number of important caveats that should be noted.

- The various approaches represent a progression of ideas, each building on from the other and adding to it. Together they provide a pattern of complementary studies into the development of management thinking. The different approaches are not in competition with each other and no one approach should be viewed as if it were the only approach, replacing or superseding earlier contributions. Many ideas of earlier writers are still of relevance today and of continuing importance in modern management practice.
- Any categorisation of individual writers into specific approaches is inevitably somewhat arbitrary and not all writers can be neatly arranged in this manner. This is only to be

expected. Such writers are expounding their current thoughts and ideas in keeping with the continual development of management theory and changes in management practice. The comment made about some management writers that they are saying different things at different times might therefore be taken more as a compliment than as a criticism.

■ Even when there is agreement on the nature of the contribution from different writers, the actual division into varying approaches may take a number of forms. In other words, while there might be acceptance of the need for a framework, there is no agreement on its shape. Different authors have adopted different formats in which to set out the developments in management thinking.

■ Some of the literature categorises management thinkers into divisions called 'schools'. The use of this term suggests a clarity of distinction between each division and a uniformity of beliefs within each division. This is perhaps an exaggeration. The distinction between these so-called schools is not clear-cut and there is not necessarily a consistency of thinking among the various contributors in each division. The term 'approaches' to management is more indicative of the obscure lines between the different categorisations and, paradoxically, it is the suggestion of vagueness that, arguably, makes it a more appropriate term to use.

> *Of course, management theories have often been the subject of discourse and criticism. Some critics see organisational philosophies as management fads that will be replaced by new ones as other theories are proposed. That may well be the case, but it is good for management theories to evolve, because organisations change, the environment changes, and as a result, management practices and techniques change . . . Theories provide us with valuable insights into how we can be more understanding, influential and ultimately more successful in managing organisations and the turbulent dynamic environments in which they operate . . . you of course, may have a different view!*
>
> Jacqueline McLean[75]

The importance of cultural contexts

A major criticism of the attempt to define generalised models of management theory is the assumption of national culture. In a review of management theory and practice, *Heller* contrasts British and American thinking with methods employed by the Japanese. In the 1960s, Western managements showed a total lack of curiosity about competition from Japan; British and European managers were still obsessed by the American example. The Japanese built hugely on what they had borrowed from the USA. However, the Japanese also practised and perfected what management scientists often only preached.[76]

Although British management has failed to live up to Japanese standards, professional standards among managers in Britain have improved greatly over the past 25 years. The potential of a widening Europe and the Japanese penchant for locating more plants in Britain provide the best reasons for brighter prospects.

Schneider and Barsoux draw attention to how the different theories on how to organise all reflect societal concerns of the times as well as the cultural backgrounds of the individuals. Different approaches reflect different cultural assumptions regarding, for example, human nature and the importance of task and relationships.[77]

Cheng, Sculli and Chan also question the universality of theories of management and organisational behaviour on the grounds that they have not adequately addressed the factor of culture. 'Traditionally, the greatest aspiration of researchers is to discover objective, universalistic principles of behaviour. The tacit assumption behind this is that these principles may be discovered without reference to cultural contexts.' They conclude that while there may be some universality to organisation structures, for example the need for some form of hierarchy whatever its shape may be, different national cultures frequently give those structures different meanings.[78]

TOWARDS A SCIENTIFIC VALUE APPROACH?

It might arguably be that the study of organisations, their structure and management is moving towards a more scientific approach. Management science can assist managers in the analysis of complex problems that are subject to quantitative constraints and in the optimisation of decisions in such problems. It may also assist in the establishment of broad theory.

> It is obvious from even a cursory glance at the history of management science that science and technology are considered to be key instruments in solving workplace problems and in controlling workplaces . . . While Taylorist scientific management may have its academic critics, management science is thriving. It is itself a large business, providing employment for management consultants whose sole concern is solving workplace problems of other corporations.[79]

Balance between philosophy and science

Miner, however, suggests that although the degree of commitment to the scientific value system is increasing, as yet there is insufficient research to move the field entirely into science, completely divorced from philosophy. At present management theory is clearly in the 'schools' phase. As discussed earlier, it is possible to argue over the use of the term 'schools'. However, whatever terminology is used, and whatever the state of our knowledge, the message from Miner is clear:

> . . . schools of management thought are very much a reality, and the management student who approaches the field without at least a minimal understanding of them does so at some risk.[80]

Whatever the moves towards a more scientific approach, many operational problems in organisations relate to the nature of human behaviour and the people–organisation relationship and do not lend themselves to the application of a scientific answer. For example, according to *Handy*:

> If there were such a thing as Management Science, presumably there would be scientific laws and rules. I was to be grievously disappointed. I read endless hypotheses that tried to explain why people and organisations behaved the way they did but no proof . . . Managing a business, or any organisation, I came to see was more practical art than applied science.[81]

BENEFITS TO THE MANAGER

Whatever the balance between philosophy and science, a knowledge and understanding of management theory will help with the complexities of management in modern work organisations.

According to *Crainer*, management is active, not theoretical. But management is nothing without ideas.

> Ideas drive management as surely as the immediate problems which land on managers' desks or which arrive via their email. Decisions have to be based on ideas, as well as instinct. Without ideas managers flit desperately from crisis to crisis. They cannot know where they are going, why they are doing something or what they will achieve, without the fuel of ideas.[82]

Crainer also suggests that as one idea after another fails to translate into sustainable practice, there is a growing disillusionment with the pedlars of managerial wisdom.

> Yet, the desire for instant solutions which tackle all managerial problems in one fell swoop remains strong . . . Amid the hard sell, the quick fixes and organisational placebos, it is true to say that there is little that's original. But, without gurus, managers would lose a rich source of inspiration, information and controversy.[83]

Reporting on a 12-year study of the knowledge and use of management concepts in technical organisations, *Flores and Utley* suggest that a look back at the theories and principles that have been taught in the past could give an indication of the success of any new approach and help prepare today's and tomorrow's managers for the future.[84] And *Stern* has this to say:

> *Management thinkers still have a lot to tell us. You don't have to believe everything they say, but they may at least offer stimulation; they might provoke senior managers into abandoning complacency and trying to see problems in a new light.*[85]

There is undoubtedly much scepticism about, and criticism of, management gurus. For example, in a cynical and provocative feature in *The Times, Billen* suggests that the tide is turning against the gurus and their gobbledegook.

> *In the past two decades, management theory, once rejected in Britain by both management and unions, has been deliberately imposed on almost every aspect of commercial and public life . . . It would be a brave new world without such gobbledegook in it but – to use a management theorist's phrase – an empowered one, too. Managers would be chosen not for their ability to bandy jargon with their superiors but for their empathy, pragmatism, experience and decisiveness with their staff.*[86]

Whatever the value of management theory, clearly no single approach to organisation and management provides all the answers. It is the comparative study of different approaches which will yield benefits to the manager. There is, of course, no shortage of new ideas on organisational behaviour and management thinking. To what extent, however, do these ideas lead to improved organisational performance? *Ghoshal et al.* suggest that:

> *There is much truth in the saying that every living practitioner is prisoner to the ideas of a dead theorist. Immunized by their daily confrontation with the 'real world' corporate managers typically exhibit a healthy distrust of theory that has, in general, served them well.*[87]

There are no definitive or final solutions to the problems of organisations. The nature of work organisations and the environment in which they operate is becoming increasingly complex and subject to continual change. However, at least we do understand more about the dynamics of management and organisational behaviour as a basis for the analysis of human behaviour in organisations.[88] *Stern* suggests that 'Management is both science and art, and the trick of it lies in separating the good ideas from the bad, knowing when to be scientific and when to be artful.'[89]

There are, then, many aspects to management. There are no simple solutions, no one best way to manage. However, the study of organisations, their structure and management is still important for the manager and remains an indispensable part of the job.

Critical reflection

'The historical study of different approaches to organisation and management and the development of organisation theory have no practical relevance for today's managers. It is really no more than a luxury for students and the time could be spent better on the study of more important topic areas.'

*How would you present a **counter** argument?*

SYNOPSIS

■ The study of organisational behaviour has to proceed on a broad front. A central part of this study is the development of management thinking and what might be termed management theory. In order to help identify main trends in the development of organisational behaviour, it is usual to categorise the work of leading writers into various 'approaches' based on their views of organisations, their structure and management. This provides a simplistic framework on which to direct study and focus attention.

■ The classical writers placed emphasis on purpose and structure, on the technical requirements of the organisation, and on the assumption of rational and logical behaviour. The human relations writers emphasised the importance of the informal organisation and the psychological and social needs of people at work. The systems approach focuses attention on the interactions between technical and social variables. The organisation is seen in continual interaction with the external environment. Contingency theory highlights possible means of differentiating between alternative forms of structures and systems of management.

■ This four-fold categorisation provides a useful starting point for the identification of main trends in the development of management thinking. Within this framework, however, it is possible to identify a number of other approaches or sub-divisions of approaches. The decision-making approach emphasises the need for good information and channels of communication. Social action writers attempt to view the organisation from the position of individual members who will each have their own interpretation of the work situation in terms of the satisfaction sought and the meaning that work has for them.

■ With the development of the information and technological age the need arises for alternative forms of corporate structure and systems. A more recent view is the idea of postmodernism. This rejects a rational systems approach to our understanding of organisations and management, and to accepted explanations of society and behaviour. Postmodernism is arguably more of a generalised sociological concept rather than a specific approach to organisation and management. Nevertheless, postmodernist organisation can arguably be seen as a healthy challenge to more traditional approaches and reminds us of the complexities in our understanding of management and organisational behaviour.

■ Whatever form of categorisation is adopted, the division of writers on organisation and management into various approaches offers a number of advantages. It helps in organisational analysis and the identification of problem areas. It enables the manager to take from the different approaches those ideas that suit best the particular requirements of the job. There are, however, a number of caveats that should also be noted, including the significance of cultural contexts.

■ It might be that the study of organisations is moving towards a more scientific value approach. However, whatever the balance between philosophy and science, a knowledge of management theory will help with the complexities of management in modern work organisations. There is much scepticism and criticism of management gurus but the study of organisation theory is an indispensable part of the job. Ideas are as important to management decisions as is instinct. It is necessary to view the interrelationships among the development of theory, behaviour in organisations and management practice.

Cases

The story of the middleman

Stefan Stern

Reports of the death of middle management were not merely exaggerated, they were wrong. Yes, organisations have de-layered. Yes, the current 'white-collar' recession is having a big impact on the middle tier of professionals within businesses. But middle managers have not been abolished. They are still here, hard at work.

That is one reason that the book *The Truth About Middle Managers* by Paul Osterman is welcome. It attempts to take a serious look at the reality of middle management. The author has made a sincere attempt to shed more light on this under-analysed cadre of managers. Sincere but also, regrettably, flawed. The author defines his terms clearly enough. 'Senior management makes the decisions that set the organisation's course, whereas middle management interprets and executes those decisions,' he writes. Based on his research, Osterman tests some of the common assumptions made about middle managers.

It is not true, he argues, that middle managers are sinking into a pit of despair as their numbers fall and job insecurity rises. In fact, in the US at any rate, there are more managers than ever. They are 'less secure, but more in demand'. Nor is it true, Osterman asserts, that middle managers are alienated from their work and have little commitment to what they do. 'Middle managers are the glue that holds organisations together,' he writes.

> Middle managers very much enjoy what they do and have what I term a strong craft commitment to their work. But it is also true they have lost their loyalty to their firm. As organisations have divested themselves of managerial levels, core managerial responsibilities have been pushed down to middle management. Middle managers are now the negotiators between different interests and are making key decisions about trade-offs.

That is certainly true, as is his other observation,

> In the past the nature of the firm was stable, whereas today it is constantly being reshaped. The continuous organisational turmoil that ensues creates an environment that seems chaotic and out of control from the perspective of middle management.

So why has he come up with some relatively sunny conclusions?

A key part of the research for this book involved in-depth interviews with 50 middle managers from two separate organisations, a bank and a high-tech company. But these interviews were conducted in 2004 and 2005. How were your prospects back then? A lot better than today, we can assume. Second, who were these managers? Osterman explains: 'The middle managers were chosen randomly from a list provided by the human resources staff in each organisation.' Did HR allow any malcontents, whingers and otherwise less-than-upbeat people to be interviewed? It seems unlikely. So we must be sceptical – insecurity is real, not imagined, and disillusionment is widespread. As one of his witnesses said, even then, 'I think if you asked people if they had a choice today whether they'd take a job or take the [redundancy] package, you'd get a fair number of people whose hands would be raised for the package – mine included.'

Source: Stern, S. 'The Story of the Middleman', *Financial Times*, 25 February 2009. Copyright © 2009 The Financial Times Limited, reproduced with permission.

Discussion questions

1 This article describes some research into management and organisational behaviour. Explain which of the approaches to organisational behaviour outlined in the chapter you think Osterman takes, and why.

2 What does the article tell us about the problems associated with researching organisational behaviour? How can such problems be minimised or avoided?

CASE STUDY

Dell Computers: the world at your fingertips

Breaking the mould

The growth of the home personal computer (PC) market is one of the most remarkable success stories of the last quarter century. If you own a home PC or an electronic notebook and you live in the United States, then there is a one in three possibility that it arrived on your doorstep packed in boxes labelled 'Dell'. Whilst Dell has a smaller proportion of the PC market outside the USA (it is locked in close competition with its nearest rival, Hewlett-Packard, which overtook Dell to become the biggest seller of PCs in late 2008) there remains a strong possibility that your new PC was assembled in Limerick, Penang or Xiamen. Any of these is a very long way from the bedroom of a campus dormitory at the University of Texas at Austin, which is where Michael Dell began to build and sell computers directly to customers in 1984 before dropping out of college to run his business full-time.

Michael Dell transformed a business run from his bedroom at university to one of the leading companies in the IT market.

Source: Rex Features

In 1984, building a PC from components was still a specialised activity, and while some people were able to assemble their own equipment in order to save money and get precisely what they wanted, the majority of domestic customers bought ready-made products from retailers. The distribution channel for the industry usually contained five components: supplier (of components, chips, software etc.), manufacturer, distributor, retailer and customer. Michael Dell's idea was to sell direct, and at the same time allow customers to have a PC partly tailored to their personal requirements by choosing options from a list of components and specifications which he would then assemble to order. This move eliminated two of the five elements of the distribution channel (the distributors and the retailers) leaving only three players: the suppliers, Dell and the customer.[90]

The opportunity to develop this new approach into a successful business was made possible by the coalescence of three trends: increased levels of consumer confidence and knowledge about the product itself; better and faster software which enabled first the phone-based and then the internet-based ordering system to run effectively; and finally technological and manufacturing advances which enabled Dell to lower the price of a PC to a level where it clearly became good value for money. Whilst Dell supplied both business and individual customers, it was in the home PC market that the approach had particular success. Each computer was assembled to order, with components purchased from suppliers as they were required, so

ability to pull together both its own efforts and those of other organisations (i.e. component manufacturers, transport and logistics organisations, delivery companies etc.), often in far-flung regions of the world, to put together a package which offered both reliability and value for money for its customers. As we have seen, its original strength was in its ability to cut out the 'middle man' and deliver that package quickly and cheaply. But the IT business is both highly competitive and a dizzyingly fast-moving environment; and in the early years of the 21st century Dell had to rebalance the content of its package. The area where the Dell operation proved most vulnerable was that of customer service and technical support. In the more traditional world of retail outlets, customers were able to discuss purchases and return faulty equipment or seek support at a store. Such a network of customer support was absent from the Dell model.

Initially Dell outsourced customer support (along with delivery), but as expectations about after-sales service rose, its call centre support lagged behind these expectations resulting in some very public criticism,[93] not least of which was in the form of a long-running critical blog by dissatisfied customer and journalist Jeff Jarvis.[94] Dell brought its technical support centres back in-house; two were based in Canada, but mostly they were 'offshored' (but not 'outsourced') to the Philippines, Malaysia and India, where Dell opened new Business Centres in 2007.[95] It also launched its own blog[96] as a means of capturing and responding to customer complaints. In July 2006, Dell's share price

Dell was able to identify and respond to customer preferences and industry trends very quickly, and without a significant amount of capital being tied up in inventory or stock (the value of which would be declining rapidly as new and better products emerged). The system had the added advantage that customers pre-paid for the goods, thus placing Dell on a firm financial footing from the outset.

While this approach to the manufacture of consumer goods is by no means unique (the 'lean manufacturing' approach is widely used in the car industry for example) and other players in the IT market adopted it, Dell was able to make it work more successfully than its competitors. The basic business model transferred readily to the internet, where the process of 'mass customisation' can be managed even more effectively on-line.[91] Dell's growth at the turn of the century took it worldwide, and it was placed first in a ranking of the 'Most Admired Companies' by *Fortune* magazine in February 2005.[92] Dell has also won accolades for ethical standards of corporate behaviour.

Not all plain sailing

The brand image which helped put Dell at the top of Fortune's list in 2005 depended very heavily on its

The soul of Dell

Dell is keen to balance business performance with responsible operations; the overall general philosophy is described by the company as 'The Soul of Dell'[98] and the Code of Conduct reflects its ambitions to

> conduct business the Dell Way – the right way, which is 'Winning with Integrity'. Simply put, we want all members of our team, along with our shareholders, customers, suppliers and other stakeholders, to understand that they can believe what we say and trust what we do.[99]

Feedback from the workforce as well as customers is clearly critical to the success of Dell, and the workforce is encouraged to get involved in the process through its 'Tell Dell' system.

> There is change happening all across Dell, creating a revolution in how we interact and drive for business results. Processes are changing, attitudes are shifting, objectives are being aligned, careers are being enhanced and people are listening. Closely. At the core of it is Tell Dell. The Tell Dell survey program has been continually refined over the past several years from being a good informational instrument to its current use as a critical analytic and diagnostic tool for making Dell a better place to work and a stronger company. Part of the Winning Culture philosophy is to engage directly with our employees, the way we do with our customers. As managers at Dell, it is critical that we support our Winning Culture by working to deliver an unbeatable employee experience each and every day.
>
> Ro Parra and Joe Marengi, Senior Vice Presidents of Americas.[100]

dropped substantially after a profit warning was issued following the decision to make a major investment in customer support systems.[97] The task then facing Dell's management was to persuade investors that the proposed plan would result in a long-term improvement of the company's ability to stay ahead of the game and ultimately deliver a good return on investment.

Why was this move necessary? To a large extent, the very success of Dell at the cheaper end of the market meant that similar low-cost operators ceased to be a major competitive threat by the end of the 1990s. However, as home computers became big business for more up-market companies and those which had previously focused on business customers, Dell found itself competing directly with the very companies it had side-stepped in the 1990s: Hewlett-Packard, Lenovo (the Chinese company which bought the IBM computer manufacturing arm in 2005) and even Sony. These organisations were not only able to provide high-quality, reliable products, but also had much stronger customer service support. This revealed a strategic weakness in Dell's operation and forced it to raise its game not only in terms of the computing power it delivers, but also in terms of its after-sales service.

Talking to Hyderabad

This case study is being written on a Dell computer. It was ordered from the front room of a terraced house in the south of England at about 10pm one March evening. Within minutes, I had an email from Sunita at the Hyderabad Customer Experience Centre to say she would be tracking my order to completion and giving me updates on its progress. I could look at the progress it was making by following events on the website, which told me that the components were on their way to Limerick, then that the PC had been assembled, then that it had been dispatched to the distribution hub where it was joined by the chosen accessories. I could see when it crossed from Ireland to the UK and when it had reached the local distribution centre, and finally Sunita phoned me to announce the delivery day and time about one week after the order was placed.

She rang again to ensure that it had arrived and was operating to my satisfaction. When I mentioned that the cooling fan seemed rather noisy, she logged a call to the technical support team (also in India) and I found myself, phone in one hand, screwdriver in the other, involved in what can only be described as the postmodern experience of running a diagnostic test on my PC, with Sunita's colleague talking me through the process of opening the operating unit, dismantling the fan and checking the nature of the fault. As a result, a local engineer was dispatched with a replacement component. Within ten days the whole operation was complete to both my and Sunita's satisfaction, and we said our farewells.

Your tasks

1 Analyse the organisational choices that Dell has made using two of the four main analytical models that are presented in Figure 2.1. Which approach do you think is more appropriate and why?

2 What are the main organisational challenges which Dell faces in order to 'conduct business the Dell Way?' What are the implications for line managers and supervisors of creating a corporate culture based on the Dell Way?

3 Dell is using technologically sophisticated methods to collect 'soft' data about its performance from both customers (Direct2Dell) and staff (Tell Dell). Evaluate these initiatives, and discuss the value of such information in relation to 'hard' data (such as sales figures, share price etc.) as a management tool.

4 Critically review the concept of postmodernism as a means of understanding the nature of highly diverse (in terms of geography, technology, organisation, technical specialisation and culture) organisations such as Dell.

Review Questions and Tests

REVIEW AND DISCUSSION QUESTIONS

1 Assess critically the relevance of scientific management to present-day organisations. Illustrate your answer with reference to your own organisation.

2 To what extent is there anything positive to be said for bureaucratic structures? Select a large-scale organisation of your choice and suggest ways in which it displays characteristics of a bureaucracy.

3 What are the main conclusions that can be drawn from the Hawthorne experiments? Discuss critically the relevance of these experiments for management and organisational behaviour today.

4 Summarise the main features of the neo-human relations approach to organisation and management. How does it differ from other approaches?

5 Evaluate the application of the systems approach to the analysis of work organisations. Suggest an example of a work situation in which the systems approach might be appropriate.

6 Contrast approaches to improving organisational performance based on attention to technical and structural requirements with those based on concern for psychological and social factors.

7 Explain what is meant by a social action approach. Assess critically the practical relevance of 'action theory'.

8 Identify, and outline briefly, major trends in management theory since the beginning of this century. Debate critically the extent to which the ideas of management gurus have any practical relevance or benefits for managers.

PERSONAL AWARENESS AND SKILLS EXERCISE

Objectives

Completing this exercise should help you to enhance the following skills:

■ Demonstrate your knowledge and understanding of scientific management techniques.

■ Write an objective set of instructions for undertaking a simple piece of work.

Exercise

Using the example from Figure 2.2 as a model, you are required to develop a *detailed* programme using scientific management techniques for any *two* of the following simple domestic tasks:

■ booking an airline ticket;

■ cooking a simple meal (for example spaghetti bolognese);

■ bathing a small child;

■ rearranging 100 CDs in some form of order, 10 to each shelf;

■ washing up after a small dinner party;

■ renewing your passport.

Discussion

■ What are the potential upsides and downsides of removing operator discretion in this way?

■ Explain with supporting reasons those tasks or activities that you believe are particularly suited to a scientific management approach.

■ How do you feel about carrying out routine tasks on an ongoing basis over which you are given little personal discretion?

Chapter 2:

The Role of the Manager

1.1   Introduction

An **entrepreneur** is someone with a new venture, project or activity, and is usually associated with creative thinking, driving innovation and championing change.

The Ryanair case illustrates several aspects of management. A group of **entrepreneurs** saw an opportunity in the market, and created an organisation to take advantage of it. They bring resources together and transform them into a service which they sell to customers. They differ from their competitors by using different resources (e.g. secondary airports) and different ways to transform these into outputs (e.g. short turnrounds). They have been innovative in the way they run the business, such as in identifying what some customers valued in a flight – cost rather than luxury – and carried a record 65 million passengers in 2009.

Innovation is usually concerned with product or service development.

Entrepreneurs such as Michael O'Leary of Ryanair are always looking for ways to **innovate** and make the most of new opportunities. Other managers face a different challenge – more demand with less resources. Those managing the United Nations World Food Programme struggle to raise funds from donor countries – aid is falling while hunger is increasing. In almost every public healthcare organisation, managers face a growing demand for treatment, but have fewer resources with which to provide it.

Organisations of all kinds – from rapidly growing operations such as Facebook to established businesses such as Royal Dutch Shell or Marks & Spencer – depend on people at all levels who can run the current business efficiently and also innovate. This book is about the knowledge and skills that enable people to meet these expectations, and so build a satisfying and rewarding management career.

Figure 1.1 illustrates the themes of this chapter. It represents the fact that people draw resources from the external environment and manage their transformation into outputs that they hope are of greater value. They pass these back to the environment, and the value they obtain in return (money, reputation, goodwill, etc.) enables them to attract new resources to continue in business (shown by the feedback arrow from output to input). If the outputs do not attract sufficient resources, the enterprise will fail.

The chapter begins by examining the significance of managed organisations in our world. It then outlines what management means, and introduces theories about the nature of managerial work. Finally, it introduces ideas on studying management.

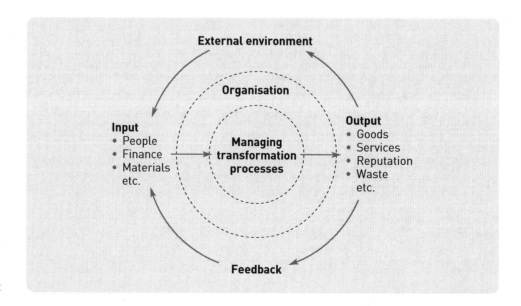

Figure 1.1
Managing organisation and environment

Activity 1.1   **What is management?**

Write a few notes summarising what you think 'management' means.

- You may find it helpful to think of instances in which you have encountered 'management' – such as when you have been managed in your school or university.
- Alternatively, reflect on an occasion when you have managed something, such as a study project. Keep the notes so you can refer to them.

1.2   Managing to add value to resources

We live in a world of managed **organisations**. We experience many every day – domestic arrangements (family or flatmates), large public organisations (the postal service), small businesses (the newsagent), well-known private companies (the jar of coffee) or a voluntary group (the club we attended). They affect us and we judge their performance. Did the transaction work smoothly or was it chaotic? Was the service good, reasonable or poor? Will you go there again?

> An **organisation** is a social arrangement for achieving controlled performance towards goals that create value.

Key ideas   Joan Magretta on the innovation of management

What were the most important innovations of the past century? Antibiotics and vaccines that doubled, or even tripled, human life spans? Automobiles and aeroplanes that redefined our idea of distance? New agents of communication, such as the telephone, or the chips, computers and networks that are propelling us into a new economy?

All of these innovations transformed our lives, yet none of them could have taken hold so rapidly or spread so widely without another. That innovation is the discipline of management, the accumulating body of thought and practice that makes organisations work. When we take stock of the productivity gains that drive our prosperity, technology gets all of the credit. In fact, management is doing a lot of the heavy lifting.

Source: Magretta (2002), p. 1.

As human societies become more specialised, we depend more on others to satisfy our needs. We meet some of these by acting individually or within family and social groups: organisations provide the rest. Good managers make things work – so that aid is delivered, roads are safe, shops have stock, hospitals function and all the rest. They do not do the work themselves, but build an organisation with the resources *and* competences to deliver what people need (Johnson *et al.*, 2008, pp. 95–6). **Tangible resources** are physical assets such as plant, people and finance – things you can see and touch. **Intangible resources** are non-physical assets such as information, reputation and knowledge.

> **Tangible resources** are the physical assets of an organisation such as plant, people and finance.

> **Intangible resources** are non-physical assets such as information, reputation and knowledge.

To transform these resources into valuable goods and services people need to work together. They need to know what to do, understand their customers, deal with enquiries properly and generally make the transaction work well. Beyond that, they look for opportunities to improve, be innovative and learn from experience. Good managers bring out the best in their staff so that they willingly 'go the extra mile': together they develop effective ways of working that become second nature. These 'ways of working' are **competences** – skills, procedures or systems that enable people to use resources productively. The managers role is to secure and retain resources and competences so that the organisation adds **value** – it is producing an output that is more valuable than the resources it has used.

> **Competences** are the skills and abilities by which resources are deployed effectively – systems, procedures and ways of working.

> **Value** is added to resources when they are transformed into goods or services that are worth more than their original cost plus the cost of transformation.

Well-managed organisations create value in many ways. If you buy a ticket from Ryanair, you can easily measure the tangible value of a cheap flight. In other purchases the value is intangible, as people judge a product by its appearance, what it feels or smells like, how trendy it is or whether it fits their image. Others value good service, or a clear set of instructions. Good managers understand what customers value and build an organisation to satisfy them.

Management in practice   Creating value at DavyMarkham   www.davymarkham.com

Kevin Parkin is Managing Director (and part-owner) of DavyMarkham, a small engineering company. Although the company has a long history, by the mid-1990s it was making regular losses, and its survival was in doubt. Since Mr Parkin joined the company he has returned it to profit, and in 2009 was predicting a 10 per cent increase in sales the following year. He has concentrated on identifying what the company is good at, and then using tough management and financial discipline to make sure staff follow the recipe for success. Mr Parkin has removed poor managers, walks the shop floor twice a day to check on progress, and engages with the workforce.

It's been essential to tell people the truth about the business, whether it's good or bad, and giving them the enthusiasm they require to make them want to succeed . . . I also ask [my 'mentors' – people I have known in previous jobs] about key strategic decisions, people issues, market penetration, capital spending and general business solutions.

Source: From an article by Peter Marsh and Andrew Bounds, *Financial Times*, 27 May 2009.

Commercial organisations of all kinds (business start-ups, small and medium-sized enterprises (SMEs), online firms and international enterprises) aim to add value and create wealth. So do voluntary and not-for-profit organisations – by educating people, counselling the troubled or caring for the sick. There are about 190,000 charities in England and Wales, with annual incoming resources of over £50 billion (equal to about 3 per cent of gross domestic product), and employing over 660,000 staff (Charities Commission Annual Report for 2008–9, at **www.charitycommission.gov.uk**). Managing a large charity is at least as demanding a job as managing a commercial business, facing similar challenges of adding value to limited resources. Donors and recipients expect them to manage resources well so that they add value to them.

Theatres, orchestras, museums and art galleries create value by offering inspiration, new perspectives or unexpected insights. Other organisations add value by serving particular interests – such as Unison, a trade union that represents workers in the UK public sector, or the Law Society, which defends the interests of lawyers. Firms in most industries create trade organisations to protect their interests by lobbying or public relations work.

While organisations aim to add value, many do not do so. If people work inefficiently they will use more resources than customers will pay for. They may create pollution and waste, and so destroy wealth. Motorway builders create value for drivers, residents of by-passed villages, and shareholders – but destroy value for some people if the route damages an ancient woodland rich in history and wildlife. The idea of creating value is subjective and relative.

Managers face some issues that are unique to the setting in which they operate (charities need to maintain the support of donors) and others which arise in most organisations (business planning or ensuring quality). Table 1.1 illustrates some of these diverse settings, and their (relatively) unique management challenges – which are in addition to challenges that are common to all.

Table 1.1 Where people manage

Setting – industry or type	Examples in this book	'Unique' challenges
Business start-ups	Innocent Drinks in the early days – Part 1 case	Securing funding to launch and enough sales of an unknown product to sustain cash-flow. Building credibility
Small and medium-sized enterprises (SMEs)	DavyMarkham – MIP feature above	Generating enough funds to survive, innovate and enter new markets
Professional business services	Hiscox (insurance) – MIP feature in Chapter 11	Managing highly-qualified staff delivering customised, innovative services
Voluntary, not-for-profit organisations and charities	Eden Project – Chapter 15 case	Providing an experience which encourages visitors to return, raising funds for educational work, fulfilling mission
Public sector organisations	Crossrail – Chapter 6 case	Managing high-profile political and commercial interests
Large private businesses	Virgin Media – Part 4 case	Controlling diverse activities
Online firms	Google – Chapter 12 case; Apple – Chapter 14 case	Maintaining constant innovation in rapidly changing market
International businesses	Starbucks – Chapter 4 case Zara – Chapter 19 case	Managing diverse activities across many cultures; balancing central control and local initiative

Note: MIP = Management in Practice

Whatever its nature, the value an organisation creates depends on how well those who work there develops its capabilities.

Activity 1.2   Focus on management settings

Choose ONE of the settings in Table 1.1 which interests you. Gather information about an organisation of that type (using, for example, case studies in this book or someone you know who works in that setting) so you can:

- Name one organisation in that setting.
- Identify how it adds value to resources, and the main management challenges it faces.
- Collect evidence about the managing in that setting.
- Compare your evidence with someone who has gathered data about a different setting, and summarise similarities or differences in the management challenges.

<table>
<tr><td></td><td></td></tr>
</table>

1.3	**Meanings of management**

Management as a universal human activity

Management as a universal human activity occurs whenever people take responsibility for an activity and consciously try to shape its progress and outcome.

As individuals we run our lives and careers: in this respect we are managing. Family members manage children, elderly dependants and households. Management is both a **universal human activity** and a distinct occupation. In the first sense, people manage an infinite range of activities:

> When human beings 'manage' their work, they take responsibility for its purpose, progress and outcome by exercising the quintessentially human capacity to stand back from experience and to regard it prospectively, in terms of what will happen; reflectively, in terms of what is happening; and retrospectively, in terms of what has happened. Thus management is an expression of human agency, the capacity actively to shape and direct the world, rather than simply react to it. (Hales, 2001, p. 2)

A **manager** is someone who gets things done with the aid of people and other resources.

Management is the activity of getting things done with the aid of people and other resources.

Rosemary Stewart (1967) expressed this idea when she described a **manager** as someone who gets things done with the aid of people and other resources, which defines **management** as the activity of getting things done with the aid of people and other resources. So described, management is a universal human activity – domestic, social and political – as well as in formally established organisations.

In pre-industrial societies people typically work alone or in family units, controlling their time and resources. They decide what to make, how to make it and where to sell it, combining work and management to create value. Self-employed craftworkers, professionals in small practices, and those in a one-person business do this every day. We all do it in household tasks or voluntary activities in which we do the work (planting trees or selling tickets for a prize draw) and the management activities (planning the winter programme).

Activity 1.3	**Think about the definition**

Choose a domestic, community or business activity you have undertaken.

- What, specifically, did you do to 'get things done with the aid of people and other resources'?
- Decide if the definition accurately describes 'management'.
- If not, how would you change it?

Management as a distinct role

Management as a distinct role develops when activities previously embedded in the work itself become the responsibility not of the employee but of owners or their agents.

Human action can also separate the 'management' element of a task from the 'work' element, thus creating 'managers' who are in some degree apart from those doing the work. **Management as a distinct role** emerges when external parties, such as a private owner of capital, or the state, gain control of a work process that a person used to complete themselves. These parties may then dictate what to make, how to make it and where to sell it. Workers become employees selling their labour, not the results of their labour. During industrialisation in Western economies, factory owners took control of the physical and financial means of production. They also tried to control the time, behaviour and skills of those who were now employees rather than autonomous workers.

The same evolution occurs when someone starts an enterprise, initially performing the *technical* aspects of the work itself – writing software, designing clothes – and also more *conceptual* tasks such as planning which markets to serve or deciding how to raise money.

If the business grows and the entrepreneur engages staff, he or she will need to spend time on *interpersonal* tasks such as training and supervising their work. The founder progressively takes on more management roles – a **role** being the expectations that others have of someone occupying a position. It expresses the specific responsibilities and requirements of the job, and what someone holding it should (or should not) do.

> A **role** is the sum of the expectations that other people have of a person occupying a position.

This separation of management and non-management work is not inevitable or permanent. People deliberately separate the roles, and they can also bring them together. As Henri Fayol (1949) (of whom you will read more in Chapter 2) observed:

> Management . . . is neither an exclusive privilege nor a particular responsibility of the head or senior members of a business; it is an activity spread, like all other activities, between head and members of the body corporate. (p. 6)

Key ideas   **Tony Watson on separating roles**

All humans are managers in some way. But some of them also take on the formal occupational work of being managers. They take on a role of shaping . . . work organisations. Managers' work involves a double . . . task: managing others and managing themselves. But the very notion of 'managers' being separate people from the 'managed', at the heart of traditional management thinking, undermines a capacity to handle this. Managers are pressured to be technical experts, devising rational and emotionally neutral systems and corporate structures to 'solve problems', 'make decisions', 'run the business'. These 'scientific' and rational–analytic practices give reassurance but can leave managers so distanced from the 'managed' that their capacity to control events is undermined. This can mean that their own emotional and security needs are not handled, with the effect that they retreat into all kinds of defensive, backbiting and ritualistic behaviour which further undermines their effectiveness.

Source: Watson (1994), pp. 12–13.

Someone in charge of part of, say, a production department will usually be treated as a manager and referred to as one. The people who operate the machines will be called something else. In a growing business such as Ryanair, the boundary between 'managers' and 'non-managers' is likely to be very fluid, with all staff being ready to perform a range of tasks, irrespective of their title. Hales' (2006) research shows how first-line managers now hold some responsibilities traditionally associated with middle managers. They are still responsible for supervising subordinates, but often also have to deal with costs and customer satisfaction – previously a middle manager's job.

1.4   Specialisation between areas of management

As an organisation grows, senior managers usually create separate functions and a hierarchy, so that management itself becomes divided (there are exceptions such as W.L. Gore Associates – see Chapter 17 – but these are still a small minority).

Functional specialisation

General managers typically head a complete unit of the organisation, such as a division or subsidiary, within which there will be several functions. The general manager is responsible for the unit's performance, and relies on the managers in charge of each function. A small

> **General managers** are responsible for the performance of a distinct unit of the organisation.

Functional managers are responsible for the performance of an area of technical or professional work.

Line managers are responsible for the performance of activities that directly meet customers' needs.

organisation will have only one or two general managers, who will also manage the functions. At Shell UK the most senior general manager in 2010 was James Smith, the Chairman.

Functional managers are responsible for an area of work – either as line managers or staff managers. **Line managers** are in charge of a function that creates value directly by supplying products or services to customers: they could be in charge of a retail store, a group of nurses, a social work department or a manufacturing area. Their performance significantly affects business performance and image, as they and their staff are in direct contact with customers or clients. At Shell, Mike Hogg was (in 2010) the General Manager of Shell Gas Direct, while Melanie Lane was General Manager, UK Retail.

Management in practice   The store manager – fundamental to success

A manager with extensive experience of retailing commented:

The store manager's job is far more complex that it may at first appear. Staff management is an important element and financial skills are required to manage a budget and the costs involved in running a store. Managers must understand what is going on behind the scenes – in terms of logistics and the supply chain – as well as what is happening on the shop floor. They must also be good with customers and increasingly they need outward-looking skills as they are encouraged to take high-profile roles in the community.

Source: Private communication from the manager.

Staff managers are responsible for the performance of activities that support line managers.

Project managers are responsible for managing a project, usually intended to change some element of an organisation or its context.

Staff managers are in charge of activities such as finance, personnel, purchasing or legal affairs which support the line managers, who are their customers. Staff in support departments are not usually in direct contact with external customers, and so do not earn income directly for the organisation. Managers of staff departments operate as line managers within their unit. At Shell, in 2010 Bob Henderson was Head of Legal, and Kate Smith was Head of UK Government Relations.

Project managers are responsible for a temporary team created to plan and implement a change, such as a new product or system. Mike Buckingham, an engineer, managed a project to implement a new manufacturing system in a van plant. He still had line responsibilities for aspects of manufacturing, but worked for most of the time on the project, helped by a team of technical specialists. When the change was complete he returned to full-time work on his line job.

Entrepreneurs are people who are able to see opportunities in a market which others have overlooked. They quickly secure the resources they need, and use them to build a profitable business. John Scott (Managing Director of Scott Timber, now the UK's largest manufacturer of wooden pallets – **www.scott-timber.co.uk**) recalls the early days – 'I went from not really knowing what I wanted to do . . . to getting thrown into having to make a plant work, employ men, lead by example. We didn't have an office – it was in my mum's house, and she did the invoicing. The house was at the top of the yard, and the saw mill was at the bottom' (*Financial Times*, 11 July 2007, p. 18).

Management hierarchies

As organisations grow, senior managers usually create a hierarchy of positions. The amount of 'management' and 'non-management' work within these positions varies, and the boundaries between them are fluid (Hales, 2006).

Performing direct operations

People who perform direct operations do the manual and mental work to make and deliver products or services. These range from low-paid cleaners or shop workers to highly-paid pilots or lawyers. The activity is likely to contain some aspects of management work, although in lower-level jobs this will be limited. People running a small business combine management work with direct work to meet customer requirements.

Supervising staff on direct operations

Sometimes called supervisors or first-line managers, they typically direct and control the daily work of a group or process,

> framed by the requirement to monitor, report and improve work performance. (Hales 2005, p. 484)

They allocate and co-ordinate work, monitor the pace and help with problems. Sometimes they become involved with middle managers in making operational decisions on staff or work methods. Examples include the supervisor of a production team, the head chef in a hotel, a nurse in charge of a hospital ward or the manager of a bank branch. They may continue to perform some direct operations, but they will spend less time on them than subordinates.

Management in practice   **Leading an army platoon**

In the British Army an officer in charge of a platoon is responsible for 30 soldiers. Captain Matt Woodward, a platoon commander, describes the job:

> As a platoon commander at a regiment you're looking after up to 30 soldiers, all of whom will have a variety of problems you'll have to deal with – helping them [sort out financial difficulties], one of them might need to go to court for something, and you might go and represent them in court, try and give them a character reference, help them as best you can. Or a soldier who has got a girl pregnant, or a soldier who has just got family problems and needs some help. Somebody else may want to take a posting back to England if they're based in Germany, or indeed if they're in England they might want to go to Germany. That's your job to try and help them out as best you can, to help manage their career to find them the best job they can but also in the place they want to be. And obviously as well as welfare and family and discipline problems we lead soldiers in the field and on operations.

Source: Based on an interview with Matt Woodward.

Managing supervisors or first-line managers

Usually referred to as middle managers, they – such as an engineering manager at Ryanair – are expected to ensure that first-line managers work in line with company policies. They translate strategy into operational tasks, mediating between senior management vision and operational reality. They may help to develop strategy by presenting information about customer expectations or suggesting alternative strategies to senior managers (Floyd and Wooldridge, 2000; Currie and Proctor, 2005). They provide a communication link – telling first-line managers what they expect, and briefing senior managers about current issues. Others face the challenge of managing volunteers. Charities depend on their time and effort, yet commonly face problems when they don't turn up, or work ineffectively – but cannot draw on the systems commonly used to reward and retain paid staff (Boezeman and Ellemers, 2007).

Managing the business

Managing the business is the work of a small group, usually called the board of directors. They establish policy and have a particular responsibility for managing relations with people and institutions in the world outside, such as shareholders, media or elected representatives. They need to know broadly about internal matters, but spend most of their time looking to the future or dealing with external affairs. Depending on local company law, the board usually includes non-executive directors – senior managers from other companies who should bring a wider, independent view to discussions. Such non-executive directors can enhance the effectiveness of the board, and give investors confidence that the board is acting in their interests. They can

> both support the executives in their leadership of the business and monitor and control executive conduct. (Roberts *et al.*, 2005, p. S6)

by challenging, questioning, discussing and debating issues with the executive members. The board will not consider operational issues.

1.5 Influencing through the process of managing

Stakeholders are individuals, groups or organisations with an interest in, or who are affected by, what the organisation does.

Whatever their role, people add value to resources by influencing others, including internal and external **stakeholders** – those parties who affect, or who are affected by, an organisation's actions and policies. The challenge is that stakeholders will have different priorities, so managers need to influence them to act in ways they believe will add value.

They do this directly and indirectly. Direct methods are the interpersonal skills (see Chapter 14) which managers use – persuading a boss to support a proposal, a subordinate to do more work, or a customer to change a delivery date. Managers also influence others indirectly through:

- the process of managing;
- the tasks of managing (Section 1.6); and
- shaping the context (Section 1.7).

Key ideas   Rosemary Stewart – how managers spend their time

What are managers' jobs like? Do they resemble an orderly, methodical process – or a constant rush from one problem to the next? One of the best-known studies was conducted by Rosemary Stewart (1967) of Oxford University, who asked 160 senior and middle managers to keep a diary for four weeks. This showed that they typically worked in a fragmented, interrupted fashion. Over the four weeks they had, on average, only nine periods of 30 minutes or more alone, with 12 brief contacts each day. They spent 36 per cent of their time on paperwork (writing, dictating, reading, calculating) and 43 per cent in informal discussion. They spent the remainder on formal meetings, telephoning and social activities.

The research team also found great variety between managers, identifying five distinct profiles based not on level or function but on how they spent their time:

- **Emissaries** spent most time out of the organisation, meeting customers, suppliers or contractors.
- **Writers** spent most time alone reading and writing, and had the fewest contacts with other managers.
- **Discussers** spent most time with other people and with their colleagues.
- **Troubleshooters** had the most fragmented work pattern, with many brief contacts, especially with subordinates.
- **Committee members** had a wide range of internal contacts, and spent much time in formal meetings.

Source: Stewart (1967).

Henry Mintzberg – ten management roles

Mintzberg (1973) observed how (five) chief executives spent their time, and used this data to create a frequently quoted model of management roles. Like Stewart he noted that managers' work was varied and fragmented (see Key Ideas), and contained ten roles in three categories – informational, interpersonal and decisional. Managers can use these roles to influence other people. Table 1.2 describes them, and illustrates each with a contemporary example provided by the manager of a school nutrition project.

Informational roles

Managing depends on obtaining information about external and internal events, and passing it to others. The *monitor role* involves seeking out, receiving and screening information to understand the organisation and its context. It comes from websites and reports, and especially from chance conversations – such as with customers or new contacts at conferences

Table 1.2 Mintzberg's ten management roles

Category	Role	Activity	Examples from a school nutrition project
Informational	Monitor	Seek and receive information, scan reports, maintain interpersonal contacts	Collect and review funding applications; set up database to monitor application process
	Disseminator	Forward information to others, send memos, make phone calls	Share content of applications with team members by email
	Spokesperson	Represent the unit to outsiders in speeches and reports	Present application process at internal and external events
Interpersonal	Figurehead	Perform ceremonial and symbolic duties, receive visitors	Sign letters of award to successful applicants
	Leader	Direct and motivate subordinates, train, advise and influence	Design and co-ordinate process with team and other managers
	Liaison	Maintain information links in and beyond the organisation	Become link person for government bodies to contact for progress reports
Decisional	Entrepreneur	Initiate new projects, spot opportunities, identify areas of business development	Use initiative to revise application process and to introduce electronic communication
	Disturbance handler	Take corrective action during crises, resolve conflicts among staff, adapt to changes	Holding face-to-face meetings with applicants when the outcome was negative; handling staff grievances
	Resource allocator	Decide who gets resources, schedule, budget, set priorities	Ensure fair distribution of grants nationally
	Negotiator	Represent unit during negotiations with unions, suppliers, and generally defend interests	Working with sponsors and government to ensure consensus during decision making

Source: Based on Mintzberg (1973) and private communication from the project manager.

and exhibitions. Much of this information is oral (gossip as well as formal meetings), or building on personal contacts. In the *disseminator role* the manager shares information by forwarding reports, passing on rumours or briefing staff. As a *spokesperson* the manager transmits information to people outside the organisation – speaking at a conference, briefing the media or giving the department's view at a company meeting. Michael O'Leary at Ryanair is renowned for flamboyant statements to the media about competitors or officials in the European Commission with whose policies he disagrees.

Interpersonal roles

Interpersonal roles arise directly from a manager's formal authority and status, and shape relationships with people within and beyond the organisation. In the *figurehead role* the manager is a symbol, representing the unit in legal and ceremonial duties such as greeting a visitor, signing legal documents, presenting retirement gifts or receiving a quality award. The *leader role* defines the manager's relationship with other people (not just subordinates), including motivating, communicating and developing their skills and confidence – as one commented:

> I am conscious that I am unable to spend as much time interacting with staff members as I would like. I try to overcome this by leaving my door open whenever I am alone, as an invitation to staff to come in and interrupt me, and encourage them to discuss any problems.

The *liaison role* focuses on contacts with people outside the immediate unit. Managers maintain a network in which they trade information and favours for mutual benefit with clients, government officials, customers and suppliers. For some managers, particularly chief executives and sales managers, the liaison role takes a high proportion of their time and energy.

Management in practice   Strengthening interpersonal roles

A company restructured its regional operations, closed a sales office in Bordeaux and transferred the work to Paris. The sales manager responsible for south-west France was now geographically distant from her immediate boss and the rest of the team. This caused severe problems of communication and loss of teamwork. She concluded that the interpersonal aspects of the role were vital as a basis for the informational and decisional roles. The decision to close the office had broken these links.

She and her boss agreed to try the following solutions:

- A 'one-to-one' session of quality time to discuss key issues during monthly visits to head office.
- Daily telephone contact to ensure speed of response and that respective communication needs were met,
- Use of fax and email at home to speed up communications.

These overcame the break in interpersonal roles caused by the location change.

Source: Private communication.

Decisional roles

Creativity is the ability to combine ideas in a unique way or to make unusual associations between ideas.

In the *entrepreneurial role* managers demonstrate **creativity** and initiate change. They see opportunities and create projects to deal with them. Managers play this role when they introduce a new product or create a major change programme – as when Lars Kolind became chief executive of Oticon (Chapter 10 case), determined to change an established and inflexible business, unable to deal with new competition. Managers play the *disturbance-handler role* when they deal with problems and changes that are unexpected.

The *resource-allocator role* involves choosing among competing demands for money, equipment, personnel and other resources. How much of her budget should the housing manager, quoted on page 22, spend on different types of project? What proportion of the budget should a company spend on advertising a product? The manager of an ambulance service regularly decides between paying overtime to staff to replace an absent team member, or letting service quality decline until a new shift starts. This is close to the *negotiator role*, in which managers seek agreement with other parties on whom they depend. Managers at Ryanair regularly negotiate with airport owners to agree on the services and fees for a subsequent period.

Mintzberg proposed that every manager's job combines these roles, with their relative importance depending on the manager's level and type of business. Managers usually recognise that they use many of the roles as they influence others.

Managers often highlight two roles missing from Mintzberg's list – manager as subordinate and manager as worker. Most managers have subordinates but, except for those at the very top, they are subordinates themselves. Part of their role is to advise, assist and influence their boss – over whom they have no formal authority. Managers often need to persuade people higher up the organisation of a proposal's value or urgency. A project manager recalled:

This is the second time we have been back to the management team, to propose how we wish to move forward, and to try and get the resources that are required. It is worth taking the time up front to get all members fully supportive of what we are trying to do. Although it takes a bit longer we should, by pressure and by other individuals demonstrating the benefits of what we are proposing, eventually move the [top team] forward.

Many managers spend time doing the work of the organisation. A director of a small property company helps with sales visits, or an engineering director helps with difficult technical problems. A lawyer running a small practice performs both professional and managerial roles.

Key ideas — Managerial work in small businesses

O'Gorman *et al.* (2005) studied the work of ten owner-managers of small growth-oriented businesses to establish empirically if the nature of their work differs from those in the large businesses studied by Mintzberg. They concluded that managerial work in these businesses is in some ways similar to that in large organisations, finding brevity, fragmentation and variety; mainly verbal communication; and an unrelenting pace.

Another observation was that managers moved frequently between roles, switching from, say, reviewing financial results to negotiating prices with a customer. They were constantly receiving, reviewing and giving information, usually by telephone or in unscheduled meetings. They reacted immediately to live information by redirecting their attention to the most pressing issues, so that their days were largely unplanned, with frequent interruptions. They spent only a quarter of their time in scheduled meetings compared with Mintzberg's finding that managers in large organisations spent almost 60 per cent of their time in this way. Finally, the owners of these small businesses spent 8 per cent of their time in non-managerial activities – twice that of those in Mintzberg's study.

The research shows that the nature of managerial work in small growth-oriented businesses is in some ways similar to, and in others different from, that in large organisations. There is the same brevity and fragmentation, but more informal communication.

Source: O'Gorman *et al.* (2005).

Managers as networkers

Does the focus of a manager's influencing activities affect performance? Mintzberg's study gave no evidence on this point, but work by Luthans (1988) showed that the relative amount of time spent on specific roles did affect outcomes. The team observed 292 managers in four organisations for two weeks, recording their behaviours in four categories – communicating, 'traditional management', networking, and human resource management. They also distinguished between levels of 'success' (relatively rapid promotion) and 'effectiveness' (work-unit performance and subordinates' satisfaction). They concluded that *successful* managers spent much more time networking (socialising, politicking, interacting with outsiders) than the less successful. *Effective* managers spent most time on communication and human resource management.

Networking refers to behaviours that aim to build, maintain and use informal relationships (internal and external) that may help work-related activities.

Wolff and Moser (2009) confirmed the link between **networking** and career success, showing building, maintaining and using internal and external contacts was associated with current salary, and with salary growth. Effective networkers seek out useful connections and contacts, and use the information and ideas they gather to create something valuable. They also look critically at their networks – are they dealing too often with people like themselves and with a similar professional background? And a network that is too extensive may take more time and energy than it is worth.

A second way in which managers influence others is when they manage the transformation of resources into more valuable outputs. Building on Figure 1.1, this involves the **management tasks** of planning, organising, leading and controlling the transformation of resources. The amount of each varies with the job and the person, and they do not perform them in sequence: they do them simultaneously, switching as the situation requires.

Figure 1.2 illustrates the elements of this definition. It expands the central 'transforming' circle of Figure 1.1 to show the tasks that together make up the transformation process.

> **Management tasks** are those of planning, organising, leading and controlling the use of resources to add value to them.

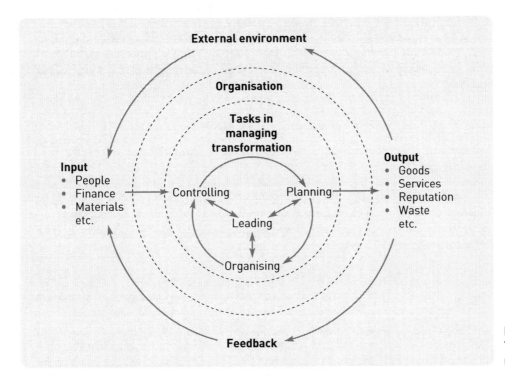

Figure 1.2
The tasks of managing

People draw inputs (resources) from the environment and transform them through the tasks of planning, organising, leading and controlling. This results in goods and services that they pass as output into the environment. The feedback loop indicates that this output is the source of future resources.

External environment

Organisations depend on the external environment for the tangible and intangible resources they need to do their work. So they depend on people in that environment being willing to buy or otherwise value their outputs. Commercial firms sell goods and services, and use the revenue to buy resources. Public bodies depend on their sponsors being sufficiently satisfied with their performance to provide their budget. Most managers are now facing the challenge of how they manage their organisations to ensure that they use natural resources not just efficiently but also sustainably. Part 2 of the book deals with the external environment.

Planning

Planning sets out the overall direction of the work to be done. It includes forecasting future trends, assessing resources and developing performance objectives. It means deciding on the scope and direction of the business, the areas of work in which to engage and how to use resources. Managers invest time and effort in developing a sense of direction for the organisation, or their part of it, and express this in a set of objective. Part 3 deals with planning.

Management in practice   Planning major rail projects   www.networkrail.co.uk

More than most civil engineering projects, rail projects depend on extensive and detailed advance planning. In 2010 the UK government announced the preferred route for the first stage of a high-speed West Coast railway line. The first stage will run from London to Birmingham, but construction is not expected to begin until 2015 at the earliest, with completion about four years later. The Crossrail project in London (see Chapter 6 case) also illustrates the scale and complexity of the planning required to build a large railway through (and below) the centre of London.

Source: Company website.

Organising

Organising moves abstract plans closer to reality by deciding how to allocate time and effort. It includes creating a structure for the enterprise, developing policies for human resource management (HRM), deciding what equipment people need, and how to implement change. Part 4 deals with organising.

Management in practice   Chris Thompson, serial entrepreneur   www.express-group.co.uk

Chris Thompson's grandfather was a shipyard worker on Tyneside and his father a draughtsman who set up Express Engineering, an engineering business, in the 1970s. While working as an apprentice toolmaker in the company, Chris Thompson also sold jeans on a market stall, and turned oil drums into barbecues in his spare time. He took over Express Engineering in 1986, and since then has created more than 40 new businesses. He has sold some to management or third parties, while remaining closely involved with about 20 of them as an investor, director or chairman, many grouped under the brand name Express Group.

The companies are in manufacturing, product development, consultancy, training and property, with many customers in relatively resilient economic sectors such as oil and gas, aerospace and defence. A senior colleague from another company says of Mr Thompson:

> He is clear and decisive. He is very considered; doesn't jump to conclusions but makes decisions very quickly. He could have simply continued with the business his father started and been very successful: he is a great example, a great role model.

As well as being closely involved with about 20 of the companies he has founded, he also takes on public sector roles, notably as deputy chair of the regional development agency:

> I enjoy the good things in life, but I'm conscious of the disparity between the haves and the have-nots.

Source: From an article by Chris Tighe and Peter March, *Financial Times*, 17 June 2009, p.12.

Leading

Leading is the activity of generating effort and commitment – influencing people of all kinds, generating commitment and motivation, and communicating – whether with individuals or in teams. These activities are directed at all of the other tasks – planning, organising and controlling – so they are placed in the middle of Figure 1.2. Part 5 deals with this topic.

Controlling

Control is the task of monitoring progress, comparing it with plan and taking corrective action. For example, managers set a budget for a housing department, an outpatients' clinic or for business travel. They then ensure that there is a system to collect information regularly on expenditure or performance – to check that they are keeping to budget. If not, they need to decide how to bring actual costs back into line with budgeted costs. Are the outcomes consistent with the objectives? If so, they can leave things alone. But if by Wednesday it is clear that staff will not meet the week's production target, then managers need to act. They may deal with the deviation by a short-term response – such as authorising overtime. Control is equally important in creative organisations. Ed Catmull, cofounder of Pixar comments:

> Because we're a creative organization, people [think that what we do can't be measured]. That's wrong. Most of our processes involve activities and deliverables that can be quantified. We keep track of the rates at which things happen, how often something had to be reworked, whether a piece of work was completely finished or not when it was sent to another department . . . Data can show things in a neutral way, which can stimulate discussion. (Catmull, 2008, p. 72)

The discussion to which Catmull refers is the way to learn from experience – an essential contributor to performance. Good managers create and use opportunities to learn from what they are doing, as the Management in Practice feature on a charity illustrates. Part 6 deals with control.

***

Management in practice **A charity which encourages learning**

The organisation is a national charity that runs residential homes for people with severe learning disabilities. It has a high reputation for the quality of the care it gives and for the way it treats the carers. Managers take whatever opportunities they can to help staff gain confidence in the difficult and often stressful work. An example:

> Staff in one area described how their manager supported their studies by creating a file for them containing information on relevant policies and legislation. The same manager recognised that a night shift worker doing a qualification was not getting the range of experience necessary to complete college assessments: 'So she took me to a review last week and also took me to a referral for a service user. I'd never seen that side before – but now I can relate to the stuff that will come up at college. It's about giving you the fuller picture, because sometimes the night shift can be quite isolating.'

Source: Unpublished research.

***

The tasks in practice

Managers typically switch between tasks many times a day. They deal with them intermittently and in parallel, touching on many different parts of the job, as this manager in a not-for-profit housing association explains:

My role involves each of these functions. Planning is an important element as I am part of a team with a budget of £8 million to spend on promoting particular forms of housing. So planning where we will spend the money is very important. Organising and leading are important too, as staff have to be clear on which projects to take forward, as well as being clear on objectives and deadlines. Controlling is also there – I have to compare the actual money spent with the planned budget and take corrective action as necessary.

And a manager in a professional services firm:

As a manager in a professional firm, each assignment involves all the elements to ensure we carry it out properly. For example, I have to set clear objectives for the assignment, organise the necessary staff and information to perform the work, supervise staff and counsel them if necessary, and evaluate the results. All the roles interrelate and there are no clear stages for each one.

Activity 1.5   **Gather evidence about the tasks of managing**

- Do the four tasks of managing cover all of your work, or did you do things that are not included? What were they?
- Give an example of something which you did in each of the tasks.
- Were there any of these to which you should have given more time? Or less?
- If possible, compare your results with other members of your course.

1.7   **Influencing through shaping the context**

A third way in which managers influence others is through changing aspects of the context in which they work. Changing an office layout, people's reporting relationships, or the rewards they obtain, alter their context and perhaps their actions. The context is both an influence on the manager and a tool with which to influence others (Johns, 2006):

It is impossible to understand human intentions by ignoring the settings in which they make sense. Such settings may be institutions, sets of practices, or some other contexts created by humans – contexts which have a history, within which both particular deeds and whole histories of individual actors can and have to be situated in order to be intelligible. (Czarniawska, 2004, p. 4)

Managers continually aim to create contexts that they hope will influence others to act in ways that meet their objectives.

Dimensions of context

Internal context

Figures 1.1 and 1.2 show the links between managers, their organisation and the external environment. Figure 1.3 enlarges the 'organisation' circle to show more fully the elements that make up the internal environment within which managers work. Any organisation contains these elements – they represent the immediate context of the manager's work. For example, as Jorma Ollila built Nokia into a major business, he and his team made many changes to technology, business processes – and, indeed, to all the elements shown in the figure (Steinbock, 2001), which later chapters examine:

- **culture** (Chapter 3) – norms, beliefs and underlying values of a unit;
- **objectives** (Chapters 6 and 8) – a desired future state of an organisation or unit;

- **structure** (Chapter 10) – how tasks are divided and co-ordinated to meet objectives;
- **technology** (Chapter 12) – facilities and equipment to turn inputs into outputs;
- **power** (Chapter 14) – the amount and distribution of power with which to influence others;
- **people** (Chapter 15) – their knowledge, skills, attitudes and goals;
- **business processes** (Chapter 18) – activities to transform materials and information; and
- **finance** (Chapter 20) – the financial resources available;

Models such as this show that managers work within constraints – they are to some degree helped or hindered by the elements in Figure 1.3. Effective managers do not accept their context passively – they initiate change to create the combination of elements to meet their objectives (Chapter 13).

Historical context

Managing takes place within the flow of history, as what people do now reflects past events and future uncertainties. Managers typically focus on current issues, ensuring that things

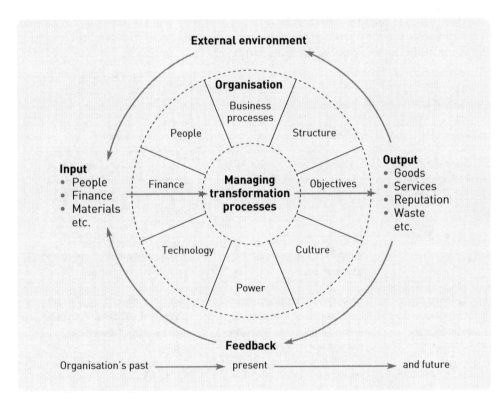

Figure 1.3 The internal and external context of management

run properly, and that the organisation works. At the same time, history influences them through the structure and culture they work within, and which affects how people respond to proposals.

Effective managers also look to the future, questioning present systems and observing external changes. Are we wasting resources? What are others doing? The arrow at the foot of Figure 1.3 represents the historical context.

External context

Chapter 3 shows that the external context includes an immediate competitive (micro) environment and a general (or macro) environment. These affect performance and part of the manager's work is to identify, and adapt to, external changes. Managers in the public sector are expected to deliver improved services with fewer resources, so they seek to influence people to change the internal context (such as how staff work) in order to meet external expectations. They also seek to influence those in the external context about both expectations and resources.

Table 1.3 summarises the last two sections and illustrates how managers can influence others as they perform tasks affecting internal, micro and macro contexts.

Managers and their context

Managers use one of three theories (even if subconsciously) of the link between their context and their action – determinism, choice or interaction.

Determinism

This describes the assumption that factors in the external context determine an organisation's performance – micro and macro factors such as the industry a company is in, the amount of competition, or the country's laws and regulations. Managers adapt to external changes and have little independent influence on the direction of the business. On this view, the context is an independent variable, as shown in Figure 1.4(a).

Table 1.3 Examples of managing tasks in each context

	Internal (organisational)	Micro (competitive)	Macro (general)
Planning	Clarifying the objectives of a business unit and communicating them clearly to all staff	Reducing prices in the hope of discouraging a potential competitor from entering the market	Lobbying for a change in a trade agreement to make it easier to enter an overseas market
Organising	Changing the role of a business unit	Reducing the number of suppliers in exchange for improved terms	Lobbying government to change planning laws to enable longer trading hours
Leading	Redesigning tasks and training staff to higher levels to improve motivation	Arranging for staff to visit customers so that they understand more fully what the customer's need	Sending staff to work in an overseas subsidiary to raise awareness of different markets
Controlling	Ensuring the information system keeps an accurate output record	Implementing an information system directly linked to customers and suppliers	Lobbying for tighter procedures to ensure all countries abide by trade agreements

Choice

An alternative assumption is that people are able to influence events and shape their context. Those in powerful positions choose which businesses to enter or leave, and in which countries they will operate. Managers in major companies lobby to influence taxation, regulations and policy generally, in order to serve their interests. On this view, the context is a dependent variable, as shown in Figure 1.4(b).

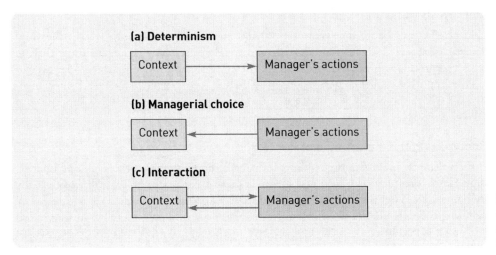

Figure 1.4
Alternative models
of managers and
their context

Interaction

The interaction approach expresses the idea that people are influenced by, and themselves influence, the context. They interpret the existing context and act to change it to promote personal, local or organisational objectives. A manager may see a change in the company's external environment, and respond by advocating that it responds by entering the market with a product that meets a perceived demand. Others interpret this proposal in the light of *their* perspective – existing suppliers may lobby government to alter some regulations to protect them from this new competitor – the players try to influence decisions in a way that best suits their interests. The outcomes from these interactions affect the context (the company enters the market or the regulations deter them from doing so) – which now provides the historical background to future action. The essential idea is that the relation between the manager and the context works both ways, as shown in Figure 1.4(c). People shape the context, and the context shapes people. Throughout the book there are examples of managers interacting with their context.

1.8   Critical thinking

Managers continually receive data, information and knowledge – but they cannot take what they receive at face value. They must test it by questioning the underlying assumptions, relating it to context, considering alternatives and recognising limitations. These are the skills of critical thinking.

Critical thinking

Brookfield (1987) stresses the benefits of thinking critically, in that it:

> involves our recognizing the assumptions underlying our beliefs and behaviors. It means we can give justifications for our ideas and actions. Most important, perhaps, it means we try to judge the rationality of these justifications . . . by comparing them to a range of varying interpretations and perspectives. (p. 13)

Critical thinking is positive activity that enables people to see more possibilities, rather than a single path. Critical thinkers 'are self-confident about their potential for changing aspects of their worlds, both as individuals and through collective action' (Brookfield, 1987, p. 5). He identifies four components of critical thinking.

Critical thinking
identifies the
assumptions behind
ideas, relates them to
their context, imagines
alternatives and
recognises limitations.

Identifying and challenging assumptions

Critical thinkers look for the assumptions that underlie taken-for-granted ideas, beliefs and values, and question their accuracy and validity. They are ready to discard those that no longer seem valid guides to action, in favour of more suitable ones. Managers who present a well-supported challenge to a theory of marketing that seems unsuitable to their business, or who question the need for a new business division, are engaging in this aspect of critical thinking.

Recognising the importance of context

Critical thinkers are aware that context influences thought and action. Thinking uncritically means assuming that ideas and methods that work in one context will work equally well in others. What we regard as an appropriate way to deal with staff reflects a specific culture: people in another culture – working in another place or at a different time – will have other expectations. Critical thinkers look for such approaches suitable for the relevant context.

Key ideas   **Techniques to help develop your ability to think critically**

1. Identifying and challenging assumptions:

   - Reflect on recent events which worked well or not-so-well; describing what happened and your reactions to it may help to identify assumptions that were confirmed or challenged by events.
   - Do the same for an achievement of which you are most proud.
   - Imagine that you have decided to leave your job and are advising the committee who will appoint your replacement: list the qualities they should look for in that person. That may indicate the assumptions you hold about the nature of your job, and what it takes to do it well.

2. Recognising the importance of context:

   - Select a practice which people in your organisation take for granted; ask people in other organisations how they deal with the matter, and see if the differences relate to context.
   - Repeat that with people who have worked in other countries.

3. Imagining and exploring alternatives:

   - Brainstorming – trying to think of as many solutions to a problem as you can in a short period, by temporarily suspending habitual judgements.
   - Gather evidence about how other businesses deal with an aspect of management that interest you: the more alternatives you find, the easier it may become to think of alternatives that could work for you.

4. Seeing limitations:

   - Acknowledging the limited evidence behind a theory or prescription.
   - Asking if it has been tested in different settings or circumstances.

Source: Based on Brookfield (1987) and Thomas (2003), p. 7.

Thinking critically will deepen your understanding of management. It does not imply a 'do-nothing' cynicism, 'treating everything and everyone with suspicion and doubt' (Thomas, 2003, p. 7). Critical thinking lays the foundation for a successful career, as it helps to ensure that proposals are supported by convincing evidence and reasoning.

Managing your studies

Studying management is itself a task to manage. Each chapter sets out some learning objectives. The text, including the activities and case questions, help you work towards these objectives, and you can check your progress by using the review questions at the end of each chapter. The questions reflect objectives of varying levels of difficulty (Anderson and Krathwohl, 2001), which Table 1.4 illustrates. Working on these will help develop your confidence to think critically in your studies and as a manager.

Table 1.4 Types of Learning Objective in the Text

Type of objective	Typical words associated with each	Examples
Remember – retrieve relevant knowledge from memory	Recognise, recall	State or write the main elements and relationships in a theory
Understand – construct meaning from information	Interpret, give examples, summarise, compare, explain, contrast	Compare two theories of motivation; contrast two strategies, and explain which theory each reflects
Apply – use a procedure in a specified situation	Demonstrate, calculate, show, experiment, illustrate, modify	Use (named theory) to show the issues which managers in the case should consider
Analyse – break material into parts, showing relation to each other and to wider purpose	Classify, separate, order, organise, differentiate, infer, connect, compare, divide	Collect evidence to support or contradict (named theory); which theory is reflected in (example of practice)?
Evaluate – make judgements based on criteria and standards	Decide, compare, check, judge	Decide if the evidence presented supports the conclusion; should the company do A or B?
Create – put parts together into a coherent whole; reorganise elements	Plan, make, present, generate, produce, design, compose	Present a marketing plan for the company; design a project proposal

Source: Adapted from Anderson and Krathwohl (2001), p. 31.

Studying is an opportunity to practice managing. You can plan what you want to achieve, organise the resources you need, generate personal commitment and check your progress. The book provides opportunities to improve your skills of literacy, reflection (analysing and evaluating evidence before acting), critical thinking, communicating, problem solving and teamwork.

The most accessible sources of ideas and theory are this book, (including the 'further reading' and websites mentioned), your lectures and tutorials. Draw on the experience of friends and relatives to help with some of the activities and questions. As you go about your educational and social lives you are experiencing organisations, and in some cases helping to manage them. Actively reflecting on these experiences will support your studies.

1.9   Integrating themes

Each chapter concludes with a section relating the topic to three integrating themes:

- achieving environmentally sustainable performance;
- meeting expectations about standards of governance and control;
- working in an increasingly international economy.

Sustainable performance

'Sustainability' features regularly in media discussion, is on the legislative agenda of most national governments, and is the subject of the Kyoto Agreement which aims to secure international action to avert climate change. Most managers are aware of the issues, and consider how changes in public opinion and legislation will affect their organisation – what are the implications for the competitive landscape, what threats and opportunities are arising, what should they do to deal with issues of sustainability so that they enhance performance? Managers in the public sector face similar pressures, being expected to provide better services with the same or fewer resources. The interest in **sustainable performance** is driven mainly by legislation, consumer concerns and employees' interest, while barriers include a lack of information on what to do, perceived difficulty in making the business case for such expenditure, and poor implementation of such proposals as are agreed (Hopkins, 2009).

Amory Lovins (Hawken *et al.,* 1999) is an influential advocate of running organisations in a sustainable way, believing that it is wrong to see it as a cost that business will need to bear. Drawing on years of advisory experience at the Rocky Mountain Institute which he helped to found, he maintains that companies who make productive use, not only of financial and physical resources but also of human and natural ones, do well. They turn waste into profit – for example, by taking a radical approach to energy efficiency in buildings, processes and vehicles, and by designing products and services so that they avoid waste.

He also acknowledges that 'turning waste into profit' does not happen easily – it needs thought and careful planning, and will change the way people throughout the organisation do things. It is no different, he suggests, from any other management innovation – people have to pay attention to the problem to find and implement a workable solution. This is likely to involve new capabilities such as being able to work on a whole system, rather than isolated parts; working with colleagues in other units; developing a culture which encourages long-term thinking; and engaging with external stakeholders. These are all part of the work of managing in organisations.

Governance and control

The shareholders of commercial companies expect to receive a return on the investment they have made in the business: unless they can be reasonably sure that a business is financially sound they will not lend money or buy shares. They can find some basic information relevant to this in the published Annual Reports, but these are inherently historical documents and cannot cover all aspects of the business. High-profile corporate collapses (see Table 5.1 on page 137 for more details) have occurred despite their Annual Reports giving the impression that all was well. There has also been widespread criticism over the pay and pensions of senior executives, especially in banks. These scandals have damaged investors and employees – and public confidence in the way managers were running these and other large companies.

Many questioned how such things could happen. Why could such apparently successful businesses get into such difficulties so quickly? Were there any warning signals that were ignored? What can be done to prevent similar events happening again? How can public confidence in these businesses be restored? These questions are all linked to corporate governance:

> a lack of effective corporate governance meant that such collapses could occur; good corporate governance can help prevent [them] happening again. (Mallin, 2007, p. 1)

Corporate governance is also relevant in the public sector. There too have been scandals about the poor delivery of service, losses of personal data, failures by staff supposed to be protecting vulnerable people, and examples of dubious expense claims and criminal charges when people award public contracts to business associates. Again people ask how this could happen, who was in charge and what can be done to put things right?

A narrow definition of corporate governance expresses it in essentially financial terms – such that it deals with the ways in which the suppliers of finance to corporations assure themselves of getting a return on their investment. Many now interpret the topic more broadly, to cover the interests of people other than shareholders, and also to include public and not-for-profit organisations. A broader view of the topic is that it is concerned with ensuring that internal controls adequately balance the needs of those with a financial interest in the organisation, and that these are balanced with the interests of other stakeholders.

Governance is an essential mechanism helping the organisation to meet its objectives, by monitoring performance towards them. It does so by:

- helping to ensure there are adequate systems of control to safeguard assets;
- preventing any single individual from becoming too powerful;
- reviewing relationships between managers, directors, shareholders and other stakeholders; and
- ensuring transparency and accountability in transactions.

Internationalisation

Developments in communications technology and changes in the regulations governing international trade have helped to steadily increase the amount of trade that crosses national borders. Managing the international activities of an organisation has become a common feature of the work of many managers – whether working as an expatriate manager in another country, being part of an international team with colleagues from many countries, or managing in an international business which works in many countries.

The international dimension is a pervasive theme of management, with implications for each of the tasks of managing – how to lead in an international environment, and the implications of an increasingly dispersed business for planning, organising and controlling the organisation. These issues will be explored not just in Chapter 4 but also as an integrating theme throughout the book.

THE ROLE OF A MANAGER

The management role is as old as history, although it only became the subject of serious study in the late nineteenth century. The organisation of the building of the pyramids in the years before 2000 BC, the exploits of generals such as Alexander the Great around 300 BC and the development of great civilisations and empires all over the world through history required management at all levels. The extent to which management is universal and involves generic skills is a point of argument and discussion. Is managing a commercial organisation all that different from managing one in the public sector? Is managing a football team very different from managing a hospital or university? There is no doubting the views of Socrates who suggested by his usual method of asking questions that successful businesspeople and generals perform much the same functions (Exhibit 20.1).

Socrates went further to argue that

> *'the management of private concerns differs only in point of number from that of public affairs. In other respects they are much alike, and particularly in this, that neither can be carried on without men, and the men employed in private and public transactions are the same.'*
>   (Adair, 1989)

The management role has always involved decision making, choice, supervision and control and has always been much more than a purely operational function. In the future, as in the past, it will include the need to forecast and plan, to organise, to command and coordinate. The role does not mean following instructions without question or carrying out routine tasks as is the case in an operational job – it does mean making decisions between different courses of action. A manager has been described as a person who decides what needs to be done and who arranges for someone to do it – and clearly a managerial job offers opportunities for making choices in what is done, how it is done and when it is done. All of this is within the context of an organisation, its corporate and ethical structure and its external environment.

It is possible to 'measure' a management job by the length of time the manager is left to work alone before the work is checked for quality. This 'time–space discretion' may be a few hours for a supervisor or foreman, a few days for junior and middle managers, up to weeks or months for senior managers. Generally speaking the more choices a manager has then the further up the management hierarchy he or she has climbed. A junior manager has a limited area of choice and limited means to manoeuvre, but the management function can be said to have clearly entered a job at the moment when a significant amount of decision making and choice enters the role.

Promotion in an organisation normally means an increase in the management function, so that decision making and choice become an increasing part of the job. The move from 'player' to 'manager' requires a considerable adjustment, one which many people find difficult to make. The brilliant salesperson, for example, may not be a good sales manager: his or her expertise is in the process of selling and making decisions within that framework not in the organising, controlling and decision making required to be a manager. At the next stage, top managers are concerned much more with planning and organising and will spend relatively little time supervising, while middle managers may spend fairly even amounts of time on planning, organising, directing and controlling. Again, the change in role will involve an adjustment which may be hard to make.

Exhibit 20.1 **Socrates**

NICOMACHIDES: Isn't it like the Athenians? They have not chosen me after all the hard work I have done since I was called up, in the command of company or regiment, though I have been so often wounded in action. They have chosen Antisthenes, who has never served in a marching regiment nor distinguished himself in the cavalry and understands nothing but money making.

SOCRATES: Isn't that a recommendation? Suppose he proves capable of supplying the men's needs?

NICOMACHIDES: Why, merchants also are capable of making money, but that doesn't make them fit to command any army.

SOCRATES: But Antisthenes also is eager for victory, and that is a good point in a general. Whenever he has been a choir-master, you know, his choir has always won.

NICOMACHIDES: No doubt, but there is no analogy between the handling of a choir and of an army.

SOCRATES: But you see, though Antisthenes knows nothing about music or choir training, he showed himself capable of finding the best experts in those activities. And therefore if he finds out and prefers the best men in warfare as in choir training, it is likely he will be victorious in that too; and probably he will be more ready to spend money on winning a battle with the whole state than on winning a choral competition with his tribe.

NICOMACHIDES: Do you mean, Socrates, that the man who succeeds with a chorus will also succeed with an army?

SOCRATES: I mean that, whatever a man controls, if he knows what he wants and can get it he will be a good controller, whether he controls a chorus, an estate, a city or an army.

NICOMACHIDES: I would never have thought to hear you say that a good business man would make a good general.

SOCRATES: For the good business man, through his knowledge that nothing profits or pays like a victory in the field, and nothing is so utterly unprofitable and entails such heavy loss as a defeat, will be eager to seek and avoid what leads to defeat, prompt to engage the enemy if he sees he is strong enough to win; and above all, will avoid an engagement when he is not ready.

Source: Adapted from J Adair (1989) *Leaders*, Guildford: Talbot Adair Press.

The so-called 'Peter principle' can come into play as people are promoted. This suggests that people tend to be promoted to their level of incompetence – that is, just above the point at which they can cope, a point where they can no longer cope. Luckily this is not always the case but it is essential for managers to discover the level at which they are confident in their ability and can be a success. This is not an easy process because ambition and higher salaries will encourage managers to seek promotion perhaps to a point where they are no longer successful. At the same time, senior managers may promote more junior managers because of their performance at that level.

Organisations have introduced training and development programmes to prepare managers for more senior levels and to attempt to assess their suitability for promotion. The armed services have had this procedure in place for many years in order to decide who should become an officer and then be promoted at every level. This type of process establishes a structured management career, which is reflected in some large companies but is becoming rarer as managers take more responsibility for their own development. John Kotter (2001) has described most US corporations at the present time as 'over-managed and underled', so that managers need to develop their capacity to exercise leadership. Kotter argues that successful corporations do not wait for leaders to emerge, they actively seek out people with leadership potential and expose them to career experiences designed to develop that potential. However, strong leadership with weak management can be worse, or no better, than strong management with weak leadership. An organisation needs both strong management and strong leadership, there needs to be an understanding of the differences between the two so that people can be developed appropriately.

Management is about coping with complexity, while leadership is about coping with change. The two overlap so that strategic management, for example, is about developing strategies that create a fit between an organisation and its environment, and ideally both leadership and management are required for this to be successful (see Zaleznik, 2004). However, while management can provide the organisation and control once a strategy has been developed, it requires leadership to decide on new strategies when the environment alters. As a result of the spread of globalisation, the development of new technology and increasing levels of competition, the organisational environment has become more volatile and major changes have become more and more necessary. This requires more leadership. A clear illustration of this difference between management and leadership is that while in peacetime an army can survive on good administration and management, in wartime an army needs leadership at all levels.

MANAGEMENT SKILLS

Managers need a diversity of skills because of the complexity of the job, including conceptual skills which involve planning and thinking, and the ability to see the organisation as a whole and the relationship of its various parts. They need to understand how their particular role fits into the total organisation. As managers are promoted, the ability to think strategically becomes more important, so that even if they find it difficult to provide leadership they can understand the leader's role. The software company Microsoft has been said to reflect, and is perhaps dependent on, the strategic decisions of Bill Gates, founder and chairman. With modern technology he is able to spread his ideas throughout the whole giant organisation via e-mail, for example the decision to move into the superhighway of communication and information technology. The senior vice-president for US sales and marketing has been quoted as saying

> *'each part of the company has a life of its own, but Bill is the glue that holds it all together.'*
> (Schlewder, 1990)

As managers are promoted into more senior positions they must develop conceptual and strategic skills or their performance will be poor and they will effectively have reached their level of incompetence, and they will not be able to become leaders. This is the problem of promoting a highly competent and successful deputy into the top position, whether this is as the CEO of a company, the head coach of a sports team or the headteacher of a school. The deputy may remain a good 'manager' but may prove to be a hopeless 'leader'. Managers have to organise, control and problem solve, while leaders have to motivate and inspire and provide direction.

In organising and controlling people, the ability to work with people is an essential skill. People management skills are demonstrated by the way a manager is able to motivate, coordinate and communicate with other people. This not only involves distributing work and resolving conflicts but also coaching and encouraging people. Managers have to relate to a wide range of people, employers, colleagues, more senior managers, customers, suppliers and members of the community – they need what has, in the last decade, been called 'emotional intelligence'. They need to have social skills to enable them to be comfortable in a range of situations, to represent the organisation confidently, to focus people's efforts on the objectives of the organisation and to encourage teamwork and a high level of motivation in order to provide for the needs of customers.

> *'Every businessperson knows a story about a highly intelligent, highly skilled executive who was promoted into a leadership position only to fail at the job.'* (Goleman, 1998)

And they may also know about someone with fewer obvious intellectual abilities and technical skills who, when promoted, has succeeded. Goleman's view is that the majority of effective leaders had one thing in common – 'emotional intelligence'. He has identified five components of this emotional intelligence and these are summarised in Exhibit 20.2.

Technical skill is the understanding of proficiency in the performance of specific tasks, whether they are concerned with product engineering, marketing or finance. These skills include specialised knowledge, analytic ability and competence in processes and procedures applied to solving problems. Such skills are more important for junior and middle managers than for senior management where human and conceptual skills are more important. However, most managers have to prove themselves in a technical area before they are given the opportunity to exhibit their conceptual and human skills. Goleman (1998) argues that IQ and technical skills are 'threshhold capabilities' in the sense that they are the entry-level requirements for executive positions. A manager can have the best training, an incisive and analytical mind and smart ideas but still not make a successful leader. A leader must have self-management skills (self-regulation and motivation) and be able to manage relationships with other people (empathy and social skills). These skills can be developed as a result of correctly focused training programmes which concentrate on changing behavioural habits and developing skills such as 'listening' and 'motivating'.

Exhibit 20.2 The components of emotional intelligence

Component	Definition	Characteristics
Self-awareness	an understanding of your own moods and their effect on others	self-confidence, realistic self-assessment
Self-regulation	the ability to control impulses and to think before acting	integrity, open to change
Motivation	a propensity to pursue goals with energy and persistence	strong drive to succeed, optimism and commitment
Empathy	the ability to understand people	expertise in retaining talent, service to customers, cross-cultural sensivity
Social skills	proficiency in managing relationships and in negotiating common ground	effectiveness in leading change and team building

Source: Based on D Goleman (1998) 'What makes a leader?', *Harvard Business Review*, November/December.

MANAGEMENT CAREERS

Management careers tend to evolve through a series of stages. These can either be seen as a fairly straightforward move from exploration through establishment and maintenance to decline; or as a more complex process of transition which occurs every five or seven years. Individual careers do not, of course, necessarily follow either of these patterns exactly, but these patterns do help in understanding where managers are in their careers and what shape the future may be.

The first stage is one of **exploration**, which occurs at the beginning of a career and is characterised by self-analysis and the exploration of the different types of available jobs. This is a stage which most people experience in their late teens and into their twenties. They may hold part-time jobs while at school or college which help them to understand about work and the type of job they may want or want to avoid if possible. The first full-time job is often not the one that people settle into these days (in contrast to the pre-1940s) and there may be some experimentation with various jobs before a career begins to be established.

A career can be seen as a sequence of work experiences which accumulate over a person's working life more or less successfully. The second stage is when the career path is **established**. This is typically when people are aged between the middle twenties and middle thirties. Jobs may now establish a pattern where the experiences of the exploration stage are put into practice and each job is sought as a progression on the previous one. Promotion is sought in the same company or in different companies and a career pattern begins to develop.

The third stage in career evolution is the **maintenance** stage where the established career pattern is maintained and nurtured. The manager's career may stabilise at this stage, grow or even stagnate. It is at this point that careers may reach a plateau where there is little further development. The last stage is the **decline** stage which usually occurs near retirement when people may not be able to maintain prior performance levels because of a loss of interest or difficulty in keeping their job skills up to date. The maintenance stage may occur at any age from the mid-thirties or forties onwards, while decline may set in during the forties, fifties or not until the sixties.

The career plateau occurs when a person becomes stuck in a particular job where the likelihood of promotion or major development is very low. In unskilled and semi-skilled work, the career plateau can start in the twenties when physical energy and motivation are at their greatest and can last until a person's forties or fifties when these factors are decreasing and the period of decline begins. In these types of work, typically seen in areas such as building and construction, earning levels may be highest in a person's twenties and thirties with a levelling off or decline thereafter. Managers hope to continue to increase their real earnings well into their fifties, but their career plateau may arrive sooner than this because of a level of ability or bad luck or poor assessment by superiors. Most people will experience it in one way or another because there is a tendency for there to be more candidates for higher-level positions than there are positions available, so that as managers rise up the hierarchical pyramid even highly successful ones eventually reach a career plateau. This is the case in terms of promotion and with flatter organisations the number of promotional steps has declined in most organisations. However, companies can no longer afford to keep large numbers of 'plateaued' managers with the consequence that redundancy and early retirement become a feature of management careers (see Figure 20.1).

Figure 20.1 **Career stages**

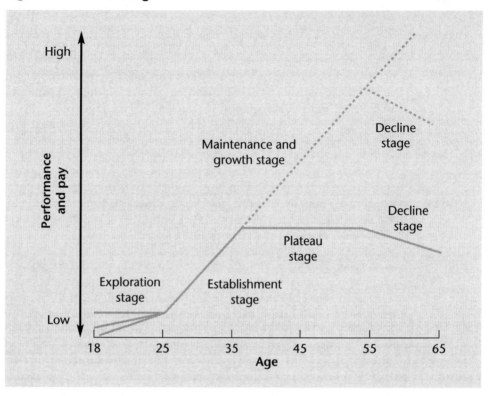

In practice, managers may reach their career plateau at any time because any promotion may prove to be the last at junior, middle or senior management level. Pay levels may reflect this situation as well so that real pay reaches a maximum as the plateau is reached. It is important for managers to recognise that they have reached this stage and to make the most of it. The plateau can be made much more interesting if sideways moves and changes in job roles are possible, or fresh opportunities open up by changing jobs or taking on new developments.

The Levinson model of career evolution (Levinson *et al.*, 1978) suggests that adult life involves a series of transitions in a fairly predictable sequence every five to seven years (see Exhibit 20.3).

The plateau in their career which managers may reach in their forties or fifties can lead to the mid-life crisis or the 'age 50 transition', and perhaps a relatively early decline. Some managers move from one job to another in an attempt to find an area of growth, while others attempt to maintain their interest in a role in which they have become expert. They have to accept that younger managers may overtake them and that they are not going to reach the top of their career path. Levinson's model may act as a guide to pitfalls and opportunities ahead, and to some extent these stages are 'proved' by the exceptional cases which are highlighted in pop music and film careers. A pop group may compress all these stages into a few short years so that they reach the top of the charts and their highest pay levels in their twenties. They then reach a brief plateau and a quick decline from which they may never recover. The more talented groups 're-create' themselves for new audiences every few years, while others move into different areas of the entertainment industry.

Exhibit 20.3 **Levinson model of career evolution**

- **Age 17–22**　**Early adult transition** – assertion of independence, breaking away from family ties. Those who prolong parental ties may underperform in their careers

- **Age 22–28**　**Entering the adult world** – a preoccupation with entering the adult world, education completed and career selection begins

- **Age 28–33**　**Age 30 transition** – review of career and life progress and feeling of last chance to change career

- **Age 33–40**　**Settling down** – job and career advancement takes precedence

- **Age 40–45**　**Mid-life transition** – another period of review, possible mid-life crisis

- **Age 45–50**　**Entering middle adulthood** – consolidation of period of review, with a possible sense of fulfilment

- **Age 50–55**　**Age 50 transition** – possible crisis or review of previous periods of transition

- **Age 55–60**　**Combination of middle adulthood** – relatively stable, with preparation for retirement

- **Age 60–65**　**Late adult transition** – retirement with review and reflection on career

- **Age 65+**　**Late adulthood** – evaluation and summing up

Source: D J Levinson, C N Darrow, E B Klein, M H Levinson and B McKee (1978) *The Seasons of a Man's Life*, New York: Knopf. Reprinted by permission of Sterling Lord Literistic Inc. Copyright © by Daniel Levinson.

It is obviously necessary for all managers to analyse their career aims and objectives, to be clear about their own abilities and shortcomings, to be realistic about the opportunities that are available and accept the fact that no one can be as interested in an individual's career as that particular person is. For an ambitious manager a career needs to be planned so that the correct steps can be taken at the right moments, but these plans are unlikely to succeed without a realistic analysis of what opportunities exist and what talents are on offer. In their study of management careers Cappelli and Hamori (2005) confirm that there have been major changes since William H Whyte wrote his 1956 classic book *The Organisation Man*, with hints of change in the 1970s clearly emerging in the 1980s and 1990s. Top executives in the top companies are now generally younger than their predecessors in the 1980s, more of them are female and they have reached the top faster increasingly moving from one company to another as their careers develop. Fewer managers are 'organisation men' employed and developed by one large corporation throughout their adult lives.

The advanced economies have changed dramatically in the last 50 years from an industrial base to a service base and towards the so-called 'knowledge economy' where companies need to be at the forefront of technology, information, knowledge sharing and learning. The typical top executives in the news today are leading companies mainly in such areas as retailing, airlines and computer software. Capelli and Hamori note that certain types of companies in general offer better chances for promotion than others. Growing companies offer the best prospects for promotion, along with young companies – and while marketing was seen as an advantageous route to the top in the 1970s, finance has been the best route since then. Companies such as

> *'General Electric, Procter & Gamble and the like provide extensive training and development opportunities. They also offer relatively long promotion ladders – hence the common notion that these "academic companies" are great to have been from.'*
>
> (Capelli and Homari, 2005)

The right time to move from a company is obviously a difficult and individual decision, but as the average age of executives falls then delays in promotion become more damaging. Other factors which can be taken into account in making decisions are such matters as the future of the company and its stage in its life cycle, along with consideration of the length of time already spent in the company:

> *'Research suggests that the odds of advancement fall as a person's tenure in a job grows. Individuals who advance to the top tend to be amongst the youngest in their cohorts – possibly because talent and ability get spotted early, possibly because of "halo" or reputation effects.'*
>
> (Capelli and Hamori, 2005)

While it may seem at first glance that the 'delayering' of company structure would provide greater opportunities for internal promotion, there may be a view that the gap between moving from one layer to another is too great in terms of experience and competencies, so that the company recruits from outside. An account manager may find that the way to the role of sales manager or sales director is blocked because there are no meaningful intermediary jobs in the company where the ability to manage people and to take responsibility for profit and loss can be proved. Small companies may provide more opportunities than large companies for proving ability in these areas.

MANAGEMENT DEVELOPMENT

In 1987 the Institute of Management (renamed the Chartered Management Institute since it received a Royal Charter in 2002) reported on the importance of managers to the economy of a country:

> *'One of the most important resources possessed by a nation is its managerial skills. Ideas can be turned into wealth when combined with effective management. The ability to create more wealth is vital if the growing expectations of society are to be met. Those services which spend the wealth must also be well managed to ensure the maximum benefit from the resources available.'*   (Constable and McCormick, 1987)

This report found that over 10 per cent of the working population were in managerial roles in Great Britain. Since then this proportion has continued to grow as more people are required to manage other people, physical resources, financial resources and information, ideas and knowledge. The report highlighted the lack of systems for management development in the UK compared to other industrial countries, a situation that has not changed dramatically in the last two decades in spite of a variety of initiatives.

In the last 20 years there have been a number of initiatives to promote management development, but the world of work has become more competitive as well as more flexible and volatile and hours of work have increased for many managers rather than fallen. An article in *Guardian Weekend* (12 June 2004) based on her book *Willing Slaves: How The Overwork Culture is Ruling Our Lives* (Bunting, 2004) asked the question 'why haven't wealth and technological development brought us leisure?' The argument is that from John Maynard Keynes to Alvin Toffler, thinkers predicted that the twenty-first century would be an 'age of leisure' and that with the expansion of automation and the rapid developments in computer technology there were concerns about how people would usefully fill their time. In fact in the last decade or so hours at work have increased rather than fallen:

> *'The office is now where the heart is, not the home, as the complexities of the workplace demand an ever larger share of our emotional resources.'*   (Bunting, 2004)

The demands of a job have been measured in terms of time and effort, to which now has to be added its emotional demands. This has partly been due to the growth of the service economy plus the emphasis on a customer focus, and partly as a result of the shake-up of the structure of enterprises and their physical organisation. An open-plan office alters the relationship between the boss and the team, while 'flatter' organisations require the individual to have qualities of empathy, persuasion and communication skills. At the same time areas of work such as call centres, with a demand for consistent politeness and friendly helpfulness, have been one of the fastest growing sources of employment. Increasing demands on people's time at work have been seen as an obstacle to initiatives in management and staff development such as Investors in People and the 'learning organisation':

> *'Often managers and employees were faced with many competing demands on their time and energy, which they had simultaneously to negotiate. These pressures can lead to role strain, or what we have described as "initiative overload."'*   (Bell *et al.*, 2002)

Initiatives in the development of managers have included those developed as a result of *The Making of British Managers* (Constable and McCormick, 1987) and *The Making of Managers* (Handy, 1987) which led to the formation of the National Forum for Management and in 1988 its executive arm, the Management Charter Initiative (MCI). Also during this period Investors in People, a state-sponsored workplace training initiative, encouraged managers to achieve a base level of good practice in the development of employees, while the 'National Targets for Education and Training' were published as a result of the Confederation of British Industry (1989) report *Towards a Skills Revolution* with the objective of making 'lifetime learning a reality throughout the workforce'. At the same time there was an increase in the number of MBAs on offer, although a report by the Chartered Management Institute (Mann, 2006) found that the boom time for MBA salaries had waned from increases of 39 per cent in 2002 to 18 per cent in 2004. This had been partly because employers who paid for their employees' MBA studies, which usually involved a contractual obligation, did not need to offer a large reward on graduation. At the same time the increase in the number of people holding MBAs may have dampened salary increases. The average age for those taking the MBA in Europe was found to be 26 to 27. A *Times* newspaper sponsored survey was reported by the CMI to have found that 'base salaries increase sharply between three and five years after graduation' and that 'average salaries three to five years after graduation were 53 per cent higher than graduates' pre-MBA salaries' (Mann, 2006).

However in spite of these and subsequent initiatives, a CMI report published in 2005 found that only 20 per cent of UK managers had a management-related qualification (Kennett, 2006). Other results showed that experience at work was more valuable for managers than natural ability, and that business performance was improved when management development was linked to business strategy. At the same time organisations such as Investors in People, the British Quality Foundation and the Learning and Skills Council supported the link between investment in management development and improved business performance.

The largest companies, such as Shell and ICI, have recognised the need for management development for a long time but there remains a difference between the demand for management development by employers and the demand by individuals. From the employers' point of view, their interest is in managers obtaining skills rather than qualifications. Some employers have been found to be opposed to qualifications because they made managers potentially more mobile. Individuals, on the other hand, want to obtain qualifications as well as skills in order to build up their curriculum vitae and to increase their opportunities in the job market. Employers have tended to emphasise job experience and innate ability as the most important factors contributing to creating an effective manager, although training would help. Education and management training has also been recognised to play an important part in broadening a manager's perspective, especially in a situation in which many managers obtain much of their experience within a single function. They may be experts in managing areas of production, or sales or finance, but may have very little knowledge across these functional borders. This not only limits the number of potential senior managers with a width of experience but can also encourage a blinkered perspective amongst managers, so that, for example, they know about production but little about the finances that provide investment and facilities.

The idea that management might become a 'profession' similar to medicine or the law has been floated at times without much support from major companies. The possibility that their managers could accumulate qualifications which might not be closely related to their actual work has sometimes been felt to be a distraction from their main occupation, so that while MBAs and other management qualifications have expanded in availability and in the number of managers obtaining them, they are often studied as a result of individual initiative rather than organisational support. In support of the Charter Group Initiative in the 1980s and 1990s, the president of the Board of Trade threw out a challenge to companies to develop the talents of their managers as an essential part of their business strategy. In practice, a survey of 258 chief executives, carried out for the *Sunday Times* (Smith, 1997), found that British managers did not have the skills to obtain the full potential from their businesses. This survey suggested that they lacked the vision and were too concerned with cost-cutting to build their businesses. The majority of the chief executives thought that the business, social and economic environment in Great Britain had created a culture in which cost-cutting was the driving force for managers instead of the development of the skills to manage growth and innovation. They believed that leadership and a strategic vision were by far the most important skills while, in practice, managers were better versed in technical and financial skills.

As managers have had to take more responsibility for and control over their careers, they have had to chart their own path through management development, balancing qualifications and courses with work experience to build up a curriculum vitae which will propel them into the first interview for a job. After this the result of subsequent interviews will depend on a manager's communication and presentational skills, the quality of the other candidates for a job and whether or not a person's 'face fits', that is whether or not the people already in a company feel that they can work with a particular candidate. A *Management Today* survey (Kennett, 2006) found that nearly half the 1000 managers surveyed from a mixture of private and public sector organisations were very ambitious and another quarter were moderately ambitious. However, over half were not actively seeking promotion and nearly 70 per cent did not want their boss's job. In five years' time, 27.1 per cent thought they would be in the same organisation in a more senior role, 19.1 per cent thought they would be running their own business, 17.4 per cent thought they would be in the same job or a similar job in another organisation and 7.7 per cent thought they would have retired. The Loyalty and Alliances Manager of BP, who had survived a radical restructuring in the company, was quoted in the survey as saying:

> *'change has become a way of life. It never stops – we have to continually reinvent ourselves. Just like Tesco. Or Madonna.'*   (Kennett, 2006)

So just as an organisation has to restructure to keep up with the competition, so ambitious managers have to make sure that their development retains their competitiveness in the job market.

Cases

Case study   Ryanair www.ryanair.com

In 2010 Ryanair, based in Dublin, was Europe's largest low-fare airline and, despite the recession, it carried almost 66 million passengers in the 12 months to the end of February: a record for that period. In 1985 the company began offering services between Dublin and London, in competition with the established national carrier, Aer Lingus. In the early years the airline changed its business several times – initially a conventional competitor for Aer Lingus, then a charter company, at times offering a cargo service. The Gulf War in 1990 discouraged air travel and deepened the company's financial problems. In 1991 senior managers decided to focus the airline as a 'no-frills' operator, in which many traditional features of air travel (free food, drink, newspapers and allocated seats) were no longer available. It aimed to serve a group of flyers who wanted a functional and efficient service, not luxury.

In 1997 changes in European Union regulations enabled new airlines to enter markets previously dominated by established national carriers such as Air France and British Airways. Ryanair quickly took advantage of this, opening new routes between Dublin and continental Europe. Although based in Ireland, 80 per cent of its routes are between airports in other countries – in contrast with established carriers that depend heavily on passengers travelling to and from the airline's home country (Barrett, 2009, p. 80).

Managers were quick to spot the potential of the internet, and in 2000 opened Ryanair.com, a booking site. Within a year it sold 75 per cent of seats online and now sells almost all seats this way. It also made a long-term deal with Boeing to purchase 150 new aircraft over the next eight years.

Several factors enable Ryanair to offer low fares:

- Simple fleet – using a single aircraft type (Boeing 737 – most of which are quite new) simplifies maintenance, training and crew scheduling.
- Secondary airports – using airports away from major cities keeps landing charges low, sometimes as little as £1 per passenger against £10 at

© Thierry Tronnel/Corbis

a major airport; it also avoids the delays and costs caused by congestion at major airports.
- Fast turnrounds – staff typically turn an aircraft round between flights in 25 minutes, compared with an hour for older airlines. This enables aircraft to spend more time in the air, earning revenue (11 hours compared with seven at British Airways).
- Simplified operations – not assigning seats at check-in simplifies ticketing and administrative processes, and also ensures that passengers arrive early to get their preferred seat.
- Flying directly between cities avoids transferring passengers and baggage between flights, where mistakes and delays are common.
- Cabin staff collect rubbish before and after landing, saving the cost of cleaning crews which established carriers choose to use.

Source: *Economist*, 10 July 2004; O'Connell and Williams (2005); Doganis (2006); and other published information.

Case questions 1.1

- What did 'management' contribute to the growth of the airline?
- Give examples of three points at which managers changed what the organisation does and how it works.

The company has continued to grow rapidly, announcing that it had carried almost 66 million passengers in the 12 months to the end of February. It now referred to itself as 'the world's largest international scheduled airline', and continued to seek new bases from which to operate its growing European network.

The airline's success depends on balancing low costs, fare levels and load factors (Malighetti *et al.*, 2009). Airline seats are what is known as a perishable good – they have no value if they are not used on the flight, so companies aim to maximise the proportion of seats sold on a flight. Ryanair uses a technique known as dynamic pricing, which means that prices change with circumstances. Typically, fares rise the nearer the passenger is to the departure date, although if a flight is under-booked, the company encourages late sales by very low fares.

Ryanair also earns a growing proportion of revenue from charges and services such as refreshments, and in 2009 it sharply increased the cost of checked-in bags: it prefers customers to carry hand baggage into the cabin. Each time a passenger rents a car or books a hotel room on the Ryanair website, it earns a commission. It sells scratch cards on board, offers in-flight gambling and online gaming over its website: the chief executive thinks that gambling could double Ryanair's profits over the next decade. The company expects revenue from ancillary activities will continue to grow more rapidly than passenger revenue.

Sources: *Economist*, 10 July 2004; *Independent*, 7 October 2006; *Financial Times*, 7 June 2006; Kumar (2006); Malighetti *et al.* (2009); and company website.

Case questions 1.2

- Which of Mintzberg's management roles can you identify being exercised in the latest stage of the Ryanair case?
- Decide which two of these roles are likely to be most critical in the next stage of the company's development, and explain why.

The company depends on securing agreements with airport operators, and also approvals from aviation authorities in the countries to which it flies. This often leads it into public disputes with airport operators and/or with the European Commission over subsidies.

In 2009 it withdrew its flights from Manchester airport when it was unable to reach agreement with the airport's owners over landing charges. Michael O'Leary takes a deliberately aggressive stance to these controversies, believing that:

> as long as its not safety-related, there's no such thing as bad publicity.

He is dismissive of traditional high-cost airlines, the European Commission, airport operators, travel agents and governments that try to protect established airlines from competition.

The Open Skies agreement reached between the European Union and the US in 2008 is intended to increase the number of flights between Europe and the US (Barrett, 2009). This offers new possibilities for Ryanair to extend the successful model from short to long flights – especially given the many people of Irish descent who live in the US.

Sources: *Business Week*, 8 May 2006; *Independent*, 7 October 2006; and other sources.

Case questions 1.3

- Which aspects of the external general environment have affected the company?
- How has the company affected these environments?
- In 2010 the company faced a strategic decision on whether to offer flights to the US. Evaluate the extent to which the factors that have supported its success would be present on these new routes.

More Than a Good Story

The management style of Life is good co-founders and brothers John (left) and Bert Jacobs is based on their personal and business philosophy of simplicity, humor, and humility.

Jake and Rocket, a cartoon guy and his cartoon dog, can be found on most of the apparel and other branded products sold by the Life is good® company.[44] With his perky beret (or other appropriate head gear), Jake has that contented look of being able to enjoy life as it is and finding reasons to be happy right now. And Rocket? Well, he's just happy to be along for the ride. And what a ride it's been for the two! They've been a part of the company's growth to over $100 million in revenues. Company co-founders and brothers, Bert and John Jacobs have a personal and business philosophy much like Jake: simplicity, humor, and humility. However, both understand that even with this philosophy, they need to be good managers and they need good managers throughout the organization in order to stay successful.

Bert and John designed their first tee shirts in 1989 and sold them door-to-door in college dorms along the East Coast and in Boston where they'd set up shop using an old card table in locations on one-way streets so they could pick up and move quickly if they needed to. They used this simple sales approach because, like many young entrepreneurs, they couldn't afford required business licenses. Although they met a lot of wonderful people and heard a lot of good stories during those early years, sales weren't that great. As the company legend goes, the brothers "lived on peanut butter and jelly, slept in their beat-up van, and showered when they could." During one of their usual post-sales-trip parties, Bert and John asked some friends for advice on an assortment of images and slogans they had put together. Those friends (some of whom now work for the company) liked the "Life is good" slogan and a drawing of Jake that had been sketched by John. So Bert and John printed up 48 Jake shirts for a local street fair in Cambridge, Massachusetts. By noon, the 48 shirts were gone, something that had never happened! The brothers were smart enough to recognize that they might be on to something. And, as the old saying goes . . . the rest is history! Since that momentous day in 1994, they've sold nearly 20 million Life is good tee shirts featuring Jake and Rocket. Bert attributes their success to his belief that "the 'Life is good' message, coupled with the carefree image of Jake, was simple enough to swallow, light enough not to be mistaken for preachy, and profound enough to matter." He goes on to say that, "Note that we don't say 'Life is great!' We say life is good, period. Three simple words. People connect with it instantly."

Another important facet of Life is good is their commitment to good causes. And those aren't just "words" to Bert and John; they act on their words. They are passionately involved with Project Joy, which is a nonprofit organization that fosters the development of at-risk children through the art of play. Bert says their partnership with Project Joy aligns with Life is good's whole philosophy. The financial commitment the company has made is supported by its Life is good Kids Foundation, which raises funds through the popular Life is good festivals and through sales of fundraising t-shirts and books at its retail stores.

Today, Life is good, based in Boston, has a product line of more than 900 items. The company continues to grow about 30 to 40 percent annually. Bert and John's style of managing is guided by another of the company's mottoes, "Do what you like. Like what you do."® As the company's Web site states, "In addition to knowledge, skills, and experience, we look to hire people who possess the same optimistic outlook on life that Jake has." It's an approach that seems to be working for Bert and John and for Jake and Rocket.

Discussion Questions

1. As the top managers of their company, what types of issues might Bert and John have to deal with? Be as specific as possible. Which management functions might be most important to them? Why?

2. Using descriptions from the case, describe Bert and John's managerial style. Would this approach work for other organizations? Why or why not?

3. How do you think the company's motto "Do what you like. Like what you do" might affect how managers manage? Be specific.

4. What managerial challenges might there be in having friends work for your business? How could these challenges be kept inconsequential?

5. Would you want to work for a company like this? Why or why not?

6. In what ways would the Life is good managers (corporate and retail store) have to deal with the challenges of customer service, innovation, and sustainability? Be specific in your description.

CASE APPLICATION

A NEW WAY OF WORKING

Being efficient and effective isn't important just for the people that managers supervise. It's also important for managers! However, that isn't always easy. A manager's job is varied, complex, and sometimes hectic. Their workdays are filled with tasks, decisions, actions, and interruptions. Just like your work on school projects, managers sometimes find that certain parts of the projects they're working on are boring and monotonous. Wouldn't it be great to have a magic button you could push to get someone else to do that boring, time-consuming stuff? At Pfizer, that "magic button" is a reality for a large number of employees.

As a global pharmaceutical company, Pfizer is continually looking for ways to help employees be more efficient and effective. The company's senior director of organizational effectiveness, Jordan Cohen (pictured above), found that the "Harvard MBA staff we hired to develop strategies and innovate were instead Googling and making PowerPoints." Indeed, internal studies conducted to find out just how much time its valuable talent was spending on menial tasks was startling. The average Pfizer employee was spending 20 percent to 40 percent of his or her time on support work (creating documents, typing notes, doing research, manipulating data, scheduling meetings) and only 60 percent to 80 percent on knowledge work (strategy, innovation, networking, collaborating, critical thinking). And the problem wasn't just at lower levels. Even the highest level employees were affected. Take, for instance, David Cain, an executive director for global engineering. He enjoys his job—assessing environmental real estate risks, managing facilities, and controlling a multimillion-dollar budget. But he didn't so much enjoy having to go through spreadsheets and put together PowerPoints. Now, however, with Pfizer's "magic button," those tasks could be passed off to individuals outside the organization.

PfizerWorks allows employees to shift tedious and time-consuming tasks with the click of a single button on their computer desktop. They describe what they need on an online form, which is then sent to one of two Indian service-outsourcing firms. When a request is received, a team member in India calls the Pfizer employee to clarify what's needed and by when. The team member then e-mails back a cost specification for the requested work. If the Pfizer employee decides to proceed, the costs involved are charged to the employee's department. About this unique arrangement, Cain said that, "He relishes working with what he prefers to call his 'personal consulting organization.'"

How beneficial has PfizerWorks been? It's estimated that 66,500 employee work hours have been saved. What about David Cain's experiences? When he gave the Indian team a complex project researching strategic actions that worked when consolidating company facilities, the team put the report together in a month, something that would have taken him six months to do alone.

Discussion Questions

1. Describe and evaluate what Pfizer is doing with its PfizerWorks.

2. We've defined managers as those individuals in an organization who direct and oversee the activities of other people in the organization. What challenges might there be for managers when those "people" are halfway around the world? How might the four management functions be useful in dealing with those challenges? What skills would managers need to be able to function effectively in this type of arrangement?

3. Do you think that PfizerWorks would work for someone who's a first-line manager? Why or why not?

4. Do you think this arrangement would work for other types of organizations? Why or why not? What types of organizations might it also work for?

Sources: M. Weinstein, "Retrain and Restructure Your Organization," *Training* (May 2009), p. 36; J. McGregor, "The Chore Goes Offshore," *BusinessWeek*, March 23 & 30, 2009, pp. 50–51; "Pfizer: Making It 'Leaner, Meaner, More Efficient,'" *BusinessWeek Online*, March 2, 2009; and A. Cohen, "Scuttling Scut Work," *Fast Company*, February 2008, pp. 42–43.

Review Questions and Tests

Review questions

1 Apart from delivering goods and services, what other functions do organisations perform?

2 What is the difference between management as a general human activity and management as a specialised occupation? How has this division happened and what are some of its effects?

3 What examples are there in the chapter of this boundary between 'management' and 'non-management' work being changed and what were the effects?

4 Describe, with examples, the differences between general, functional, line, staff and project managers.

5 Give examples from your experience or observation of each of the four tasks of management.

6 How does Mintzberg's theory of management roles complement that which identifies the tasks of management?

7 What is the significance to someone starting a career in management of Luthans' theory about roles and performance?

8 How can thinking critically help managers do their job more effectively?

9 Review and revise the definition of management that you gave in Activity 1.1.

Think about the way managers in your company, or one with which you are familiar, go about their work. If you are a full-time student, draw on any jobs you have held, or on the management of your studies at school or university. Review the material in the chapter and make notes on the following questions:

● Which of the issues discussed in this chapter are most relevant to the way you and your colleagues manage?

● What **assumptions** about the role of management appear to guide the way you, or others, manage? Are these assumptions supported by the evidence of recent events – have they worked or not? Which aspects of the content and process of managing are you expected to focus on – or are you unsure? Does your observation support, or contradict, Luthans' theory?

● What aspects of the historical or current **context** of the company appear to influence how you, and others, interpret your management role? Do people have different interpretations?

● Can you compare and contrast your role with that of colleagues on your course? Does this suggest any plausible **alternative** ways of constructing your management role, in terms of where you devote your time and energy? How much scope do you have to change it?

● What **limitations** can you see in the theories and evidence presented in the chapter? For example, how valid might Mintzberg's theory (developed in large commercial firms) be for those managing in a small business or in the public sector? Can you think of ways of improving the model – e.g. by adding elements to it, or being more precise about the circumstance to which it applies?

SECTION 2:
STRATEGY AND PLANNING

Chapter 3:

Planning

A Manager's Dilemma

A massive earthquake struck Haiti on January 12, 2010, causing catastrophic damage.[1] Mobilizing all the resources and people for the relief effort required considerable planning. The World Food Program (WFP), the world's largest humanitarian relief organization, immediately assembled land, sea, and air resources to move hundreds of tons of emergency supplies.

Lou Policastro, executive vice president of Geodis Wilson, which manages WFP's logistics, was contacted initially over the Martin Luther King holiday weekend when "nothing was open." It took four days to mobilize, load, and deliver trailers of food to Miami where it was loaded onto a ship. WFP already had moved more than 400 tons of emergency food aboard 747s and smaller aircraft, encountering delays at Port-au-Prince's airport because of all the relief flights. All told, the WFP delivered nearly 3 million meals in the first days after the quake—enough to feed the population of Port-au-Prince for one day. Policastro said, "This is the most complex operation that WFP has ever launched. Haiti presented a unique problem: an isolated island and heavily populated in the central location that was hit hardest by the quake." What types of plans might be needed to ensure that efficient and effective aid efforts continue?

What Would You Do?

You may think that "planning" isn't something that's relevant to you right now. But when you figure out your class schedule for the next term or when you decide what you need to do to finish a class project on time, you're planning. And planning is something that all managers, such as Lou Policastro and others who responded to the Haiti relief effort, need to do. Although what they plan and how they plan may differ, it's still important that they do plan. In this chapter we present the basics: what planning is, why managers plan, and how they plan.

LEARNING OUTCOME
8.1
Define the nature and purposes of planning.

The What and Why of Planning

Boeing called its new 787 aircraft the Dreamliner, but the project turned into more of a nightmare for managers. The new plane was the company's most popular product ever, mostly because of its innovations, especially in fuel efficiency. However, the plane is two and a half years behind schedule. The first airplanes are scheduled to be delivered to ANA (All Nippon Airways) in the fourth quarter of 2010. Boeing admitted that the project's timeline was way too ambitious even though every detail had been meticulously planned.[2] Some customers (the airlines who ordered the jets)—around 60 in total—got tired of waiting or responded to the changing economic environment and canceled their orders. Could Boeing's managers have planned better?

What Is Planning?

As we stated in Chapter 1, **planning** involves defining the organization's goals, establishing strategies for achieving those goals, and developing plans to integrate and coordinate work activities. It's concerned with both ends (what) and means (how).

When we use the term *planning*, we mean *formal* planning. In formal planning, specific goals covering a specific time period are defined. These goals are written and shared with organizational members to reduce ambiguity and create a common understanding about what needs to be done. Finally, specific plans exist for achieving these goals.

Why Do Managers Plan?

Planning seems to take a lot of effort. So why should managers plan? We can give you at least four reasons. First, planning *provides direction* to managers and nonmanagers alike. When employees know what their organization or work unit is trying to accomplish and what they must contribute to reach goals, they can coordinate their activities, cooperate with each other, and do what it takes to accomplish those goals. Without planning, departments and individuals might work at cross-purposes and prevent the organization from efficiently achieving its goals.

Next, planning *reduces uncertainty* by forcing managers to look ahead, anticipate change, consider the impact of change, and develop appropriate responses. Although planning won't eliminate uncertainty, managers plan so they can respond effectively.

In addition, planning *minimizes waste and redundancy*. When work activities are coordinated around plans, inefficiencies become obvious and can be corrected or eliminated.

Finally, planning *establishes the goals or standards used in controlling*. When managers plan, they develop goals and plans. When they control, they see whether the plans have been carried out and the goals met. Without planning, there would be no goals against which to measure work effort.

Planning and Performance

Is planning worthwhile? Numerous studies have looked at the relationship between planning and performance.[3] Although most showed generally positive relationships, we can't say that organizations that formally plan *always* outperform those that don't plan. What *can* we conclude?

First, generally speaking, formal planning is associated with positive financial results—higher profits, higher return on assets, and so forth. Second, it seems that doing a good job planning and implementing those plans play a bigger part in high performance than does how much planning is done. Next, in those studies where formal planning didn't lead to higher performance, the external environment often was the culprit. When external forces—think governmental regulations or powerful labor unions—constrain managers' options, it reduces the impact planning has on an organization's performance. Finally, the planning-performance relationship seems to be influenced by the planning time frame. It seems that at least four years of formal planning is required before it begins to affect performance.

Goals and Plans

8.2

LEARNING OUTCOME
Classify the types of goals organizations might have and the plans they use.

Planning is often called the primary management function because it establishes the basis for all the other things managers do as they organize, lead, and control. It involves two important aspects: goals and plans.

Goals (objectives) are desired outcomes or targets.[4] They guide management decisions and form the criterion against which work results are measured. That's why they're often described as the essential elements of planning. You have to know the desired target or outcome before you can establish plans for reaching it. **Plans** are documents that outline how goals are going to be met. They usually include resource allocations, schedules, and other necessary actions to accomplish the goals. As managers plan, they develop both goals and plans.

---

planning
Defining the organization's goals, establishing strategies for achieving those goals, and developing plans to integrate and coordinate work activities

goals (objectives)
Desired outcomes or targets

plans
Documents that outline how goals are going to be met

The goal that guides management decisions at Sykes Enterprises is that every client will be more efficient, more profitable, and have stronger loyalty to the company brands due to the services provided by Sykes. As a global outsourcing and consulting service, Sykes operates more than 40 technical help and customer support centers in the Americas, Asia, Europe, and Africa. One of the plans Sykes has for achieving its goal is to employ the best individuals in the industry and to reward them for their commitment to excellence. For example, the well-trained technicians shown here at Sykes' multilingual call center in Manila speak fluent English in responding to clients' questions and providing comprehensive service that ensures customer satisfaction.

Types of Goals

It might seem that organizations have a single goal. Businesses want to make a profit and not-for-profit organizations want to meet the needs of some constituent group(s). However, a single goal can't adequately define an organization's success. And if managers emphasize only one goal, other goals essential for long-term success are ignored. Also, as we discussed in Chapter 5, using a single goal such as profit may result in unethical behaviors because managers and employees will ignore other aspects of their jobs in order to look good on that one measure.[5] In reality, all organizations have multiple goals. For instance, businesses may want to increase market share, keep employees enthused about working for the organization, and work toward more environmentally sustainable practices. And a church provides a place for religious practices, but also assists economically disadvantaged individuals in its community and acts as a social gathering place for church members.

We can classify most company's goals as either strategic or financial. Financial goals are related to the financial performance of the organization, while strategic goals are related to all other areas of an organization's performance. For instance, McDonald's states that its financial targets are 3 to 5 percent average annual sales and revenue growth, 6 to 7 percent average annual operating income growth, and returns on invested capital in the high teens.[6] Here's an example of a strategic goal from Bloomberg L.P.: "We want to be the world's most influential news organization."[7]

The goals just described are **stated goals**—official statements of what an organization says, and what it wants its stakeholders to believe, its goals are. However, stated goals—which can be found in an organization's charter, annual report, public relations announcements, or in public statements made by managers—are often conflicting and influenced by what various stakeholders think organizations should do. For instance, Nike's goal is "delivering inspiration and innovation to every athlete." Canadian company EnCana's vision is to "be the world's high performance benchmark independent oil and gas company." Deutsche Bank's goal is "to be the leading global provider of financial solutions, creating lasting value for our clients, our shareholders and people and the communities in which we operate."[8] Such statements are vague and probably better represent management's public relations skills than being meaningful guides to what the organization is actually trying to accomplish. It shouldn't be surprising then to find that an organization's stated goals are often irrelevant to what actually goes on.[9]

If you want to know an organization's **real goals**—those goals an organization actually pursues—observe what organizational members are doing. Actions define priorities. For example, universities may say their goal is limiting class sizes, facilitating close student-faculty relations, and actively involving students in the learning process, but then they put students into 300+ student lecture classes! Knowing that real and stated goals may differ is important for recognizing what you might otherwise think are inconsistencies.

Let's Get Real

F2F

Goals are important because *they set priorities for which managers and employees should strive. Goals are often set higher than expectations, making a clear and concise plan even more important.*

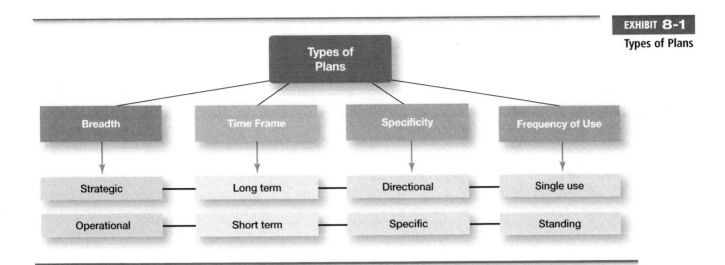

EXHIBIT 8-1

Types of Plans

Types of Plans

The most popular ways to describe organizational plans are breadth (strategic versus operational), time frame (short term versus long term), specificity (directional versus specific), and frequency of use (single use versus standing). As Exhibit 8-1 shows, these types of plans aren't independent. That is, strategic plans are usually long term, directional, and single use whereas operational plans are usually short term, specific, and standing. What does each include?

Strategic plans are plans that apply to the entire organization and establish the organization's overall goals. Plans that encompass a particular operational area of the organization are called **operational plans**. These two types of plans differ because strategic plans are broad while operational plans are narrow.

The number of years used to define short-term and long-term plans has declined considerably because of environmental uncertainty. Long-term used to mean anything over seven years. Try to imagine what you're likely to be doing in seven years and you can begin to appreciate how difficult it would be for managers to establish plans that far in the future. We define **long-term plans** as those with a time frame beyond three years.[10] **Short-term plans** cover one year or less. Any time period in between would be an intermediate plan. Although these time classifications are fairly common, an organization can use any planning time frame it wants.

Intuitively, it would seem that specific plans would be preferable to directional, or loosely guided, plans. **Specific plans** are clearly defined and leave no room for interpretation. A specific plan states its objectives in a way that eliminates ambiguity and problems with misunderstanding. For example, a manager who seeks to increase his or her unit's work output by 8 percent over a given 12-month period might establish specific procedures, budget allocations, and schedules of activities to reach that goal.

However, when uncertainty is high and managers must be flexible in order to respond to unexpected changes, directional plans are preferable. **Directional plans** are flexible plans that set out general guidelines. They provide focus but don't lock managers into

LEADER who made a difference

Jeff Bezos, founder and CEO of Amazon.com, understands the importance of goals and plans. As a leader, he exudes energy, enthusiasm, and drive.[12] He's fun loving (his legendary laugh has been described as a flock of Canadian geese on nitrous oxide) but has pursued his vision for Amazon with serious intensity and has demonstrated an ability to inspire his employees through the ups and downs of a rapidly growing company. When Bezos founded the company as on online bookstore, his goal was to be the leader in online retailing. Now fifteen years later, Amazon is quickly becoming the world's general store, selling not only books, CDs, and DVDs, but LEGOs, power drills, and Jackalope Buck taxidermy mounts, to name a few of the thousands of products you can buy.

specific goals or courses of action. For example, Sylvia Rhone, president of Motown Records, said she has a simple goal—to "sign great artists."[11] So instead of creating a specific plan to produce and market 10 albums from new artists this year, she might formulate a directional plan to use a network of people around the world to alert her to new and promising talent so she can increase the number of new artists she has under contract. Keep in mind, however, that the flexibility of directional plans must be weighed against the lack of clarity of specific plans.

Some plans that managers develop are ongoing while others are used only once. A **single-use plan** is a one-time plan specifically designed to meet the needs of a unique situation. For instance, when Walmart wanted to expand the number of its stores in China, top-level executives formulated a single-use plan as a guide. In contrast, **standing plans** are ongoing plans that provide guidance for activities performed repeatedly. Standing plans include policies, rules, and procedures, which we defined in Chapter 7. An example of a standing plan is the sexual harassment policy developed by the University of Arizona. It provides guidance to university administrators, faculty, and staff as they make hiring plans.

8.3

LEARNING OUTCOME
Compare and contrast approaches to goal setting and planning.

Setting Goals and Developing Plans

Taylor Haines has just been elected president of her business school's honorary fraternity. She wants the organization to be more actively involved in the business school than it has been. Francisco Garza graduated from Tecnologico de Monterrey with a degree in marketing and computers three years ago and went to work for a regional consulting services firm. He recently was promoted to manager of an eight-person e-business development team and hopes to strengthen the team's financial contributions to the firm. What should Taylor and Francisco do now? Their first step should be to set goals.

Approaches to Setting Goals

As we stated earlier, goals provide the direction for all management decisions and actions and form the criterion against which actual accomplishments are measured. Everything organizational members do should be oriented toward achieving goals. These goals can be set either through a traditional process or by using management by objectives.

In **traditional goal setting**, goals set by top managers flow down through the organization and become subgoals for each organizational area. This traditional perspective assumes that top managers know what's best because they see the "big picture." And the goals passed down to each succeeding level guide individual employees as they work to achieve those assigned goals. If Taylor were to use this approach, she would see what goals the dean or director of the school of business had set and develop goals for her group that would contribute to achieving those goals. Or take a manufacturing business, for example. The president tells the vice president of production what he expects manufacturing costs to be for the coming year and tells the marketing vice president what level he expects sales to reach for the year. These goals are passed to the next organizational level and written to reflect the responsibilities of that level, passed to the next level, and so forth. Then, at some later time, performance is evaluated to determine whether the assigned goals have been achieved. Although the process is supposed to happen in this way, in reality it doesn't always do so. Turning broad strategic goals into departmental, team, and individual goals can be a difficult and frustrating process.

Another problem with traditional goal setting is that when top managers define the organization's goals in broad terms—such as achieving "sufficient" profits or increasing "market

EXHIBIT 8-2

The Downside of Traditional Goal Setting

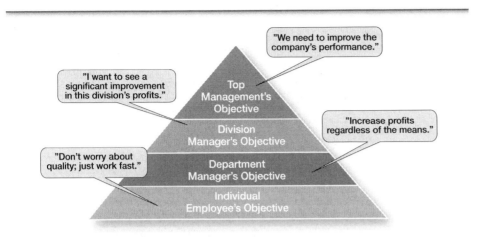

leadership"—these ambiguous goals have to be made more specific as they flow down through the organization. Managers at each level define the goals and apply their own interpretations and biases as they make them more specific. However, what often happens is that clarity is lost as the goals make their way down from the top of the organization to lower levels. Exhibit 8-2 illustrates what can happen. But it doesn't have to be that way. For example, at the Carrier-Carlyle Compressor Facility in Stone Mountain, Georgia, employees and managers focus their work efforts around goals. Those goals encompass meeting and exceeding customer needs, concentrating on continuous improvement efforts, and engaging the workforce. To keep everyone focused on those goals, a "thermostat"—a 3-foot-by-4-foot metric indicator—found at the employee entrance communicates what factory performance is at any given time and where attention is needed. "The thermostat outlines plant goals across a range of metrics as well as monthly performance against those goals." Company executives state, "We have found that well-executed pre-planning drives improved results." Does their goal approach work? In the past three years, the facility has experienced a nearly 76 percent reduction in customer reject rates and a 54.5 percent reduction in OSHA-recordable injury and illness cases.[13]

When the hierarchy of organizational goals *is* clearly defined, as it is at Carrier-Carlyle Compressor, it forms an integrated network of goals, or a **means-ends chain**. Higher-level goals (or ends) are linked to lower-level goals, which serve as the means for their accomplishment. In other words, the goals achieved at lower levels become the means to reach the goals (ends) at the next level. And the accomplishment of goals at that level becomes the means to achieve the goals (ends) at the next level and on up through the different organizational levels. That's how traditional goal setting is supposed to work.

Instead of using traditional goal setting, many organizations use **management by objectives (MBO)**, a process of setting mutually agreed-upon goals and using those goals to evaluate employee performance. If Francisco were to use this approach, he would sit down with each member of his team and set goals and periodically review whether progress was being made toward achieving those goals. MBO programs have four elements: goal specificity, participative decision making, an explicit time period, and performance feedback.[14] Instead of using goals to make sure employees are doing what they're supposed to be doing,

single-use plan
A one-time plan specifically designed to meet the needs of a unique situation

standing plans
Ongoing plans that provide guidance for activities performed repeatedly

traditional goal setting
An approach to setting goals in which top managers set goals that then flow down through the organization and become subgoals for each organizational area

means-ends chain
An integrated network of goals in which the accomplishment of goals at one level serves as the means for achieving the goals, or ends, at the next level

management by objectives (MBO)
A process of setting mutually agreed-upon goals and using those goals to evaluate employee performance

EXHIBIT **8-3**

Steps in MBO

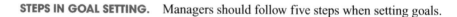

1. The organization's *overall objectives and strategies* are formulated.
2. Major objectives are allocated among *divisional and departmental units*.
3. Unit managers *collaboratively set specific objectives* for their units with their managers.
4. Specific objectives are collaboratively set with *all department members*.
5. *Action plans*, defining how objectives are to be achieved, are specified and agreed upon by managers and employees.
6. The action plans are *implemented*.
7. Progress toward objectives is *periodically reviewed*, and *feedback is provided*.
8. Successful achievement of objectives is reinforced by *performance-based rewards*.

Let's Get Real

I set goals by *carefully studying historic business data and realistically exceeding our past performance by adding incentives and making use of new and innovative marketing approaches.*

MBO uses goals to motivate them as well. The appeal is that it focuses on employees working to accomplish goals they've had a hand in setting. Exhibit 8-3 lists the steps in a typical MBO program.

Does MBO work? Studies have shown that it can increase employee performance and organizational productivity. For example, one review of MBO programs found productivity gains in almost all of them.[15] But is MBO relevant for today's organizations? If it's viewed as a way of setting goals, then yes, because research shows that goal setting can be an effective approach to motivating employees.[16]

CHARACTERISTICS OF WELL-WRITTEN GOALS.   Goals aren't all written the same way. Some are better than others at making the desired outcomes clear. For instance, the CEO of Procter & Gamble said that he wants to see the company add close to 548,000 new customers a day, every day, for the next five years.[17] It's an ambitious but specific goal. Managers should be able to write well-written goals. What makes a "well-written" goal?[18] Exhibit 8-4 lists the characteristics.

STEPS IN GOAL SETTING.   Managers should follow five steps when setting goals.

1. *Review the organization's* **mission**, *or purpose*. A mission is a broad statement of an organization's purpose that provides an overall guide to what organizational members think is important. Managers should review the mission before writing goals because goals should reflect that mission.
2. *Evaluate available resources*. You don't want to set goals that are impossible to achieve given your available resources. Even though goals should be challenging, they should be realistic. After all, if the resources you have to work with won't allow you to achieve a goal no matter how hard you try or how much effort is exerted, you shouldn't set that goal. That would be like the person with a $50,000 annual income and no other financial resources setting a goal of building an investment portfolio worth $1 million in three years. No matter how hard he or she works at it, it's not going to happen.
3. *Determine the goals individually or with input from others*. The goals reflect desired outcomes and should be congruent with the organizational mission and goals in other organizational areas. These goals should be measurable, specific, and include a time frame for accomplishment.

EXHIBIT **8-4**

Well-Written Goals

- Written in terms of outcomes rather than actions
- Measurable and quantifiable
- Clear as to a time frame
- Challenging yet attainable
- Written down
- Communicated to all necessary organizational members

4. *Write down the goals and communicate them to all who need to know.* Writing down and communicating goals forces people to think them through. The written goals also become visible evidence of the importance of working toward something.

5. *Review results and whether goals are being met.* If goals aren't being met, change them as needed.

Once the goals have been established, written down, and communicated, a manager is ready to develop plans for pursuing the goals.

Developing Plans

The process of developing plans is influenced by three contingency factors and by the planning approach followed.

CONTINGENCY FACTORS IN PLANNING. Look back at our chapter-opening "A Manager's Dilemma." How will Lou Policastro and other aid relief managers know what types of plans to develop for what needs to get done in responding to the Haiti disaster? Three contingency factors affect the choice of plans: organizational level, degree of environmental uncertainty, and length of future commitments.[20]

Exhibit 8-5 shows the relationship between a manager's level in the organization and the type of planning done. For the most part, lower-level managers do operational planning while upper-level managers do strategic planning.

The second contingency factor is environmental uncertainty, a factor that was quite obvious in the chapter-opening Haitian relief effort example. When uncertainty is high, plans should be specific, but flexible. Managers must be prepared to change or amend plans as they're implemented. At times, they may even have to abandon the plans.[21] For example, prior to Continental Airlines' merger with United Airlines, the former CEO and his management team established a specific goal of focusing on what customers wanted most—on-time flights—to help the company become more competitive in the highly uncertain airline industry. Because of the high level of uncertainty, the management team identified a "destination, but not a flight plan," and changed plans as necessary to achieve that goal of on-time service.

The last contingency factor also is related to the time frame of plans. The **commitment concept** says that plans should extend far enough to meet those commitments made when the plans were developed. Planning for too long or too short a time period is inefficient and ineffective. What happened at AT&T with the iPhone is a good example of why it's important to

EXHIBIT 8-5

Planning and Organizational Level

Strategic Planning

Top Executives

Middle-Level Managers

First-Level Managers

Operational Planning

mission
The purpose of an organization

commitment concept
Plans should extend far enough to meet those commitments made when the plans were developed

understand the commitment concept. When it secured exclusive rights to support the iPhone on its wireless network in June 2007, both Apple and AT&T vastly underestimated the phone's popularity—some 42.4 million have been sold. And then there's all those apps—at least 140,000 different ones that have been downloaded some 3 billion times—many of which consume bandwidth. AT&T's network "simply can't handle the traffic." AT&T's Operations president John Stankey said, "We missed on our usage estimates." As the company discovered, the bandwidth-hungry super-phone has created serious challenges.[22] How does this illustrate the commitment concept? In becoming the primary provider of the iPhone, AT&T "committed" to whatever future expenses are generated by that planned decision. And they have to live with the decision and its consequences, good and bad.

Approaches to Planning

Federal, state, and local government officials are working together on a plan to boost populations of wild salmon in the northwestern United States. Managers in the Global Fleet Graphics division of the 3M Company are developing detailed plans to satisfy increasingly demanding customers and to battle more aggressive competitors. Emilio Azcárraga Jean, chairman, president, and CEO of Grupo Televisa, gets input from many different people before setting company goals and then turns over the planning for achieving the goals to various executives. In each of these situations, planning is done a little differently. *How* an organization plans can best be understood by looking at *who* does the planning.

In the traditional approach, planning is done entirely by top-level managers who often are assisted by a **formal planning department**, a group of planning specialists whose sole responsibility is to help write the various organizational plans. Under this approach, plans developed by top-level managers flow down through other organizational levels, much like the traditional approach to goal-setting. As they flow down through the organization, the plans are tailored to the particular needs of each level. Although this approach makes managerial planning thorough, systematic, and coordinated, all too often the focus is on developing "the plan," a thick binder (or binders) full of meaningless information that's stuck away on a shelf and never used by anyone for guiding or coordinating work efforts. In fact, in a survey of managers about formal top-down organizational planning processes, over 75 percent said that their company's planning approach was unsatisfactory.[23] A common complaint was that, "plans are documents that you prepare for the corporate planning staff and later forget." Although this traditional top-down approach to planning is used by many organizations, it can be effective only if managers understand the importance of creating documents that organizational members actually use, not documents that look impressive but are never used.

Another approach to planning is to involve more organizational members in the process. In this approach, plans aren't handed down from one level to the next, but instead are developed by organizational members at the various levels and in the various work units to meet their specific needs. For instance, at Dell, employees from production, supply management, and channel management meet weekly to make plans based on current product demand and supply. In addition, work teams set their own daily schedules and track their progress against those schedules. If a team falls behind, team members develop "recovery" plans to try to get back on schedule.[24] When organizational members are more actively involved in planning, they see that the plans are more than just something written down on paper. They can actually see that the plans are used in directing and coordinating work.

LEARNING OUTCOME 8.4
Discuss contemporary issues in planning.

Contemporary Issues in Planning

The second floor of the 21-story Hyundai Motor headquarters buzzes with data 24 hours a day. That's where you'd find the company's Global Command and Control Center (GCCC), which is modeled after the CNN newsroom with "dozens of computer screens relaying video and data keeping watch on Hyundai operations around the world." Managers get information on parts shipments from suppliers to factories. Cameras watch assembly lines and "keep a close watch on Hyundai's giant Ulsan, Korea, plant, the world's largest integrated auto factory" looking for competitors' spies and any hints of labor unrest. The GCCC also keeps tabs on the company's R&D activities in Europe, Japan, and North America. Hyundai can identify problems in an instant and react quickly. The company is all about aggressiveness and speed and is representative of how a successful twenty-first-century company approaches planning.[25]

We conclude this chapter by addressing two contemporary issues in planning. Specifically, we're going to look at planning effectively in dynamic environments and then at how managers can use environmental scanning, especially competitive intelligence.

How Can Managers Plan Effectively in Dynamic Environments?

As we saw in Chapter 2, the external environment is continually changing. For instance, cloud computing storage is revolutionizing all kinds of industries from financial services to health care to engineering.[26] Social networking sites are being used by companies to connect with customers, employees, and potential employees. Amounts spent on eating out instead of cooking at home are predicted to decline. And experts believe that China and India are transforming the twenty-first-century global economy.

How can managers effectively plan when the external environment is continually changing? We already discussed uncertain environments as one of the contingency factors that affect the types of plans managers develop. Because dynamic environments are more the norm than the exception, let's look at how managers can effectively plan in such environments.

In an uncertain environment, managers should develop plans that are specific, but flexible. Although this may seem contradictory, it's not. To be useful, plans need some specificity, but the plans should not be set in stone. Managers need to recognize that planning is an ongoing process. The plans serve as a road map although the destination may change due to dynamic market conditions. They should be ready to change directions if environmental conditions warrant. This flexibility is particularly important as plans are implemented. Managers need to stay alert to environmental changes that may impact implementation and respond as needed. Keep in mind, also, that even when the environment is highly uncertain, it's important to continue formal planning in order to see any effect on organizational performance. It's the persistence in planning that contributes to significant performance improvement. Why? It seems that, as with most activities, managers "learn to plan" and the quality of their planning improves when they continue to do it.[27] Finally, make the organizational hierarchy flatter to effectively plan in dynamic environments. This means allowing lower organizational levels to set goals and develop plans because there's little time for goals and plans to flow down from the top. Managers should teach their employees how to set goals and to plan and then trust them to do it. And you need look no further than Bangalore, India, to find a company that effectively understands this. Just a decade ago, Wipro Limited was "an anonymous conglomerate selling cooking oil and personal computers, mostly in India." Today, it's a $6 billion-a-year global company with much of its business coming from information-technology services.[28] Accenture, Hewlett-Packard, IBM, and the big U.S. accounting firms know all too well the competitive threat Wipro represents. Not only are Wipro's employees economical, they're knowledgeable and skilled. And they play an important role in the company's planning. Because the information services industry is continually changing, employees are taught to analyze situations and to define the scale and scope of a client's problems in order to offer the best solutions. These employees are the ones on the front line with the clients and it's their responsibility to establish what to do and how to do it. It's an approach that positions Wipro for success no matter how the industry changes.

Let's Get Real

You can be a better planner by *not being far-sighted. Don't lose sight of what is happening right now by planning too far in the future. If you take care of the now, the long term will take care of itself. Be prepared to react and adjust to short-term changes and fluctuations in the economy and in your industry.*

formal planning department
A group of planning specialists whose sole responsibility is helping to write organizational plans

Scanning the environment helps Toyota Motor Corporation managers detect emerging trends that influence the company's future plans. Based on trends in computing and communications technology plus demographic trends such as a rapidly aging population and a decreasing birthrate in Japan and other developing nations, Toyota sees robotics as a key business in coming years. Its violin-playing robot, with 17 joints in each hand and arm, has the precise control and coordination to achieve humanlike agility for performing domestic chores like folding laundry and medical tasks such as dispensing medicine. Toyota and competitors such as Honda and Hitachi are racing to build robots that will serve the needs of the elderly in Japan, where 40 percent of the population is expected to be older than 65 by 2055, and in other global markets.

How Can Managers Use Environmental Scanning?

Crammed into a small Shanghai apartment that houses four generations of a Chinese family, Indra Nooyi, Chairman and CEO of PepsiCo Inc., asked the inhabitants several questions about "China's rapid development, their shopping habits, and how they feel about Western brands." This visit was part of an "immersion" tour of China for Ms. Nooyi, who hopes to strengthen PepsiCo's business in emerging markets. She said, "I wanted to look at how people live, how they eat, what the growth possibilities are."[29] The information gleaned from her research—a prime example of environmental scanning up close and personal—will help in establishing PepsiCo's future goals and plans.

A manager's analysis of the external environment may be improved by **environmental scanning**, which involves screening information to detect emerging trends. One of the fastest-growing forms of environmental scanning is **competitor intelligence**, which is gathering information about competitors that allows managers to anticipate competitors' actions rather than merely react to them.[30] It seeks basic information about competitors: Who are they? What are they doing? How will what they're doing affect us?

Many who study competitive intelligence suggest that much of the competitor-related information managers need to make crucial strategic decisions is available and accessible to the public.[31] In other words, competitive intelligence isn't corporate espionage. Advertisements, promotional materials, press releases, reports filed with government agencies, annual reports, want ads, newspaper reports, information on the Internet, and industry studies are readily accessible sources of information. Specific information on an industry and associated organizations is increasingly available through electronic databases. Managers can literally tap into this wealth of competitive information by purchasing access to databases. Attending trade shows and debriefing your own sales staff also can be good sources of information on competitors. In addition, many organizations even regularly buy competitors' products and ask their own employees to evaluate them to learn about new technical innovations.[32]

In a changing global business environment, environmental scanning and obtaining competitive intelligence can be quite complex, especially since information must be gathered

environmental scanning
Screening information to detect emerging trends

competitor intelligence
Gathering information about competitors that allows managers to anticipate competitors' actions rather than merely react to them

from around the world. However, one thing managers could do is subscribe to news services that review newspapers and magazines from around the globe and provide summaries to client companies.

Managers do need to be careful about the way information, especially competitive intelligence, is gathered to prevent any concerns about whether it's legal or ethical.[33] For instance, Starwood Hotels recently sued Hilton Hotels alleging that two former employees stole trade secrets and helped Hilton develop a new line of luxury, trendy hotels designed to appeal to a young demographic.[34] The court filing said, "This is the clearest imaginable case of corporate espionage, theft of trade secrets, unfair competition, and computer fraud." Competitive intelligence becomes illegal corporate spying when it involves the theft of proprietary materials or trade secrets by any means. The Economic Espionage Act makes it a crime in the United States to engage in economic espionage or to steal a trade secret. Difficult decisions about competitive intelligence arise because often there's a fine line between what's considered *legal and ethical* and what's considered *legal but unethical.* Although the top manager at one competitive intelligence firm contends that 99.9 percent of intelligence gathering is legal, there's no question that some people or companies will go to any lengths—some unethical—to get information about competitors.[35]

Let's Get Real:
My Response to *A Manager's Dilemma, page 232*

What Would You Do?

A crisis the magnitude of the Haitian earthquake requires a global response, which is exactly what happened. The timing of the disaster on a holiday weekend was unfortunate, but no one can fault the herculean efforts of the WFP in their response to the crisis. In the shadow of Hurricane Katrina, agencies such as the WFP were intensely scrutinized and obviously had fairly well laid out action plans for disasters such as this. That being said, no amount of planning can prepare for the devastation that the relief teams found in Haiti.

Getting the military involved from the outset was a key factor. They are at a constant state of readiness and are trained first responders. The military command should take control of damage assessment, procuring local equipment, and mobilizing shipments of additional equipment necessary to get runways repaired and open and seaports in working order. The WFP should immediately take the lead and begin centralizing food and relief supplies from the myriad of relief agencies across the country and begin scheduling shipments accordingly.

In general, the actual relief operation was impressive and efficient and argues well for the effectiveness of good planning.

Chuck Pick
President
**Chuck's Parking
Service, Inc.
Sherman Oaks, CA**

Cases

CASE APPLICATION 1
Short-Term and Long-Term Planning in the UK Construction Industry

In 2010 it was reported that the UK construction industry was experiencing its worst slump in 30 years.

Between 1992 and 2007, house prices in England rose by a staggering 250 percent. The average age of a first-time buyer (without family or state assistance) was now 37 years of age. Four out of ten Britons between the ages of 18 and 30 said they would delay having children until after they bought their first property. In 2010 it was reported that the UK construction industry was experiencing its worst slump in 30 years. About 118,000 homes were built in England in 2009, down from 175,000 in 2007. It was less than half of the 240,000 needed annually to meet the government's goal to build 3 million homes from mid-2007 to 2020. The lack of new properties is affecting both private buyers and those seeking state housing. Nearly 5 million people are on waiting lists for government-subsidized housing and first-time home buyers are struggling to enter the market because of prohibitively high prices and more limitations on mortgages.

What is the cause of the housing slump? The global recession certainly played a major part as construction projects were abandoned resulting in a lower number of new homes. Poor planning perhaps contributed to the problem as well. The amount of land approved for development has been decreasing steadily over the last 10 years. Moreover, there was not enough land available to meet the short-term and long-term demand, according to the Home Builders Federation, the industry's main lobby group. Consequently, Citigroup has predicted a possible shortage of 1.2 million homes by 2016. Peter Redfern, chief executive officer of Taylor Wimpey Plc, the country's second-largest home builder, feels that with a scarcity of readily available land and a growing population, a radical change is needed to enable planning to be granted on more sites.

The previous Labour government set its home-building target following a 2004 report that concluded there was a shortfall of about 450,000 homes (later the decline in building during the recession had pushed that figure closer to 1 million). Regional governing bodies set their own housing targets. Local councils that failed to meet both of these goals would potentially lose their state funding. The government also planned to provide financial incentives to local councils to encourage them to grant planning permission.

Former Labour Housing Minister John Healey believes that central planning is necessary for coordinating infrastructure work that helps promote investment, boost economic growth and deliver homes. From another perspective, the Home Builders Federation argues that the government needs to reduce the cost, complexity, and uncertainty of regulation that is preventing the building of more homes. At the same time, the Conservatives, the opposition party at the time, argued that more planning authority should be given to local councils. Bearing all this in mind, market fragility and supply uncertainty in the UK housing sector is still making planning a complex task for any government.[38]

Discussion Questions

1. Why have plans failed to achieve the targets in the UK housing industry?

2. What short-term and long-term plans does the UK construction sector need?

3. Do you think advanced techniques like management by objectives (MBO) can help the UK housing industry?

Understanding Yourself

What Are My Course Performance Goals?

INSTRUMENT   Using the following scale, select the answer for each of the 12 statements that best expresses why you study for a course.

1 = Never
2 = Rarely
3 = Sometimes
4 = Often
5 = Always

I study because:

		1	2	3	4	5
1.	I want to be praised by my professors and parents.	1	2	3	4	5
2.	I want to be noticed by my friends.	1	2	3	4	5
3.	I don't want my classmates to make fun of me.	1	2	3	4	5
4.	I don't want to be disliked by a professor.	1	2	3	4	5
5.	I want people to see how smart I am.	1	2	3	4	5
6.	I wish to get better grades than my peers.	1	2	3	4	5
7.	I want to get good grades.	1	2	3	4	5
8.	I want to be proud of getting good grades.	1	2	3	4	5
9.	I don't want to fail final exams.	1	2	3	4	5
10.	I wish to be admitted to graduate school.	1	2	3	4	5
11.	I want to get a good job in the future.	1	2	3	4	5
12.	I want to attain status in the future.	1	2	3	4	5

SCORING KEY   Total up the number of 4 and 5 responses. This will be between zero and 12.

ANALYSIS AND INTERPRETATION   What drives you to study? What goals are you trying to achieve? This questionnaire measures goal orientation as related to your course work.

There are no "right" goals. But having clear goals can help you better understand your studying behavior. If you had no responses in the 4 or 5 categories, your course performance is likely to suffer because you have no strong reasons for studying. This suggests a need for you to reassess your goals and consider what you want from your course work. If you had a number of responses in the 4 or 5 categories, you appear to have specific goals that will motivate you to study and achieve high performance.

Source: Based on T. Hayamizu and B. Weiner, "A Test of Dweck's Model of Achievement Goals as Related to Perceptions of Ability," *Journal of Experimental Education*, vol. 59, 1991, pp. 226–34. Modified per C. Dupeyrat and E. V. Smith Jr., "Toward Establishing a Unified Metric for Performance and Learning Goal Orientations," *Journal of Applied Measurement*, vol. 2, no. 4, 2001, pp. 312–36.

Review Questions and Tests

REVIEW AND DISCUSSION QUESTIONS

1. Explain what studies have shown about the relationship between planning and performance.

2. Discuss the contingency factors that affect planning.

3. Describe how managers can effectively plan in today's dynamic environment.

4. Will planning become more or less important to managers in the future? Why?

5. If planning is so crucial, why do some managers choose not to do it? What would you tell these managers?

6. Explain how planning involves making decisions today that will have an impact later.

7. How might planning in a not-for-profit organization such as the American Cancer Society differ from planning in a for-profit organization such as Coca-Cola?

8. What types of planning do you do in your personal life? Describe these plans in terms of being (a) strategic or operational, (b) short term or long term, and (c) specific or directional.

9. The late Peter Drucker, an eminent management author, coined the SMART format for setting goals back in 1954: S (specific), M (measurable), A (attainable), R (relevant), and T (time-bound). Are these still relevant today? Discuss.

10. Many companies have a goal of becoming more environmentally sustainable. One of the most important steps they can take is controlling paper waste. Choose a company—any type, any size. You've been put in charge of creating a program to do this for your company. Set goals and develop plans. Prepare a report for your boss (that is, your professor) outlining these goals and plans.

Chapter 4:

Strategic Management Overview

The importance of having good strategies can be seen by what Kate Connally has accomplished with AddictingGames. By recognizing game opportunities in current news stories and in new formats and formulating effective strategies to exploit these opportunities, her company has become the leader in online gaming. As she continues expanding access to those games, strategic management will continue to play an important role in the company's ability to continue to be the most popular online games site. An underlying theme in this chapter is that effective strategies result in high organizational performance.

LEARNING OUTCOME 9.1
Define strategic management and explain why it's important.

Strategic Management

▶ Vente-privee.com, one of Europe's top e-tailers, is looking to expand in Europe, but not in the United States, where competition from outlet malls and discounters is too great.

▶ Facing intense pressure from users over privacy issues, Facebook CEO Mark Zuckerberg unveiled a new set of controls to help people better understand what information they are sharing online.

▶ Charles Schwab, chairman and founder of his namesake financial services company, is worried about his customers, especially since his company's success depends on his financial advisers' ability to keep those customers "engaged" in equities markets.

▶ The private equity firm, C. Dean Metropoulos & Company, has reached an agreement to buy Pabst Blue Ribbon, a once-popular beer brand, with hopes of rebuilding its share in a competitive market.[2]

These are just a few of the business news stories from a single week, and each one is about a company's strategies. Strategic management is very much a part of what managers do. In this section, we want to look at what strategic management is and why it's important.

What Is Strategic Management?

The discount retail industry is a good place to see what strategic management is all about. Walmart and Kmart Corporation (now part of Sears Holdings) have battled for market dominance since 1962, the year both companies were founded. The two chains have other similarities: store atmosphere, names, markets served, and organizational purpose. Yet, Walmart's performance (financial and otherwise) has far surpassed that of Kmart. Walmart is the world's largest retailer and Kmart was the largest retailer ever to seek Chapter 11 bankruptcy protection. Why the difference in performance? Because of different strategies and competitive abilities.[3] Walmart has excelled by using strategic management effectively while Kmart has struggled by failing to use strategic management effectively.

Strategic management is what managers do to develop the organization's strategies. It's an important task involving all the basic management functions—planning, organizing, leading, and controlling. What are an organization's **strategies**? They're the plans for how the organization will do whatever it's in business to do, how it will compete successfully, and how it will attract and satisfy its customers in order to achieve its goals.[4]

One term often used in strategic management is **business model**, which simply is how a company is going to make money. It focuses on two things: (1) whether customers will value what the company is providing, and (2) whether the company can make any money doing that.[5] For instance, Dell pioneered a new business model for selling computers to consumers directly online instead of selling through computer retailers like other manufacturers. Did customers "value" that? Absolutely! Did Dell make money doing it that way? Absolutely! As managers think about strategies, they need to think about the economic viability of their company's business model.

Why Is Strategic Management Important?

In the summer of 2002, a British television show spin-off called *American Idol* became one of the biggest shows in American television history. Nine seasons later, it's still the most-watched show on television although its audience has declined for four seasons. However, the show's executive producer said, "If we're smart about it, there's no reason why 'Idol' wouldn't keep going. Just look at 'Price is Right.' It's been on for over 35 years."[6] The managers behind *Idol* seem to understand the importance of strategic management as they've developed and exploited every aspect of the *Idol* business—the television show, the music, the concerts, and all the other associated licensed products. Now, their challenge is to keep the franchise a strong presence in the market by making strategic changes.

Why is strategic management so important? There are three reasons. The most significant one is that it can make a difference in how well an organization performs. Why do some

Wang Chuanfu recognizes the importance of strategic management to improve organizational performance. Chuanfu is the CEO of BYD, a firm he started in 1995 in Shenzhen, China, to make and sell rechargeable batteries for computers. Today BYD is a top battery supplier to both computer and cell phone makers. Recognizing an opportunity to build profits by entering a new market, Chuanfu bought a struggling car company in China and applied his core technology of rechargeable batteries to producing electric cars. Chuanfu, shown here with his e6 fuel-efficient and environmentally friendly electric car, hopes to capture a good part of the worldwide global market for electric cars that's predicted to be as big as 10 million cars per year by 2016.

strategic management	**strategies**	**business model**
What managers do to develop the organization's strategies	The plans for how the organization will do what it's in business to do, how it will compete successfully, and how it will attract and satisfy its customers in order to achieve its goals	How a company is going to make money

businesses succeed and others fail, even when faced with the same environmental conditions? (Remember our Walmart and Kmart example.) Research has found a generally positive relationship between strategic planning and performance.[7] In other words, it appears that organizations that use strategic management do have higher levels of performance. And that fact makes it pretty important for managers!

Another reason it's important has to do with the fact that managers in organizations of all types and sizes face continually changing situations (as we discussed in Chapter 6). They cope with this uncertainty by using the strategic management process to examine relevant factors and decide what actions to take. For instance, as business executives across a wide spectrum of industries coped with the global recession, they focused on making their strategies more flexible. At Office Depot, for example, store managers throughout the company told CEO Steve Odland that cash-strapped consumers no longer wanted to buy pens or printer paper in bulk. So the company created special displays promoting single Sharpie pens and introduced five-ream packages of paper, half the size of the normal big box of paper.[8]

Finally, strategic management is important because organizations are complex and diverse. Each part needs to work together toward achieving the organization's goals; strategic management helps do this. For example, with more than 2.1 million employees worldwide working in various departments, functional areas, and stores, Walmart Stores, Inc., uses strategic management to help coordinate and focus employees' efforts on what's important as determined by its goals.

Today, both business organizations and not-for-profit organizations use strategic management. For instance, the U.S. Postal Service (USPS) is locked in competitive battles with overnight package delivery companies, telecommunications companies' e-mail and text messaging services, and private mailing facilities. In 2006, 213 billion pieces of mail were handled by the postal service. In 2009, that total had dropped to 177 billion, a decline of almost 17 percent. John Potter, USPS's CEO (the U.S. Postmaster General), is using strategic management to come up with a response. One possible action plan, which many critics consider drastic, is discontinuing Saturday mail delivery. However, some strategic changes are needed as the USPS faces losses of $238 billion over the next decade.[9] Strategic management will continue to be important to its operation. Check out the organization's *Vision 2013,* which outlines its internal plan for the future.[10] Although strategic management in not-for-profits hasn't been as well researched as it has in for-profit organizations, we know it's important for these organizations as well.

9.2

The Strategic Management Process

The **strategic management process** (see Exhibit 9-1) is a six-step process that encompasses strategy planning, implementation, and evaluation. Although the first four steps describe the planning that must take place, implementation and evaluation are just as important! Even the best strategies can fail if management doesn't implement or evaluate them properly.

EXHIBIT 9-1

Strategic Management Process

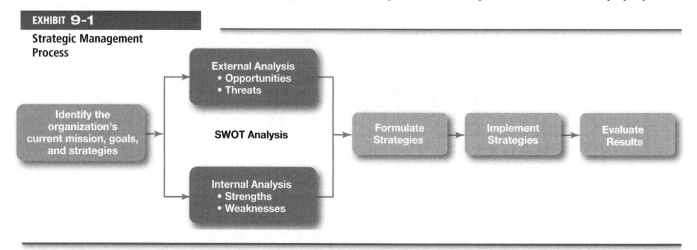

Step 1: Identifying the Organization's Current Mission, Goals, and Strategies

Every organization needs a mission—a statement of its purpose. Defining the mission forces managers to identify what it's in business to do. For instance, the mission of Avon is "To be the company that best understands and satisfies the product, service, and self-fulfillment needs of women on a global level." The mission of Facebook is "a social utility that connects you with the people around you." The mission of the National Heart Foundation of Australia is to "reduce suffering and death from heart, stroke, and blood vessel disease in Australia." These statements provide clues to what these organizations see as their purpose. What should a mission statement include? Exhibit 9-2 describes some typical components.

Step 2: Doing an External Analysis

What impact might the following trends have for businesses?

▶ With the passage of the national health care legislation, every big restaurant chain will now be required to post calorie information on their menus and drive-through signs.
▶ Cell phones are now used by customers more for data transmittal and retrieval than for phone calls.
▶ The share of new high-school graduates enrolled in college hit a record high in 2009 and continues to climb.[11]

We described the external environment in Chapter 2 as an important constraint on a manager's actions. Analyzing that environment is a critical step in the strategic management process. Managers do an external analysis so they know, for instance, what the competition is doing, what pending legislation might affect the organization, or what the labor supply is like in locations where it operates. In an external analysis, managers should examine the economic, demographic, political/legal, sociocultural, technological, and global components to see the trends and changes.

Once they've analyzed the environment, managers need to pinpoint opportunities that the organization can exploit and threats that it must counteract or buffer against. Opportunities are positive trends in the external environment; threats are negative trends.

EXHIBIT 9-2

Components of a Mission Statement

Customers: Who are the firm's customers?

Markets: Where does the firm compete geographically?

Concern for survival, growth, and profitability: Is the firm committed to growth and financial stability?

Philosophy: What are the firm's basic beliefs, values, and ethical priorities?

Concern for public image: How responsive is the firm to societal and environmental concerns?

Products or services: What are the firm's major products or services?

Technology: Is the firm technologically current?

Self-concept: What are the firm's major competitive advantage and core competencies?

Concern for employees: Are employees a valuable asset of the firm?

Source: Based on F. David, *Strategic Management,* 13th ed. (Upper Saddle River, NJ: Prentice Hall, 2011), p. 51.

strategic management process
A six-step process that encompasses strategic planning, implementation, and evaluation

mission
A statement of an organization's purpose

opportunities
Positive trends in the external environment

threats
Negative trends in the external environment

Step 3: Doing an Internal Analysis

Now we move to the internal analysis, which provides important information about an organization's specific resources and capabilities. An organization's **resources** are its assets—financial, physical, human, and intangible—that it uses to develop, manufacture, and deliver products to its customers. They're "what" the organization has. On the other hand, its **capabilities** are its skills and abilities in doing the work activities needed in its business—"how" it does its work. The major value-creating capabilities of the organization are known as its **core competencies.**[12] Both resources and core competencies determine the organization's competitive weapons.

After completing an internal analysis, managers should be able to identify organizational strengths and weaknesses. Any activities the organization does well or any unique resources that it has are called **strengths. Weaknesses** are activities the organization doesn't do well or resources it needs but doesn't possess.

The combined external and internal analyses are called the **SWOT analysis**, which is an analysis of the organization's *s*trengths, *w*eaknesses, *o*pportunities, and *t*hreats. After completing the SWOT analysis, managers are ready to formulate appropriate strategies—that is, strategies that (1) exploit an organization's strengths and external opportunities, (2) buffer or protect the organization from external threats, or (3) correct critical weaknesses.

Step 4: Formulating Strategies

As managers formulate strategies, they should consider the realities of the external environment and their available resources and capabilities in order to design strategies that will help an organization achieve its goals. The three main types of strategies managers will formulate include corporate, competitive, and functional. We'll describe each shortly.

Step 5: Implementing Strategies

Once strategies are formulated, they must be implemented. No matter how effectively an organization has planned its strategies, performance will suffer if the strategies aren't implemented properly.

Step 6: Evaluating Results

The final step in the strategic management process is evaluating results. How effective have the strategies been at helping the organization reach its goals? What adjustments are necessary? After assessing the results of previous strategies and determining that changes were needed, Ursula Burns, Xerox's CEO, made strategic adjustments to regain market share and improve her company's bottom line. The company cut jobs, sold assets, and reorganized management. (See Leader Who Made a Difference box on p. 258.)

LEARNING OUTCOME **9.3**
Describe the three types of corporate strategies.

Corporate Strategies

As we said earlier, organizations use three types of strategies: corporate, competitive, and functional. (See Exhibit 9-3.) Top-level managers typically are responsible for corporate strategies, middle-level managers for competitive strategies, and lower-level managers for the functional strategies. In this section, we'll look at corporate strategies.

What Is Corporate Strategy?

A **corporate strategy** is one that determines what businesses a company is in or wants to be in, and what it wants to do with those businesses. It's based on the mission and goals of the organization and the roles that each business unit of the organization will play. We can see both of these aspects with PepsiCo, for instance. Its mission: To be the world's premier consumer products company focused on convenient foods and beverages. It pursues that mission with a

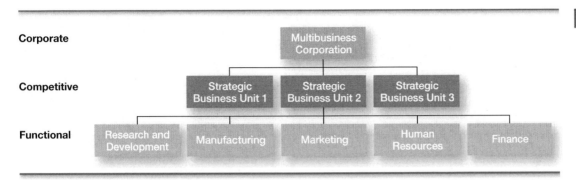

EXHIBIT 9-3

Types of
Organizational
Strategies

corporate strategy that has put it in different businesses including PepsiCo Americas Beverages (which includes Pepsi, Gatorade, and other beverages), PepsiCo Americas Foods (which includes Frito-Lay North America, Quaker Foods North America, and Latin American Foods), and PepsiCo International (which includes all PepsiCo's other international products). The other part of corporate strategy is when top managers decide what to do with those businesses: grow them, keep them the same, or renew them.

What Are the Types of Corporate Strategy?

The three main types of corporate strategies are growth, stability, and renewal. Let's look at each type.

GROWTH.   Even though Walmart is the world's largest retailer, it continues to grow internationally and in the United States. A **growth strategy** is when an organization expands the number of markets served or products offered, either through its current business(es) or through new business(es). Because of its growth strategy, an organization may increase revenues, number of employees, or market share. Organizations grow by using concentration, vertical integration, horizontal integration, or diversification.

An organization that grows using *concentration* focuses on its primary line of business and increases the number of products offered or markets served in this primary business. For instance, Beckman Coulter, Inc., a Fullerton, California-based organization with annual revenues over $3.2 billion, has used concentration to become one of the world's largest medical diagnostics and research equipment companies. Another example of a company using concentration is Bose Corporation of Framingham, Massachusetts, which focuses on developing innovative audio products and has become one of the world's leading manufacturers of speakers for home entertainment, automotive, and pro audio markets with sales of more than $2 billion.

A company also might choose to grow by *vertical integration*, either backward, forward, or both. In backward vertical integration, the organization becomes its own supplier so it can control its inputs. For instance, eBay owns an online payment business that helps it provide more secure transactions and control one of its most critical processes. In forward vertical integration, the organization becomes its own distributor and is able to control its outputs. For example, Apple has more than 287 retail stores worldwide to distribute its product.

In *horizontal integration*, a company grows by combining with competitors. For instance, French cosmetics giant L'Oreal acquired The Body Shop. Another example is Live Nation,

LEADER who made a **difference**

She's the first African American woman to lead a *Fortune* 500 company.[13] Ursula Burns, who joined Xerox as a summer engineering intern more than 30 years ago, has a reputation for being bold. As a mechanical engineer, she got noticed at Xerox because she wasn't afraid to speak up bluntly in a culture that's known more for being polite, courteous, and discreet than for being outspoken. But that bold approach is serving Burns well in a challenging environment. Just weeks after taking over as CEO, she announced the biggest deal in the firm's history—a $6.4 billion acquisition of Affiliated Computer Services, an outsourcing firm that most people had never heard of. Although the action was criticized, Burns recognized that Xerox needed dramatic action. Her challenge at Xerox is crafting strategies that will help it prosper and be an industry leader in a digital age where change is continual.

the largest concert promoter in the United States, which combined operations with competitor HOB Entertainment, the operator of the House of Blues Clubs. Horizontal integration has been used in a number of industries in the last few years—financial services, consumer products, airlines, department stores, and software, among others. The U.S. Federal Trade Commission usually scrutinizes these combinations closely to see if consumers might be harmed by decreased competition. Other countries may have similar restrictions. For instance, the European Commission, the "watchdog" for the European Union, conducted an in-depth investigation into Unilever's acquisition of the body and laundry care units of Sara Lee.

Finally, an organization can grow through *diversification*, either related or unrelated. Related diversification happens when a company combines with other companies in different, but related, industries. For example, American Standard Cos., based in Piscataway, New Jersey, is in a variety of businesses including bathroom fixtures, air conditioning and heating units, plumbing parts, and pneumatic brakes for trucks. Although this mix of businesses seems odd, the company's "strategic fit" is the efficiency-oriented manufacturing techniques developed in its primary business of bathroom fixtures, which it has transferred to all its other businesses. Unrelated diversification is when a company combines with firms in different and unrelated industries. For instance, the Tata Group of India has businesses in chemicals, communications and IT, consumer products, energy, engineering, materials, and services. Again, an odd mix. But in this case, there's no strategic fit among the businesses.

STABILITY. As the global recession dragged on and U.S. sales of candy and chocolate slowed down, Cadbury Schweppes—with almost half of its confectionary sales coming from chocolate—is maintaining things as they are. A **stability strategy** is a corporate strategy in which an organization continues to do what it is currently doing. Examples of this strategy include continuing to serve the same clients by offering the same product or service, maintaining market share, and sustaining the organization's current business operations. The organization doesn't grow, but doesn't fall behind, either.

RENEWAL. In 2009, Symantec lost $6.7 billion. Sprint-Nextel lost $2.4 billion, and many financial services and real-estate-related companies faced serious financial issues with huge losses. When an organization is in trouble, something needs to be done. Managers need to develop strategies, called **renewal strategies**, that address declining performance. The two main types of renewal strategies are retrenchment and turnaround strategies. A *retrenchment strategy* is a short-run renewal strategy used for minor performance problems. This strategy helps an organization stabilize operations, revitalize organizational resources and capabilities, and prepare to compete once again. When an organization's problems are more serious, more drastic action—the *turnaround strategy*—is needed. Managers do two things for both renewal strategies: cut costs and restructure organizational operations. However, in a turnaround strategy, these measures are more extensive than in a retrenchment strategy.

How Are Corporate Strategies Managed?

When an organization's corporate strategy encompasses a number of businesses, managers can manage this collection, or portfolio, of businesses using a tool called a corporate portfolio matrix. This matrix provides a framework for understanding diverse businesses and helps managers establish priorities for allocating resources.[14] The first portfolio matrix—the **BCG matrix**—was developed by the Boston Consulting Group and introduced the idea that an organization's various businesses could be evaluated and plotted using a 2 × 2 matrix

EXHIBIT 9-4

BCG Matrix

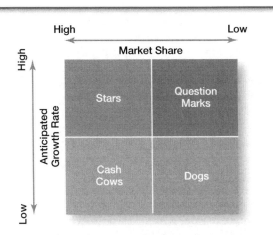

(see Exhibit 9-4) to identify which ones offered high potential and which were a drain on organizational resources.[15] The horizontal axis represents market share (low or high) and the vertical axis indicates anticipated market growth (low or high). A business unit is evaluated using a SWOT analysis and placed in one of the four categories.

What are the strategic implications of the BCG matrix? The dogs should be sold off or liquidated as they have low market share in markets with low growth potential. Managers should "milk" cash cows for as much as they can, limit any new investment in them, and use the large amounts of cash generated to invest in stars and question marks with strong potential to improve market share. Heavy investment in stars will help take advantage of the market's growth and help maintain high market share. The stars, of course, will eventually develop into cash cows as their markets mature and sales growth slows. The hardest decision for managers relates to the question marks. After careful analysis, some will be sold off and others strategically nurtured into stars.

Competitive Strategies

9.4

LEARNING OUTCOME
Describe competitive advantage and the competitive strategies organizations use to get it.

A **competitive strategy** is a strategy for how an organization will compete in its business(es). For a small organization in only one line of business or a large organization that has not diversified into different products or markets, its competitive strategy describes how it will compete in its primary or main market. For organizations in multiple businesses, however, each business will have its own competitive strategy that defines its competitive advantage, the products or services it will offer, the customers it wants to reach, and the like. For example, the French company LVMH-Moët Hennessy Louis Vuitton SA has different competitive strategies for its businesses, which include Donna Karan fashions, Louis Vuitton leather goods, Guerlain perfume, TAG Heuer watches, Dom Perignon champagne, and other luxury products. When an organization is in several different businesses, those single businesses that are independent and that have their own competitive strategies are referred to as **strategic business units (SBUs)**.

The Role of Competitive Advantage

Michelin has mastered a complex technological process for making superior radial tires. Coca-Cola has created the world's best and most powerful brand using specialized marketing and

---

stability strategy
A corporate strategy in which an organization continues to do what it is currently doing

renewal strategy
A corporate strategy designed to address declining performance

BCG matrix
A strategy tool that guides resource allocation decisions on the basis of market share and growth rate of SBUs

competitive strategy
An organizational strategy for how an organization will compete in its business(es)

strategic business unit (SBU)
The single independent businesses of an organization that formulate their own competitive strategies

merchandising capabilities.[16] The Ritz Carlton hotels have a unique ability to deliver personalized customer service. Each of these companies has created a competitive advantage.

Developing an effective competitive strategy requires an understanding of **competitive advantage**, which is what sets an organization apart—that is, its distinctive edge.[17] That distinctive edge can come from the organization's core competencies by doing something that others cannot do or doing it better than others can do it. For example, Southwest Airlines has a competitive advantage because of its skills at giving passengers what they want—convenient and inexpensive air passenger service. Or competitive advantage can come from the company's resources because the organization has something that its competitors do not have. For instance, Walmart's state-of-the-art information system allows it to monitor and control inventories and supplier relations more efficiently than its competitors, which Walmart has turned into a cost advantage.

QUALITY AS A COMPETITIVE ADVANTAGE.   When W. K. Kellogg started manufacturing his cornflake cereal in 1906, his goal was to provide his customers with a high-quality, nutritious product that was enjoyable to eat. That emphasis on quality is still important today. Every employee has a responsibility to maintain the high quality of Kellogg products. If implemented properly, quality can be a way for an organization to create a sustainable competitive advantage.[18] That's why many organizations apply quality management concepts in an attempt to set themselves apart from competitors. If a business is able to continuously improve the quality and reliability of its products, it may have a competitive advantage that can't be taken away.[19]

SUSTAINING COMPETITIVE ADVANTAGE.   Every organization has resources (assets) and capabilities (how work gets done). So what makes some organizations more successful than others? Why do some professional baseball teams consistently win championships or draw large crowds? Why do some organizations have consistent and continuous growth in revenues and profits? Why do some colleges, universities, or departments experience continually increasing enrollments? Why do some companies consistently appear at the top of lists ranking the "best," or the "most admired," or the "most profitable"? The answer is that not every organization is able to effectively exploit its resources and to develop the core competencies that can provide it with a competitive advantage. And it's not enough simply to create a competitive advantage. The organization must be able to sustain that advantage; that is, to keep its edge despite competitors' actions or evolutionary changes in the industry. But that's not easy to do! Market instabilities, new technology, and other changes can challenge managers' attempts at creating a long-term, sustainable competitive advantage. However, by using strategic management, managers can better position their organizations to get a sustainable competitive advantage.

Many important ideas in strategic management have come from the work of Michael Porter.[20] One of his major contributions was explaining how managers can create a sustainable competitive advantage. An important part of doing this is an industry analysis, which is done using the five forces model.

Kellogg has developed a competitive advantage by creating and maintaining high-quality products for more than a century. Quality management at Kellogg includes making each employee responsible for maintaining quality and conducting quality control tests of the company's raw materials, processing, and packaging operations. Quality assurance personnel regularly visit suppliers' plants to assure that proper sanitation procedures are followed and that raw materials meet Kellogg's rigid specifications. A Quality Division at company headquarters establishes quality practices that are carried out by employees at the manufacturing facilities.

EXHIBIT 9-5

Five Forces Model

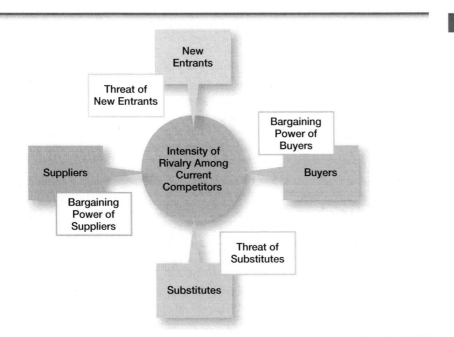

Source: Based on M. E. Porter, *Competitive Strategy: Techniques for Analyzing Industries and Competitors.* New York: The Free Press, 1980.

FIVE FORCES MODEL.   In any industry, five competitive forces dictate the rules of competition. Together, these five forces (see Exhibit 9-5) determine industry attractiveness and profitability, which managers assess using these five factors:

1. *Threat of new entrants.* How likely is it that new competitors will come into the industry?
2. *Threat of substitutes.* How likely is it that other industries' products can be substituted for our industry's products?
3. *Bargaining power of buyers.* How much bargaining power do buyers (customers) have?
4. *Bargaining power of suppliers.* How much bargaining power do suppliers have?
5. *Current rivalry.* How intense is the rivalry among current industry competitors?

Choosing a Competitive Strategy

Once managers have assessed the five forces and done a SWOT analysis, they're ready to select an appropriate competitive strategy—that is, one that fits the competitive strengths (resources and capabilities) of the organization and the industry it's in. According to Porter, no firm can be successful by trying to be all things to all people. He proposed that managers select a strategy that will give the organization a competitive advantage, either from having lower costs than all other industry competitors or by being significantly different from competitors.

When an organization competes on the basis of having the lowest costs (costs or expenses, not prices) in its industry, it's following a *cost leadership strategy*. A low-cost leader is highly efficient. Overhead is kept to a minimum, and the firm does everything it can to cut costs. You won't find expensive art or interior décor at offices of low-cost leaders. For example, at Walmart's headquarters in Bentonville, Arkansas, office furnishings are functional, not elaborate, maybe not what you'd expect for the world's largest retailer. Although a low-cost leader doesn't place a lot of emphasis on "frills," its product must be perceived as comparable in quality to that offered by rivals or at least be acceptable to buyers.

competitive advantage
What sets an organization apart; its distinctive edge

A company that competes by offering unique products that are widely valued by customers is following a *differentiation strategy*. Product differences might come from exceptionally high quality, extraordinary service, innovative design, technological capability, or an unusually positive brand image. Practically any successful consumer product or service can be identified as an example of the differentiation strategy; for instance, Nordstrom (customer service); 3M Corporation (product quality and innovative design); Coach (design and brand image); and Apple (product design).

Although these two competitive strategies are aimed at the broad market, the final type of competitive strategy—the *focus strategy*—involves a cost advantage (cost focus) or a differentiation advantage (differentiation focus) in a narrow segment or niche. Segments can be based on product variety, customer type, distribution channel, or geographical location. For example, Denmark's Bang & Olufsen, whose revenues are over $527 million, focuses on high-end audio equipment sales. Whether a focus strategy is feasible depends on the size of the segment and whether the organization can make money serving that segment.

What happens if an organization can't develop a cost or a differentiation advantage? Porter called that being *stuck in the middle* and warned that's not a good place to be. An organization becomes stuck in the middle when its costs are too high to compete with the low-cost leader or when its products and services aren't differentiated enough to compete with the differentiator. Getting unstuck means choosing which competitive advantage to pursue and then doing so by aligning resource, capabilities, and core competencies.

Although Porter said that you had to pursue either the low cost or the differentiation advantage to prevent being stuck in the middle, more recent research has shown that organizations *can* successfully pursue both a low cost and a differentiation advantage and achieve high performance.[22] Needless to say, it's not easy to pull off! You have to keep costs low *and* be truly differentiated. But companies such as Hewlett-Packard, FedEx, Intel, and Coca-Cola have been able to do it.

Before we leave this section, we want to point out the final type of organizational strategy, the **functional strategies**, which are the strategies used by an organization's various functional departments to support the competitive strategy. For example, when R. R. Donnelley & Sons Company, a Chicago-based printer, wanted to become more competitive and invested in high-tech digital printing methods, its marketing department had to develop new sales plans and promotional pieces, the production department had to incorporate the digital equipment in the printing plants, and the human resources department had to update its employee selection and training programs. We don't cover specific functional strategies in this book because you'll cover them in other business courses you take.

LEARNING OUTCOME 9.5
Discuss current strategic management issues.

Let's Get Real

F2F

Skills needed by a good strategic leader include:
- Ability to listen
- Determination
- Flexibility
- Able to affect change and buy-in from employees
- Patience
- Planning

Current Strategic Management Issues

There's no better example of the strategic challenges faced by managers in today's environment than the recorded music industry. Overall sales of CDs have plummeted in the last decade and are down about 50 percent from their peak. Not only has this trend impacted the music companies, but it's affected music retailers as well. "Retailers have been forced to adjust, often by devoting some shelf space to other products." For instance, Best Buy, the national electronics retailer, decided to experiment with selling musical instruments. During spring 2010, the company opened its 100th musical instrument department. Other major music retailers, such as Walmart, have shifted selling space used for CDs to other departments. "At music specialty stores, however, diversification has become a matter of survival." Managers are struggling to find strategies that will help their organizations succeed in such an environment. Many have had to shift into whole new areas of business.[23] But it isn't just the music industry that's dealing with strategic challenges. Managers everywhere face increasingly intense global competition and high performance expectations by investors and customers. How have they responded to these new realities? In this section we look at three current strategic management issues including the need for strategic leadership, the need for strategic flexibility, and how managers design strategies to emphasize e-business, customer service, and innovation.

The Need for Strategic Leadership

Pablo Isa, CEO of Spain's Inditex (owner of clothing chain Zara), is overseeing an aggressive expansion. The company is adding as many as 450 stores a year, including a three-level store on Chicago's Michigan Avenue. With so much prime retail space available in the United States, Isa is exploiting the opportunity to negotiate better deals.[24]

An organization's strategies are usually developed and overseen by its top managers. An organization's top manager is typically the CEO (chief executive officer). This individual usually works with a top management team that includes other executive or senior managers such as a COO (chief operating officer), CFO (chief financial officer), CIO (chief information officer), and other individuals who may have various titles. Traditional descriptions of the CEO's role in strategic management include being the "chief" strategist, structural architect, and developer of the organization's information/control systems.[25] Other descriptions of the strategic role of the "chief executive" include key decision maker, visionary leader, political actor, monitor and interpreter of environment changes, and strategy designer.[26]

No matter how top management's job is described, you can be certain that from their perspective at the organization's upper levels, it's like no other job in the organization. By definition, top managers are ultimately responsible for every decision and action of every organizational employee. One important role that top managers play is that of strategic leader. Organizational researchers study leadership in relation to strategic management because an organization's top managers must provide effective strategic leadership. What is strategic leadership? It's the ability to anticipate, envision, maintain flexibility, think strategically, and work with others in the organization to initiate changes that will create a viable and valuable future for the organization.[27] How can top managers provide effective strategic leadership? Eight key dimensions have been identified.[28] (See Exhibit 9-6.) These dimensions include determining the organization's purpose or vision, exploiting and maintaining the organization's core

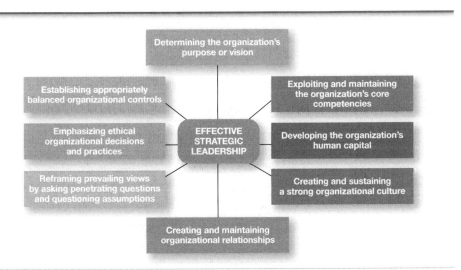

EXHIBIT 9-6
Effective Strategic Leadership

Sources: Based on J. P. Wallman, "Strategic Transactions and Managing the Future: A Druckerian Perspective," *Management Decision*, vol. 48, no. 4, 2010, pp. 485–499; D. E. Zand, "Drucker's Strategic Thinking Process: Three Key Techniques," *Strategy & Leadership*, vol. 38, no. 3, 2010, pp. 23–28; and R. D. Ireland and M. A. Hitt, "Achieving and Maintaining Strategic Competitiveness in the 21st Century: The Role of Strategic Leadership," *Academy of Management Executive*, February 1999, pp. 43–57.

functional strategy
The strategies used by an organization's various functional departments to support the competitive strategy

strategic leadership
The ability to anticipate, envision, maintain flexibility, think strategically, and work with others in the organization to initiate changes that will create a viable and valuable future for the organization

competencies, developing the organization's human capital, creating and sustaining a strong organizational culture, creating and maintaining organizational relationships, reframing prevailing views by asking penetrating questions and questioning assumptions, emphasizing ethical organizational decisions and practices, and establishing appropriately balanced organizational controls. Each dimension encompasses an important part of the strategic management process.

The Need for Strategic Flexibility

Not surprisingly, the economic recession changed the way that many companies approached strategic planning.[29] For instance, at Spartan Motors, a maker of specialty vehicles, managers used to draft a one-year strategic plan and a three-year financial plan, reviewing each one every financial quarter. However, CEO John Sztykiel said, "that relatively inflexible method bears some of the blame for Spartan's sharp drop in sales and gross profit." He also said that the company didn't "respond quickly enough to shifting demand." Now, the company uses a three-year strategic plan that the top management team updates every month. And at J.C. Penney Company, an ambitious five-year strategic growth plan rolled out in 2007 had to be put on hold as the economy floundered.[30] In its place, CEO Mike Ullman III crafted a tentative "bridge" plan to guide the company. This plan worked as the company improved its profit margins and did not have to lay off any employees.

Jürgen Schrempp, former CEO of Daimler AG, stated, "My principle always was . . . move as fast as you can and [if] you indeed make mistakes, you have to correct them. . . . It's much better to move fast, and make mistakes occasionally, than move too slowly."[31] You wouldn't think that smart individuals who are paid lots of money to manage organizations would make mistakes when it comes to strategic decisions. But even when managers use the strategic management process, there's no guarantee that the chosen strategies will lead to positive outcomes. Reading any of the current business periodicals would certainly support this assertion! But the key is responding quickly when it's obvious that the strategy isn't working. In other words, they need **strategic flexibility**—that is, the ability to recognize major external changes, to quickly commit resources, and to recognize when a strategic decision isn't working. Given the highly uncertain environment that managers face today, strategic flexibility seems absolutely necessary! Exhibit 9-7 provides suggestions for developing such strategic flexibility.

Important Organizational Strategies for Today's Environment

ESPN.com gets more than 16 million unique users a month. 16 million! That's almost twice the population of New York City. And its popular online business is just one of many businesses that ESPN is in. Originally founded as a television channel, ESPN is now into original programming,

---

EXHIBIT 9-7

Developing Strategic Flexibility

- *Encourage leadership unity* by making sure everyone is on the same page.
- *Keep resources fluid* and move them as circumstances warrant.
- *Have the right mindset* to explore and understand issues and challenges.
- Know what's happening with strategies currently being used by *monitoring and measuring results*.
- Encourage employees to *be open about disclosing and sharing negative information*.
- *Get new ideas and perspectives from outside* the organization.
- Have *multiple alternatives* when making strategic decisions.
- *Learn from mistakes.*

Sources: Based on Y. L. Doz and M. Kosonen, "Embedding Strategic Agility: A Leadership Agenda for Accelerating Business Model Renewal," *Long Range Planning,* April 2010, pp. 370–382; E. Lewis, D. Romanaggi, and A. Chapple, "Successfully Managing Change During Uncertain Times," *Strategic HR Review,* vol. 9, no. 2, 2010, pp. 12–18; and K. Shimizu and M. Hitt, "Strategic Flexibility: Organizational Preparedness to Reverse Ineffective Strategic Decisions," *Academy of Management Executive,* November 2004, pp. 44–59.

radio, online, publishing, gaming, X games, ESPY awards, ESPN Zones, global, and is looking to move into more local sports coverage.[32] Company president George Bodenheimer "runs one of the most successful and envied franchises in entertainment," and obviously understands how to successfully manage its various strategies in today's environment! We think three strategies are important in today's environment: e-business, customer service, and innovation.

e-BUSINESS STRATEGIES.   Managers use e-business strategies to develop a sustainable competitive advantage.[33] A cost leader can use e-business to lower costs in a variety of ways. For instance, it might use online bidding and order processing to eliminate the need for sales calls and to decrease sales force expenses; it could use Web-based inventory control systems that reduce storage costs; or it might use online testing and evaluation of job applicants.

A differentiator needs to offer products or services that customers perceive and value as unique. For instance, a business might use Internet-based knowledge systems to shorten customer response times, provide rapid online responses to service requests, or automate purchasing and payment systems so that customers have detailed status reports and purchasing histories.

Finally, because the focuser targets a narrow market segment with customized products, it might provide chat rooms or discussion boards for customers to interact with others who have common interests, design niche Web sites that target specific groups with specific interests, or use Web sites to perform standardized office functions such as payroll or budgeting.

Research also has shown that an important e-business strategy might be a clicks-and-bricks strategy. A clicks-and-bricks firm is one that uses both online (clicks) and traditional stand-alone locations (bricks).[34] For example, Walgreen's established an online site for ordering prescriptions, but some 90 percent of its customers who placed orders on the Web preferred to pick up their prescriptions at a nearby store rather than have them shipped to their home. So its "clicks-and-bricks" strategy has worked well!

CUSTOMER SERVICE STRATEGIES.   Companies emphasizing excellent customer service need strategies that cultivate that atmosphere from top to bottom. Such strategies involve giving customers what they want, communicating effectively with them, and providing employees with customer service training. Let's look first at the strategy of giving customers what they want.

It shouldn't surprise you that an important customer service strategy is giving customers what they want, which is a major aspect of an organization's overall marketing strategy. For

Trader Joe's customer service strategy centers on giving customers what they want and having an effective customer communication system. The specialty grocery uses face-to-face conversations, listening to customers and getting their feedback. Spending most of their day on the retail floor, store managers are available to interact with customers, and the company gives them authority to set up their store to meet local needs. Trader Joe's lets employees open products shoppers want to taste and encourages them to recommend products they like and to be honest about products they don't like. At Trader Joe's, a permanent store section that offers free samples also gives employees another chance to listen and respond to what customers want.

strategic flexibility
The ability to recognize major external changes, to quickly commit resources, and to recognize when a strategic decision was a mistake

instance, New Balance Athletic Shoes gives customers a truly unique product: shoes in varying widths. No other athletic shoe manufacturer has shoes for narrow or wide feet and in practically any size.[35]

Having an effective customer communication system is an important customer service strategy. Managers should know what's going on with customers. They need to find out what customers liked and didn't like about their purchase encounter—from their interactions with employees to their experience with the actual product or service. It's also important to let customers know what's going on with the company that might affect future purchase decisions. For instance, Retailer Hot Topic is fanatical about customer feedback, which it gets in the form of shopper "report cards." The company's CEO, Betsy McLaughlin, pores over more than 1,000 of them each week.[36]

Finally, an organization's culture is important to providing excellent customer service. This typically requires that employees be trained to provide exceptional customer service. For example, Singapore Airlines is well-known for its customer treatment. "On everything facing the customer, they do not scrimp," says an analyst based in Singapore.[37] Employees are expected to "get service right," leaving employees with no doubt about the expectations as far as how to treat customers.

INNOVATION STRATEGIES.   When Procter & Gamble purchased the Iams pet-food business, it did what it always does—used its renowned research division to look for ways to transfer technology from its other divisions to make new products.[38] One outcome of this cross-divisional combination: a new tartar-fighting ingredient from toothpaste that's included in all of its dry adult pet foods.

As this example shows, innovation strategies aren't necessarily focused on just the radical, breakthrough products. They can include applying existing technology to new uses. And organizations have successfully used both approaches. What types of innovation strategies do organizations need in today's environment? Those strategies should reflect their innovation philosophy, which is shaped by two strategic decisions: innovation emphasis and innovation timing.

Managers must first decide where the emphasis of their innovation efforts will be. Is the organization going to focus on basic scientific research, product development, or process improvement? Basic scientific research requires the most resource commitment because it involves the nuts-and-bolts work of scientific research. In numerous industries (for instance, genetics engineering, pharmaceuticals, information technology, or cosmetics), an organization's expertise in basic research is the key to a sustainable competitive advantage. However, not every organization requires this extensive commitment to scientific research to achieve high performance levels. Instead, many depend on product development strategies. Although this strategy also requires a significant resource investment, it's not in areas associated with scientific research. Instead, the organization takes existing technology and improves on it or applies it in new ways, just as Procter & Gamble did when it applied tartar-fighting knowledge to pet food products. Both of these first two strategic approaches to innovation (basic scientific research and product development) can help an organization achieve high levels of differentiation, which can be a significant source of competitive advantage.

Finally, the last strategic approach to innovation emphasis is a focus on process development. Using this strategy, an organization looks for ways to improve and enhance its work processes. The organization innovates new and improved ways for employees to do their work in all organizational areas. This innovation strategy can lead to lower costs, which, as we know, also can be a significant source of competitive advantage.

Once managers have determined the focus of their innovation efforts, they must decide their innovation timing strategy. Some organizations want to be the first with innovations whereas others are content to follow or mimic the innovations. An organization that's first to bring a product innovation to the market or to use a new process innovation is called a **first mover**. Being a

first mover
An organization that's first to bring a product innovation to the market or to use a new process innovation

Advantages	Disadvantages
• Reputation for being innovative and industry leader • Cost and learning benefits • Control over scarce resources and keeping competitors from having access to them • Opportunity to begin building customer relationships and customer loyalty	• Uncertainty over exact direction technology and market will go • Risk of competitors imitating innovations • Financial and strategic risks • High development costs

EXHIBIT 9-8

First-Mover Advantages and Disadvantages

first mover has certain strategic advantages and disadvantages as shown in Exhibit 9-8. Some organizations pursue this route, hoping to develop a sustainable competitive advantage. Others have successfully developed a sustainable competitive advantage by being the followers in the industry. They let the first movers pioneer the innovations and then mimic their products or processes. Which approach managers choose depends on their organization's innovation philosophy and specific resources and capabilities.

Let's Get Real:
My Response *to A Manager's Dilemma, page 252*

What Would You Do?

We need to get our strategic leaders together to analyze our SWOT to see how we can leverage ourselves in this marketplace. Since we don't have experience with iPhones, we need to gain expertise in that area—the technical area, perhaps tapping into our current global technological network. Action steps include:

• Forming a focus group of our core users to see how they would use the iPhone (if at all)

  • Do our current customers (teens) use iPhones and how can we retain their loyalty in the future?

• Examining how other companies are bringing games/applications to the iPhone

• Testing games with heavy iPhone users to see what appeals to them

  • Are iPhone users looking for convenience and are they in the working environment?

Sid Gokhale
President
**Dowden Custom Media
Montvale, NJ**

Chapter 5:

Strategic Management in Detail

8.1   Introduction

HMV illustrates the value of managing strategy. For many years it was a leading player in the UK music retailing industry, but in 2005 its performance declined. Management successfully resisted a hostile takeover bid, arguing that it undervalued the company and was not in the shareholders' interests. They then had to deliver on that promise: the board appointed a new chief executive, who set out a three-year strategic plan to improve performance. Managers know that entrepreneurs could again use any trading weakness as an opportunity to buy the company.

All organisations (not just those in trouble) face strategic issues. Established businesses such as BT are in a growing and diversifying telecommunications market, but they face new competition that threatens their core business. Should the company try to compete in all areas, or concentrate on one sector, as Vodafone has done? Should Virgin continue to extend the brand into ever more diverse areas of activity, or would it gain more by building profits in the existing areas, and achieving more synergies across the group? Some charities face declining income: should their managers continue as they are now, or will they serve their cause better by initiating a radical review of their strategy? Strategic management enables companies to be clear about how they will add value to resources, even though much is changing in their world. Strategy links the organisation to the outside world, where changes in the competitive (micro) and wider (macro) environment bring opportunities and threats. Table 8.1 gives some examples of organisations managing their strategies.

Table 8.1 Examples of organisations making strategic changes

Organisation and strategic issue	Strategic decisions or moves
MySpace – in 2010 facing competition from Facebook and a slow growth in advertising revenues. Owner (News Corporation) seeking better financial return. **www.MySpace.com**	New management abandon international expansion strategy, and close several overseas offices, making about 30 per cent of staff redundant. Also scrap plans for a new corporate campus in Los Angeles
Procter and Gamble (world's largest supplier of consumer goods, such as soap and toothpaste) – how to ensure long-term growth. **www.pg.com**	Changed from focus on people in rich economies to those in poor countries; affects R&D, market research and manufacturing to identify and make suitable products
Nestlé (global food and beverage company) – how to stimulate sales and profits in a mature business. **www.nestle.com**	Increased emphasis on healthy foods, by adapting current products and taking over companies with established reputations for healthy products

The first sections of the chapter give you some ideas about the strategy process: how managers develop their strategy, and the tools they use to analyse their external and internal environments. The following two sections then present models with which to analyse corporate and business unit strategies, followed by a presentation of the ways in which managers choose to deliver their strategy.

8.2   Strategy – process, content and context

What is strategy?

Strategy is about how people decide to organise major resources to enhance the performance of an enterprise. It is about resource decisions that are large, relatively long term, expensive and visible – with correspondingly large implications for performance: decisions that are not strategic are operational or tactical. Elaborating on the definition:

Strategy is about how people decide to organise major resources to enhance performance of an enterprise.

- **People** Strategy is typically the responsibility of senior management, but some believe that in conditions of rapid change enabling more people to contribute will improve the result.
- **Decide** In formal planning processes and/or informal conversations among managers.
- **Organise** How to divide and co-ordinate activities to add most value.
- **Major** Significant, expensive, visible – decisions with long-term implications.
- **Resources** Inputs the enterprise needs, including those in other organizations.
- **Enhance performance** The intended outcome of strategic decisions.
- **Enterprise** All types of organisations can benefit from managing their strategy.

The definition is consistent with the view of Johnson *et al.* (2007), who suggest that strategy is something people do (their strategy process) *and* that organisations have (their strategy content).

Process

People, usually senior managers, talk, email and argue about their present and future strategy: this is their strategy process. In this sense, strategy is something that people do (Johnson *et al.*, 2007). Understanding this perspective implies finding out who takes part in strategy formation, what information they gather and how they use the tools available. Do they work in formal settings leading to rationally based plans, or is the process more fluid and iterative? Are strategies set for years, or do they emerge, alter and disappear, sometimes very quickly? Sections 8.3 and 8.4 introduce ideas on strategic processes.

Content

The existing strategy is the starting point of, and the new one is the result of, the strategy process, so in this sense strategy is something that organisations have (Johnson *et al.*, 2007). Something stimulates managers to question current strategy (such as the takeover bid for HMV) or the emergence of a new service which customers may value, but which will require strategic investment. Most managers develop strategy to perform well against competitors. They try to identify what gives their enterprise an edge, so that they can define their **competitive strategy.** This includes deciding what to offer, to which markets, using what resources. Sections 8.5 and 8.6 will deal with these topics.

Competitive strategy explains how an organisation (or unit within it) intends to achieve competitive advantage in its market.

Context

Context here refers to the setting in which the organisation works, which affects the issues those managing it will face. Not-for-profit (NFP) or public sector organisations share some characteristics with commercial businesses (they need to attract and retain enthusiastic and capable staff) and differ in others (their performance criteria and sources of funding). Table 8.2 illustrates these differences between some familiar types of organisation.

Table 8.2 Strategic issues in different settings

Type of organisation	Distinctive strategic issues	Examples in this text
Large MNCs	Structure and control of global activities Allocating resources between units	Procter and Gamble (this chapter); BP (Part 2 case)
SMEs	Strongly influenced by founders or owners; lack of capital limits choices	Linn Products (Section 18.3)
Manufacturing	Relative contribution to competitive advantage of the manufacturing (physical product) or service aspect (delivery, customer support) of the offer	BMW (Chapter 11)
Firms in innovative sectors	Adding value depends on rapid innovation, so strategy aims to create a culture of questioning and challenge	Nokia (Chapter 3); Oticon (Chapter 10)
Public sector	Competing for resources, and so aim to demonstrate best value in outputs; most problems require co-operation between agencies, thus complicating strategy	Crossrail (Chapter 6)
Voluntary and NFP sector	Balancing ideology and values with interests of funding sources; balancing central control (consistency) with local commitment (volunteers and local staff).	The Eden Project (Chapter 15)

Whatever their context, strategists hope that their work will enhance performance by clarifying and unifying purpose, reducing uncertainty, linking short-term actions to long-term goals and providing control – since setting goals provides standards against which to measure performance.

Activity 8.2   Think about the definition

Reflect on an organisation you have worked in, or ask a friend or relative who works in an organisation to help.

- Can you/they identify examples of people in that organisation working on some or all of the items in the definition of strategy?
- Did you/they do other things that were seen as 'managing strategy' but which are not mentioned?
- Decide if the definition accurately describes 'strategy'.
- If not, how would you change it?

8.3   Planning, learning and political perspectives on strategy

Table 8.3 shows three perspectives on the strategy process, comparing their approach, content, nature and outcomes – and the context in which they may be suitable.

Planning

The 'planning view' is prescriptive and based on a belief that the complexity of strategic decisions requires an explicit and formalised approach to guide management through the

Table 8.3 Alternative perspectives on the strategy process

	Planning	Learning	Political
Approach	Prescriptive; assumes rationality	Descriptive; based on bounded rationality	Descriptive; based on bounded rationality
Content	Analytical tools and techniques; forecasting; search for alternatives, each evaluated in detail	Limited use of tools and techniques; limited search for options: time and resources don't permit	As learning view, but some objectives and options disregarded as politically unacceptable
Nature of process	Formalised, systematic, analytical; top down – centralised planning teams	Adaptive, learning by doing; top down and bottom up	Bargaining; use of power to shape strategies; top down and bottom up
Outcomes	Extensive plans made before work begins; plans assumed to be achieved with small changes	Plans are made but not all are 'realised'; some strategies are not planned but emerge in course of 'doing'	Plans may be left ambiguous to secure agreement; need interpretation during implementation; compromises
Context/environment	Stable environment; assumption that future can be predicted; if complex, use of more sophisticated tools	Complex, dynamic, future unpredictable	Stable or dynamic, but complex; stakeholders have diverging values, objectives and solutions

process. In the 1960s and 1970s a wide literature, most notably the work of Ansoff (1965), took this approach, presenting strategy development as a systematic process, following a pre-scribed sequence of steps and making extensive use of analytical tools and techniques (shown in Figure 8.1). Those favouring this perspective assume that events and facts can be expressed or observed objectively and that people respond rationally to information.

Those who challenge these assumptions of objectivity and rationality advocate two alternative views: the learning and the political (Brews and Hunt, 1999).

Learning

This sees strategy as an *emergent* or adaptive process. Mintzberg (1994a, 1994b) regards for-mal strategic planning as a system developed during a period of stability, and designed mainly for the centralised bureaucracies typical of the Western manufacturing industry in the

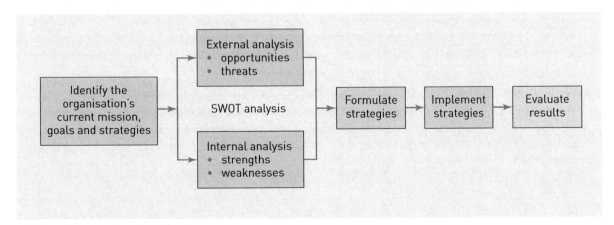

Figure 8.1 The planning view of strategy

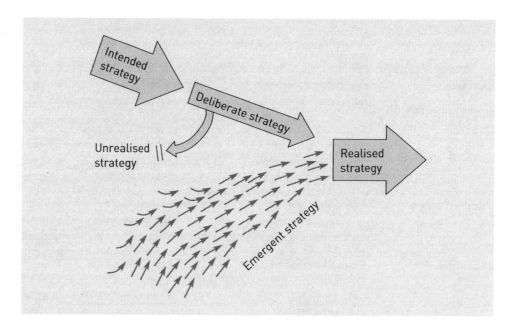

Figure 8.2
Forms of strategy

Source: Mintzberg
(1994a).

mid-twentieth century. This style of planning is appropriate for those conditions, but not for businesses in rapidly changing sectors: they require a more flexible approach.

He therefore distinguished between intended and **emergent strategy** (Figure 8.2). He acknowledges the validity of strategy as a plan, setting out intended courses of action, and recognises that some deliberate intentions may be realised. But it is also likely that some plans are not implemented (unrealised strategies) and that others which he describes as 'emergent strategies' were not expressly intended. They resulted from:

Emergent strategies
are those that result from
actions taken one by one
that converge in time in
some sort of consistency
pattern.

> actions taken one by one, which converged in time in some sort of consistency or pattern.
> (Mintzberg, 1994a, p. 25)

| **Management in practice** | **Emergent strategy at Ikea** www.ikea.com |

Barthélemy (2006) offers an insight into the strategy process at Ikea (Chapter 7 case). Ikea's strategy has clearly been highly successful, but how did it come about? A close examination of the company's history shows that many of the specifics of the strategy were not brought about through a process of deliberate formulation followed by implementation:

> **Instead, the founder, Ingvar Kamprad started with a very general vision. Ikea's specific strategy then emerged as he both proactively developed a viable course of action and reacted to unfolding circumstances.** (p. 81)

Examples include:

- The decision to sell furniture was an adaptation to the market, not a deliberate strategy – furniture was initially a small part of the retail business, but was so successful that he soon dropped all other products.
- The flat pack method which symbolises the group was introduced to reduce insurance claims on the mail order business – its true potential only became clear when the company started opening stores, and realised that customers valued this type of product.
- The company only began to design its own furniture because other retailers put pressure on established furniture companies not to sell to Ikea.

Source: Barthélemy (2006).

A flexible approach to strategy recognises that:

the real world inevitably involves some thinking ahead of time as well as some adaptation *en route*. (Mintzberg, 1994a, p. 26)

The essence of the learning view is adaptation, reacting to unexpected events, experimenting with new ideas 'on the ground'. Mintzberg gives the example of a salesperson coming up with the idea of selling an existing product to some new customers. Soon all the other salespeople begin to do the same, and

one day, months later, management discovers that the company has entered a new market. (Mintzberg, 1994a, p. 26)

This was not planned but learned, collectively, during implementation.

Political view

Strategy as an emergent process has much in common with political perspectives, since both draw on the concepts of bounded rationality and satisficing behaviour (Chapter 7). While the learning view reflects the logic that planning can never give complete foresight, the political view adds dimensions of power, conflict and ambiguity.

Drawing on his experience in the public policy sphere, Lindblom (1959) was an early proponent of the political view (see also Chapter 7). He drew attention to the way value judgements influence policy and to the way in which conflicting interests of stakeholders frustrate attempts to agree strategy. He concluded that strategic management is not a scientific, comprehensive or rational process, but is an iterative, incremental process, characterised by restricted analysis and bargaining between the players. Lindblom (1959) called this the method of 'successive limited comparisons' whereby 'new' strategy is made by marginal adjustments to existing strategy:

Policy is not made once and for all; it is made and remade endlessly . . . [through] . . . a process of successive approximation to some desired objectives.

It is not a comprehensive, objective process but a limited comparison of options, restricted to those that are politically acceptable and possible to implement.

While advocating a learning view, Mintzberg also stresses the value of planning:

Too much planning may lead us to chaos, but so too would too little, more directly. (Mintzberg, 1994a, p. 416)

The planning style suited the relative stability of the 1960s. Uncertain business conditions probably require a different approach, of which the next section provides some evidence.

Activity 8.3   Gather evidence about the three perspectives

Read one of these case studies – Crossrail (Chapter 6), Apple (Chapter 14), or any other organisation will be suitable for this activity.

- Identify two or three strategic moves made by the company, and write a brief note on each.
- Can you find evidence to show which of the three perspectives on strategy they used: planning, learning or political?
- On reflection, does that seem to have been the best method for the situation?
- Compare your answers with other students on your course, and try to identify any common or contrasting themes.

8.4 How do managers develop strategies?

Grant (2003) gives some insights into the way managers develop strategy from his study in eight major oil companies, especially how the greater uncertainty in their business environment had affected them. In the relatively stable conditions of the 1970s they had developed formal planning systems which were conducted by staff at corporate HQ, with much emphasis on analysis, detailed forecasts of energy demand and price, and documents setting out long-term plans for the businesses to follow.

At the time of Grant's study, all oil companies used a clear planning process – the details varied between them but Figure 8.3 shows the common components. Corporate HQ set the overall strategic direction, which provided a framework within which business unit staff developed their strategic proposals. They discussed these with corporate staff, and the revised plans then informed both the annual financial budget, and the corporate plan. After Board approval, the corporate plan formed the context for annual performance targets, and for appraising their achievement.

As expected, all the companies said that the more turbulent environment (volatile oil prices, economic uncertainty and competition) had changed the strategy process. There was now:

- less detailed forecasting, more broad scenario planning (see below), more making assumptions about significant variables;
- less formality and documentation, more face-to-face discussion between corporate and business unit staff;
- shorter planning meetings;
- a shift in responsibility from corporate to business management, and from planning staff to line management.

The content of strategic plans had also changed in that they now covered shorter periods, were more concerned with direction than with detail, and emphasised performance planning by setting:

- financial targets;
- operating targets;

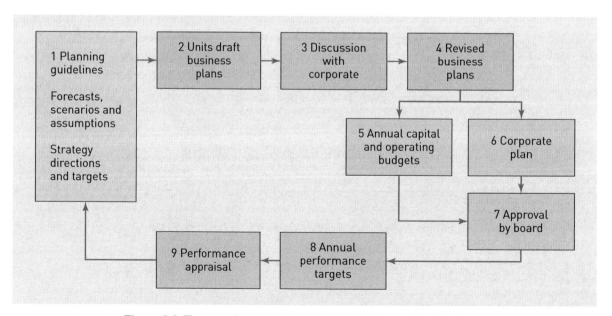

Figure 8.3 The generic strategic planning cycle among the oil majors
Source: Based on Grant (2003), p. 499.

- safety and environmental targets;
- strategic mileposts; and
- capital expenditure limits.

Grant's final conclusion was that the strategic planning processes in these companies were mainly concerned with co-ordinating the strategies emerging from the business units, and with monitoring and controlling their implementation:

> Strategic planning has become less about strategic decision making and more a mechanism for coordination and performance managing . . . permitting increased decentralization of decision making and greater adaptability and responsiveness to external change. (p. 515)

The eight oil companies are not typical organisations – but studies in other sectors of the economy present a similar picture of contemporary strategic planning as a process combining elements of formality and informality, of demanding targets and intelligent flexibility. Whittington *et al.* (2006) and Johnson *et al.* (2007) add to this with their view of 'strategy as practice', showing what people do as they craft strategy, and how their context influences this (see Key Ideas).

Key ideas Strategy as practice

Whittington *et al.* (2006) conducted qualitative research in 10 organisations to examine how they developed their strategies. They conclude that in a world of accelerating change the linked activities of formulating strategy and designing organisation are best conducted as tightly linked practical activities. They focused on three specific tools; strategy workshops or away-days, strategic change projects, and symbolic artifacts (things that people develop to represent and communicate strategy). Their observations showed the transitory nature of strategies and organisational forms leading them to suggest that verbs ('strategising' and 'organising' respectively) capture the nature of the work people do as they work on strategy.

They also found that practical crafts of strategising and organising were as important as the formal tools of analysis:

> Formal strategy can be renewed by a greater appreciation of the everyday, practical, non-analytical skills required to carry it out [especially those of coordination, communication and control]. (p. 616) Strategists run workshops and video-conferences, draw flip-charts, design PowerPoints, manipulate spreadsheets, manage projects, write reports, monitor metrics and talk endlessly: their skills at these activities can mean success or failure for entire strategy processes. (p. 625)

Source: Whittington *et al.* (2006).

Hodgkinson *et al.* (2006) studied the use of strategy workshops, a common management practice in which senior managers take time out from daily activities to deliberate on the longer-term direction of the concern, especially on formulating and implementing changes in strategy. Their research showed that workshops did indeed play an important role in the strategic planning process, were more discursive than analytical, and were typically for top managers. They also found that:

- most companies held strategy workshops once a year, as part of their formal planning process, usually lasting between one and three days;
- most participants spent less than one day preparing for them – rather than detailed information gathering and analysis, they were designed to allow participants to share experience and ideas;
- tools most commonly used to help structure the discussion were SWOT analysis, stakeholder analysis, scenario planning, market segmentation, competence analysis, PESTEL and Value Chain Analysis; and
- top managers were more likely to attend than middle managers.

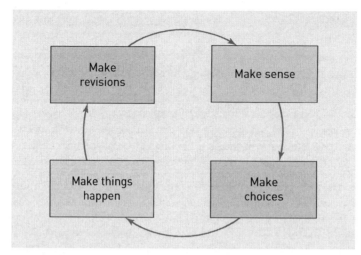

They observed that since the main benefit of such workshops was to communicate and co-ordinate strategy, the absence of middle managers made this difficult to achieve.

Sull (2007) believes that since volatile markets throw out a steady stream of opportunities and threats, managers cannot predict the form, magnitude or timing of events. This makes the planning view of strategy inadequate, as it may deter people from incorporating new information into action. He therefore sees the strategy process as inherently iterative – a loop instead of a line:

> According to this view, every strategy is a work in progress that is subject to revision in light of ongoing interactions between the organization and its shifting environment. To accommodate those interactions, the strategy loop consists of four major steps: making sense of a situation, making choices on what to do (and what not to do), making those things happen and making revisions based on new information (p. 31).

Figure 8.4 shows the strategy loop, the most important feature of which is that it implies that managers incorporate and use new information as it becomes available, closely linking strategy formation and implementation.

Sull stresses the importance of conversations – formal and informal, short and long, one-on-one and in groups – as the key mechanism for co-ordinating activity inside a company. To put the strategy loop into practice, managers at every level must be able to lead discussions about the four steps. The following sections provide ideas and examples about each of these:

- making sense – using information about external and internal environments;
- making choices – deciding strategy at corporate and business unit levels;
- making things happen – ways to deliver strategy; and
- making revisions – reflecting on results, and taking in new information.

8.5   Making sense – external and internal analysis

External analysis

Chapter 3 outlined Porter's five forces model, showing the forces which affect the profitability of an industry (see Key Ideas).

Using Porter's five forces in strategic analysis

Analysing the likely effects on a company of the five forces which Michael Porter (1980a, 2008) identified can show the action points which managers need to consider in their strategy.

- **Threat of entry**: what are the barriers that new entrants need to overcome if they are to compete successfully? High barriers are good for incumbents: they fear barriers that are becoming lower, as this exposes them to more competition. Government legislation in the 1980s reduced the barriers protecting banks from competition, and allowed other companies to enter the industry.
- **Threat of substitutes**: what alternative products and services may customers choose? Many people choose to receive their news online rather than in print, seriously threatening print newspapers, which need to build strategies for survival.
- **Power of buyers**: if they have strong bargaining power they force down prices and reduce profitability. Small food companies are attracted by the prospect of doing business with large retailers, but are wary of the power of the retailers to dictate prices.
- **Power of suppliers**: if suppliers have few competitors they can raise prices at the expense of customers. Companies that have few alternative sources of energy or raw materials are exposed when stocks are low.
- **Competitive rivalry**: the four forces combine to affect the intensity of rivalry between an organisation and its rivals. Factors such as industry growth or the ease with which companies can leave it also affect this.

The model remains popular, and Porter published a revised version in 2008, mainly by adding current examples: the five forces remain the same. They help strategists to understand the fundamental conditions of their industry, and to work out how to make their company less vulnerable and more profitable.

Source: Porter (1980a, 2008).

At the macro-level of the general environment, the PESTEL framework helps to identify the major drivers of change affecting their strategy. These may conflict: an aging population might seem like good news for businesses such as Southern Cross or Care UK, but budget problems in local authorities, which buy most of the places in care homes, mean that they prefer, whenever they can, to provide care in an elderly person's home, rather than admitting him/her to a residential home. A company may also, like Motorola, miss signals about changes in the outside world (see the following Management in Practice).

Motorola misreads the market www.motorola.com

In 2009 Greg Brown, Motorola's joint chief executive, explained the dramatic decline in the company's mobile phone business. He said that the company did not spot quickly enough how mobiles were evolving from simple devices for making phone calls into sophisticated handsets for surfing the internet and sending email. Smartphones have thrived with the arrival of third-generation mobile technology, and Motorola has been weak in that area. As Brown says:

> Motorola didn't see the trends coming in smartphone and 3G with the kind of foresight and customer attention it should have.

He went on to describe Motorola's failure to anticipate the growing importance of mobile software rather than handset design – accepting that most of the challenges the company faces were their own doing.

The company was the world's largest mobile maker in the 1990s until Nokia stole that mantle in 1998. It then followed a strategy of selling cheap handsets in developing countries, but abandoned that as it was unprofitable. In the fourth quarter of 2006 the company's market share of mobile sales was 23.3 per cent – in the same quarter of 2008 it was 6.6 per cent.

Source: *Financial Times*, 2 March 2009.

Kay (1996) defined strategy as the match between the organisation's external relationships and its internal capabilities, describing 'how it responds to its suppliers, its customers, its competitors, and the social and economic environment within which it operates'. Before establishing a direction, managers need an internal analysis to show how well they can cope with external changes.

Internal analysis: resources, capabilities and dynamic capabilities

Managers analyse the internal environment to identify the organisation's strengths and weaknesses. This means identifying what the organisation does well, where it might do better and whether it has the resources and competences to deliver a preferred strategy. Those that are considered essential to outperforming the competition constitute critical success factors.

Chapter 1 introduced the idea of strategic capability as the ability to perform at the level required to survive and prosper, and showed how this depends on the resources available to the organisation, and its competence in using them. Tangible resources are the physical assets such as buildings, equipment, people or finance, while intangible resources include reputation, knowledge or information. **Unique resources** are those which others cannot obtain: a powerful brand, access to raw material or a distinctive culture.

Unique resources are resources that are vital to competitive advantage and which others cannot obtain.

Organisations also need to develop *competences* – activities and processes which enable it to deploy resources effectively. Joe Morris, operations director at TJ Morris, a Liverpool-based chain of discount stores (in 2010 the second largest independent grocer in the UK) claims that its IT system (which his brother Ed designed) gives them a competitive advantage:

> It is our own bespoke product. It is extremely reliable and simple. We can do what we want to do very quickly.

While the amount and quality of these resources matter, how people use them matters more. If managers encourage staff to develop higher skills, co-operate with each other, be innovative and creative, the company is likely to perform better than one where managers treat staff indifferently.

Understanding competitive advantage requires a further distinction:

- **Threshold capabilities** (resources and competences) – an organisation must have these to be in a market (adequate IT systems, for example).
- **Core capabilities** (resources and competencies) – an organisation can deploy these to gain a competitive advantage, because others cannot imitate them.

Ryanair has prospered not because it has resources (a fleet of modern, standard aircraft) – other airlines have similar resources but are unprofitable. The difference is that Ryanair has developed competencies, such as quick turnrounds which enable it to use aircraft more efficiently. GlaxoSmithKline has a strategy to acquire half of its new drugs from other organisations: for this to work, it will need to develop a **core competence** of identifying and working with suitable partners.

> **Core competences** are the activities and processes through which resources are deployed to achieve competitive advantage in ways that others cannot imitate or obtain.

Management's task in internal analysis is to identify those capabilities (resources and competencies) that distinguish it to the customer. At the *corporate level*, this could be the overall balance of activities that it undertakes – the product or service portfolio. Does it have sufficient capabilities in growing rather than declining markets? Does it have too many new products (which drain resources) relative to established ones? Are there useful synergies between the different lines of business? At the *divisional or strategic business unit level*, performance depends on having adequate resources (physical, human, financial and so on) and competences (such as design, production or marketing).

In highly uncertain business conditions the factors which once enabled an organisation to prosper may no longer be enough. It may need to create new capabilities which enable it to remain competitive in the new conditions, such as the ability to bring new products to the market more rapidly than competitors, or to develop skills of developing alliances with other businesses. These are called **dynamic capabilities**, which enable it to renew and recreate its strategic capabilities to meet the needs of a changing environment. These capabilities may be relatively formal, such as systems for developing new products or procedures for acquiring firms with valuable skills or products. They may also be informal, such as the ability to reach decisions quickly when required, or the ability of staff to work well in multi-professional teams.

> **Dynamic capabilities** are an organisation's abilities to renew and recreate its strategic capabilities to meet the needs of a changing environment.

> A **value chain** 'divides a firm into the discrete activities it performs in designing, producing, marketing and distributing its product. It is the basic tool for diagnosing competitive advantage and finding ways to enhance it' (Porter, 1985).

Value chain analysis

The concept of the **value chain**, introduced by Porter (1985), is derived from an accounting practice that calculates the value added at each stage of a manufacturing or service process. Porter applied this idea to the activities of the whole organisation, as an analysis of each activity could identify sources of competitive advantage.

Figure 8.5 shows primary and support activities. *Primary* activities transform inputs into outputs and deliver them to the customer:

- **inbound logistics**: receiving, storing and distributing the inputs to the product or service; also material handling and stock control, etc.;
- **operations**: transforming inputs into the final product or service, by machining, mixing and packing;
- **outbound logistics**: moving the product to the buyer – collecting, storing and distributing; in some services (a sports event) these activities will include bringing the customers to the venue;
- **marketing and sales**: activities to make consumers aware of the product;
- **service**: enhancing or maintaining the product – installation, training, repairs.

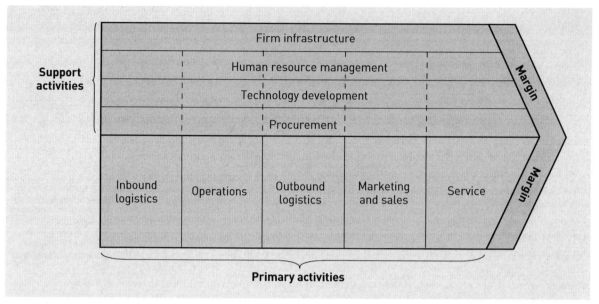

Figure 8.5 The value chain

Source: Reprinted with the permission of The Free Press, a Division of Simon & Schuster, Inc., from *COMPETITIVE ADVANTAGE: Creating and Sustaining Superior Performance* by Michael E. Porter, copyright © 1985, 1998 by Michael E. Porter. All rights reserved.

These depend on four *support* activities:

- **firm infrastructure:** organisational structure, together with planning, financial and quality systems;
- **human resource management:** recruitment, training, rewards, etc.;
- **technology development:** relate to inputs, operational processes or outputs;
- **procurement:** acquiring materials and other resources.

> ### Case questions 8.4
>
> As part of the recovery plan, HMV is widening the range of products it stocks, and changing the ways it receives these and delivers them to customers. Use the value chain to analyse these changes, doing it separately for HMV and Waterstone's when necessary.
>
> - How do these changes fit into the value chain?
> - What new challenges may they have raised for the linkages between stages in the chain?

Value chain analysis enables managers to consider which activities benefit customers and which are more troublesome – perhaps destroying value rather than creating it. The business might, say, be good at marketing, outbound logistics and technology development, but poor at operations and human resource management. That awareness may lead managers to consider which activities it should do, and which it should outsource to other firms. Each activity in the chain:

> can contribute to a firm's relative cost position and create a basis for differentiation. (Porter, 1985)

the two main sources of competitive advantage. Analysing the value chain helps management to consider:

- Which activities have most effect on reducing cost or adding value? If customers value quality more than costs, then that implies a focus on ensuring quality of suppliers.
- What linkages do most to reduce cost, enhance value or discourage imitation?
- How do these linkages relate to the cost and value drivers?

SWOT analysis

Strategy follows a 'fit' between internal capabilities and external changes – managers try to identify key issues from each and draw out the strategic implications. A SWOT analysis (see Chapter 6) summarises the internal and external issues and helps identify potentially useful developments, which are shown schematically in Figure 8.6.

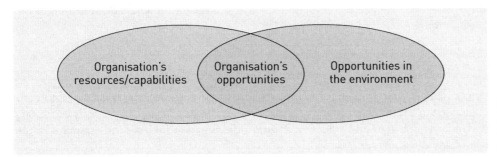

Figure 8.6
Identifying the organisation's opportunities

Hodgkinson *et al.* (2006) found that managers often use the technique in strategy workshops, although like any technique the value depends on how thoroughly people use it; for example by taking time to gather evidence about the relative significance of factors identified, rather than simply making a long list of items without challenge.

Case questions 8.5

Drawing on your answers to previous questions:

- Make a summary SWOT analysis for the two businesses in the HMV Group.
- Consult the HMV Group's website to read recent statements from the CEO and other information.

If the SWOT analysis is done thoroughly, managers can use the output to develop and evaluate strategic alternatives, aiming to select those that make the most of internal strengths and external opportunities. Managers in large enterprises develop strategies at corporate, business and functional levels, although in smaller organisations there will be less complexity. Figure 8.7 shows this.

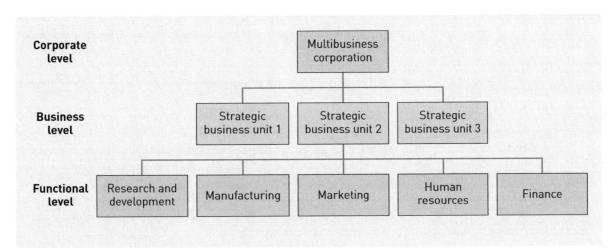

Figure 8.7 Levels of strategy

> ### 8.6   Making choices – deciding strategy at corporate level

At corporate level the strategy reflects the overall direction of the organisation, and the part which the respective business units will play in that. What is the overall mission and purpose? Should it focus on a small range of activities or diversify? Should it remain a local or national business, or seek to operate internationally? These decisions establish the direction of the organisation.

The corporate mission

A **mission statement** is a broad statement of an organisation's scope and purpose, aiming to distinguish it from similar organisations.

Defining the mission is intended to provide a focus for work. A broad **mission statement** can guide those setting more specific goals and the strategies to achieve them, by expressing the underlying beliefs and values held within the organisation (see the examples in the following Management in Practice).

Management in practice   Examples of missions and visions

Ikea (www.ikea.com)
A better everyday life.
Google (www.google.com)
To organize the world's information.
Royal Society for the Protection of Birds (www.rspb.org.uk)
To secure a healthy environment for birds and wildlife, helping to create a better world for us all.
Cancer Research UK (www.cancerresearchuk.org)
Together we will beat cancer
Nokia (www.nokia.com)
To connect people in new and better ways.

Mission statements may be idealistic aspirations rather than guides to action. Employees only believe, and act upon, the mission statement if they see managers doing so. The mission needs to be cascaded through the structure to ensure it guides day-to-day actions.

Setting a strategic direction

Strategies can aim for growth, stability or renewal. Growth strategies try to expand the number of products offered or markets served. Stability is when the organisation offers the same products and services to much the same group of customers. Renewal often follows a period of trouble and involves significant changes to the business to secure the required turnaround.

Management in practice   A new strategy at ABB   www.abb.com

ABB is a Swiss-Swedish electrical engineering group, which in 2009 surprised observers by appointing a new chief executive, Joe Hogan, who had spent over 20 years at the US giant, General Electric. He had taken a low-key approach to managing the business in his early months in the job, preferring to move carefully. A few months into the job he had made three big strategic adjustments:

Boosting services. ABB is already active in areas such as facilities management and energy conservation, but he wants to increase services revenue from 16 per cent of total sales to 25 per cent: 'the great thing about services is that it also gets you much closer to your customer, helping you understand their needs'.

A sharper sales culture. 'I want to see more of an external focus. Like many engineering companies ABB has tended to be inward looking.' It must become more sensitive to market signals and immediate customer needs.

Plugging geographic weaknesses. ABB is admired for having moved early into China and India. Mr Hogan believes the group can deepen its activities in existing markets and grow where it is weak. 'We need to improve our global footprint. ABB has always been heavily focused on Europe.'

Source: *Financial Times*, 8 June 2009.

Managers can decide how to achieve their chosen option by using the product/market matrix, shown in Figure 8.8. They can achieve growth by focusing on one or more of the

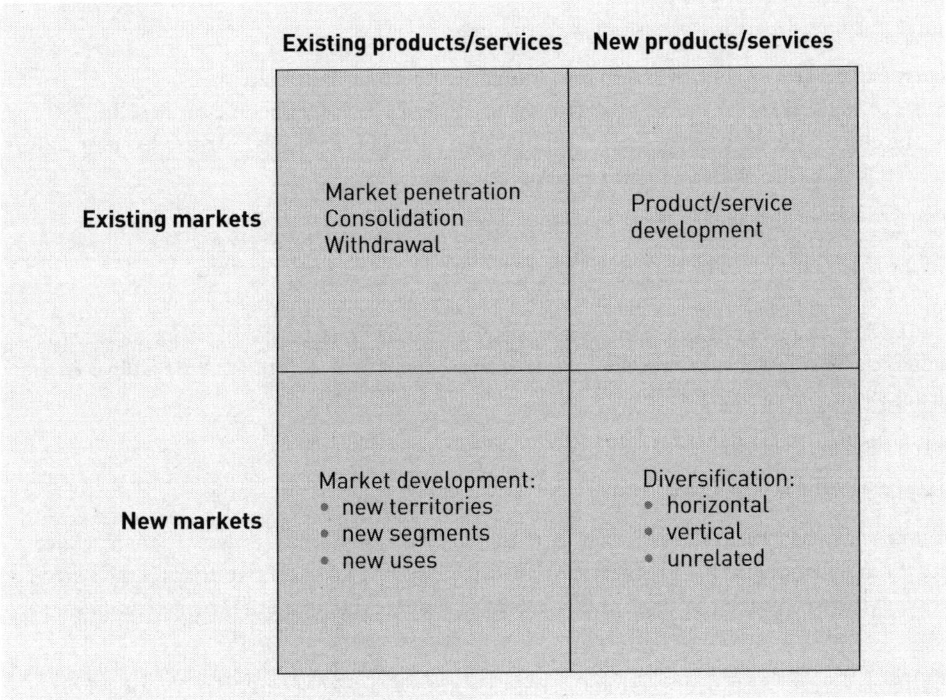

	Existing products/services	**New products/services**
Existing markets	Market penetration Consolidation Withdrawal	Product/service development
New markets	Market development: • new territories • new segments • new uses	Diversification: • horizontal • vertical • unrelated

Figure 8.8
Strategy development directions – the product/market matrix

Source: As adapted in Johnson *et al.* (2008) from Chapter 6 of H. Ansoff, *Corporate Strategy* published by Penguin 1988.

quadrants: stability by remaining with existing products and services; and renewal by leaving some markets followed by entry into others.

Existing markets, existing product/service

Choice within this segment depends on whether the market is growing, mature or in decline, or has reached maturity. Each box shows several possibilities:

- A market penetration strategy aims to increase market share, which will be easier in a growing than in a mature market. It could be achieved by reducing price, increasing advertising or improving distribution.
- Consolidation aims to protect the company's share in existing markets. In growing or mature markets this could mean improving efficiency and/or service to retain custom. In declining markets management might consolidate by acquisition of other companies.

- Withdrawal is a wise option when, for instance, competition is intense and the organisation is unable to match its rivals; staying in that line of business would destroy value, not create it. In the public sector, changing priorities lead to the redeployment of resources. Health boards have withdrawn accident and emergency services from some hospitals to make better use of limited resources.

Existing markets, new products/services

A strategy of product or service development allows a company to retain the relative security of its present markets while altering products or developing new ones. In retail sectors such as fashion, consumer electronics and financial services, companies continually change products to meet perceived changes in consumer preferences. Car manufacturers compete by adding features and extending their model range. Some new products, such as 'stakeholder pensions' in the UK, arise out of changes in government policy. Many new ideas fail commercially, so that product development is risky and costly.

New markets, existing products/services

Market development aims to find new outlets by:

- extending geographically (from local to national or international);
- targeting new market segments (groups of customers, by age, income or lifestyle); or
- finding new uses for a product (a lightweight material developed for use in spacecraft is also used in the manufacture of golf clubs).

Management in practice   P&G targets poorer customers www.pg.com

Procter & Gamble, the world's largest consumer goods company, has built its success on selling detergent, toothpaste and beauty products to the world's wealthiest 1 billion consumers. When chief executive A.G. Lafley arrived in 2002 and said

> We're going to serve the world's consumers'

he surprised the company's staff. One recalled:

> We realised that we didn't have the product strategy or the cost structure to be effective in serving lower income consumers. What's happened in the last five years has been one of the most dramatic transformations I've seen in my career. We now have all of our functions focused on meeting the needs of poorer consumers.

By 2005 it was devoting 30 per cent of the annual research and development budget to low-income markets, a 50 per cent increase on five years earlier. Developing markets are expected to grow twice as fast as developed markets over the next five years. The transformation has been evident in three areas:

- how the company finds out what customers want;
- how this affects R&D; and
- manufacturing facilities.

Sources: Published sources; company website.

New markets, new products/services

Often described as diversification, this can take three forms:

- **Horizontal integration** Developing related or complementary activities, such as when mortgage lenders extend into the insurance business, using their knowledge of, and contact with, existing customers to offer them an additional service. The advantages include the ability to expand by using existing resources and skills, such as Kwik-Fit's use of its database of depot customers to create a motor insurance business.

- **Vertical integration** Moving either backwards or forwards into activities related to the organisation's products and services. A manufacturer might decide to make its own components rather than buy them from elsewhere. Equally, it could develop forward, for instance into distribution.

- **Unrelated diversification** Developing into new markets outside the present industry. Virgin has used its strong brand to create complementary activities in sectors as diverse as airlines, trains, insurance and soft drinks. The extension by some retailers into financial services is another example. It is a way to spread risk where demand patterns fluctuate at different stages of the economic cycle, and to maintain growth when existing markets become saturated.

Alternative development directions are not mutually exclusive: companies can follow several at the same time. Apple Inc. has a clear strategy to move away from being a computer manufacturer and into areas which would give their products a very wide appeal. One observer predicted, at the time of the iPad launch in 2010:

> Get on any train in five years' time, and people will be reading the newspaper (downloaded at home or automatically when they walk through Waterloo Station on the way home), books, watching TV, playing games (quite possibly with fellow passengers!) on their iPads.

8.7 | Making choices – deciding strategy at business unit level

At the business unit level, firms face a choice about how to compete. Porter (1980b, 1985) identified two types of competitive advantage: low cost or differentiation. From this he developed the idea that there are three generic strategies a firm can use to develop and maintain competitive advantage: cost leadership, differentiation and focus. Figure 8.9 shows these strategies. The horizontal axis shows the two bases of competitive advantage. Competitive scope, on the vertical axis, shows whether company's target market is broad or narrow in scope.

Cost leadership

Cost leadership is when a firm aims to compete on price rather than, say, advanced features or excellent customer service. They will typically sell a standard no-frills product and try to minimize costs. This requires **economies of scale** in production and close attention to efficiency and operating costs, although other sources of cost advantage, such as preferential access to raw materials, also help. However, a low cost base will not in itself bring competitive advantage – consumers must see that the product represents value for money. Retailers that have used this strategy include Wal-Mart (Asda in the UK), Argos and Superdrug; Dell Computers is another example, as is Ryanair (Chapter 1 case).

A cost leadership strategy is one in which a firm uses low price as the main competitive weapon.

Economies of scale are achieved when producing something in large quantities reduces the cost of each unit.

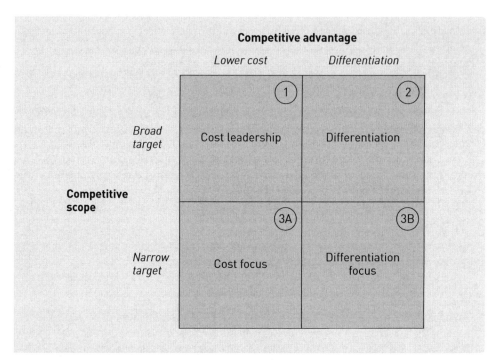

Figure 8.9
Generic
competitive
strategies

| Key ideas | The experience curve |

An important feature of cost leadership is the effect of the experience curve, in which the unit cost of manufacturing a product or delivering a service falls as experience increases. In the same way that a person learning to knit or play the piano improves with practice, so 'the unit cost of value added to a standard product declines by a constant percentage (typically 20–30 per cent) each time cumulative output doubles' (Grant, 2003). This allows firms to set initial low selling prices in the knowledge that margins will increase as output grows and costs fall. The rate of travel down the cost experience curve is a crucial aspect of staying ahead of the competition in an undifferentiated market and underlines the importance of market share – if high volumes are not sold, the cost advantage is lost. Examples of products where costs have fallen as volumes have risen are semiconductors, watches, cars and online reservations.

Differentiation

Differentiation strategy
consists of offering a
product or service that is
perceived as unique or
distinctive on a basis
other than price.

A **differentiation strategy** is seen when a company offers a service that is distinct from its competitors, and which customers value. It is 'something unique beyond simply offering a low price' (Porter, 1985) that allows firms to charge a high price or retain customer loyalty. Chatterjee (2005) shows the strategic benefits of identifying very clearly the outcomes that customers value, and Sharp and Dawes (2001) contrast companies' methods of differentiation:

- Nokia achieves differentiation through the individual design of its product;
- Sony achieves it by offering superior reliability, service and technology;
- BMW differentiates by stressing a distinctive product/service image;
- Coca-Cola differentiates by building a widely recognised brand.

The form of differentiation varies. In construction equipment durability, spare parts availability and service will feature in a differentiation strategy, while in cosmetics differentiation is based on images of sophistication, exclusivity and eternal youth. Cities compete by stressing differentiation in areas such as cultural facilities, available land or good transport links.

Focus

A **focus strategy** involves targeting a narrow market segment, either by consumer group (teenagers, over-60s, doctors) or geography. The two variants – cost focus and differentiation focus – are simply narrow applications of the broad strategies. Examples include:

A **focus strategy** is when a company competes by targeting very specific segments of the market.

- Saga offers travel and insurance for those over 50;
- Rolls-Royce offers luxury transport to the wealthy;
- NFU Mutual offers insurance for farmers, Female Direct offers insurance for women;
- Cooperative Financial Services appeals to consumers with social concerns.

Management in Practice — Strategic focus at Maersk www.maersk.com

I think because of the size of our organisation now, our strategy is really targeted to focus on certain segments. One of the things we did this year was start a brand new service from Costa Rica to the UK, specifically bringing in bananas. That was a new service for us and provided a different service for the customer, whereas before they've always been shipped in bulk vessels, and now we've containerised them. So we try and be very specific about the marketing. Once the customer is on board, then we have small teams of customer service people looking after specific customers, both here and elsewhere in the world.

Once we've locked them into the customer experience, what we want to do then is build a long term relationship with the customer, get to know the business, get to know where we can improve them. Not just on the service but also from a cost point of view, because obviously cost is very important in this market. So we like to go into partnerships. Some of the biggest retailers in the UK for instance we have long-term relationships with, one of those being Tesco, where we've been able to take a lot of costs out of their supply chain by giving them a personalised service by actually knowing their business.

Source: Interview with Brian Godsafe, Customer Services Manager.

Activity 8.5 — Critical reflection on strategy

- Select two companies you are familiar with and, in each case, gather evidence to help you decide which generic strategy they are following.
- Then consider what features you would expect to see if the company decided to follow the opposite strategy.

Porter initially suggested that firms had to choose between cost leadership and differentiation. Many disagreed, observing how companies often appeared to follow both strategies simultaneously. By controlling costs better than competitors, companies can reinvest the savings in features that differentiate them. Porter (1994) later clarified his view:

> Every strategy must consider both relative cost and relative differentiation . . . a company cannot completely ignore quality and differentiation in the pursuit of cost advantage, and vice versa . . . Progress can be made against both types of advantage simultaneously. (p. 271)

However, he notes there are trade-offs between the two and that companies should 'maintain a clear commitment to superiority in one of them'.

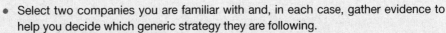

Functional-level strategy

Business-level strategies need the support of suitable functional level strategies - Chapters 9, 11 and 12 give examples.

> ## 8.8 Making things happen – deciding how to deliver strategy

Organisations deliver their strategies internal development, acquisition, or alliance – or a combination of these.

Internal development

The organisation delivers the strategy by expanding or redeploying relevant resources that it has or can employ. This enables managers to retain control of all aspects of the development of new products or services, especially where the product has technologically advanced features. Microsoft develops its Windows operating system in-house.

Public sector organisations typically favour internal development, traditionally providing services through staff whom they employ directly. Changes in the wider political agenda have meant that these are often required to compete with external providers, while some, such as France Telecom, Deutsche Post or the UK Stationery Office, have been partially or wholly sold to private investors.

Merger and acquisition

One firm merging with, or acquiring, another allows rapid entry into new product or market areas and is a quick way to build market share. It is also used where the acquiring company can use the other company's products to offer new services or enter new markets. Companies such as Microsoft and Cisco Systems frequently buy small, entrepreneurial companies and incorporate their products within the acquiring company's range. A company might be taken over for its expertise in research or its knowledge of a local market. Financial motives are often strong, particularly where the merger leads to cost-cutting. When The Royal Bank of Scotland acquired NatWest it achieved major economies by merging the two companies' computer systems. Other mergers extend the range of activities. Vodafone made several large acquisitions in its quest to become the world's largest mobile phone company.

Mergers and acquisitions frequently fail, destroying rather than adding value. When Sir Roy Gardner took over as chairman of Compass (a UK catering company) at which profits and the share price had fallen rapidly, he was critical of the previous management:

> (They) concentrated far too much on growing the business through acquisition. They should have stopped and made sure (that) what they had acquired delivered the expected results. Compass was being run by its divisional mangers, which resulted in a total lack of consistency. (*Financial Times*, 19 January 2007, p. 19)

Joint developments and alliances

Organisations sometimes turn to partners to co-operate in developing products or services. Arrangements vary from highly formal contractual relationships to looser forms of co-operation, but there are usually advantages to be gained by both parties. One attraction of this method is that it limits risk. UK construction firm John Laing has a joint venture with the Commonwealth Bank of Australia to invest in UK hospital and European road projects: rather than borrow funds for a project, Laing shares the risk (and the reward) with the bank. HMV acquired a 50 per cent equity stake in 7digital in September 2009, as this will enable it to use that company's technological expertise to enhance its own digital offers in entertainment and e-books.

Management in practice   GSK's drug development strategy www.gsk.com

Half of the new drug discovery projects at GlaxoSmithKline may be undertaken by external partners by the turn of the decade as part of a radical overhaul designed to improve the pipeline of new drugs at the group. The research and development will be co-ordinated by GSK's Centre of Excellence for External Drug Discovery (CEEDD) which the company created in 2005 to boost innovation. The company's research director estimated that between one-quarter to one-third of GSK's existing research pipeline of new drugs already involved work conducted with external partners and a growing role would be played by the CEEDD, managing a 'virtual' portfolio of research run by such companies:

In the future we are going to have many more external projects.

Source: *Financial Times*, 31 May 2006, p. 22.

A second reason for JVs is to learn about new technologies or markets. Alliances also arise where governments want to keep sensitive sectors, such as aerospace, defence and aviation, under national control. Airbus, which competes with Boeing in aircraft manufacture, was originally a JV between French, German, British and Spanish manufacturers. Alliances, such as the Star Alliance led by United Airlines of the United States and Lufthansa of Germany, are also common in the airline industry, where companies share revenues and costs over certain routes. As governments often prevent foreign ownership, such alliances avoid that barrier.

Other forms of joint development include franchising (common in many retailing activities – Ikea uses this method), licensing and long-term collaboration between manufacturers and their suppliers.

Alliances and partnership working have also become commonplace in the public sector. In many cities alliances or partnerships have been created between major public bodies, business and community interests. Their main purpose is to foster a coherent approach to planning and delivering services. Public bodies often act as service commissioners rather than as direct providers, developing partnerships with organisations to deliver services on their behalf.

Activity 8.6   Critical reflection on delivering strategy

- Select two companies you are familiar with, and in each case gather evidence to help you decide which of the available options (or a combination) they have chosen to deliver their strategy.
- What are the advantages of the route they have chosen compared to the alternatives?
- Compare your evidence with other students on your course and identify any common themes.

8.9   Making revisions – implementing and evaluating

Implementation turns strategy into action, moving from corporate to operational levels. Many strategies fail to be implemented, or fail to achieve as much as management expected. A common mistake is to assume that formulating a strategy will lead to painless implementation. Sometimes there is an 'implementation deficit', when strategies are not implemented at all, or are only partially successful. A common reason for this is that while formulating strategy may appear to be a rational process, it is often a political one. Those who were content with the earlier strategy may oppose the new one if it affects their status, power or career prospects. Chapter 13 shows how implementing change is a complex, often conflicting process.

Evaluate results

Managers, shareholders (current and potential) and financial analysts routinely compare a company's performance with its published plans. Only by tracking results can these and other interested parties decide if performance is in line with expectations or if the company needs to take some corrective action. Many targets focus on financial and other quantitative aspects of performance, such as sales, operating costs and profit.

Although monitoring is shown as the last stage in the strategy model, it is not the end of the process. This is continuous as organisations adjust to changes in their business environment. Regular monitoring alerts management to the possibility that targets might not be achieved and that operational adjustments are needed. Equally, and in conjunction with continuous scanning of the external environment, performance monitoring can prompt wider changes to the organisation's corporate and competitive strategies.

Donald Sull (2007) advises that in any discussions to revise strategy, people should treat actions as experiments:

> they should analyse what's happened and use the results to revise their assumptions, priorities and promises. As such, the appropriate time to have such conversations is after the team has reached a significant milestone in making things happen . . . Managers must acknowledge that that their mental models are merely simplified maps of complex terrain based on provisional knowledge that is subject to revision in the light of new information (pp. 36–37)

8.10   Integrating themes

Sustainable performance

If managers are to enhance the sustainability of their activities, they will need to ensure that it becomes part of their strategic discussions. Chapter 5 contrasted the 'Friedmanite' and 'stakeholder' perspectives: the former arguing that the business leaders should focus on the financial interests of shareholders, while the latter believe that managers have responsibilities to a wider constituency. Claims for and against the idea that corporations should act responsibly often reflect deeply-held moral and ethical principles, and this makes it a challenge to relate them to a company's strategic decisions.

A perspective that can help to clarify the issue was suggested by Vogel (2005), who concludes that while advocates of corporate responsibility (in this context, sustainability) are genuinely motivated by a commitment to social goals, it is only sustainable if 'virtue pays off'. Responsible action is both made possible and constrained by market forces.

Virtuous behaviour can make business sense for some firms in some areas in some circumstances, but does not in itself ensure commercial success. Companies that base their strategy on acting responsibly may be commercially successful, but equally they may fail – responsible behaviour carries the same risks as any other kind of business behaviour. While some consumers or investors will give their business to companies that appear to be acting responsibly, others will not. Some customers place a higher priority on price, appearance or any other feature than they do on whether goods are produced and delivered in a sustainable way. As Vogel (2005) observes:

> There *is* a place in the market economy for responsible firms. But there is also a large place for their less responsible competitors. (p. 3)

While some companies can benefit from a strategy based on acting responsibly, market forces alone cannot prevent others from having a less responsible strategy, and profiting from doing so. Hawken *et al.* (1999) and Senge *et al.* (2008) provide abundant evidence that sustainable performance can be both good for the planet and good for profits.

Governance and control

Pye (2002) sees a close link between what she terms the process of governing and strategising. Having conducted long-term research with the boards of several large companies she notes:

i. in 1987–89, no one talked of corporate governance, whereas now most contributors raise this subject of their own volition, implying greater awareness of and sensitivity to such issues; and

ii. relationships with major shareholders have changed considerably across the decade and directors now see accounting for their *strategic direction* as crucial in this context. (p. 154, emphasis added)

She distinguished between governance and governing:

Corporate governance is often identified through indicators such as board composition, committee structure, executive compensation schemes, and risk assessment procedures etc, which offer a snapshot view of governance practice, rather than the dynamic process of governing. To explore governing, i.e. how governance is enacted, means unraveling the complex network of relationships amongst [the board] *as well as* relationships with 'outsiders' who observe [the board's] governance. (p. 156)

She refers to strategising as the process by which directors go about deciding the strategic direction of the organisation, although this is primarily shaped by the executive directors. She found that almost all directors agreed that what is crucial is not so much the words on paper as the process of dialogue and debate by which those words are created – the strategising process is more important than the final document.

Internationalisation

As the business world becomes ever more international, companies inevitably face difficult strategic choices about the extent to which they develop an international presence, and the way in which they develop their international strategy. The nature of the challenge is shown by the fact that, while many companies have done very well from international expansions, many overseas ventures fail, destroying value rather than creating it.

Chapter 4 outlines the nature of the challenges faced as companies respond to what they perceive to be international opportunities. They need, for example, to deal with complex structural and logistical issues when products are made and sold in several countries, ensure that there are adequate links between research, marketing and production to speed the introduction of new products, and facilitate the rapid transfer of knowledge and ideas between the national components of the business. These are complex enough issues in themselves, but the extra dimension is that solutions that work in one national context may not work as well in another. Differences in national culture mean that people will respond in perhaps unexpected ways to strategies and plans, especially if these are perceived in some way to be inconsistent with the local culture (as the examples cited in Chapter 4 testify).

The content of an international strategy will be shaped by the process of its production, and the extent to which different players in the global enterprise take part in it.

Cases

CASE APPLICATION **1**
Gaga Over Gaga

Just now in her mid-twenties, Lady Gaga has taken the music world by storm with a unique blend of business savvy, interesting hair and wardrobe choices, and a fabulous sound with a "spacey Euro vibe."[41] Five years ago, Lady Gaga did not exist. But the individual who is Lady Gaga, Stefani Germanotta, was waitressing and singing in drab and dingy New York clubs. She was ambitious and had bigger goals. After being signed and dropped from one label, Def Jam (turns out that may not have been the best decision by them), she joined forces with a hand-picked core team of creative advisers she called "Haus of Gaga." Behind all that glitz, glamour, and unusual fashion choices is a "case study of what it takes to succeed in the music business today."

Lady Gaga and her team of creative advisors crafted a strategy consisting of a unique persona, a 360-degree deal, and the use of digital media to achieve phenomenal success in the music industry and extreme loyalty from millions of Little Monsters to her brand that spans music, video, design, and marketing.

Gaga's impact on the music world in the span of a year has been nothing short of phenomenal. Writing her own material, she's sold more than 10 million albums. Her debut album generated four No.1 songs. She also topped the digital sales chart in 2009 with 15.3 million tracks sold, most on iTunes. She's had more than 1 billion Web views. Some 3.8 million "Little Monsters"—Gaga's nickname for her fans—follow her on Twitter and she has over 6.4 million "fans" on Facebook. She was the most-Googled image in 2009. And then in recognition of the fact that she's been deemed worthy of the success she's had, she opened the Grammy's award show in early 2010 with music legend Sir Elton John. She "reigns over a brand that spans music, video, design, and marketing." One advertising executive said, "No other artist commands the kind of attention that Gaga does. If she does something with your brand, it's like *bam!*—a million eyeballs." For instance, together with MAC Cosmetics, she created a shade of Viva Glam lipstick that has raised $2.2 million for AIDS awareness—Viva Glam's most successful launch ever. What strategies has she used to navigate the turbulent industry and become a star?

One important component to her success is her savvy awareness of the power of digital media and her exceptional ability to exploit it. "Her persona is built for the online generation." Even though much of Gaga's audience has got her music online legally for free, "being embedded on the Web can pay dividends in exposure and the loyalty of fans." Gaga keeps her Little Monsters engaged with personal musings and real-time thank-yous.

Another important aspect to Gaga's success is what's called in the music business the 360-degree deal. The major upheaval in the music industry over the last decade led major record companies to look for ways to replace declining revenues. In a 360-degree deal, a label invests more money upfront—on marketing, for example—but in return, gets a piece of merchandise sales, touring revenue, and other earnings artists usually kept for themselves. This arrangement has been wildly successful for Gaga.

Finally, Gaga's persona has been a calculated strategy. "Gaga's allure is that of a misfit run amok in the system, a role that has helped her cut across disparate subcultures, including teens, finicky hipsters and gays." Her look isn't considered shocking like it was say, for instance, when rockers Alice Cooper or Gene Simmons first appeared. It's unique and keeps her audiences eager to see what her next image might be.

Gaga is determined to not be a niche artist. However, her "now-trendy sound won't last forever." Her ability to remain a music industry mainstay will depend on her ability to evolve.

Discussion Questions

1. How is strategic management illustrated by this case story?
2. How might SWOT analysis be helpful to Lady Gaga as she and her advisors manage her career?
3. What competitive advantage do you think Lady Gaga is pursuing? How is she exploiting that competitive advantage?
4. Do you think Lady Gaga's success is due to external or internal factors or both? Explain.
5. What strategic implications does the suggestion that her ability to remain a music industry mainstay depends on her ability to evolve have?

MANAGING THE MAGIC

Magic happens at the happiest place on earth. At least that's what the folks at the Walt Disney Company (Disney) work hard to make us believe. However, the difficult business climate in 2008 and 2009 challenged Disney, as it did many other well-managed companies. CEO Bob Iger and his top management team are working hard to conjure up their own magic; that is, to find the best way to strategically maneuver the company to prosper despite the environmental uncertainties.

Disney has had a long record of successes and the "Disney Difference" is noticeably apparent. What is the Disney Difference? It's "high-quality creative content, backed up by a clear strategy for maximizing that content's value across platforms and markets." From books, toys, and games to online media, soundtracks, and DVDs, Disney exploits its rich legacy of products through quality creative content and exceptional storytelling. Some of these products include, among many others, *The Lion King, Toy Story, The Jungle Book, Cars,* Disney-ABC Television, and ESPN programming. Although Disney is a U.S.-based company, its businesses span the globe with operations in North America, Europe, Asia Pacific, and Latin America. Its latest push is Russia, a large untapped media market, where it's planning a broadcast version of the Disney Channel. The president of Walt Disney International says, "We believe there is vast growth to come out of this market, despite the near-term economic turmoil." The company is also funding a $452 million expansion of the Disneyland theme park in Hong Kong in hopes of boosting poor attendance figures. One of the new themed areas called Grizzly Trail is "set in an American frontier gold-mining town and features a roller coaster patterned after a runaway mine train." Despite its magical touch, just a few short years ago, Disney wasn't such a happy place.

When Bob Iger was named CEO in 2005, analysts believed that the Disney brand had become dated. And, there was this sense that Disney's target audience was young and that its products couldn't possibly be of interest to older kids. Iger, who views himself as the steward of the entire Disney brand, immediately recognized the importance of leveraging the company's vast media content on different platforms. His strategic approach had been working well until the economy slowed and the decline in global consumer spending made things even more precarious. Now, Iger and his management team will have to use all the strategic tools they have to guide the company and keep the magic coming.

Discussion Questions

1. What is the Disney Difference and how will it affect the company's corporate, competitive, and functional strategies?

2. What challenges do you think Disney might face in doing business in Russia? How could Iger and his top management team use planning to best prepare for those challenges?

3. With the announced expansion of Disney's Hong Kong Disneyland, what goals might the company set? What type of planning will be necessary?

4. How might Iger and his top management team use the strategic management process to "keep the magic coming" in the current economic climate?

Sources: C. Yung and J. Ng, "In Asia, Disney's World Will Get Bigger," *Wall Street Journal,* July 1, 2009, p. B5; P. Sanders, "Disney Profit Falls Sharply but Clouds Are Parting," *Wall Street Journal,* May 6, 2009, p. B1; R. Siklos, "Bob Iger Rocks Disney," *CNN Online,* http://www.cnnmoney.com (January 5, 2009); B. Barnes, "Disney Plans a Channel for Russian TV," *New York Times Online,* December 17, 2008; P. Sanders, "Disney Net Slips as Slump Hits Home," *Wall Street Journal,* November 17, 2008, p. B1; R. Siklos, "Q&A: The Iger Difference," *Fortune,* April 28, 2008, pp. 90–94; R. Grover, "A Star Is Born, Disney Style," *BusinessWeek,* April 21, 2008, pp. 50–51; and The Walt Disney Company *2007 Fact Book,* http://corporate. disney.go.com/investors/fact_books.html.

Case study   HMV Group www.hmv.com

HMV and Waterstone's are two familiar retailing brands, specialising in music, films, games and books. The business began in 1921 when 'His Master's Voice' opened a store in London's Oxford Street: the HMV Group now has over 400 entertainment stores and websites in the UK, Ireland, Canada, Hong Kong and Singapore, and Waterstone's. This is the UK's only specialist bookchain, and includes most of the 130 Ottakar's stores acquired when it took over that company in 2006.

The music side of the business was part of EMI Group, but in 2002 the company demerged from that company to create a purely retail company, rather than being part of the diversified EMI Group, which also owned Dillon's, another bookselling chain. HMV Group then bought Waterstone's from WH Smith.

In 2006 the company itself faced a takeover threat from Permira, an investment company. The company rejected this bid, believing that it seriously undervalued the company. HMV had experienced severe losses the previous year, which gave Permira the opportunity to mount a takeover bid. HMV had suffered from the growth of illegal music downloads, and the consequent fall in sales of CDs. Management were confident that they could recover from a poor year's trading, but the bid is a constant reminder that if management does not meet investors' expectations, they will again be vulnerable to a takeover.

This episode prompted the management team, led by chief executive Simon Fox, to develop a transformation strategy for the group. This has three strands; *revitalising the HMV and Waterstone's stores; growing revenue* from new channels; and *becoming more efficient*. The next paragraphs outline the strategy for the stores: the other strands are on later pages.

In the HMV *stores* the company is changing the mix of products to offset the decline in physical music sales. They are stocking more games software and consoles, as well as introducing MP3/4 players and accessories. They expect market growth at Waterstone's to come mainly from non-book sales, so are extending the range of high-quality gift stationery, and concentrating on the book categories

By kind permission, HMV

that are growing most rapidly, such as fiction and children's books.

To help understand customers' needs and to encourage sales to the most loyal and high spending, the company launched the Pure HMV loyalty card. Customers can exchange the points earned – at Waterstone's for future purchases, and at HMV for entertainment-related rewards. It is also developing the HMV store format to become a more inspiring shopping venue, with more interactive features.

The recession which began in 2008 affected the industry: in 2008 music retailers Zavvi and Woolworth's collapsed, followed in 2009 by Borders Bookshops. HMV issued additional shares which enabled it to buy about 20 of the Zavvi stores.

Case questions 8.1

Visit an HMV or Waterstone's store and the group website (**www.hmvgroup.com**) – navigate to the section on 'the company'.

- Note the sales and profit performance in the most recent period compared with an earlier one.
- What do the chairman and chief executive write about the company's current strategy?
- What challenges do they say the company is facing?

The second strand in the new strategy is to *grow revenue* from new channels, instead of relying on physical purchases in the stores. HMV Group is therefore investing in both stores' online sites. Customers can purchase music through the hmv.com site, giving the choice of a digital download or a physical album. The company plans to extend the site to offer video downloads as soon as this becomes worthwhile to customers and the company. They are also planning to grow revenue from live music events and ticket sales.

On becoming *more efficient*, the company is changing major parts of the cost base. For example, Waterstone's had invested in a centralised book hub, to which all book suppliers deliver their products. These are then sorted and delivered to each store as a single daily delivery, rather than having several deliveries to a store each day by individual suppliers. They are also centralising their purchasing to reduce costs, and consolidating many back-office functions of the two store chains.

Source: Group website.

Case questions 8.2

- What developments in the external environment are reflected in the company's strategy?
- What internal changes do you think this may have led to in the way the company operates?

In late 2009 the company expanded its already small presence in the live music market by buying venue owner Mama Group for £46 million. Mama runs 11 concert venues in the UK including the Hammersmith Apollo, and has other interests including an artist management business. HMV chief executive said he was delighted with the deal as the two companies were already partners in the Mean Fiddler joint venture, which runs venues in London, Birmingham, Edinburgh and Aberdeen. Mr Fox believed the deal would enable HMV to accelerate the growth into live music.

In early 2010 the company reported that it expected the total live music market to be around a third larger than recorded music by 2012. The group is able to benefit from this channel change through its acquisition of Mama Group which, apart from its venues, is also a leading operator of live music festivals. It expects this new division to grow organically through driving utilisation, occupancy and related sales at the existing venues, and adding new venues at the rate of two to three per year.

In the festival market, new events will be added to the range. It also believes a significant opportunity exists in the market for tickets, and aims to sell 3 million tickets for Mama and third-party venues in 2012/13.

Sources: Company website.

Case questions 8.6

- Use the product/market matrix to classify the elements of HMV's current strategy.
- How has the company chosen to deliver the next stage of the strategy?

Review Questions and Tests

REVIEW AND DISCUSSION QUESTIONS

1. Explain why strategic management is important.
2. Describe the six steps in the strategic management process.
3. How could the Internet be helpful to managers as they follow the steps in the strategic management process?
4. How might the process of strategy formulation, implementation, and evaluation differ for (a) large businesses, (b) small businesses, (c) not-for-profit organizations, and (d) global businesses?
5. Should ethical considerations be included in analyses of an organization's internal and external environments? Why or why not?
6. Describe the three major types of corporate strategies and how the BCG matrix is used to manage those corporate strategies.
7. Describe the role of competitive advantage and how Porter's competitive strategies help an organization develop competitive advantage.
8. "The concept of competitive advantage is as important for not-for-profit organizations as it is for for-profit organizations." Do you agree or disagree with this statement? Explain, using examples to make your case.
9. Explain why strategic leadership and strategic flexibility are important.
10. Describe e-business, customer service, and innovation strategies.

Review questions

1. Why do managers develop strategies for their organisation?
2. How does the planning view of strategy differ from the learning and political views respectively?
3. Describe the main features of the ways in which recent research suggests managers develop strategy.
4. Draw Sull's strategy loop and explain each of the elements.
5. Discuss with a manager from an organisation how his/her organisation developed its present strategy. Compare this practice with the ideas in this chapter. What conclusions do you draw?
6. What are the main steps to take in analysing the organisation's environment? Why is it necessary to do this?
7. Describe each stage in value chain analysis and illustrate each one with an example. Why is the model useful to management?
8. The chapter describes three generic strategies that organisations can follow. Give examples of three companies each following one of these strategies.
9. Give examples of company strategies corresponding to each box in the product/market matrix.
10. What are the main ways of delivering strategy?
11. Summarise an idea from the chapter that adds to your understanding of the integrating themes.

SECTION 3:
MARKETING, ENVIRONMENT AND ETHICS

Chapter 6:

Organisation Environment

    3.1   Introduction

Nokia's success depends on the ability of its managers to spot and interpret signals from consumers in the mobile phone market, and to ensure that the organisation responds more effectively than competitors. It also depends on identifying ideas emerging within the organisation (such as from the research laboratories) that have commercial potential – and working to ensure that consumers are aware of and receptive to the idea when it is incorporated into the next generation of products. The early success of the company was helped by recognising that many users see a mobile as a fashion item, and by using its design skills to meet that need. It also gained when the EU established common standards for mobile telephony, which the Finnish government supported.

All managers work within a context which both constrains and supports them. How well they understand, interpret and interact with that context affects their performance. Finkelstein (2003) (especially pp. 63–68) shows how Motorola, an early market leader in mobile communications, failed to take account of changes in consumer preferences (for digital rather than the older analogue mobile phones). By the time managers realised the new environment, Nokia had a commanding lead in the market. Each business is unique, so the forces with which they interact differ: those who are able to identify and shape them (Nokia) will perform better than those who are not (Motorola).

Figure 3.1 shows four environmental forces. The inner circle represents the organisation's **internal environment (or context)** – which Chapter 1 introduced. That includes its culture,

The **internal environment (or context)** consists of elements within the organisation such as its technology, structure or business processes.

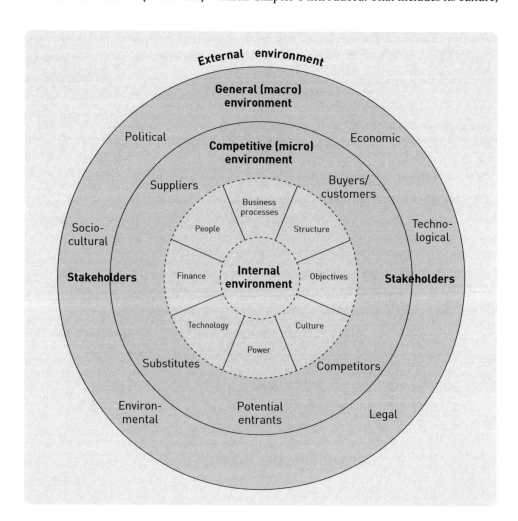

Figure 3.1
Environmental
influences on the
organisation

which many now regard as a major contextual feature. Beyond that is the immediate **competitive environment (or context),** sometimes known as the micro-environment. This is the industry-specific environment of customers, suppliers, competitors and potential substitute products. The outer circle shows the **general environment (or context),** sometimes known as the macro-environment – political, economic, social, technological, (natural) environmental and legal factors that affect all organisations. Forces in the internal and competitive environments usually have more impact on, and are more open to influence by, the organisation than those in the general environment.

Together these make up an organisation's **external environment (or context)** – a constantly changing source of threats and opportunities: how well people cope with these affects performance.

Forces in the external environment do not affect practice of their own accord. They become part of the agenda only when internal or external stakeholders act to place them on the management agenda. In terms of Figure 3.1, they are a fourth force. Managers (who are themselves stakeholders) balance conflicting interpretations of their context. They work within an internal context, and look outside for actual and potential changes that may affect the centre of Figure 3.1. The figure implies a constant interaction between an organisation's culture and its external environment.

Managers do not passively accept their business environment, but try to shape it by actively persuading governments and other agencies to act in their favour (known as 'lobbying'). Car makers and airlines, for example, regularly seek subsidies, cheap loans or new regulations to help their businesses, while most industry bodies (such as the European Automobile Manufacturers' Association – **www.acea.be**) lobby international bodies such as the European Commission – often employing a professional lobbying business to support their case.

The next section presents ideas on organisational culture, which is an immediate aspect of a manager's context. Beyond that managers need to interact intelligently with their competitive and general environments. The chapter contrasts stable and dynamic environments, outlines stakeholder expectations and introduces ideas on governance and control.

> A **competitive environment (or context)** is the industry-specific environment comprising the organisation's customers, suppliers and competitors.

> The **general environment (or context)** (sometimes known as the macro-environment) includes political, economic, social technological, (natural) environmental and legal factors that affect all organisations.

> The **external environment (or context)** consists of elements beyond the organisation – it combines the competitive and general environments.

Activity 3.1 — Which elements of the business environment matter?

- Write a few notes summarising aspects of the business environment of which you are aware. You may find it helpful to think of a manager you have worked with, or when you have been managing an activity.
- Identify two instances when they (or you) were discussing aspects of the wider context of the job – such as the culture of the organisation or the world outside.
- How did this aspect of the context affect the job of managing?
- How did the way people dealt with the issue affect performance?

3.2 — Cultures and their components

Developing cultures

Interest in organisation **culture** has grown as academics and managers have come to believe that it influences behaviour. Several claim that a strong and distinct culture helps to integrate individuals into the team or organisation (Deal and Kennedy, 1982; Peters and Waterman, 1982). Deal and Kennedy (1982) refer to culture as 'the way we do things around here' and Hofstede (1991) sees it as the 'collective programming of the mind', distinguishing one

> **Culture** is a pattern of shared basic assumptions that was learned by a group as it solved its problems of external adaptation and internal integration, and that has worked well enough to be considered valid and transmitted to new members (Schein, 2004, p. 17).

group from another. They claim that having the right culture explains the success of high-performing organisations.

Someone entering a department or organisation for the first time can usually sense and observe the surface elements of the culture. Some buzz with life and activity, others seem asleep; some welcome and look after visitors, others seem inward looking; some work by the rules, while others are entrepreneurial and risk taking; some have regular social occasions while in others staff rarely meet except at work.

Management in practice   **A culture of complaint in a bank**

John Weeks (2004) spent six years working in a UK bank (believed to be NatWest, which the Royal Bank of Scotland acquired in 2000) as part of his doctoral research. He observed and recorded the bank's distinctive culture – which he described as one of 'complaint'.

No-one liked the culture – from the most senior managers to the most junior counter staff – people spent much of their time complaining about it. Weeks realised that this was a ritual, a form of solidarity among the staff: complaining about the culture *was* the culture. He noticed that most complaints were directed at other parts of the bank – not at the unit in which the complainer worked. He noted:

> Local sub-cultures are sometimes described positively – usually to contrast them with the mainstream – but I never heard anyone [describe the bank's culture in positive terms]. It is described as too bureaucratic, too rules driven, not customer-focused enough, not entrepreneurial enough, too inflexible, too prone to navel gazing, too centralized. (p. 53)

His detailed narrative shows, with many examples, how people in the bank made sense of their culture – using it to achieve their goals, while others did the same to them.

Source: Weeks (2004).

Figure 3.2 illustrates how a distinctive culture develops; as people develop and share common values they use these to establish beliefs and norms which guide their behaviour towards each other and to outsiders. Positive outcomes reinforce their belief in the values underlying their behaviour, which then become a stronger influence on how people should work and relate to each other: should people have job titles? How should they dress? Should meetings be confrontational or supportive?

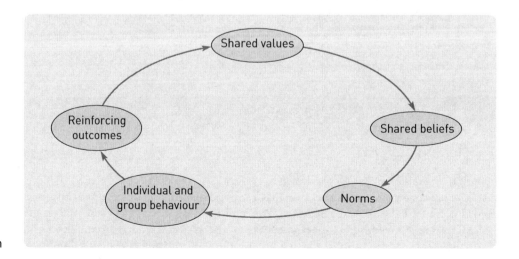

Figure 3.2
The stages of
cultural formation

A shared culture provides members with guidelines about how they can best contribute. The more they work on these issues to develop a common understanding, the better they will perform.

Components of cultures

Schein (2004) identifies three levels of a culture, 'level' referring to the degree to which the observer can see its components.

- **Artifacts** represent the visible level – elements such as the language or etiquette which someone coming into contact with a culture can observe:
  - architecture (open-plan offices without doors or private space)
  - technology and equipment
  - style (clothing, manner of address, emotional displays)
  - rituals and ceremonies (leaving events, awards ceremonies and away-days)
  - courses (to induct employees in the culture as well as the content).

  While it is easy to observe artifacts, it is difficult for outsiders to decipher what they mean to the group, or what underlying assumptions they reflect. That requires an analysis of beliefs and values.

- **Espoused beliefs and values** are the accumulated beliefs that members hold about their work. As a group develops, members refine their ideas about what works in this business: how people make decisions, how teams work together, and how they solve problems. Practices that work become the accepted way to behave:
  - 'Quality pays.'
  - 'We should stick to our core business.'
  - 'Cultivate a sense of personal responsibility.'
  - 'We depend on close team work.'
  - 'Everyone is expected to challenge a proposal – whoever made it,'

  Some companies codify and publish their beliefs and values, to help induct new members and to reinforce them among existing staff. Such beliefs and values shape the visible artifacts, though companies vary in the degree to which employees internalise them. The extent to which they do so depends on how clearly they derive from shared basic underlying assumptions.

- **Basic underlying assumptions** are deeply held by members of the group as being the way to work together. As they act in accordance with their values and beliefs, those that work become embedded as basic underlying assumptions. When the group strongly holds these, members will act in accordance with them, and reject actions based on others:
  - 'We need to satisfy customers to survive as a business.'
  - 'Our business is to help people with X problem live better with X problem.'
  - 'People can make mistakes, as long as they learn from them.'
  - 'We employ highly motivated and competent adults.'
  - 'Financial markets worry about the short term: we are here for the long term.'

  Difficulties arise when people with assumptions developed in one group work with people from another. Mergers sometimes experience difficulty when staff who have to work together realise they are from different cultures.

Management in practice   **A strong culture at Bosch**   www.bosch.com

Franz Fehrenbach is chief executive of Bosch, Germany's largest privately owned engineering group, and the world's largest supplier of car parts. In 2009 he said:

> The company culture, especially our high credibility, is one of our greatest assets. Our competitors cannot match us on that because it takes decades to build up.

The cultural traditions include a rigid control on costs, an emphasis on team thinking, employees taking responsibility for their errors, cautious financial policies, and long-term thinking. For example, to cope with the recession in 2009 Mr Fehrenbach explained that:

We have to cut costs in all areas. We will reduce spending in the ongoing business, but we will not cut back on research and development for important future projects.

Source: Based on an article by Daniel Schaefer, *Financial Times*, 2 March 2009, p. 16.

Activity 3.2   Culture spotting

- Identify as many components of culture (artifacts, beliefs and values, underlying assumptions) in an organisation or unit as you can.
- What may the artifacts suggest about the deeper beliefs and values, or underlying assumptions?
- Gather evidence (preferably by asking people) about how the culture affects behaviour, and whether they think it helps or hinders performance.
- Analyse your results and decide which of the four types in the competing values framework most closely reflects that organisation's culture.

3.3   Types of culture

This section outlines three ways of describing and comparing cultures.

Competing values framework

The competing values model developed by Quinn *et al.* (2003) reflects inherent tensions between flexibility or control and between an internal or an external focus. Figure 3.3 (based on Figure 2.2) shows four cultural types.

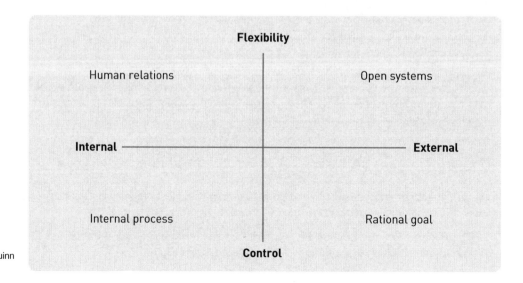

Figure 3.3
Types of organisational culture

Source: Based on Quinn *et al.* (2003).

Open systems

This represents an open systems view, in which people recognise that the external environment plays a significant role, and is a vital source of ideas, energy and resources. It also sees the environment as complex and turbulent, requiring entrepreneurial, visionary leadership and flexible, responsive behaviour. Key motivating factors are growth, stimulation, creativity and variety. Examples are start-up firms and new business units – organic, flexible operations.

Rational goal

Members see the organisation as a rational, efficiency-seeking unit. They define effectiveness in terms of production or economic goals that satisfy external requirements. Managers create structures to deal with the outside world. Leadership tends to be directive, goal-oriented and functional. Key motivating factors include competition and the achievement of goals. Examples are large, established businesses – mechanistic.

Internal process

Here members focus on internal matters. Their goal is to make the unit efficient, stable and controlled. Tasks are repetitive and methods stress specialisation, rules and procedures. Leaders tend to be cautious and spend time on technical issues. Motivating factors include security, stability and order. Examples include utilities and public authorities – suspicious of change.

Human relations

People emphasise the value of informal interpersonal relations rather than formal structures. They try to maintain the organisation and nurture its members, defining effectiveness in terms of their well-being and commitment. Leaders tend to be participative, considerate and supportive. Motivating factors include attachment, cohesiveness and membership. Examples include voluntary groups, professional service firms and some internal support functions.

Charles Handy's cultural types

Charles Handy (1993) distinguished four cultures – **power, role, task** and **person**.

Power

A dominant central figure holds power: others follow the centre's policy and interpret new situations in the way the leader would. Many entrepreneurial firms operate in this way, with few rules but with well-understood, implicit codes on how to behave and work. The firm relies on the individual rather than on seeking consensus through discussion.

Role

Typical characteristics of this culture are the job description or the procedure. Managers define what they expect in clear, detailed job descriptions. They select people for a job if they meet the specified requirements. Procedures guide how people and departments interact. If all follow the rules, co-ordination is straightforward. People's position in the hierarchy determines their power.

Task

People focus on completing the task or project rather than their formal role. They value each other for what they can contribute and expect everyone to help as needed. The emphasis is on getting the resources and people for the job and then relying on their commitment and enthusiasm. People will typically work in teams, to combine diverse skills into a common purpose.

A **power culture** is one in which people's activities are strongly influenced by a dominant central figure.

A **role culture** is one in which people's activities are strongly influenced by clear and detailed job descriptions and other formal signals as to what is expected from them.

A **task culture** is one in which the focus of activity is towards completing a task or project using whatever means are appropriate.

A **person culture** is one in which activity is strongly influenced by the wishes of the individuals who are part of the organisation.

Person

The individual is at the centre and any structure or system is there to serve them. The form is unusual – small professional and artistic organisations are probably closest to it, and perhaps experiments in communal living. They exist to meet the needs of the professionals or the members, rather than some larger organisational goal.

Activity 3.3   Cultural examples

For each of Handy's four cultural types, identify an example from within this text that seems to correspond most closely to that form.

- What clues about the company have you used to decide that allocation?
- Why do you think that culture is suitable for that organisation?
- What evidence would you seek to decide if that culture was suitable?
- Compare the similarities and differences in the competing values and Handy models.

Multiple cultures

Martin (2002) proposed that organisations have not one, but several cultures: observers take one of three perspectives towards a culture:

- **Integration** – a focus on identifying consistencies in the data, and using those common patterns to explain events.
- **Differentiation** – a focus on conflict, identifying different and possibly conflicting views of members towards events.
- **Fragmentation** – a focus on the fluid nature of organisations, and on the interplay and change of views about events.

Ogbonna and Harris (1998, 2002) provided empirical support for this view, based on interviews with staff in a retail company. They found that a person's position in the hierarchy determined his/her perspective on the culture (see Table 3.1). As consensus on culture was unlikely, they advised managers to recognise the range of sub-cultures within their organisation, and

Table 3.1 Hierarchical position and cultural perspectives

Position in hierarchy	Cultural perspective	Description	Example
Head office managers	Integration	Cultural values should be shared across the organisation. Unified culture both desirable and attainable	'If we can get every . . . part of the company doing what they should be doing, we'll beat everybody'
Store managers	Differentiation	Reconciling conflicting views of head office and shop floor. See cultural pluralism as inevitable	'People up at head office are all pushing us in different directions. Jill in Marketing wants customer focus, June in Finance wants lower costs'
Store employees	Fragmented	Confused by contradictory nature of the espoused values. See organisation as complex and unpredictable	'One minute it's this, the next it's that. You can't keep up with the flavour of the month'

Source: Based on Ogbonna and Harris (1998).

only seek to reconcile those differences that were essential to policy. They also observed that culture remains a highly subjective idea, largely in the eye of the beholder

> and is radically different according to an individual's position in the hierarchy. (Ogbonna and Harris, 1998, p. 45)

Culture and performance

Peters and Waterman (1982) believed that an organisation's culture affected performance, and implied that managers should try to change their culture towards a more productive one. Others are more skeptical about the effects on performance and question whether, even if a suitable culture has a positive effect, managers can consciously change it. Kotter and Heskett (1992) studied 207 companies to assess the link between culture and economic performance. Although they were positively correlated, the relationship was much weaker than advocates of culture as a factor in performance had predicted.

Thompson and McHugh (2002), while also critical of much writing on the topic, observe the potential benefits which a suitable culture can bring to not-for-profit organisations:

> Creating a culture resonant with the overall goals is relevant to any organisation, whether it be a trade union, voluntary group or producer co-operative. Indeed, it is more important in such consensual groupings. Co-operatives, for example, can degenerate organisationally because they fail to develop adequate mechanisms for transmitting the original ideals from founders to new members and sustaining them through shared experiences. (pp. 208–209)

As managers work within an organisational culture, they also work within an external context – whose members will have expectations from the organisation. They need some tools with which to analyse that external world.

3.4   The competitive environment – Porter's five forces

Managers are most directly affected by forces in their immediate competitive environment. According to Porter (1980a, 1985), the ability of a firm to earn an acceptable return depends on five forces – the ability of new competitors to enter the industry, the threat of substitute products, the bargaining power of buyers, the bargaining power of suppliers and the rivalry among existing competitors. Figure 3.4 shows Porter's **five forces analysis**.

Porter believes that the *collective* strength of the five forces determines industry profitability, through their effects on prices, costs and investment requirements. Buyer power influences the prices a firm can charge, as does the threat of substitutes. The bargaining power of suppliers determines the cost of raw materials and other inputs. The greater the collective strength of the forces, the less profitable the industry: the weaker they are, the more profitable they are. Managers can use their knowledge of these forces to shape strategy.

Five forces analysis is a technique for identifying and listing those aspects of the five forces most relevant to the profitability of an organisation at that time.

Threat of new entrants

The extent of this threat depends on how easily new entrants can overcome barriers such as:

- the need for economies of scale (to compete on cost), which are difficult to achieve quickly;
- high capital investment required;
- lack of distribution channels;
- subsidies which benefit existing firms at the expense of potential new entrants;
- cost advantages of existing firms, such as access to raw materials or know-how;
- strong customer loyalty to incumbent companies.

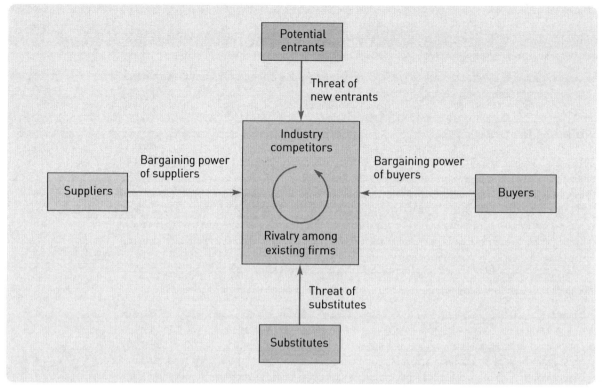

Figure 3.4 The five forces of industry competition

Nokia faces competition from new entrants to the mobile phone industry especially Apple and Research in Motion (BlackBerry) at the top end of the market. The Chinese ZTE Corporation is supplying cheap mobiles to consumers in emerging markets.

Intensity of rivalry among competitors

Strong competitive rivalry lowers profitability, and occurs when:

- there are many firms in an industry;
- there is slow market growth, so companies fight for market share;
- fixed costs are high, so firms use capacity and overproduce;
- exit costs are high; specialised assets (hard to sell) or management loyalty (in old family firms) deter firms from leaving the industry, which prolongs excess capacity and low profitability;
- products are similar, so customers can easily switch to other suppliers.

A highly competitive market will also be one in which the threat of new entrants is high. While Nokia still dominated the mobile phone industry in 2010, it continued to face pressure from established competitors Motorola, Siemens and Ericsson, and from new entrants in Asia.

Management in practice   Competition amongst Chinese brewers

SABMiller and Anheuser-Busch both sought to enter the Chinese market by buying an existing major player, Harbin (with Anheuser-Busch quickly winning the contest). They were attracted by the fact that China is the world's largest market for beer, growing at 6–8 per cent a year. However, it is also fiercely competitive as there are over 400 brewers competing for sales: this keeps prices down, and profits are on average less than 0.5 per cent of sales.

Source: *The Economist*, 15 May 2004.

Power of buyers (customers)

Buyers (customers) seek lower prices or higher quality at constant prices, thus forcing down prices and profitability. Buyer power is high when:

- the buyer purchases a large part of a supplier's output;
- there are many substitute products, allowing easy switching;
- the product is a large part of the buyers' costs, encouraging them to seek lower prices;
- buyers can plausibly threaten to supply their needs internally.

Management in practice   **Wal-Mart's power as a buyer**   www.walmart.com

Wal-Mart (which owns Asda in the UK) is the world's largest company, being three times the size of the second largest retailer, the French company Carrefour. Growth has enabled it to become the largest purchaser in America, controlling much of the business done by almost every major consumer-products company. It accounts for 30 per cent of hair care products sold, 26 per cent of toothpaste, 20 per cent of pet food, and 20 per cent of all sales of CDs, videos and DVDs. This gives it great power over companies in these industries, since their dependence on Wal-Mart reduces their bargaining power.

Source: *Business Week*, 6 October 2003, pp. 48–53; and other sources.

Bargaining power of suppliers

Conditions that increase the bargaining power of suppliers are the opposite of those applying to buyers. The power of suppliers relative to customers is high when:

- there are few suppliers;
- the product is distinctive, so that customers are reluctant to switch;
- the cost of switching is high (e.g. if a company has invested in a supplier's software);
- suppliers can plausibly threaten to extend their business to compete with the customer;
- the customer is a small or irregular purchaser.

Threat of substitutes

In Porter's model, substitutes refer to products in other industries that can perform the same function, e.g. using cans instead of bottles. Close substitutes constrain the ability of firms to raise prices, and the threat is high when buyers are able and willing to change their habits. Technological change and the risk of obsolescence pose a further threat: online news services (such as that freely available from the BBC) and recruitment sites threaten print newspapers.

Analysing the forces in the competitive environment enables managers to seize opportunities, counter threats and generally improve their position relative to competitors. They can consider how to alter the strength of the forces to improve their position by, for example, building barriers to entry or increasing their power over suppliers or buyers. Chapter 8 (Strategy) examines how managers can position their organisation within the competitive environment.

Activity 3.4   **Critical reflection on the five forces**

Conduct a five forces analysis for an organisation with which you are familiar. Discuss with a manager of the organisation how useful he/she finds the technique.

- Evaluate whether it captures the main competitive variables in his/her industry?
- Compare your analysis with one done for Nokia, and present a summary of similarities and differences in the forces affecting the companies.

| 3.5 | The general environment – PESTEL |

Forces in the wider world also shape management policies, and a **PESTEL analysis** (short for political, economic, socio-cultural, technological, environmental and legal) helps to identify these – which Figure 3.5 summarises. When these forces combine their effect is more pronounced – pharmaceutical companies face problems located in slower progress in transferring scientific knowledge into commercial products, more risk-averse regulators who require longer and more costly trials, challenges from companies making cheap generic alternatives to patented drugs, and governments trying to reduce the costs of drugs supplied to citizens.

Political factors

Political systems vary between countries and often shape what managers can and cannot do. Governments often regulate industries such as power supply, telecommunications, postal services and transport by specifying, among other things, who can offer services, the conditions they must meet and what they can charge. Regulations differ between countries and are a major factor in managers' decisions.

When the UK and most European governments altered the law on financial services, non-financial companies such as Virgin and Sainsbury's quickly began to offer banking services. Deregulating air transport stimulated the growth of low-cost airlines, especially in the US

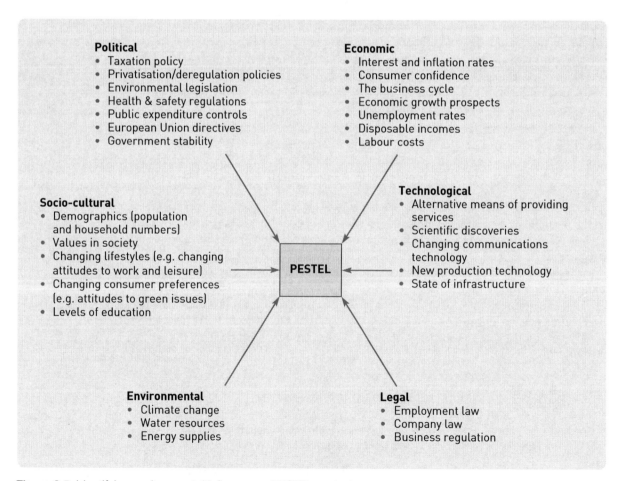

Figure 3.5 Identifying environmental influences – PESTEL analysis

(e.g. Southwest Airlines), Europe (easyJet), Australia (Virgin Blue) and parts of Asia (Air Asia), although as the Ryanair case in Chapter 1 shows, these companies still work in a political environment. The EU is developing regulations to try to manage the environmentally friendly disposal of the millions of personal computers and mobile phones that consumers scrap each year.

Managers aim to influence these political decisions by employing professional lobbyists, especially at international institutions. The European Commission (which performs the detailed analysis behind EU policy) relies on contributions from interested parties to inform its decisions, and lobbying firms provide this. They focus on those people who have decision-making power, often members of the European parliament.

Management in practice   **VT Group depends on government** www.vtplc.com

The UK government is the biggest customer of VT Group, the defence, education and engineering outsourcer. Current contracts include broadcasting the BBC's World Service and managing the Metropolitan Police's vehicle fleet. Contracts with the UK public sector represented 67 per cent of VT's revenues in 2008, and the US public sector made up much of the rest. The company sees both danger and opportunity in this. While shifts in demand for an existing service are usually gradual and predictable, future government policy is often unknown – especially before elections. Paul Lester, who in 2009 was chief executive of the group, maintains close contact with government ministers and leading members of the main opposition party.

Source: *Financial Times*, 29 June 2009.

Economic factors

Economic factors such as wage levels, inflation and interest rates affect an organisation's costs. During the 2009 recession Unilever (**www.unilever.com**) detected significant changes in shopping habits, with many doing without expensive bubble baths, body moisturisers and upmarket cleaning products in favour of less expensive purchases. The consumer goods company said that sales of stock cubes were growing very rapidly as more people 'cooked from scratch' instead of buying prepared meals.

Increasing competition and the search for cost advantages drive globalisation. Ford (**www.ford.com**) has invested in plant to make small cars in India, where demand is growing rapidly as people there become more prosperous. The same economic trend encouraged Tata (**www.tata.com**), the Indian conglomerate, to launch a low-cost car, the Nano: Renault/Nissan (**www.renault.com**) expect to be selling more cars in emerging markets than in developed countries by 2015.

The state of the economy is a major influence on consumer spending, which affects firms meeting those needs. Managers planning capital investments follow economic forecasts: if these suggest slower growth, they may postpone the project.

Socio-cultural factors

Demographic change affects most organisations, apart from those most clearly affected by the ageing population – healthcare and pharmaceuticals businesses. A growing number of single people affects the design of housing, holidays and life assurance. Demographic change affects an organisation's publicity to ensure, for example, that advertising acknowledges racial diversity. Leading banks develop investment and saving schemes that comply with *sharia* law, to attract devout Muslim investors. The growth in spending on live music encouraged HMV Group (**www.hmv.com**) to enter this market in addition to selling music through the stores (see Chapter 8 Case).

Consumer tastes and preferences change. Commenting on a decision to increase the number of healthier products, the chief executive of Nestlé said:

> I think this shows you where the future direction of the company is. This emphasis on (healthier products) is a strategic decision, reflecting changing economic and demographic conditions.

Technological factors

Companies pay close attention to the physical infrastructure – such as the adequacy of power supplies and transport systems. Even more, they monitor advances in information technology, which are dramatically changing the business environment of many companies. Advances in technology do not only affect data systems. Computers traditionally handled data, while other systems handled voice (telephones) and pictures (film and video). These components of the information revolution are familiar as separate devices, but their use of common digital technology greatly increases their ability to exchange information. Digitisation – the packaging of images and sounds into digital form – has profound implications for many industries, as Table 3.2 illustrates.

Table 3.2 Examples of digital technologies affecting established businesses

Technology	Application	Businesses affected
Digital Versatile Discs (DVDs)	Store sound and visual images	Sales of stereophonic sound systems decline sharply
IPOD, MP3 and smartphones	Digital downloads of talking books	New markets created for talking books, with titles to suit new audience
Broadband services delivering online content	Enables advertisers to use online media rather than print or television	Media companies (some of whom have now moved online – NewsCorp acquired MySpace)
Voice over Internet Protocol (VoIP)	Enables telephone calls over the internet at very low cost	Threat to revenues of traditional phone companies
Digital photography	Enables people to store pictures electronically and order prints online	Photographic retailers such as Jessops lose significant part of business

Bernoff and Li (2008) show how social networking (Facebook) and user-generated content sites (YouTube) change the technological context – to which companies are in turn responding: see Chapter 12.

Environmental factors

The natural resources available in an economy – including minerals, agricultural land and the prevailing climate – affect the kind of businesses that managers create: the mills at New Lanark (Chapter 2 case) were built beside a source of water power.

Many senior managers know that climate change will have major implications for their organisations, and are working out how best to respond. It will put most businesses at risk, with the probability of more droughts, floods, storms and heat waves – less rainfall in some places, more in others. For some it represents a threat – insurance companies, house builders and water companies are only the most visible examples of companies that are being affected. For others, sustainability brings opportunities – alternative energy suppliers, emission control businesses and waste management companies are all seeing more interest in their products and services.

Legal factors

Governments create the legal framework within which companies operate, most obviously in areas such as health and safety, employment, consumer protection and pollution control. They also create the legal basis for business – such as when the UK parliament passed the Joint Stock Companies Act in 1862. Previously people were discouraged from putting their money into a business as they were personally liable for the whole of a company's debts if it failed. The Act of 1862 limited their liability to the value of the shares they held in the company – they could lose their investment, but not the rest of their wealth. This stimulated company formation and other countries soon passed similar legislation, paving the way for the countless 'limited liability' companies that exist today (Micklethwait and Wooldridge, 2003).

The PESTEL analysis is just as relevant to public and voluntary sector organisations. Many public service organisations are in business to do things that the market does not, so a PESTEL analysis can identify emerging issues that need attention. An example is the age structure of the population: a country with growing numbers of elderly people has to finance changes in community care services, social services and hospitals. Public sector organisations are often unable to expand their operations where new problems or needs are identified, but the results can be used to lobby for increased funding or to target their existing budgets.

The PESTEL framework is a useful starting point for analysis if managers use it to identify factors that are relevant to their business and how they are changing.

Activity 3.5 **Critical reflection on a PESTEL analysis**

Conduct a PESTEL analysis for your organisation, or one with which you are familiar.

- Which of the external forces you have identified has the most implications for the business?
- Evaluate the extent to which the organisation's policy has taken account of these forces.
- Compare your analysis with that which you did for Nokia, and present a summary of similarities and differences in the forces affecting the companies.

3.6 Types of environment and stakeholders

Perceptions of environments

The axes in Figure 3.6 show two variables (Duncan, 1972) which affect how people see their environment – the degree of complexity and the degree of dynamism. Complexity refers to the number and similarity of factors which people take into consideration when making a decision – the more of these, and the more different they are, the more complex the situation. Dynamism refers to the degree to which these factors remain the same or change.

To consider only the most contrasting cells in Figure 3.6, those who perceive themselves to be in a *simple-static* environment will experience little uncertainty. Competitors offer similar products, newcomers rarely enter the market and there are few technological breakthroughs. Examples could include routine legal work such as house sales and wills, or trades such as joinery. The information required for a decision is likely to be available, so people can assess the outcome of a decision quickly and accurately. They can use past trends to predict the future with a reasonable degree of confidence. Some aspects of health and education, where demand is driven largely by demographic change, may also fit this pattern: the capacity needed in primary and secondary schools is easy to predict several years ahead.

Key ideas **Donald Sull – active waiting in unpredictable markets**

Donald Sull (2005) has studied more than 20 pairs of comparable companies in unpredictable industries such as airlines, telecommunications and software development. By comparing similar companies he was able to show how they responded differently to unforeseen threats and opportunities. Successful companies regularly responded more effectively to unexpected shifts in regulation, technology, competitive or macro-environments. They did this by what he termed 'actively waiting', using techniques which included:

- Keeping priorities clear to avoid dissipating energy and resources.
- Conducting reconnaissance to identify gaps in the market.
- Keeping a reserve of cash to fund major opportunities when they emerge.
- Using lulls to push through operational improvements.
- Declare that an opportunity is the company's main effort to seize it faster than rivals.

Source: Based on Sull (2005).

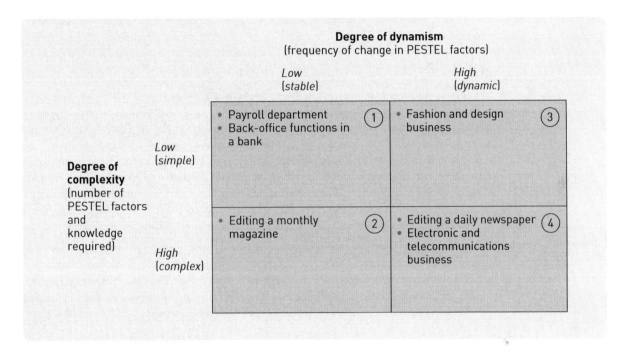

Figure 3.6 Types of environment

At the other extreme, those working in complex-dynamic environments face great uncertainty. They have to monitor many diverse and changing factors. Companies in the mobile phone or entertainment industries are like this. Multinationals such as Shell and BP experience great complexity, operating across diverse political, legal and cultural systems. Eric Schmidt (Chief Executive of Google) has said that in many high tech and other industries:

the environment is changing so fast that it requires improvisation in terms of strategy, products and even day-to-day operations. Just when you think you understand the technology landscape, you see a major disruption.

Activity 3.6   Critical reflection on type of environment

Use Figure 3.6 to analyse the environment in which your unit of the organisation works. Then try to do the same analysis for one or two other units of the organisation.

- Compare the nature of these environments.
- What are the implications of that for managing these departments, and for the organisation?

Most managers claim to work in dynamic and complex situations. This implies that they face great uncertainty over how the future will unfold. In these circumstances historical analysis is likely to be a less useful guide to the future and managers need to develop different ways of anticipating what may lie ahead.

Case question 3.4

● How would you classify the environment in which Nokia operates? Which factors contributed to your answer?

Stakeholders

All managers need to deal with stakeholders – individuals, groups or other organisations with an interest in, or who are affected by, what the enterprise does (Freeman, 1984). Organisations depend on their micro and macro environments (see Figure 3.1) for the resources they need. Stakeholders in these environments make resources available or withhold them, depending on their view of the organisation. Managers in any sector need to pay attention to stakeholder expectations, and meet these to an acceptable degree to ensure a positive view.

Stakeholders may be internal (employees, managers, different departments or professional groups, owners, shareholders) or external (customers, competitors, bankers, local communities, members of the public, pressure groups and government). The challenge is that:

> Different stakeholders do not generally share the same definition of an organization's 'problems', and hence, they do not in general share the same 'solutions.' As a result, the typical approaches to organizational problem solving, which generally pre-suppose prior consensus or agreement among parties, cannot be used; they break down. Instead a method is needed that builds off a starting point of disagreement . . . (Mitroff, 1983, p. 5)

Stakeholders have expectations of organisations and managers choose whether or not to take account of these. Nutt (2002) shows the dangers of ignoring them: he studied 400 strategic decisions and found that half of them 'failed' – in the sense that they were not implemented or produced poor results – largely because managers failed to attend to stakeholders.

Faced with evidence of excessive risk-taking in banks, shareholders have begun to become more active in criticising directors over the pay and bonus systems through which they reward senior managers in their companies. This has led to changes in corporate governance arrangements.

Figure 3.7 indicates what stakeholders may expect.

Shareholders
● Growth in dividend payments
● Growth in share price
● Growth in asset value

Customers
● Competitive price
● Quality product or service
● Guarantee provisions

Suppliers
● Timely payment of debt
● Adequate liquidity
● Integrity of directors
● Trustworthy purchasing manager

Employees
● Good pay and benefits
● Job security
● Sense of purpose in the job
● Opportunities for personal development

Government
● Adhering to the country's laws
● Paying taxes
● Providing employment
● Value for money in using public funds

Lenders
● Financial strength of the company
● Quality of management
● Quality of assets available for security
● Ability to repay interest and capital

Figure 3.7
Examples of possible stakeholder expectations

3.7   Corporate governance

Why have governance systems?

Scandals and failures in prominent organisations lead people to question the adequacy of their systems of **corporate governance**. They show that senior managers cannot always be trusted to act in the best interests of the company and the shareholders. To reduce this risk, owners have developed rules and processes which are intended to guide and control those responsible for managing public and private organisations, ensuring that they act in the interests of influential stakeholders. Governance systems are based on the principle that those managing an organisation are accountable for their actions, and create mechanisms to do that.

In capitalist economies, ownership typically becomes separated from control. The founder provides the initial capital but growth requires further finance – which investors provide in exchange for an income. They cannot supervise management decisions, but need to be confident that the business is secure before they provide further funds.

Berle and Means (1932) highlighted the dilemma facing owners who become separated from the managers they appoint to run the business:

> The corporation is a means by which the wealth of innumerable individuals has been concentrated into huge aggregates and whereby control over this wealth has been surrendered to a unified direction . . . The direction of industry other than by persons who have ventured their wealth has raised the question . . . of the distribution of the returns from business enterprise. (p. 4)

Their observations led others to develop what is now termed 'agency theory', which seeks to explain what happens when one party (the principal) delegates work to another party (the agent). In this case the shareholders (principals) have financed, and own, the business, but they delegate the work of running it to managers (agents). The principals then face the risk that managers may not act in their (the principals') best interests: they may take excessive investment risks, or withhold information so that the state of the business appears to be better than it is. The principal is then at a disadvantage to the agent, who may use this to personal advantage. Failures at major financial institutions, caused in part by lending money to risky borrowers in the hope of high returns, show that the separation of ownership from management, of principal from agent, is as relevant as ever.

Corporate governance refers to the rules and processes intended to control those responsible for managing an organisation.

Management in practice   The interests of managers and shareholders

While senior managers often claim to be trying to align their interests with those of shareholders, the two often conflict. Mergers often appear to benefit senior managers and their professional advisers rather than shareholders. Acquiring companies often pay too much for the target, but executives inside the enlarged company receive higher pay. Professional advisers (investment bankers) make money on both the merger and the break-up.

Using company money to buy the company's shares in the market uses money that can't be spent on dividends. From the vantage point of many CEOs, paying dividends is about the last thing they would want to do with corporate earnings. In theory, a CEO is carrying out shareholder wishes. In practice, as the spate of recent scandals has shown, the interests of chief executives and their shareholders can widely diverge.

Source: Based on extracts from an article by Robert Kuttner, *Business Week,* 9 September 2002.

Similar issues arise in the public sector, where elected members are nominally in charge of local authorities, health boards and other agencies – and who appoint professional managers to run the organisation on behalf of the citizens. Elected members face the risk that the people they have appointed act in their narrow professional or personal interests, rather than of those of the electorate. Hartley *et al.* (2008) point out:

> a new awareness of the social, economic and cultural contribution of government, public organizations and public services has resulted in a significant period of reform and experimentation. At the heart of these initiatives is the idea that improvements to the way public services can be governed, managed and delivered will produce improved outcomes for citizens. (p. 3)

Stakeholder theory is also relevant, as it tries to explain the evolving relationship between an organisation and its stakeholders. Many believe that governance systems should take account of the interests of this wider group, as well as those of shareholders with only a financial interest.

The substance of corporate governance

Mallin (2007) suggests that to provide an adequate oversight of managers, governance systems should have:

- an adequate system of internal controls which safeguards assets;
- mechanisms to prevent any one person having too much influence;
- processes to manage relationships between managers, directors, shareholders and other stakeholders;
- the aim of managing the company in the interests of shareholders and other stakeholders; and
- the aim of encouraging transparency and accountability, which investors and many external stakeholders expect.

Proposals to deal with these issues affect the context in which managers work, and this book will examine the topic as an integrating theme at the end of each chapter.

3.8 Integrating themes

Sustainable performance

Nicholas Stern advises the UK government on climate change, and his latest book (Stern, 2009) calls for urgent action to mitigate the effects. The paragraphs below summarise some of his points.

Climate change is not a theory struggling to maintain itself in the face of problematic evidence. The opposite is true: as new information comes in, it reinforces our understanding across a whole spectrum of indicators. The subject is full of uncertainty, but there is no serious doubt that emissions are growing as a result of human activity and that more greenhouse gases will lead to further warming.

The last 20 years have seen special and focused attention from the Intergovernmental Panel on Climate Change (IPCC) (**www.ipcc.ch**), which has now published four assessments, the most recent in 2007. With each new report, the evidence on the strength and source of the effects, and the magnitude of the implications and risks, has become stronger. The basic scientific conclusions on climate change are very robust and for good reason. The greenhouse effect is simple science: greenhouse gases trap heat, and humans are emitting ever more greenhouse gases. There will be oscillations, there will be uncertainties. But the logic of the greenhouse effect is rock-solid and the long-term trends associated with the effects of human emissions are clear in the data.

In 2010 a report by the UK Meteorological Office (Stott, 2010) confirmed these conclusions, saying that the evidence was stronger now than when the IPCC carried out its last assessment in 2007. The analysis assessed 110 research papers on the subject, concluding that the earth is changing rapidly, probably because of greenhouse gases. The study found that changes in Arctic sea ice, atmospheric moisture, saltiness of parts of the Atlantic Ocean and temperature changes in the Antarctic are consistent with human influence on our climate.

Governance and control

This chapter has examined the culture of organisations and their external contexts: governance links the two. There are high-profile examples of organisations whose culture has encouraged managers and staff to act in their interests, rather than in the interests of those they were expected to serve. This has focused attention on corporate governance arrangements, which are part of the context within which managers of all organisations work: most of the time these will be far in the background, but they become visible at times of difficulty.

The Cadbury Report (1992) has influenced the development of corporate governance systems around the world, including the UK. Set up following a series of UK financial scandals it made recommendations about the operation of the main board, the establishment and operation of board committees, the roles of non-executive directors, and on reporting and control mechanisms. These recommendations have been combined with the outcomes of related reports into what is known as the Combined Code – the latest version of which was published in 2006 (Financial Reporting Council, 2006). This is a voluntary Code of Best Practice, with which the boards of all companies listed on the London Stock Exchange are expected to comply – or to explain why they have not done so. It includes guidance on matters such as:

The Board. Every company should be headed by an effective board, which is collectively responsible for the success of the company;

Chairman and chief executive. There should be a clear division of responsibilities . . . between the running of the board and the executive responsible [for running the business]. No one individual should have unfettered powers of decision.

Board balance. The board should include a balance of executive and [independent] non-executive directors so that no individual or small group can dominate the board's decision taking

Board appointments. There should be a formal, rigorous and transparent procedure for appointing new directors to the board.

Internationalisation

Models of national culture (see Chapter 4) are highly generalised summaries of diverse populations. Their value is to give some clues about broad differences between the places in which those managing internationally will be working. They encourage people to be ready to adapt the way they work to local circumstances. Others take a more robust view of cultural differences and try to eliminate their influence within the organisation. Steve Chang founded Trend Micro, an anti-virus software company operating in many countries:

The curse is that national cultures are very different. We have to figure out how to convert everybody to one business culture – no matter where they're from. (*Business Week*, 22 September 2003)

The following Management in Practice feature shows how Iris, a rapidly growing advertising agency with a very strong and distinctive company culture AND many global clients, seeks to gain the benefits of the diversity of its international staff and combine this to add more value for the client.

Management in practice — Gaining from cultural differences — www.irisnation.com

Iris was founded in 1999 and has established a distinctive position as an independent media and advertising agency, with a growing international business. An innovative technique which is very popular with global clients is 'Project 72'. Steve Bell, chief executive of Iris London, and one of the founding partners, explains:

> Project 72 is a very simple concept, and probably the purest way of bringing different agencies in the group together as one with a common goal and a common vision. [Suppose] Iris Miami is working on a brief for a client: they say 'right, let's engage a Project 72 on this one'. So the brief will go to the other agencies around the world, it will be handed to London, for example, we will work on it for 12 hours, we will then [hand the baton] to Sydney, they will work on it for 12 hours, baton change to Singapore, so you can see how within 72 hours we've got the best freshest brains working on a brief to the common goal of developing the best creative work that we possibly can do. It's been fantastic . . .
>
> Project 72 benefits hugely from the cultural differences, and when I say cultural differences I don't mean within the agency but the societal cultural differences that happen within different areas around the world. So tapping into the fact that Singapore has a certain view around mobile telecomms enables us to look at things in a slightly different way, so it just allows fresh thinking, fresh outlooks, fresh cultures to inject some pace and some innovation around a particular brief at a given time.

Source: Interview with Steve Bell.

ENVIRONMENTAL MANAGEMENT

Over the last 40 years there has been a growing interest in the environment, or more specifically in the damage being inflicted on the environment by human activity worldwide. In Europe the process of integration has brought the transnational nature of the environmental problem to the forefront of the social, political and corporate agenda. Environmental problems and issues such as the hole in the ozone layer, climate change and global warming are the result of not one country's action but that of many. Acid rain, which is polluting rivers and lakes and damaging forests, often emanates from one country and is deposited in another.

The effects of different industrial sectors on the environment vary enormously. At one end of the spectrum might be multinational oil companies, whose very business is environmentally damaging, and at the other end might be retailers and the service sector, who have less of a direct impact on the environment – although, in most cases, they could still make environmental improvements through recycling and improved transportation policies. There is still much confusion for both consumers and companies about what constitutes an environmentally friendly product or operation, and the 'green revolution' to date has provided few answers, although many misrepresentations, particularly in the area of product marketing, have been exposed.

At the root of some of the environmental problems is the growth in consumerism and materialism. The notion that 'the consumer is king' may drive the market mechanism but the overemphasis placed on the satisfaction of customers' wants in the developed economies of the world has had a profound effect on the planet's ability to sustain life and on biodiversity. It is generally accepted that the world cannot go on using the resources of the planet at the present rate. But there is a 'free-rider problem' at work – everyone thinks that something should happen to mitigate the problem but many people just assume that everyone else will do it, and anyway their individual impact is minute so it will make no difference to the environment. This is illustrated by Exhibit 18.1.

Everything that consumers, companies and other institutions do will have some impact on the environment, but for *sustainable* development the emphasis needs to be on the strategies that organisations can follow to improve their environmental performance. Even substances which, in their final form, are environmentally benign may have been unfriendly in their manufacture, especially if that manufacture was

Exhibit 18.1 **Packaging in the UK**

'Now we know buying fruit and vegetables packed in unwanted plastic – destined for landfill sites – is not just environmentally unsound, but expensive'
(*Evening Standard*, Comment 18 April 2007)

The paper's report suggests that packaging adds 20 per cent to the cost of fruit in Waitrose, bearing out the Women's Institute finding that packaging adds about £8 to every £50 spent on food. The answer was to buy loose and for retailers to reduce packaging: 'most fruit, after all, comes ready-wrapped by nature.' A green pressure group, WRAP, was reported to be drawing up plans for industry-wide labelling on packaging disposal, while a spokesman for Waitrose declared that 'reducing packaging is a key priority for us and we have reduced the weight of product packaging by 33 per cent since 2000.'

energy-greedy. They may have been produced using non-renewable resources and may also pose problems after they have been used and it comes to their disposal. If a 'cradle-to-the-grave' view of products is taken, where their environmental impact is examined through their life cycle from raw materials and through usage to disposal then there are few, if any, products which will fail to have a negative impact on the environment. The key question, therefore, is not how environmental damage is completely eliminated but how it is reduced it over time, and how a state of balance is achieved such that the amount of environmental damage is repairable and therefore sustainable.

Industry, particularly in the developed world, must increasingly take into account the costs of the effects of its operations on the environment as opposed to regarding the planet as a free resource. In the past, few companies counted the costs of the pollution they discharged into the atmosphere and the debate has now turned to legislation aimed at forcing companies to comply with certain standards and taxing those which pollute. The so-called 'polluter pays' principle is now central to legislation in the developed countries. The implication here is clearly that prices will rise for consumers as organisations experience increased costs associated with environmental improvements. Lower energy consumption and more efficient use of resources are obvious targets for improvement and should not conflict with industry's aims, since their attainment can actually reduce costs. Many materials are already recycled and a thriving, and at times profitable, recycling industry has been established across Europe (see Exhibit 18.2).

Many of the products now considered to be environmentally hazardous were, at the time of their discovery, regarded as an invaluable resource. The best example of this has been the use of chlorofluorocarbons in refrigerators, which have since been found to be a major ozone-depleting agent. Predicting a product's long-term impact on the environment is a difficult process and, until recently, has rarely been done. This will change as firms are forced to consider cradle-to-grave management of their products and as the benefit of doubt is increasingly given to the welfare of the planet. Moreover, industry has a responsibility to ensure that its products are less harmful to the environment and there is a need to push along a very steep environmental learning curve.

Many governments across Europe have been implementing increasingly stringent environmental legislation. At the level of the European Union there has been an emphasis on the provision of information about products and processes to the public. However, a common problem is that the statutory bodies which do exist with

Exhibit 18.2 Organisational commitment in the UK

'As a responsible member of the business community we are working to reduce our impact on the environment. Climate change is one of the greatest challenges of modern times and the Society has and will continue to take action to tackle climate change by reducing our carbon emissions.'

(The Coventry Building Society TLC,
Annual General Meeting report, 2007 *Investing in Your Future*)

Practical steps to do this included purchasing greener electricity, working with the Carbon Trust to identify ways of reducing energy consumption, recycling waste paper and printer cartridges and where possible using paper that 'comes from greener sources'.

responsibility for monitoring the environmental performance of organisations have limited resources and powers in most cases. Organisations themselves have often been shown to be ignorant of current environmental legislation, particularly with regard to EU environmental directives and legislation on issues such as waste disposal, air pollution and water quality. However, such ignorance is not an excuse for non-compliance. Moreover, non-compliance which can be attributed to negligence can not only result in fines but occasionally in imprisonment for company directors.

In the USA the Environmental Protection Agency (EPA) is an independent environmental body with significant power. In 1980 the US Congress passed the Comprehensive Environmental Response, Compensation and Liability Act, better known as 'Superfund'. Under the provisions of the Act, companies must report potentially toxic spills and releases greater than a clearly defined minimum. Violations of this are criminal offences with penalties of up to one year in jail and a significant fine. Superfund also deals with uncontrolled hazardous waste sites where previous or present owners and operators of a site must help to pay for whatever remedial action is necessary. If the previous firm has gone out of business, the EPA has often managed to obtain funds from the companies which sent the waste there for treatment or disposal in the first instance. In the UK, by contrast, local authority regulators and pollution inspectors all adopt an approach of constructive engagement with companies rather than fining them in the first instance for pollution violations.

The rapid growth of public environmental awareness in recent years has placed new pressures on industry. These pressures can take many forms as individuals collectively exercise their environmental conscience as customers, employees, investors, voters, neighbours and fellow citizens. However, whether it is due to intellectual fatigue with environmental issues, a lack of conviction that an individual's own actions will have an impact or a reluctance to reduce private consumption for public welfare, it seems that many individuals prefer to pass their responsibilities on to those parties that they feel can make a significant impact. The two major parties that the public perceive as being able to make a difference are government and industry. Given the public's inherent reluctance to reduce its own levels of consumption, it is apparent that government and industry must respond in order to protect the environment effectively.

In this area of management there are frequent changes in regulations, legislation, treaties and agreements and in the details that apply to particular industries; the regulations and agreements discussed in this Chapter are examples of these.

USING THE PRICE MECHANISM TO ALLEVIATE POLLUTION

The use of the market mechanism to distribute goods and services in the West, with its consequent stress on property rights, has contributed to the environmental degradation which we have experienced. Much of the environment (particularly the air and atmosphere) is treated as a free good since no individual owns it and there are no assigned property rights to it. Firms and consumers have therefore made excessive use of environmental resources both as an input and as a source of output (or sink). This is illustrated in Figure 18.1.

Suppose that a firm produces a good and in the process of doing so it pollutes the air around it. Traditionally, and ignoring legislation which might or might not exist, the firm can do this freely since no one owns the air. Assume that the demand for the product is D_1 and the production and marketing costs of the firm imply that it is willing to sell along a supply curve given by S_1. Essentially S_1 is drawn based on only the private costs of the firm, that is, those which it must pay

Figure 18.1 Using the market mechanism to deal with environmental damage

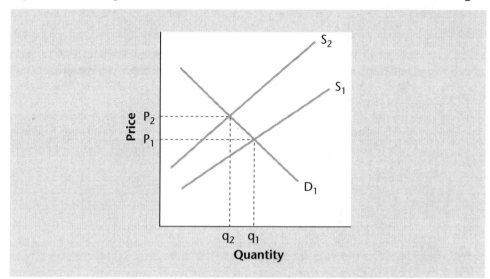

in a monetary form, but the pollution caused to the local community imposes a cost on them and on society as a whole. If the firm was required to internalise those costs either by paying a tax-to-pollute based on an estimate of the social cost that that pollution caused (the tax might subsequently be used to clean up the pollution), or by the use of legislation banning the pollution (meaning that the firm would have to invest in a new non-polluting process) then its own costs would rise. The firm's willingness to supply at any particular price would be reduced and S_1 would shift backwards to S_2. The equilibrium in the market would shift from P_1q_1 to P_2q_2. Thus less of the good would be produced and at a higher price.

The premise on which most developed countries' environmental legislation has largely been based is the 'polluter pays' principle. In other words this is a notion that public money should not be used in clearing up or avoiding pollution but, as described above, the polluters themselves should face those costs. From a welfare point of view, the difference between a firm compensating a local community for the pollution it creates and the community paying the firm not to pollute is purely distributional, but from an ethical perspective it is often argued that the 'polluter pays' principle is superior.

The sort of analysis described by Figure 18.1 can be extended to the economy as a whole. Since most processes will impose at least some negative impact on the environment, the fact that the environment has not been properly costed and treated as a free good over time has meant that too many goods have been produced. Moreover, it can be argued that mass-production techniques which have enabled firms to produce more and more goods and to charge lower prices have been particularly damaging.

SUSTAINABLE DEVELOPMENT

The belief which lies behind the concept of sustainable development is that there is a trade-off between continuous economic growth and the sustainability of the environment. Over time, growth causes pollution and atmospheric damage. The concept of sustainable development stresses the interdependence between economic growth and environmental quality. It is possible to make development and environmental protection compatible by following sustainable strategies and by not developing the particular areas of economic activity that are most damaging to the environment.

The Brundtland Report (World Commission on Environment and Development, 1987), commissioned by the United Nations to examine long-term environmental strategies, argued that economic development and environmental protection could be made compatible but that this would require quite radical changes in economic practices throughout the world. They defined sustainable development as:

'development that meets the needs of the present without compromising the ability of future generations to meet their own needs.'

In other words mass consumption is not possible indefinitely and if society today acts as if all non-renewable resources are plentiful then eventually there will be nothing left for the future. More importantly than that, however, mass consumption may cause such irreparable damage that humans may not even be able to live on the planet in the future.

The challenge that faces the economic system is how to continue to fulfil its vital role within modern society while working towards sustainability. Complying with the principles of sustainability cannot be achieved overnight. However, both for entire economies and for individual businesses there is hope that it can be achieved within the time scales which appear to be necessary if environmental catastrophe is to be avoided.

According to Welford (1993), sustainable development is made up of three closely connected issues and associated conditions.

- **Environment** – this must be valued as an integral part of the economic process and not treated as a free good. The environmental stock has to be protected, which implies minimal use of non-renewable resources and minimal emission of pollutants. The ecosystem has to be protected so the loss of plant and animal species has to be avoided.

- **Equity** – one of the biggest threats facing the world is that the developing countries want to grow rapidly to achieve the same standards of living as those in the West. That in itself would cause a major environmental disaster if it were modelled on the same sort of growth as experienced in post-war Europe. Therefore, there needs to be a greater degree of equity and the key issue of poverty has to be addressed, but it seems hypocritical for the West to tell the Third World that it cannot attain the same standards of living and consumption.

- **Futurity** – sustainable development requires that society, businesses and individuals operate on a different time scale than that which currently operates in the economy. While companies commonly operate under competitive pressures to achieve short-term gains, long-term environmental protection is often compromised. To ensure that longer-term, intergenerational considerations are observed, longer planning horizons need to be adopted and business policy needs to be proactive rather than reactive.

The Brundtland Report concludes that these three conditions are not being met. The industrialised world has already used much of the planet's ecological capital and many of the development paths of the industrialised nations are clearly unsustainable. Non-renewable resources are being depleted, while renewable resources such as soil, water and the atmosphere are being degraded. This has been caused by economic development but in time will undermine the very foundations of that development.

Like the Brundtland Report, more recent initiatives by the United Nations, including the Earth Summit held in Rio in 1992 and the World Summit on Sustainable Development (Rio+10) held in Johannesburg in 2002, call for development which is environmentally and socially sustainable rather than the current situation of unplanned, undifferentiated growth. This means reconsidering the current measures of growth, such as gross national product (GNP), which fail to take account of environmental debits such as pollution or the depletion of the natural capital stock. While concern about the depletion of materials and energy resources has diminished since the 1970s, there is nevertheless concern surrounding the environment's capacity to act as a sink for waste. For example, bringing developing countries' energy use up to the level of the developing world's would mean an increase in consumption by a factor of five. Using present energy-generation methods the planet could not cope with the impact of sulphur dioxide and carbon dioxide emissions and the consequential acidification and global warming of the environment.

One major obstacle preventing sustainability from being achieved is the overall level of consumption. However, Western consumers are apparently reluctant to significantly reduce their own levels of consumption. While governments are increasingly adopting economic instruments such as taxes, subsidies and product-labelling schemes to reduce and channel consumption towards more environmentally friendly alternatives, industry itself must be encouraged further to increase environmental efficiency.

Sustainability challenges industry to produce higher levels of output while using lower levels of input and generating less waste. The problem that remains is that while relative environmental impact per unit of output has fallen, increases in the absolute level of output, and hence environmental impact, have more than offset any gains in relative environmental efficiency. However, if we examine the ways in which environmental efficiency has been improved then we can begin to understand some of the key practical elements with which sustainability may be better promoted.

CORPORATE RESPONSES TO SUSTAINABLE DEVELOPMENT

Organisations are faced with a challenge of integrating environmental considerations into their production and marketing plans. There is always an incentive, however, for profit-maximising firms seeking short-term rewards to opt out and become a free-rider (assuming that everyone else will be environmentally conscious such that their own pollution will become negligible). However, European Union environmental legislation is increasingly plugging the gaps which allow this to happen and firms attempting to hide their illegal pollution are now subject to severe penalties. In many cases individual company directors can also be prosecuted and imprisoned for negligence which leads to environmental damage. Even before then businesses should recognise that it is not only ethical to be environmentally friendly but, with the growth of consumer awareness in the environmental area, that it will also be good business.

Organisations clearly have a role to play in the development of substitutes for non-renewable resources and innovations which reduce waste and use energy more efficiently. They also have a role in processing those materials in a way which brings about environmental improvements. For many products (e.g. cars and wash-

Exhibit 18.3 Company commitment in the UK

'Five years. Five commitments. One world. And 100 things we want to change'.

- **Climate change** – we'll aim to make all our UK operations carbon neutral within five years. We'll maximize our use of renewable energy and only use offsetting as a last resort. And, we'll be helping our customers and suppliers to cut their carbon emissions too.

- **Waste** – we'll significantly reduce the amount of packaging and carrier bags that we use and find new ways to recycle materials. By 2012 we aim to ensure that none of our clothing or packaging need end up as landfill.

- **Sustainable raw materials** – from fish to forests, our goal is to make sure our key raw materials come from the most sustainable sources available to us, protecting the environment and the world's natural resources for future generations.

- **Fair partner** – by being a fair partner we'll help to improve the lives of hundreds of thousands of people in our worldwide supply chain and local communities.

- **Health** – we'll continue to expand our healthy eating ranges and help customers and employees to choose healthier lifestyles through clear labelling and easily accessible information.

Source: Marks & Spencer plc, *the Guardian*, 19 March 2007

ing machines) the major area of environmental damage occurs in their usage. Organisations often have the opportunity of reducing this damage at the design stage, and when new products are being developed there is a whole new opportunity for considering both the use and disposal of the product. According to the American Marketing Association (Luo and Bhattacharya, 2006) as many as 90 per cent of 'Fortune 500' companies (i.e. the foremost American companies) have explicit corporate social responsibility initiatives. The increasing importance of CSR in practice has been seen in marketing studies which found that these programmes have a significant influence on several customer-related outcomes (Luo and Bhattacharya, 2006). Specifically, CSR affects consumer product responses, customer-company identification and customers' product attitude directly or indirectly and it can contribute positively to market value.

Given the internal and external demands to improve the environmental performance of organisations, those that achieve high standards of environmental performance will benefit in a number of ways. In order to realise this competitive advantage organisations must seek to develop management strategies which will improve their environmental performance and address the environmental demands placed on them by government, the EU and stakeholders. By incorporating the increasingly important environmental dimension into the decision-making processes of the organisation, managers can seek to reduce costs and exploit the opportunities offered by increased public environmental concern within a dynamic marketplace (see Exhibit 18.3). Such a strategy must be proactive and honest. It may also involve a degree of education and campaigning, such as that undertaken by The Body Shop – but more than anything it must be ethical.

The general principles of such a strategy are embodied within the International Chamber of Commerce (ICC)/World Business Council for Sustainable Development (WBCSD) *Business Charter for Sustainable Development*. The key elements to this strategy are embodied in 16 'principles for environmental management' – organisations are encouraged to endorse these following aims.

- **Corporate priority** – to recognise environmental management as among the highest corporate priorities and as a key determinant to sustainable development; to establish policies, programmes and practices for conducting operations in an environmentally sound manner.

- **Integrated management** – to integrate these policies, programmes and practices fully into each business as an essential element of management in all its functions.

- **Process of improvement** – to continue to improve corporate policies, programmes and environmental performance taking into account technical developments, scientific understanding, consumer needs and community expectations, with legal regulations as a starting point; and to apply the same environmental criteria internationally.

- **Employee education** – to educate, train and motivate employees to conduct their activities in an environmentally responsible manner.

- **Prior assessment** – to assess environmental impacts before starting a new activity or project and before decommissioning a facility or leaving a site.

- **Products and services** – to develop and provide products and services that have no undue environmental impact and are safe in their intended use, that are efficient in their consumption of energy and natural resources and that can be recycled, reused or disposed of safely.

- **Customer advice** – to advise and, where relevant, educate customers, distributors and the public in the safe use, transportation, storage and disposal of products provided; to apply similar considerations to the provision of services.

- **Facilities and operations** – to develop, design and operate facilities and conduct activities taking into consideration the efficient use of energy and raw materials, the sustainable use of renewable resources, the minimisation of adverse environmental impact and waste generation, and the safe and responsible disposal of residual wastes.

- **Research** – to conduct or support research on the environmental impacts of raw materials, products, processes, emissions and wastes associated with the enterprise and on the means of minimising such adverse impacts.

- **Precautionary approach** – to modify the manufacture, marketing or use of products or services to the conduct of activities consistent with scientific and technical understanding, to prevent serious or irreversible environmental degradation.

- **Contractors and suppliers** – to promote the adoption of these principles by contractors acting on behalf of the enterprise encouraging and, where appropriate, requiring improvements in their practices to make them consistent with those of the enterprise; to encourage the wider adoption of these principles by suppliers.

- **Emergency preparedness** – to develop and maintain, where appropriate hazards exist, emergency preparedness plans in conjunction with the emergency services, relevant authorities and the local community recognising potential cross-boundary impacts.

- **Transfer of technology** – to contribute to the transfer of environmentally sound technology and management methods throughout the industrial and public sectors.

- **Contributing to the common effort** – to contribute to the development of public policy and to business, governmental and intergovernmental programmes and educational initiatives that will enhance environmental awareness and protection.

- **Openness to concerns** – to foster openness and dialogue with employees and the public, anticipating and responding to their concerns about the potential hazards and impacts of operations, products, wastes or services, including those of trans-boundary or global significance.

- **Compliance and reporting** – to measure environmental performance, to conduct regular environmental audits and assessments of compliance with company requirements and these principles; periodically to provide appropriate information to the board of directors, shareholders, employees, the authorities and the public.

This Business Charter for Sustainable Development is one of the most widely supported business and environment charters, with over 1500 signatories worldwide, including leading companies such as Shell, BOC, British Airways, ICI, British Gas, Samsung, General Motors and Ford. Many of these companies have implemented the charter's recommendations within existing environmental initiatives and management systems.

THE EUROPEAN INTEGRATION PROCESS AND CORPORATE ENVIRONMENTAL MANAGEMENT

The original Treaty of Rome was concerned with stimulating economic growth and made no specific reference to the environment. Since then, however, EU environmental policy has developed in line with general concern in Europe and the deteriorating environmental position in which Europe finds itself. By 2003, over 300 pieces of environmental legislation had been passed covering pollution of the air and water, noise pollution, chemicals, waste, environmental impact assessment, the prevention of industrial accidents and wildlife protection. Exhibit 18.4 outlines the principal EU landmarks up to 2003.

However, few member states have been able to enforce EU legislation fully. Denmark is probably the only country with a consistently good record and the southern European countries have consistently bad records. Once again, this highlights the emphasis often given to economic growth rather than environmental protection, with the primary aim of countries such as Spain and Portugal being the attainment of similar living standards to the rest of the Union.

The Single European Act gave environmental policy a boost, stating that there is not only a need for such legislation but that the laws should meet three key objectives:

- **preservation, protection and improvement of the quality of the environment;**
- **protection of human health;**
- **prudent and rational use of natural resources.**

These objectives must be met by applying four principles:

- **prevention of harm to the environment;**
- **control of pollution at source;**

Exhibit 18.4 **Examples of important EU landmarks**

1967	First Environmental Directive, on classification, packaging and labelling of dangerous substances (67/548)
1970	Directive establishing framework for measures to combat air pollution from motor vehicles (70/220)
1973	Launch of first European environment action programme 1973–76
1979	Birds Directive, on the protection of birds and their habitats (79/409)
1980	Directive laying down minimum standards for drinking water (80/778)
1985	Directive on Environmental Impact Assessment (85/337)
1990	Directives to limit the use and release of genetically modified organisms (GMOs) (90/219 and 90/220)
1991	Maastricht Treaty Article 6 lays down that all EU policies and activities must integrate environmental protection
1992	Habitats Directive, on the conservation of natural habitats and wild flora and fauna (92/43)
1994	European Environment Agency established
1999	Start of Green Week, the annual EU environmental conferences
2000	Framework Directive for European policy on water (2000/60)
2001	Launch of the Sixth Environmental Action Programme 2001–10: Environment 2010, Our Future, Our Choice
2002	Ratification of the Kyoto Protocol on Climate Change

Source: European Commission (2002) *Choices for a Greener Future: The European Union and the Environment*, Brussels: European Commission Directorate-General for press and communications.

■ the polluter should pay;

■ integration of environmental considerations into other European Union policies (all EU policies are now required to take the environment into account).

The Internal Market Programme has added a new note of urgency to environmental problems. The relationship between economic growth and the environment has returned to centre stage. Clearly, there exists a major opportunity with industrial and legislative restructuring to put into place the appropriate financial and regulatory mechanisms that would make the internal market environmentally sustainable. The extent to which this happens will be seen over time, but the Single European Act also provides the necessary constitutional basis for a forceful environmental response. Perhaps the strongest part of this is the requirement that policy makers should make environmental considerations a component of all the European Union's other policies.

In 2001 the European Union introduced its Sixth Environmental Action Programme setting out priorities for action, practical objectives and the means to achieve them in the areas of climate change, nature and biodiversity, environment and health and quality of life, and natural resources and waste. The Sixth Environmental Action Programme provides the environmental component of the European Union's strategy for sustainable development until 2010, with the objectives being set out in Exhibit 18.5.

The First Environmental Action Programme, launched in 1973, set out a number of principles which have formed the basis of environmental action in the EU ever since – these remain important when examining the strategic aims of EU environmental policy more broadly. The aims are set out in Exhibit 18.6.

Exhibit 18.5 Objectives of the EU's sixth environmental action programme

- To stabilise the atmospheric concentrations of greenhouse gases at a level that will not cause unnatural variations of the earth's climate.

- To protect and restore the functioning of natural systems and halt the loss of biodiversity in the European Union and globally. To protect soils against erosion and pollution.

- To achieve a quality of the environment where the levels of man-made contaminants, including different types of radiation, do not give rise to significant impacts or risks to human health.

- To ensure that the consumption of renewable and non-renewable resources does not exceed the carrying capacity of the environment. To achieve a decoupling of resource use from economic growth through significantly improved resource efficiency, dematerialisation of the economy, and waste prevention.

Source: European Commission (2001) *Environment 2010: Our Future, Our Choice*, Brussels: European Commission.

Exhibit 18.6 The EU's environmental principles

- Prevention is better than cure.

- Environmental effects should be taken into account at the earliest possible stage in decision making.

- Exploitation of nature and natural resources which causes significant damage to the ecological balance must be avoided. The natural environment can only absorb pollution to a limited extent. Nature is an asset which may be used but not abused.

- Scientific knowledge should be improved to enable action to be taken.

- The 'polluter pays' principle – the polluter should pay for preventing and eliminating environmental nuisance.

- Activities in one member state should not cause environmental deterioration in another.

- Environmental policies of member states must take account of the interests of developing countries.

- The EU and member states should act together in international organisations and in promoting international environmental policy.

- Education of citizens is necessary as the protection of the environment is a matter for everyone.

- The principle of action at the appropriate level – for each type of pollution it is necessary to establish the level of action which is best suited for achieving the protection required, be it local, regional, national, EU-wide or international.

- National environmental policies must be coordinated within the EU without impinging on progress at the national level. It is intended that implementation of the action programme and gathering of environmental information by the proposed European Environment Agency will secure this.

Source: Official Journal of the European Communities: C112, 20 December 1973.

The main activities of the EU in the environmental policy arena, until 1987, were centred on the application of nearly 200 command and control directives in areas as diverse as lead in petrol and aircraft noise. More recently, realising that environmental policy is of little use unless enforced, EU environmental policy has given increased emphasis to the improved enforcement of existing legislation, with this being an important component of the Sixth Environmental Action Programme. Emphasis has also shifted from the use of traditional command-and-control instruments in environmental policy to the application of economic market-based instruments such as the proposed carbon tax and voluntary initiatives such as the eco-labelling and eco-management and audit schemes (see later in this chapter). The aim of such measures is to encourage change in all sectors of industry and society in a more general way than can be achieved through the use of tightly defined legislative instruments. Economic instruments and voluntary measures are seen as complementing rather than substituting for the more traditional application of command-and-control measures.

The EU view of the future of environmental policy and its interface with industrial development is clear. With over 400 million inhabitants the European Union is the largest trading bloc in the world and so is in a critical position to take the lead in moving towards sustainability. The Commission accepts that tighter environmental policy will have an impact on the costs of industry. However, a high level of environmental protection has increasingly become not only a policy objective of its own but also a precondition of industrial expansion. In this respect a new impetus towards a better integration of policies aiming at consolidating industrial competitiveness and at achieving a high level of protection of the environment is necessary in order to make the two objectives fully mutually supportive.

These views are given more substance within the Sixth Environmental Action Programme, and a number of specific measures relating to industry are included. Perhaps most importantly, the commitment of the EU to strengthen environmental policy is underlined. The EU shares the view that urgent action is needed for environmental protection and that many of the great environmental struggles will be won or lost in the next ten years. Further, it states that achieving sustainability will demand practical and political commitment over an extended period and that the EU, as the largest trading bloc in the world, must exercise its responsibility and commit itself to that goal.

For industries and companies that are facing a rising tide of environmental legislation, it is essential that attempts are made to find out about and then positively address the legislative pressures which they are under. However, the Sixth Environmental Action Programme primarily focuses on the improved enforcement of existing legislation as a key objective rather than the adoption of new legislation. To some extent this should allow industry to take stock of the rapid increase in environmental legislation that has taken place in recent years and to focus on achieving compliance with existing legislation. Despite the stated objective to concentrate on the effective implementation of existing policy, there are many pieces of environmental legislation in the EU policy pipeline which are awaiting final adoption. Many of these measures have fundamental implications for business and it therefore remains essential to track forthcoming legislation.

Furthermore, the Sixth Environmental Action Programme reiterates the aspiration that environmental policy should be fully incorporated into all other European Union policies (sometimes known as 'mainstreaming'). Therefore, while it may become easier to track the development of policies which are explicitly environmental, it will become more difficult to monitor the development of environmental policy throughout the activities of the Commission as a whole. The European Environment Agency now collects data and monitors compliance throughout the European Union and disseminates information to all interested parties. It is being proactive in encouraging all firms (including smaller enterprises) to take environmental issues more seriously.

The strategic significance of the EU's views cannot be overstated. By taking a long-term, EU-wide perspective and accepting that industrial competitiveness is enhanced by tight environmental legislation, the policy framework within which all European organisations must participate will reflect these views. Some organisations, some regions and some nations will benefit. If the views of the EU are correct then the economic prospects of the European Union as a whole will benefit and the environment will certainly benefit. However, realising these benefits will not be automatic at the organisation level and strategic planning and proactive responses to the changing policy climate are imperative if success is to be secured. Information must be gathered, its implications assessed and the necessary action taken in a systematic and integrated way.

Tackling environmental problems always requires a concerted and cooperative effort. In the EU success will depend on the extent to which member states are politically committed to the environmental philosophy and the extent to which they are willing to cooperate. The balancing of the economic growth/environment trade-off is likely to determine the Europe-wide success of any policies but there also need to be concerted and cooperative political motivations. It can be argued that the attainment of an effective and concerted environmental policy in Europe will require political and economic union. However, since the EU and national governments legislate over environmental protection and police offenders, significant environmental improvement will only be attained with the cooperation and commitment of producers. There is, therefore, a need for firms to institute environmental management practices.

Cases

Case study   Nokia   www.nokia.com

Nokia is the world's leading manufacturer of mobile phones. With an almost 40 per cent share of the market, it sold twice as many handsets in 2009 as second-placed Motorola and many times the number of other rivals such as Samsung and Ericsson. A Finnish company, founded in 1895 as a paper manufacturer, Nokia grew into a conglomerate with interests including electronics, cable manufacture, rubber, chemicals, electricity generation and, by the 1960s, telephone equipment. In the early 1990s senior managers decided to focus on the new mobile phone industry.

Two factors favoured this move. First, the Finnish government had taken a lead in telecoms deregulation and Nokia was already competing vigorously with other manufacturers supplying equipment to the national phone company. Second, the European Union (EU) adopted a single standard – the Global System for Mobile Telephony (GSM) – for Europe's second generation (digital) phones. Two-thirds of the world's mobile phone subscribers use this standard. Finland's links with its Nordic neighbours also helped, as people in these sparsely populated countries adopted mobile phones enthusiastically.

Nokia has strong design skills, but above all managers were quick to recognise that mobile phones are not a commodity but a fashion accessory. By offering smart designs, different ring tones and coloured covers Nokia became the 'cool' mobile brand for fashion-conscious people. Nokia has also mastered the logistics of getting millions of phones to customers around the world.

While many competitors subcontract the manufacture of handsets, Nokia assembles most of its own, with factories in many countries across the world. Managers believe this gives them a better understanding of the market and the manufacturing process. Nokia buys about 80 billion components a year, and has close relationships with its most important suppliers.

While all of these factors helped Nokia, managers believe there was a further reason. Although competitors such as Motorola and Ericsson already had advantages of scale, experience and distribution networks, the arrival of the new digital technology

Courtesy of Nokia

changed the rules of the game, forcing all players to start from scratch. Managers acknowledge that some external factors helped Nokia, but comment that 'good luck favours the prepared mind'.

The company's leading position in the industry owes much to Jorma Ollila, who became chief executive in 1992. He helped to shape the mobile phone industry by pursuing his vision of a mass market for voice communication while on the move. As he prepared to hand over to a new chief executive (Olli-Pekka Kallasvuo) in 2006, he observed that the next challenge would be to enable users to access the internet, videos, music, games and emails through a new generation of 'smart' phones and hand-held devices.

Source: Based on *The Economist*, 16 June 2001; *Financial Times*, 29 June 2001 and 10 October 2005.

Case questions 3.1

- How has the environment favoured the development of Nokia?
- How could the same factors turn to the disadvantage of the company?
- Visit Nokia's website and read its most recent trading statement (under investor relations). What have been the main developments in the last year?

In March 2010 Nokia estimated that it had maintained its market share at 34 per cent of total device sales of 1.14 billion units. It is continuing to add value to its devices, by integrating them with innovative services providing music, maps, apps and email. It also believes that its wide range of handsets means it will be able to meet demand if customers begin to prefer cheaper handsets. It also saw growth opportunities in areas of the world, such as the US and Korea, where it had little or no market share, and in smartphones where the company's products had been weak.

The company had also been reducing its reliance on selling handsets, by diversifying into new growth areas. In 2006 it reached a deal with Siemens to merge their network businesses, creating the world's third largest network equipment supplier. In 2008 it concluded that success depended not just on good quality handsets, but also on the quality of the services and applications. It therefore grouped all handset products into a Device Unit, while applications and services became part of a new Mobile Services and Software unit. Both were supported by a Marketing unit which provided sales, marketing and operational support.

One factor in the company's sustained success appears to have been a culture which encourages co-operation within teams, and across internal and external boundaries. Jorma Ollila, CEO until 2006, believed that Nokia's innovative capacity springs from multi-functional teams working together to bring new insights to products and services. Staff in the four divisions work in teams which may remain constant for many years – but sometimes combine with other teams to work on a common task.

Informal mentoring begins as soon as someone steps into a new job. Within a few days, the employee's manager lists the people in the organisation whom it would be useful for the employee to meet. He/she also reviews what topics the newcomer should discuss with the suggested contact, and why establishing a relationship with each one is important. The gift of time – in the form of hours spent on coaching and building networks – is a crucial part of the collaborative culture.

Nokia also encourages a culture of communication by creating small groups from around the company to work on a strategic issue for four months. This helps them to build ties with many parts of the company – some of which continue during later work. The induction process for new employees also encourages team-building and co-operation: the newcomer's manager must introduce him/her to at least 15 people within and outside the team.

Sources: Grattan and Erickson (2007); Doz and Kosonen (2008); company website.

Case questions 3.2

- Which of the cultural types identified by Quinn *et al.* (2003) would you expect to find within Nokia's handset business?

- How will the practices to encourage communication help a culture to develop? (Refer to Figure 3.2.)

While Nokia, like all mobile phone companies, regularly introduces more technically sophisticated devices, these account for a small proportion of the units which the industry sells each year. However, the 'smartphone' segment of the market is growing rapidly, with almost 55 million units sold in the first quarter of 2010 – a 57 per cent increase on the same quarter of 2009. Observers expected that, as prices for phones and services continue to drop, demand for more basic devices will continue to grow rapidly in the large markets of China, India, Brazil and Russia.

Nokia has been particularly successful in meeting this demand, making great efforts to secure first-time buyers and then build lifelong loyalty to the brand. Moreover, status-conscious buyers in the third world disdain unknown brands:

Brazilians want brand names and are willing to pay a bit more for Nokia or Motorola (Quoted in *Business Week,* 7 November 2005, p. 21)

More than any other handset maker, the Finnish company has connected with consumers in China and India. Greater China (the mainland, Hong Kong and Taiwan) is the company's biggest market: in 2005 it supplied 31 per cent of all sets sold there, well ahead of the 10 per cent from second-place Motorola. It has about 60 per cent of the market in India, which it expects will be the company's biggest market by 2010. It owes its strong position in both countries in part to a decentralised organisation which can spot local sales trend very quickly, together with an ability to produce sets tailored to local tastes and languages.

It also competes at the top end of the market: in October 2008 it launched a new service – Comes With Music (CWM) as a rival to Apple's iPhone. The CWM devices consist of a mobile handset which also includes a year's free unlimited subscription to Nokia's music catalogue. The company pays music publishers and artists a share of handset sales, depending on the amount of music downloaded.

Chief executive Olli-Pekka Kallasvuo set a target of 300 million users of its mobile services by the end of 2011. This is part of the company's wider strategy to offer mobile services, investing large sums in buying companies to support that – such as Navteq, a digital maps company. Such a move would help it gain higher margins from the sales of these more expensive handsets.

Sources: *Business Week*, 27 March 2006; *Financial Times*, 17 July 2009; International Data Corporation, 7 May 2010.

Case questions 3.3

Gather some information about current developments in the mobile phone industry. Also collect information on Nokia.

- Use Porter's five forces model to outline the competitive environment of the industry.
- Which of these factors may have contributed to Nokia's success?
- Which PESTEL factors are most affecting the development of the industry?

The manufacture of components for mobile phones is being moved rapidly out of the Nordic country to low-cost locations. Early in 2006 three of its subcontractors announced that they were cutting more than 1,100 jobs in Finland, underlining the dramatic shift in the global telecoms business, in which a rapidly growing share of revenue comes from cost-conscious emerging markets.

This is leading the Finns to reassess their high dependence on the industry. An economist at the Bank of Finland slated:

> Nokia's profits, and the tax revenues they have generated for Finland, have exceeded our wildest dreams in the past ten years. But it is disappointing that the production has not provided the highly-paid, large-scale source of employment we hoped for.

The company is also collaborating on long-term technical projects with Intel, whose microprocessors run about 80 per sent of the world's computers. They plan to create a type of mobile computing device beyond today's smartphones and netbooks. Kai Oistamo, Nokia's vice-president in charge of devices said:

> The mobile and computing industries are coming together, and we as leaders in our respective industries, are taking the responsibility to really be the enablers to create this brave new world.

Source: *Financial Times*, 13 March 2006 and 24 June 2009.

Case questions 3.5

- Who are the main stakeholders in Nokia?
- What are their interests in the success of the company?
- How can management ensure it maintains the support of the most important stakeholders?

MANAGEMENT IN THE NEWS

Watch out for an epidemic of petty fraud

FT

Luke Johnson

The economist J. K. Galbraith asserted that fraud rose in a bull market and shrank in a slump. The discovery of Bernard Madoff's Ponzi scheme suggests Galbraith may be right about large-scale embezzlement, but my experience is the opposite when it comes to petty larceny. I suspect industry is enduring an epidemic of crime right now, as integrity becomes a casualty of the recession.

At one of our restaurant companies, we have suffered a disturbing rise in insurance claims. This is not because we are careless: we take health and safety seriously. Several of these actions relate to apparent falls by suppliers' workers, for example. The curious thing is that in more than one case the victim appears to have waited more than 15 months before notifying us of the injury. After talking to other operators, it seems the hospitality trade is suffering a plague of legal letters from claimants looking for free money. No doubt some are genuine; but others are trying it on, I am sure, because they are feeling the pinch, and think negligence claims are easy money.

Last year, the Association of British Insurers reported a 17 per cent rise in fraudulent insurance claims. I fear the increase this year will be even greater. Unfortunately, insurers often settle small claims even if they are doubtful, simply to save legal fees and administrative bother. But this policy of expediency only encourages others to try the same con. Similarly, at another retail business we have had trouble with several thefts of large sums of cash from branches this year, all carried out by insiders.

It is very depressing to have to deal with employee dishonesty. One feels a despairing sense of betrayal, especially if senior staff are involved, and too often all that happens to the perpetrators is that they lose their job. As with all such lawless behaviour, these incidents can destroy trust in the workplace, and lead to unhealthy suspicion between owners and staff. The answer is to have excellent systems and thorough checks and balances. But no method of prevention is perfect, and crooks are ingenious at inventing ways round what appears to be foolproof security.

In Britain at least, fiddling expenses will never be seen in the same forgiving light after the recent month of political exposés in Westminster. In the wake of the parliamentary scandal, now is the perfect time for organisations to review their staff expense account

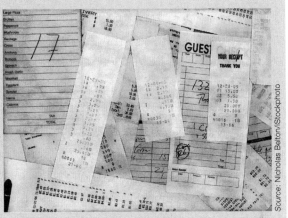

Does fraud rise in a bull market and shrink in a slump – or has integrity become a casualty of the recession?

Source: Nicholas Belton/iStockphoto

procedures and stop all abuse in its tracks. Those who cheat on their expenses will find it harder to rationalise their corruption.

I suppose the motivation behind the spike in fraud is obvious. Normally trustworthy people are desperate because they have been living beyond their means, and their income has fallen with the economy. The heightened threat of wrongdoing means business as normal is harder than ever. Vigilance and a proportionate response are required of leaders. Perhaps the most important thing is to avoid slipping into a sense of paranoia, and hope that the vast majority of people are honest, whatever the conditions.

Source: Johnson, L. 'Watch Out for an Epidemic of Petty Fraud', *Financial Times*, 2 June 2009.

Discussion questions

1 Using the checklist for a PESTEL analysis in Figure 3.7 explain the influences which the author believes to be affecting the behaviour of customers and employees.

2 How can managers guard against fraud committed by both customers and staff?

3 What impact do you think both the fraud, and the preventive measures you suggest, are likely to have on levels of organisational conflict and work related stress? Explain your views.

Review Questions and Tests

Review questions

1   Describe an educational or commercial organisation that you know in terms of the competing values model of cultures.

2   What is the significance of the idea of 'fragmented cultures' for those who wish to change a culture to support performance?

3   Identify the relative influence of Porter's five forces on an organisation of your choice and compare your results with a colleague's. What can you learn from that comparison?

4   How should managers decide which of the many factors easily identified in a PESTEL analysis they should attend to? If they have to be selective, what is the value of the PESTEL method?

5   Since people interpret the nature of environmental forces from unique perspectives, what meaning can people attach to statements about external pressures?

6   Illustrate the stakeholder idea with an example of your own, showing their expectations of an organisation.

7   Explain at least two of the mechanisms which Mallin (2007) recommends should be part of a corporate governance system.

8   Summarise an idea from the chapter that adds to your understanding of the integrating themes.

Chapter 7:

Marketing Management

9.1   Introduction

Manchester United (MU) depends on good marketing to ensure the continued loyalty and support of its customers – who all seek different things. An MU football fan might buy a season ticket to fulfil a psychological need to be part of a group with a common purpose: someone with no interest in football might use an MU mobile phone because he/she trusts the product, based on the MU reputation. Someone who buys a replica MU jersey is making a statement about his/her personality, and is not sensitive to price: he/she pays up to £40 for something that costs less than £2 to supply.

How should MU management manage the brand in these often unrelated markets? How best to understand the needs of different customers, so as to offer them profitable goods and services? How to manage relationships with customers to encourage long-term loyalty – even if the club does badly on the field? What can it do in the way it presents its goods and services to make as much revenue from them as it can?

All organisations face the challenge of understanding what customers want, and ensuring that they can meet those expectations. Managers of successful firms often attribute their success to placing marketing at the heart of their strategy. Ikea, the Swedish furniture retailer,

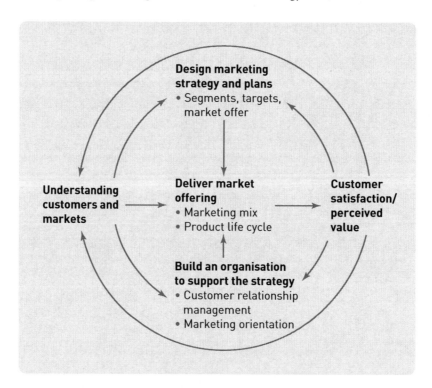

Figure 9.1
The marketing management process

has found and refined a formula that appeals to its target market, growing in 40 years from a single store to a business with over 300 stores in 38 countries. Virgin has also grown from a single store to become a global brand – by offering a wide range of products and services. Successful not-for-profit organisations such as the Eden Project demonstrate the benefits of understanding and communicating with a market. All need to give value for money, by understanding and meeting supporters' needs.

This chapter clarifies 'marketing' and shows how it can add value to resources. It explains how marketers try to understand customers' needs, in order to decide which segments of a market to target. Doing so effectively depends on developing close customer relations, building a marketing orientation and using specific marketing capabilities – known as the 'marketing mix'. Figure 9.1 gives an overview of the tasks of managing marketing.

9.2 What is marketing?

We are all familiar with the techniques of advertising and selling, when companies:

- distribute brochures;
- offer promotional prices;
- sponsor television programmes;
- persuade celebrities to endorse their products or services; or
- send advertisements to mobiles.

These selling techniques are only the most visible part of a wider **marketing** process, through which organisations aim to identify and satisfy customer needs in a way that brings value to both parties. This depends on skills in researching customers, designing products, setting prices, communicating with potential customers, ensuring delivery and evaluating customer reaction. These diverse activities bring marketing staff into contact with most parts of their organisation.

> **Marketing** is the process by which organisations create value for customers in order to receive value from them in return.

The underlying idea is that if managers understand what current and potential **customers** value, they find it easier to develop products that ensure **customer satisfaction**. In commercial businesses this means that customers are willing to pay a price that earns the company a profit. In public or not-for-profit organisations it means they are willing to make donations, use the service or otherwise support it. Managers can then secure the resources they need to maintain and grow the enterprise. Those who neglect marketing will not understand their customers, will not satisfy them and will have trouble securing resources. Organisations fail when staff do what they prefer, not what customers or service-users expect. Kotler *et al.* (2008) describe marketing as:

> **Customers** are individuals, households, organisations, institutions, resellers and governments that purchase products from other organisations.

> **Customer satisfaction** is the extent a customer perceives that a product matches their expectations.

> the homework which managers undertake to assess needs, measure their extent and intensity and determine whether a profitable opportunity exits. Marketing continues throughout the product's life, trying to find new customers and keep current customers by improving product appeal and performance, learning from product sales results and managing repeat performance. (pp. 6–7)

Peter Drucker (1999) places the activity even more firmly at the centre of business:

> Because the purpose of business is to create and keep customers, it has only two central functions – marketing and innovation. The basic function of marketing is to attract and retain customers at a profit.

While many organisations have a designated 'Marketing Department', people throughout the enterprise can contribute by, for example, telling marketing staff what customers think of the product, or what competitors are doing. The more that employees understand what customers want, and the more the organisation's systems and processes help staff to meet those expectations, the more they will satisfy them. As David Packard, co-founder of Hewlett-Packard, said:

> Marketing is too important to be left to the marketing department, i.e. the entire organis-ation should be marketing the company, from the company receptionist as 'Director of First Impressions' to the chief executive as 'Director of Shareholder Interests'.

Key ideas   **Consumer marketing and organisational (B2B) marketing**

There are two categories of marketing: (a) consumer marketing, which concerns creating and delivering prod-ucts to satisfy consumers; and (b) industrial or business-to-business (B2B) marketing, which aims to satisfy the needs of other businesses and organisations, including national and local government. Companies such as Rio Tinto Zinc (mining), Maersk (freight shipping) or PricewaterhouseCoopers (consultancy services) are solely engaged in B2B marketing. The underlying concepts are similar, but the buying behaviour of pro-fessional purchasing staff is quite different from the individual consumer – and so requires a different market-ing approach.

This chapter is mainly concerned with consumer marketing.

Managers in all types of organisations can use marketing to increase the value they offer. Local authority services such as libraries, museums or concert halls routinely survey samples of actual and potential users to evaluate their satisfaction with existing services. They also assess likely demand for new ones, before they incur the expense of providing them.

Management in practice   **Marketing in the voluntary sector**

Many staff and volunteers in charities are uncomfortable with the idea that they are in marketing – preferring to see themselves as helpers or carers. Yet

> – donors, local authorities, opinion formers, the media, all have the choice of whether or not to support a charity . . . They make up the markets within which the charity operates. Without knowledge and understanding of those markets, the charity . . . will fail . . . By knowing themselves and their mission, and by knowing the markets they . . . serve or work in, charities can match their activities to external needs and make sure that they achieve as much as possible for their beneficiaries. (Keaveney and Kaufmann, 2001, p. 2)

Source: Keaveney and Kaufmann (2001).

9.3   Understanding customers and markets

Marketing begins with trying to understand customers and what influence them.

Needs, wants and demands

Needs are states of felt deprivation, reflecting biological and social influences.

Psychologists have developed theories of human **needs** – states of felt deprivation – that people try to satisfy. Chapter 15 presents several such theories (Maslow, 1970; McClelland, 1961) which identify needs ranging from basic necessities to those that are intangible: knowl-edge, achievement or public image. They also show that their strength varies between people – some are content to satisfy basic needs, while some find that once they have satisfied their

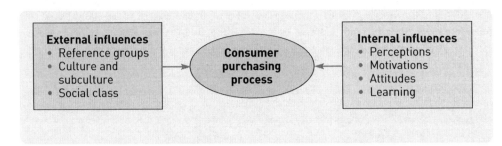

Figure 9.2
Influences on buyer behaviour

basic needs they seek opportunities to satisfy other needs – such as physical or intellectual challenge.

Wants are the form which human needs take, as they are shaped by someone's personality and the culture in which they live (Hofstede and Hofstede, 2005). Everyone needs food, but satisfy that need in many ways – which they express by describing objects or experiences that will satisfy their need.

People have limited resources, so needs and wants only become relevant to a supplier when the person can pay – when a want becomes a **demand**. Given their needs, wants and resources, people demand products and services they believe will satisfy them. The more effort an enterprise makes to understand these, the better it will satisfy them. This involves investing in research and development to create an attractive market offering.

Internal and external factors influence consumers' willingness to pay the expected price for a product – which Figure 9.2 illustrates and Table 9.1 summarises. Social factors clearly

Wants are the form which human needs take as they are shaped by local culture and individual personality.

Demands are human wants backed by the ability to buy.

Table 9.1 Influences on buying behaviour

Influence	Description	How marketers use this influence
Internal influences **Perception**	How people collect and interpret information	Design promotional material so that the images, colours and words attract the attention of intended consumers
Motivation	Internal forces that shape purchasing decisions to satisfy need	Design products to meet needs. Insurers remind people of dangers against which a policy will protect
Attitudes	Opinions and points of view that people have of other people and institutions	Design products to conform. Increasing stress on environmental benefits of products and services
Learning	How people learn affects what they know about a product, and hence their purchasing decisions	Associate product with unique colours or images (Coca-Cola with red and white)
External influences **Reference groups**	Other people with whom the consumer identifies	Marketers establish the reference groups of their consumers, and allude to them in promotions, e.g. sponsoring athletes in return for product endorsement
Culture	The culture to which a consumer belongs affects their values and behaviour	Subcultures associated with music or cars influence buying behaviour – which marketers use in positioning products for those markets
Social class	People identify with a class based on income, education or locality.	Purchase decisions reaffirm class affinities or aspirations. Marketers design promotional material to suit

shape demand for mobile phones – teenagers display them as a sign of social standing, so the appearance and functions of the device become status symbols – which marketers try to satisfy. To track how factors in the table affect attitudes to their products, marketers use marketing information systems.

Activity 9.2   What influenced you to buy?

Identify a significant purchase you have made: either a physical product or a service.

- Which, if any, of the factors in Table 9.1 affected your decision? Write down what you find.
- Can you identify any factors which influenced your decision that are not in the list?
- Compare your lists with other students, and try to identify which factors appear most frequently as influences on your purchases. Do they vary between goods and services?

Marketing information systems

A marketing information system is the systematic process for the collection, analysis and distribution of marketing information.

Marketing managers need a **marketing information system** – clear processes to collect and analyse information about the marketing environment – and to distribute it through the organisation. Figure 9.3 details the typical components. A marketing information system contains internal and external sources of data, and mechanisms to analyse and interpret the data so that marketing staff can use the information. It includes information about customers and the market as a whole, for example its size, rate of growth and the main competitors.

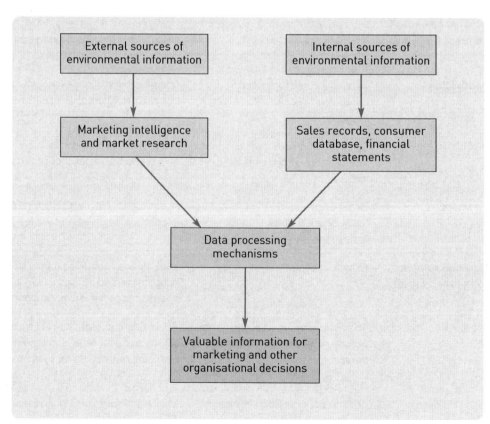

Figure 9.3
A marketing information system

Table 9.2 Sources of marketing information

Source	Description and examples
Internal records	Records of sales, costs, customer transactions, demographics, buyer behaviour, customer satisfaction, quality trends, reports from the sales force
Marketing intelligence	Data on micro- and macro-environments. For example, who are the main competitors, potential new entrants and substitute products? What economic and social changes are likely to affect demand; what political or legislative changes that may affect the market? Data is usually based on secondary sources – websites, newspapers, trade associations and industry reports. Informal sources – staff or customers – are valuable guides to competitors or market trends
Market research	Involves five stages: 1 Defining the problem and research objectives (how many people with X income, living in place Y are aware of product Z?) 2 Developing hypotheses (is awareness higher or lower in area B where the product has been advertised than in C?) 3 Developing the research plan to collect data to refute or confirm hypotheses 4 Implementing the research plan – collecting and analysing the data 5 Interpreting and reporting the findings

Management in practice   **Market information from the Tesco Clubcard**
www.tesco.com

The Tesco Clubcard scheme (Part 6 Case) has over 11 million active holders. Shoppers join the scheme by completing a simple form with some personal information about their age and where they live. Their purchases earn vouchers based on the amount they spend. Every purchase they make at Tesco is electronically recorded, and the data analysed to identify their shopping preferences. This is then used to design a package of special offers which are most likely to appeal to that customer, based on an analysis of what they have bought. These offers are mailed to customers with their quarterly vouchers, and each mailing brings a large increase in business.

The company also analyses the data to identify the kind of people the Clubcard holders are – whether they have a new baby, young children, whether they like cooking, and so on. Each product is also ascribed a set of attributes – expensive or cheap? An ethnic recipe or a traditional dish? Tesco own-label or an upmarket brand? The information on customers, shopping habits and product attributes is used to support all aspects of the business – identifying possible gaps in the product range, assessing the effect of promotional offers, noting variations in taste in different parts of the country.

Source: Part 6 case.

Figure 9.4 shows the steps in completing a market research project.

As well as gathering data about a specific product or service, marketers also gather **marketing intelligence** about competitors and other developments in the wider marketing environment.

Marketing intelligence is information about developments in the marketing environment.

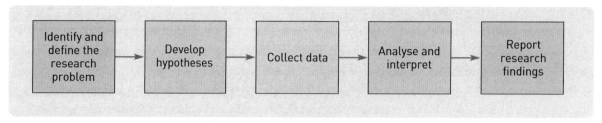

Figure 9.4 Market research process

Identifying trends in the marketing environment

The **marketing environment** consists of the actors and forces outside marketing that affect the marketing manager's ability to develop and maintain successful relationships with its target consumers.

In order to take these decisions, managers need information about consumer demands, competitor strategies and changes in the **marketing environment** that are likely to impact upon consumer demands. This part of the organisation's environment presented in Chapter 3, Figure 3.1, partially repeated as Figure 9.5, shows the micro- and macro-environments. The competitive (micro-) environment is that part of an organisation's marketing environment within which it operates. Each organisation has a unique micro-environment, including suppliers, distributors, customers and competitors. All organisations have some influence over their competitive environment and the likely impact this will have upon their marketing activities. Marketers have been quick to see that young people are big users of mobiles, which offer a possible way of advertising to young consumers who are hard to reach by traditional means such as TV or direct mail.

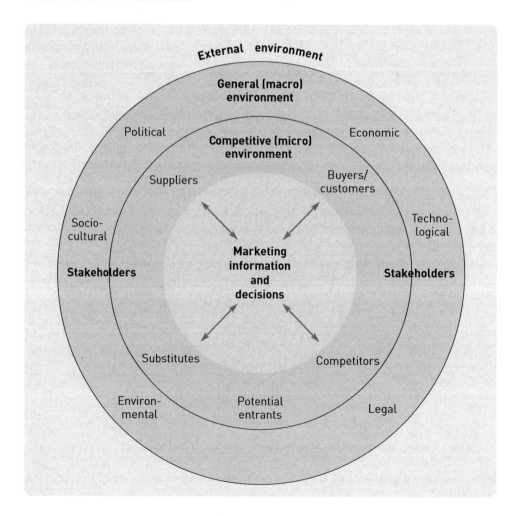

Figure 9.5
The marketing environment

The general, or macro component of an organisation's marketing environment is more remote and will be similar for all those in the same industry. Organisations have little direct influence over their macro-environment, which consists of the PESTEL factors shown in Figure 9.5

Activity 9.3   Identifying the marketing environment

- Use Figure 9.5 to identify, for each of these organisations, those parts of their micro- and macro-environments that have most impact upon their marketing activities: Ryanair, the BBC, Innocent Drinks.
- How have they responded to these environmental influences?

Such frameworks can help managers identify opportunities and threats for the organisation from external changes – for an example of a company that missed a trend, see the Management Practice featuring Motorola in Chapter 8 (page 236).

Case study   Manchester United – the case continues – what makes people buy?

A football game is not a tangible product. A regular and significant intangible purchase by a Manchester United football fan is the £27–£49 ticket to see a home game at Old Trafford or £10 on a pay-per-view TV basis. There is no guarantee of satisfaction and no exchange or refund. No promotional advertising is needed and the ticket demand is relatively 'inelastic', i.e. prices can increase without sales volumes necessarily falling.

An important question for a marketing manager is 'how does a fan reach the decision to buy this experience and how is value measured?'. The buyer behaviour framework described above can help: domestic UK fans are typically lifelong, acquiring perceptions of and loyalty to the Club at school or in the home. Influencers would include peers and older pupils. Although football was formerly male-dominated, young females are an increasing part of the market. Most fans travel in groups of two or more, so this is a segment attribute that can be managed in raising awareness and favourability. Publicity photos can depict fans celebrating or commiserating together and the whole emphasis of attending a football match can be positioned away from 'did we win?' to 'did we have a good time?'. This approach is one of MU's declared marketing strategies.

Case questions 9.2

- What customer demands were MU seeking to satisfy at the time of the case study?
- What other demands does the business have to satisfy?
- What marketing tools are mentioned in the case?

Table 9.1 shows the factors that influence individual purchasing decisions: to the extent that several individuals share these influences, marketers identify distinct segments within a population, rather than seeing a market as homogenous.

9.4   Segments, targets and the market offer

Organisations use **market segmentation** to satisfy the needs of different people within a market. Airlines offer first, business, economy or budget flights: while the basic service attribute (transport from A to B) is the same for all, the total offering is not: those in

> **Market segmentation** is the process of dividing markets comprising the heterogeneous needs of many consumers into segments comprising the homogeneous needs of smaller groups.

first will receive superior service at all stages of their journey. Universities offer degrees by full-time, part-time and distance learning study. Athletic shoe companies offer shoes specifically for running, aerobics, tennis and squash, as well as 'cross' trainers for the needs of all these sports.

Customers are more likely to respond positively to offerings that appeal to the needs of their particular segment of the market, from product design through to promotion and advertising. The personal computer market consists of all those who need a PC, but contains distinct segments of people with similar needs: travellers needing a laptop; parents wanting a cheap machine for their children; or corporate customers requiring a large number of standard machines.

Key ideas **Young consumers keep spending**

Advertising agency JWT asked 18- to 29-year-olds in several countries which items they would never cut back on, no matter how bad their finances. Brits ranked 'buying new clothes' as fourth on the list – higher than any other country in the poll. Above that, they prioritised the internet, mobile phones and satellite television. While young people in the US also said they could not do without home entertainment, they ranked alcohol consumption as the fifth most cherished area of spending. Brits put boozing at only 16 on their list. Half of the Brazilians said paying for college was their most important outgoing.

A separate survey conducted by a retailer in May 2009 found that 70 per cent of customers between 18 and 35 said they were spending the same amount or more on clothes and eating out, despite the recession:

Slaves to fashion and free of financial commitments, young people have kept spending during the economic downturn, while others have cut back. As a result, retailers geared towards the youth market – particularly clothing chains – have been basking in their good fortune. (p. 14)

Source: *Financial Times*, 9 July 2009.

Segmenting depends on identifying variables that distinguish consumers with similar needs:

- **Demography** The easiest way to segment a consumer market is by using demographic variables such as age, gender and education level. Magazine companies use gender and age to ensure that within their portfolio they have titles suitable for females, males and those of different ages. Local authorities use information on age and family structures to help decide the distribution of facilities in their area.
- **Geography** This segment markets by country or region, enabling multinational companies to 'think global but act local'. While maintaining uniform global standards of service and a common promotional theme, they vary the product to suit local tastes.
- **Socioeconomic** This segments markets by variables such as income, social class and lifestyle. Lifestyle segmentation means identifying groups of consumers that share similar values about the ways in which they wish to live.

When segmenting consumer markets, marketers typically use a mix of these variables to provide an accurate profile of distinct groups. *Marie Claire* uses age, gender, education, lifestyle and social class to attract a readership of educated, independently minded women between the ages of 25 and 35, in income brackets ABC1. Pubs aim for particular segments: sophisticated city centre, food-led, urban community, country – each aiming to meet the needs of different people.

Having segmented a market using these variables, marketers have to decide which to select as their **target market**, usually based on the criteria that it:

- contains demands they can satisfy;
- is large enough to provide a financial return;
- is likely to grow.

> A **target market** is the segment of the market selected by the organisation as the focus of its activities.

The market offer – products, services and experiences

Information about customers' wants and demands helps companies to develop a **market offering**: a combination of products, services and experiences that they hope will satisfy their customers. While the features of a physical product are part of the value for the customer, service and experience also affect this: how staff treat the customer, their ability to answer questions and the quality of after-sales service. The experience of using the product also matters – both the thing itself (good to use?), and how others react (does it boost your image?). Effective marketers look beyond the basic attributes of their products, aiming to create brands that mean something significant for their customers. They are then willing to pay a higher price.

> A **market offering** is the combination of products, services, information or experiences that an enterprise offers to a market to satisfy a need or want.

9.5   Customer relationship management

People aim to satisfy needs and wants through **exchange** – the act of obtaining a desired object from someone by offering something in return – a process that is at the core of many human activities, including marketing. It only happens if both parties can offer something of value to the other, and if they can communicate this. If both agree, this leads to a **transaction** in which they exchange things of value at a specified time and place. Countless transactions take place without further contact between buyer and seller – such as buying a newspaper or petrol during a journey. Some marketers are content if they achieve a satisfactory number of transactions, if this achieves their financial or other targets.

Others choose to focus on what is called **customer relationship management (CRM)** – they aim to develop long-term profitable relationships with customers in the hope that this will add more value to both parties. By increasing customer satisfaction they hope to build their loyalty to the product or service, so that they continue to make purchases over many years. This of course depends on understanding what features of the service will not only attract current purchases, but also encourage return visits, which are quite different things.

> **Exchange** is the act of obtaining a desired object from someone by offering something in return.

> A **transaction** occurs when two parties exchange things of value to each at a specified time and place.

> **Customer relationship management (CRM)** is a process of creating and maintaining long-term relationships with customers.

A narrow interpretation of CRM is to gather data on individual customers, and use that to build customer loyalty. Many hotels, airlines and retailers use loyalty schemes whereby every purchase earns points, which customers exchange for other benefits (see Smith and Sparks (2009) for a study of how these work, and of the different ways in which consumers redeem their points).

Others use CRM technologies that enable sales staff to build relationships with customers as they complete transactions. These are typically portable devices which sales staff use to share market information with colleagues, manage their customer contacts, create sales presentations, prepare quotations during a sales call and submit call reports.

Management in practice · How banks assess customers

Banks are becoming more skilful in identifying people to whom it may be unwise to lend money. According to the British Bankers' Association (BBA), banks now collect four kinds of data to assess client risk: 'negative' data, such as court fines and convictions; 'positive' data on commitments; income data; and reports on spending. The banks acquire this data from three sources – the electoral roll; their own systems which link to payment organisations such as Visa; and credit-checking agencies. A spokesman for the BBAs said:

> People are creatures of habit. You put your salary into your account once a month and may go to the supermarket weekly. From that analysis, you see the ability of someone to repay. Banks all look at the same data.

Source: *Financial Times*, 3 October 2007.

CRM also has a broader meaning that includes all aspects of building and maintaining close relations with customers by understanding their needs, and delivering superior value to them. Simple techniques are listed below – the following Key Ideas feature illustrates a more substantial approach, with greater implications for the organisational changes needed to support it:

- involving customers in product review and development;
- sponsoring consumer clubs and especially online communities;
- inviting customers to corporate sporting or cultural events;
- inviting online comments;
- sending promotional offers to a customers' mobiles.

More significant approaches to CRM involve a substantial commitment to organisational change (see Key Ideas).

Key ideas · Elements of CRM

After reviewing of the spread of customer relationship management, Plakoyiannaki *et al.* (2008) say that in essence its aim is to add value by creating and maintaining relationships with customers. While the approach promises many benefits, it depends on the critical role of employees in delivering enhanced value, and so on policies which encourage that contribution. They find that CRM consists of four sub-processes:

- **Strategic planning sub-system** – provides the direction for CRM, and cultivates a strategic orientation around the organisation that sees CRM as a priority.
- **Information sub-system** – to acquire, disseminate and use information from customer contacts to understand their preferences and to improve the dialogue with customers across the organisation.

- **Value creation sub-system** – design and delivery of products and services that enhance value to the customer, thus ensuring they experience positive benefits throughout the interaction.
- **Performance measurement sub-system** – monitoring, evaluating and continuously improving the whole CRM experience, to ensure it has met the goals.

Their study of a CRM programme in an automotive repair company showed that the benefits depended heavily on managing employees in ways that encouraged them to develop an appropriate attitude to customers. It also depended on ensuring that the four sub-systems were in place and working satisfactorily.

Source: Plakoyiannaki *et al.* (2008).

The intention behind these diverse activities is to build the sponsoring company's knowledge of the customer's current and emerging needs, so that they can try to meet those needs profitably. As always, managers continually seek for evidence about the effectiveness of such expenditure, and what aspects are most effective in building close relationships (see the following Key Ideas).

Key ideas   What makes an online community effective?

Porter and Donthu (2008) noted that while many companies have launched virtual communities for their customers, many received little benefit. They therefore conducted a study to help managers understand how sponsoring virtual communities could add more value. Trust is essential for successful online marketing, so their central premise was that a community's value to the sponsoring firm depends on the sponsor's ability to cultivate trust with the community's members. They predicted that three factors would most affect a community's trust in a site:

- providing quality content (e.g. relevant content, frequently updated);
- fostering member embeddedness (e.g. seek opinions about community policies);
- fostering member interaction (e.g. encourage members to share information);

    and that trust in turn would increase members' willingness to:

- share personal information;
- co-operate in new product development; and
- express loyalty intentions.

Their empirical study (based on 663 responses from users of online communities) concluded that fostering member embeddedness in the community had more effect on trust than the other two factors. It also led the authors to stress the importance of using technology to build relationships with customers, rather than only to generate transactions – especially as many customers use the internet for activities other than shopping.

Source: Porter and Donthu (2008).

While there are evidently potential benefits from developing long-term relationships with customers, this is not the case in all markets. Zolkiewski (2004) shows that relationship marketing is not suitable for all organisations, and that not all relationships are beneficial or necessary.

Case questions 9.3

- Use the frameworks in this section to identify segments in the MU market.
- Visit the website to find specific examples of products the company offers to each segment.
- List your segments and examples, and exchange what you have found with other students.
- Can you identify any segments which may represent new target markets for the company?

Activity 9.4 Examples of customer relationship management

Select an organisation in which you have an interest, ideally as a customer, which tries to build relationships with its customers.

- Which of the tools mentioned above (using customer data; CRM technologies; sponsored online communities; or those mentioned in the Key Ideas feature) does it use?
- How have they affected your attitude and behaviour towards the company?
- If it sponsors an online community, which of the three practices suggested in the Key Ideas feature does it use?
- Is there any evidence about their effects?

9.6 A marketing orientation

Chapter 3 outlines the idea of organisational culture, and how it influences where people focus their efforts and attention. Four such cultures (or 'orientations') relevant in marketing are: product, production, sales and marketing.

Four orientations

- **Product.** In units with a product orientation people focus on the design and perhaps the perfection of the product itself. This could mean focusing on developing highly sophisticated products using the latest scientific developments; or it could mean continuing to deliver a familiar product in a familiar way. This can work well in small or protected markets which others find hard to enter, but risk missing external changes in what people want to buy. Burgers *et al.* (2008) show how Polaroid (whose successful business sold cameras cheaply, and made money from selling film) used their *technical* skills to develop digital cameras. Unfortunately they lacked the *market* skills to generate revenues from the new (film-free) cameras, and failed to establish a position in this business.
- **Production.** Here the aim is to produce large quantities of a limited range of products efficiently and economically. This works well in situations where few goods and services are available, as customers have little choice. Companies with a production focus may suffer if conditions change towards greater competition and wide choice. A focus on volume production may make it hard to meet the needs of customers who expect variety and change.
- **Sales.** Units with this orientation aim to turn available products into cash, often using aggressive sales techniques. This may be the only way to sell products (sometimes called 'distress purchases') which people do not enjoy buying, such as tyres or insurance, or

where a concert has unsold seats a few days before the show. Companies also use this approach when they must raise cash urgently to meet pressing financial commitments.

- **Marketing.** Here the focus is on understanding and satisfying customer needs and demands. This approach is likely to be especially useful when the supply of goods exceeds demand, so that competition is intense. Many believe this is the situation most commonly facing modern organisations, and advocate that managers develop this approach in preference to the others. The next sub-section outlines the features of the approach, while Table 9.3 summarises the alternatives.

Marketing orientation

Most commercial organisations have a marketing function – a group of people who work on market research, competitor analysis and product strategy or promotion. A **marketing orientation** means much more than this, in that it refers to a situation where the significance of marketing is deeply embedded throughout the organisation. This means, among other things, that staff who are not in direct contact with customers nevertheless understand their needs, and give time and effort to satisfy them. While all the orientations in Table 9.3 work in some business conditions, many commentators believe that a marketing orientation is best suited to modern competitive environments (see, for example, Kirca *et al.,* 2005; Morgan *et al.,* 2009).

> **Marketing orientation** refers to an organisational culture that encourages people to behave in ways that offer high-value goods and services to customers.

Levitt pointed out many years ago the danger of focusing on the features of the product, at the expense of its ability to satisfy needs and wants. A marketing orientation is hard to achieve, as it depends on developing a culture that encourages appropriate behaviour in relation to:

- customers – understanding and anticipating their needs and demands;
- competitors – identifying and anticipating their marketing plans;
- co-ordination – ensuring that all the separate functions within the organisation work together to meet customer needs in a way that adds value to both parties.

It seems plausible that companies which pay attention to these factors will perform well, and this seems, on balance, to be supported by evidence of staff being in such organisations being willing to support the marketing focus. Kirca *et al.* (2005) reviewed 114 quantitative studies of the relationship between firms claiming to have a marketing orientation and their performance. They found that, especially in manufacturing firms, there was a positive and significant link between marketing orientation and innovativeness, and customer loyalty and quality: this in turn enhanced business performance.

Table 9.3 Alternative organisational orientations

Organisational orientations	Focus	Benefits	Risks
Product	Technological skills and product features	High-quality, innovative products	Does not meet customer needs, so sales are poor
Production	Efficient, high volume, low-cost production	Low price may build sales	Competition from lower cost producers. Inflexible
Sales	Seller's need to convert product into cash	May work for 'unsought goods' (insurance) and in cash-flow crises	Sales techniques may damage future sales prospects
Marketing	Understanding and meeting consumers' needs	Satisfying consumer needs improves firm performance	High costs of building and maintaining a marketing orientation

Theodore Levitt and marketing myopia

Levitt (1960) sets out with great clarity the case for a customer orientation. Beginning with the example of great industries which had suffered dramatic declines in demand, he claimed this was not because their market was saturated, but because their senior managers suffered from 'marketing myopia'. That is, they defined their businesses too narrowly: railway businesses saw themselves as providing railways, not transportation; Hollywood film companies saw themselves as producing films, not providing entertainment. In each case this prevented them from quickly seizing opportunities to enter new markets – road and air transport, or TV production, respectively.

Levitt gives examples of companies that were indeed product focused, yet that prospered: not because of their product focus, but because they *also* had a strong customer-orientation. They constantly looked for opportunities to apply their acknowledged technical expertise to satisfy new customers. He concludes by proposing that managers must view the entire corporation as a customer-satisfying organism – not as producing products, but as providing customer satisfaction:

It must put this into every nook and cranny of the organisation, continuously, and with the flair that excites and stimulates the people in it. (p. 56)

Source: Levitt (1960).

Morgan *et al.* (2009) developed this line of research by showing the specific processes by which firms deploy a marketing orientation to improve performance. Their marketing orientation means they are skilled at generating, disseminating and responding to market information, and are then able to put this information to good use through their marketing capabilities – a set of 'marketing mix' practices (see Section 9.7) such as product management, pricing, communication and distribution.

> **A customer-centred organisation** is focused upon, and structured around, identifying and satisfying the demands of its consumers.

Concentrating on the market and being a **customer-centred organisation** enables managers to discover what consumers want. They can then decide how best to use the strengths of the organisation to *return* to the market with a product for which a demand exists. They use information about demand and the price that consumers will pay to decide how much to produce and at what cost. While the sales orientation focuses on shifting products, the marketing orientation focuses on satisfying consumers and building mutually satisfying relationships – they anticipate changing demands and develop new products to meet them. For a study of two fashion retailers with different approaches, see Newman and Patel (2004), and for some further insight consider the views of Tim Smit of the Eden Project (Chapter 15 Case), who says:

> Of course we have to give people a good day out, a cup of tea they enjoy, and all that. But I think we have actually struck a vein which has got deeper and more important to us as a society, which is people are not just looking for leisure: what many are looking for is a purpose in their lives, and I think the combination of a great day out, with something meaningful, learning about your environment, learning about your relationship with nature, was a killer proposition. That's why I think we get the numbers we do.

Customer-oriented activities in manufacturing

Bowen *et al.* (1989) found that two sets of customer-oriented activities enhanced competitiveness:

Augmenting products by:

- designing products that have characteristics that enhance customer satisfaction;
- delivering products safely and reliably;
- providing responsive and friendly after-sales service.

Incorporating customer focus into strategy by:

- understanding customer needs and using that to develop innovative products;
- increasing customer involvement early in design;
- tracking and communicating customer satisfaction and loyalty metrics across the organisation.

All of these activities require that employees throughout the business embrace the idea of customer orientation, and use it to guide their day-to-day activities.

Source: Bowen *et al.* (1989).

Management in practice   Unilever reconnects with customers www.unilever.com

After several years of performing less well than other consumer goods companies such as Nestlé and Procter & Gamble, Unilever appointed a new chief executive in 2009. Commenting on his task, Paul Polman said:

> We need to move increasingly from an efficiency-driven, manufacturing-driven supply chain. At the end what counts is to get the right product, at the right place, at the right price.

To help achieve that, he is creating 'customer innovation centres' in the US, Europe and Asia as hubs for testing new products and conducting consumer research. Most exciting, potentially, is the new product pipeline. Mr Polman wants Unilever to develop fewer products but to commercialise them faster.

Underpinning the whole cultural reinvention of Unilever, Mr Polman is trying to create a more performance-based culture among staff, with six-monthly, instead of annual, evaluations and bonus targets linked to volume growth and operating margins.

Source: *Financial Times*, 7 May 2009.

Activity 9.5   Gathering examples

Select an organisation (or unit) with which you are familiar, or about which you can find out.

- Which of the four cultural types in Table 9.3 most closely describes it?
- Describe briefly the features which best describes the way it works.
- If it has a marketing orientation, what examples can you give of the way people throughout the organisation work?
- Compare what you have found with other students, and identify any common themes.

Developing a marketing orientation

While a marketing orientation is a desirable goal for companies in volatile markets, such cultural change is hard to achieve. Staff at all levels and in all functions need to share a common commitment to work together in the interests of customers. It requires consistent and sustained effort by senior managers to clarify and implement the direction, sometimes replacing staff who are unable or unwilling to work in new ways (see Gebhardt *et al.* (2007) for a comprehensive empirical analysis of the scale of the task required). Chapter 13 contains ideas about implementing large organisational changes, of which developing a marketing orientation is an example.

9.7

9.7   Using the marketing mix

The **marketing mix** is the set of marketing tools – product, price, promotion and place – that an organisation uses to satisfy consumers' needs.

Marketing managers select the tools to satisfy the customers in their target market – everything they can do to influence demand. There are many of these, depending on the product or service being delivered. A convenient way to group the factors in the **marketing mix** is known as the 'four Ps' – product, price, promotion and place – which Figure 9.6 illustrates by showing some components in each

---

Key ideas   **Marketing mix – strengths and limitations**

The marketing mix comprises four levers which marketing managers can control. The mix *positions* products in the market in a way that makes them attractive to the target consumers. A product's position reflects what consumers think of it, in comparisons with competitors – classy and desirable, cheap and affordable, pricey but reliable and so on. Marketers aim to position their products *within the minds of their target consumers* as better able to satisfy their needs than competing products. To position products effectively, the marketing manager develops a co-ordinated, coherent marketing mix.

The 'four Ps' are of course an over-simplification, and it is not hard to add other dimensions. However, the aim should not be to seek an (unattainable) precision about the list of factors, but to have a reasonably simple framework about the factors to manage in trying to meet customer needs.

Product

Product refers to the range of goods and services which the company offers the target market. Some are physical products, others intangible services and most are a mixture of the two since the full experience of a product includes services such as delivery, customer advice and after-sales service. Figure 9.6 shows that it also includes items such as packaging, maintenance and insurance.

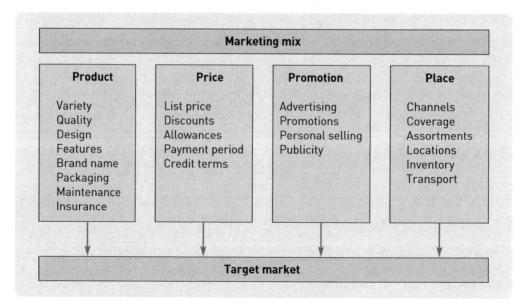

Figure 9.6 The four Ps in the marketing mix

Source: KOTLER, PHILIP; ARMSTRONG, GARY, *PRINCIPLES OF MARKETING*, 13th ed. © 2010, p. 52. Reprinted by permission of Pearson Education, Inc., Upper Saddle River, NJ.

The development and introduction of Swatch is a classic example of marketing techniques being used by a traditional industry to launch a new product. Faced with competition from low-cost producers SMH, an established Swiss watchmaker (whose brands include Longines and Omega), urgently needed a new product line. Its engineers developed a radically new product – the Swatch – which combined high quality with an affordable price. The company worked closely with advertising agencies in the US on product positioning and advertising strategy. In addition to the name 'Swatch', a snappy contraction of 'Swiss' and 'watch', this research generated the idea of downplaying the product's practical benefits and positioning it as a 'fashion accessory that happens to tell the time'. Swatch would be a second or third watch used to adapt to different situations without replacing the traditional 'status symbol' watch.

Swatch is now the world's largest watch company and continues to reposition itself through new products (such as Snowpass). It has been appointed official timekeeper of the Olympic Games until 2020.

Sources: Based on 'Swatch', Case No. 589-005-1, INSEAD-Cedep, Fontainebleau; and company website.

The extent to which offerings are tangible or intangible affects how marketing staff deal with them. Services present marketing with particular challenges because they are perishable and intangible, heterogeneous and inseparable.

Perishable

Perishable services cannot be held in stock for even the shortest amount of time. Empty seats on a flight, unoccupied rooms in a hotel or unsold newspapers are permanently lost sales.

Intangible

Intangible services are those that cannot usually be viewed, touched or tried before their purchase, so it is difficult for the customers to know what they are getting before their purchase – holidays, concerts, health clubs would be examples. Consumers have difficulty assessing whether the product will meet their needs, so many providers of such services build customer groups where users can share experiences with others, and encourage current members to invite friends and family with trial memberships.

Heterogeneous and inseparable

Services rely on the skills, competences and experiences of the people who provide them, and this creates particular marketing challenges. Services are *heterogeneous* in that their personal nature means the customer may experience a slightly different product each time, even though it is essentially the same meal or dental treatment that is being provided. Services are *inseparable* in that the customer interacts with the producer during delivery: it is consumed as it is produced, as in a medical appointment. Providers and consumers have personalities, opinions and values that make them unique, so the service delivered is always unique.

Organisations operating through branch systems such as banks or fast-food restaurants have to overcome these hazards to ensure that staff deliver consistent standards, otherwise customers will be dissatisfied. Organisations such as Pizza Hut and UCI cinemas try to minimise differences by providing staff with company uniforms, decorating premises in a similar way and setting firm guidelines for the way staff deliver the service.

Consumer products (both goods and services) can be classified as convenience, shopping, speciality or unsought products. Each poses a different marketing challenge, which Table 9.4 summarises.

Price

Price is the value placed upon the goods, services and ideas exchanged between organisations and consumers. The money price is the commonest measure, although this part of the mix also

Table 9.4 Market challenges by type of product, using the marketing mix

Type of product	Examples	Marketing challenge
Convenience	Regular purchases, low price – bread, milk, magazines	Widely available and easy to switch brands. Managers counter this by heavy advertising or distinct packaging of the brand
Shopping	Relatively expensive, infrequent purchase – washing machines, televisions, clothes	Brand name, product features, design and price are important, and managers will spend time searching for the best mix. Managers spend heavily on advertising and on training sales staff
Speciality	Less frequent, often luxury purchases – cars, jewellery, perfumes	Consumers need much information. Sales staff vital to a sale – management invest heavily in them, and in protecting the image of a product by restricting outlets. Also focused advertising and distinctive packaging
Unsought	Consumers need to buy – but don't get much pleasure from – insurance, a car exhaust	Managers need to make customers aware that they supply a product that meets this need

includes discounts, trade-in allowances payment period and credit terms. Airlines often levy charges for elements of the service, which they formerly offered as part of an inclusive fare.

In selecting the price that will position a product competitively within consumers' minds, the marketing manager must be aware of the image that consumers have of the product. Consumers have expected price ranges for certain types of product. For children's products and those associated with their health or self-image, consumers have a *minimum* price they expect to pay. A price below this will discourage a purchase, as customers will associate that with poor quality or low value.

Dynamic pricing was initially used by hotels and airlines, which face the problem that since their services are provided at a specified time, they have no value if they are not used by then. Companies try to raise revenue in this situation by varying prices in response to demand for a particular day. Airlines usually start with low prices, rising as the date of travel approaches: sometimes falling sharply if there is spare capacity just before the date of travel. They hope in this way to reallocate demand across time (those who can be flexible will learn to avoid peak times) and so make better use of a limited supply. Some suppliers of clothing, mobile phones and consumer electronics now use the practice, partly to dispose of stocks whose value depreciates as newer versions become available (Sahay, 2007).

Promotion

Properly referred to as marketing communications, this element of the marketing mix involves informing customers about the merits of the product, and persuading them to buy. Technological developments are increasing the number of ways in which organisations can communicate with their target markets. Packaging can provide information, a company logo may transmit a particular message, and sponsoring a football team or concert indicates an organisation's values and attitudes. Common ways to encourage consumers to buy are advertising, sales promotions, personal selling and publicity.

- *Advertising* is used to transmit a message to a large audience. It is impersonal, as it does not involve direct communication between an organisation and a potential consumer. Advertising is effective in creating awareness of the offering but is less effective in persuading consumers to buy.

Table 9.5 Top five companies in the Bowen Craggs Index of corporate websites, 2010

Company	Construction	Message	Contact	Serving society	Serving investors	Serving media	Serving job seekers	Serving customers	Total
Maximum score	60	38	12	32	28	32	32	32	280
Royal Dutch Shell	44	38	9	27	28	21	24	22	213
BP	43	35	10	25	27	21	24	25	210
Siemens	43	42	10	26	20	27	20	22	210
Roche	42	40	8	24	22	27	23	23	209
Rio Tinto	42	35	7	25	24	20	25	23	201

Source: FT Bowen Craggs & Co Index of Corporate Website Effectiveness 2010.

- *Sales promotions* encourage consumers who are considering a product to take the next step and buy it. They also use promotions to encourage repeat purchases and to try new products.
- *Personal selling* provides consumers with first-hand information before they buy. It is most useful for infrequently purchased products such as DVD players and cars. Personal selling is a direct transfer of product information to potential consumers: it is able to respond to questions that consumers might have and to explain complicated or technical product features.
- *Publicity* or public relations (PR) aims to build a positive image of the organisation. It depends on good working relationships with the media to ensure that positive events such as launching a new product are fully reported, and that negative ones do as little damage as possible.
- *Websites* have rapidly become the first place that many users go to check products, prices and availability, and are probably the most-read publication a company produces. The FT Bowen Craggs & Co Index of corporate website effectiveness evaluates the websites of the world's largest companies against eight criteria (such as 'serving customers' and 'serving the media'). The scores of the top five companies in the 2010 index are shown in Table 9.5.
- *Online communities* enable users of a product to share experiences. These are often formed independently, but others are sponsored by the company as a way to build relationships.

Management in practice   Online retailing – the benefits of user-generated content

Many people enjoy telling others about their shopping experiences, whether good or bad, which has helped to increase the popularity of online shopping communities. If people find they cannot air their views on a retailer's website, they will soon do so elsewhere on the internet.

Companies can eavesdrop on these conversations to gain valuable marketing information, and some now host these conversations by opening their websites to what is called 'user-generated content'. The most common type of content is when users provide product reviews. Negative comments may indicate genuine problems with a product that the company needs to deal with: good ones may be a signal to increase stocks to be ready for higher demand.

There is also evidence that shoppers are more likely to buy on a site that contains user-generated content, and that they have more trust in brands that offer product reviews.

Place

This refers to how products can best be distributed to the final consumer, either directly or through intermediaries. Some, especially those in luxury goods or fashion markets, take great care to ensure that products are only available through carefully controlled distributors, to help ensure consistent quality or promote their market image. One company developed an e-book service which can sell full 'e-books', highlights or chapters to users – probably onto their laptops, mobiles or iPads. It decided to sell the device through publishers, rather than to individual consumers. Many companies debate whether how to combine online distribution with traditional channels – partly influenced by their understanding of why people buy the product. As one publisher observed:

> Music is only there to be listened to, but books are also shared, given as presents, used as furniture. (*Financial Times*, 13 April 2009, p. 17)

In developing a marketing mix that will place products competitively within the minds of consumers, marketing managers aim for coherence. In positioning a supermarket chain as, for example, value for money, they ensure that each part of the mix supports and reinforces this image. This means familiar products features, relatively low prices and promotion messages that stress the value for money. The stores should be simple, to avoid sending a message that the costs of creating a smart place will raise prices. An effective marketing mix is one where there is coherence among the elements, giving the customer a consistent positive experience.

Management in practice   **Using the marketing mix in the pub business**

The UK pub business has experienced significant changes, with legislation on drink-driving and smoking, together with competition from supermarkets selling cheap alcoholic drinks, thus reducing revenues. Many have responded by changing the product, offering food and a wide range of entertainment, especially live big-screen sport. They have also segmented the market, with pubs being developed in ways that appeal to different groups of drinkers.

Source: Pratten and Scoffield (2007).

Case questions 9.4

- Use the frameworks in this section to identify how MU uses the marketing mix.
- Visit the website and identify two significant target markets for the company.
- For each market, analyse how the company has used the market mix to construct its market offering.
- List your markets and examples of the 'four Ps', and exchange what you have found with other students. Can you identify any significant aspects of the offering that are not covered by one the '4 Ps'?

9.8   The product lifecycle

The **product lifecycle** suggests that products pass through the stages of introduction, growth, maturity and decline.

In managing the organisation's product decisions, marketing managers use a concept called the **product lifecycle** (Figure 9.7). The central assumption is that all products have a limited life, varying from months to decades. Depending on the stage reached in its lifecycle, a known set of competitive conditions exists that can guide the marketing activities for that stage.

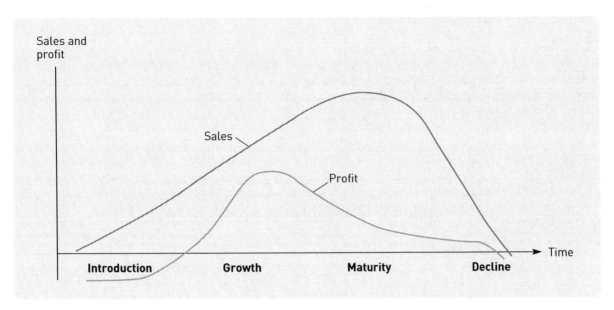

Figure 9.7 The product lifecycle

Mapping the sales and profit generated, the product lifecycle suggests that products pass through five stages – development, introduction, growth, maturity and decline.

Development

In many commercial markets, companies only survive if they can show a steady stream of new products, a small proportion of which will be profitable. Sometimes they acquire already developed products from other companies, as a way of quickly filling a perceived gap in their product range. Alternatively, they depend on their own research and development department to develop new products – whether these are completely new devices or modifications and improvements to an earlier design. This is an expensive process, during which the company is spending large sums with no immediate return.

Introduction

This is the stage at which products enter the marketplace. Profits are still negative because sales from the early adopters have not reached the level needed to pay back investment in R&D. Few consumers are aware of – and therefore interested in – buying the product and few organisations are involved in producing and distributing it. The aim of the marketing manager at this stage is to invest in marketing communication and make as many potential consumers as possible aware of the product's entry into the marketplace.

Growth

At this stage consumers have become aware of and started buying the product. Sales rise quickly and profits peak. As people buy the product, more consumers become aware of it and the high profit levels attract new competitors into the industry. The aim of the marketing manager at this stage is to fight off existing competitors and new entrants. This can be done by (a) encouraging consumer loyalty, (b) distributing the product as widely as is demanded by consumers, and (c) cutting selling prices: production costs fall as the total units increase, due to the learning curve effect. Competitors arriving later have not had time to cut costs, so may baulk at entering the market.

Maturity

With profits peaking during the growth stage, profit and sales start to plateau and then decline towards the end of this stage. By this stage in a product's lifecycle, many consumers are aware of and have bought the product and there are many organisations competing for a decreasing amount of consumer demand for the product. The aim of the marketing manager is to fight competition by reducing the price of the product or by differentiating it by, for example, altering its packaging and design. Swatch continues to add value to its product in the later stages of its product lifecycle with items such as the Infinity Concept watch launched in early 2007.

At this stage product differentiation can successfully reposition products to an earlier stage in their lifecycle. It is also important that the marketing manager begins to consider ideas for replacement products and to select ideas for research and development.

Decline

In the decline phase, there is little consumer demand and all competing organisations are considering removing the product from the marketplace. It is important that, by this stage, the marketing manager has a new product ready to enter the marketplace and replace the product that is being removed. Certain rarity products can still generate profits in the decline phase, e.g. spare parts for old cars.

An awareness of the stage which a product is at in its lifecycle can assist the marketing manager in deciding upon a course of action. Aware that a product is in maturity, the marketing manager might decide to reposition the product by changing the packaging or image created by the branding of the product. Lucozade was traditionally marketed as a health drink for older people, but product changes, new packaging and celebrity endorsement have repositioned it as a youth sports drink (**www.lucozade.com**).

Activity 9.6   **Using the product lifecycle**

- State the stage that you believe each of the following products to be in and comment on how long, in years, you believe their lifecycle to be: drawing pins, iPods, umbrellas, hand soap.

Some products appear not have a limited lifespan and others have been repositioned to an earlier stage. Despite these criticisms, the product lifecycle offers the marketing manager a useful aid to many product decisions.

Case study   **Manchester United – the case continues**

One of the challenges facing Manchester United is the best organisational marketing structure to design and the internal culture to induce in managing its huge operation. At corporate level, the Glazer family owns football-related and non-football-related businesses, and is involved with various joint ventures in TV, financial services and mobile phones. At business and product levels, management have to deal directly with their target segments. Promotional campaigns for individual products have to be sensitive to the image of sister MU products. Hoarding adverts of a noisy football crowd having a good time will be exciting to other potential fans but could be off-putting for someone who has to produce their MU credit card at local stores.

Preserving the perceived value of the brand is also important: the replica jersey product manager will not want stores such as Tesco to sell them at a discount. This raises important questions of channel management and relationship with companies whose strategy might be more cost focused than differentiated. In 2009 MU signed a deal worth £80 million over four years with Aon, an American financial services group, to be its principal sponsor: this was the largest-ever football sponsorship deal. They also signed a three-year deal with Turkish Airlines to be their official carrier.

9.9 Integrating themes

Sustainable performance

Marketing is both part of the problem and part of the solution to sustainability. Companies in many areas of the economy have used the skills of marketing to promote the greater consumption of goods and services that have contributed to the current situation. Some are now using those same skills to identify segments of their markets in which there are customers willing to switch to products that use more sustainable methods of production, and to that extent have less environmental impact. As Chapter 5 shows, such responsible practices are limited by market circumstances, and are themselves only sustainable if they are commercially viable in the face of competition from other suppliers who may feel less constrained to meet these demands.

Key ideas — Naomi Klein's No Logo: Taking aim at the brand bullies

Klein (2000) presents a powerful argument against the growing dominance of some global brands in consumer markets, and how many use advertising to exploit impressionable teenagers. She argues that companies such as Microsoft, Gap and Starbucks now present themselves as purveyors of lifestyles, images and dreams rather than products. In doing so they harm both the cultures in which they operate and the workers they employ. She also reports a growing backlash by ethical shareholders, human rights activists and McUnion organisers demanding a citizen-centred alternative to the rule of the brands.

However, not everyone agrees that Klein is correct. She is accused of overstating her case, and brand advocates point out the many positives that brands have for consumers, manufacturers and retailers. What is not in dispute, however, is that companies are now facing up to social and ethical responsibility as never before.

Source: Klein (2000).

The discipline of marketing could also be part of the solution of achieving a sustainable economic system, since any set of proposals about the changes needed in the way people live and work will only work if they are widely accepted by members of the public. Surveys regularly show that even among the (minority) who accept the problem, many are unwilling to commit to the personal changes required. Marketing skills in the area of understanding attitudes and interests, and in developing policies intended to change behaviour, have been applied to many areas of policy, such as public health, alcohol abuse and domestic violence. The same skills may be relevant in promoting widespread acceptance of more sustainable lifestyles.

Governance and control

One aspect of governance is that of assessing risks – indeed it is one of the requirements of The Combined Code (2006) that Boards appoint a risk assessment committee. While this would normally focus on the financial or perhaps technological risks potentially embodied in a strategy, reputational risk will sometimes also be worth evaluating as new products or services are developed. This is where a company acts in a way that many believe to be unethical, leading to long-term damage to its reputation. A clear example of this would be the way in which companies in financial services, in the years before the 2008 financial crisis, encouraged people to support their lifestyles on debt which they could not afford.

While governance has traditionally been concerned primarily with the immediate financial arrangements of a company, some now suggest that part of the governance process should include an assessment of the risks to which the company is exposed through the way it conducts the business. In some lines of business, especially financial services, governance and control could arguably include the role of marketing in shaping the risks to which the company is exposed.

Internationalisation

The majority of the top 100 most valuable brands are global, which derive their value from making strong emotional connections with customers across countries and cultures. With some exceptions, such as Google and Amazon which have achieved global status very quickly, most did so by following three principles:

- Adapt to local needs and culture – spend time finding out which features of the product can remain constant, and which will need to be adapted.
- Seek to tap a universal truth – strong brands are founded on a promise that resonates with consumers, so identify some essential aspect of human nature with which to associate the brand.
- align the organisation around the global strategy – people at all levels need to be clear about how their work supports the brand, and how it could equally be how inconsistent actions would undermine it.

Activity 9.7   Revising your definition

- Having completed this chapter, how would you define marketing?

- Compare this definition with the one that you were asked to make in Activity 9.1 and comment on any changes.

Cases

Case study   Manchester United FC www.manutd.com

With over 50 million fans across the globe, Manchester United Football Club (MU) is one of the best-known soccer clubs. Founded in 1878, it rose to prominence in the early 1950s. Since then, the club has never been out of the sports headlines, hiring a series of almost legendary managers (including Sir Matt Busby and, since 1986, Sir Alex Ferguson) and buying or developing world-recognised players (including David Beckham, Ruud van Nistelrooy and Wayne Rooney).

In May 2005 the club was taken over in a £790 million pound bid by American sports tycoon Malcolm Glazer in a deal that was heavily financed by debt. *Forbes* magazine ranked it in 2009 as the world's wealthiest club, valuing it $1,870 million, well ahead of nearest rivals Real Madrid and Arsenal. In early 2010 it issued bonds worth £500 (paying interest at 9 per cent), mainly to repay loans from international banks.

The 2009 operating income was £516 million, generated from a wide range of football-related businesses (gate and TV revenues, sports clothes, etc.) and brand-related activities (MUTV, mobiles, travel and finance). MU is only a part of the worldwide operations. The holding company (Manchester United plc) owns MU, Manchester United Catering (Agency Company) and Manchester United Interactive. MUTV, the club's official channel, is a joint venture between Manchester United plc, Granada, and BSkyB.

The Club's ambition is to be the most successful team in football. Its business strategy is to do this by having the football and commercial operations work hand-in-hand, both in current and new domestic markets, and in the potential markets represented by the Club's global fan base, especially Asia. The marketing strategy is built on maintaining success on the field and leveraging global brand awareness through new products and partnered services designed to appeal to MU's worldwide fans. A substantial partner is Nike, whose development and marketing channels are used to generate new value from the MU trademarks (for example, replica kits) by supplying the millions of MU fans in the UK and Asia.

PA Photos:Kin Cheung/AP.

MU attempts to control and develop its own routes to market for media rights (for example, MUTV), thereby exploiting the Club's own performance and reputation rather than relying on the collective appeal of competition football. The management believes this enhances the ability to deliver branded services to customers anywhere in the world. They rely strongly on IT-based CRM (customer relationship management) technology to convert fans to customers.

Sources: Based on material from Butterworth Heinemann Case 0181, *Manchester United and British Soccer: Beautiful game, brutal industry*; 'Can football be saved?'; other published material.

Case questions 9.1

- Consider the marketing implications of MU's activities. What is MU offering to customers?
- What groups would MU see as competitors? Are they simply other successful football clubs?
- What distinctive challenges do you think may arise in marketing a football club?

A football game is not a tangible product. A regular and significant intangible purchase by a Manchester United football fan is the £27–£49 ticket to see a home game at Old Trafford or £10 on a pay-per-view TV basis. There is no guarantee of satisfaction and no exchange or refund. No promotional advertising is needed and the ticket demand is relatively 'inelastic', i.e. prices can increase without sales volumes necessarily falling.

An important question for a marketing manager is 'how does a fan reach the decision to buy this experience and how is value measured?'. The buyer behaviour framework described above can help: domestic UK fans are typically lifelong, acquiring perceptions of and loyalty to the Club at school or in the home. Influencers would include peers and older pupils. Although football was formerly male-dominated, young females are an increasing part of the market. Most fans travel in groups of two or more, so this is a segment attribute that can be managed in raising awareness and favourability. Publicity photos can depict fans celebrating or commiserating together and the whole emphasis of attending a football match can be positioned away from 'did we win?' to 'did we have a good time?'. This approach is one of MU's declared marketing strategies.

Case questions 9.2

- What customer demands were MU seeking to satisfy at the time of the case study?
- What other demands does the business have to satisfy?
- What marketing tools are mentioned in the case?

One of the challenges facing Manchester United is the best organisational marketing structure to design and the internal culture to induce in managing its huge operation. At corporate level, the Glazer family owns football-related and non-football-related businesses, and is involved with various joint ventures in TV, financial services and mobile phones. At business and product levels, management have to deal directly with their target segments. Promotional campaigns for individual products have to be sensitive to the image of sister MU products. Hoarding adverts of a noisy football crowd having a good time will be exciting to other potential fans but could be off-putting for someone who has to produce their MU credit card at local stores.

Preserving the perceived value of the brand is also important: the replica jersey product manager will not want stores such as Tesco to sell them at a discount. This raises important questions of channel management and relationship with companies whose strategy might be more cost focused than differentiated. In 2009 MU signed a deal worth £80 million over four years with Aon, an American financial services group, to be its principal sponsor: this was the largest-ever football sponsorship deal. They also signed a three-year deal with Turkish Airlines to be their official carrier.

PART 3 CASE
THE VIRGIN GROUP
www.virgin.com

Virgin is a branded venture capital organisation, known all over the world and seen as standing for value for money, quality, innovation and fun. Founded by Richard Branson, it has created over 200 companies worldwide, employing about 50,000 people in 30 countries.

The first record shop was opened in 1971 and the record label launched in 1973. Virgin Atlantic Airways began operating in 1984, quickly followed by Virgin Holidays. In 1995 the company entered a joint venture offering financial services. By 1997 it was an established global corporation with airline, retailing and travel operations. In 2010 its main activities are grouped into Travel, Lifestyle, Media and Mobile, Music, Money, and People and Planet.

The original record business was launched shortly after the UK government had abolished retail price maintenance, a practice that had limited competition and kept prices high. Richard Branson saw the opportunity and began a mail order business offering popular records at prices about 15 per cent below those charged by shops.

The business prospered until there was a postal strike. Branson's response was to open a retail outlet, which was an immediate success, and the start of Virgin Retail. These retail interests were later consolidated around the Megastore concept in a joint venture with a major retailer. At prestige locations in major cities, Megastores began to sell home entertainment products – music, videos and books – on a large scale. The success of the Megastore concept was exported to major cities throughout the world, frequently through joint ventures.

In the early 1980s Branson was approached by Randolph Fields, who was seeking additional finance for his cut-price airline. The airline business then was tightly regulated, with routes, landing rights, prices and service levels established and maintained by intergovernmental arrangements. These regulations were mainly used to protect inefficient, often state-owned, national 'flag carriers', keeping fares high. After three months of intense activity, Branson and Fields had gained permission to fly, arranged to lease an aircraft and recruited staff. The first flight was in June 1984. To grow, Branson needed more landing rights, and would need to persuade government ministers to secure them at both ends of each route. Those ministers would also

Visual Media

be lobbied by the established airlines, to persuade them not to approve the low fares that Branson was proposing. Alternatively, they could undercut his fares and subsidise the losses from profits on other routes.

Virgin Atlantic grew successfully and by 1990, although still a relatively small player, it competed with the major carriers on the main routes from London, winning awards for innovation and service. The airline was now the focus of Branson's interests and was becoming a serious threat to the established airlines. It now serves 30 destinations around the world. Virgin America (created in 2007) is based in California and offers high-quality, innovative services. The company is also involved in the low-cost airline business through Virgin Blue (founded 1997) in Australia.

The Virgin brand

Research on the Virgin brand name demonstrated the impact over time of quirky advertising and publicity stunts. The brand was recognised by 96 per cent of UK consumers, and Richard Branson was correctly identified by 95 per cent as the company's founder. The Virgin name was associated by respondents with words such as fun, innovation, success and trust, and identified with a range of businesses, confirming what Branson and others had believed: in principle there were no product or service boundaries limiting a brand name, provided it was associated with a quality offering.

Encouraged by the research, Virgin began entering new sectors outside its core activities of travel and retail. Virgin businesses as diverse as radio broadcasting, book publishing and computer games found a home in the same stable, as well as hotels, railways, personal computers, cola drinks, cinemas and financial services. Branson continued to work at the centre, supported by a small business development group, a press office, and advisers on strategy and finance. The early Virgin style of informality and openness remains – ties are rarely worn, denim jeans are common and everybody is on first-name terms.

The Virgin organisation

Having a centre did not mean a centralised operation. Each operating unit was expected to stand alone, having little interaction with either head office or other units. Unit managers networked informally (usually at parties or similar events), but were not obliged to follow prescriptive corporate policies; these were 'understood' rather than codified. For example, there was no common human resource policy. Managers knew that employees must be treated 'fairly' since 'that is what Richard would want', and they complied in their own way. Similarly there was no group information technology strategist or central purchasing function, because Branson believed that those roles would constitute interference and discourage managerial creativity. Nor was there any systematic seeking out of synergy, either at the centre or by unit managers.

At the centre is Virgin Management Ltd (VML), providing advisory and management support to all of the Virgin companies and to specialist Sector teams around the world. In conjunction with the Sector teams (such as those for Travel or Finance) VML manages Virgin's assets around the world. While finance, marketing and human resource management policies are guided by the centre, the businesses have a high degree of autonomy in how they work. The company describes the style as a collaborative and supportive relationship between the centre and the businesses.

Criteria for investing in new ventures

When they start a new venture they base it on hard research and analysis. Typically they review the industry from the perspective of the customer, and try to see what they could do to improve the experience. They ask questions such as:

- Is this an opportunity for restructuring the market and creating competitive advantage?
- What are competitors doing?
- Is the customer confused or badly served?
- Is this an opportunity for the Virgin brand?
- Can we add value?
- Will it interact with our other business?

New ventures are often steered by managers seconded from other parts of the business, who bring with them the distinctive management style, skills and experience. The company frequently works by creating partnerships to combine industry specific skills with the Virgin style. Managers in the companies are empowered to run the businesses without VML interfering, but are also expected to help one another to overcome problems.

The Virgin Charter is an agreement between VML (in effect the holding company) and the subsidiaries. It defines the role of the centre in relation to the subsidiaries in such matters as taxation, legal affairs, intellectual property and real estate. It also outlines closer links in areas previously left to individual units: IT, people, purchasing. Thus the Charter sets out ways for the many Virgin companies to tackle common activities with a common approach. Nearly all are private and owned entirely by the Virgin Group or Branson's family trusts. Business should be 'shaped around people', Branson believes, citing his experience of subdividing the record company as it grew. Each new record label was given to up-and-coming managers, creating in-house entrepreneurs who were highly motivated to build a business with which they identified.

He believes that expanding by creating discrete legal entities gives people a sense of involvement with, and loyalty to, the small unit to which they belong. He gives substantial autonomy to those running the subsidiaries and offers them share options – Virgin has produced many millionaires. Branson does not want his best people to leave the company to start a venture outside; he prefers to make millionaires within. He has created a structure of numerous small companies around the world, each operated quasi-independently. Both systems embody the maxims 'small is beautiful' and 'people matter'.

Virgin.com

During one significant management meeting participants realised that, more by chance than planning, Virgin was in businesses 'that were ideally suited to e-commerce and in which growth is expected to occur – travel, financial services, publishing, music, entertainment'. To exploit this potential the participants decided to streamline their online services with a single Virgin web address: Virgin.com.

Branson believes that the Virgin name, known for its consumer-friendly image and good service, would translate well across a range of businesses – 'Virgin isn't a company, it's a brand', commented one senior manager in the company. This is attractive to partners, who provide the expertise and capital for a joint venture in their area of business (such as insurance or share trading), while Virgin provides the brand image. By putting all Virgin's business on one easily accessible site, Branson hopes to cross-promote a wide range of offerings. The site groups these under headings such as online shopping, finance and money, media and telecommunications, leisure and pleasure, travel and tourism, and health. Throughout the group, the company claims that it aims to deliver a quality service by empowering employees, and by facilitating and monitoring customer feedback to continually improve the customer's experience though innovation.

In October 2006 Richard Branson, at a meeting of the Clinton Global Initiative, announced that he would invest all future profits of the Virgin Group's transportation businesses – mainly airlines and trains – into renewable energy initiatives. These would be within the Virgin transportation companies and in new biofuel research and development projects.

In 2010 Virgin Galactica announced that the first commercial manned spaceship, VSS Enterprise, had made its first test flight. The craft is intended to carry six fare-paying passengers on sub-orbital space flights: the company has already taken $45 million in deposits from 330 people who want to share the experience. Virgin Media, the UK's dominant cable television operator, claimed to be the only company able to exploit the market for superfast broadband, although it faced intense competition from BT.

Sources: Based on material from INSEAD Case 400-002-1, *The House that Branson Built: Virgin's entry into the new millennium; Financial Times*, 15 December 2008; company website.

Part case questions

- What examples does the case give of links between Branson's strategy for Virgin and the environment in which it operates?
- Which of these are similar to, and which are different from, those facing HMV?
- Are the decisions mentioned in the case programmed or non-programmed? How do you sense, from the information in the case, that the company ensures the quality of those decisions?
- What common themes link the different businesses in the group?
- Which generic strategy has Virgin followed at different periods in its history?
- On balance, does the Virgin story support the planned or the emergent view of strategy?
- Why does Branson use joint ventures with other companies to realise the Virgin strategy? Are there any disadvantages in this method of working?
- To what extent has Virgin implemented a marketing orientation?
- Visit Virgin's website and comment on how it has used this to support its marketing activities.
- Where do Richard Branson's publicity stunts fit into the company's marketing strategy?

Review Questions and Tests

Review questions

1 Why do charities and local authorities need to devote resources to marketing?

2 Explain why understanding what customers want is a valuable investment.

3 Outline sources of marketing information and illustrate each with an example.

4 In what way is an organisation's micro-environment different from its macro-environment? How do these environments affect marketing activities?

5 What are the main stages in conducting a market research project?

6 What are the advantages of market segmentation and what variables do marketers typically use to segment consumer markets?

7 What are the two broad approaches to customer relationship management?

8 Does the marketing orientation have advantages over product, production or sales philosophies?

9 Illustrate each element in the marketing mix with an original example.

10 Use a product of your choice to illustrate all or part of the product lifecycle.

11 Summarise an idea from the chapter that adds to your understanding of the integrating themes.

Chapter 8:

Social Responsibility and Ethics

A Manager's Dilemma

It's an incredibly simple but potentially world-changing idea.[1] For each pair of shoes sold, a pair is donated to a child in need. That's the business model followed by TOMS Shoes. During a visit to Argentina in 2006 as a contestant on the CBS reality show *The Amazing Race*, Blake Mycoskie, founder of TOMS, "saw lots of kids with no shoes who were suffering from injuries to their feet." Just think what it would be like to be barefoot, not by choice, but from lack of availability and ability to own a pair. He was so moved by the experience that he wanted to do something. That something is what TOMS does now by blending charity with commerce. (The name TOMS is actually short for a "better tomorrow.") And a better tomorrow is what Blake wanted to provide to shoeless children around the world.

Those shoe donations have been central to the success of the TOMS brand, which is popular among tweens, teens, and twenty-somethings. And 400,000 pairs of shoes had been donated as of early 2010. Put yourself in Blake's position. How can he balance being socially responsible *and* being focused on profits?

What Would You Do?

Deciding how socially responsible an organization needs to be is just one example of the complicated types of ethical and social responsibility issues that managers, such as Blake Mycoskie, may have to cope with as they plan, organize, lead, and control. As managers manage, these issues can and do influence their actions.

LEARNING OUTCOME **5.1**
Discuss what it means to be socially responsible and what factors influence that decision.

What Is Social Responsibility?

By using digital technology and file-sharing Web sites, music and video users all over the world often obtain and share many of their favorite recordings for free. Large global corporations lower their costs by outsourcing to countries where human rights are not a high priority and justify it by saying they're bringing in jobs and helping strengthen the local economies. Businesses facing a drastically changed economic environment offer employees reduced hours and early retirement packages. Are these companies being socially responsible? Managers regularly face decisions that have a dimension of social responsibility in areas such as employee relations, philanthropy, pricing, resource conservation, product quality and safety, and doing business in countries that devalue human rights. What does it mean to be socially responsible?

From Obligations to Responsiveness to Responsibility

The concept of *social responsibility* has been described in different ways. For instance, it's been called "profit making only," "going beyond profit making," "any discretionary corporate activity intended to further social welfare," and "improving social or environmental conditions."[2] We can understand it better if we first compare it to two similar concepts: social obligation and social responsiveness.[3] **Social obligation** is when a firm engages in social actions because of its obligation to meet certain economic and legal responsibilities. The organization does what it's obligated to do and nothing more. This idea reflects the **classical view** of social responsibility, which says that management's only social responsibility is to maximize profits. The most outspoken advocate of this approach is economist and Nobel laureate Milton Friedman. He argued that managers' primary responsibility is to operate the business in the best interests of the stockholders, whose primary concerns are financial.[4] He also argued that when managers decide to spend the organization's resources for "social good," they add to the costs of doing business, which have to be passed on to consumers through higher prices or absorbed by stockholders through smaller dividends. You need to understand that Friedman doesn't say that organizations shouldn't be socially responsible. But his interpretation of social responsibility is to maximize profits for stockholders.

The other two concepts—social responsiveness and social responsibility—reflect the socioeconomic view, which says that managers' social responsibilities go beyond making profits to include protecting and improving society's welfare. This view is based on the belief that corporations are *not* independent entities responsible only to stockholders, but have an obligation to the larger society. Organizations around the world have embraced this view as shown by a survey of global executives in which 84 percent said that companies must balance obligations to shareholders with obligations to the public good.[5] But how do these two concepts differ?

Social responsiveness is when a company engages in social actions in response to some popular social need. Managers are guided by social norms and values and make practical, market-oriented decisions about their actions.[6] For instance, Ford Motor Company became the first automaker to endorse a federal ban on sending text messages while driving. A company spokesperson said that, "The most complete and most recent research shows that activity that draws drivers' eyes away from the road for an extended period while driving, such as text messaging, substantially increases the risk of accidents."[7] By supporting this ban, company managers "responded" to what they felt was an important social need. When the disastrous earthquake hit Haiti in January 2010, many companies responded to the immense needs in that region. For instance, UPS has a company-wide policy that urges employees to volunteer during natural disasters and other crises. In support of this policy, UPS maintains a 20-person Logistics Emergency Team in Asia, Europe, and the Americas that's trained in humanitarian relief.[8]

A socially *responsible* organization views things differently. It goes beyond what it's obligated to do or chooses to do because of some popular social need and does what it can to help improve society because it's the right thing to do. We define social responsibility as a business's intention, beyond its legal and economic obligations, to do the right things and act in ways that are good for society.[9] Our definition assumes that a business obeys the law and cares for its stockholders, but adds an ethical imperative to do those things that make society better and not to do those that make it worse. A socially responsible organization does what is right because it feels it has an ethical responsibility to do so. For example, Abt Electronics in Glenview, Illinois, would be described as socially responsible according to our definition. As one of the largest single-store electronics retailers in the United States, it responded to soaring energy costs and environmental concerns by shutting off lights more frequently and reducing air conditioning and heating. However, an Abt family member said, "These actions weren't just about costs, but about doing the right thing. We don't do everything just because of money."[10]

So, how should we view an organization's social actions? A U.S. business that meets federal pollution control standards or that doesn't discriminate against employees over the age of 40 in job promotion decisions is meeting its social obligation because laws mandate these actions. However, when it provides on-site child-care facilities for employees or packages products using recycled paper, it's being socially responsive. Why? Working parents and environmentalists have voiced these social concerns and demanded such actions.

For many businesses, their social actions are better viewed as being socially responsive than socially responsible (at least according to our definition). However, such actions are still good for society. For example, Walmart sponsored a program to address a serious social problem—hunger. Customers donated money to America's Second Harvest by purchasing puzzle pieces and Walmart matched the first $5 million raised. As part of this program, the company ran advertisements in major newspapers showing the word H_NGER and the tag line, "The problem can't be solved without You."[11]

social obligation
When a firm engages in social actions because of its obligation to meet certain economic and legal responsibilities

classical view
The view that management's only social responsibility is to maximize profits

socioeconomic view
The view that management's social responsibility goes beyond making profits to include protecting and improving society's welfare

social responsiveness
When a firm engages in social actions in response to some popular social need

social responsibility
A business's intention, beyond its legal and economic obligations, to do the right things and act in ways that are good for society

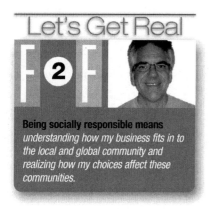

Should Organizations Be Socially Involved?

Other than meeting their social obligations (which they *must* do), should organizations be socially involved? One way to look at this question is by examining arguments for and against social involvement. Several points are outlined in Exhibit 5-1.[12]

Numerous studies have examined whether social involvement affects a company's economic performance.[13] Although most found a small positive relationship, no generalizable conclusions can be made because these studies have shown that relationship is affected by various contextual factors such as firm size, industry, economic conditions, and regulatory environment.[14] Another concern was causation. If a study showed that social involvement and economic performance were positively related, this correlation didn't necessarily mean that social involvement *caused* higher economic performance. It could simply mean that high profits afforded companies the "luxury" of being socially involved.[15] Such methodological concerns can't be taken lightly. In fact, one study found that if the flawed empirical analyses in these studies were "corrected," social responsibility had a neutral impact on a company's financial performance.[16] Another found that participating in social issues not related to the organization's primary stakeholders was negatively associated with shareholder value.[17] A re-analysis of several studies concluded that managers can afford to be (and should be) socially responsible.[18]

EXHIBIT 5-1

Arguments For and Against Social Responsibility

For	Against
Public expectations Public opinion now supports businesses pursuing economic and social goals.	**Violation of profit maximization** Business is being socially responsible only when it pursues its economic interests.
Long-run profits Socially responsible companies tend to have more secure long-run profits.	**Dilution of purpose** Pursuing social goals dilutes business's primary purpose—economic productivity.
Ethical obligation Businesses should be socially responsible because responsible actions are the right thing to do.	**Costs** Many socially responsible actions do not cover their costs and someone must pay those costs.
Public image Businesses can create a favorable public image by pursuing social goals.	**Too much power** Businesses have a lot of power already and if they pursue social goals they will have even more.
Better environment Business involvement can help solve difficult social problems.	**Lack of skills** Business leaders lack the necessary skills to address social issues.
Discouragement of further governmental regulation By becoming socially responsible, businesses can expect less government regulation.	**Lack of accountability** There are no direct lines of accountability for social actions.
Balance of responsibility and power Businesses have a lot of power and an equally large amount of responsibility is needed to balance against that power.	
Stockholder interests Social responsibility will improve a business's stock price in the long run.	
Possession of resources Businesses have the resources to support public and charitable projects that need assistance.	
Superiority of prevention over cures Businesses should address social problems before they become serious and costly to correct.	

Another way to view social involvement and economic performance is by looking at socially responsible investing (SRI) funds, which provide a way for individual investors to support socially responsible companies. (You can find a list of SRI funds at [www.socialfunds.com].) Typically, these funds use some type of social screening; that is, they apply social and environmental criteria to investment decisions. For instance, SRI funds usually will not invest in companies that are involved in liquor, gambling, tobacco, nuclear power, weapons, price fixing, fraud, or in companies that have poor product safety, employee relations, and environmental track records. The number of socially screened mutual funds has grown from 55 to 260 and assets in these funds have grown to more than $2.7 trillion—about 11 percent of total assets in managed funds in the United States.[19] But more important than the total amount invested in these funds is that the Social Investment Forum reports that the performance of most SRI funds is comparable to that of non-SRI funds.[20]

So, what can we conclude about social involvement and economic performance? It appears that a company's social actions *don't hurt* its economic performance. Given political and societal pressures to be socially involved, managers probably need to take social issues and goals into consideration as they plan, organize, lead, and control.

Green Management and Sustainability

5.2

LEARNING OUTCOME
Explain green management and how organizations can go green.

Coca-Cola, the world's largest soft drink company, announced that 100 percent of its new vending machines and coolers would be hydrofluorocarbon-free (HFC-free) by 2015. This initiative alone would have the same effect on global carbon emissions as taking 11 million cars off the road for a single year.[21] The Fairmont Hotel chain has generated a lot of buzz over its decision to set up rooftop beehives to try and help strengthen the population of honeybees, which have been mysteriously abandoning their hives and dying off by the millions worldwide. This Colony Collapse Disorder could have potentially disastrous consequences since one-third of the food we eat comes from plants that depend on bee pollination. At Toronto's Fairmont Royal York, six hives are home to some 360,000 bees that forage in and around the city *and* produce a supply of award-winning honey.[22] In 2004, top executives at General Electric Company voted against CEO Jeffrey Immelt's plan for a green business initiative. However, Immelt refused to take "no" for an answer and today that initiative, called Ecomagination, is one of the most widely recognized corporate green programs. It led to $100 million in cost savings and reduced the company's greenhouse emissions by 30 percent. And the program fostered the development of 80 new products and services that generate some $17 billion in annual revenue. Immelt said, "Going green has been 10 times better than I ever imagined."[23] Being green is in!

Until the late 1960s, few people (and organizations) paid attention to the environmental consequences of their decisions and actions. Although some groups were concerned with conserving natural resources, about the only reference to saving the environment was the ubiquitous printed request "Please Don't Litter." However, a number of environmental disasters brought a new spirit of environmentalism to individuals, groups, and organizations. Increasingly, managers have begun to consider the impact of their organization on the natural environment, which we call green management. What do managers need to know about going green?

How Organizations Go Green

Managers and organizations can do many things to protect and preserve the natural environment.[24] Some do no more than what is required by law—that is, they fulfill their social obligation. However, others have radically changed their products and production processes. For instance, Fiji Water is using renewable energy sources, preserving forests,

---

social screening
Applying social criteria (screens) to investment decisions

green management
Managers consider the impact of their organization on the natural environment

LEADER
difference who made a

Yvon Chouinard is a self-taught blacksmith who, in 1957, started crafting mountain climbing pitons used by himself and other climbing enthusiasts as anchors on risky climbs.[26] His hardware became so popular that he would go on to found the outdoor-clothing company Patagonia. As his company grew, Chouinard realized that everything his company did had an effect—mostly negative—on the environment. Today, he defines the company's mission in eco-driven terms: "To use business to inspire and implement solutions to the environmental crisis." Chouinard has put environmental activism at the forefront of his company. Since 1985, Patagonia has donated 1 percent of its annual sales to grassroots environmental groups and has gotten more than 1,200 companies to follow its lead as part of its "1% for the Planet" group. He recognizes that "every product, no matter how much thought goes into it, has a destructive impact on Earth." But nonetheless, he keeps doing what he does because "it's the right thing to do."

and conserving water. Carpet-maker Mohawk Industries uses recycled plastic containers to produce fiber used in its carpets. Google and Intel initiated an effort to get computer makers and customers to adopt technologies that reduce energy consumption. Paris-based TOTAL, SA, one of the world's largest integrated oil companies, is going green by implementing tough new rules on oil tanker safety and working with groups such as Global Witness and Greenpeace. UPS, the world's largest package delivery company, has done several things—from retrofitting its aircraft with advanced technology and fuel-efficient engines to developing a computer network that efficiently dispatches its fleet of brown trucks to using alternative fuel to run those trucks. Although interesting, these examples don't tell us much about how organizations go green. One model uses the terms *shades of green* to describe the different environmental approaches that organizations may take.[25] (See Exhibit 5-2.)

The first approach, the *legal (or light green) approach,* is simply doing what is required legally. In this approach, which illustrates social obligation, organizations exhibit little environmental sensitivity. They obey laws, rules, and regulations without legal challenge and that's the extent of their being green.

As an organization becomes more sensitive to environmental issues, it may adopt the *market approach,* and respond to environmental preferences of customers. Whatever customers demand in terms of environmentally friendly products will be what the organization provides. For example, DuPont developed a new type of herbicide that helped farmers around the world reduce their annual use of chemicals by more than 45 million pounds. By developing this product, the company was responding to the demands of its customers (farmers) who wanted to minimize the use of chemicals on their crops. This is a good example of social responsiveness, as is the next approach.

In the *stakeholder approach,* an organization works to meet the environmental demands of multiple stakeholders such as employees, suppliers, or community. For instance, Hewlett-Packard has several corporate environmental programs in place for its supply chain (suppliers), product design and product recycling (customers and society), and work operations (employees and community).

Finally, if an organization pursues an *activist (or dark green) approach,* it looks for ways to protect the earth's natural resources. The activist approach reflects the highest degree of environmental sensitivity and illustrates social responsibility. For example, Belgian company Ecover produces ecological cleaning products in a near-zero-emissions factory. This factory (the world's first ecological one) is an engineering marvel with a huge grass roof that keeps things cool in summer and warm in winter and a water treatment system that runs on wind and solar energy. The company chose to build this facility because of its deep commitment to the environment.

EXHIBIT 5-2

Green Approaches

Source: Based on R. E. Freeman, J. Pierce, and R. Dodd, *Shades of Green: Business Ethics and the Environment* (New York: Oxford University Press, 1995).

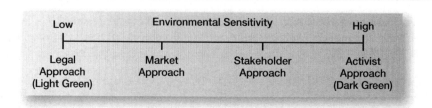

Low	Environmental Sensitivity		High
Legal Approach (Light Green)	Market Approach	Stakeholder Approach	Activist Approach (Dark Green)

At New Zealand's largest wind farm, these wind turbines made by Siemens Windpower generate clean electricity for 100,000 households. One of the most sustainable corporations in the world, Germany-based Siemens pursues an activist approach to the environment from its factories and buildings that consume only small amounts of power to its power plants that generate electricity from the sun. As a good corporate citizen and as a business enterprise, Siemens management and employees are committed to provide products, systems, and technologies that protect the environment, foster human health, and help conserve natural resources.

Evaluating Green Management Actions

As businesses become "greener," they often release detailed reports on their environmental performance. More than 1,300 companies around the globe voluntarily report their efforts in promoting environmental sustainability using the guidelines developed by the Global Reporting Initiative (GRI). These reports, which can be found on the GRI Web site [www.globalreporting.org], describe the numerous green actions of these organizations.

Another way that organizations show their commitment to being green is through pursuing standards developed by the nongovernmental International Organization for Standardization (ISO). Although ISO has developed more than 18,000 international standards, it's probably best known for its ISO 9000 (quality management) and ISO 14000 (environmental management) standards. Organizations that want to become ISO 14000 compliant must develop a total management system for meeting environmental challenges. In other words, it must minimize the effects of its activities on the environment and continually improve its environmental performance. If an organization can meet these standards, it can state that it's ISO 14000 compliant, an accomplishment that organizations in 155 countries have achieved.

One final way to evaluate a company's green actions is to use the Global 100 list of the most sustainable corporations in the world [www.global100.org].[27] To be named to this list, which is announced each year at the renowned World Economic Forum in Davos, Switzerland, a company has displayed a superior ability to effectively manage environmental and social factors. In 2010, the United Kingdom led the list with 21 Global 100 companies. The United States followed with 12, and both Australia and Canada had 9 companies on the list. Some companies on the 2010 list included Siemens (Germany), Pearson PLC (U.K.), Westpac Banking Corp. (Australia), Encana Corp. (Canada), and Starbucks (U.S.).

Managers and Ethical Behavior

5.3

LEARNING OUTCOME
Discuss the factors that lead to ethical and unethical behavior.

One hundred fifty years. That was the maximum prison sentence handed to financier Bernard Madoff, who stole billions of dollars from his clients, by a U.S. district judge who called his crimes "evil." In Britain, which has been characterized by some critics as a "nanny state because of its purported high level of social control and surveillance," a controversy is brewing over the monitoring of garbage cans. Many local governments have installed monitoring chips in municipally distributed trash bans. These chips match cans with owners and can be used to track the weight of the bins, leading some critics to fear that the country is moving to a pay-as-you go system, which they believe will discriminate against large families. A government report says that Iceland, hit hard by both the global economic meltdown and a

pesky volcano, was "victimized by politicians, bankers, and regulators who engaged in acts of extreme negligence."[28] When you hear about such behaviors—especially after the high-profile financial misconduct at companies such as Enron, Worldcom, Lehman Brothers, and others—you might conclude that businesses aren't ethical. Although that's not the case, managers—at all levels, in all areas, in all sizes, and in all kinds of organizations—do face ethical issues and dilemmas. For instance, is it ethical for a sales representative to bribe a purchasing agent as an inducement to buy? Would it make a difference if the bribe came out of the sales rep's commission? Is it ethical for someone to use a company car for private use? How about using company e-mail for personal correspondence or using the company phone to make personal phone calls? What if you managed an employee who worked all weekend on an emergency situation and you told him to take off two days sometime later and mark it down as "sick days" because your company had a clear policy that overtime would not be compensated for any reason?[29] Would that be okay? How will you handle such situations? As managers plan, organize, lead, and control, they must consider ethical dimensions.

What do we mean by **ethics**? We're defining it as the principles, values, and beliefs that define right and wrong decisions and behavior.[30] Many decisions that managers make require them to consider both the process and who's affected by the result.[31] To better understand the ethical issues involved in such decisions, let's look at the factors that determine whether a person acts ethically or unethically.

Factors That Determine Ethical and Unethical Behavior

Whether someone behaves ethically or unethically when faced with an ethical dilemma is influenced by several things: his or her stage of moral development and other moderating variables including individual characteristics, the organization's structural design, the organization's culture, and the intensity of the ethical issue. (See Exhibit 5-3.) People who lack a strong moral sense are much less likely to do the wrong things if they're constrained by rules, policies, job descriptions, or strong cultural norms that disapprove of such behaviors. Conversely, intensely moral individuals can be corrupted by an organizational structure and culture that permits or encourages unethical practices. Let's look more closely at these factors.

STAGE OF MORAL DEVELOPMENT.   Research divides moral development into three levels, each having two stages.[32] At each successive stage, an individual's moral judgment becomes less dependent on outside influences and more internalized.

At the first level, the *preconventional* level, a person's choice between right or wrong is based on personal consequences from outside sources, such as physical punishment, reward, or exchange of favors. At the second level, the *conventional* level, ethical decisions rely on maintaining expected standards and living up to the expectations of others. At the *principled* level, individuals define moral values apart from the authority of the groups to which they belong or society in general. The three levels and six stages are described in Exhibit 5-4.

EXHIBIT 5-3

Factors that Determine Ethical and Unethical Behavior

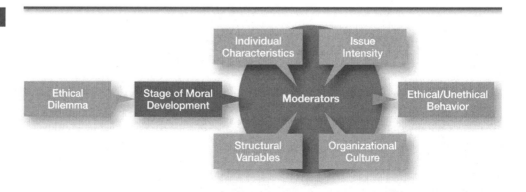

Level	Description of Stage
Principled	6. Following self-chosen ethical principles even if they violate the law
	5. Valuing rights of others and upholding absolute values and rights regardless of the majority's opinion
Conventional	4. Maintaining conventional order by fulfilling obligations to which you have agreed
	3. Living up to what is expected by people close to you
Preconventional	2. Following rules only when doing so is in your immediate interest
	1. Sticking to rules to avoid physical punishment

EXHIBIT 5-4

Stages of Moral Development

Source: Based on L. Kohlberg, "Moral Stages and Moralization: The Cognitive-Development Approach," in T. Lickona (ed.), *Moral Development and Behavior: Theory, Research, and Social Issues* (New York: Holt, Rinehart & Winston, 1976), pp. 34–35.

What can we conclude about moral development?[33] First, people proceed through the six stages sequentially. Second, there is no guarantee of continued moral development. Third, the majority of adults are at Stage 4: They're limited to obeying the rules and will be inclined to behave ethically, although for different reasons. A manager at stage 3 is likely to make decisions based on peer approval; a manager at stage 4 will try to be a "good corporate citizen" by making decisions that respect the organization's rules and procedures; and a stage 5 manager is likely to challenge organizational practices that he or she believes to be wrong.

INDIVIDUAL CHARACTERISTICS. Two individual characteristics—values and personality—play a role in determining whether a person behaves ethically. Each person comes to an organization with a relatively entrenched set of personal **values**, which represent basic convictions about what is right and wrong. Our values develop from a young age based on what we see and hear from parents, teachers, friends, and others. Thus, employees in the same organization often possess very different values.[34] Although *values* and *stage of moral development* may seem similar, they're not. Values are broad and cover a wide range of issues; the stage of moral development is a measure of independence from outside influences.

Two personality variables have been found to influence an individual's actions according to his or her beliefs about what is right or wrong: ego strength and locus of control. **Ego strength** measures the strength of a person's convictions. People with high ego strength are likely to resist impulses to act unethically and instead follow their convictions. That is, individuals high in ego strength are more likely to do what they think is right and be more consistent in their moral judgments and actions than those with low ego strength.

Locus of control is the degree to which people believe they control their own fate. People with an *internal* locus of control believe they control their own destinies. They're more likely to take responsibility for consequences and rely on their own internal standards of right and wrong to guide their behavior. They're also more likely to be consistent in their moral judgments and actions. People with an *external* locus believe what happens to them is due to luck or chance. They're less likely to take personal responsibility for the consequences of their behavior and more likely to rely on external forces.[35]

STRUCTURAL VARIABLES. An organization's structural design can influence whether employees behave ethically. Those structures that minimize ambiguity and uncertainty with

ethics
Principles, values, and beliefs that define what is right and wrong behavior

values
Basic convictions about what is right and wrong

ego strength
A personality measure of the strength of a person's convictions

locus of control
A personality attribute that measures the degree to which people believe they control their own fate

Let's Get Real

F 2 F

My company's values include
supporting local nonprofit organizations and groups by donating leftover food and gift certificates.

formal rules and regulations and those that continuously remind employees of what is ethical are more likely to encourage ethical behavior. Other structural variables that influence ethical choices include goals, performance appraisal systems, and reward allocation procedures.

Although many organizations use goals to guide and motivate employees, those goals can create some unexpected problems. One study found that people who don't reach set goals are more likely to engage in unethical behavior, even if they do or don't have economic incentives to do so. The researchers concluded that "goal setting can lead to unethical behavior."[36] Examples of such behaviors abound—from companies shipping unfinished products just to reach sales goals or "managing earnings" to meet financial analysts' expectations, to schools excluding certain groups of students when reporting standardized test scores to make their "pass" rate look better.[37]

An organization's performance appraisal system also can influence ethical behavior. Some systems focus exclusively on outcomes, while others evaluate means as well as ends. When employees are evaluated only on outcomes, they may be pressured to do whatever is necessary to look good on the outcomes, and not be concerned with how they got those results. Research suggests that "success may serve to excuse unethical behaviors."[38] The danger of such thinking is that if managers are more lenient in correcting unethical behaviors of successful employees, other employees will model their behavior on what they see.

Closely related to the organization's appraisal system is how rewards are allocated. The more that rewards or punishment depend on specific goal outcomes, the more employees are pressured to do whatever they must to reach those goals, perhaps to the point of compromising their ethical standards.

ORGANIZATION'S CULTURE. As Exhibit 5-3 showed, the content and strength of an organization's culture also influence ethical behavior.[40] We learned in Chapter 2 that an organization's culture consists of the shared organizational values. These values reflect what the organization stands for and what it believes in as well as create an environment that influences employee behavior ethically or unethically. When it comes to ethical behavior, a culture most likely to encourage high ethical standards is one that's high in risk tolerance, control, and conflict tolerance. Employees in such a culture are encouraged to be aggressive and innovative, are aware that unethical practices will be discovered, and feel free to openly challenge expectations they consider to be unrealistic or personally undesirable.

Because shared values can be powerful influences, many organizations are using **values-based management**, in which the organization's values guide employees in the way they do their jobs. For instance, Timberland is an example of a company using values-based management. With a simple statement, "Make It Better," employees at Timberland know what's expected and valued; that is, find ways to "make it better"—whether it's creating quality products for customers, performing community service activities, designing employee training programs, or figuring out ways to make the company's packaging more environmentally friendly. As CEO Jeffrey Swartz says on the company's Web site, "Everything we do at Timberland grows out of our relentless pursuit to find a way to make it better." At Corning, one of the core values guiding employee behavior is integrity. Employees are expected to work in ways that are honest, decent, and fair. Timberland and Corning aren't alone in their use of values-based management. A survey of global companies found that a large number (more than 89%) said they had a written corporate values statement.[41] This survey also found that most of the companies believed that their values influenced relationships and reputation, the top-performing companies consciously connected values with the way employees did their work, and top managers were important to reinforcing the importance of the values throughout the organization.

Thus, an organization's managers do play an important role here. They're responsible for creating an environment that encourages employees to embrace the culture and the desired values as they do their jobs. In fact, research shows that the behavior of managers is the single most important influence on an individual's decision to act ethically or unethically.[42] People look to see what those in authority are doing and use that as a benchmark for acceptable practices and expectations.

Finally, as we discussed in Chapter 2, a strong culture exerts more influence on employees than a weak one. If a culture is strong and supports high ethical standards, it has a powerful and positive influence on the decision to act ethically or unethically. For example, IBM has a strong culture that has long stressed ethical dealings with customers, employees, business partners, and communities.[43] To reinforce the importance of ethical behaviors, the company developed an explicitly detailed set of guidelines for business conduct and ethics. And the penalty for violating the guidelines: disciplinary actions including dismissal. IBM's managers continually reinforce the importance of ethical behavior and reinforce the fact that a person's actions and decisions are important to the way the organization is viewed.

ISSUE INTENSITY.   A student who would never consider breaking into an instructor's office to steal an accounting exam doesn't think twice about asking a friend who took the same course from the same instructor last semester what questions were on an exam. Similarly, a manager might think nothing about taking home a few office supplies yet be highly concerned about the possible embezzlement of company funds. These examples illustrate the final factor that influences ethical behavior: the intensity of the ethical issue itself.[44]

As Exhibit 5-5 shows, six characteristics determine issue intensity or how important an ethical issue is to an individual: greatness of harm, consensus of wrong, probability of harm, immediacy of consequences, proximity to victim(s), and concentration of effect. These factors suggest that the larger the number of people harmed, the more agreement that the action is wrong, the greater the likelihood that the action will cause harm, the more immediately that the consequences of the action will be felt, the closer the person feels to the victim(s), and the more concentrated the effect of the action on the victim(s), the greater the issue intensity or importance. When an ethical issue is important, employees are more likely to behave ethically.

Ethics in an International Context

Are ethical standards universal? Although some common moral beliefs exist, social and cultural differences between countries are important factors that determine ethical and unethical

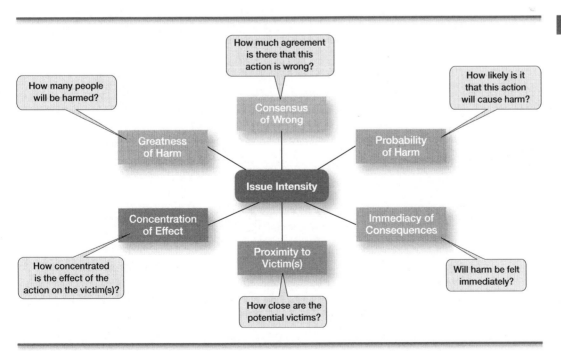

EXHIBIT 5-5

Issue Intensity

values-based management
The organization's values guide employees in
the way they do their jobs

behavior.[45] For example, the manager of a Mexican firm bribes several high-ranking government officials in Mexico City to secure a profitable government contract. Although this business practice is acceptable in Mexico, it's unethical (and illegal) in the United States.

Should Coca-Cola employees in Saudi Arabia adhere to U.S. ethical standards, or should they follow local standards of acceptable behavior? If Airbus (a European company) pays a "broker's fee" to an intermediary to get a major contract with a Middle Eastern airline, should Boeing be restricted from doing the same because such practices are considered improper in the United States? (Note: In the United Kingdom, the Law Commission, a governmental advisory body, has said that bribing officials in foreign countries should be a criminal offense. It said that claims of "it's local custom" should not be a reason for allowing it.[46]) Recently, British defense giant BAE, which has been the target of various bribery and corruption allegations, was ordered to "submit to the supervision of an ethics monitor and pay nearly $500 million to resolve the corruption allegations."[47]

In the case of payments to influence foreign officials or politicians, U.S. mangers are guided by the Foreign Corrupt Practices Act (FCPA), which makes it illegal to knowingly corrupt a foreign official. However, even this law doesn't always reduce ethical dilemmas to black and white. In some countries, government bureaucrat salaries are low because custom dictates that they receive small payments from those they serve. Payoffs to these bureaucrats "grease the machinery" and ensure that things get done. The FCPA does not expressly prohibit small payoffs to foreign government employees whose duties are primarily administrative or clerical *when* such payoffs are an accepted part of doing business in that country. Any action other than this is illegal. In 2009, the U.S. Department of Justice brought 11 FCPA enforcement actions against corporations and 33 against individuals.[48]

It's important for individual managers working in foreign cultures to recognize the social, cultural, and political-legal influences on what is appropriate and acceptable behavior.[49] And international businesses must clarify their ethical guidelines so that employees know what's expected of them while working in a foreign location, which adds another dimension to making ethical judgments.

Another guide to being ethical in international business is the Global Compact, which is a document created by the United Nations outlining principles for doing business globally in the areas of human rights, labor, the environment, and anticorruption. (See Exhibit 5-6.)

EXHIBIT 5-6

Ten Principles of the UN Global Compact

Human Rights

Principle 1:	Support and respect the protection of international human rights within their sphere of influence.
Principle 2:	Make sure business corporations are not complicit in human rights abuses.

Labor Standards

Principle 3:	Freedom of association and the effective recognition of the right to collective bargaining.
Principle 4:	The elimination of all forms of forced and compulsory labor.
Principle 5:	The effective abolition of child labor.
Principle 6:	The elimination of discrimination in respect to employment and occupation.

Environment

Principle 7:	Support a precautionary approach to environmental challenges.
Principle 8:	Undertake initiatives to promote greater environmental responsibility.
Principle 9:	Encourage the development and diffusion of environmentally friendly technologies.

Anti-Corruption

Principle 10:	Businesses should work against corruption in all its forms, including extortion and bribery.

Source: Courtesy of UN Global Compact.

More than 7,700 corporate participants and stakeholders from over 130 countries have signed the Compact, making it the world's largest voluntary corporate citizenship initiative.[50] The goal of the Compact is a more sustainable and inclusive global economy. Organizations making this commitment do so because they believe that the world business community plays a significant role in improving economic and social conditions. In addition, the Organization for Economic Co-operation and Development (OECD) has made fighting bribery and corruption in international business a high priority. The centerpiece of its efforts is the Anti-Bribery Convention (or set of rules and guidelines), which was the first global instrument to combat corruption in cross-border business deals. To date, significant gains have been made in fighting corruption in the 38 countries that have ratified it.[51]

Encouraging Ethical Behavior

5.4

LEARNING OUTCOME

Describe management's role in encouraging ethical behavior.

At a Senate hearing exploring the accusations that Wall Street firm Goldman Sachs deceived its clients during the housing-market meltdown, Arizona senator John McCain said, "I don't know if Goldman has done anything illegal, but there's no doubt their behavior was unethical."[52] You have to wonder what the firm's managers were thinking or doing while such ethically questionable decisions and actions were occurring.

Managers can do a number of things if they're serious about encouraging ethical behaviors—hire employees with high ethical standards, establish codes of ethics, lead by example, and so forth. By themselves, such actions won't have much of an impact. But if an organization has a comprehensive ethics program in place, it can potentially improve an organization's ethical climate. The key variable, however, is *potentially*. There are no guarantees that a well-designed ethics program will lead to the desired outcome. Sometimes corporate ethics programs are little more than public relations gestures that do little to influence managers and employees. For instance, Sears had a long history of encouraging ethical business practices through its corporate Office of Ethics and Business Practices. However, its ethics programs didn't stop managers from illegally trying to collect payments from bankrupt charge account holders or from routinely deceiving automotive service center customers into thinking they needed unnecessary repairs. Even Enron, often referred to as the "poster child" of corporate wrongdoing, outlined values in its final annual report that most would consider ethical—communication, respect, integrity, and excellence. Yet the way top managers behaved didn't reflect those values at all.[53] Let's look at some specific ways that managers can encourage ethical behavior and create a comprehensive ethics program.

Employee Selection

The selection process (interviews, tests, background checks, and so forth) should be viewed as an opportunity to learn about an individual's level of moral development, personal values, ego strength, and locus of control.[54] However, a carefully designed selection process isn't foolproof and, even under the best circumstances, individuals with questionable standards of right and wrong may be hired. Such an issue can be overcome if other ethics controls are in place.

Codes of Ethics and Decision Rules

George David, former CEO and chairman of Hartford, Connecticut-based United Technologies Corporation, believed in the power of a code of ethics. That's why UTC has always had one that was quite explicit and detailed. Employees know the behavioral expectations, especially when it comes to ethics. UBS AG, the Swiss bank, also has an explicit employee code crafted by CEO Oswald Grübel that bans staff from helping clients cheat on their taxes.[55] However, not all organizations have such explicit ethical guidelines.

Uncertainty about what is and is not ethical can be a problem for employees. A **code of ethics**, a formal statement of an organization's values and the ethical rules it expects employees to follow, is a popular choice for reducing that ambiguity. Research shows that 97 percent of organizations with more than 10,000 employees have a written code of ethics. Even in smaller organizations, nearly 93 percent have one.[56] And codes of ethics are becoming more popular globally. Research by the Institute for Global Ethics says that shared values such as honesty, fairness, respect, responsibility, and caring are pretty much universally embraced.[57] In addition, a survey of businesses in 22 countries found that 78 percent have formally stated ethics standards and codes of ethics; and more than 85 percent of *Fortune* Global 200 companies have a business code of ethics.[58]

What should a code of ethics look like? It should be specific enough to show employees the spirit in which they're supposed to do things yet loose enough to allow for freedom of judgment. A survey of companies' codes of ethics found their content tended to fall into three categories as shown in Exhibit 5-7.[59]

Unfortunately, codes of ethics may not work as well as we think they should. A survey of employees in U.S. businesses found that 49 percent of those surveyed had observed ethical or legal violations in the previous 12 months including such things as conflicts of interest,

---

EXHIBIT 5-7

Codes of Ethics

Cluster 1. Be a Dependable Organizational Citizen

1. Comply with safety, health, and security regulations.
2. Demonstrate courtesy, respect, honesty, and fairness.
3. Illegal drugs and alcohol at work are prohibited.
4. Manage personal finances well.
5. Exhibit good attendance and punctuality.
6. Follow directives of supervisors.
7. Do not use abusive language.
8. Dress in business attire.
9. Firearms at work are prohibited.

Cluster 2. Do Not Do Anything Unlawful or Improper That Will Harm the Organization

1. Conduct business in compliance with all laws.
2. Payments for unlawful purposes are prohibited.
3. Bribes are prohibited.
4. Avoid outside activities that impair duties.
5. Maintain confidentiality of records.
6. Comply with all antitrust and trade regulations.
7. Comply with all accounting rules and controls.
8. Do not use company property for personal benefit.
9. Employees are personally accountable for company funds.
10. Do not propagate false or misleading information.
11. Make decisions without regard for personal gain.

Cluster 3. Be Good to Customers

1. Convey true claims in product advertisements.
2. Perform assigned duties to the best of your ability.
3. Provide products and services of the highest quality.

Source: F. R. David, "An Empirical Study of Codes of Business Ethics: A Strategic Perspective," paper presented at the 48th Annual Academy of Management Conference, Anaheim, California, August 1988. Used with permission of Fred David.

EXHIBIT 5-8

A Process for Addressing Ethical Dilemmas

Step 1: What is the **ethical dilemma**?

Step 2: Who are the **affected stakeholders**?

Step 3: What **personal**, **organizational**, and **external factors** are important in this decision?

Step 4: What are possible **alternatives**?

Step 5: What is my **decision** and how will I act on it?

abusive or intimidating behavior, and lying to employees. And 37 percent of those employees didn't report observed misconduct.[60] Does this mean that codes of ethics shouldn't be developed? No. However, in doing so, managers should use these suggestions:[61]

1. Organizational leaders should model appropriate behavior and reward those who act ethically.
2. All managers should continually reaffirm the importance of the ethics code and consistently discipline those who break it.
3. The organization's stakeholders (employees, customers, and so forth) should be considered as an ethics code is developed or improved.
4. Managers should communicate and reinforce the ethics code regularly.
5. Managers should use the five-step process (see Exhibit 5-8) to guide employees when faced with ethical dilemmas.

Leadership

In 2007, Peter Löscher was hired as CEO of German company Siemens to clean up a global bribery scandal that cost the company a record-setting $1.34 billion in fines. His approach: "Stick to your principles. Have a clear ethical north. Be trusted and be the role model of your company . . . true leaders have a set of core values they publicly commit to and live by in good times and bad."[62] Doing business ethically requires a commitment from top managers. Why? Because they're the ones who uphold the shared values and set the cultural tone. They're role models in terms of both words and actions, though what they *do* is far more important than what they *say*. If top managers, for example, take company resources for their personal use, inflate their expense accounts, or give favored treatment to friends, they imply that such behavior is acceptable for all employees.

Top managers also set the tone by their reward and punishment practices. The choices of whom and what are rewarded with pay increases and promotions send a strong signal to employees. As we said earlier, when an employee is rewarded for achieving impressive results in an ethically questionable manner, it indicates to others that those ways are acceptable. When an employee does something unethical, managers must punish the offender and publicize the fact by making the outcome visible to everyone in the organization. This practice sends a message that doing wrong has a price and it's not in employees' best interests to act unethically!

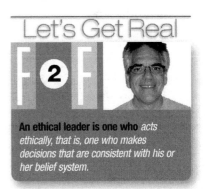

Let's Get Real

An ethical leader is one who *acts ethically, that is, one who makes decisions that are consistent with his or her belief system.*

Job Goals and Performance Appraisal

Employees in three Internal Revenue Service offices were found in the bathrooms flushing tax returns and other related documents down the toilets. When questioned, they openly admitted doing it, but offered an interesting explanation for their behavior. The employees' supervisors had been pressuring them to complete more work in less time. If the piles of tax returns weren't processed and moved off their desks more quickly, they were told their performance reviews and salary raises would be adversely affected. Frustrated by few resources

code of ethics
A formal statement of an organization's primary values and the ethical rules it expects its employees to follow

and an overworked computer system, the employees decided to "flush away" the paperwork on their desks. Although these employees knew what they did was wrong, it illustrates how powerful unrealistic goals and performance appraisals can be.[63] Under the stress of unrealistic goals, otherwise ethical employees may feel they have no choice but to do whatever is necessary to meet those goals. Also, goal achievement is usually a key issue in performance appraisal. If performance appraisals focus only on economic goals, ends will begin to justify means. To encourage ethical behavior, both ends *and* means should be evaluated. For example, a manager's annual review of employees might include a point-by-point evaluation of how their decisions measured up against the company's code of ethics as well as how well goals were met.

Ethics Training

More organizations are setting up seminars, workshops, and similar ethics training programs to encourage ethical behavior. Such training programs aren't without controversy as the primary concern is whether ethics can be taught. Critics stress that the effort is pointless because people establish their individual value systems when they're young. Proponents note, however, several studies have shown that values can be learned after early childhood. In addition, they cite evidence that shows that teaching ethical problem solving can make an actual difference in ethical behaviors;[64] that training has increased individuals' level of moral development;[65] and that, if nothing else, ethics training increases awareness of ethical issues in business.[66]

How can ethics be taught? Let's look at an example involving global defense contractor Lockheed Martin, one of the pioneers in the case-based approach to ethics training.[67] Lockheed Martin's employees take annual ethics training courses delivered by their managers. The main focus of these short courses is Lockheed Martin–specific case situations "chosen for their relevance to department or job-specific issues." In each department, employee teams review and discuss the cases and then apply an "Ethics Meter" to "rate whether the real-life decisions were ethical, unethical, or somewhere in between." For example, one of the possible ratings on the Ethics Meter, "On Thin Ice," is explained as "bordering on unethical and should raise a red flag." After the teams have applied their ratings, managers lead discussions about the ratings and examine "which of the company's core ethics principles were applied or ignored in the cases." In addition to its ethics training, Lockheed Martin has a widely used written code of ethics, an ethics helpline that employees can call for guidance on ethical issues, and ethics officers based in the company's various business units.

Cisco Systems' ethics training program teaches employees such as the software engineers in this photo how to deal with ethical problems they encounter every day. Based on its own risk analysis and designed to fit the company's corporate culture, the training parodies the *American Idol* TV show. The Web-based program shows cartoon contestants singing about various ethical workplace scenarios included in Cisco's Code of Business Conduct and then poses questions to employees as to which judge's answer they agree with. Employees can provide feedback, see how other employees respond, and view the official Cisco answer to help them learn how to make good ethical decisions that apply to their day-to-day jobs.

Independent Social Audits

The fear of being caught can be an important deterrent to unethical behavior. Independent social audits, which evaluate decisions and management practices in terms of the organization's code of ethics, increase that likelihood. Such audits can be regular evaluations or they can occur randomly with no prior announcement. An effective ethics program probably needs both. To maintain integrity, auditors should be responsible to the company's board of directors and present their findings directly to the board. This arrangement gives the auditors clout and lessens the opportunity for retaliation from those being audited. Because the Sarbanes-Oxley Act holds businesses to more rigorous standards of financial disclosure and corporate governance, more organizations are finding the idea of independent social audits appealing. As the publisher of *Business Ethics* magazine stated, "The debate has shifted from *whether* to be ethical to *how* to be ethical."[68]

Protective Mechanisms

Employees who face ethical dilemmas need protective mechanisms so they can do what's right without fear of reprimand. An organization might designate ethical counselors for employees facing an ethics dilemma. These advisors also might advocate the ethically "right" alternatives. Other organizations have appointed ethics officers who design, direct, and modify the organization's ethics programs as needed.[69] The Ethics and Compliance Officer Association is the world's largest group of ethics and compliance practitioners with a total membership topping 1,100 (including more than half of the *Fortune* 100 companies) and covering several countries including, among others, the United States, Germany, India, Japan, and Canada.[70]

Social Responsibility and Ethics Issues in Today's World

5.5

LEARNING OUTCOME
Discuss current social responsibility and ethics issues.

Today's managers continue to face challenges in being socially responsible and ethical. Next we examine three current issues: managing ethical lapses and social irresponsibility, social entrepreneurship, and promoting positive social change.

Managing Ethical Lapses and Social Irresponsibility

Even after public outrage over the Enron-era misdeeds, irresponsible and unethical practices by managers in all kinds of organizations haven't gone away, as you've observed with some of the questionable behaviors that took place at financial services firms such as Goldman Sachs and Lehman Brothers. But what's more alarming is what's going on "in the trenches" in offices, warehouses, and stores. One survey reported that among 5,000 employees: 45 percent admitted falling asleep at work; 22 percent said they spread a rumor about a coworker; 18 percent said they snooped after hours; and 2 percent said they took credit for someone else's work.[71]

Unfortunately, it's not just at work that we see such behaviors. They're prevalent throughout society. Studies conducted by the Center for Academic Integrity showed that 26 percent of college and university business majors admitted to "serious cheating" on exams and 54 percent admitted to cheating on written assignments. But business students weren't the worst cheaters—that distinction belonged to journalism majors, of whom 27 percent said they had cheated.[72] And a survey by Students in Free Enterprise (SIFE) found that only 19 percent of students would report a classmate who cheated.[73] But even more frightening is what today's teenagers say is "acceptable." In a survey, 23 percent said they thought violence toward another person is acceptable on some level.[74] What do such statistics say about what managers may have to deal with in the future? It's not too far-fetched to say that organizations may have difficulty upholding high ethical standards when their future employees so readily accept unethical behavior.

What can managers do? Two actions seem to be particularly important: ethical leadership and protecting those who report wrongdoing.

ETHICAL LEADERSHIP.   Not long after Herb Baum took over as CEO of Dial Corporation, he got a call from Reuben Mark, the CEO of competitor Colgate-Palmolive, who told him he had a copy of Dial's strategic marketing plan that had come from a former Dial salesperson who recently had joined Colgate-Palmolive. Mark told Baum that he had not looked at it, didn't intend to look at, and was returning it. In addition, he himself was going to deal appropriately with the new salesperson.[75] As this example illustrates, managers must provide ethical leadership. As we said earlier, what managers *do* has a strong influence on employees' decisions whether to behave ethically. When managers cheat, lie, steal, manipulate, take advantage of situations or people, or treat others unfairly, what kind of signal are they sending to employees (or other stakeholders)? Probably not the one they want to send. Exhibit 5-9 gives some suggestions on how managers can provide ethical leadership.

PROTECTION OF EMPLOYEES WHO RAISE ETHICAL ISSUES.   What would you do if you saw other employees doing something illegal, immoral, or unethical? Would you step forward? Many of us wouldn't because of the perceived risks. That's why it's important for managers to assure employees who raise ethical concerns or issues that they will face no personal or career risks. These individuals, often called **whistle-blowers**, can be a key part of any company's ethics program. For example, Sherron Watkins, who was a vice president at Enron, clearly outlined her concerns about the company's accounting practices in a letter to chairman Ken Lay. Her statement that, "I am incredibly nervous that we will implode in a wave of accounting scandals" couldn't have been more prophetic.[76] However, surveys show that most observers of wrongdoing don't report it and that's the attitude managers have to address.[77] How can they protect employees so they're willing to step up if they see unethical or illegal things occurring?

One way is to set up toll-free ethics hotlines. For instance, Dell has an ethics hotline that employees can call anonymously to report infractions that the company will then investigate.[78] In addition, managers need to create a culture where bad news can be heard and acted on before it's too late. Michael Josephson, founder of the Josephson Institute of Ethics [www.josephsoninstitute.org] said, "It is absolutely and unequivocally important to establish a culture where it is possible for employees to complain and protest and to get heard."[79] Even if some whistle-blowers have a personal agenda they're pursuing, it's important to take them seriously. Finally, the federal legislation Sarbanes-Oxley offers some legal protection. Any manager who retaliates against an employee for reporting violations faces a stiff penalty: a 10-year jail sentence.[80] Unfortunately, despite this protection, hundreds of employees who have stepped forward and revealed wrongdoings at their companies have been fired or let go from their jobs.[81] So at the present time, it's not a perfect solution, but is a step in the right direction.

Social Entrepreneurship

The world's social problems are many and viable solutions are few. But numerous people and organizations are trying to do something. For instance, Reed Paget, founder and CEO

EXHIBIT 5-9
 	
Being an Ethical Leader
	• Be a good role model by being ethical and honest.
	
	   • Tell the truth always.
	
	   • Don't hide or manipulate information.
	
	   • Be willing to admit your failures.
	
	• Share your personal values by regularly communicating them to employees.
	
	• Stress the organization's or team's important shared values.
	
	• Use the reward system to hold everyone accountable to the values.

of British bottled water company Belu, made his company the world's first to become carbon-neutral. Its bottles are made from corn and can be composted into soil.
Also, Belu's profits go toward projects that bring clean
water to parts of the world that lack access to it. Paget
has chosen to pursue a purpose as well as a profit.[82] He
is an example of a **social entrepreneur**, an individual
or organization who seeks out opportunities to improve
society by using practical, innovative, and sustainable
approaches.[83] "What business entrepreneurs are to the
economy, social entrepreneurs are to social change."[84]
Social entrepreneurs want to make the world a better
place and have a driving passion to make that happen.
For example, AgSquared aims to help small farmers,
who make up 90 percent of the farms in the United States, keep better track of critical
information such as basic accounting of seeds, soil data and weather mapping, and even
best practices from the farm community.[85] Also, social entrepreneurs use creativity and
ingenuity to solve problems. For instance, Seattle-based PATH (Program for Appropriate
Technology in Health) is an international nonprofit organization that uses low-cost technology to provide needed health-care solutions for poor, developing countries. By collaborating with public groups and for-profit businesses, PATH has developed simple life-saving
solutions, such as clean birthing kits, credit-card sized lab test kits, and disposable vaccina-
tion syringes that can't be reused. PATH has pioneered innovative approaches to solving
global medical problems.[86]

Matt Flannery (right) and Premel Shah
are trying to do something about the
world's social problems. Social
entrepreneurs Flannery, cofounder and
CEO, and Shah, president, operate their
nonprofit organization Kiva.org by
combining microfinance with the
Internet to create a global community of
lenders for entrepreneurs in developing
nations and the United States. Kiva's
mission is to connect people, through
lending, for the sake of alleviating
poverty. Practical and innovative, Kiva
promotes partnership relationships that
are characterized by mutual dignity and
respect rather than benefactor
relationships.

What can we learn from these social entrepreneurs? Although many organizations have
committed to doing business ethically and responsibly, perhaps there is more they can do,
as these social entrepreneurs show. Maybe, as in the case of PATH, it's simply a matter of
business organizations collaborating with public groups or nonprofit organizations to address a social issue. Or maybe, as in the case of AgSquared, it's providing expertise where
needed. Or it may involve nurturing individuals who passionately and unwaveringly believe
they have an idea that could make the world a better place and simply need the organizational
support to pursue it.

Businesses Promoting Positive Social Change

Since 1946, Target has contributed 5 percent of its annual income to support community
needs, an amount that adds up to more than $3 million a week. And it's not alone in those
efforts. "Over the past two decades, a growing number of corporations, both within and beyond the United States, have been engaging in activities that promote positive social
change."[87] Businesses can do this in a couple of ways: through corporate philanthropy and
through employee volunteering efforts.

CORPORATE PHILANTHROPY.   Corporate philanthropy can be an effective way for companies to address societal problems.[88] For instance, the breast cancer "pink" campaign
and the global AIDS Red campaign (started by Bono) are ways that companies support
social causes.[89] Many organizations also donate money to various causes that employees
and customers care about. In 2008 (latest numbers available), the three largest cash
givers—Walmart, Bank of America, and ExxonMobil—donated more than $734 million.[90]
Others have funded their own foundations to support various social issues. For example,
Google's foundation—called DotOrg by its employees—has about $2 billion in assets that

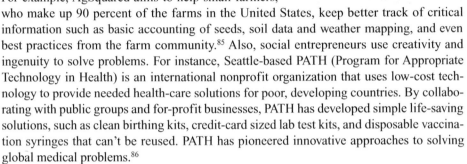

whistle-blower
Individuals who raise ethical concerns or issues
to others

social entrepreneur
An individual or organization who seeks out
opportunities to improve society by using
practical, innovative, and sustainable
approaches

it will use to support five areas: developing systems to help predict and prevent disease pandemics, empowering the poor with information about public services, creating jobs by investing in small and midsized businesses in the developing world, accelerating the commercialization of plug-in cars, and making renewable energy cheaper than coal.[91]

EMPLOYEE VOLUNTEERING EFFORTS.   Employee volunteering is another popular way for businesses to be involved in promoting social change. For instance, Molson-Coors' eleven-member executive team spent a full day at their annual team-building retreat building a house in Las Vegas with Habitat for Humanity. PricewaterhouseCoopers employees renovated an abandoned school in Newark, New Jersey. Every Wachovia employee is given six paid days off from work each year to volunteer in his or her community. Other businesses are encouraging their employees to volunteer in various ways. The Committee to Encourage Corporate Philanthropy says that more than 90 percent of its members had volunteer programs and almost half encouraged volunteerism by providing paid time off or by creating volunteer events.[92] Many businesses have found that such efforts not only benefit communities, but enhance employees' work efforts and motivation.

What Would You Do?

Owner
**The Stone Oven
Bakery & Café
Cleveland, OH**

Let's Get Real:

My Response *to A Manager's Dilemma, page 152*

TOMS is doing a great act of charity and kindness. The challenge is to stay profitable while continuing to do good humanitarian work. Presumably, TOMS shoes are priced somewhat higher than those of their competition in order to pay for the donated shoes. The question then becomes how much more would people be willing to pay for a pair of shoes knowing that they are helping someone on the other side of the globe. 10 percent? 20 percent?

The answer to this question depends on the market(s) that TOMS serves. Certainly, a globally conscious person would be willing to pay the higher price. The company should therefore direct their marketing and advertising efforts toward this sector of the market. The focus, of course, must be on educating the consumer on the importance of sending shoes to South America and the good that results from this act of generosity.

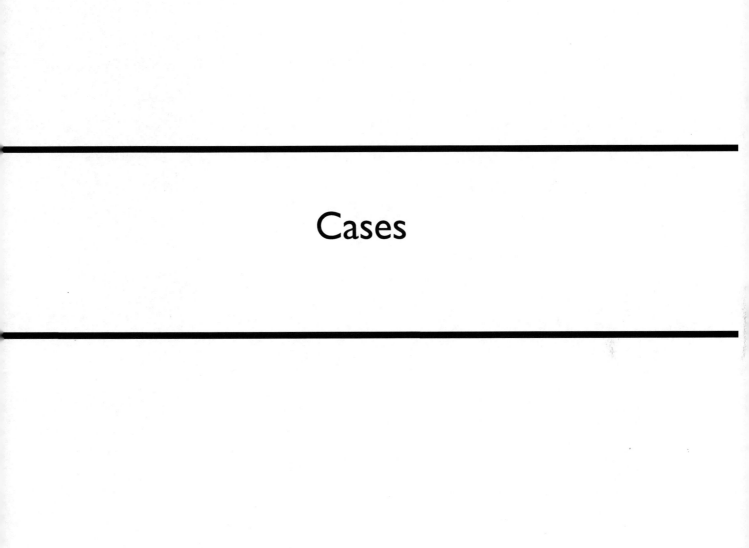

Cases

CASE APPLICATION **1**
Lessons from Lehman Brothers: Will We Ever Learn?

On September 15, 2008, financial services firm Lehman Brothers filed for bankruptcy with the U.S. Bankruptcy Court in the Southern District of New York.[95] That action—the largest Chapter 11 filing in financial history—unleashed a "crisis of confidence that threw financial markets worldwide into turmoil, sparking the worst crisis since the Great Depression." The fall of this Wall Street icon is, unfortunately, not a new one, as we've seen in the stories of Enron, WorldCom, and others. In a report released by bankruptcy court-appointed examiner Anton Valukas, Lehman executives and the firm's auditor, Ernst & Young, were lambasted for actions that led to the firm's collapse. He said, "Lehman repeatedly exceeded its own internal risk limits and controls, and a wide range of bad calls by its management led to the bank's failure." Let's look behind the scenes at some of the issues.

One of the major problems at Lehman was its culture and reward structure. Excessive risk taking by employees was openly lauded and rewarded handsomely. Individuals making questionable deals were hailed and treated as "conquering heroes." On the other hand, anyone who questioned decisions was often ignored or overruled. For instance, Oliver Budde, who served as an associate general counsel at Lehman for nine years, was responsible for preparing the firm's public filings on executive compensation. Infuriated by what he felt was the firm's "intentional under-representation of how much top executives were paid," Budde argued with his bosses for years about that matter, to no avail. Then, one time he objected to a tax deal that an outside accounting firm had proposed to lower medical insurance costs saying, "My gut feeling was that this was just reshuffling some papers to get an expense off the balance sheet. It was not the right thing, and I told them." However, Budde's bosses disagreed and okayed the deal.

Another problem at Lehman was the firm's top leadership. Valukas's report was highly critical of Lehman's executives who "should have done more, done better." He pointed out that the executives made the company's problems worse by their conduct, which ranged from "serious but nonculpable errors of business judgment to actionable balance sheet manipulation." Valukas went on to say that "former chief executive Richard Fuld was at least grossly negligent in causing Lehman to file misleading periodic reports." These reports were part of an accounting device called "Repo 105." Lehman used this device to get some $50 billion of undesirable assets off its balance sheet at the end of the first and second quarters of 2008, instead of selling those assets at a loss. The examiner's report "included e-mails from Lehman's global financial controller confirming that the only purpose or motive for Repo 105 transactions was reduction in the balance sheet, adding that there was no substance to the transactions." Lehman's auditor was aware of the use of Repo 105 but did not challenge or question it. Sufficient evidence indicated that Fuld knew about the use of it as well; however, he signed off on quarterly reports that made no mention of it. Fuld's attorney said, "Mr. Fuld did not know what these

"Greed" and "Crooks" are a sampling of comments recorded on a rendering of Lehman's chief executive Richard Fuld by artist Geoffrey Raymond, who placed his painting outside of Lehman's New York City offices and handed out markers to employees and pedestrians so they could write a message regarding the firm's announcement that it was filing for bankruptcy.

transactions were—he didn't structure or negotiate them, nor was he aware of their accounting treatment." A spokesperson from Ernst & Young (the auditor) said that, "Lehman's bankruptcy was the result of a series of unprecedented adverse events in the financial markets."

Discussion Questions

1. Describe the situation at Lehman Brothers from an ethics perspective. What's your opinion of what happened here?

2. What was the culture at Lehman Brothers like? How did this culture contribute to the company's downfall?

3. What role did Lehman's executives play in the company's collapse? Were they being responsible and ethical? Discuss.

4. Could anything have been done differently at Lehman Brothers to prevent what happened? Explain.

5. After all the public uproar over Enron and then the passage of the Sarbanes-Oxley Act to protect shareholders, why do you think we still continue to see these types of situations? Is it unreasonable to expect that businesses can and should act ethically?

CASE APPLICATION 2
Green Up on Aisle Two

It's probably the last company that you'd think of as going green.[96] As the world's largest retailer with more than 8,400 stores globally, Walmart moves massive amounts of products and uses massive amounts of power and other resources to operate its business. But it's also striving to transform itself into a company that's seen as environmentally friendly. That's why the company's announcement that it would cut some 20 million metric tons of greenhouse gas emissions from its supply chain—the equivalent of removing more than 3.8 million cars from the road for a year—got widespread attention. This announcement came a few months after the company said that it would be creating a sustainability index of just how green its products are.

The first part of Walmart's three-phase plan was getting information from its more than 100,000 suppliers using a 15-question survey about their greenhouse gas emissions, water and solid waste reduction efforts, and other details about business practices. That information was received by October 2009, and the second-phase process of entering it into a massive database began. The third phase involves getting all that data eventually condensed into an easily understood universal rating system, similar to a nutrition label but focused on details about environmental and social sustainability. However, it's likely that this effort won't be complete until 2013.

This isn't the company's first push toward being green. Walmart has started many environmental initiatives in recent years including improving the efficiency of its truck fleet and working with 20th Century Fox Home Entertainment, which produces DVDs, to cut greenhouse gas emissions by eliminating the plastic knob in the center of its CD cases. The most difficult part of this latest green initiative has been persuading its suppliers to spend the time and money tracking and lessening their environmental impact. Essentially, suppliers are being asked to "examine the carbon lifecycle of their products, from the raw materials used in manufacturing all the way through to the recycling phase." Although supplier participation was not mandatory, Walmart made it clear that it was interested in doing business only with suppliers that shared its goals. The company is also collaborating with organizations such as the Environmental Defense Fund, ClearCarbon, the Applied Sustainability Center at the University of Arkansas, and the Carbon Disclosure Project. These groups will advise Walmart and its suppliers and help in evaluating and measuring reductions.

MANAGEMENT IN THE NEWS

Trade-offs in the moral maze

Adam Jones

In today's climate of corporate scandal and recrimination, there is a tendency to look at business ethics in black or white terms. Not in Michel Anteby's classroom. An assistant professor of organisational behaviour at Harvard Business School, he specialises in looking at moral grey areas in the workplace. Building on an innovative study of an aerospace factory he carried out in France, Professor Anteby is adept at exploring situations in which employees break house rules with the tacit or explicit agreement of their supervisors.

Such shady behaviour can sometimes benefit an organisation, he argues – a conclusion that evades the polarised, good or evil certainties of the post-Madoff age. The aerospace study examined a tradition found in many factories in which craftsmen pinched raw materials from their employer in order to make objects for personal use in company time, using company tools. The objects they made at the factory – retirement gifts, lamps, stools, chandeliers – were examples of what the French call perruques, which is also the word for 'wig' (the two usages have concealment in common).

> 'Under the eye of supervisors, the more desirable discounted items are removed from the shop floor and hidden for purchase later.'

Higher-ups tended to turn a blind eye because, far from damaging the company, the perruques helped to make the workforce more cohesive by providing an outlet for individual flair that could not always flourish in the rigidly controlled manufacture of aircraft engines.

> 'They were gaining identity and gaining recognition as craftsmen,' says Professor Anteby. 'For them, it is who they are.'

Moreover, he adds, the practice involved an implicit social contract between workers and supervisors that meant the skilled perruque-makers were particularly flexible and helpful during exceptionally busy periods at the plant.

But, when Professor Anteby helps to teach the first-year leadership and organisational behaviour component of the Harvard MBA, the Frenchman is not trying to topple entirely the conventional view that staff pilfering is to be discouraged. When he goes through examples of grey areas, Professor Anteby is instead trying to make his students alive to the nuances of each situation, so they are better equipped to figure out if flexibility is appropriate when they encounter their own morally tangled situations. In addition, he recognises that grey areas of the type that seemed to work well in the French aerospace factory can also make participants vulnerable to disciplinary action if the prevailing mood of indulgence changes. For that reason, some French unions advise their members not to make perruques even if they are unofficially tolerated by their employer, he says.

Professor Anteby's current research project takes his fascination with moral ambiguity into a new realm: the supply of corpses for medical training. He is looking at what medical faculties do when they realise that they do not have enough bodies for students to dissect. Are they willing to source them through a third party? It is another grey area – and one most managers will be grateful to have avoided in their own careers.

Source: Jones, A. 'Trade-offs in the Moral Maze', *Financial Times*, 9 March 2009. Copyright © 2009 The Financial Times Limited, reproduced with permission.

Discussion questions

1 Explain what sort of ethical reasoning is used by the supervisors in the example of the aerospace company to justify ignoring 'perruques'.

2 What are the arguments for and against managers tolerating this type of behaviour? On balance, would you personally 'turn a blind eye' to such conduct or not, and why?

Review Questions and Tests

REVIEW AND DISCUSSION QUESTIONS

1. Differentiate between social obligation, social responsiveness, and social responsibility.

2. What does social responsibility mean to you personally? Do *you* think business organizations should be socially responsible? Explain.

3. What is green management and how can organizations go green?

4. What factors influence whether a person behaves ethically or unethically? Explain all relevant factors.

5. Do you think values-based management is just a "do-gooder" ploy? Explain your answer.

6. Discuss specific ways managers can encourage ethical behavior.

7. Internet file sharing programs are popular among college students. These programs work by allowing non-organizational users to access any local network where desired files are located. Because these types of file sharing programs tend to clog bandwidth, local users' ability to access and use a local network is reduced. What ethical and social responsibilities does a university have in this situation? To whom do they have a responsibility? What guidelines might you suggest for university decision makers?

8. What are some problems that could be associated with employee whistle-blowing for (a) the whistle-blower and (b) the organization?

9. Describe the characteristics and behaviors of someone you consider to be an ethical person. How could the types of decisions and actions this person engages in be encouraged in a workplace?

10. Explain the ethical and social responsibility issues facing managers today.

SECTION 4:
ORGANISATION STRUCTURE

Chapter 9:
Organisation Structure

1. Why Study Organizational Structure?

Most of this book is about how you can be most effective personally while helping your organization succeed. You've learned how to be a good leader (regardless of your role at work), how to motivate, and how effective communication will set you apart. You've also learned that excellent planning, strategizing, decision making, and critical thinking are essential for your success. You now know how to deal with change in life and at work, and how creativity, innovation, and a spirit of entrepreneurship are some of the more exciting and important aspects of work today.

But regardless of how well you lead, motivate, or inspire others, the context in which you work—your organization's structure—will have a tremendous impact on you and your organization. Organizational structure affects your behavior, your accomplishments, and your attitude about work. Organizational structure affects your organization's agility, efficiency, and effectiveness. We study organizational structure because it is so crucial to the overall performance and well-being of organizations and employees.

Think about a few companies you know: a favorite clothing store, restaurant, or mobile phone store, for example. Imagine what it is like to work in these organizations. What do employees do every day? When you are in the store, can you tell who is a manager and who is not? How? How many people seem to report to the manager? How many employees are in the store? How many employees are in the company? Are there senior managers? What do they do? What would the leaders of these organizations be responsible for? What sorts of jobs does the organization have, and what tasks do people do? All of these questions and more are related to how the organization is structured.

Understanding how organizations are structured—who does what; how people, groups, and divisions work together; and how jobs are designed—will help you be a better leader, manager, and employee. As an introduction to this chapter, we will examine several key concepts that are traditionally important in organizational structure and design. Then we will analyze several intriguing and modern concepts that pertain to how we can understand organizations and their structures today. Following this, we will explore how organizations are classified and learn about business ownership models. In the remainder of the chapter, you will learn about some popular contemporary organizational structures and how jobs fit into them. You will study the factors that managers and leaders consider when designing an organizational structure, such as the organization's strategy, the environment in which the organization operates, and its technology, size, and geographic dispersion. Finally, the chapter concludes with a look at what HR and all of us can do to create and sustain a healthy organizational structure.

Most Popular » Discussion Questions

1. Think about your family as an organization. Who is/are the leader(s)? Who makes major decisions? How does your family organize household work?
2. How does the way your family is organized affect you?

---

2. How Do Traditional Concepts Affect Our Views about Organizational Structure Today?

An **organization** is a group of people assembled to perform activities that will allow the entity to accomplish a set of strategic and tactical goals and to realize its mission. The term **organizational structure** refers to the way in which the division of labor, communication, and movement of resources among the parts of an organization are coordinated to accom-

Organization
A group of people assembled to perform activities that will allow the entity to accomplish a set of strategic and tactical goals and to realize its mission.

Organizational structure
The way in which the division of labor, communication, and movement of resources among the parts of an organization are coordinated to accomplish tasks and goals.

Organization design
The process of creating an organizational structure.

plish tasks and goals. A broader definition of organizational structure includes all of the physical, social, and legal mechanisms that enable an organization to accomplish its goals.

Organizational structure and organization design are two terms that are often used interchangeably, but they really mean two different things. **Organization design** is the process of creating an organizational structure. Said another way, organizational structure is the outcome of organization design.

To illustrate these three concepts, consider your school. Your school is an organization. Within its geographic and virtual structure, groups of people are organized in ways that enable them to advance and share knowledge, among other things. Your school's mission includes educating students, and it has a strategy to fulfill that mission. The strategy likely includes processes for identifying students who fit the mission, enrolling them, and ensuring that they receive a good education. All of these activities require that work, communication, and resources be coordinated.

Over the years, your school's employees have engaged in organization design to create an organizational structure that can support the school in implementing its strategy through finding, enrolling, and educating students. For instance, it is likely that your school has an admissions department. Within this part of the organizational structure, employees select potential students who meet the school's standards for entering the institution. In many schools, selecting students is a process conducted by an admissions committee. This committee is a team structure within a departmental structure. Imagine if the admissions department did not exist: How would the school select students who fit the school's mission? Would the president select students? Would students have to write to an instructor and ask to be admitted?

Your school no doubt also has a registration department and a finance department. Whereas the registrar coordinates enrollment for the entire school and for individual classes, the finance department collects tuition, pays employees, and manages financial aid. Imagine the chaos that would ensue if there were no registrar. How would students enroll in classes? How would class sizes be controlled? What if 500 students wanted to attend a particular course and there was only room for 30? Whose problem would that be? Would each instructor have to collect tuition and fees from every student each semester? How would employees get paid? How would financial aid be dispersed?

Finally, your school has academic departments. Academic departments foster ease of communication among faculty whose jobs and interests are similar. These departments are structured to provide a sense of identity for both students and faculty. They house classes, study groups, and research projects that enable faculty members to advance and share knowledge and support students in furthering their education.

In this example, you can see how your school—an organization—has been designed in ways that allow people to simplify, divide, and coordinate work processes. Many of our organizations (likely including your school) have designed their organizational structures around three traditional concepts: hierarchy, span of control, and centralization of decision making, all of which we consider next.

Hierarchy in Organizational Structures

Hierarchy
A way of organizing people and groups according to formal authority.

In an organization, a **hierarchy** is a way of organizing people and groups according to formal authority. A simple organizational hierarchy looks like a pyramid, with one person on the top (e.g., the president), a few below him or her (vice presidents), several beneath each of them (managers), and on down until you get to first-level employees at the bottom.

Organizational hierarchies can be "tall" or "flat." Tall organizational structures have many layers of management, whereas flat organizations have few. We will discuss the implications of how tall or flat a structure is later in the chapter. For now, you can see an example of a typical organizational hierarchy in ▪Exhibit 9.1, which depicts part of the Dallas Independent School District Service Centers.[1]

The Dallas Independent School District Service Centers organizational chart illustrates a hierarchy.

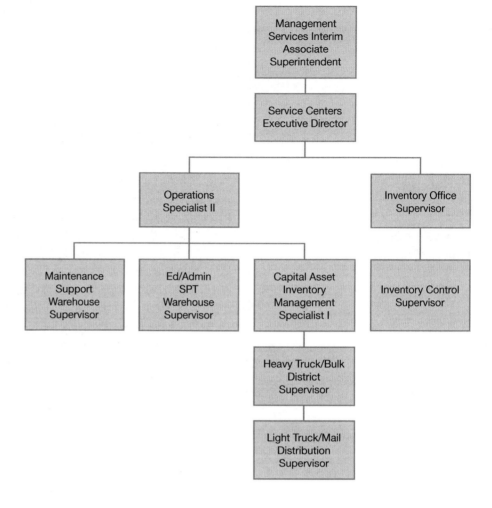

A hierarchy includes reporting relationships—who reports to whom. This is sometimes called the *chain of command*. Three concepts related to hierarchies and reporting relationships are important when it comes to how people behave within a hierarchical structure: authority, responsibility, and accountability.

Authority

Authority

The legitimate right of a person in a particular job to make certain decisions, allocate resources, and direct certain other people's activities.

Authority in an organization is defined as the legitimate right of a person in a particular job to make certain decisions, allocate resources, and direct certain other people's activities. Note that in this definition, we mention a job—that is because in the traditional sense, authority is associated with jobs, not people. If, for example, you were called by the university president today and told you'd been hired to teach this course, you would have the authority to ask students to complete assignments and grade them. This example shows why it is important to understand the person–job fit, which we will discuss later in the chapter.

Within a traditional organizational hierarchy, the job at the top of the structure has the most authority, and the jobs at the bottom have the least. Everyone within the hierarchy accepts his or her level of authority and honors others' levels of authority both above and below their own. For instance, in this management class, your professor is at the top of the hierarchy. Maybe there is a teaching assistant who is one step below the professor in the hierarchy. Then there is you (and the other students), located below the teaching assistant. If this is a "perfect" hierarchy, you will know exactly what level of authority the teaching assistant has compared to your professor. This knowledge allows you to honor the hierarchy by, for example, approaching the teaching assistant with certain questions, rather than your professor.

Responsibility
The obligation to satisfactorily accomplish the tasks associated with a job.

Accountability
An individual's willingness to report job success or failure regarding expected job outcomes to his or her manager or other superiors in the chain of command.

Span of control
The number of jobs that report to a position at the next higher level in a hierarchy.

Span of leadership
The number of jobs reporting to a person who is responsible for influencing, inspiring, and developing the people who hold those jobs.

Responsibility

A second important traditional concept related to organizational hierarchy is responsibility. In an organization, **responsibility** is defined as the obligation to satisfactorily accomplish the tasks associated with a job. As a student, you are likely responsible for reading the assignments and preparing for and attending class. Similarly, your professor is responsible for sharing information with you in a manner that will enable you to learn.

Accountability

Along with authority and responsibility comes accountability. **Accountability** is an individual's willingness to report success or failure regarding expected job outcomes to his or her manager or other superiors in the chain of command.[2] For example, say you are a manager in a bookstore. You are responsible for managing the daily finances of the shop, which in turn means overseeing the cashiers and ensuring that they balance their registers correctly every evening. If one of the cashiers is short or over, *you* are accountable for the situation and must report it to your manager.

Accountability has received a great deal of attention recently in terms of one particular aspect of work: ethical conduct on the job. Many senior-level jobs explicitly include ethical guidelines, and many organizations have explicit ethical codes of conduct as well. Partly as a result of gross ethical transgressions in some businesses, employees, managers, and leaders are now being held increasingly accountable for transparent and ethical behavior.

Span of Control in Organizational Structures

The second key traditional consideration in organizational structure is span of control. The term **span of control** refers to the number of jobs that report to a position at the next higher level in a hierarchy. Let's go back to the college classroom example: In a very large class, a professor might have five teaching assistants (TAs) reporting to him or her. This means that the professor's span of control is five. Similarly, if each teaching assistant is responsible for twenty students, each TA's span of control is twenty.

But does the professor *really* control the teaching assistants? Do the teaching assistants control the students? In both cases, this is unlikely. A more realistic way of describing this concept might be span of management, or even better, span of leadership. **Span of leadership** refers to the number of jobs reporting to a person who is responsible for influencing, inspiring, and developing the people who hold those jobs.

A key question related to span of leadership is how many jobs/people should report to any one job/individual. The practical consideration is clear: How many individuals can one leader actually influence, inspire, and develop? Twenty employees? One hundred? One thousand? Most research indicates that when aspects of the leader's responsibility include direct in-person supervision in a traditional hierarchy, a reasonable expectation for span of leadership is probably around ten jobs/people.

Although this formula might hold true in many cases, today's organizational designers must address at least two serious issues when considering span of leadership. First, in many organizations, maintaining a span of leadership that small is simply too expensive. Second, in recent years, the trend has been to move away from many layers of hierarchy, to fewer levels and more empowered employees. By definition, this means that span of leadership is much larger than in the past.

These changes lead to several conclusions: Organizations will need to provide managers with the skills to lead more people; organizational structures will need to be created that support individuals and groups working autonomously; and/or people at all levels will need to use critical thinking skills to make more and better decisions on their own. Whereas in the past, many of the most important decisions were made at the top of an organization, in many cases, this is no longer true in organizations today. This means we need to understand yet another traditional concept—the degree to which decision making is centralized in an organization.

Centralization of Decision Making in Organizational Structures

Centralized decision making
Structural model in which the vast majority of decision-making power is concentrated, typically among those at the top of the organizational hierarchy.

Centralized decision making refers to a structural model in which the vast majority of decision-making power is concentrated, typically among those at the top of the organizational hierarchy. One advantage of this model is that responsibility and accountability are very clear—everyone knows who can decide what. Another advantage is greater consistency within an organization around key processes. For example, if leadership development is centralized in the senior HR group, it is more likely that the organization will have one leadership model, one set of training programs, and so forth. A downside of centralized decision making is that it can be extremely inefficient, slow, and unresponsive to internal organizational needs or to changes in the external environment. For this reason, many organizations adapt a decentralized decision-making approach when possible.

Decentralized decision making
Structural model in which decision-making power is distributed among the people closest to the relevant information, those who will be affected by the decision, or those who will have to implement the decision.

Decentralized decision making is a structural model in which decision-making power is distributed among the people closest to the relevant information, those who will be affected by the decision, or those who will have to implement the decision. In an organizational structure, then, decentralizing decision making means that people lower in the hierarchy and most directly involved in a given situation are empowered to make decisions. Decentralization is characterized by a more dispersed and shared decision-making process—a "leaderless" or distributed leadership model.

Decentralized decision making offers many advantages. First, most people enjoy having some control over their actions and decisions. Empowered employees are committed employees. Second, employees closest to the problems and opportunities often have the best solutions and ideas. For example, say the chairs in your classroom are extremely uncomfortable. Who would make a better decision about criteria for new chairs—students, or administrators who never sit in these chairs?

A third advantage of decentralized decision making is that things can happen *fast*. This is important in many organizations today because the environment changes rapidly, calling for new and better responses. Related to this, decentralized decision making allows an organization to decipher and respond to customers' actual needs in a timely manner, rather than waiting for far-away research teams to collect data, analyze trends, and begin the process of adjusting products or services.

Decentralized decision making also has disadvantages. First, the quality of such decisions is wholly dependent on the individuals making them. This means that these employees must have excellent critical thinking skills and highly developed competencies such as pattern recognition, systems thinking, and social awareness. They need to be able to see the big picture, and how their decisions fit into the organization. If employees do not have these skills, serious errors will occur.

Second, decentralized decision making can result in the development of practices at the local level that should be—but are not—consistent with organization-wide systems, such as ethics policies, financial management processes, human resource processes, customer service and leadership models, and so forth.

For this reason, and also to ensure that decision-making models fit the organization's strategy, leaders need to pay careful attention to which kinds of decisions are centralized and which are decentralized. Employees, managers, and leaders can be more effective in their jobs if they understand and learn how to navigate an organization's structure. In the next section, we will examine a visual tool that helps us simplify this structure in order to study it.

1. Imagine that you have taken a job for which the typical span of leadership is 30 people. You find yourself reporting to a manager who can't possibly train you directly. Brainstorm some ways to get the training and attention you need.
2. Have you ever worked in an environment that used centralized decision making? If so, what did you like and dislike about it? Similarly, have you ever worked in an environment in which decision making was decentralized? If so, what did you like and dislike about it?

3. What Is an Organizational Chart?

An organizational chart depicts the hierarchy and areas of responsibility within an organization. In other words, an **organizational chart** is a visual representation of how roles, jobs, authority, and responsibility are distributed within an organization. ■Exhibit 9.2 shows a simple organizational chart for a small restaurant.

Organizational chart
A visual representation of how roles, jobs, authority, and responsibility are distributed within an organization.

As you can see, the general manager is at the top of the chart. This person is responsible for the entire organization. The general manager is accountable to the owners for realizing the restaurant's mission (to serve healthy and delicious food), making the business profitable, and leading an organization in which employees can be and do their best while learning and having fun (also part of the restaurant's mission). The general manager has the authority to make, approve, or disapprove all decisions. Two managers report to the general manager, and various other positions report to those managers.

Each of the boxes on this chart represents a job that includes certain responsibilities and is granted a certain level of authority. The people doing these jobs hold roles (e.g., busser, server, head chef, etc.) that are distinct and different. For example, bussers may pour water, clear tables, and support servers in delivering food. They have the authority to determine when a customer needs water and to provide it. Servers are responsible for taking and delivering orders. They are not responsible for cooking the food—the chefs are. Among the chefs, the assistant chefs are responsible for prepping and cooking food. They have the authority to decide if food is spoiled and to replace a certain amount as necessary, but they do not have the authority to change the menu—the head chef has the authority to do this for certain items, and the general manager has authority for significant changes to the menu. A shift manager is responsible for coordinating all activities during his or her shift and preparing the restaurant for the next shift. He or she has the authority to schedule workers but shares this authority with the other shift managers.

■Exhibit **9.2**

An organizational chart for a restaurant depicts the business's reporting structure.

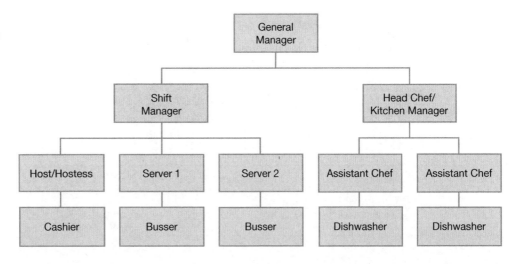

This hierarchy facilitates communication, organization of tasks and resources, and management and leadership of people in different functions (i.e., the restaurant floor and the kitchen). Organizational charts are helpful because they show hierarchy, jobs, and roles. However, the picture an organizational chart portrays doesn't tell even half the story about how an organization is really structured. To illustrate this, look at ■Exhibit 9.3. This organizational chart includes the U.S. Department of Homeland Security's mission statement at the top.

Considering what the Department of Homeland Security does, do you think this chart represents the way things actually work? What about when the director of the Domestic Nuclear Detection Office needs to put a team together with people in the Coast Guard? Can that director call the commandant? Or does the director ask his or her boss: the secretary or deputy secretary? Who is her boss, anyway? You can see that a line from the secretary goes all the way through each level. In a flat organizational structure like this, all of the positions technically report to the secretary. So how can the secretary manage the 27 people who report to him or her? Or, what if one of the directors is close to the president of the United States? Would that affect this director's power in the organization? Or, say two individuals worked their way "up" in the government and have had interpersonal problems. Would this get in the way of interdivisional coordination?

The questions one could ask about the Department of Homeland Security illustrate that reporting relationships are only one determinant for how people work and coordinate tasks. Formal and informal communication, power relationships, and even phys-

■Exhibit **9.3**

The complete organizational chart for the U.S. Department of Homeland Security is 25 pages long.

"This Department of Homeland Security's overriding and urgent mission is to lead the unified national effort to secure the country and preserve our freedoms. While the Department was created to secure our country against those who seek to disrupt the American way of life, our charter also includes preparation for and response to all hazards and disasters. The citizens of the United States must have the utmost confidence that the Department can execute both of these missions."

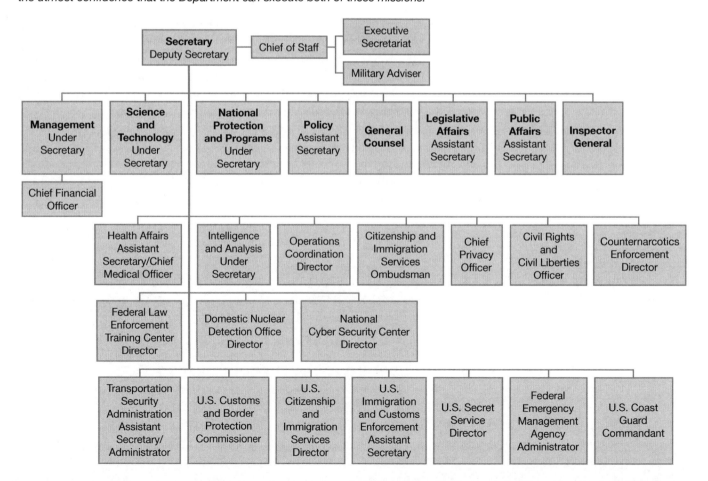

ical proximity are examples of some of the complex factors that also affect how work is coordinated and accomplished. An organizational chart can help us talk about some aspects of structure, but in the end, it is only a two-dimensional picture of jobs, roles, and hierarchical reporting relationships—nothing more, nothing less.

In this section, we have covered important concepts that claim a rightful place in the study of how organizations are designed. As helpful as these ideas are, however, they don't tell the whole story. Organizations are groups of *people*, and people are complicated. Accordingly, in the next section, we will explore several models and metaphors that allow us to consider organizational structure in more sophisticated and creative ways.

Most Popular » Discussion Questions

1. Draw an organizational chart for your family. In what ways does this chart demonstrate "how things really work" in the family? In what ways does it not capture things like communication, power relationships, and coordination of work and chores?
2. Join together with three other people. Without looking at each others' work, draw the organizational chart for your school. Now compare the charts: Are your hierarchies the same or different? If they are different, why might that be?

---

6. What Are Common Contemporary Organizational Structures?

In this section, we will look at several common organizational structures in use today. One reason we focus on specific structures is that at some point in your career, you are likely going to need to weigh in on how to structure your organization, or at least the part of the organization in which you work. In fact, employees at all levels are more and more likely to be asked to weigh in on decisions like these—especially in flatter organizations, which we will explain later in this section.

Another reason why it is important to recognize typical organizational structures is that you will probably feel more or less comfortable working within some organizational structures than others. For example, you may prefer more or less guidance, autonomy, certainty, ambiguity, or change. You might prefer very clear lines of authority, or you might like more networked and informal authority. Recognizing which kinds of organizational structures foster the kind of conditions you enjoy and where you can be at your best will result in making better choices about the organizations you join and the jobs you accept.

We will start this section by looking more deeply at the differences between "tall" and "flat" organizational structures. Then we will discuss departmentalization and how structures differ when jobs are grouped by division, function, product, process, customer, and geography. Finally, we'll conclude by looking at several structures that have emerged in recent years to support organizations in dealing with today's complex environment: matrix, hybrid, and networked structures.

"Tall" and "Flat" Organizational Structures

A vertical organizational structure can be "tall" with several levels of hierarchy, or it can be "flat" with few levels of hierarchy. In theory, tall vertical structures support fluid movement of information and resources up and down the hierarchy, whereas flatter structures facilitate faster and more effective communication horizontally across and among groups in the organization.

Tall vertical structures involve a chain of command that forms a pyramid-type organizational chart, extending from boards of directors and the most senior leaders at or near the top, to managers, supervisors, and then lower-level employees at the bottom. Tall structures can be understood purely in terms of hierarchy, as in the rank system of the U.S. Army. As you can see in ▪Exhibit 9.11, enlisted soldiers are classified into 13 hierarchical

▪Exhibit **9.11**

The U.S. Army uses 24 rank designations for enlisted soldiers and officers.*

Enlisted Soldiers*			Commissioned Officers		
Insignia	**Rank**	**Designation**	**Insignia**	**Rank**	**Designation**
	Sergeant Major of the Army	E–9		General of the Army (GOA)	0–11
	Command Sgt Major (CSM)	E–9		General (GEN)	0–10
	Sergeant Major (SGM)	E–9		Lieutenant General (LTG)	0–9
	First Sergeant (1SG)	E–8		Major General (MG)	0–8
	Master Sergeant (MSG)	E–8		Brigadier General (BG)	0–7
	Sergeant First Class (SFC)	E–7		Colonel (COL)	0–6
	Staff Sergeant (SSG)	E–6		Lieutenant Colonel (LTC)	0–5
	Sergeant (SGT)	E–5		Major (MAJ)	0–4
	Corporal (CPL)	E–4		Captain (CPT)	0–3
	Specialist (SPC)	E–4		First Lieutenant (1LT)	0–2
	Private-First Class (PFC)	E–3		Second Lieutenant (2LT)	0–1
	Private (PVT2)	E–2			
NO INSIGNIA	Private (PVT)	E–1			

*Among enlisted soldiers, corporal and above are referred to as non-commissioned officers.

ranks, 9 of which represent the category of "non-commissioned officers" (NCOs). The hierarchy of "commissioned officers" (the lowest of which technically outranks the highest ranking enlisted soldier) has 11 different ranks, for a total of 24 hierarchical levels.

A major benefit of clear vertical structures is that the hierarchy tends to work as a cohesive whole, and information sharing up and down the chain of command can be efficient.[67] One drawback is that different vertical structures within an organization (e.g., marketing, finance, manufacturing) can develop a "silo mentality." The term *silos* is often used to describe parts of an organization that are isolated from and interact less with other parts of the organization.[68]

Many organizations will try to minimize the negative impact of silos by creating cross-functional teams for important organization-wide projects. **Cross-functional teams** consist of individuals from many parts of an organization who are brought together to provide different points of view and skills in the service of organization-wide challenges and opportunities, innovations, and special projects.

Another potential problem in a tall vertical structure is that more managers and executives are needed to make decisions, allocate resources, and the like. This is expensive and can be highly inefficient. That is why in recent decades, many organizations have "downsized" by reorganizing their hierarchies so that fewer managers are needed to oversee operations. In other words, organizations are becoming "flatter." An organization is referred to as "flat" when there are few levels of hierarchy in the organizational structure. Think of a pyramid that is very wide at its base and not very high, and you have the basic concept of what a flat organization is like (Exhibit 9.12).

In flat organizations, communication can be more effective horizontally across teams, work groups, and departments. Theoretically, resources can flow more easily across the organization. To this end, flat organizations often have team-based structures, less specialization, and wider spans of control and leadership.[69] A flat structure can potentially result in decreased costs and increased speed because there are fewer layers of management to involve in the decision-making process.

A truly flat structure is rare and would only be found in very small organizations. Moreover, many people have a hard time imaging what it would be like to work in a flat organization. Members of the Boston Consulting Group published an article pointing out that contemporary thinking about career paths and peer groups tends to be very much the same as in the past—and both of these are linked to hierarchal models of organizational structure. People want to move "up." In addition, metrics, planning, and budgeting all continue to support the vertical, hierarchical organization.[70]

Cross-functional teams
Teams that consist of individuals from many parts of an organization who are brought together to provide different points of view and skills in the service of organization-wide challenges and opportunities, innovations, and special projects.

Exhibit **9.12**
Organizations may be tall or flat.

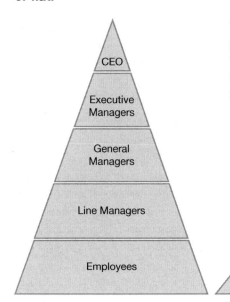

IDEO

Business Case

Empowering Employees

Companies are not limited to traditional organizational structures. Innovative firms often bypass these structures and create new configurations that allow more freedom for creativity, innovation, and teamwork. Consider the example of IDEO, a global design consultancy firm with over 500 employees worldwide. The word "ideo" is Greek for idea, and one of the company's founders, David Kelley, has become well known as an innovator.

His inventive style in designing products can also be seen in IDEO's unique organizational structure. Kelley recalls working for large corporations early in his career and finding them oppressive. In his words, "You could feel the weight of the organizational chart. My boss was a person I didn't know, who was making decisions about my life." Therefore, when he later started his own company, Kelley wanted to do something different—something he refers to as "employee empowerment."[71]

Continued on next page>>

IDEO **Continued**

The result of Kelley's innovative thinking was IDEO's current structure. Although the firm's employees can be described as a flat team, they also form "studios" and multidisciplinary "hot teams." Studios are departments that vary in size from 15 to 25 people, with each studio head responsible for the profit and loss of his or her particular group. Studio heads are not hired from the outside but are instead groomed from within IDEO. Hot teams are groups of people with multidisciplinary backgrounds who work together for a certain period of time. The leaders of the hot teams come from within the teams and are not hired to be leaders; rather, these individuals have worked at IDEO for some time and have come to be respected by their colleagues.

Clients and thinkers from outside IDEO are also vital participants in the company's hot teams. This cross-disciplinary approach has contributed to IDEO's success in the completion of

Hot teams spark innovation

design projects such as the Palm V, the Apple mouse, and the Crest Neat-Squeeze Tube for toothpaste. In fact, IDEO has won more *Business Week*/IDSA Industrial Design Excellence Awards than any other firm and has been ranked among the 25 most innovative companies by both *Fast Company* and Boston Consulting Group.[72] David Kelley attributes his company's success partly to its use of teams: "We have the advantage of working in multiple industries. Let's say we are working on a chair, but we've learned something in the automobile industry before. Maybe we learned about a certain kind of spring in the automobile industry. We just cross-pollinate that into the chair, and now we have an innovation in the furniture industry."[73]

Source: Case written by Laura Town; **Photo Source:** Shutterstock

---

Departmentalization
The process by which individuals or activities are grouped together into departments according to function, geography, product, process, or customer, as well as how the departments are coordinated and how they fit within the larger organization.

■Exhibit **9.13**
General Electric's organizational chart illustrates its divisional structure.

When a flat structure is implemented, the changes in employee attitudes and organizational culture can be both beneficial and challenging. For instance, researchers have found that when a firm "flattens," employees feel empowered but have less access to feedback. Additionally, involvement increases, but identification with the organization can suffer. Finally, intrinsic motivation tends to rise dramatically, but this can be at the cost of decreased satisfaction in important extrinsic motivators such as pay and job security.[74]

Departmentalization and Organizational Structure

Within an organizational hierarchy, jobs are often grouped in ways that allow people, resources, and processes to be coordinated for efficiency and effectiveness. This is called departmentalization. **Departmentalization** is the process by which individuals or activities are grouped together into departments according to function, geography, product, process, or customer, as well as how the departments are coordinated and how they fit within the larger organization. Departmentalization can also support matrix, hybrid, and network structures. Let's examine each of these departmental groupings in turn.

Divisional Structures

Divisions are structures within a company that include all of the departments necessary to achieve particular organizational goals. For example, a global consumer goods company might have a "Foods Division" that is a self-contained organization including departments such as marketing, sales, human resources, and supply chain—everything that is needed to produce, distribute, market, and sell the company's products. In some cases, each division operates as if it is a separate business with its own hierarchy, top leaders, and even board of directors.[75] As you can see in ■Exhibit 9.13, a large company may also choose a divisional structure to support separate and self-contained structures for the production of a certain product or service line. In

General Electric Company
- GE Capital Services
  - Capital Real Estate
  - Commercial Lending and Leasing
- GE Industrial
  - Consumer and Industrial
    - Lighting LLC (Kentucky)
    - Lighting Ltd (UK)
  - Sensing and Inspection Technologies

Exhibit 9.13, the top two levels of the company, GE Capital Services and GE Industrial, are divisions. Within each division are departments necessary to manage the entire production-to-market cycle.

"Pure" divisional structures would not need or have any hierarchical or reporting relationships with the parent company, except through the division's leader. In practice, however, it is more common for certain business units and functional groups such as HR and finance to have secondary "dotted line" reporting relationships into the central organization to ensure consistency in vital organizational processes.[76]

Functional Departmentalization

Functional departmentalization is a method of grouping jobs based on the nature of the work being performed. Most organizations have five functional areas: operations (all the jobs related to what the organization does, produces, or provides), marketing, sales, human resources, and finance. Many organizations also have other functions that support their particular business or institution. ■Exhibit 9.14 illustrates functional departmentalization at the executive level of an organization, showing the president at the top of the organization and five vice presidents (VPs) of each functional area.

Functional departmentalization
Method of grouping jobs based on the nature of the work being performed.

■Exhibit **9.14**
Functional departmentalization groups jobs based on the type of work being performed.

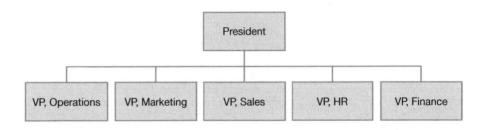

One benefit of functional departmentalization is that each functional area works as a cohesive whole, and information sharing within each function can be efficient.[77] A drawback is that the different functions can develop the "silo mentality" mentioned earlier because they may interact less with other functions of the organization.[78]

Product Departmentalization

In some larger corporations, departmentalization occurs along product lines. For example, Fortune Brands owns various brands of alcohol including Jim Beam, Canadian Club, and Maker's Mark. The company also manufactures kitchen and bath faucets under the brand name Moen and produces Titleist golf balls.[79] This diversified company uses a product departmentalization structure. **Product departmentalization** is a method of grouping jobs based on the products made or services offered.

Product departmentalization
A method of grouping jobs based on the products made or services offered.

■Exhibit **9.15**
Product departmentalization groups jobs based on the products or services offered.

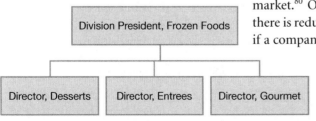

In a large diversified organization, having separate departments devoted to particular products or services helps cut costs related to getting goods and services to market.[80] One drawback to this type of departmentalization, however, is that there is redundancy in the jobs being done across the organization. For example, if a company has an entire division devoted to making soap, another to making shampoo, a third to toothpaste, and a fourth to hair gel, each of those divisions will need HR professionals, a finance group, and a marketing group. ■Exhibit 9.15 shows an example of product departmentalization for a frozen food company.

Process departmentalization
A method of grouping jobs based on the sequential steps of the work people do to produce products or services or engage in other business activities.

Process Departmentalization

Process departmentalization is a method of grouping jobs based on the sequential steps of the work people do to produce products or services or engage in other business activities. Let's say you work in a manufacturing plant where soda is produced, bottled, and prepared for market. Using process departmentalization, one department would have all the jobs

■Exhibit **9.16**
Process departmentalization groups jobs based on the sequential steps required to create a good or provide a service.

Plant Manager

Mixing | Bottle/Cap Production | Filling | Labeling | Inspection | Packing and Shipping

associated with mixing the soda. Another department would be involved in manufacturing the glass bottles and metal caps. A third would involve pouring the soda into individual bottles and capping those bottles. The fourth department would include all jobs related to labeling the bottles, and the fifth department would be responsible for inspection and quality control. Finally, one department would be responsible for packing the bottles into boxes and shipping them out. ■Exhibit 9.16 illustrates this particular process structure.

Customer Departmentalization

Customer departmentalization
A method of grouping jobs based on the needs of customers, consumers, or clients.

Customer departmentalization is a method of grouping jobs based on the needs of customers, consumers, or clients. Focusing attention on the specific customers who purchase products or services can enhance customer satisfaction because it often means a team of individuals—or an entire division—is devoted to the best customers. For example, Newell Rubbermaid has teams of sales representatives dedicated to their largest customers, such as Home Depot and Lowe's. As with some other types of departmentalization, however, this structure suffers from job redundancy. ■Exhibit 9.17 shows an example of customer departmentalization for a management consulting firm.

■Exhibit **9.17**
Customer departmentalization is a structure that groups jobs based on the needs of customers, consumers, or clients.

Managing Director Manufacturing Clients | Managing Director Retail Clients | Managing Director Governmental Clients

VP Tax Services

Geographic Departmentalization

Geographic departmentalization
A method of grouping jobs based on their physical location.

Geographic departmentalization is a method of grouping jobs based on their physical location. This is often seen within sales divisions of large organizations (■Exhibit 9.18).

Matrix
A structure in which departments within an organization are linked directly to one unit in the vertical organization and to another unit in the horizontal organization.

Departmentalization structures are complex, no matter what form they take, because it is always challenging to coordinate complex vertical structures (e.g., the hierarchy) and even more daunting to coordinate among departments, because they have inherent "walls" between them. Nevertheless, several popular new structures have been developed to eliminate some of the problems inherent in structures that hamper communication, creativity, and speed. We look at three of these structures next: matrix, hybrid, and networked structures.

Matrix Structure

■Exhibit **9.18**
Geographic departmentalization groups jobs based on their physical location.

A **matrix** is a structure in which departments within an organization are linked directly to one unit in the vertical organization and to another unit in the horizontal organization. The purpose of a matrix structure is to maximize the positive attributes of vertical structures while also supporting effective coordination, communication and agility across the organization. A common type of matrix is organized by function and geography, as shown in ■Exhibit 9.19.

The horizontal and vertical dimensions of a matrix structure can be any of the structures

Southwest Regional Sales Manager

Sales Representative, TX | Sales Representative, AZ | Sales Representative, NM

■Exhibit **9.19**

A basic matrix structure combines vertical and horizontal structures.

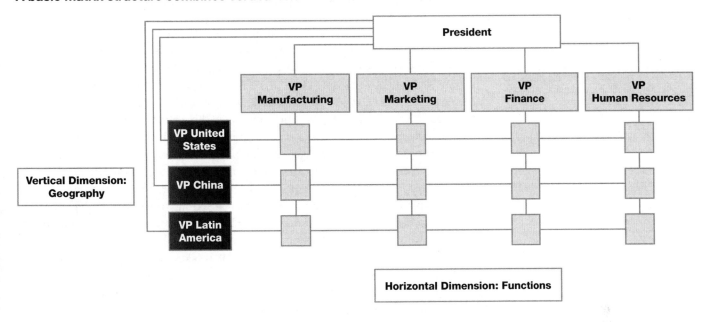

studied so far: divisional, functional, product, process, customer, or geographic. Sometimes, organizations will create a matrix structure for special projects, innovation teams, or any group that needs the support and control inherent in a vertical chain of command as well as the expertise from a department in the horizontal organization.

A matrix structure often helps shift the organizational culture away from a silo mentality in which each department or division is isolated from the rest of the organization. At its best, this type of structure allows for optimal control in the hierarchical organization while also ensuring maximum efficiency and effective coordination of the horizontal organization.

The downside of the matrix structure is that it can be very confusing. Most people are used to working within a single hierarchy. In a basic matrix structure, people often report formally to two bosses. Even if the structure does not have everyone reporting formally to two bosses, the department itself is responsible for the outcomes required by two distinct and different parts of the organization—each of which has its own goals. Sometimes, the required outcomes can be in conflict with one another. This can cause a great deal of tension in the organization and result in overburdening the senior leader or leaders who have to resolve conflicts.

Hybrid structure
A structure that incorporates more than one type of structure in the overall organization.

■Exhibit **9.20**

The hybrid structure in this cancer center incorporates more than one type of structure.

Hybrid Structure

A **hybrid structure** incorporates more than one type of structure in the overall organization. For example, ■Exhibit 9.20 depicts part of the structure of a large cancer center. The structure is divisional, but it also includes flat team structures within the clinical investigations and clinical affairs divisions.

As many variations of hybrid structures exist as there are combinations of organizational structures. One structure that is worth mentioning because it hardly ever shows up on an organizational chart is the vertical structure created within a team. As mentioned earlier in the chapter, many people have been socialized to view hierarchy as the most important aspect of organizational structure. We tend to be most comfortable with the rules of hierarchies (even if we don't like them). For this and other reasons, people often gravitate toward implementing a hierarchy, even when it is not officially called for in the organizational structure.

You may have experienced this on a project team in the past. When you started to work together, members were equal, with the exception that there was a designated leader. Maybe the work was complicated, it was hard to meet the deadlines, or your leader was busy or unavailable. Suddenly (it seemed to you), one of the other members was now the "project manager"—he or she was organizing work, delegating tasks, and reporting back to the team leader. Not everyone on the team appreciated this, so two people designated themselves as "subgroup leaders." They began organizing the work of the remaining members and reporting to the project manager. At this point, you had a team of eight people, four of whom were organizing and delegating, and four of whom were actually doing the work. This obviously makes no sense—especially for the four people doing the work!

It is surprising how often this happens in real settings at work. This dynamic may arise in part because some people resist being led and need to learn the art of followership. It may also arise because of poor team leadership—flat structures such as teams are not easy to lead, as you will see in Chapter 10. It takes special skills and a high level of self-confidence to let people work collaboratively without micromanagement.

As more and more organizations adopt flat and hybrid structures, it will serve you well to learn to recognize the signs that a flat structure is turning into a dysfunctional hierarchy. It will also serve you well to learn how to manage and lead groups without the benefit of a formal hierarchical structure. This is particularly true when it comes to flat, networked structures—in which power dynamics are an important part of the overall structure that must be understood and tracked.

Networked Organizational Structures and Power Dynamics

All of the structures we have looked at so far have been described primarily in terms of formal authority, responsibility, and accountability. In other words, these structures revolve around formal and position power. This is not the only important dimension, however, when it comes to organizational structure. Other increasingly important dimensions of organizational success include access to resources, information, and social networks.

An organization is a social network. People are linked in many ways: by similarity in jobs, similarity in level of authority, personal relationships, the need to work together, or common interests, to name just a few. By virtue of where you "sit" in an organization and how you interact with others, you will have more or less access to information. Typically, we think of people in higher-level jobs as having access to more organizational knowledge and resources. This can be true, but take the example of an executive assistant. This person has little position power but might hold a great deal of social power because she constantly makes decisions about who gets access to what information, who has access to her boss, and so forth. Her boss, who has tremendous position power, may have little power in the sense that his information is filtered through a small group of people in the organization.[81]

Organizations can tailor social networks to improve the flow of information, facilitate the spread of innovation, improve decision making, strengthen organizational culture, and remove information "bottlenecks," which occur when too much information is passing through too few individuals.[82] As shown in ∎Exhibit 9.21, the networked structure of an organization can also be mapped out in terms of communication and interaction between departments, boards, teams, functional divisions, and so forth. In this case, the focus is not on which individuals are interacting, but rather on which parts of the organization are interacting and in what way.

In this section, we have described numerous contemporary organizational structures, as well as a few of the pros and cons of these structures. One form of organiza-

■Exhibit **9.21**

The network structure at Indymedia.

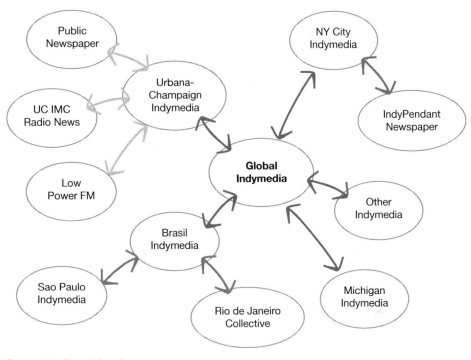

Source: http://www.indymedia.org

tion we have not yet discussed is the virtual organization. Because of advances in information and communication technologies, a vast number of organizations are now at least partially virtual. For this reason, Chapter 11 is entirely dedicated to this topic. Now, let's turn our attention to what happens within all of these structures: work.

Most Popular » Discussion Questions

1. Organizational structure is not always easy to see when we interact with a company, but it is important to understand when taking a job. Brainstorm a list of questions you could ask an interviewer about the company's organizational structure that would help you to determine if it is a place you would like to work. *Note:* "What is this organization's structure?" is a given. See what else you can come up with.

2. How do you think the structure and functions of hot teams contribute to IDEO's success?

3. In a matrix organization, you could have two bosses. What problems might arise in this situation? How could you deal with these problems?

4. In this section, we pointed out that people often feel comfortable with hierarchical structures and will create a mini-hierarchy around themselves, even if the formal structure does not call for it. In addition to our explanations, why do you think people do this?

---

7. How Is Work Structured?

You can consider overarching organizational structures, such as those described in the previous section, as "templates" within which smaller units and functions operate, jobs get done, and tasks are accomplished. As we have stressed throughout this chapter, organizational structure is an important concept to understand, but as you read on, please remember that numerous other factors, such as leadership, management practices, and organizational culture, are also extremely powerful in determining *how* work gets done, jobs are defined, and organizational goals are accomplished (or not). Let's look briefly at how tasks and jobs fit into the study of organizational structure.

Tasks

Within an organizational structure, *tasks* are the activities that people do regularly as part of their jobs. For example, an administrative assistant answers his boss's phone—this is a task. His job, on the other hand, is to provide support to his boss in a variety of ways, including managing his boss's calendar, editing written materials, arranging travel, and preparing speech and presentations materials. Likewise, a sales representative that completes her monthly expense report is doing a task for which she is responsible. This person's job is to sell products to certain customers within a geographical region.

Jobs

Job
A group of tasks and responsibilities related to accomplishing organizational objectives.

A **job** is defined as a group of tasks and responsibilities related to accomplishing organizational objectives. Like organizations, jobs can be classified in many ways. For example, jobs can be classified by profession or industry, type of workplace, associated tasks, grade or pay level, union or nonunion status, public or private sector status, or paid or unpaid status. As discussed earlier in the chapter, job specialization and division of labor describe how narrowly focused tasks and jobs are. For example, Henry Ford's assembly line in the early twentieth century used division of labor (as do many assembly lines today). Workers were assigned to very few tasks—even just one, which they did over and over—efficient, perhaps, but also mind-numbing.[83]

Job specialization is an old topic. Plato discussed it extensively in his famous work *The Republic*.[84] Centuries later, famed economist Adam Smith explained that specialization increased production output and wealth.[85] In the twentieth century, functional job specialization was explained as a core concept of scientific management by industrial researcher Frederick Taylor.[86] Job specialization, in this sense, has been linked to the movement to subdivide labor into its smallest units, such as what you might see on an assembly line. Organizational design will of course be affected by such processes, but so are people.

Highly specialized work, when taken to the extreme, can result in highly efficient but extremely boring and repetitive tasks and a mechanistic view of the organization.[87] It can lead to feelings of alienation.[88] On the other hand, employee satisfaction can be improved if job enlargement is pursued (i.e., by adding more and more interesting tasks).[89] In advanced industrial societies, scholars have recommended that functional specialization can give way to "flexible specialization," or the ability to quickly and efficiently manufacture customized products at low volume.[90] When this happens, employees are given the opportunity to vary the types of tasks and their order. This flexible specialization has been seen, for instance, in computer assembly based on customer input, which gave Dell Computers a strategic edge at the beginning of the twenty-first century.

When a course of job specialization is pursued, markets for each specialized job tend to emerge. When this occurs, jobs begin to develop outside the firm, and this can lead to outsourcing.[91] Additionally, "integration" of various specialties in organizational design can itself become a specialized function in the firm.[92]

Researchers have suggested that although job specialization is often intended to increase efficiency, it also may create more motivation by requiring deep "expert" knowledge in a specific work area.[93] Other researchers have noted that job specialization is beneficial in high-tech industries. Although in the past, job rotation had been adopted to alleviate the burnout associated with highly specialized work, in high-tech work, deep knowledge of one area of work increases self-efficacy and decreases burnout.[94]

While some jobs are highly specialized, other jobs are broader and include more tasks and activities. For example, the HR director in a manufacturing facility may perform most tasks associated with that position. She may coordinate all of the recruiting, hiring, pay practices, benefits administration, training, employee relations, and safety practices, and she may even craft policies and procedures.

A person who performs a wide variety of tasks is known as a generalist. A specialist, on the other hand, is someone who has a very narrowly focused set of job tasks. Using the HR analogy, in a large corporate center you may have one person responsible for benefits, several people responsible for payroll, a team of corporate trainers, and so forth. These are specialists.

Now that you know quite a lot about jobs, organizations, and how they can be structured, let's look at a few important factors leaders must consider when determining just how to structure—or restructure—an organization.

Most Popular » Discussion Questions

1. Have you ever done a highly specialized job? What was it? What did you like and what did you dislike about it?
2. Would you prefer to be a generalist or a specialist? Why?

---

8. What Factors Affect the Design of Organizational Structures?

We have been discussing structure as if it is something that already exists, something we can see and evaluate—which of course you can. You can step into any one of the types of businesses discussed in the previous section and "see" the structure that exists at that moment in time. But how did it get that way? When the organizational design process is deliberate, leaders and HR professionals consider several important factors: the organization's strategy, the external environment, technology, size, and geography.

The Relationship between Structure and Strategy

Over the years, scholars have debated the relationship between strategy and structure. You will often hear people in organizations say "Structure follows strategy," as if it is a known and unquestionable fact. It's a little more complicated than that, however.

Structure Follows Strategy

Organizational scholar Alfred Chandler was one of the first to propose that structure must follow strategy. The argument is pretty straightforward: An organization exists in a particular environment from which it draws its resources and within which it provides products or services. The decisions about how to position the organization in the environment are part of the organization's strategy. To implement that strategy, the organization makes certain choices about structure. In other words, the organization's structure is part of the outcome of the strategic decision-making process. Hence, structure follows strategy.[95]

Strategy Can Be Determined by Structure

Others have argued just the opposite—that structure *determines* strategy. This argument states that the benefits and limitations of the structure will determine what types of strategies are viable. Because structures can limit the implementation of certain strategies, it is important for organizations to develop a proactive approach to strategy formation. In a proactive organization, strategy and structure are constantly influencing each other. When this is not the case, the strategy is in danger of becoming "the lackey of the structure."[96]

Structure and Strategy: An Iterative Process

Now, let's consider the issue from another perspective. Tactics are actions that are implemented to try to achieve a strategic goal. A particular tactic, however, can only be used if the existing structure allows it (i.e., resources cannot be used by one part of the organization if they are controlled by another in a tall, siloed organization). At the same time, a tactic can be chosen because it is instrumental in changing organizational structure. If this works, different tactical choices become possible down the road. In other words, tactics are the interface between strategy and structure. More scholars are coming to recognize the importance of putting strategy and structure in an iterative relationship—a relationship in which strategy influences structure, structure influences strategy, and both are constantly improving.[97]

The External Environment

The external environment in which an organization operates also plays a key role in the structure of the organization. For example, Nautilus, a Vancouver, Washington–based company that manufactures fitness equipment, recently went through a major restructuring as a result of adverse economic conditions in the business environment. Facing a tough economic environment in 2008, including an $8.9 million loss in just one quarter, the company examined its strategies and structure in an attempt to become more aligned with external conditions.[98]

In an effort to cut costs, Nautilus closed one of its manufacturing facilities and combined two distribution centers. This change in structure meant that other areas of the company would need to handle an increased workload. Additionally, teams were established and given authority and responsibility for specific business units. The company also launched a strategic initiative supporting new product development, to keep the company's products fresh for the market.[99] Thanks to these changes, by the third quarter of 2009, the company was able to reduce its losses, and by the fourth quarter, it began showing profit.[100]

What the company had found was that its business of selling to exercise clubs and hotels was struggling, while consumer sales were doing well. So, in March 2010, Nautilus decided to shed its commercial sales in order to more effectively focus on the portion of the company that was generating profit—direct consumer sales.[101] In response to a changing environment, Nautilus continues to restructure the organization and to refocus its strategy.

How quickly and how well an organization adapts to the environment is also important. The national trucking company Vitran Express immediately took action when fuel prices rose in 2008. They began purchasing biodiesel fuels and ensured that drivers did not exceed 65 miles per hour. This quick adaptation saved the company $375,000 in their Chicago area terminals alone.[102]

In both of these cases, changes in the external environment happened *fast*. This situation is very common today. Positive changes such as advances in technology and the emergence of new markets are the norm, and companies need to be ready to take advantage of these changes. These examples illustrate a fact of organizational life today: The global environment is volatile and uncertain. Major changes can and do happen very quickly.

Environmental uncertainty
A situation in which market conditions are changing rapidly or are unclear.

Environmental uncertainty refers to a situation in which market conditions are changing rapidly or are unclear. Environmental uncertainty can be the result of political instability or changes such as elections or regime changes in influential countries. As another example, when resources are controlled for political reasons (as happens with oil), entire industries can be forced to change what they are doing overnight.

Social changes such as how people are using technology to share information can also cause a good deal of uncertainty. For example, only a few years ago news reporters were usually the ones to find and report stories. Now, anyone with a cell phone camera can do this work. This means that the news industry needs to change dramatically. And because of our increasingly interconnected world, other environmental conditions such as wars, conflicts or potential conflicts, regional environmental regulations, and even local laws can cause environmental uncertainty in places far from an organization's activities.

Competition on a global scale can also create environmental uncertainty. The recession in the late 2000s combined with increased international competition in the auto industry hit U.S. automotive companies especially hard. Since 1990, the 30,000 companies involved in supplying the auto industry have consolidated into 10,000 as a result of failures, mergers, and acquisitions.[103] In the auto industry and many others, environmental uncertainty will continue to affect business profoundly, in turn affecting how businesses and organizations structure people and operations.

Technology

We will discuss the effects of technology on individuals and organizations in depth in Chapter 11. For now, let us simply say that the level of technology in an organization impacts both the structure and strategy. As early as the 1950s, British researcher Joan Woodward found that the structure of an organization is influenced by the technology that it employs. For example, if a manufacturing company uses mass production, the structure might be one in which managers supervise more employees than in a custom manufacturing environment, where there may be fewer employees reporting to each manager.[104] In more modern times, computer technologies have greatly influenced the structure of organizations. Communication within the organizational structure has also adapted to these new technologies.

Company Size and Geography

In addition to strategy, the environment, and technology, numerous other factors can affect how leaders design or redesign an organization. Two that we will mention here are the organization's size and geography.

Company Size

An organization's size affects its structure in obvious ways. If your company has 20 people, you would not have 20 departments—you probably wouldn't even want four departments. If you differentiated that much, you would certainly be wasting resources. Similarly, if your organization has 20,000 people, you wouldn't organize them all in one department. Doing so would be chaotic and unmanageable.

There are no rules that dictate how leaders should design organizations of various sizes. However, in traditional vertical organizations, there seem to be some trends as organizations grow: Power becomes less concentrated; there are increasingly more levels of management, but this levels off as the organization becomes quite large; and more formal policies tend to emerge as a company grows.

Most research on how size affects structure has concentrated on traditional organizations in which the people counted are employees. Considering the fact that there has been a rapid increase in different employment relationships (such as contractors and temporary workers), we now need to look at the relationship of size to structure differently. As social networking continues to affect the "virtual" size of an organization, more research will be conducted as to what actually constitutes a small, medium, or large business, and how the various internal and external groups work together to impact structure—and vice versa.

Geography

How geographically dispersed employees and customers are will have an impact on organizational design. For example, national restaurant chains have hundreds of locations, and thousands of employees are needed to staff the individual restaurant sites. Each restaurant has a manager, but each manager also reports to a district manager. The reason why these district managers are responsible for specific geographical areas is because it would be too difficult to manage thousands of staff from one central corporate office. It would be challenging to maintain consistency, and controls on operations would be very limited.

In addition to the geographical dispersion of employees, geographical distribution of customers is key when it comes to structure. Large consumer products companies such as Procter & Gamble and Black & Decker have sales representatives in territories corresponding to the locations of major customer bases such as Walmart, Home Depot, and Target.

All of the topics presented so far in this section have an effect on organizational design. One would imagine, then, that leaders would always consider such factors before deciding to design, or redesign, an organization. That is not always the case, however, as we will see next.

Organizational Design: It's Not Always Deliberate!

As organizations grow, strategies change, or technology changes, organizational structures often *emerge* without much conscious planning or design. Individual managers and business leaders often make structure decisions for "their" parts of the organization, resulting in something of a hodgepodge over time. This emergent process can support adaptability. On the other hand, it can also result in chaos and redundancy of tasks and functions.

For example, in one very large company we know, the HR function was decentralized in the late 1990s. What this meant was that HR leaders were empowered within each division to make decisions that suited their particular needs with regard to leadership development, hiring practices, and the like. About five years later, the organization bought another large company that had to be integrated into the current organization. Numerous problems were discovered, including the fact that there was no centralized technology system to track "hiring" the employees from the acquired organization— every division used different software. It was impossible to track who went where.

Second, the acquiring organization wisely wanted to ensure that this new, bigger entity's managers and leaders would share a common approach to leadership, values, and culture. As the central HR team began investigating the leadership models that were in use around the business, they found that over the five years of decentralization, no less than 187 new leadership models had been adopted and taught in as many regions and divisions! Imagine trying to coordinate communication about leadership and culture under those circumstances.

As much as empowerment and adaptability are key to success, so is ensuring that the structure used across the organization is coherent. In most organizations, this is accomplished through centralized planning around key issues related to the environment and technology, as well as a host of factors such as the organization's size, geographical dispersion of locations, degree of specialization, and the like.

Most Popular » Discussion Questions

1. In what ways does the external environment influence the structure of your school as an organization?
2. Are there any new technologies that are affecting how work gets done in your school or place of work? If so, what are they, and what impact do they have on work processes?
3. Use the Internet to find the biggest company you can, in terms of number of employees. Now, study the company's structure. How do you think the size of this organization impacted decisions about its structure?

Chapter 10:
Structure Advantages and Disadvantages

ORGANISATIONAL DESIGN AND STRUCTURE

The outcome of a company's organising activities can be depicted in organisational design. The object of the design is to create an organisational structure which fits with its objectives, its resources and its environment because the structure describes the relationship between the different parts of the organisation and the people in it. It specifies the division of work, the hierarchy and authority structure, and the formal links that exist between people within the organisation. In practice, of course, there are cross-functional relationships, networks and informal links which are not described by a formal structure but may be of equal importance. A management or organisation chart is a diagram of an organisation's formal structure describing the functions, departments and positions of people within the organisation and how they are related.

An organisation chart usually consists of a line diagram showing the chain of command and official channels of communication (see Figures 1.6 and 1.7). A hierarchical structure will usually be described in terms of the organisation of line management and reporting, while a matrix structure will be described more in terms of relationships between units and people and processes of coordination. In order both to describe company structure and reflect the company priorities other forms of diagram may be designed, or more than one diagram may be felt to be appropriate. For example, in order to focus on the importance of customers, a diagram such as an inverted triangle (see Figure 9.2 opposite, above) may be felt to be appropriate.

In Figure 9.3, opposite, the teams and employees closest to the organisation's customers are at the top of the triangle in order to emphasise the supporting role of functional departments and senior management (see also Figure 3.1). Of course, much greater detail can be included in this type of diagram and it can simply consist of an inverted management chart. Figure 9.3 shows a more traditional chart with senior managers at the top, middle managers below them and operational staff at the bottom. At the same time the chart is divided into functional groupings with line management and responsibility flowing down the functions. It is difficult in this type of diagram to show functional links, coordination of projects and informal relationships. Some attempt can be made to do this by using dotted lines.

Figure 9.2 **Inverted triangle**

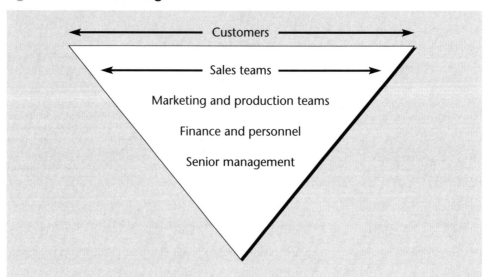

Figure 9.3 **Organisation chart**

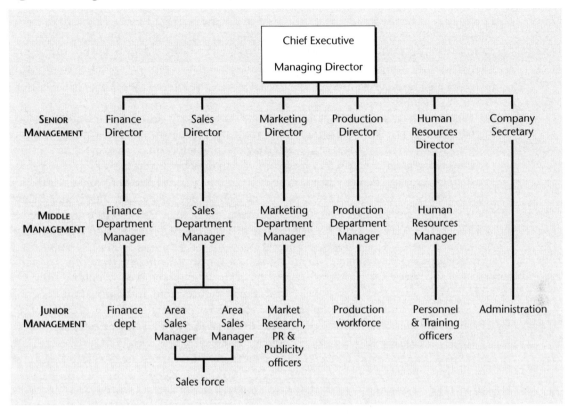

Functional structure

The functional structure illustrated in Figure 9.4 brings together all those engaged in related activities into one department. The production director and the production department are responsible for all the products manufactured by the company and the sales managers are responsible for all the sales of these products. This 'traditional' structure is often seen as the most logical method for dividing up the work of the organisation. It is used in small and medium organisations and in an adapted form it may be used in large organisations. However, the disadvantage of this structure becomes more obvious as an organisation grows in size (Table 9.2 summarises advantages and disadvantages).

This functional structure can bring together specialists and specialist equipment in order to develop high-quality products and services from their particular department. The staff in these departments can provide support for each other and their teamwork can help innovation to develop within their relatively narrow area. Line management control, leadership and authority are all very easily understood within this structure, and employees can develop considerable loyalty towards their department which may be more difficult to create for the whole company. This loyalty may develop some suspicion and even antagonism towards other departments. Other departments may be blamed when things go wrong or they may appear to be favoured by senior management and to receive more than their fair share of resources.

The advantages for managers and employees of a functional structure are that they can develop their expertise, they have a clear promotion path within the department and they can communicate easily with other people with similar backgrounds and working on similar tasks. These departments can develop a paternalistic form of leadership and management which may favour some people at the expense of others. At the same time the differences between the 'home' department and the others may be manifested in a variety of ways. Particular jargon may develop which makes it difficult for people from other departments to understand what is being said, stereotypes may be used to describe people working in other departments, company policies may be interpreted and put into practice differently in the various departments and jealousies may develop over working space, equipment levels and so on.

Functional departments can encourage bureaucracy and empire building. The department may feel that it is more important the greater the resources it uses and the larger its staff. Managers and other staff may become reluctant to pass specialised information to people not in their department. There may be slow responses to changes in customer needs, particularly from those departments which have little contact with the final customer. Tasks which cut across departments may take a long time because they have to move sequentially from one department to another. This can be exacerbated by a lack of clear responsibility for such tasks with each department able to lay blame for any delay on another department. For example, all employees may be appointed through the personnel department and if it is slow in this process then other departments may have a long wait for salespeople or production workers. Genuine conflicts may develop over priorities so that, for example, new designs and innovation may not be seen as particularly important by the production department, whereas the marketing department considers that new designs are essential to meet customer needs.

As organisations grow in size, either by broadening their products and services or by expanding geographically, the disadvantages of a functional structure become apparent. It becomes more difficult to obtain quick decisions on actions because functional managers have to report to central headquarters in order to have decisions endorsed. At the same time, control over the departments becomes more difficult, and coordination may not be able to create a situation where the organisation's objectives can be achieved. These developments cause large organisations to consider other forms of structure to reflect their new requirements. The most extreme of these is the matrix structure.

Table 9.2 **Functional organisation**

ADVANTAGES	DISADVANTAGES
Efficient use of specialised resources	Empire building and bureaucracy
Responsibility, authority and control are clear	Slow response to customer needs
Encourages specialised management	Narrow perspective and limited innovation
Promotes employee loyalty to small unit	Obscures responsibility for overall tasks
Clear promotion path	Limits scope for development of general managers and employees to move into new areas
Good 'vertical' communication	Poor networks and 'horizontal' communication

Matrix structure

The usual matrix structure is designed to answer the main problems of the functional structure. It combines a vertical chain of command, through functions and departments or units, with a horizontal 'project', 'business unit' or 'product' team. The purpose of the matrix structure is to promote across the company groupings of people and skills to provide a team in order to produce a product or service. This lateral structure is led by a project or group manager who is expert in the team's assigned area of specialisation. The individual therefore has two bosses, a functional manager and a project or group manager. This is the basis for the use of the term 'matrix' which in mathematics applies to an array of vertical columns and horizontal rows.

An example of a matrix structure is shown in Figure 9.4 (see also Figure 1.7). Staff from production, marketing, sales, human resources and administration are divided into four project (or product/service) teams which consist of staff from all five functions under project managers who report to the chief executive. An individual employee in production, for instance, will be in a project team manufacturing a product and reporting to a project manager. The project manager is responsible for making sure that the team not only makes the product as specified but also markets it and sells it. Personnel, training or administrative staff may also be allocated to the team. The production employee will report to the production manager of the company, who will be responsible for initially allocating the employee to this specific project and also for the career of the employee in the organisation. The production manager is, in fact, the employee's line and functional manager, while the project manager is the task or activity manager.

In a similar way members of teams or units may have separate functional managers on a vertical scale, while the whole team moves together from one project to the next. Research teams in science and engineering often work in this way because the skills of the team may be complementary and essential for the completion of the task. At the same time the functional managers provide the specialist support and career path which may not be available through the team. In this way the matrix structure is intended to combine the advantages of functional specialisation with product or project specialisation. The matrix team works on relatively narrowly defined projects, while individuals retain the link with the functional structure of the organisation.

In some organisations a particular unit or section has a matrix structure, while the rest of the organisation has a functional structure. It has proved quite difficult in fact to organise on a full matrix in a large organisation, while small consultancies, research teams, advertising agencies and so on are able to work within this structure very easily. This is because an effective matrix structure requires a high degree of cooperation and flexibility from everybody at all levels. There must be open and direct lines of communication horizontally and vertically and a high level of confidence between managers and between employees. For these reasons matrix structures can work well where staff members have similar qualifications and share common goals, and where teamwork is more important than authority. Consultancies and research teams are good examples of this situation, and organisations such as advertising agencies may also operate in this way because everybody is working together on a variety of accounts.

Figure 9.4 **Matrix structure**

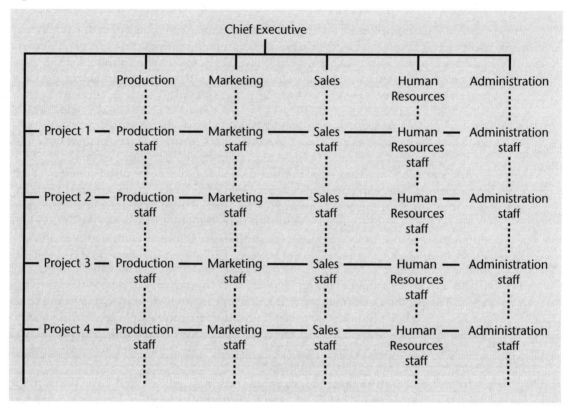

The matrix structure can be an effective means of bringing together people with the diverse skills required to solve a complex problem, such as in research teams and consultancies. It throws the focus on the project to be completed. This provides a common purpose with a well-defined objective for which the whole team or group can be responsible, while the functional structure can too easily fragment the clarity of this aim. By working together, people from various functions can understand the demands placed on other people from different areas of work. For example, preconceptions of marketing personnel about engineers can be overcome in this way, and vice versa. This understanding can produce a more realistic approach to each other's work. If the structure is sufficiently flexible and has not become rigid then it can help to keep down the costs of an organisation, because managers need only assign the number of people needed to complete a particular project (see Table 9.3).

Although the matrix structure may be easy to design and appears to have great advantages over the functional structure, it may be difficult to implement. Problems can arise over shared responsibility, the use of resources in common and the question of priorities. One manager may be played off against another by employees, so that the project manager, for example, is told that the functional manager has decided to pull an individual out of the team to work elsewhere. If this happens without proper consultation it can cause great problems for the project team.

Product, market and geographical structures

As a company diversifies so that its products and services penetrate a range of markets and expands to cover broad geographical areas, its structure needs to reflect these changes. The functional structure is usually felt to be inadequate for these circumstances. Functional managers can find themselves responsible for the production or marketing of numerous and vastly different products and services, and senior managers can become responsible for coordinating areas which are beyond their capacity to monitor and control. At the same time the matrix structure may not be suitable because it does not provide the necessary control over wide-ranging areas of work and too many people of different qualifications, experiences and backgrounds will be involved.

There are a number of different approaches to the problem of finding a structure to match the requirements of a company in this situation but the usual approach is to develop divisions or units which, unlike a functional department, resemble a separate business. There is a divisional head who is responsible for the operation of the division and may be accountable for its profitability. However, unlike a separate business, the division has to conform to the company requirements and is accountable to it.

The company may establish the rules and policies for its divisions in connection with such areas as finance, training, personnel, advertising and so on. Some 'divisions' are given a high degree of autonomy in, say, a geographical area, so that they become satellite companies run as almost separate entities but owned by the parent company and responsible to it. For example, Rank Xerox UK plc is owned by the parent North American company but enjoys a high degree of autonomy within the UK and Europe. The creation of divisional structures has been advantageous in geographically distinct areas. A local company can produce products for its geographically local markets, it can develop marketing and sales techniques which are tailor-made for the local area and it can develop a culture which is sympathetic to the locality. For example, Ford UK produces motor cars aimed specifically at the UK and European markets and adapts its marketing and sales techniques to the requirements of these markets. Through this process the UK can be treated as a distinct market requiring clear focus in the approach to it.

Of course, these factors are true also where there are clearly different markets for the same product or service, or where a company is producing clearly different products or services for the same market. For example, many publishers have an education division for publishing educational and training books and a general or fiction division for publishing novels. This may be subdivided by age group, so that a children's book division concentrates on that market. Some books will cross the divisional lines and may be sold as a children's book by one division, as an educational reader by another and as a general work of fiction by a third.

Table 9.3 **Advantages and disadvantages of a matrix structure**

ADVANTAGES	DISADVANTAGES
Focuses on end product	Requires excellent communications
Stimulates creativity	Encourages power struggles
Provides challenges	Risks duplication of effort
Enables flexibility in an organisation	Confuses lines of responsibility
Improves communication and understanding	Requires high levels of interpersonal skills
	May lead to more discussion than action

A divisional-type structure (see Table 9.4) has the advantage of combining all the activities, skills and expertise required to produce and market particular products or a product in a particular marketplace. The whole process can be coordinated easily and the speed of decision making can be increased because divisional decisions are made relatively close to the point of implementation. Divisions are able to focus on the needs of their particular customers and managers have a degree of autonomy in meeting these needs. On the other hand, of course, there may be disadvantages to this structure. The interests of the division can be placed above those of the whole organisation. The division may not place organisational objectives in quite the same order of priority as the central organisation, and may place its short-term interests above the longer-term interests of the whole company.

Table 9.4 **Divisional structure**

ADVANTAGES	DISADVANTAGES
Focus on a product/service/market	May develop a conflict of interests
Clearly defines responsibilities and accountability	Possibility of a drift in meeting corporate objectives
Provides autonomy to managers	May produce neglect of long-term priorities
Provides supporting services from the centre to divisions	Central control may stifle local innovation

Divisional structures can lead to a conflict of interest between divisions which develop different objectives and priorities and it is the role of the central organisation to be responsible for coordinating the work of divisions. This is not the same as the federal organisation described in Chapter 3 (p. 97) where a number of separate organisations or companies come together out of mutual interest, although one of their objectives is to gain some of the advantages of a division of a large organisation in terms of support. Chapter 3 describes changes to organisational structure brought about by greater flexibility in the labour force – this flexibility needs to be reflected in whichever management structure is chosen.

→ Ch. 3

→ Ch. 3

Cases

MANAGEMENT IN THE NEWS

A taxing merger

Vanessa Houlder

When a UK government department lost computer discs carrying the personal data of 25m people – members of 7m families in receipt of child benefit – in 2008, the incident was blamed on mistakes by junior officials. But a report just published on the debacle focuses its criticism not so much on individuals as on the 'unsuitable organisational design' of Her Majesty's Revenue and Customs (HMRC), the department formed by the merger of the Inland Revenue and Customs & Excise three years before.

In the report of the investigation Kieran Poynter, chairman of City of London professional services firm PwC, expresses dismay at HMRC's 'muddled accountabilities'. In a swipe at the complex structure adopted for the 2005 merger, he says HMRC should have opted for a traditional, hierarchical structure: '[HMRC] is not suited to the so-called "constructive friction" matrix type organisation [that was] in place at the time of the data loss.'

So did HMRC really get it so wrong – and if so, why?

Both outside and inside HMRC, the management structure has been condemned. Even before the discs were lost, at least one professional institute – the tax faculty of the ICAEW, the UK chartered accountants'

body – blamed the 'matrix management' for lack of accountability, ownership of issues and clarity of vision. Soon after, a Cabinet Office report highlighted the 'proliferation of committees' at HMRC and criticised 'the complex management structure'.

At the time of the merger, however, HMRC's top managers faced a traditional management problem of finding a way to integrate two entities without forcing one partner to mould itself to the other. They had two big organisations with different cultures: Inland Revenue was pragmatic and intellectual; Customs & Excise more confrontational. Costs had to be cut 5 per cent a year, with the consent of the unions and without alienating staff.

Around the time the HMRC was formed, Sir David Varney, the chairman (a senior industrialist who had worked at Shell, British Gas and BT) explained that senior managers' responsibilities would not correspond with the former structures of the two legacy organisations, so enabling a new culture to develop. 'We didn't want an organisation that was split along lines of customers, operations or policies or infrastructure,' he said. But was the matrix structure a fundamental flaw? The idea of a grid-like structure with multiple reporting lines first became popular in

→

Management in the news – continued

the 1970s for encouraging speed and innovation. At best, it helps top management understand the consequences of a course of action. But it has often been criticised for causing loyalty clashes and turf battles.

Professor Nelson Phillips, head of the organisation and management group at Tanaka Business School at Imperial College, London says matrix structures remain essential for multinationals. But he says a hierarchical structure has advantages for transaction-processing organisations such as HMRC that need clear lines of communication. He suspects the adoption of a complex structure in cases such as HMRC might be a way of avoiding hard decisions: 'Who is the boss? You can both be the boss in a matrix,' he says. In the aftermath, HMRC has moved

to a simpler structure that makes responsibilities clear. But in the long run, creating a common culture may prove a hard task.

Source: Houlder, V. 'A Taxing Merger', *Financial Times*, 10 July 2008. Copyright © 2008 The Financial Times Limited, reproduced with permission.

Discussion questions

1 What lessons can be drawn from the article about the importance of organisational structure?

2 Why might the management of the newly created HMRC have chosen a matrix style (as shown in Figure 14.12), rather than a hierarchy? Explain the benefits and drawbacks of each for both employees and for the government.

CASE APPLICATION 2

A New Kind of Structure

Admit it. Sometimes the projects you're working on (school, work, or both) can get pretty boring and monotonous. Wouldn't it be great to have a magic button you could push to get someone else to do that boring, time-consuming stuff? At Pfizer, that "magic button" is a reality for a large number of employees.[44]

As a global pharmaceutical company, Pfizer is continually looking for ways to help employees be more efficient and effective. The company's senior director of organizational effectiveness found that the "Harvard MBA staff we hired to develop strategies and innovate were instead Googling and making PowerPoints." Indeed, internal studies conducted to find out just how much time its valuable talent was spending on menial tasks was startling. The average Pfizer employee was spending 20 percent to 40 percent of his or her time on support work (creating documents, typing notes, doing research, manipulating data, scheduling meetings) and only 60 percent to 80 percent on knowledge work (strategy, innovation, networking, collaborating, critical thinking). And the problem wasn't just at lower levels. Even the highest-level employees were affected. Take, for instance, David Cain, an executive director for global engineering. He enjoys his job—assessing environmental real estate risks, managing facilities, and controlling a multimillion-dollar budget. But he didn't so much enjoy having to go through spreadsheets and put together PowerPoints. Now, however, with Pfizer's "magic button," those tasks are passed off to individuals outside the organization.

Just what is this "magic button?" Originally called the Office of the Future (OOF), the renamed PfizerWorks allows employees to shift tedious and time-consuming tasks with the click of a single button on their computer desktop. They describe what they need on an online form, which is then sent to one of two Indian service-outsourcing firms. When a request is received, a team member in India calls the Pfizer employee to clarify what's needed and by when. The team member then e-mails back a cost specification for the requested work. If the Pfizer employee decides to proceed, the costs involved are charged to the employee's department. About this unique arrangement, Cain said that he relishes working with what he prefers to call his "personal consulting organization."

The number 66,500 illustrates just how beneficial PfizerWorks has been for the company. That's the number of work hours estimated to have been saved by employees who've used PfizerWorks. What about Joe Cain's experiences? When he gave the Indian team a complex project researching strategic actions that worked when consolidating company facilities, the team put the report together in a month, something that would have taken him six months to do alone. He says, "Pfizer pays me not to work tactically, but to work strategically."

Discussion Questions

1. Describe and evaluate what Pfizer is doing with its PfizerWorks.
2. What structural implications—good and bad—does this approach have? (Think in terms of the six organizational design elements.)
3. Do you think this arrangement would work for other types of organizations? Why or why not? What types of organizations might it also work for?
4. What role do you think organizational structure plays in an organization's efficiency and effectiveness? Explain.

anish company Bang & Olufsen (B&O) is known globally for its high-end audio and video equipment. Many of its incredibly beautiful and artistic products—most of which are made in Denmark—are part of the collection at New York's Museum of Modern Art. Needless to say, product design is critically important to B&O. What's even more unique than its futuristic products, however, is the company's approach to the design process, which is a critical strategic capability of the organization. CEO Kalle Hvidt Nielsen says, "Our mission is to make complex technology very simple to use."

Unlike the conventional design approach used by most organizations in which marketing employees conduct consumer market research and then decide design direction, B&O uses contract designers, not organizational design employees, to create the company's products. And these designers have been empowered to veto any product they don't like. The company's lead designer, David Lewis, has freelanced for the company since the early 1960s. He spends just two or three days per month at the company's headquarters in Struer and says that, "It's a great, concentrated way of working...I see things in a different way because I am not at all part of the system here." Lewis and his team of six designers, who all are external freelancers, don't ever meet.

The design process isn't really a process. Lewis says that, "Every time we design a new product, it's like starting all over. Time frames, technology, and demands are different each time." However, he and his team do have an approach. They don't use sketches; they model the new product out of cardboard, pieces of paper, little bits of plastic, or whatever's on hand. Working like a sculptor, the team builds the model. They stand around it, talk about it, and modify it as needed. Once the model is complete, Lewis takes it to headquarters where company executives can see what the design is about. And being able to see and feel the new product in three dimensions, it's easy for top-level decision makers to see all the details and really feel the design.

Giving such power to individuals who aren't employees would frighten most managers. However, it works well for B&O. This "business-by-genius model depends on the instincts of a handful of quirky and creative individuals and the ability of executives to manage them."

Discussion Questions

1. Describe and evaluate what B&O is doing.
2. What structural implications—good and bad—does this approach have? (Think in terms of the six organizational design elements.)
3. Do you think this arrangement would work for other types of organizations? Why or why not?
4. The B&O design approach depends on "the ability of executives to manage" the designers. What abilities would managers need in managing in this type of organizational design?
5. What role do you think organizational structure plays in an organization's strategic capabilities, especially in innovation efforts?

Sources: D. A. Keeps, "Out of-the-Box Offices," *Fortune,* January 19, 2009, pp. 45–50; D. Steinbom, "Talking About Design: An Interview with David Lewis," *Wall Street Journal,* June 23, 2008, p. R6; D. Steinbom, "A Speaker That Was Decades in the Making," *Wall Street Journal,* June 23, 2008, p. R6; and J. Greene, "Where Designers Rule," *BusinessWeek,* November 5, 2007, pp. 46–51.

Case Study: *StarCars*

StarCars was formed in 1994 by Ernie Anderson. He started by purchasing a Porsche 911 and hiring it out in his home town of Oxford. Demand for the car was unbelievable. By 1996 he had bought another Porsche, a Ferrari and an Aston Martin and was beginning to develop a profitable business. By 2002 he had five car hire centres - a head office and centre in Oxford, centres in Reading and Watford, and two others in London. The business was organised as shown in Figure 3.

By 2008 StarCars had another 14 centres, as shown on Figure 4. But some serious problems had arisen.

- There were communication problems. Staff in other centres often found it difficult to sort out wage queries with Oxford. Also, when a centre had a problem, such as a customer dispute, it

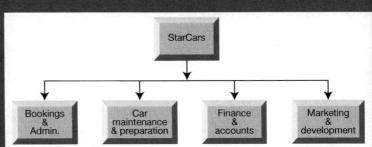

Figure 3: Organisation chart for StarCars

- **Bookings & Admin**. Each centre had one full-time and two part-time staff handling bookings and administration. They dealt with customers when they booked cars, picked them up and dropped them off.
- **Car maintenance and preparation**. A 'mobile' mechanic was based at Oxford, but dealt with maintenance work on all of the cars. In each centre one person cleaned the cars and prepared them for customers before they were picked up.
- **Finance and accounts**. Two people were employed at Oxford to process wages, deal with staff problems, record business transactions, produce accounts and carry out purchasing.
- **Marketing and business development**. This section was set up when the business started to expand. Ernie played an important role, but also hired two other staff to help him. This part of the business bought the cars. It was time consuming because the cars were expensive and required research, comprehensive knowledge, sound negotiation skills and careful judgment. The role of one of the staff was to advertise the business and find suitable sites for new centres.

→

Figure 4: StarCar centres in 2004

Thirsk
York
Leeds
Liverpool
Chester
Birmingham
Coventry
Statford-upon-Avon
Cambridge
Watford
Oxford
Reading
London
Exeter
Torquay
Plymouth

was difficult to settle because no one seemed to have any authority. Ernie, who made all the key decisions, was often unavailable.

- Because of the distances involved, the mobile mechanic found it impossible to maintain cars all over the country. The mechanic was overworked, even though eventually an assistant was employed.

- Ernie worried about the accountability of each centre. Although he trusted the majority of his staff, he felt that there was not enough incentive for each centre to maximise performance.

- Because of the geographical distance between centres, staff felt isolated. There was often a lack of leadership and some staff became demotivated. Staff turnover had also risen, particularly in the centres away from the South East.

Ernie felt that the solution was to organise the company geographically. Looking at Figure 5, he thought that the company could be divided into six areas. It would be necessary to appoint a manager responsible for each region and delegate a lot more responsibility. Regional managers would make daily visits to each centre in the region, recruit staff, and attend a management meeting with Ernie every two weeks in Birmingham. Managers could take decisions on behalf of their region without consulting Ernie.

Ernie decided to outsource all car maintenance to another business and to allow managers to buy cars for their region based on regional demand. However, managers would have to be carefully trained in this task. Ernie also decided to pay managers a low basic salary, but offer an incentive package based on the amount of time cars were hired out. If cars were hired out 80 per cent of the time an annual bonus of £10,000 would be paid. If this rose to 95 per cent a further £17,000 would be paid. Ernie expected all managers to reach the first target and the company would make a reasonable profit based on this performance. However, the second target was likely to be more of a challenge.

(a) **Explain why you think Ernie organised StarCars by function initially. (6 marks)**

(b) **Draw the new organisational chart suggested by Ernie, based on geographical location in Figure 4. (8 marks)**

(c) **Explain why organisation by product might be inappropriate for StarCars. (6 marks)**

(d) **Explain why accountability is likely to improve after the reorganisation. (12 marks)**

(e) **To what extent will the new organisation structure help overcome the problems StarCars is experiencing? (18 marks)**

Review Questions and Tests

KNOWLEDGE

1. What is meant by organisation by function?
2. Why might a business be organised in more than one way?
3. State two advantages and two disadvantages of a functional organisational structure.
4. Describe the advantages of a company organising itself by product.
5. When is regional organisation likely to be an appropriate method of organisation for a business?
6. Why might solicitors organise themselves according to customer group?
7. What is meant by organisation by process?
8. Suggest two types of business that may organise themselves by process.

SECTION 5:
ORGANISATION CULTURE

Chapter 11:
Organisation Culture

1. What Is Culture?

Culture
Everything that the people in a society have learned and share through traditions, pass on to children, and teach new members; this includes religion, beliefs, political ideologies, values, customs, foods, language, gender roles, sexuality, and many other aspects of everyday life.

Exhibit **13.1**

Anthropologist Margaret Mead was best known for her study of Samoan culture.

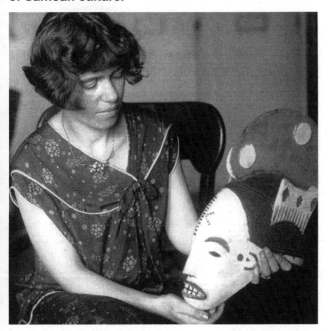

Pictorial Press/Alamy Images

The famous anthropologist Margaret Mead defined **culture** as everything that people in a society have learned and share through traditions, pass on to children, and teach new members (Exhibit 13.1). According to this view, culture includes religion, beliefs, political ideologies, values, customs, foods, language, gender roles, sexuality, and many other aspects of everyday life.[1]

Culture is a powerful force in our lives because it guides our beliefs, our values, and almost everything we do at home, in our communities, and at work. We learn about culture from the moment we are born. The language we learn is part of our culture. The food we eat is part of our culture. Our manners and how we behave are part of our culture. Culture and cultural expectations affect how we think, feel, and act. Often invisible, culture is so much a part of us that we may not realize we are following its "rules." Rather, these "rules" are simply the way things are supposed to be. As organizational scholar Geert Hofstede puts it, culture is the "collective programming of the mind."[2]

To be an effective leader, manager, or employee, you must appreciate how culture affects people, influences relationships, and impacts organizations. In this chapter, you will study aspects of culture that affect people at work and in other relationships. You will also learn about models of culture in organizations. In addition, you'll evaluate the types of organizational cultures that are important today, HR's role in creating and maintaining healthy cultures, and what we can all do to create powerful organizational cultures. Let's start by developing a deeper understanding of the ways in which values, attitudes, and commonly held expectations of behavior relate to culture.

Values

Values are ideas that a person or a group believes to be right or wrong, good or bad, attractive or undesirable.[3] Values related to a society's culture often include ideas about principles like freedom, democracy, truth, and justice. Values also include ideas about things such as sex, marriage, and raising children. For example, you might have certain values associated with family life: Should you be married before having children? Should adult children care for elderly parents at home, rather than moving them to a nursing facility? Should family members be loyal no matter what someone does? You may have strong opinions about these questions and feel less intensely about others. That's because values aren't just abstract ideas—they often help to define who we are and can therefore produce very strong emotions.

Deeply held values are profound drivers of our behavior at work and in life. People will fight and even die for values that are important to them, such as justice, freedom, or those linked with religious beliefs. Do you know which values are most important to you and why? Do you know how your values affect you at work? Understanding your values will help you in life and at work.

One example of a personal value that can impact how people feel and behave in the workplace is "fairness." People who place a high value on fairness will often act in ways that enhance justice and equality. Individuals who hold this value typically favor use of the merit system, and they believe that employees should be rewarded for their performance. In addition, these people are generally on the alert for any signs of injustice. If such signs are detected, people who value fairness may become angry, frustrated, and demoralized at work.

Organizations often promote specific values that guide behavior among employees, customers, stakeholders, and behavior related to property and the natural environment. One example of an organizational value that is commonly espoused in companies goes something like this: "People are our greatest asset." Companies that hold this value tend to place special emphasis on supporting people's learning, development, health, and well-being.

In companies that put a high value on people, you might expect that managers who mistreat employees would be chastised and maybe even let go. Indeed, this was recently the case in one U.S. law firm. This firm was a partnership—meaning that the senior lawyers owned the business together. In this sort of business structure, it is very difficult to fire people. Nevertheless, this particular company decided that some of its partners were not living up to the firm's values when it came to how to treat people. These partners were not supporting the young attorneys' development, they often communicated in harsh and unprofessional ways, and they were causing employees to burn out. The firm's leadership felt that this violation of values was serious—and they fired several senior partners as a result.

Attitudes

Sometimes we hear people say things like "He has a bad attitude" or "Her attitude is so positive!" These types of statements are often shorthand for any number of beliefs, values, and behaviors that affect a person, how he or she relates to others, and how he or she is seen at work. When we hear statements like these, it is important for us to go beyond the shorthand and find out exactly what the speaker means.

Attitudes are a group of ideas, values, beliefs, and feelings that predispose a person to react to a thing, a situation, another person, or a group in a certain way.[4] What is your attitude toward school? Do you value learning and feel generally positive about your classes, and do you usually see the benefits of attending school? Or do you resent having to go to school? How does your attitude about school affect your study habits?

Attitudes matter when it comes to how we perceive situations and judge people, and, in turn, how those people see and judge us. Strongly held attitudes evoke strong emotions in people in much the same way that values do. Many people don't spend much time thinking about their values or attitudes, or about which of these are most important and which are less so. That's because values and attitudes are so much a part of "who we are" that they often go unexamined.

Good leaders, however, do not leave values or attitudes unexamined. They constantly push themselves to understand what is driving them, which values are sacrosanct, and which attitudes may need to change. Understanding our own values and attitudes—and the emotions we attach to them—is critical because it helps us understand our behavior and develop a personal code of ethics. Knowing our values also helps us better understand other peoples' values, and it permits us to examine the values that our organizations ask us to uphold. Values and attitudes are also important because they affect behaviors and norms.

Norms

Norms are internalized standards for behavior that support agreed-upon ways of doing things and what people expect of one another within a cultural group. For example, norms guide how we dress and behave at a formal dinner, how we greet one another, and how we behave with friends versus family versus coworkers.

Norms are often unspoken, and in some cases, people may not even recognize them until they are violated. For instance, in the United States, people go to the end of the line at a counter in a store and wait until it is their turn to pay for their merchandise. No one has to tell us to do that—it's just what happens. Now, imagine what you would think and feel if someone walked to the front of the line and pulled out his wallet. You'd probably be irritated, because the person was violating a norm. Or, imagine how you would feel if someone joined you on an elevator and stood several inches closer than normal. What

Attitudes
A group of ideas, values, beliefs, and feelings that predispose a person to react to a thing, a situation, another person, or a group in a certain way.

Norms
Internalized standards for behavior that support agreed-upon ways of doing things and what people expect of one another within a cultural group.

would you do? What would you think of the person? Your thoughts and feelings would be in part related to the fact that the person was violating norms about personal space.

Some norms function like guidelines, whereas others are more like social rules. Accordingly, scholars have identified two distinct categories of norms: folkways, which are like guidelines, and mores, which are stricter social rules. **Folkways** are the routine conventions of everyday life. They include aspects of culture such as appropriate dress and good social manners. People who violate folkways may be perceived as odd or weird, but not necessarily as evil or bad (■Exhibit 13.2). For example, if you jumped fully dressed into a crowded pool, others would view you as an oddball. Folkways also exist at work, and they might include such things as how you greet senior managers, how you are expected to behave at an office party (e.g., don't drink too much), or how carefully you attend to the start and end times of meetings.

As opposed to folkways, **mores** (pronounced "morays") are norms that are central to the functioning of society or a group. More like rules than guidelines, mores might include a society's stance on murder, rape, sexuality, or childrearing practices. When people violate mores, they can face serious reprisals, often because many of our mores are codified into laws. For example, in many societies, people face trial and possible jail time for theft, murder, or incest.

Societies differ, of course, and mores are not universal from one culture to the next. For instance, several countries, including the United States, have laws that prohibit polygamy. The nation of Senegal, however, does not have mores prohibiting polygamy. In Senegal, polygamy is allowed and practiced alongside marriages between one man and one woman. Indeed, one researcher found that 15 percent of Christian men and 28 percent of Muslim men in Senegal reported having polygamous marriages in the year 2000. This equaled about 29 percent of the country's population at the time.[5]

Within the work environment, mores often revolve around core business practices and ethics. For example, many businesses expect their employees to refuse to take or offer bribes for any reason or in any situation. Another example of a more might relate to the protection of corporate secrets, such as the formulas involved in preparing products like Kentucky Fried Chicken or Coca-Cola.

Understanding how values and norms differ in cultures is critical in business today. That's because so many businesses—both domestic and international—conduct operations outside their home country and/or employ people whose cultures differ.

To work effectively together, people need to understand and respect one another's norms and values. For example, it is often said that the failure of the auto industry merger between Daimler-Benz (maker of Mercedes-Benz) and Chrysler was linked to irreconcilable differences in culture and the inability of the company's leaders to bridge these gaps.[6] In the next section, we will look at other aspects of culture and how they affect us at work.

Folkways
The routine conventions of everyday life.

Mores
Norms that are central to the functioning of society.

■Exhibit **13.2**
Unusual haircuts are often seen as a violation of folkways.

blickwinkel/Teister/Alamy

Most Popular » Discussion Questions

1. Brainstorm a list of things that you believe define your national culture, such as beliefs, values, traditions, foods, and religion. Share with others from your own culture and from another. How are your lists the same? How are they different?
2. Give two examples of folkways at your school.
3. Have you ever experienced a new and different culture? If so, how did you learn about the norms of that culture?
4. What are your core values—those values that define who you are as a person and guide you in some of the most important arenas of your life, including family, relationships, and work?

5. How Can We Study Organizational Culture?

Culture is often difficult to understand. However, it's critical to learn how to study organizational culture because it has such a powerful effect on people's values, attitudes, and behaviors. Culture also affects organizational results. In this section, you'll begin by considering two ways to "look" at culture. The first method enables you to see three levels of culture—from more obvious to less. The second method draws your attention to stories, traditions, taboos, and the way in which language is used in organizations—all of which are powerful indicators of culture. After that, we discuss practical methods for studying culture—methods that managers can actually use.

Exhibit **13.7**

We can observe some parts of culture, but other parts are less obvious.

Observable Artifacts

Values and Attitudes

Basic Assumptions

Edgar Schein's Levels of Culture

The respected scholar Edgar Schein has done much to help us understand how culture develops in organizations, how it is maintained, and how it can be improved.[50] Schein notes that some aspects of culture can be directly observed, including language, dress, and behavioral norms such as how late or early people are for meetings. These aspects are what Schein calls *observable artifacts*, as depicted in Exhibit 13.7. Other aspects of culture—values, for example—are not as easy to see, and even less visible are what Schein calls *basic assumptions*.[51] Let's look at each of these levels of culture and how they might play out in an organization.

Observable Artifacts: The Top Level of Schein's Organizational Culture Model

Observable artifacts are those aspects of a culture that can be seen, heard, or experienced by an organization's members. Observable artifacts can often be easily determined just by asking questions. Some common examples of observable artifacts:

• *Dress code:* An organization's dress code may be written or unwritten, but in either case the organization has a clear expectation of how employees should dress for work. To determine a company's dress code, try asking the following types of questions: Can you wear jeans to work, or would that be cause for dismissal? Do men wear ties? Do people pay a lot of attention to things like polished shoes? Do some people wear uniforms but other people wear their own clothes?

• *Language and jargon:* Language and jargon are clues to what people value and pay attention to in a culture. When studying language and jargon, ask yourself the following questions: Do people use words that have meaning only to organization members? Are acronyms frequently used? Is slang used? By whom and how? In a multicultural organization, is one language the norm for senior leaders?

• *Interpersonal relationships:* Organizations have cultural "rules" about how people relate to one another. When determining the relational norms, you can start by asking: Do people know much about one another's personal lives? Do people do things together outside of work? Do people treat each other with respect and consideration, or do they relate more instrumentally around tasks?

• *Technology:* How people use technology is linked to beliefs and norms around work. To explore how technology relates to people's beliefs, ask the following sorts of questions: Are Macs or PCs used? Do employees communicate mainly through e-mail, or do they talk to each other directly?

- *Workspace:* Where people do their work is an indication of communication norms, power dynamics, and the like. You can study this by asking: Do the big bosses have special offices? Is management close to staff or far away? Does everyone have a desk in an open space? If it's a virtual organization, does technology support group work?
- *Ceremonies, rituals, and awards:* Ceremonies, rituals, and awards indicate what is valued in a culture. To explore this, you can ask: Are there events that can't be missed and that people will cancel vacations to attend? Do managers always bring food to early morning meetings? Are there "prizes" for certain outcomes, such as hitting sales targets?

There are many observable indicators of culture. Learning how to question what you see will enable you to draw conclusions about some of the less visible and yet very powerful aspects of organizational culture, such as values.

Values: The Middle Level of Schein's Organizational Culture Model

Espoused values

Explicit values that are preferred by an organization and communicated deliberately to the organization's members.

The **espoused values** of an organization are explicit values that are preferred by the organization and communicated deliberately to the organization's members. Founders and leaders have an important role in shaping these values, which are often listed in the company's marketing materials, mission statement, and employee training materials. Note, however, that the term *espoused values* refers only to what is said, and not necessarily to what is actually done. For example, a company can communicate to its employees and customers that one of its core values is quality, but if the organization does not have a quality control department and does not measure defects, then these values are merely espoused (rather than enacted).

Enacted values

The values that are actually exhibited in an organization.

Enacted values are the values that are actually exhibited in an organization. These values can be seen, for example, in how people treat customers or how people treat each other at work. Enacted values are also often evident in people's ethics, in policies regarding sustainability, and in the behaviors for which employees are rewarded.

Basic Assumptions: The Deepest Level of Schein's Organizational Culture Model

In Schein's system the deepest level of organizational culture consists of basic assumptions, or the *core* beliefs that are deeply embedded in the organization and that are largely invisible. Organization members are usually unaware of these assumptions or how they guide behavior, and they are often taken for granted. For example, a basic assumption may be that people are opportunists and will steal when given the opportunity. In this situation, you may never hear anyone say that people are untrustworthy, and if asked, people might not admit to this basic assumption. You would see, however, that managers are highly vigilant, inventory is checked regularly, security is tight, and monitoring cameras are used throughout the organization's facilities. Another example of a common basic assumption is that only leaders can fix organizational problems. Again, people would not say this directly and if asked would not necessarily agree. But the basic assumption would be evident in things like the number of small decisions made at senior meetings.

This brings us back to the importance of carefully observing and interpreting observable artifacts. These, and both espoused and enacted values, are the clues to "what's really going on around here." To deepen your understanding, you can also look at other indicators of culture: organizational myths and heroes, taboos, sacred symbols, and language.

Myths and Heroes, Taboos, Sacred Symbols, and Language

Culture is rarely communicated directly. More often, it is conveyed through the stories people tell about themselves, through what is considered good or evil, and through the ways in which language is used. When seeking to learn about an organization's culture, therefore, it is especially helpful to consider the organization's myths, heroes, taboos, sacred symbols, and language. These types of cultural expression are linked to values and basic assumptions, and they drive members' behavior because they are part of what people look to when they make decisions about what to think, believe, and do.[52]

Myths and Heroes

Myths
Exaggerated stories that are told and retold to communicate values and to emphasize norms.

In anthropology, myths are stories that describe ideologies.[53] An organization's **myths** are exaggerated stories that are told and retold to communicate values and to emphasize norms. These stories usually involve important events or people, such as the founder of the organization, setbacks that occurred long ago, heroes who overcame problems, or even examples of "perfect" or "evil" behavior.[54] Myths point to what an organization values, and they also communicate which behaviors are desirable and which are considered taboo. Because they bind people together around a common vision of good and bad behavior, myths demonstrate what it takes to succeed in a company.

Hero
A legendary person who embodies the highest values of a culture.

Myths often center on the actions of a hero. Here, a **hero** is defined as a legendary person who embodies the highest values of a culture. He or she defends the organization against external or internal forces that threaten values, beliefs, or the best way to do things. Schein notes that in the mythologies of many organizations, stories are told of managers and engineers who have fallen into disfavor for bucking an organizational norm only to later become heroes in some other context.[55]

For example, author William Rogers relates a story about a low-level IBM employee who refused to admit the chairman of the board to a secure area without proper identification. When others in the group verbally assaulted the employee, the chairman rewarded his behavior by silencing the critics and obtaining the requested identification.[56] This particular story communicates the idea that rule breaking is unacceptable, even for the highest status members of IBM.[57] The employee who challenged the chairman became elevated to the status of folk hero through the telling and retelling of the story. Stories like this show how heroes uphold organizational values even when facing danger. Heroes are courageous and bigger than life.

How do you know a hero story when you hear one? Chances are, the person at the center of the story will be talked about a lot in the organization. In addition, people tend to employ strong language when talking about heroes, using words like *amazing, incredible, brilliant, unbelievably creative,* and *charismatic.* He or she will be referred to with respect and perhaps even reverence.

Socialization
The process of teaching new members about a culture.

Myths and hero stories are important because they support **socialization**, or the process of teaching new members about a culture. They also provide a way to explain current practices and shape the future.[58]

Taboos

Taboos
Strong prohibitions against certain activities.

Hero stories frequently describe what people should do in organizations. In contrast, taboos tell people what *not* to do. **Taboos** are strong prohibitions against certain activities, and they are often associated with what a group considers sacred or profane.[59] In many societies' cultures, they involve such things as food, sexuality, religious practice, and death. Taboos essentially act as unwritten laws that forbid various activities, thoughts, and even feelings. Violations can lead to severe sanctions, such as shaming, ostracism, or, in some societies, losing one's life.

Every culture has taboos, and this includes organizational cultures. For instance, some organizational cultures include an unspoken rule that you should never get mad at your boss. Other common examples include taboos around whom employees can date—sometimes, other employees are off limits, and oftentimes, clients are as well. In addition, some scholars who study conflict between men and women believe that many cultures have strong taboos against men and women arguing or disagreeing with one another.[60] You can see how this would not be helpful in organizations, because disagreement often leads to better solutions.

Other researchers have focused specifically on taboos related to an organization's willingness to engage in socially responsible behavior. One scholar has identified three taboos that inhibit corporate social responsibility: the taboo against seeing business as having moral responsibility; the taboo against questioning the goal of continuous economic growth; and the taboo against becoming involved in the "politics" around social responsibility.[61] Of the three, the taboo against interfering with continuous economic growth is perhaps strongest. For most of the twentieth century, growth was the "Holy Grail" and anything that interfered with it seemed to be taboo.[62]

Sacred Symbols

Sacred symbols
Things, people, and events that are untouchable and unquestionable within a culture.

A culture's **sacred symbols** are the things, people, and events that are untouchable and unquestionable. Consider how people sometimes feel about their nation's flag: It's just a piece of cloth, really, but it holds such special meaning that it is often protected from harm by laws and taboos (■Exhibit 13.8). Thus, to some people in some cultures, the flag is sacred.

The same sort of thing happens in organizations. Certain objects, people, or events take on such special meaning that they cannot be harmed, removed, or changed. Consider the proverbial "corner office." In some organizations, status and power come with sacred trappings like the corner office, or perhaps a private washroom or a special cafeteria. These privileges are viewed as sacred symbols of having "made it" in the organization.

When something becomes sacred, it is extremely difficult to change. This can even apply to products, such as Coca-Cola. Coca-Cola company's management found out the hard way that consumers weren't going to tolerate any changes to their beloved drink. When "New Coke" was introduced in the mid-1980s consumers rebelled. In fact, some people actually stockpiled "real" Coke before the change, and many people felt betrayed by the company.

What's especially interesting about the "New Coke" example is that the Coca-Cola Company had changed Coke's recipe numerous times since the product was first introduced in the mid-1880s. Back then, the drink was known as "Cocawine," and its recipe included both alcohol and derivatives of coca leaves, which are used in the production of cocaine. By the 1930s, however, the company had phased out these ingredients, eventually arriving at the formula we know today.

Few people complained when the company adjusted its recipe between 1880 and 1930, yet when Coke's formula was changed in the mid-1980s, people rebelled. Maybe

■Exhibit **13.8**

Many Americans consider the flag to be sacred and are disturbed when it is burned in protest.

Sergey Kamshylin/Shutterstock

it was because the recipe had been the same for more than 50 years, and two or three generations had grown up with the "old" taste, logo, bottles, and packaging. Or maybe it was because Coke had become a symbol of something much more profound than a sweetened drink—it had become an American icon, and for some a symbol of freedom. Indeed, before the end of the Cold War in the late 1980s, whenever Coke's advertising appeared on the streets of a Communist country, some people believed that progress was being made toward establishment of a less restrictive society.[63]

Whatever the reason, one thing remained certain: New Coke wasn't Coke, and it really didn't matter if the updated version was "better" or not. Ultimately, this public outcry convinced the Coca-Cola Company to switch back to the previous formula.[64] In doing so, the company had to take on the cost and time burdens associated with two major changes in production and marketing within a short time frame.

Sometimes events unfold in the opposite direction of the "New Coke" debacle. In such cases, companies refuse to change their products or services or wait too long to do so because their products or services have historically been part of the company's image. These products and services are therefore viewed by the company as sacred and untouchable, even when the market no longer wants or needs them. For example, for some years now there has been more awareness that fast-food restaurants often serve foods that are high in fats, sugar, and the like, and that these are not good for you. One would think that these restaurants would have paid attention to the trend. In fact, they appeared to do so when, in the late 1990s, we started seeing things like "chicken Caesar salads" appear on menus. Customers soon discovered, however, that these salads often had more fat and more calories than burgers! It is only recently that truly healthy foods have begun to show up on fast-food menus.

Language

How people use words, which native language is paramount in multicultural organizations, and even body language are powerful indicators of culture. An organization's culture can therefore be studied by looking at how language and symbols relate to ideologies and practices that unify an organization.[65]

Because spoken language is a key form of communication, familiarity with the sayings, slang, jargon, and/or acronyms specific to an organization is useful when seeking to understand that organization's culture. Consider the following expression: *"I can't believe the butterbar went VFR direct to the Old Man!"*[66]

Can you translate this? Unless you belong or have belonged to a military subculture that uses this language, you probably won't have a clue what is meant. In this case, a butterbar is a second lieutenant, the lowest officer rank in the army. The derogatory term refers to the yellow color of the single bar insignia. VFR is an acronym for "visual flight rules" and means to take the most visually direct path. Here, VFR becomes a metaphor for circumventing the chain of command to reach the top (the "Old Man") officer, a taboo in the military and many other cultures. This illustrates problems related to the use of slang, jargon, and the like: Although this language tends to unify members inside an organization, it also serves to keep other people out. In addition, unique language can establish a barrier between an organization and its customers, consumers, and vendors. In today's flat, complex, international organizations, this can be destructive.

Many companies today have a much bigger problem than simply controlling the use of jargon and acronyms: today, members of many organizations speak different native languages. Consider the example of a large European financial services company with senior managers whose native languages are Italian, German, and English. Several managers prefer using their native Italian, several others prefer doing business in German, and one or two prefer English. In most subsidiaries, employees speak only the local language. How does a company like this manage language—and how can language be effective in supporting culture if people can't speak to one another? Situations like this are common today. Thus, in recent years, many organizations have had to develop "language policies" to guide which language(s) are used on the job and what language(s) employees must learn in order to be promoted.[67]

The intricate and inseparable relationship between language and culture means that a choice of one language over others has an organization-wide impact on how power is perceived and who has access to it. To return to the previous example, the company's leaders eventually decided that English was the preferred language for business. This decision caused a great deal of conflict and disagreement, because it was seen as a sign that the company was going to adopt more British and/or American ways of doing business. Many of the Italian and German managers were highly displeased with the decision and the implications for the organization's culture.

Nonverbal communication provides us with another means for understanding a culture. By examining people's facial expressions, body language, posture, tone of voice, and so forth, you can gain a significant amount of information. For example, if you notice that people tend to lower their eyes and speak softly when talking with senior managers, this might indicate high power distance—or a large status differentiation between lower level employees and upper management.

Language, nonverbal communication, and the stories people tell about their cultures are powerful in that they can help maintain and strengthen that culture. This is fine when the culture supports the goals of the organization—but that isn't always the case, especially in today's rapidly changing world. For instance, when myths are really just questionable beliefs that are protected by taboos, or when heroes' behavior is actually harmful, myths and hero stories can be destructive.[68] Similarly, when things that are sacred really need to be changed, or when taboos prevent people from doing the right things, culture becomes a barrier to success. Accordingly, one powerful way to begin to change a culture is to examine the various aspects of that culture, then consciously use those aspects that support positive outcomes and change those that don't. In the next section of the chapter, you'll learn how to study culture to better understand which aspects of culture help an organization and which get in the way.

Leaders and Managers as Ethnographers

Observing, myths, heroes, taboos, sacred symbols, and language can help tremendously in understanding a culture. Sometimes, however, you need to go beyond simple observation and interpretation. You need to also find out from people themselves about their culture. Most of the time you can't simply ask questions because peoples' culture is so deeply buried that they don't consciously recognize it. For that reason, students of organizational culture—and good managers and leaders—must become ethnographers.

Ethnography is the systematic study of human cultures. An ethnographic approach includes observation and co-inquiry. In a co-inquiry process, people observe and collaborate with one another to truly understand what is happening within their group or organization. This is sometimes called *participant observation*, and it isn't necessarily comfortable.[69] It's hard to really look at your culture. That's because when we co-inquire into an organization's culture, we attempt to explore the unspoken aspects of the culture—things that are a part of "who we are" but that might need to change. When faced with this challenge, good leaders can remember a quote widely attributed to Plato: "We can easily forgive a child who is afraid of the dark. The real tragedy of life is when men are afraid of the light."[70]

Through observation and inquiry, we can literally shine a light on an organization's culture. Dynamic inquiry is a co-inquiry approach developed by scholars Annie McKee and Cecilia McMillen. This process enables organization members to uncover cultural values and the basic assumptions that drive people's behavior as well as how leadership practices affect people and the organization.[71] Authors Daniel Goleman, Richard Boyatzis, and Annie McKee describe the process this way:

Ethnography
The systematic study of human cultures.

> *Many large companies have processes in place for systematically evaluating employee attitudes, values, and beliefs—a kind of proxy for the emotional reality. These processes can be very helpful, but the problem is that surveys measure only what they set out to measure—and they rarely tap the more subtle layer of . . . complex norms*

that flow through an organization. This blind spot can result in simply measuring what people want to know, but not what they don't want known. . . .

Dynamic inquiry offset[s] the "find what you look for" effect of most surveys and enable[s] leaders to begin to address the underlying cultural issues that are getting in their way. . . . Through the process of discovering the truth about their organization, people begin to create a shared language about what's really going on as well as what they'd like to see—their ideal vision of the company.

Dynamic inquiry involves focused conversations and open-ended questions intended to get at people's feelings. . . . It is only when people talk about their feelings that they begin to uncover root causes of problems in the culture and the true sources of inspiration around them. . . . They create a language that captures the real truth about the forces that affect people's day-to-day lives in the organization as well as their hopes for the future. . . . Once people are engaged in this kind of open dialogue about their culture and their dreams, it is very difficult to put the lid back on the box. . . . The creation of a shared language that is based on feelings as well as facts is a powerful driver of change. This shared language provides a sense of unity and resonance, and the resulting momentum helps people to move from talk to action. They feel inspired and empowered, willing to work together to address their collective concerns.[72]

Another ethnographic method often used to discover the underlying attributes of culture focuses exclusively on what's working in a group or organization. Developed by David Cooperrider, *appreciative inquiry* is a process that explores people's and the organization's strengths—in other words, everything that stimulates both people and the organization to become healthy and productive.[73] Appreciative inquiry is a form of ethnographic research that often includes interviews and large-group meetings where people can identify cultural and organizational strengths and opportunities and explore these together. This method can be particularly powerful when a company's employees have lost sight of what their unique contributions are, or when morale is so low that people need to build psychological strength to face challenges.

Methods such as dynamic inquiry and appreciative inquiry are built on the assumption that as a *study* of an organization is conducted, *change will begin to occur.* In other words, these methods are forms of action research, or research that seeks to effect organizational change as part of the study process.[74] With this type of research, all people who are involved in the interview process are also viewed as active participants in change management.[75]

Studying culture isn't reserved for experts or consultants—we all need to learn how to do it—employees, managers, and leaders alike. Understanding an organization's culture can help us to make the right choice about joining a company. Equally important is the fact that understanding culture can help us to be effective in a company. In the next section, we will look at what kinds of cultures leaders are attempting to create and foster in order to help their companies to be successful in today's complex environment.

Most Popular » Discussion Questions

1. How do things like dress, language, spatial arrangement, technology, relationships, and rituals reflect the cultural values of your school or place of work?
2. Articulate several core values for a group to which you belong. Now, try to determine the underlying basic assumptions that drive these values.
3. Think about some taboos in your family, workplace, or at school. How do these taboos affect how people interact and/or how effective the group is?
4. Using a co-inquiry approach, interview a classmate about the culture of your school, then have him or her interview you. Together, identify themes that relate to the culture of your school.

6. Organizational Culture: What's Important Today?

Today's managers and leaders are increasingly struggling with issues related to organizational culture. One reason for this is that many organizational cultures have developed with very little guidance. Indeed, for much of the last century, managers and leaders paid little attention to the "people issues" in their organizations, including culture. Many organizational cultures, therefore, have been developed in haphazard ways. Many current cultures are also problematic in that they feature norms, values, and attitudes that supported simpler ways of doing business that worked a few decades ago but do not adequately support the complexity of today's business environment.

For these and other reasons many leaders are struggling to change their organizational cultures to better support long-term organizational sustainability, excellence, and success in today's environment. The next few sections explore organizational cultures that focus in turn on innovation, customer service, diversity, ethics, sustainability, and supporting employees in becoming the best they can be.

Innovative Cultures

Organizations must be innovative to remain competitive in today's global marketplace. An innovative culture can support employees in creative problem solving, formulating breakthrough ideas, developing new products and services, and finding more effective and efficient ways to work. Research demonstrates that when a culture has little bureaucracy, gives people autonomy, and allows them to take risks, then innovation flourishes.[76] Furthermore, when employees perceive their work environments to be original and imaginative, there is an increased level of creativity in their own work.[77] Of course, an innovative culture must be supported by management and organizational reward systems, and employees must not be burdened by excessive workloads and pressures, because these can inhibit development of this type of culture.[78]

Customer Service Cultures

Another way companies can distinguish themselves from their competitors is by providing superior service to their customers. For example, the Ritz-Carlton Hotel Company's credo includes the following statement: "We are ladies and gentlemen serving ladies and gentlemen"[79] (Exhibit 13.9). This philosophy highlights that Ritz-Carlton's goal is to excel at providing service with a high degree of professionalism.

In a study of best practices in the U.S. lodging industry, one common characteristic shared by all of the leading companies was that their hotels created a service culture. Consider the Four Seasons & Regent Hotel and Resorts, for instance.[80] This company has a comprehensive orientation and training program designed to teach its employees the value of personal service. Then, to support employees in delivering such service, the company keeps a higher than normal ratio of employees to guests. Finally, senior management collects data from focus groups, guests, and managers to ensure that a service culture is not just created, but successfully maintained.

Many organizations far removed from the lodging industry also focus on creating cultures that support excellent customer service. In businesses ranging from banks to clothing stores to software companies, service has become a priority. Interestingly, researchers

Exhibit **13.9**

The Ritz-Carlton employees follow a credo.

note that successful customer and market orientation—and the cultures that support these characteristics—are highly dependent on good leadership.[81]

Diversity Cultures

Innovation and customer service can capture customers' attention—as well as their business. Even innovation and great customer service, however, aren't enough to make a business successful over the long term. To achieve lasting success, people must be able to effectively work together inside the organization—and one potential challenge to this ability lies in the area of demographics.

The demographics in many business organizations have changed rapidly in recent years, and they continue to change today. For example, according to the research organization Catalyst, in 2008 more than half of management and professional occupations were held by women.[82] However, only 6.2 percent of top earners at Fortune 500 companies were women, and only 3 percent of Fortune 500 CEO positions were held by females. Still, in 2008, women held 15.2 percent of Fortune 500 board seats, compared to only 11.7 percent in 2000.[83]

Companies are also becoming increasingly diverse in terms of ethnicity and race. According to U.S. Bureau of Labor Statistics (BLS) projections, 68.3 percent of entrants into the labor force from 2006 to 2016 will be people of color or women, and 22.3 percent of this total will be Hispanic.[84] It is expected that the fastest rate of growth will be among Asian and Hispanic employees.[85] Also, many modern organizations—even small- and medium-sized companies—are international and have employees, suppliers, and vendors from more than one country, as well as customers and consumers all over the world. Finally, diversity in the workplace also includes differences in sexual orientation, religion, and physical abilities.[86]

Given the realities of the current business environment, it is essential that leaders and managers take steps to create more inclusive and diverse workplaces. Research indicates that diverse perspectives lead to better decisions, and they also help companies attract the best employees. Nonetheless, diversity can also be a source of conflict—when people have different ways of engaging with each other, different ways of working, or different cultures, clashes sometimes ensue. Thus, diversity is more likely to produce benefits if an organization focuses on integration and learning, which can help people better understand these sorts of differences.[87]

Some companies already know how to leverage diversity in the workforce to ensure that both employees and the company thrive. For one example of a culture that promotes diversity, consider the efforts of Johnson & Johnson, a global pharmaceutical company based in the United States. Chairman and CEO William C. Weldon and his management team believe that diversity increases competitive advantage, and their efforts have propelled Johnson & Johnson to the number-one spot on Diversity Inc.'s list of the Top 50 Most Diverse Companies of 2009.[88]

Weldon and his team are vitally involved in the company's many concrete efforts to build a culture that supports diversity, as depicted in ■Exhibit 13.10. For example, Weldon meets regularly with employees to discuss diversity initiatives. These types of meetings between the CEO and rank-and-file employees are rare in most companies. Another notable example of the company's diversity efforts is that Johnson & Johnson offers benefits to employees' same-sex partners.

Companies like Johnson & Johnson aren't leaving the development of a diverse workforce up to chance. Rather, they are actively engaged in building cultures that support everyone in contributing their best, and they also help employees develop the skills necessary to work effectively across cultural boundaries. In today's global business environment, this isn't just a "nice-to-have" characteristic—it's a must.

Ethical Cultures

Yet another attribute that distinguishes companies from one another is their commitment to ethics. Social pressure for people and companies to act in an ethical manner has

■Exhibit **13.10**

Johnson & Johnson's Diversity Efforts[89]	
Diversity Area	Johnson & Johnson's Efforts
CEO commitment	Chairman and CEO William Weldon regularly meets with employee-resource groups. Weldon has the company's chief diversity officer as a direct report. More than 6 percent of the bonuses for Weldon's direct reports are tied to meeting the diversity targets set forth in their goals and strategies. Johnson & Johnson has a diverse board of directors: among the 11 directors, African Americans, Asians, Latinos, and women are represented.
Company-wide commitment	Johnson & Johnson gets a perfect score on work/life benefits and on the benefits it offers to employees' same-sex domestic partners. Both the company's overall workforce and its management populations reflect the demographics of the communities Johnson & Johnson serves in the United States. Thirty-one percent of the most senior-level executives (CEO and direct reports) and nearly half of the company's top 10 percent, highest paid employees were women. Johnson & Johnson has excellent employee resource groups, including a group for employees of Middle Eastern and North African heritage.
Supplier diversity	Johnson & Johnson sponsors business-school programs for key diverse suppliers. The company also sponsors memberships and other professional development for diverse suppliers, such as participation in the National Minority Manufacturing Institute.

been increasing steadily for years, and recent high-profile cases of business leaders acting unethically have caused this movement to gain momentum.

Employees today are faced with numerous dilemmas, and for many of them, working in an organization that rewards ethical decisions is important. That's one reason why having an ethical culture is critical: When values and norms support ethical behavior, there is pressure for employees throughout a company to behave ethically in all circumstances.[90]

Research suggests that it is important for ethics to be institutionalized—but what does this mean? For some organizations, the process of institutionalizing ethics means explicitly encoding ethics in rules and guidelines. For example, companies may prohibit bribery, have rules about how to dispose of toxic waste, or set policies for investing employees' retirement funds. These rules protect the companies' ethical stance on a variety of social issues. However, explicit institutionalization of ethics is not enough. If an organization adopts guidelines that support ethical decision making but its managers don't follow these guidelines or not everyone has to observe them, then the organization's employees are bound to receive mixed signals.

This is why implicit institutionalization of ethics is important. Implicit institutionalization is the integration of ethics into the organizational culture. This process must include having management make a commitment to ethical leadership, as well as promoting a culture of personal responsibility when making ethical choices. To give an example, consider the previous example where the IBM employee refused to admit the chairman because he lacked the required credentials. He was following the rules, but in doing so potentially violating a company norm (deference to leaders). Facing an ethical dilemma, he chose to do the "right thing," in part because he had internalized the company's stance on security.

Scholars have found that when ethics are not mandated but are instead internalized, they have a much more powerful effect on employees' belief that the workplace is ethical.[91] This is linked to another reason to focus on implicit institutionalization of an ethical culture: Research suggests that implicit institutionalization leads to job satisfaction and high morale, whereas explicit institutionalization alone does not.[92]

How, then, can companies build an ethical culture? Luis Ramos, CEO of The Network, a company that provides ethics and compliance services, suggests the following:[93]

- A company's ethical code should be thought of as a living document—historical, yet modern. The code of ethics should therefore be an accessible resource which can easily be read by others.
- Ethics is a way of doing business; it is not a "program," which means it is a dynamic and continuous process.
- Ethics training is always relevant and, with the right attitude, it can be fun. If a company's ethics training is relevant, employees will more likely be interested in participating.
- Make sure that employees are actively engaged members of the organization and are aligned with the company's culture.

These actions support both ethical values and ethical behavior, two key aspects of an ethical culture.[94]

So, what types of companies carry out these activities successfully? One example is Cisco Systems, a firm that creates and supplies network management products for the Internet. Cisco wants its more than 65,000 employees to know that ethics are at the core of its business practices. In support of this goal Cisco rewrote its code of ethics to make it more user-friendly, and the company helps promote ethics and two-way communication by having monthly meetings for employees.

When a culture does not support ethical behavior people can get away with bad behavior. Consider Bernie Madoff, former non-executive chairman of the NASDAQ stock exchange, who was recently exposed for defrauding thousands of investors out of more than $60 billion. Although Madoff claimed that he was solely responsible for this scheme, authorities questioned whether he could have conducted such a vast fraud on his own. On August 11, 2009, Frank DiPascali, Jr., a former Madoff deputy, was taken into custody after admitting guilt to 10 felony counts of fraud. DiPascali was a cooperating witness in the Madoff trial, and he was the second insider to admit criminal responsibility in Madoff's scheme. Although Madoff insisted that he acted by himself, DiPascali implicated others in the criminal enterprise.[95]

Managing the details of a fraud of this magnitude would have been a monumental job, and it is not likely that one person, or even two or three, could have done it alone. So, although we can only speculate, it is certainly possible that Madoff's company had developed a culture that supported actions that ultimately resulted in fraud. One can easily imagine some of the unspoken norms and beliefs in such a culture—perhaps "Don't ask questions," "Do as you are told," or "The founder can do no wrong."

Cultures That Support Sustainability and Service

Today, companies of all types are choosing—or being forced—to reduce their impact on the environment and to do business in a socially responsible manner. Many companies are finding that to become responsible stewards of the environment and to be socially responsible they need to change their cultures. What might such a culture look like? Unilever, the Dutch/British manufacturer of consumer goods including Lipton tea and Dove soap, is an example of a company that infuses its business projects with a focus on sustainability. One Unilever project that reflects this commitment is the company's Cleaner Planet Plan. As a result of this plan, since 1995, Unilever claims to have reduced energy-related greenhouse gas emissions from its laundry product factories by 44 percent, disposal waste by 70 percent, and water consumption by 76 percent per metric ton of production.[96] Indeed, Unilever is currently ranked by an organization called "Global 100" as one of the top 100 global companies with regard to sustainability."[97]

Yet another Unilever project highlights the corporation's focus on a socially responsible approach to marketing. Specifically, in its "Campaign for Real Beauty," Unilever has deliberately moved away from traditional stereotypes of women and attractiveness. One element in this campaign is the now-famous "Dove Evolution," a short documentary film produced by the Dove Self-Esteem Fund.[98] This short film and the marketing campaign for Dove soaps and beauty products depict women of all ages, races, and sizes as beautiful and strong—which is markedly different from some of the more typical marketing images that limit beauty to the young and slender.

The movement toward sustainable business practices and social responsibility requires significant cultural changes. Instead of viewing the world as "us and them," people must come to visualize the entire planet as "us." Also, the practice of seeking individual success at any cost must end. To thrive, an organization's culture will have to support both success *and* acceptable practices, especially with respect to the natural environment and the wider communities within which an organization exists.

Cultures That Support the Whole Person: Mind, Body, Heart, and Spirit

In recent years, the amount of attention paid to employees' health, psychological well-being, work/life balance, and even spirituality has increased dramatically. The idea that companies should support employees in reaching their full potential as both workers and unique individuals has been embraced by a wide variety of organizations. One primary reason behind this focus on the "whole person" is that our society is changing, and people now have different expectations about what work—and the culture of the workplace—can and should provide. Also, during the past 50 years, women have entered the workforce in unprecedented numbers. This means that work is now a family affair. In addition, people are living longer than ever before in many parts in the world. Today, individuals frequently work well into their seventies, so being employed is no longer something to do while you wait to retire.

Moreover, technology has made it possible to work around the clock from almost anywhere. This is both good and bad—theoretically more can be done, but people can easily burn out, too. Finally, the global workforce is far more mobile now than in the past. People move more often, change jobs more often, and even change careers more often than in the past. One of the outcomes of these changes is that people don't have to stay in organizations that treat them poorly.

When employees feel satisfied, fulfilled, physically resilient, and committed to their work and the organization, results can soar. It makes good business sense for leaders to create cultures that focus on the mind, the body, the heart, and the spirit. In practical terms, focusing on "the mind" might mean creating a culture that enables people to learn and grow and to develop their intellect and their talents. Similarly, focusing on "the body" might mean ensuring that the culture supports physical health.

But what about focusing on "the heart" and "the spirit"? A culture that supports people's "hearts" is one that values productive relationships, positive and effective communication, respect, and compassion. Recent research in psychology and neuroscience indicates that when people are excited, appropriately challenged, and experiencing positive emotions, they are more creative, flexible, and resilient.[99] In comparison, a culture that supports spirituality is one that focuses on ensuring that work is meaningful and that people feel connected in working together toward an important mission.[100] People naturally seek meaning in life, so a sense of meaningfulness in the workplace can be highly motivating. As more and more businesses have recognized this fact, the term *workforce spirituality* has become increasingly popular in recent years. An important note—the term workforce spirituality refers to meaningfulness in work and the organization's goals, not religion. At the time of this writing, searching Google for "workforce spirituality" resulted in more than 222,000 links.[101] But why is workplace spirituality important? Scholars highlight the following points:[102]

1. Workplace spirituality can facilitate organizational effectiveness and productivity. For instance, one study revealed that employees who experienced workplace spirituality were more likely to increase their work unit performance.[103]
2. Workplace spirituality may facilitate ethical behavior. When employees are focused on connectedness as opposed to individual self-interest, they may be more likely to think about how their decisions influence others and whether they are ethical.[104]
3. The incorporation of spirituality in the workplace can be increasingly important in providing employees with feelings of connectedness, empowerment, and work/family balance. These conditions are becoming increasingly important to people today.[105]

Research therefore proves that people seek meaning in their work, and leadership that seeks to integrate ways for people to feel deeply fulfilled in the workplace can have a significant impact on employee motivation.[106] Creating a culture that supports people in finding meaning in their work will support positive organizational performance.

Most Popular » Discussion Questions

1. Of the types of cultures discussed in this section (innovation, customer service, diversity, ethics, sustainability, and cultures that support the whole person) which is the most appealing to you? Why?
2. Discuss the role of ethics and spirituality in your life at school or at work.
3. Consider a team with which you have worked in recent months. Examine the cultures and backgrounds of each team member. What was the nature of the diversity on this team? How did the team deal with diversity?

ORGANISATIONAL CULTURE

Although most of us will understand in our own minds what is meant by **organisational culture**, it is a general concept with many different meanings and difficult to define or explain precisely. The concept of culture has developed from anthropology. Although people may not be aware consciously of culture, it still has a pervasive influence over their behaviour and actions. There is, however, no consensus on its meaning or its applications to the analysis of work organisations.[8] Furthermore, there is sometimes confusion over the difference between the interpretation of organisational culture and organisational climate (discussed later in this chapter). A popular and simple way of defining culture is 'how things are done around here'. For example, *Atkinson* explains organisational culture as reflecting the underlying assumptions about the way work is performed; what is 'acceptable and not acceptable'; and what behaviour and actions are encouraged and discouraged.[9]

A more detailed definition is:

> *The collection of traditions, values, policies, beliefs, and attitudes that constitute a pervasive context for everything we do and think in an organisation.*[10]

The culture of an organisation is also often likened to the personality of an individual[11] (*see* Assignment 1 at the end of this chapter).

Charters questions the extent to which the concept of 'folklore' offers the potential to explore the existence of company myths and legends. Dictionary definitions, and discussions of the term in research papers, point to its close connection with culture.

> *Elements of folklore include myths and legends, and hence the concept of folklore appears to validate the exploration of organisational stories as part of cultural research . . . If folklore really is an expression of culture, then it could be argued that it should be possible to discern aspects of the culture of an organisation through the legends and myths of that organisation, the stories told which may or may not have a foundation in history.*[12]

System of management authority

Cartwright sees culture as a system of management authority. When accepted by employees, cultural values increase the power and authority of management in three ways. Employees

- identify themselves with their organisation and accept its rules when 'it is the right thing to do';
- internalise the organisation's values when they believe they are right; and
- are motivated to achieve the organisation's objectives.[13]

Levels of culture

Schein suggests a view of organisational culture based on distinguishing three levels of culture, from the shallowest to the deepest: artefacts and creations; values; and basic assumptions.[14]

- **Level 1: Artefacts**. The most visible level of the culture is artefacts and creations – the constructed physical and social environment. This includes physical space and layout, the technological output, written and spoken language and the overt behaviour of group members.
- **Level 2: Espoused values**. Cultural learning reflects someone's original values. Solutions about how to deal with a new task, issue or problem are based on convictions of reality. If the solution works, the value can transform into a belief. Values and beliefs become part of the conceptual process by which group members justify actions and behaviour.
- **Level 3: Basic underlying assumptions**. When a solution to a problem works repeatedly it comes to be taken for granted. Basic assumptions are unconsciously held learned responses. They are implicit assumptions that actually guide behaviour and determine how group members perceive, think and feel about things.

Schein suggests that the basic assumptions are treated as the essence – what culture really is – and values and behaviours are treated as observed manifestations of the culture essence.

TYPES OF ORGANISATIONAL CULTURE

There are a number of ways to classify different types of organisational culture. Developing the ideas of *Harrison*,[15] *Handy* describes four main types of organisational cultures: power culture; role culture; task culture; and person culture.[16]

- **Power culture** depends on a central power source with rays of influence from the central figure throughout the organisation. A power culture is frequently found in small entrepreneurial organisations and relies on trust, empathy and personal communications for its effectiveness. Control is exercised from the centre by the selection of key individuals. There are few rules and procedures, and little bureaucracy. It is a political organisation with decisions taken largely on the balance of influence.

- **Role culture** is often stereotyped as a bureaucracy and works by logic and rationality. Role culture rests on the strength of strong organisational 'pillars' – the functions of specialists in, for example, finance, purchasing and production. The work of, and interaction between, the pillars is controlled by procedures and rules, and co-ordinated by the pediment of a small band of senior managers. Role or job description is often more important than the individual, and position is the main source of power.

- **Task culture** is job-oriented or project-oriented. In terms of structure the task culture can be likened to a net, some strands of which are stronger than others, and with much of the power and influence at the interstices. An example is the matrix organisation. Task culture seeks to bring together the right resources and people, and utilises the unifying power of the group. Influence is widely spread and based more on expert power than on position or personal power.

- **Person culture** is where the individual is the central focus and any structure exists to serve the individuals within it. When a group of people decide that it is in their own interests to band together to do their own thing and share office space, equipment or clerical assistance, then the resulting organisation would have a person culture. Examples are groups of barristers, architects, doctors or consultants. Although it is found in only a few organisations, many individuals have a preference for person culture, for example university professors and specialists. Management hierarchies and control mechanisms are possible only by mutual consent. Individuals have almost complete autonomy and any influence over them is likely to be on the basis of personal power.

Every organisation will have its own unique culture and most large businesses are likely to be something of a mix of cultures with examples for each of the four types in varying areas of the organisation. Different people enjoy working in different types of organisation culture and they are more likely to be happy and satisfied at work if their attributes and personalities are consistent with the culture of that part of the organisation in which they are employed.

Four generic types of culture

From an examination of hundreds of business organisations and their environments, *Deal and Kennedy* categorise corporate cultures according to two determining factors in the marketplace:

- the degree of risk associated with the organisation's activities; and
- the speed at which organisations and their employees receive feedback on the success of decisions or strategies.

These factors give rise to four generic types of culture: the tough-guy, macho culture; the work-hard/play-hard culture; the bet-your-company culture; and the process culture.[17]

- **Tough-guy, macho culture** – an organisation of individualists who frequently take high risks and receive quick feedback on the right or wrong of their actions. Examples cited include police departments, surgeons, construction, cosmetics, management consulting and the entertainment industry. Financial stakes are high and there is a focus on speed. The intense pressure and frenetic pace often results in early 'burn-out'. Internal competition and conflict are normal, stars are temperamental but tolerated. A high staff turnover can create difficulties in building a strong cohesive culture.

- **Work-hard/play-hard culture** – characterised by fun and action where employees take few risks, all with quick feedback. There is a high level of relatively low-risk activity. Examples include sales organisations such as estate agents and computer companies, mass consumer companies such as McDonald's, office equipment manufacturers and retail stores. Organisations tend to be highly dynamic and the primary value centres on customers and their needs. It is the team who produce the volume, and the culture encourages games, meetings, promotions and conventions to help maintain motivation. However, although a lot gets done, volume can be at the expense of quality.

- **Bet-your-company culture** – where there are large-stake decisions with a high risk but slow feedback so that it may be years before employees know if decisions were successful. Examples include oil companies, investment banks, architectural firms and the military. The focus is on the future and the importance of investing in it. There is a sense of deliberateness throughout the organisation typified by the ritual of the business meeting. There is a hierarchical system of authority with decision-making from the top down. The culture leads to high-quality inventions and scientific breakthroughs, but moves only very slowly and is vulnerable to short-term fluctuations.

- **Process culture** – a low-risk, slow-feedback culture where employees find difficulty in measuring what they do. Typical examples include banks, insurance companies, financial services and the civil service. The individual financial stakes are low and employees get very little feedback on their effectiveness. Their memos and reports seem to disappear into a void. Lack of feedback forces employees to focus on how they do something, not what they do. People tend to develop a 'cover your back' mentality. Bureaucracy results with attention to trivial events, minor detail, formality and technical perfection. Process cultures can be effective when there is a need for order and predictability.

Note, however that in a subsequent publication, *Deal and Kennedy* suggest revisions to the original typology. For example, under process cultures, banks might not yet fit into the work-hard/play-hard culture but have evolved more into sales-type organisations.[18]

Critical reflection

'Attempting to analyse culture in terms of different levels or generic typologies is too simplistic and prescriptive and serves no useful purpose in evaluating applications of management and organisational behaviour.'

What do you think? How would you analyse organisation culture?

INFLUENCES ON THE DEVELOPMENT OF CULTURE

The culture and structure of an organisation develop over time and in response to a complex set of factors. We can, however, identify a number of key influences that are likely to play an important role in the development of any corporate culture. These include history, primary function and technology, strategy, size, location, management and leadership, and the environment.[19]

- **History**. The reason, and manner in which, the organisation was originally formed, its age, and the philosophy and values of its owners and first senior managers will affect culture. A key event in the organisation's history such as a merger or major reorganisation, or a new generation of top management, may bring about a change in culture. Corporate history can be an effective induction tool to assist a growth programme, and to help integrate acquisitions and new employees by infusion with the organisation's culture and identity.[20] Failure in mergers and acquisitions can arise from cultural clashes and failure to integrate different cultures.[21]

- **Primary function and technology**. The nature of the organisation's 'business' and its primary function have an important influence on its culture. This includes the range and quality of products and services provided, the importance of reputation and the type of customers. The primary function of the organisation will determine the nature of the technological processes and methods of undertaking work, which in turn also affect structure and culture.

- **Strategy**. Although a business organisation may pursue profitability, this is not by itself very clear or a sufficient criterion for its effective management. For example, to what extent is emphasis placed on long-term survival or growth and development? How much attention is given to avoiding risks and uncertainties? Or how much concern is shown for broader social responsibilities? The organisation must give attention to objectives in all key areas of its operations. The combination of objectives and resultant strategies will influence culture, and may itself be influenced by changes in culture. (See also Chapter 14 and Chapter 18.)

- **Size**. Usually larger organisations have more formalised structures and cultures. Increased size is likely to result in separate departments and possibly split-site operations. This may cause difficulties in communication and inter-departmental rivalries with the need for effective co-ordination. A rapid expansion, or decline, in size and rate of growth, and resultant changes in staffing will influence structure and culture.

- **Location**. Geographical location and the physical characteristics can have a major influence on culture – for example, whether an organisation is located in a quiet rural location or a busy city centre can influence the types of customers and the staff employed. An example could be a hotel or restaurant. Location can also affect the nature of services provided, the sense of 'boundary' and distinctive identity, and opportunities for development.

- **Management and leadership**. Top executives can have considerable influence on the nature of corporate culture. Examples are the key roles played by Sir Richard Branson, Anita Roddick, founder of The Body Shop,[22] and Marjorie Scardino and her change of style when she took over as the new chief executive of Pearson.

  Her candour works . . . As an example of straight talking winning over a sceptical City and press, it is brilliant. As an example of just how much a company's culture can change under a new chief executive, it is breathtaking.[23]

Another example is *Louis Gerstner*, who defined a strategy for the computing giant IBM and remade the ossified culture bred by the company's success, rebuilt the leadership team and gave the workforce a renewed sense of purpose.[24]

However, all members of staff help to shape the dominant culture of an organisation, irrespective of what senior management feel it should be. Culture is also determined by the nature of staff employed and the extent to which they accept management philosophy and policies or pay only 'lip service'. Another important influence is the match between corporate culture and employees' perception of the psychological contract (discussed in Chapter 1).

■ **The environment.** In order to be effective, the organisation must be responsive to external environmental influences. For example, if the organisation operates within a dynamic environment it requires a structure and culture that are sensitive and readily adaptable to change. An organic structure is more likely to respond effectively to new opportunities and challenges, and risks and limitations presented by the external environment.

THE CULTURAL WEB

In order to help describe and understand the culture of an organisation, *Johnson, Scholes and Whittington* present a cultural web, which brings together different aspects for the analysis of organisational culture (*see* Figure 19.1).

Figure 19.1	The cultural web of an organisation

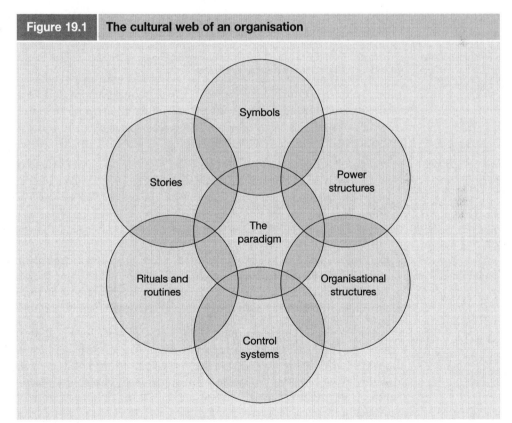

Source: Johnson, G., Scholes, K. and Whittington, R. *Exploring Corporate* Strategy, seventh edition, Financial Times Prentice Hall (2005), p. 202. Reproduced with permission from Pearson Education Ltd.

- **Routine behaviours** – the ways in which members of the organisation behave towards each other and towards those outside the organisation and which make up how things are done or how things should happen.
- **Rituals** – the particular activities or special events through which the organisation emphasises what is particularly important; can include formal organisational processes and informal processes.
- **Stories** told by members of the organisation that embed the present and flag up important events and personalities, and typically have to do with successes, failures, heroes, villains and mavericks.
- **Symbols** – such as logos, offices, cars, titles, type of language or terminology commonly used – which become a shorthand representation of the nature of the organisation.
- **Power structures** – the power of the most powerful individuals or groups in the organisation may be based on management position and seniority, but in some organisations power can be lodged with other levels or functions.
- **Control systems** – the measurement and reward systems that emphasise what it is important to monitor, and to focus attention and activity upon – for example, stewardship of funds or quality of service.
- **Organisation structure** – which reflects power structures and delineates important relationships and activities within the organisation, and involves both formal structure and control and less formal systems.
- **The paradigm** of the organisation, which encapsulates and reinforces the behaviours observed in other elements of the cultural web.[25]

Other interpretations of culture

There are, however, many other ways in which people attempt to describe and understand what constitutes organisational culture, and different areas of attention for analysing the elements of culture. *Wilson* suggests that culture is a characteristic of the organisation, not of individuals.

> One way of examining the culture of an organization is to look at its corporate image to see what and who is valued in the organization. A corporate image is the mental picture the clients, customers, employees, and others have of an organization. The impression is the combination of unconscious, unintended, conscious, and intended factors that arise.[26]

ACAS distinguishes two different organisation cultures and different ways of doing things:

- **Control culture** with the emphasis on rules and procedures, control and compliance with precedent providing guidelines; and
- **Quality of working life culture** with the emphasis on core values, with mission statements providing guidance and commitment via shared goals, values and traditions.[27]

Naylor suggests that seeing quite what forms organisational culture is difficult, and to make a start we need to recognise both the visible and invisible layers. On the surface is the visible layer made up of elements such as artefacts, symbols, languages, stories and activities which can be collected, compared and assembled into a description of the organisation. Underpinning this 'visible culture' is the invisible layer of beliefs, values, norms, basic assumptions and understanding.[28]

THE IMPORTANCE OF CULTURE

Applications of organisational behaviour and the effective management of human resources are dependent not only upon the nature of the industry or business, but also upon the characteristic features of the individual organisation – and its culture. The pervasive nature of culture in terms of 'how things are done around here' and common values, beliefs and attitudes will therefore have a significant effect on organisational processes such as decision-making, design of structure, group behaviour, work organisation, motivation and job satisfaction, and management control. For example, many managers claim that their organisation's culture contributes considerably to their stress.[29]

Harrison and Stokes maintain that organisational culture influences the behaviour of all individuals and groups within the organisation.

> *Culture impacts most aspects of organizational life, such as how decisions are made, who makes them, how rewards are distributed, who is promoted, how people are treated, how the organization responds to its environment, and so on.*[30]

A similar point is made by *Reigle*, who refers to culture as an important factor in successful technology implementation, innovation, mergers, acquisitions, job satisfaction, organisational success and team effectiveness, and to the importance of determining whether organisations exhibit organic or mechanistic cultures.[31]

Culture and organisation control

Egan refers to culture as the largest organisational control system that dictates how crazy or idiosyncratic people can be. Companies and institutions have both an overt and covert culture that influences both business and organisational behaviour.

> *The covert set can be quite dysfunctional and costly. Culture – the assumptions, beliefs, values and norms that drive 'the way we do things here' – is the largest and most controlling of the systems because it affects not only overt organisational behaviour but also the shadow-side behaviour . . . Culture lays down norms for the social system. In one institution you had to be an engineer to rise to the top. There was no published rule, of course, it was just the way things were. In one bank you could never be made an officer of the company if you wore polyester clothes. Culture tells us what kind of politics are allowed and just how members of an organisation are allowed to play the political game.*[32]

Egan also distinguishes between the 'preferred culture' which serves the business and the 'culture-in-use'. This culture-behind-the-culture carries the real beliefs, values and norms that drive patterns of behaviour within the company. These remain unnamed, undiscussed and unmentionable and these covert cultures lie outside ordinary managerial control. The first step in changing such limiting behaviour features is to identify the preferred culture and to ensure that the company's way of operating effectively serves the business right now.[33]

Culture and work ethic

Culture can influence people's attitudes and behaviour at work. For example a report from the Chartered Management Institute found that one in three managers felt that in their organisation there was a culture of not taking time off for sickness and nearly half felt they would not be treated sympathetically if they took sick leave.[34] *Bunting* draws attention to the link between work ethic (discussed in Chapter 1) and culture, and the extent to which people have a choice over how hard they work. Although some people have no choice, for the vast majority of people there is a degree of choice but the choices are not made in isolation:

> *they are the product of the particular organisational culture of our workplaces, which promote concepts of success, of team spirit so that we don't let colleagues down, and a powerful work ethic. We are also influenced by a culture that reinforces that work ethic and its cycle of continual achievement and consumption as measures of self-worth.*

Bunting maintains that it is through work that we seek to satisfy our craving for a sense of control, mastery and security and that clever organisations exploit this cultural context by designing corporate cultures that meet the emotional needs of their employees.[35]

Culture in short-life organisations

The importance of culture raises interesting questions relating to its nature and influence in 'short-life' organisations – that is, organisations created to run for only a short period of time such as arts festivals or national garden festivals. For example, how does culture develop when the organisation has little or no prior history, has short-term goals and objectives and has only limited time for top management to exercise influence? How do managers in such organisations attempt to inculcate culture? From a study of Garden Festival Wales, *Meudell and Gadd* found that success in creating a culture occurred as a direct result of their recruitment and training initiatives. However, it is not only culture but climate that is important for organisational effectiveness.

> *Rigorous training in customer care/corporate culture might produce an automatic 'Have a nice day' but only the engendering of a suitable climate will encourage people to say it and mean it.*[36]

Culture and organisational performance

Culture is clearly an important ingredient of effective organisational performance. In commenting, in a study of Europe's top companies, on Heineken's superiority in world markets, *Heller* makes the point that it rests in part on its remarkable corporate culture:

> *There is nothing accidental about cultural strengths . . . There is a relationship between an organisation's culture and its performance.*[37]

In their original study of highly successful companies, *Goldsmith and Clutterbuck* identified eight characteristics built into the day-to-day culture of the organisation. From their subsequent study of the world's top companies, it appears that a key characteristic of high-performing companies is a challenge culture. All the companies are very demanding of the people who work for them but this is balanced by a nurturing culture that shows that they also care for their employees in numerous ways.[38]

And according to *Cummings and Worley*:

> *An organization's culture is the pattern of assumptions, values and norms that are more or less shared by an organization's members. A growing body of research has shown that culture can affect strategy formulation and implementation as well as a firm's ability to achieve high levels of excellence.*[39]

Use of managerial tools

Chatman and Cha suggest that every company has a culture – good or bad. However, there is more to a good culture than happy staff. In order to aid long-term performance, there are three main criteria needed to develop a suitable culture:

- it must be strategically relevant;
- it needs to be strong in order that people care about what is important; and
- the culture must have an intrinsic ability to adapt to changing circumstances.

In order that leaders can develop, manage and change their culture for better performance, Chatman and Cha refer to the use of three managerial tools:

- **Recruitment and selection** – hire people who fit the company's culture even if this may involve overlooking some technical skills for a better cultural fit. Look carefully at the characteristics of your recruiters and consider your selection decision in the light of culture.
- **Social tools and training** – develop practices that enable new people to understand the values, abilities, expected behaviour and social knowledge in order to participate fully as an employee, and to create strong bonds among members.
- **Reward system** – culture is an organisation's informal reward system but it needs to be intricately connected to formal rewards. Examples include staff meetings where the seating arrangement is in accordance with level of sales, name badges that include inventory losses, and payments of large commissions in front of customers and other staff.[40]

Culture change

The pervasive nature of organisational culture means that if change is to be brought about successfully, this is likely to involve changes to culture. For example, *Stewart* makes the following comment on the relationship between culture and change:

> In recent years attention has shifted from the effects of the organization of work on people's behavior to how behavior is influenced by the organizational culture. What is much more common today is the widespread recognition that organizational change is not just, or even necessarily mainly, about changing the structure but often requires changing the culture too.[41]

A similar view is held by *Naylor*, who points out that 'In the holistic system, any change will affect the culture and the culture will affect or constrain the change . . . Cultural change is intimately bound up with the process of organisational change.'[42]

However, although attention is often given to shifting the prevailing activities and atmosphere of an organisation to a brighter future, changing the ethos and culture of an organisation is not easy. In practice, organisations usually appear to alter their underlying ethos only on a gradual basis and the complexity of environmental pressures may itself hinder rapid change. Culture is often deep-rooted and commitment to the objectives and policies of the organisation, people's cognitive limitations and their uncertainties and fears, may mean a reluctance to accept a change in behaviour. Culture is reinforced through the system of rites and rituals, patterns of communication, the informal organisation, expected patterns of behaviour and perceptions of the psychological contract.

> *Clearly most organisations are not the stable, predictable structures of the past. Keeping followers motivated and committed in an era of unrelenting change, means that leaders must be able to create organisational cultures that foster not only performance, but also a sense of pride and fun. Because cultures evolve over many years and are usually deep-rooted, they can be difficult to change. Some commentators have observed that it is easier to change behaviour by changing processes and systems in an organisation than it is to change people's attitudes. While goals change in the course of a person's life, values tend to remain constant and help determine an employee's attitudes to their employer.*
>
> DTI (2004)[43]

The nature of organisational change is discussed later in this chapter.

National and international culture

Culture helps to account for variations among organisations and managers, both nationally and internationally. It helps to explain why different groups of people perceive things in their own way and perform things differently from other groups.[44] With greater international competition, an understanding of national culture has become of increasing importance for managers. According to *Siddall*, for example, 'International business, the issue of culture and the need for better understanding have become major parts of organisational behaviour.'[45] Cultural practices vary widely among different countries and because of our own values may be difficult to understand.

Schneider and Barsoux suggest that cultural beliefs and values influence the meaning of management and also show up differences in conceptions of organisations. National differences and cultural reasons raise concerns about the transferability of organisational structures, systems and processes and question the logic of universal 'best practice'.[46] *Cheng, Sculli and Chan* also question the universality of theories of management and organisational behaviour on the grounds that they have not adequately addressed the factor of culture.[47] Those fortunate enough to have shared the experience of the author in visiting both Walt Disney World Resort in Florida and Disneyland Resort Paris would probably have witnessed the cultural differences in the attitudes to, and acceptance of, the Disney approach and procedures between American and French employees.

According to *Francesco and Gold*, culture has recently been accepted as an explanation of organisational behaviour. One reason is the increase in competitiveness of nations and a second reason is that managers encounter different cultures in their contacts with people from other nations. However, there are limits to the use of culture to explain organisational behaviour, and the relationship between national cultural values and actual behaviour in organisations is complex.[48]

Recall also the discussion on the international context of management and organisational behaviour in Chapter 1.

Critical reflection

'The proliferation of definitions and explanations of culture, its anthropological origins and lack of clarity undermines its value to our understanding of organisational behaviour. It is too ambigious a concept for the effective day-to-day management of the organisation.'

Do you agree? What role do you think culture plays in the management of modern work organisations?

Cases

CASE APPLICATION 1
Out of Control

Toyota Motor Company President Akio Toyoda, grandson of the company's founder, bows in apology during a press conference where he announced a global vehicle recall. Toyoda's gesture of bowing is the Japanese way of publicly expressing remorse as an act of contrition to restore faith in the company's brands.

With a worldwide recall of some 8 million cars and 51 deaths that U.S. regulators say have been caused by mechanical failures in its cars, Toyota Motor Corporation faces a corporate crisis of epic proportions.[58] What happened at the car company that had finally achieved the title of world's largest car maker? (It overtook General Motors in 2008.) What factors contributed to the mess it now found itself in?

At the core of Toyota's manufacturing prowess is the Toyota Production System (TPS), which has long been touted and revered as a model of corporate efficiency and quality. Four management principles (the 4P model) were at the core of TPS and guided employees: problem solving, people and partners, process, and philosophy. The idea behind these principles was that "Good Thinking Means Good Product." Taiichi Ohno, a long-time Toyota executive, is widely credited as the innovative genius behind TPS. During the 1950s, Ohno, along with a small core of other Toyota executives, developed several principles of car-making efficiency that became what is now known as lean manufacturing and just-in-time inventory management. "Ohno's ideas not only changed the auto industry, they changed late-twentieth-century manufacturing." At the very core of these concepts were attention to detail and a "noble frugality." However, over the years, it appears that Toyota's executives slowly lost the "purity" of that approach as the once-strong commitment to quality embedded in Toyota's corporate culture became lost in its aggressive moves to grow market share and achieve productivity gains.

From about 1995 to 2009, Toyota embarked on the "most aggressive overseas expansions in automotive history" and at the same time had a laser-like unparalleled focus on cutting costs. Four major cost-cutting and expansion initiatives severely strained organizational processes and employees. One initiative was localized manufacturing. Starting in the late 1990s, Toyota established manufacturing hubs in Asia, North America, and Europe. Such an approach meant relying more on local suppliers and design teams to tailor cars to local tastes. Another initiative was called Construction of Cost Competitiveness for the 21st Century, or CCC21. It was a massive cost reduction program. Through an ongoing process of redesigning parts and working with suppliers, more than $10 billion of savings were achieved. The Value Innovation initiative was a more ambitious version of CCC21. Under this program, more savings were achieved by making the entire development process cheaper and by further cutting parts and production costs. And finally, the Global 15 initiative was a master global plan for attaining a 15 percent share of the global car market by 2010. As of mid-2010, Toyota had an 11.7 percent share of the worldwide car market. However, this "combination of high-speed global growth and ambitious cost cuts led to the quality lapses that tarnished the once-mighty brand." Toyota's president, Akio Toyoda apologized for the company's actions and said, "We pursued growth over the speed at which we were able to develop our people and our organization. I regret that this has resulted in the safety issues described in the recalls we face today, and I am deeply sorry for any accidents that Toyota drivers have experienced."

So what is Toyota doing to remedy its problems? In addition to the massive recall, the company's president says that it is setting up a system to respond more quickly to complaints. In fact, the automaker has promised to give regional executives a bigger role in issuing recalls based on local consumer complaints, although Mr. Toyoda says that the final decisions regarding recalls will continue to be made in Japan. The company is also holding twice-yearly global quality meetings and more frequent regional quality meetings. And finally, the company is re-committing itself to better training employees in quality control.

Discussion Questions

1. Using Exhibit 2-5 and the information from the case, describe the culture at Toyota Motor Corporation. Why do you think this type of culture might be important to a car maker?

2. How do you think a long-standing culture that had such a strong commitment to quality lost its ability to influence employee behaviors and actions? What lesson can be learned about organizational culture from this?

3. Do you think it was important for Mr. Toyoda to apologize for the company's decisions? Why? (Think in terms of the company's stakeholders.)

4. What could other organizations learn from Toyota's experiences about the importance of organizational culture?

SECTION 6:
CHANGE MANAGEMENT

Chapter 12:
Change Management

The managerial challenges facing NASA'S leaders in encouraging continued innovative efforts among all the agency's employees during uncertain times is certainly not unique. Big companies and small businesses, universities and colleges, state and city governments, and even the military are forced to be innovative. Although innovation has always been a part of the manager's job, it has become even more important in recent years. We'll describe why innovation is important and how managers can manage innovation in this chapter. Because innovation is often closely tied to an organization's change efforts, we'll start by looking at change and how managers manage change.

LEARNING OUTCOME
6.1
Compare and contrast views on the change process.

The Change Process

When John Lechleiter assumed the CEO's job at Eli Lilly, he sent each of his senior executives a gift—"a digital clock counting down, second by second, to October 23, 2011. That's the day Lilly's $5 billion-a-year schizophrenia pill, Zyprexa, is no longer under patent." Between 2010 and the end of 2016, Lilly stands to lose $10 billion in annual revenues as patents on three of its key drugs expire. Needless to say, the company has had to make some organizational changes as it picks up the pace of drug development.[2] Lilly's managers are doing what managers everywhere must do—implement change!

If it weren't for change, a manager's job would be relatively easy. Planning would be simple because tomorrow would be no different from today. The issue of effective organizational design would also be resolved because the environment would not be uncertain and there would be no need to redesign the structure. Similarly, decision making would be dramatically streamlined because the outcome of each alternative could be predicted with almost certain accuracy. But that's not the way it is. Change is an organizational reality.[3] Organizations face change because external and internal factors create the need for change (see Exhibit 6-1). When managers recognize that change is needed, then what? How do they respond?

Two Views of the Change Process

Two very different metaphors can be used to describe the change process.[4] One metaphor envisions the organization as a large ship crossing a calm sea. The ship's captain and crew know exactly where they're going because they've made the trip many times before. Change comes in the form of an occasional storm, a brief distraction in an otherwise calm and predictable trip.

EXHIBIT 6-1

External and Internal Forces for Change

External

- Changing consumer needs and wants
- New governmental laws
- Changing technology
- Economic changes

Internal

- New organizational strategy
- Change in composition of workforce
- New equipment
- Changing employee attitudes

In the calm waters metaphor, change is seen as an occasional disruption in the normal flow of events. In the other metaphor, the organization is seen as a small raft navigating a raging river with uninterrupted white-water rapids. Aboard the raft are half-a-dozen people who have never worked together before, who are totally unfamiliar with the river, who are unsure of their eventual destination, and who, as if things weren't bad enough, are traveling at night. In the white-water rapids metaphor, change is normal and expected and managing it is a continual process. These two metaphors present very different approaches to understanding and responding to change. Let's take a closer look at each one.

THE CALM WATERS METAPHOR. At one time, the calm waters metaphor was fairly descriptive of the situation that managers faced. It's best discussed using Kurt Lewin's three-step change process.[5] (See Exhibit 6-2.)

According to Lewin, successful change can be planned and requires *unfreezing* the status quo, *changing* to a new state, and *refreezing* to make the change permanent. The status quo is considered equilibrium. To move away from this equilibrium, unfreezing is necessary. Unfreezing can be thought of as preparing for the needed change. It can be done by increasing the *driving forces,* which are forces pushing for change; by decreasing the *restraining forces*, which are forces that resist change; or by combining the two approaches.

Once unfreezing is done, the change itself can be implemented. However, merely introducing change doesn't ensure that it will take hold. The new situation needs to be *refrozen* so that it can be sustained over time. Unless this last step is done, there's a strong chance that employees will revert back to the old equilibrium state—that is, the old ways of doing things. The objective of refreezing, then, is to stabilize the new situation by reinforcing the new behaviors.

Lewin's three-step process treats change as a move away from the organization's current equilibrium state. It's a calm waters scenario where an occasional disruption (a "storm") means changing to deal with the disruption. Once the disruption has been dealt with, however, things can continue on under the new changed situation. This type of environment isn't what most managers face today.

EXHIBIT 6-2

The Three-Step Change Process

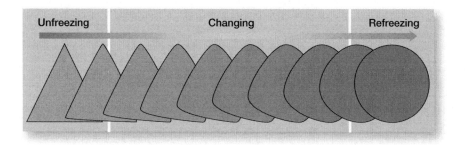

| Unfreezing | Changing | Refreezing |

WHITE-WATER RAPIDS METAPHOR. Susan Whiting is CEO of Nielsen Media Research, the company best known for its television ratings, which are frequently used to determine how much advertisers pay for TV commercials. The media research business isn't what it used to be, however, as the Internet, video on demand, cell phones, iPods, digital video recorders, and other changing technologies have made data collection much more challenging. Whiting says, "If you look at a typical week I have, it's a combination of trying to lead a company in change in an industry in change."[6] That's a pretty accurate description of what change is like in our second change metaphor—white-water rapids. It's also consistent with a world that's increasingly dominated by information, ideas, and knowledge.[7]

To get a feeling of what managing change might be like in a white-water rapids environment, consider attending a college that had the following rules: Courses vary in length. When you sign up, you don't know how long a course will run. It might go for 2 weeks or 15 weeks. Furthermore, the instructor can end a course at any time with no prior warning. If that isn't challenging enough, the length of the class changes each time it meets: Sometimes the class lasts 20 minutes; other times it runs for 3 hours. And the time of the next class meeting is set by the instructor during this class. There's one more thing: All exams are unannounced, so you have to be ready for a test at any time. To succeed in this type of environment, you'd have to respond quickly to changing conditions. Students who are overly structured or uncomfortable with change wouldn't succeed.

Increasingly, managers are realizing that their job is much like what a student would face in such a college. The stability and predictability of the calm waters metaphor don't exist. Disruptions in the status quo are not occasional and temporary, and they are not followed by a return to calm waters. Many managers never get out of the rapids. Like Susan Whiting, they face constant change.

Is the white-water rapids metaphor an exaggeration? Probably not! Although you'd expect a chaotic and dynamic environment in high-tech industries, even organizations in non-high-tech industries are faced with constant change. Take the case of Swedish home appliance company Electrolux. You might think that the home appliances industry couldn't be all that difficult—after all, most households need the products, which are fairly uncomplicated—but that impression would be wrong. Electrolux's chief executive Hans Straberg has had several challenges to confront.[8] First, there's the challenge of developing products that will appeal to a wide range of global customers. Then, there's the challenge of cheaper alternatives flooding the market. In addition, Electrolux faces intense competition in the United States, where it gets 40 percent of its sales. Because approximately 80 percent of the workforce in Sweden belongs to a labor union, companies certainly face expectations as far as how they treat their employees. However, Straberg recognized that his company was going to have to change if it was going to survive and prosper. One thing he did was to shift production to lower-cost facilities in Asia and Eastern Europe. Then, to better grasp what today's consumers are thinking, the company held in-depth interviews with 160,000 customers from around the world. Using this information, a group of Electrolux employees gathered in Stockholm for a weeklong brainstorming session to search for insights on what hot new products to pursue. Finally, to make the new product development process speedier, Straberg eliminated the structural divisions between departments. Designers, engineers, and marketers have to work together to come up with ideas. These changes were essential if Electrolux wanted to survive the white-water rapids environment in which it operated.

Today, any organization that treats change as the occasional disturbance in an otherwise calm and stable world runs a great risk. Too much is changing too fast for an organization or its managers to be complacent. It's no longer business as usual. And managers must be ready to efficiently and effectively manage the changes facing their organization or their work area.

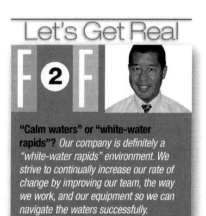

Let's Get Real

F2F

"Calm waters" or "white-water rapids"? *Our company is definitely a "white-water rapids" environment. We strive to continually increase our rate of change by improving our team, the way we work, and our equipment so we can navigate the waters successfully.*

LEARNING OUTCOME **6.2**
Classify types of organizational change.

Types of Organizational Change

Managers at Verizon Wireless know what change is all about. "Even in an industry where rapid change is the status quo, it takes a special kind of company to handle the challenges posed by a major corporate acquisition and massive product rollout."[9] Verizon was up for the challenges and focused its change efforts on its people and processes.

What Is Organizational Change?

Most managers, at one point or another, will have to change some things in their workplace. We classify these changes as **organizational change**, which is any alteration of people, structure, or technology. Organizational changes often need someone to act as a catalyst and assume the responsibility for managing the change process—that is, a **change agent**. Change agents can be a manager within the organization, but could be a nonmanager—for example, a change specialist from the HR department or even an outside consultant. For major changes, an organization often hires outside consultants to provide advice and assistance. Because they're from the outside, they have an objective perspective that insiders may lack. But outside consultants have a limited understanding of the organization's history, culture, operating procedures, and people. They're also more likely to initiate drastic change than insiders would because they don't have to live with the repercussions after the change is implemented. In contrast, internal managers may be more thoughtful, but possibly overcautious, because they must live with the consequences of their decisions.

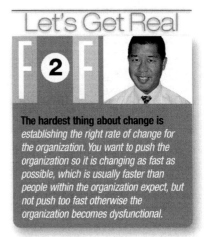

Let's Get Real

F | 2 | F

The hardest thing about change is *establishing the right rate of change for the organization. You want to push the organization so it is changing as fast as possible, which is usually faster than people within the organization expect, but not push too fast otherwise the organization becomes dysfunctional.*

Types of Change

Managers face three main types of change: structure, technology, and people (see Exhibit 6-3). Changing *structure* includes any change in structural variables such as reporting relationships, coordination mechanisms, employee empowerment, or job redesign. Changing *technology* encompasses modifications in the way work is performed or the methods and equipment that are used. Changing *people* refers to changes in attitudes, expectations, perceptions, and behavior of individuals or groups.

CHANGING STRUCTURE.   Changes in the external environment or in organizational strategies often lead to changes in the organizational structure. Because an organization's structure is defined by how work gets done and who does it, managers can alter one or both of these *structural components*. For instance, departmental responsibilities could be combined, organizational levels eliminated, or the number of persons a manager supervises could be increased. More rules and procedures could be implemented to increase standardization. Or employees could be empowered to make decisions so decision making could be faster.

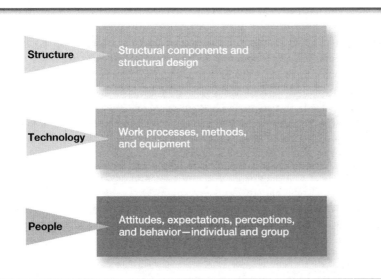

Structure — Structural components and structural design

Technology — Work processes, methods, and equipment

People — Attitudes, expectations, perceptions, and behavior—individual and group

EXHIBIT 6-3

Three Types of Change

---

organizational change
Any alteration of people, structure, or technology in an organization

change agent
Someone who acts as a catalyst and assumes the responsibility for managing the change process

Another option would be to make major changes in the actual *structural design*. For instance, when Hewlett-Packard acquired Compaq Computer, product divisions were dropped, merged, or expanded. Structural design changes also might include, for instance, a shift from a functional to a product structure or the creation of a project structure design. Avery-Dennis Corporation, for example, revamped its structure to a new design that arranges work around teams.

CHANGING TECHNOLOGY. Managers can also change the technology used to convert inputs into outputs. Most early management studies dealt with changing technology. For instance, scientific management techniques involved implementing changes that would increase production efficiency. Today, technological changes usually involve the introduction of new equipment, tools, or methods; automation; or computerization.

Competitive factors or new innovations within an industry often require managers to introduce *new equipment, tools,* or *operating methods*. For example, coal mining companies in New South Wales updated operational methods, installed more efficient coal handling equipment, and made changes in work practices to be more productive.

Automation is a technological change that replaces certain tasks done by people with tasks done by machines. Automation has been introduced in organizations such as the U.S. Postal Service where automatic mail sorters are used, and in automobile assembly lines, where robots are programmed to do jobs that workers used to perform.

The most visible technological changes have come from *computerization*. Most organizations have sophisticated information systems. For instance, supermarkets and other retailers use scanners that provide instant inventory information. Also, most offices are computerized. At BP p.l.c., for example, employees had to learn how to deal with the personal visibility and accountability brought about by an enterprise-wide information system. The integrative nature of this system meant that what any employee did on his or her computer automatically affected other computer systems on the internal network.[10] At the Benetton Group SpA, computers link its manufacturing plants outside Treviso, Italy, with the company's various sales outlets and a highly automated warehouse. Now, product information can be transmitted and shared instantaneously, a real plus in today's environment.[11]

CHANGING PEOPLE. Changing people involves changing attitudes, expectations, perceptions, and behaviors, something that's not easy to do. **Organizational development (OD)** is the term used to describe change methods that focus on people and the nature and quality of interpersonal work relationships.[12] The most popular OD techniques are described in Exhibit 6-4. Each seeks to bring about changes in the organization's people and make them work together better. For example, executives at Scotiabank, one of Canada's Big Five banks, knew that the success of a new customer sales and service strategy depended on changing employee attitudes and behaviors. Managers used different OD techniques during the strategic change including team building, survey feedback, and intergroup development. One indicator of how well these techniques worked in getting people to change was that every branch in Canada implemented the new strategy on or ahead of schedule.[13]

Much of what we know about OD practices has come from North American research. However, managers need to recognize that some techniques that work for U.S. organizations

EXHIBIT 6-4

Popular OD Techniques

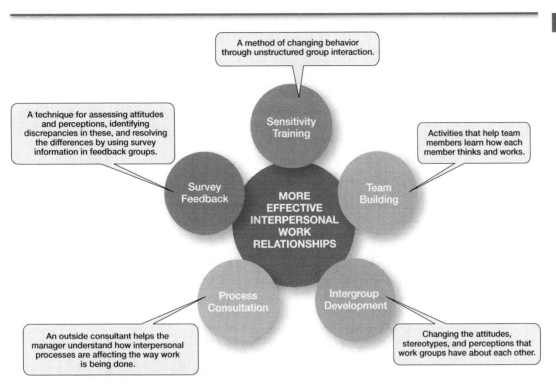

A method of changing behavior through unstructured group interaction.

A technique for assessing attitudes and perceptions, identifying discrepancies in these, and resolving the differences by using survey information in feedback groups.

Activities that help team members learn how each member thinks and works.

Sensitivity Training

Survey Feedback

Team Building

MORE EFFECTIVE INTERPERSONAL WORK RELATIONSHIPS

Process Consultation

Intergroup Development

An outside consultant helps the manager understand how interpersonal processes are affecting the way work is being done.

Changing the attitudes, stereotypes, and perceptions that work groups have about each other.

may not be appropriate for organizations or organizational divisions based in other countries.[14] For instance, a study of OD interventions showed that "multirater [survey] feedback as practiced in the United States is not embraced in Taiwan" because the cultural value of "saving face is simply more powerful than the value of receiving feedback from subordinates."[15] What's the lesson for managers? Before using the same OD techniques to implement behavioral changes, especially across different countries, managers need to be sure that they've taken into account cultural characteristics and whether the techniques "make sense for the local culture."

Changing technology allows physicians to visit patients online rather than at a doctor's office or hospital emergency room. Advances in video-conferencing equipment, high-speed communication links by satellite, and more dependable Internet security are fueling the growth of interactive telemedicine businesses such as NuPhysicia, a start-up launched by Dr. Oscar Boultinghouse, an emergency medicine physician, and two colleagues. Dr. Boultinghouse is shown in this photo at his office in Houston talking to a patient who is a crane operator working on an oil rig in the South China Sea. Via two-way video, he used an electronic stethoscope that a paramedic on the rig held in place as part of diagnosing the patient's illness.

organizational development (OD)
Change methods that focus on people and the nature and quality of interpersonal work relationships

LEARNING OUTCOME
Explain how to manage
resistance to change.

6.3

Managing Resistance to Change

We know that it's better for us to eat healthy and to be active, yet few of us follow that advice. We resist making changes in our lifestyle. Volkswagen Sweden and ad agency DDB Stockholm did an experiment to see if they could get people to change their behavior and take the healthier option of using the stairs instead of riding an escalator.[16] How? They put a working piano keyboard on a stairway in a Stockholm subway station (you can see a video of it on YouTube) to see if commuters would use it. The experiment was a resounding success as stair traffic rose 66 percent. The lesson—people can change if you make the change appealing.

Change can be a threat to people in an organization. Organizations can build up inertia that motivates people to resist changing their status quo, even though change might be beneficial. Why do people resist change and what can be done to minimize their resistance?

Why Do People Resist Change?

It's often said that most people hate any change that doesn't jingle in their pockets. This resistance to change is well documented.[17] Why *do* people resist change? The main reasons include uncertainty, habit, concern over personal loss, and the belief that the change is not in the organization's best interest.[18]

Change replaces the known with uncertainty. No matter how much you may dislike attending college, at least you know what's expected of you. When you leave college for the world of full-time employment, you'll trade the known for the unknown. Employees in organizations are faced with similar uncertainty. For example, when quality control methods based on statistical models are introduced into manufacturing plants, many quality control inspectors have to learn the new methods. Some may fear that they will be unable to do so and may develop a negative attitude toward the change or behave poorly if required to use them.

Another cause of resistance is that we do things out of habit. Every day when you go to school or work you probably go the same way, if you're like most people. We're creatures of habit. Life is complex enough—we don't want to have to consider the full range of options for the hundreds of decisions we make every day. To cope with this complexity, we rely on habits or programmed responses. But when confronted with change, our tendency to respond in our accustomed ways becomes a source of resistance.

The third cause of resistance is the fear of losing something already possessed. Change threatens the investment you've already made in the status quo. The more that people have invested in the current system, the more they resist change. Why? They fear the loss of status, money, authority, friendships, personal convenience, or other economic benefits that they value. This fear helps explain why older workers tend to resist change more than younger workers. Older employees generally have more invested in the current system and thus have more to lose by changing.

A final cause of resistance is a person's belief that the change is incompatible with the goals and interests of the organization. For instance, an employee who believes that a proposed new job procedure will reduce product quality can be expected to resist the change. This type of resistance actually can be beneficial to the organization if expressed in a positive way.

Let's Get Real

I manage resistance to change by *communicating and making people understand "why" the change is required and "what-is-in-it-for-me."*

Techniques for Reducing Resistance to Change

When managers see resistance to change as dysfunctional, what can they do? Several strategies have been suggested in dealing with resistance to change. These approaches include education and communication, participation, facilitation and support, negotiation, manipulation and co-optation, and coercion. These tactics are summarized here and described in Exhibit 6-5. Managers should view these techniques as tools and use the most appropriate one depending on the type and source of the resistance.

Education and communication can help reduce resistance to change by helping employees see the logic of the change effort. This technique, of course, assumes that much of the resistance lies in misinformation or poor communication.

Technique	When Used	Advantage	Disadvantage
Education and communication	When resistance is due to misinformation	Clear up misunderstandings	May not work when mutual trust and credibility are lacking
Participation	When resisters have the expertise to make a contribution	Increase involvement and acceptance	Time-consuming; has potential for a poor solution
Facilitation and support	When resisters are fearful and anxiety ridden	Can facilitate needed adjustments	Expensive; no guarantee of success
Negotiation	When resistance comes from a powerful group	Can "buy" commitment	Potentially high cost; opens doors for others to apply pressure too
Manipulation and co-optation	When a powerful group's endorsement is needed	Inexpensive, easy way to gain support	Can backfire, causing change agent to lose credibility
Coercion	When a powerful group's endorsement is needed	Inexpensive, easy way to gain support	May be illegal; may undermine change agent's credibility

EXHIBIT 6-5

Techniques for Reducing Resistance to Change

Participation involves bringing those individuals directly affected by the proposed change into the decision-making process. Their participation allows these individuals to express their feelings, increase the quality of the process, and increase employee commitment to the final decision.

Facilitation and support involve helping employees deal with the fear and anxiety associated with the change effort. This help may include employee counseling, therapy, new skills training, or a short paid leave of absence.

Negotiation involves exchanging something of value for an agreement to lessen the resistance to the change effort. This resistance technique may be quite useful when the resistance comes from a powerful source.

Manipulation and co-optation refer to covert attempts to influence others about the change. It may involve distorting facts to make the change appear more attractive.

Finally, *coercion* can be used to deal with resistance to change. Coercion involves the use of direct threats or force against the resisters.

Contemporary Issues in Managing Change

6.4

LEARNING OUTCOME
Discuss contemporary issues in managing change.

When CEO David Gray joined Daxko, a small software vendor based in Birmingham, Alabama, he wanted a more collegial workplace and he wanted to relieve employee stress. Now with a Wii console and a 52-inch plasma TV in the work/play lounge and an open-office layout, the company's "casual but driven environment now resembles Silicon Valley more than the Deep South." One employee said, "It's pretty intense here. Expectations for what I need to accomplish are clearly set. And if I can play the Wii while doing it, that's even better."[19] Employee stress is one of the major critical concerns for managers today. In this section, we're going to discuss stress and two other critical concerns—changing organizational culture and making change happen successfully. Let's look first at changing culture.

Changing Organizational Culture

Korean Air CEO Cho Yang-Ho had a challenging change situation facing him. He wanted to transform his airline's image of being an accident-prone airline from a developing country to that of a strong international competitor.[20] His main focus was on improving safety above all else, which meant making significant changes to the organization's culture. What made his task even more challenging was Korea's hierarchical culture that teaches Koreans to be deferential toward their elders and superiors. Cho says, "It (the hierarchical culture) exists in all Oriental culture." His approach to changing his company's culture involved implementing a "systems approach aimed at minimizing the personality-driven, top-down culture that is a legacy of Korean business managers who place emphasis on intuition and responding to orders." The cultural change must have worked. Korean Air is now the world's largest commercial cargo carrier and it has earned a four-star rating (out of five possible stars) from a London aviation firm that rates airlines on quality.

The fact that an organization's culture is made up of relatively stable and permanent characteristics tends to make it very resistant to change.[21] A culture takes a long time to form, and once established it tends to become entrenched. Strong cultures are particularly resistant to change because employees have become so committed to them. For instance, it didn't take long for Lou Gerstner, who was CEO of IBM from 1993 to 2002, to discover the power of a strong culture. Gerstner, the first outsider to lead IBM, needed to overhaul the ailing, tradition-bound company if it was going to regain its role as the dominant player in the computer industry. However, accomplishing that feat in an organization that prided itself on its long-standing culture was Gerstner's biggest challenge. He said, "I came to see in my decade at IBM that culture isn't just one aspect of the game—it *is* the game."[22] Over time, if a certain culture becomes a handicap, a manager might be able to do little to change it, especially in the short run. Even under the most favorable conditions, cultural changes have to be viewed in years, not weeks or even months.

UNDERSTANDING THE SITUATIONAL FACTORS. What "favorable conditions" facilitate cultural change? One is that *a dramatic crisis occurs,* such as an unexpected financial setback, the loss of a major customer, or a dramatic technological innovation by a competitor. Such a shock can weaken the status quo and make people start thinking about the relevance of the current culture. Another condition may be that *leadership changes hands.* New top leadership can provide an alternative set of key values and may be perceived as more capable of responding to the crisis than the old leaders were. Another is that *the organization is young and small.* The younger the organization, the less entrenched its culture. It's easier for managers to communicate new values in a small organization than in a large one. Finally, the *culture is weak.* Weak cultures are more receptive to change than are strong ones.[23]

MAKING CHANGES IN CULTURE. If conditions are right, how do managers change culture? No single action is likely to have the impact necessary to change something ingrained and highly valued. Managers need a strategy for managing cultural change, as described in Exhibit 6-6. These suggestions focus on specific actions that managers can take. Following them, however, is no guarantee that the cultural change efforts will succeed. Organizational members don't quickly let go of values that they understand and that have worked well for them in the past. Change, if it comes, will be slow. Also, managers must stay alert to protect against any return to old, familiar traditions.

EXHIBIT 6-6

Changing Culture

- *Set the tone through management behavior;* top managers, particularly, need to be positive role models.
- Create *new stories, symbols, and rituals* to replace those currently in use.
- Select, promote, and support employees who *adopt the new values.*
- *Redesign socialization processes* to align with the new values.
- To encourage acceptance of the new values, *change the reward system.*
- Replace unwritten norms with *clearly specified expectations.*
- *Shake up current subcultures* through job transfers, job rotation, and/or terminations.
- Work to get consensus through *employee participation* and creating a climate with a high level of trust

Employee Stress

"Most weekdays at 5:30 p.m., after putting in eight hours as an insurance agent in Lawrenceville, Georgia, April Hamby scurries about 100 yards to the Kroger supermarket two doors away. She's not there to pick up some milk and bread, but instead to work an additional six hours as a cashier before driving home 35 miles and slipping into bed by 2 a.m. so she can get up at 7 a.m. and begin the grind anew."[24] And April's situation isn't all that unusual. During the economic downturn, many people found themselves working two or more jobs and battling stress.[25]

As a student, you've probably experienced stress—class projects, exams, even juggling a job and school. Then, there's the stress associated with getting a decent job after graduation. But even after you've landed that job, stress isn't likely to stop. For many employees, organizational change creates stress. An uncertain environment characterized by time pressures, increasing workloads, mergers, and restructuring has created a large number of employees who are overworked and stressed.[26] In fact, depending on which survey you look at, the number of employees experiencing job stress in the United States ranges anywhere from 40 percent to 80 percent.[27] However, workplace stress isn't just an American problem. Global studies indicate that some 50 percent of workers surveyed in 16 European countries reported that stress and job responsibility have risen significantly over a five-year period; 35 percent of Canadian workers surveyed said they are under high job stress; in Australia, cases of occupational stress jumped 21 percent in a one-year period; more than 57 percent of Japanese employees suffer from work-related stress; some 83 percent of call-center workers in India suffer from sleeping disorders; and a study of stress in China showed that managers are experiencing more stress.[28] Another interesting study found that stress was the leading cause of people quitting their jobs. Surprisingly, however, employers were clueless. They said that stress wasn't even among the top five reasons why people leave and instead wrongly believed that insufficient pay was the main reason.[29]

Providing a frustration venting room where factory workers can slam inflatable punching bags is one way that management of Foxconn Technology Group is helping its employees in China reduce personal and work-related stress. Because of severe labor shortages in China, Foxconn's factory employees work long days and are under extreme pressure to produce products. Many employees are young migrant workers living away from their families and other support groups. Foxconn has also set up a help line and hired psychiatrists to assist lonely and depressed workers and has recruited singers, dancers, and gym trainers to teach all employees how to relax and relieve stress.

WHAT IS STRESS?   Stress is the adverse reaction people have to excessive pressure placed on them from extraordinary demands, constraints, or opportunities.[30] Stress isn't always bad. Although it's often discussed in a negative context, stress can be positive, especially when it offers a potential gain. For instance, functional stress allows an athlete, stage performer, or employee to perform at his or her highest level at crucial times.

However, stress is more often associated with constraints and demands. A constraint prevents you from doing what you desire; demands refer to the loss of something desired. When you take a test at school or have your annual performance review at work, you feel stress because you confront opportunity, constraints, and demands. A good performance review may lead to a promotion, greater responsibilities, and a higher salary. But a poor review may keep you from getting the promotion. An extremely poor review might lead to your being fired.

One other thing to understand about stress is that just because the conditions are right for stress to surface doesn't always mean it will. Two conditions are necessary for *potential* stress to become *actual* stress.[31] First, there must be uncertainty over the outcome, and second, the outcome must be important.

WHAT CAUSES STRESS?   Stress can be caused by personal factors and by job-related factors called **stressors**. Clearly, change of any kind—personal or job-related—has the potential to cause stress because it can involve demands, constraints, or opportunities.

---

stress
The adverse reaction people have to excessive pressure placed on them from extraordinary demands, constraints, or opportunities

stressors
Factors that cause stress

Organizations have no shortage of factors that can cause stress. Pressures to avoid errors or complete tasks in a limited time period, changes in the way reports are filed, a demanding supervisor, and unpleasant coworkers are a few examples. Let's look at five categories of organizational stressors: task demands, role demands, interpersonal demands, organization structure, and organizational leadership.

Task demands are factors related to an employee's job. They include the design of a person's job (autonomy, task variety, degree of automation), working conditions, and the physical work layout. Work quotas can put pressure on employees when their "outcomes" are perceived as excessive.[33] The more interdependence between an employee's tasks and the tasks of others, the greater the potential for stress. *Autonomy*, on the other hand, tends to lessen stress. Jobs in which temperatures, noise, or other working conditions are dangerous or undesirable can increase anxiety. So, too, can working in an overcrowded room or in a visible location where interruptions are constant.

Role demands relate to pressures placed on an employee as a function of the particular role he or she plays in the organization. **Role conflicts** create expectations that may be hard to reconcile or satisfy. **Role overload** is experienced when the employee is expected to do more than time permits. **Role ambiguity** is created when role expectations are not clearly understood and the employee is not sure what he or she is to do.

Interpersonal demands are pressures created by other employees. Lack of social support from colleagues and poor interpersonal relationships can cause considerable stress, especially among employees with a high social need.

Organization structure can increase stress. Excessive rules and an employee's lack of opportunity to participate in decisions that affect him or her are examples of structural variables that might be potential sources of stress.

Organizational leadership represents the supervisory style of the organization's managers. Some managers create a culture characterized by tension, fear, and anxiety. They establish unrealistic pressures to perform in the short run, impose excessively tight controls, and routinely fire employees who don't measure up. This style of leadership filters down through the organization and affects all employees.

Personal factors that can create stress include family issues, personal economic problems, and inherent personality characteristics. Because employees bring their personal problems to work with them, a full understanding of employee stress requires a manager to be understanding of these personal factors.[34] Evidence also indicates that employees' personalities have an effect on how susceptible they are to stress. The most commonly used labels for these personality traits are Type A and Type B.

Type A personality is characterized by chronic feelings of a sense of time urgency, an excessive competitive drive, and difficulty accepting and enjoying leisure time. The opposite of Type A is **Type B personality**. Type Bs don't suffer from time urgency or impatience. Until quite recently, it was believed that Type As were more likely to experience stress on and off the job. A closer analysis of the evidence, however, has produced new conclusions. Studies show that only the hostility and anger associated with Type A behavior are actually associated with the negative effects of stress. And Type Bs are just as susceptible to the same anxiety-producing elements. For managers, what is important is to recognize that Type A employees are more likely to show symptoms of stress, even if organizational and personal stressors are low.

WHAT ARE THE SYMPTOMS OF STRESS?   We see stress in a number of ways. For instance, an employee who is experiencing high stress may become depressed, accident prone, or argumentative; may have difficulty making routine decisions; may be easily distracted, and so on. As Exhibit 6-7 shows, stress symptoms can be grouped under three general categories: physical, psychological, and behavioral. All of these can significantly affect an employee's work.

In Japan, there's a stress phenomenon called *karoshi* (pronounced kah-roe-she), which is translated literally as "death from overwork." During the late 1980s, "several high-ranking Japanese executives still in their prime years suddenly died without any previous sign of illness."[35] As public concern increased, even the Japanese Ministry of Labor got involved,

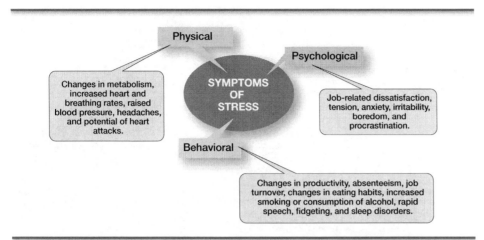

EXHIBIT 6-7

Symptoms of Stress

and it now publishes statistics on the number of karoshi deaths. As Japanese multinational companies expand operations to China, Korea, and Taiwan, it's feared that the karoshi culture may follow.

HOW CAN STRESS BE REDUCED?   As mentioned earlier, not all stress is dysfunctional. Because stress can never be totally eliminated from a person's life, managers want to reduce the stress that leads to dysfunctional work behavior. How? Through controlling certain organizational factors to reduce job-related stress, and to a more limited extent, offering help for personal stress.

Things that managers can do in terms of job-related factors begin with employee selection. Managers need to make sure that an employee's abilities match the job requirements. When employees are in over their heads, their stress levels are typically high. A realistic job preview during the selection process can minimize stress by reducing ambiguity over job expectations. Improved organizational communications will keep ambiguity-induced stress to a minimum. Similarly, a performance planning program such as MBO will clarify job responsibilities, provide clear performance goals, and reduce ambiguity through feedback. Job redesign is also a way to reduce stress. If stress can be traced to boredom or to work overload, jobs should be redesigned to increase challenge or to reduce the workload. Redesigns that increase opportunities for employees to participate in decisions and to gain social support also have been found to reduce stress.[36] For instance, at U.K. pharmaceutical maker GlaxoSmithKline, a team-resilience program in which employees can shift assignments, depending on people's workload and deadlines, has helped reduce work-related stress by 60 percent.[37]

Stress from an employee's personal life raises two problems. First, it's difficult for the manager to control directly. Second, ethical considerations include whether the manager has the right to intrude—even in the most subtle ways—in an employee's personal life? If a manager believes it's ethical and the employee is receptive, the manager might consider several approaches. Employee *counseling* can provide stress relief. Employees often want to talk to someone about their problems, and the organization—through its managers, in-house human resource counselors, or free or low-cost outside professional help—can meet that need. Companies such as Citicorp, AT&T, and Johnson & Johnson provide extensive counseling services for their employees. A *time management program* can help employees whose personal lives suffer from a lack of planning to sort out their priorities.[38] Still another

role conflicts
Work expectations that are hard to satisfy
role overload
Having more work to accomplish than time permits

role ambiguity
When role expectations are not clearly understood
Type A personality
People who have a chronic sense of urgency and an excessive competitive drive

Type B personality
People who are relaxed and easygoing and accept change easily

Because of its willingness to adapt to changing market conditions, UPS has evolved from its founding in 1907 as a private messenger and delivery service in Seattle to a global service provider that handles 15.1 million packages each day. As a change-capable organization, UPS considered future business expansion and factored it into management's decision making for adding air service, entering the overnight air delivery business, and starting international air service. After receiving FAA authorization to operate its own aircraft, the company officially became an airline—UPS Airlines— with computerized operations systems for flight planning, scheduling, and load handling that can create optimum flight plans up to six years in advance.

approach is organizationally sponsored *wellness programs*. For example, Wellmark Blue Cross Blue Shield of Des Moines, Iowa, offers employees an onsite health and fitness facility that is open six days a week. Employees at Cianbro, a general contracting company located in the northeastern United States, are provided a wellness program tailored to the unique demands of the construction environment.[39]

Making Change Happen Successfully

Organizational change is an ongoing daily challenge facing managers in the United States *and* around the globe. In a global study of organizational changes in more than 2,000 organizations in Europe, Japan, the United States, and the United Kingdom, 82 percent of the respondents had implemented major information systems changes, 74 percent had created horizontal sharing of services and information, 65 percent had implemented flexible human resource practices, and 62 percent had decentralized operational decisions.[40] Each of these major changes entailed numerous other changes in structure, technology, and people. When changes are needed, who makes them happen? Who manages them? Although you may think that it's just top-level managers, actually managers at *all* organizational levels are involved in the change process.

Even with the involvement of all levels of managers, change efforts don't always work the way they should. In fact, a global study of organizational change concluded that "Hundreds of managers from scores of U.S. and European companies [are] satisfied with their operating prowess . . . [but] dissatisfied with their ability to implement change."[41] How can managers make change happen successfully? They can (1) make the organization change capable, (2) understand their own role in the process, and (3) give individual employees a role in the change process. Let's look at each of these suggestions.

In an industry where growth is slowing and competitors are becoming stronger, United Parcel Service (UPS) prospers. How? By embracing change! Managers spent a decade creating new worldwide logistics businesses because they anticipated slowing domestic shipping demand. They continue change efforts in order to exploit new opportunities.[42] UPS is what we call a change-capable organization. What does it take to be a change-capable organization? Exhibit 6-8 summarizes the characteristics.

The second component of making change happen successfully is for managers to recognize their own important role in the process. Managers can, and do, act as change agents. But their role in the change process includes more than being catalysts for change; they must also be change leaders. When organizational members resist change, it's the manager's responsibility to lead the change effort. But even when there's no resistance to the change, someone has to assume leadership. That someone is managers.

EXHIBIT 6-8

Change-Capable Organizations

- *Link the present and the future*. Think of work as more than an extension of the past; think about future opportunities and issues and factor them into today's decisions.
- *Make learning a way of life*. Change-friendly organizations excel at knowledge sharing and management.
- *Actively support and encourage day-to-day improvements and changes*. Successful change can come from the small changes as well as the big ones.
- *Ensure diverse teams*. Diversity ensures that things won't be done like they've always been done.
- *Encourage mavericks*. Because their ideas and approaches are outside the mainstream, mavericks can help bring about radical change.
- *Shelter breakthroughs*. Change-friendly organizations have found ways to protect those breakthrough ideas.
- *Integrate technology*. Use technology to implement changes.
- *Build and deepen trust*. People are more likely to support changes when the organization's culture is trusting and managers have credibility and integrity.
- *Couple permanence with perpetual change*. Because change is the only constant, companies need to figure out how to protect their core strengths during times of change.
- *Support an entrepreneurial mindset*. Many younger employees bring a more entrepreneurial mindset to organizations and can serve as catalysts for radical change.

Sources: Based on S. Ante, "Change Is Good—So Get Used to It," *BusinessWeek*, June 22, 2009, pp. 69–70; and P. A. McLagan, "The Change-Capable Organization," *T&D*, January 2003, pp. 50–59.

The final aspect of making change happen successfully revolves around getting all organizational members involved. Successful organizational change is not a one-person job. Individual employees are a powerful resource in identifying and addressing change issues. "If you develop a program for change and simply hand it to your people, saying, 'Here, implement this,' it's unlikely to work. But when people help to build something, they will support it and make it work."[43] Managers need to encourage employees to be change agents—to look for those day-to-day improvements and changes that individuals and teams can make. For instance, a study of organizational change found that 77 percent of changes at the work group level were reactions to a specific, current problem or to a suggestion from someone outside the work group; and 68 percent of those changes occurred in the course of employees' day-to-day work.[44]

Stimulating Innovation

6.5

LEARNING OUTCOME
Describe techniques for stimulating innovation.

"Innovation is the key to continued success." "We innovate today to secure the future."[45] These two quotes (the first by Ajay Banga, the newly appointed CEO of MasterCard, and the second by Sophie Vandebroek, chief technology officer of Xerox Innovation Group) reflect how important innovation is to organizations. Success in business today demands innovation. In the dynamic, chaotic world of global competition, organizations must create new products and services and adopt state-of-the-art technology if they're going to compete successfully.[46]

What companies come to mind when you think of successful innovators? Maybe it's Apple with its iPad, iPhone, iPod, and wide array of computers. Maybe it's Google with its continually evolving web platform. Google, for instance, is a good example of the new, faster face of innovation. The company runs 50 to 200 online search experiments with users at any given time. In one instance, Google asked selected users how many search results they'd like to see on a single screen. The reply from the users was more, many more. So Google ran an experiment that tripled the number of search results per screen to 30. The result: traffic declined because "it took about a third of a second longer for search results to appear—a seemingly insignificant delay that nonetheless upset many of the users."[47] Google tried something new and quickly found out it wasn't something they wanted to pursue. Even Procter & Gamble, the global household and personal products giant, is doing the

EXHIBIT **6-9**

World's Most Innovative Companies

Fast Company's Top 10 List	Bloomberg BusinessWeek's Top 10 List
Facebook	Apple
Amazon.com	Google
Apple	Microsoft
Google	IBM
Huawei	Toyota Motor
First Solar	Amazon.com
Pacific Gas &Electric	LG Electronics
Novartis	BYD
Walmart	General Electric
Hewlett-Packard	Sony

Sources: *Fast Company* Staff, "The World's 50 Most Innovative Companies," *Fast Company*, March 2010, pp. 52+; and M. Arndt and B. Einhorn, "The 50 Most Innovative Companies," *Bloomberg BusinessWeek*, April 25, 2010, pp. 34–40.

Let's Get Real

F2F

Innovation is important because *it is a necessity to survive in a global competitive environment. Companies must constantly innovate to be in front of and respond to market opportunities, competitive threats, and changes in the business environment.*

"vast majority of our concept testing online, which has created truly substantial savings in money and time," according to the company's global consumer and market knowledge officer.[48] (See Exhibit 6-9 for a list of companies named as most innovative in the world.) What's the secret to the success of these innovator champions? What can other managers do to make their organizations more innovative? In the following pages, we'll try to answer those questions as we discuss the factors behind innovation.

Creativity Versus Innovation

Creativity refers to the ability to combine ideas in a unique way or to make unusual associations between ideas.[49] A creative organization develops unique ways of working or novel solutions to problems. But creativity by itself isn't enough. The outcomes of the creative process need to be turned into useful products or work methods, which is defined as **innovation**. Thus, the innovative organization is characterized by its ability to channel creativity into useful outcomes. When managers talk about changing an organization to make it more creative, they usually mean they want to stimulate and nurture innovation.

Stimulating and Nurturing Innovation

The systems model can help us understand how organizations become more innovative.[50] Getting the desired outputs (innovative products and work methods) involves transforming inputs. These inputs include creative people and groups within the organization. But having creative people isn't enough. It takes the right environment to help transform those inputs into innovative products or work methods. This "right" environment—that is, an environment that stimulates innovation—includes three variables: the organization's structure, culture, and human resource practices. (See Exhibit 6-10.)

STRUCTURAL VARIABLES. When Carol Bartz joined Yahoo! Inc. as CEO, one of the first things she noticed was how the organization's structure got in the way of innovation. Employees who wanted to try something different were unsure about whether they got to make the decision or somebody else did and what would happen if they went for it. Bartz's philosophy was that "There's a freedom when you organize around the idea that you're clearly in charge and go for it." Today, Yahoo!'s structure has been changed so that it provides clearer lines of responsibility and the freedom to make mistakes.[51]

An organization's structure can have a huge impact on innovativeness. Research into the effect of structural variables on innovation shows five things.[52] First, an organic-type structure

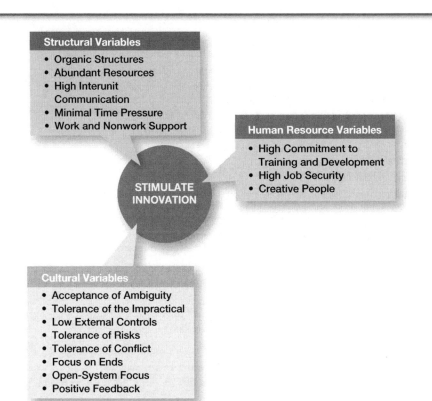

EXHIBIT 6-10

Innovation Variables

positively influences innovation. Because this structure is low in formalization, centralization, and work specialization, it facilitates the flexibility and sharing of ideas that are critical to innovation. Second, the availability of plentiful resources provides a key building block for innovation. With an abundance of resources, managers can afford to purchase innovations, can afford the cost of instituting innovations, and can absorb failures. For example, at Smart Balance Inc., the heart-healthy food developer uses its resources efficiently by focusing on product development and outsourcing almost everything else including manufacturing, product distribution, and sales. The company's CEO says that this approach allows them to be "a pretty aggressive innovator" even during economic downturns.[53] Third, frequent communication between organizational units helps break down barriers to innovation.[54] Cross-functional teams, task forces, and other such organizational designs facilitate interaction across departmental lines and are widely used in innovative organizations. For instance, Pitney Bowes, the mail and documents company, uses an electronic meeting place called IdeaNet where its 35,000-plus employees can collaborate and provide comments and input on any idea they think will help create new sources of revenue, improve profitability, or add new value for customers. IdeaNet isn't just an electronic suggestion box or open forum; employees are presented with specific idea challenges. A recent one involved how to expand its mail service business into new segments. Hundreds of employees from multiple functions and business units weighed in with ideas and eight promising ideas were generated.[55] Fourth, innovative organizations try to minimize extreme time pressures on creative activities despite the demands of white-water rapids environments. Although time pressures may spur people to work harder and may make them feel more creative, studies show that it actually causes them to be less creative.[56] Companies such as Google, 3M, and Hewlett-Packard actually urge staff researchers to spend a chunk of their workweek on self-initiated projects, even if those

creativity
The ability to combine ideas in a unique way or to make unusual associations between ideas

innovation
Taking creative ideas and turning them into useful products or work methods

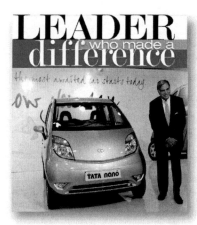

Ratan Tata, chairman of both Tata Group and Tata Motors, has built one of the world's largest conglomerates.[59] When India's long-protected economy was opened in 1981, Tata decided that for his myriad companies to survive and thrive in a global economy, he had to "make innovation a priority and build it into the DNA of the Tata Group so that every employee at every company might think and act like an innovator." One unique way innovation is encouraged at Tata is an internal innovation competition. Teams from units of the Indian conglomerate are presented with a challenge and prepare projects that are presented at the global finals at headquarters in Mumbai. Last year, 1,700 employee teams registered for the competition. The winners get no cash, only awards such as the Tata's Promising Innovation Award or the Dare to Try Award. The real prize for employees is the respect and recognition of Tata's leadership. However, the biggest winner is probably the company itself.

projects are outside the individual's work area of expertise.[57] Finally, studies have shown that an employee's creative performance was enhanced when an organization's structure explicitly supported creativity. Beneficial kinds of support included things like encouragement, open communication, readiness to listen, and useful feedback.[58]

CULTURAL VARIABLES. "Throw the bunny" is part of the lingo used by a product development team at toy company Mattel. It refers to a juggling lesson where team members learn to juggle two balls and a stuffed bunny. Most people easily learn to juggle two balls but can't let go of that third object. Creativity, like juggling, is learning to let go—that is, to "throw the bunny." And for Mattel, having a culture where people are encouraged to "throw the bunny" is important to its continued product innovations.[60]

Innovative organizations tend to have similar cultures.[61] They encourage experimentation, reward both successes and failures, and celebrate mistakes. An innovative organization is likely to have the following characteristics.

▶ *Accept ambiguity.* Too much emphasis on objectivity and specificity constrains creativity.
▶ *Tolerate the impractical.* Individuals who offer impractical, even foolish, answers to what-if questions are not stifled. What at first seems impractical might lead to innovative solutions.
▶ *Keep external controls minimal.* Rules, regulations, policies, and similar organizational controls are kept to a minimum.
▶ *Tolerate risk.* Employees are encouraged to experiment without fear of consequences should they fail. Mistakes are treated as learning opportunities. You don't want your employees to fear putting forth new ideas. A recent study found that one fear employees have is that their coworkers will think negatively of them if they try to come up with better ways of doing things. Another fear is that they'll "provoke anger among others who are comfortable with the status quo."[62] In an innovative culture, such fears are not an issue.
▶ *Tolerate conflict.* Diversity of opinions is encouraged. Harmony and agreement between individuals or units are *not* assumed to be evidence of high performance.
▶ *Focus on ends rather than means.* Goals are made clear, and individuals are encouraged to consider alternative routes toward meeting the goals. Focusing on ends suggests that several right answers might be possible for any given problem.
▶ *Use an open-system focus.* Managers closely monitor the environment and respond to changes as they occur. For example, at Starbucks, product development depends on "inspiration field trips to view customers and trends." Michelle Gass, now the company's senior vice president of global strategy, "took her team to Paris, Düsseldorf, and London to visit local Starbucks and other restaurants to get a better sense of local cultures, behaviors, and fashions." She says, "You come back just full of different ideas and different ways to think about things than you would had you read about it in a magazine or e-mail."[63]
▶ *Provide positive feedback.* Managers provide positive feedback, encouragement, and support so employees feel that their creative ideas receive attention. For instance, at

idea champion
Individuals who actively and enthusiastically support new ideas, build support, overcome resistance, and ensure that innovations are implemented

Research in Motion, Mike Lazaridis, president and co-CEO says, "I think we have a culture of innovation here, and [engineers] have absolute access to me. I live a life that tries to promote innovation."[64]

▶ *Exhibit empowering leadership.* Be a leader who lets organizational members know that the work they do is significant. Provide organizational members the opportunity to participate in decision making. Show them that you're confident they can achieve high performance levels and outcomes. Being this type of leader will have a positive influence on creativity.[65]

HUMAN RESOURCE VARIABLES.   In this category, we find that innovative organizations actively promote the training and development of their members so their knowledge remains current; offer their employees high job security to reduce the fear of getting fired for making mistakes; and encourage individuals to become **idea champions**, actively and enthusiastically supporting new ideas, building support, overcoming resistance, and ensuring that innovations are implemented. Research finds that idea champions have common personality characteristics: extremely high self-confidence, persistence, energy, and a tendency toward risk taking. They also display characteristics associated with dynamic leadership. They inspire and energize others with their vision of the potential of an innovation and through their strong personal conviction in their mission. They're also good at gaining the commitment of others to support their mission. In addition, idea champions have jobs that provide considerable decision-making discretion. This autonomy helps them introduce and implement innovations in organizations.[66]

Let's Get Real:

My Response *to A Manager's Dilemma, page 180*

to A Manager's Dilemma, page 180

I would motivate the employees by invoking cultural icons that they readily recognize: (1) NASA employees are familiar with the concept of a strategic mission, e.g. "going to the moon"; and (2) United States is known for its entrepreneurial spirit. I would explain to the staff that this is not the end of an era but the beginning of a new and exciting era of commercialized space travel. Their experience with the space program gives them a unique position to capitalize on this next era. Their personal mission should be to continue to do their job to their best of their abilities while looking for entrepreneurial opportunities.

I would then enable their personal mission by organizing business planning and management training at night, forums for investors and advanced technology companies to meet employees, and so on.

One potential risk with this approach is that if the strategy is too successful, employees may want to leave early. To mitigate the risk, you can create a bonus plan to motivate people to stay until the end of the space shuttle program.

What Would You Do?

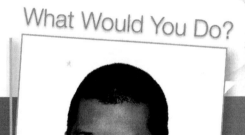

Reginald Lo
Vice President of
Professional Services
Third Sky, Inc.
Alameda, CA

Cases

CASE APPLICATION **1**
Too Big to Change?

GM's former CEO Ed Whitacre celebrates with employees during his announcement that the company repaid its government loans in full and ahead of schedule as a result of management's efforts to change GM's bureaucratic culture.

No one could have imagined it. After all these years, many thought it was too big to fail. Yet, on June 1, 2009, General Motors Corporation (GM) filed for Chapter 11 bankruptcy protection, the second-largest industrial bankruptcy in history (WorldCom was the largest).[70] GM, which hadn't made a profit since 2004, declared in its filing that it had $172 billion in debt and $82 billion in assets. As any competent business student could tell you, that ratio doesn't make a balance sheet balance, especially when the company's equity is worth little.

Fritz Henderson, who was named CEO of GM on March 30, 2009, was a numbers guy, but he knew the company's culture had to change. His vision of the new organizational culture revolved around four guidelines: risk taking, accountability, speed, and customer-product focus. The problem was that GM had tried before to reinvent itself, with mixed success. "GM's past is littered with the buzzwords of culture change. . . . It has struggled to impose cultural change across the highly bureaucratic company in which brands, departments, and regions operated like self-governing and competing states within a federation." But, GM's executives said, this time would be different. After all, there was the bankruptcy and the selective elimination of entrenched leadership. Were things really changing, though? Despite his well-intentioned plans, Henderson was fired by the board on December 1, 2009. Some felt he wasn't radical enough to change the company. His replacement was the person appointed by the Obama administration's car czar to oversee the automaker's revival after bankruptcy, Ed Whitacre, the well-respected retired chairman and CEO of AT&T.

The challenges Whitacre faces in changing GM's "plodding" culture are vast. A recent meeting of the CEO and other top executives illustrates why. The meeting was called to approve plans for a new generation of cars and trucks. Before the executives could go through all the pictures, charts, and financial projections they had prepared, Whitacre stopped them to ask why they were having the meeting in the first place. "Y'all have checked all this out pretty thoroughly. I imagine you're not going to approve something that's bad or unprofitable, so why don't you make the final decisions?" He let the plans stand and suggested that the group disband its regular Friday sessions. And it's not just the top executives who did this. In the past, even minor decisions were mulled over by committee after committee. Whitacre's trying to change that. Pushing authority and decision making down into GM's multilayered organization and slicing away at the bureaucracy are big parts of the cultural changes Whitacre is attempting. Changing GM's entrenched corporate culture isn't going to be easy, but it is necessary if GM is going to become the automotive icon it once was.

With the changes Whitacre initiated, GM achieved profitability in the first two quarters of 2010. As was his intent all along, Whitacre stepped down as CEO in early August 2010 and was replaced by Daniel Akerson, a member of the company's board of directors.

Discussion Questions

1. How would you describe the organizational culture at GM? Why was decision making so slow—"plodding" as one analyst described it?

2. Why do you think the previous CEO's (Mr. Henderson) attempts to change the organizational culture might have been lacking?

3. What changes is Mr. Whitacre making to the culture of GM?

4. What types of resistance is he likely to encounter? Using Exhibit 6-5, what would be the best ways to address that resistance? Be specific.

CASE APPLICATION 2

The Port of Rotterdam

The Port of Rotterdam is one of the world's largest seaports. It functions as an important transit point for the transport of bulk and other goods between the European continent and other parts of the world. The port also handles a large quantity of chemicals and other hazardous materials. Handling such substances has potential risks for both the port and its workers. The increase in the number of ships calling at the port can also lead to dangerous jobs, such as cleaning tanks containing hazardous substances. Due to the high risks associated with the hazardous material, any accidents are reported to the port's central command intelligence room and multiple public agencies are prompted to form a response team, or Commando Place Incident (CoPI).

CoPI is made up of firefighters, the police, the port authority, medical/ambulance workers, the Municipality of Rotterdam and managers. One challenge of having so many different organizations within the team is that as separate entities they do not share information and communication systems. Instead, CoPI team members collaborate in face-to-face settings supported by relatively limited access to information sources. The main networks used are radio Porto phones and mobile phone networks that connect the different members of the team to their respective Emergency Control Centers (ECC).

In order to make effective decisions rapidly, CoPI needs accurate information in a timely manner, but poor communication and limited information exchange makes this difficult. One response to the crisis management process was the comprehensive change management plan, which sought to enhance collaboration and communication between the different organizations within CoPI resulting in a quicker and more efficient response unit. Why doesn't the Port of Rotterdam adopt an IT system to support crisis management decisions? The problem is the need for accurate information, a difficulty in getting it on time, and also an overwhelming amount of available, heterogeneous sources of potential data.

Will the comprehensive change management plan be a success? The end-users (i.e., CoPI members) are reluctant to adopt the IT-based decision support system particularly as it does not fit in with their current procedures. Therefore, the main challenge will be convincing the crisis management team members that their procedures should change first. In other words, IT-based systems could potentially cause more problems if they are not installed on the correct platforms. Change needs to occur on three different levels: information exchange, decision-making procedures, and the level and scope of responsibilities and authorities. These are the critical parts of the change plan that CoPI members and other related bodies may not accept easily.[71]

Discussion Questions

1. How would you describe the crisis management team's organizational culture? What problems do they have in making decisions quickly? Explain.

2. What changes are they making to accelerate the crisis management decision-making procedures at the Port of Rotterdam?

3. What challenges to the plan might the Port of Rotterdam crisis management team face?

CASE APPLICATION

CLP POWER IN HONG KONG

Founded in Hong Kong in 1901, CLP Power Hong Kong Ltd. is one of the largest electricity investor-operators in the Asia Pacific region; in 2008, it had a market capitalization of approximately HK$127 billion (US$16.3 billion). It operates a vertically integrated electricity generation, transmission, and distribution business that is regulated by the government under a Scheme of Control (SOC).[50] However, this public power utility has been faced with external challenges such as a potential review of the regulatory regime, increasing environmental concerns, and tariff pressure from the public. In the early 2000s, an internal analysis also identified the need to boost key business indicators such as competitiveness and cost-efficiency. The company has thus decided to reinvent its business to become more "competitive."

For example, since 2004 one of its business groups, the Generation Business Group, has initiated various change management initiatives. Full-time members from different functional areas convened to form a continuous improvement team (CIT) to collect employee opinions and identify areas of change. But the success of change initiatives is dependent on support from the top management. A steering committee met and agreed on the change by committing to the vision of a "commercial model." A series of unconventional communication sessions, open forums, and "big-bang" workshops were organized in order to collect employee opinions.

Traditionally, a hierarchical organizational structure and reporting relationship existed in the power utility. While lower levels of employees were reluctant to make decisions, an "upward delegation" workflow prevailed. A "silo mentality" was also common among the engineers and technicians. Cross-departmental communications were always found to be difficult, particularly between the operations and maintenance departments. In view of such difficulties, the company instilled a sense of empowerment in the employees. The organizational structure was streamlined to have fewer layers of staff. In parallel, existing channels of communication such as broadcasts, e-mails, notice boards, and so on, were reviewed to allow faster decision making. In addition, a Partnership Charter was signed between employees of different departments to foster stronger teamwork. A new culture of "doing more with less," "doing smarter," and "just enough" was cascaded down to all employees so that there was continuous improvement and less waste.

Despite these change management initiatives and support from the top management, resistance was sometimes found among the staff who were accustomed to a stable and paternalistic working culture. Most of them were engineers who were familiar with technical operations only. In the beginning, because staff could not envisage the need for change in such a profitable business, they challenged some changes. Through continuous education and support, the top management and CIT members managed to explain the rationale and benefits of change. Also, they invited ambassadors to tap the pulse and sentiments of various staff groups by collecting opinions and promoting various change initiatives to the rest. Eventually, it received strong support from the staff, and 120 ambassadors (among 700 employees) were willing to take up the role. These ambassadors were seeded members of the CIT, and they later became an important part of the impetus for ongoing customized change initiatives in different departments.

Change has been successful, and the program entered into its second phase in 2006. Now, the human resources management department has taken over the role of the CIT, but change management initiatives have continued.

Discussion Questions

1. What types of change have taken place in CLP Power Hong Kong Ltd.?
2. What external and internal forces could create the need for the company to change?
3. Use Lewin's change model to illustrate the phases of change.
4. Why do people resist the change? How did CLP cope with the resistance?

Sources: Interviews with the human resource manager and public affairs manager of Generation Business Group; and CLP Group Web site. http://www.clpgroup.com.

Review Questions and Tests

REVIEW AND DISCUSSION QUESTIONS

1. Contrast the calm waters and white-water rapids metaphors of change.

2. Explain Lewin's three-step model of the change process.

3. Describe how managers might change structure, technology, and people.

4. Can a low-level employee be a change agent? Explain your answer.

5. Why do people resist change? How can resistance to change be reduced?

6. How are opportunities, constraints, and demands related to stress? Give an example of each.

7. Planned change is often thought to be the best approach to take in organizations. Can unplanned change ever be effective? Explain.

8. Organizations typically have limits to how much change they can absorb. As a manager, what signs would you look for that might suggest that your organization has exceeded its capacity to change?

9. Describe the structural, cultural, and human resources variables that are necessary for innovation.

10. Innovation requires allowing people to make mistakes. However, being wrong too many times can be disastrous to your career. Do you agree? Why or why not? What are the implications for nurturing innovation?

Understanding Yourself

Am I Burned Out?

Burnout is when you've reached an overwhelming level of chronic and long-term stress. It can lead to exhaustion and diminished interest in activities, both work and personal. This instrument was designed to provide insights into whether you're suffering from burnout.

INSTRUMENT Respond to each of the 21 items using the following scale:

1 = Never
2 = Once in a while
3 = Rarely
4 = Sometimes
5 = Often
6 = Usually
7 = Always

How often do you have any of the following experiences?

		1	2	3	4	5	6	7
1.	Being tired	1	2	3	4	5	6	7
2.	Feeling depressed	1	2	3	4	5	6	7
3.	Having a good day	1	2	3	4	5	6	7
4.	Being physically exhausted	1	2	3	4	5	6	7
5.	Being emotionally exhausted	1	2	3	4	5	6	7
6.	Being happy	1	2	3	4	5	6	7
7.	Being "wiped out"	1	2	3	4	5	6	7
8.	"Can't take it anymore"	1	2	3	4	5	6	7
9.	Being unhappy	1	2	3	4	5	6	7
10.	Feeling run-down	1	2	3	4	5	6	7
11.	Feeling trapped	1	2	3	4	5	6	7
12.	Feeling worthless	1	2	3	4	5	6	7
13.	Being weary	1	2	3	4	5	6	7
14.	Being troubled	1	2	3	4	5	6	7
15.	Feeling disillusioned and resentful	1	2	3	4	5	6	7
16.	Being weak and susceptible to illness	1	2	3	4	5	6	7
17.	Feeling hopeless	1	2	3	4	5	6	7
18.	Feeling rejected	1	2	3	4	5	6	7
19.	Feeling optimistic	1	2	3	4	5	6	7
20.	Feeling energetic	1	2	3	4	5	6	7
21.	Feeling anxious	1	2	3	4	5	6	7

SCORING KEY To calculate your burnout score, add up your score for items 3, 6, 19, and 20. Then subtract that total from 32. To this number, add your direct scores for the remaining 17 items. Finally, divide this combined number by 21.

ANALYSIS AND INTERPRETATION Your burnout score will be somewhere between 1 and 7. The higher your number, the closer you are to burnout. The authors claim that scores below 3 indicate few signs of burnout. Scores between 3 and 4 suggest the need to examine your work life and reevaluate priorities with the intent of making changes. If your score is higher than 4, you are experiencing a number of signs associated with burnout. You need to take some action to address your problems. Scores above 5 indicate an acute state, requiring immediate professional attention.

Source: A. Pines and E. Aronson, "Why Managers Burn Out," *Sales & Marketing Management* (February 1989), p. 38.

SECTION 7:
TEAMS

Chapter 13:
Teams

THE MEANING AND IMPORTANCE OF GROUPS AND TEAMS

Work is a group-based activity and if the organisation is to function effectively it requires collaboration and co-operation among its members. **Groups** are an essential feature of any organisation. Individuals seldom work in isolation from others. Although there is no single accepted definition, most people will readily understand what constitutes a group. The essential feature is that its members regard themselves as belonging to the group. A popular definition defines the group in psychological terms as:

> *any number of people who (1) interact with one another; (2) are psychologically aware of one another; and (3) perceive themselves to be a group.*[1]

Another useful way of defining a work group is a collection of people who share most, if not all, of the following characteristics:

- a definable membership
- group consciousness
- a sense of shared purpose
- interdependence
- interaction
- ability to act in a unitary manner.[2]

Groups are a characteristic of all social situations and almost everyone in an organisation will be a member of one or more groups. The working of groups and the influence they exert over their membership is an essential feature of human behaviour and of organisational performance. Members of a group must co-operate in order for work to be carried out, and managers themselves will work within these groups. People in groups influence each other in many ways and groups may develop their own hierarchies and leaders. Group pressures can have a major influence over the behaviour of individual members and their work performance.

DIFFERENCES BETWEEN GROUPS AND TEAMS

The use of the word 'teams' has become increasingly fashionable in recent years. *Crainer* refers to the use of 'teamworking' as a side effect of increasing concentration on working across functional divides and fits neatly with the trend towards empowerment. However, despite the extensive literature about teams and teamworking, the basic dynamics of teamworking often remain clouded and uncertain.

> *Teams occur when a number of people have a common goal and recognise that their personal success is dependent on the success of others. They are all interdependent. In practice, this means that in most teams people will contribute individual skills many of which will be different. It also means that the full tensions and counter-balance of human behaviour will need to be demonstrated in the team.*[3]

In common usage and literature, including to some extent in this book, there is a tendency for the terms 'groups' and 'teams' to be used interchangeably. It is not easy to distinguish clearly between a group and a team. According to ACAS: 'the term "team" is used loosely to describe many different groupings and a variety of labels are given to the types of teams. It is doubtful whether any definitions of types of teams would be universally acceptable.'[4]

According to *Holpp*, while many people are still paying homage to teams, teamwork, empowerment and self-management, others have become disillusioned. Holpp poses the question: What are teams?

> *It's a simple enough question, but one that's seldom asked. We all think we know intuitively what teams are. Guess again. Here are some questions to help define team configurations.*

- *Are teams going to be natural work groups, or project-and-task oriented?*
- *Will they be self-managed or directed?*
- *How many people will be on the teams; who's in charge?*
- *How will the teams fit into the organisation's structure if it shows only boxes and not circles or other new organisational forms?*

Holpp also poses the question: why do you want teams?

If teams are just a convenient way to group under one manager a lot of people who used to work for several downsized supervisors, don't bother. But if teams can truly take ownership of work areas and provide the kind of up-close knowledge that's unavailable elsewhere, then full speed ahead.[5]

Teamwork as a fashionable term

Cane suggests that organisations are sometimes unsure whether they have teams or simply groups of people working together.

It is certainly true to say that any group of people who do not know they are a team cannot be one. To become a team, a group of individuals needs to have a strong common purpose and to work towards that purpose rather than individually. They need also to believe that they will achieve more by co-operation than working individually.[6]

Whereas all teams are, by definition, groups, it does not necessarily follow that all groups are teams.

Belbin points out that to the extent that teamwork was becoming a fashionable term, it began to replace the more usual reference to groups and every activity was now being described as 'teamwork'. He questions whether it matters whether one is talking about groups or teams and maintains that the confusion in vocabulary should be addressed if the principles of good teamwork are to be retained. Belbin suggests there are several factors that characterise the difference between groups and teams (*see* Figure 8.1). The best differentiator is size: groups can comprise any number of people but teams are smaller with a membership between (ideally) four and six. The quintessential feature of a small, well-balanced team is that leadership is shared or rotates whereas large groups typically throw up solo leaders.[7]

Figure 8.1	Differences between a team and a group	
	Team	**Group**
Size	Limited	Medium or large
Selection	Crucial	Immaterial
Leadership	Shared or rotating	Solo
Perception	Mutual knowledge understanding	Focus on leader
Style	Role spread co-ordination	Convergence conformism
Spirit	Dynamic interaction	Togetherness persecution of opponents

Source: Belbin, R. M. *Beyond the Team*, Butterworth-Heinemann (2000). Copyright © 2000. Reproduced with permission from Elsevier Ltd.

While acknowledging the work of Belbin it appears that the term 'group' is often used in a more general sense and 'team' in a more specific context. We continue to refer to 'group' or 'team' according to the particular focus of attention and the vocabulary of the quoted authors.

Another possible distinction is based on the development and maturity of the 'group'. For example, in terms of Tuckman's model (discussed later in this chapter), not until a group proceeds beyond the stages of forming, norming and storming and successfully reaches the performing stage does it become a team.

GROUP VALUES AND NORMS

The classical approach to organisation and management tended to ignore the importance of groups and the social factors at work. The ideas of people such as F. W. Taylor popularised the concept of the 'rabble hypothesis' and the assumption that people carried out their work, and could be motivated, as solitary individuals unaffected by others. The human relations approach, however (discussed in Chapter 2), gave recognition to the work organisation as a social organisation and to the importance of the group, and group values and norms, in influencing behaviour at work.

One experiment involved the observation of a group of 14 men working in the bank wiring room. The men formed their own sub-groups or cliques, with natural leaders emerging with the consent of the members. Despite a financial incentive scheme where workers could receive more money the more work they did, the group decided on 6,000 units a day as a fair level of output. This was well below the level they were capable of producing. Group pressures on individual workers were stronger than financial incentives offered by management.

Informal social relations

The group developed its own pattern of informal social relations and codes and practices ('norms') of what constituted proper group behaviour.

- **Not to be a 'rate buster'** – not to produce at too high a rate of output compared with other members or to exceed the production restriction of the group.
- **Not to be a 'chiseller'** – not to shirk production or to produce at too low a rate of output compared with other members of the group.
- **Not to be a 'squealer'** – not to say anything to the supervisor or management which might be harmful to other members of the group.
- **Not to be 'officious'** – people with authority over members of the group, for example inspectors, should not take advantage of their seniority or maintain a social distance from the group.

The group had their own system of sanctions including sarcasm, damaging completed work, hiding tools, playing tricks on the inspectors and ostracising those members who did not conform with the **group norms**. Threats of physical violence were also made and the group developed a system of punishing offenders by 'binging' that involved striking someone a fairly hard blow on the upper part of the arm. This process of binging also became a recognised method of controlling conflict within the group.

Team performance

According to *Riches*, one way to improve team performance is to establish agreed norms or rules for how the team is to operate and rigorously stick to them. Norms could address the obligations of individual members to the team, how it will assess its performance, how it will work together, what motivation systems will be used, how it will relate to customers, and the mechanisms to facilitate an honest exchange about the team norms and behaviour.[8]

Figure 8.2 Concept map of group norms

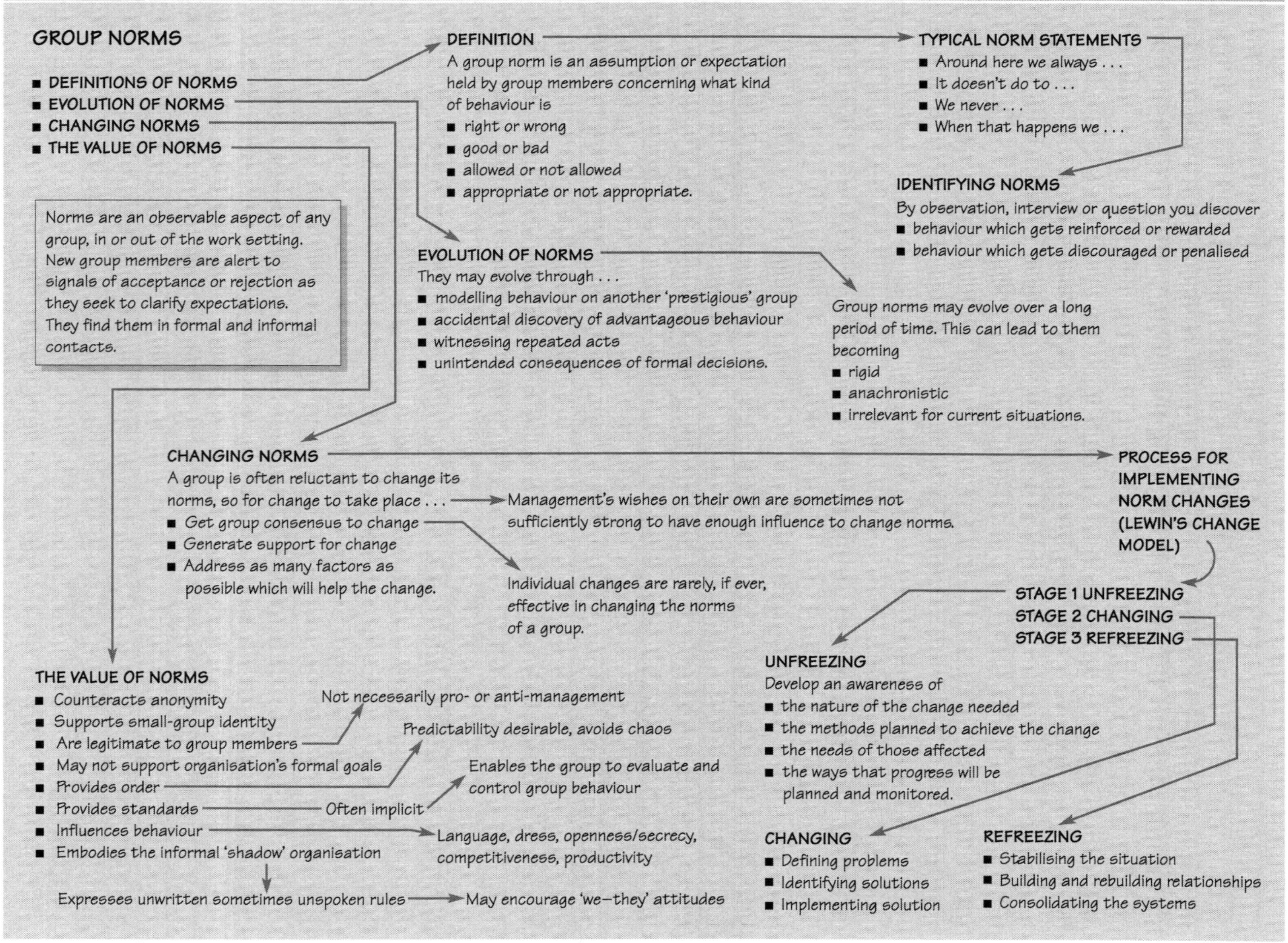
GROUP NORMS
■ DEFINITIONS OF NORMS
■ EVOLUTION OF NORMS
■ CHANGING NORMS
■ THE VALUE OF NORMS
Norms are an observable aspect of any group, in or out of the work setting. New group members are alert to signals of acceptance or rejection as they seek to clarify expectations. They find them in formal and informal contacts.
DEFINITION
A group norm is an assumption or expectation held by group members concerning what kind of behaviour is
■ right or wrong
■ good or bad
■ allowed or not allowed
■ appropriate or not appropriate.
TYPICAL NORM STATEMENTS
■ Around here we always . . .
■ It doesn't do to . . .
■ We never . . .
■ When that happens we . . .
IDENTIFYING NORMS
By observation, interview or question you discover
■ behaviour which gets reinforced or rewarded
■ behaviour which gets discouraged or penalised
EVOLUTION OF NORMS
They may evolve through . . .
■ modelling behaviour on another 'prestigious' group
■ accidental discovery of advantageous behaviour
■ witnessing repeated acts
■ unintended consequences of formal decisions.
Group norms may evolve over a long period of time. This can lead to them becoming
■ rigid
■ anachronistic
■ irrelevant for current situations.
CHANGING NORMS
A group is often reluctant to change its norms, so for change to take place . . .
■ Get group consensus to change
■ Generate support for change
■ Address as many factors as possible which will help the change.
Management's wishes on their own are sometimes not sufficiently strong to have enough influence to change norms.
Individual changes are rarely, if ever, effective in changing the norms of a group.
PROCESS FOR IMPLEMENTING NORM CHANGES (LEWIN'S CHANGE MODEL)
STAGE 1 UNFREEZING
STAGE 2 CHANGING
STAGE 3 REFREEZING
UNFREEZING
Develop an awareness of
■ the nature of the change needed
■ the methods planned to achieve the change
■ the needs of those affected
■ the ways that progress will be planned and monitored.
CHANGING
■ Defining problems
■ Identifying solutions
■ Implementing solution
REFREEZING
■ Stabilising the situation
■ Building and rebuilding relationships
■ Consolidating the systems
THE VALUE OF NORMS
■ Counteracts anonymity
■ Supports small-group identity
■ Are legitimate to group members
■ May not support organisation's formal goals
■ Provides order
■ Provides standards
■ Influences behaviour
■ Embodies the informal 'shadow' organisation
Not necessarily pro- or anti-management
Predictability desirable, avoids chaos
Enables the group to evaluate and control group behaviour
Often implicit
Language, dress, openness/secrecy, competitiveness, productivity
Expresses unwritten sometimes unspoken rules
May encourage 'we–they' attitudes

Source: Copyright © 2008 The Virtual Learning Materials Workshop. Reproduced with permission.

A 2003 study by the Economic & Social Research Council draws attention to the importance of social norms among employees and questions whether employees are guided not only by monetary incentives but also by peer pressure towards social efficiency for the workers as a group. 'Intuitively, social norms among workers must be important if they work in teams where bonuses are dependent on group rather than individual effort.'[9] (You may see some similarity here with the bank wiring room experiment, discussed above.)

A concept map of group norms is set out in Figure 8.2.

FORMAL AND INFORMAL GROUPS

Groups are deliberately planned and created by management as part of the formal organisation structure. However, groups will also arise from social processes and the informal organisation that was discussed in Chapter 3. The informal organisation arises from the interaction of people working within the organisation and the development of groups with their own relationships and norms of behaviour, irrespective of those defined within the formal structure. This leads to a major distinction between formal and informal groups.

Formal groups

Groups are formed as a consequence of the pattern of organisation structure and arrangements for the division of work, for example the grouping together of common activities into sections. Groups may result from the nature of technology employed and the way in which work is carried out, for example the bringing together of a number of people to carry out a sequence of operations on an assembly line. Groups may also develop when a number of people of the same level or status within the organisation see themselves as a group, for example departmental heads of an industrial organisation or chief officers of a local authority. **Formal groups** are created to achieve specific organisational objectives and are concerned with the **co-ordination of work activities**. People are brought together on the basis of defined roles within the structure of the organisation. The nature of the tasks to be undertaken is a predominant feature of the formal group. Goals are identified by management, and certain rules, relationships and norms of behaviour established.

Formal groups tend to be relatively permanent, although there may be changes in actual membership. However, temporary formal groups may also be created by management, as with for example the use of project teams in a matrix organisation. Formal work groups can be differentiated in a number of ways, for example on the basis of membership, the task to be performed, the nature of technology, or position within the organisation structure.

Virtuoso teams

Boynton and Fischer draw attention to '**virtuoso teams**' that are formed specifically for big change in organisations. They are comprised of individual superstars or virtuosos with a single clear, ambitious mandate and are not intended to remain together over multiple initiatives or projects. Virtuoso teams require a special kind of leadership and to be managed in a manner that unleashes the maximum contribution from each individual superstar. Although most organisations rarely form such teams, they are required for radical change opportunities that represent a significant departure from prior practice and/or how an organisation conducts its business. Examples of big changes that required a virtuoso team are the Manhattan Project, Thomas Edison's inventory factory and Roald Amundsen's polar expedition.[10]

Informal groups

The formal structure of the organisation, and system of role relationships, rules and procedures, will always be augmented by interpretation and development at the informal level.

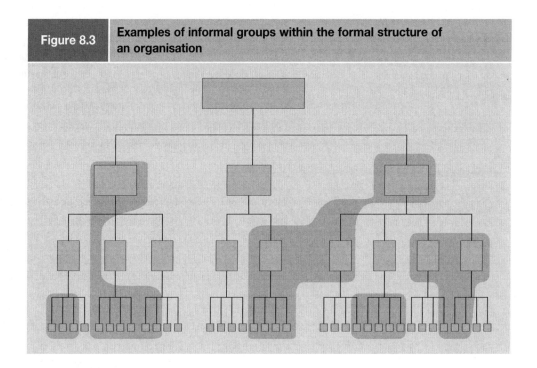

Figure 8.3 Examples of informal groups within the formal structure of an organisation

Informal groups are based more on personal relationships and agreement of group members than on defined role relationships. They serve to satisfy psychological and social needs not related necessarily to the tasks to be undertaken. Groups may devise ways of attempting to satisfy members' affiliation and other social motivations lacking in the work situation. Membership of informal groups can cut across the formal structure. They may comprise individuals from different parts of the organisation and/or from different levels of the organisation, both vertically and diagonally, as well as from the same horizontal level. An informal group could also be the same as the formal group, or it might comprise a part only of the formal group (*see* Figure 8.3).

Members of an informal group may appoint their own leader who exercises authority by the consent of the members themselves. The informal leader may be chosen as the person who reflects the attitudes and values of the members, helps to resolve conflict, leads the group in satisfying its goals, or liaises with management or other people outside the group. The informal leader may often change according to the particular situation facing the group. Although not usually the case, it is possible for the informal leader to be the same person as the formal leader appointed officially by management.

Major functions of informal groups

Lysons suggests four main reasons for informal groups:

- **The perpetuation of the informal group 'culture'.** Culture in this context means a set of values, norms and beliefs which form a guide to group acceptance and group behaviour. Unless you broadly subscribe to the group culture, you will not belong and will be an 'outsider' or 'isolate'.
- **The maintenance of a communication system.** Groups want all the information that affects their welfare, either negatively or positively. If groups are not apprised of policies and motives behind actions, they will seek to tap into formal communication channels and spread information among group members.
- **The implementation of social control.** Conformity to group culture is enforced by such techniques as ridicule, ostracism and violence. This is illustrated, for example, by the enforcement of group norms in the bank wiring room discussed in the previous section.

■ **The provision of interest and fun in work life.** Many jobs are monotonous and fail to hold workers' attention. Work may also offer few prospects. Workers may try to compensate by interpersonal relations provided by the group and in such activities as time wasting by talking, gambling, practical joking and drinking.[11]

> *We humans are a gregarious lot. We like to gather together and establish our own social networks, which are often the real key to creativity and innovation in organisations . . . But many managers are unaware that seemingly pointless social networking does in fact play a crucial part in the way people interact with each other and get work done.*
>
> Sue Law[12]

An example of informal groups

A lack of direction and clear information flow within the formal structure can give rise to uncertainty and suspicion. In the absence of specific knowledge, the grapevine takes on an important role, rumours start and the informal part of the organisation is highlighted, often with negative results. A typical example concerned an industrial organisation in a highly competitive market and experiencing a drop in sales. Two top managers had suddenly lost their jobs without any apparent explanation and there were board meetings seemingly every other day. Although there was no specific information or statements from top management, the general feeling among the staff was that whatever was about to happen was most unlikely to be good news.

At lunchtime three junior members of staff, one female and two male, each from different departments, were having a chat. With a half smile the female member said to the others that she could well be seeing a lot more of both or at least one of them before long. She said that she had heard, unofficially, from her manager that the department was about to be awarded a very profitable order. She surmised that other departments, which she had also heard had lost their parts of the same contracts and not had many orders recently, would have to integrate into the successful department with the possible loss of certain jobs. The other two members both believed this and talked about it within their own departments as if it were a fact. The result? Even more uncertainty throughout the organisation, increased gloom and distraction from the task. In fact, no such integration did take place, only a minor restructuring of the organisation with no direct loss of jobs other than through voluntary early retirement. However, it proved very difficult for top management to quash effectively the rumour and restore trust and morale.

Critical reflection

'Given the obvious importance of social networks and interpersonal relationships for both the morale and job satisfaction of staff and their levels of work performance, the main focus in the study of organisational behaviour should be on the operations and management of the informal organisation.'

Can you present a counter argument to this contention?

17.5 Stages of team development

Putting people into a team does not mean that they perform well immediately, as teams need to go through stages of growth. Some never perform well. Tuckman and Jensen (1977) developed a theory that groups can potentially pass through five fairly clearly defined stages of development. Figure 17.3 shows these.

Teams need to have the chance to grow up and to develop trust among the members. As the work makes progress people learn about each other, and how they can work well together. The closer they get, the easier it becomes to develop mutual trust.

Forming

Forming is the stage at which members choose, or are told, to join a team. Managers may select them for their functional and technical expertise or for some other skill. They come together and begin to find out who the other members are, exchanging fairly superficial information about themselves, and beginning to offer ideas about what the group should do. People are trying to make an impression on the group and to establish their identity with the other members.

Storming

Conflicts may occur at the storming stage, so it can be an uncomfortable time for the group. As the group begins the actual work members begin to express differences of interest that they withheld, or did not recognise, at the forming stage. People realise that others want different things from the group, have other priorities and, perhaps, have hidden agendas.

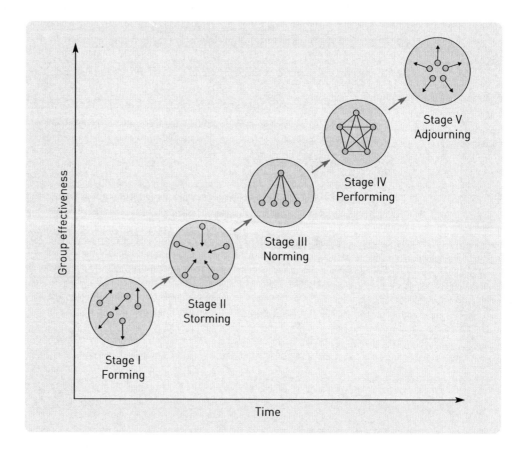

Figure 17.3
Stages of team
development

Different personalities emerge, with contrasting attitudes towards the group and how it should work. Some experience conflicts between the time they are spending with the group and other duties. Differences in values and norms emerge.

Some groups never pass this stage. There may be little open conflict and members may believe the group is performing well – but may be deluding themselves. If the group does not confront disagreements it will remain at the forming or storming stage, and will do no significant work. Performance depends on someone doing or saying something to move the group to the next stage.

Norming

Here the members are beginning to accommodate differences constructively and to establish adequate ways of working together. They develop a set of shared norms – expected ways of behaving – about how they should interact with each other, how they should approach the task, how they should deal with differences. People create or accept roles so that responsibilities are clear. The leader may set those roles formally or members may accept them implicitly during early meetings. Members may establish a common language to guide the group and allow members to work together effectively.

Performing

Here the group is working well, gets on with the job to the required standard and achieves its objectives. Not all groups get this far.

Adjourning

The team completes its task and disbands. Members may reflect on how the group performed and identify lessons for future tasks. Some groups disband because they are clearly not able to do the job and agree to stop meeting.

Key ideas | **Managing the virtual team lifecycle**

Furst *et al.* (2004) noted the benefits of virtual teams in eliminating boundaries of time and space, but also found that they more often fail than succeed. To explain this they tracked the evolution of six virtual teams in a company, using the Tuckman and Jensen model. They found that virtual teams faced additional problems at each stage of the model, compared with those working in the same place.

- **Forming** is more difficult, and takes longer, as there is less frequent communication, especially the informal chat between workers who meet regularly. This reduces the speed at which people make friendships and increases the risk of forming false impressions or stereotypes about other team members.
- **Storming** can also be more fraught, as the absence of frequent non-verbal clues increases the risks of misunderstanding. Disagreements can be exacerbated or prolonged if people do not respond quickly to electronic communication – even if caused by differences in working times or poor technology.
- **Norming** in virtual teams needs to clarify how to co-ordinate work, how to communicate and how quickly to respond to requests. The process of norming itself is made more complex with electronic communication, as it is harder to try out ideas tentatively and to gauge reactions.
- **Performing** depends on sharing information, integrating ideas and seeking creative solutions. The challenges of virtual working at this stage include competing pressure from local assignments, losing focus, and the fear of a failure that would damage a career.

Furst *et al.* use their analysis to suggest what those managing a virtual team could do at each stage to increase the chances of virtual teams reliably adding value.

Source: Furst *et al.* (2004).

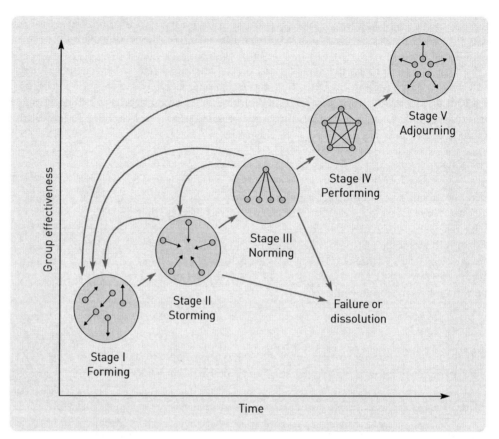

Figure 17.4
Modified model of
the stages of team
development

A team that survives will go through these stages many times. As new members join, as others leave, as circumstances or the task change, new tensions arise that take the group back to an earlier stage. A new member implies that the team needs to revisit, however briefly, the forming and norming stages. This ensures the new members are brought psychologically into the team and understand how they are expected to behave. A change in task or a conflict over priorities can take a team back to the storming stage, from which it needs to work forward again. The process will be more like Figure 17.4 than the linear progression implied by the original theory.

17.6   Team processes

Effective teams, often with the help of skilled team coaches (Hackman and Wageman, 2005), develop working methods, or team processes, that help them to accomplish their tasks. These include developing a common approach, understanding categories of communication and observing team practices.

Common approach

A primary outcome of an effective 'norming' stage is that members agree both the administrative and social aspects of working together. This includes deciding who does which jobs, what skills members need to develop, and how the group should make and modify decisions. In other words the group needs to agree the work required and how it will fit together. It needs to decide how to integrate the skills of the group and use them co-operatively to advance performance.

The common approach includes supporting and integrating new members into the team. It also includes practices of remembering and summarising agreements. Working together on these tasks helps to promote the mutual trust and constructive conflict necessary to team success. Groups need to spend as much time on developing a common approach as they do on developing a shared purpose.

Team members need to control their meetings effectively – whether face to face or at a distance. That involves ensuring they are conducted in a way that suits the purpose of the task, without participants feeling that they are being manipulated. Table 17.4 is an example of the advice widely available to managers about effective and ineffective meetings.

Categories of communication

Group members depend on information and ideas from others to help them perform the group task; a useful skill is to be able to identify the kind of contribution that people make (Chapter 16 illustrated patterns of group communication), and whether this helps the group to manage the task. To study and learn how people behave in groups we need a precise and reliable way to describe events. There are many such models, each suited to a purpose: Table 17.5 illustrates one such list of behaviours. The significance of this is the evidence that how a group uses its time between these categories of communication will affect performance. A group that devotes most of its time to proposing ideas and disagreeing with them will not progress far. A more effective group will spend more time proposing and building, which of course implies developing better listening skills.

Table 17.4 Five tips for effective meetings

Meetings are likely to succeed if:	Meetings are likely to fail if:
• they are scheduled well in advance	• they are fixed at short notice (absentees)
• they have an agenda, with relevant papers distributed in advance and invite additions at the start	• they have no agenda or papers (no preparation, lack of focus, discussion longer)
• they have a starting and finishing time and follow prearranged time limits on each item	• they are of indefinite length (discussion drifts), time is lost and important items are not dealt with (delay, and require a further meeting)
• decisions and responsibilities for action are recorded and circulated within 24 hours	• decisions lack clarity (misunderstanding what was agreed, delay, reopening issues)
• they keep subgroups or members of related teams informed of progress	• the team is not aware of work going on in other teams that is relevant to its work

Observing the team

Members can develop the skill of assessing how well a team is performing a task. There are many guides to help them do this, and anyone can develop their ability to **observe** groups by concentrating on this aspect rather than on the **content** of the immediate task. They work

Observation is the activity of concentrating on how a team works rather than taking part in the activity itself.

Content is the specific substantive task that the group is undertaking.

Table 17.5 Categories of communication within a group

Category	Explanation
Proposing	Putting forward a suggestion, idea or course of action
Supporting	Declaring agreement or support for an individual or their idea
Building	Developing or extending an idea or suggestion from someone else
Disagreeing	Criticising another person's statement
Giving information	Giving or clarifying facts, ideas or opinions
Seeking information	Seeking facts, ideas or opinions from others

slightly apart from the team for a short time and keep a careful record of what members say or do. They also note how other members react, and how that affects the performance of the team. At the very least, members can reflect on these questions at the end of a task:

- What did people do or say that helped or hindered the group's performance?
- What went well during that task, which we should try to repeat?
- What did not go well, which we could improve?

With practice, skilled members of a team are able to observe what is happening as they work on the task. They can do this more easily and powerfully if they focus their observations on certain behaviour categories – such as those shown in Table 17.8 – but only those suited to the purpose of the observation.

Teams have outcomes that can benefit the members, the organisation – and perhaps both.

INTERACTIONS AMONG MEMBERS

If groups are to be successful and perform effectively, there must be a spirit of unity and co-operation. In the previous chapter we mentioned that how people behave and perform as members of a group is as important as their behaviour or performance as individuals, and drew attention to the importance of effective teamwork. The main focus of attention in this chapter is the actual roles, behaviours and performance of people working in groups or teams. Once again, however, we should be aware of the tendency for the terms 'groups' and 'teams' to be used interchangeably. Members of a group must work well together as a team. As *Crainer* reminds us, in most teams people will contribute individual skills, many of which will be different. However, referring to the work of *Obeng*,[1] Crainer points out that it is not enough to have a rag-bag collection of individual skills.

> *The various behaviours of the team members must mesh together in order to achieve objectives. For people to work successfully in teams, you need people to behave in certain ways. You need some people to concentrate on the task at hand (doers). You need some people to provide specialist knowledge (knowers) and some to solve problems as they arise (solvers). You need some people to make sure that it is going as well as it can and that the whole team is contributing fully (checkers). And you need some people to make sure that the team is operating as a cohesive social unit (carers).*[2]

Co-operation and interactions

As ACAS points out: 'In a general sense people talk of teamwork when they want to emphasise the virtues of co-operation and the need to make use of the various strengths of employees . . . To remain competitive organisations need to make optimum use of equipment and people if they are to thrive or even survive.'[3]

In order to understand the functions and processes of a group, it is necessary to understand what happens when people meet; the actions and behaviour of individual members; the parts people play; the patterns of interactions and forces within the group; and influences on individual and group performance. According to *Guirdham*, for example:

> *Many of the concepts that have helped us understand interactive behaviour in work relationships are also needed for understanding it in groups, including role behaviour, norms and co-operation, competition, conflict and conflict resolution. Most of what there is to understand about group work applies equally to both decision-making groups and teams but there are some further issues particular to the two different kinds of groups. There is, however, no suggestion that teams do not have to solve problems!*[4]

BELBIN'S TEAM ROLES

One of the most popular and widely used analyses of individual roles within a work group or team is that developed by *Meredith Belbin*. Following years of research and empirical study, Belbin concludes that groups composed entirely of clever people, or of people with similar personalities, display a number of negative results and lack creativity. The most consistently successful groups comprise a range of roles undertaken by various members. The constitution of the group itself is an important variable in its success.[5] Initially, Belbin identified eight useful types of contribution – or team roles.

A **team role** is described as a pattern of behaviour, characteristic of the way in which one team member interacts with another whose performance serves to facilitate the progress of the team as a whole. In a follow-up publication, Belbin discusses the continual evolution of team roles, which differ in a few respects from those originally identified, and adds a ninth role.[6] Strength of contribution in any one role is commonly associated with particular weaknesses. These are called allowable weaknesses. Members are seldom strong in all nine team roles. A description of the evolved nine team roles is given in Table 9.1.

The types of people identified are useful team members and form a comprehensive list. These are the key team roles and the primary characters for successful teams. Creative teams

Table 9.1	Belbin's evolved nine team roles	
Roles and descriptions – team-role contribution		**Allowable weaknesses**
Plant	Creative, imaginative, unorthodox. Solves difficult problems.	Ignores details. Too preoccupied to communicate effectively.
Resource investigator	Extravert, enthusiastic, communicative. Explores opportunities. Develops contacts.	Over-optimistic. Loses interest once initial enthusiasm has passed.
Co-ordinator	Mature, confident, a good chairperson. Clarifies goals, promotes decision-making. Delegates well.	Can be seen as manipulative. Offloads personal work.
Shaper	Challenging, dynamic, thrives on pressure. Has the drive and courage to overcome obstacles.	Can provoke others. Hurts people's feelings.
Monitor-Evaluator	Sober, strategic and discerning. Sees all options. Judges accurately.	Lacks drive and ability to inspire others.
Teamworker	Co-operative, mild, perceptive and diplomatic. Listens, builds, averts friction.	Indecisive in crunch situations.
Implementer	Disciplined, reliable, conservative and efficient. Turns ideas into practical actions.	Somewhat inflexible. Slow to respond to new possibilities.
Completer	Painstaking, conscientious, anxious. Searches out errors and omissions. Delivers on time.	Inclined to worry unduly. Reluctant to delegate.
Specialist	Single-minded, self-sharing, dedicated. Provides knowledge and skills in rare supply.	Contributes on only a narrow front. Dwells on technicalities.

Source: Belbin, R. M. *Team Roles at Work*, Butterworth-Heinemann (a division of Reed Elsevier UK Ltd) and Belbin Associates (1993), p. 23. Reproduced with permission.

require a balance of all these roles and comprise members who have characteristics complementary to each other. 'No one's perfect, but a team can be.' Belbin claims that good examples of each type would prove adequate for any challenge, although not all types are necessarily needed. Other members may be welcome for their personal qualities, for example a sense of humour, but experience suggests there is no other team role that it would be useful to add.

Back-up team roles

The most consistently successful teams were 'mixed' with a balance of team roles. The role that a person undertakes in a group is not fixed and may change according to circumstances.

Individuals may have a 'back-up team role' with which they have some affinity other than their primary team role. If certain roles were missing, members would call upon their back-up roles. Team roles differ from what Belbin calls 'functional roles'. These are the roles that members of a team perform in terms of the specifically technical demands placed upon them. Team members are typically chosen for functional roles on the basis of experience and not personal characteristics or aptitudes.

Belbin has developed a Self-Perception Inventory designed to provide members of a group with a simple means of assessing their best team roles.

The value of Belbin's team-roles inventory

Despite possible doubts about the value of Belbin's Self-Perception Inventory, it remains a popular means of examining and comparing team roles. For example, in order to explore whether local government managers were distinctively different from the model of private sector management, *Arroba and Wedgwood-Oppenheim* compared samples of the two groups of managers and Belbin's key team roles. There were noticeable similarities between the two groups, with the noticeable exception of the marked difference between private sector managers and local government officers in the score for teamworkers and the team roles they preferred to adopt. The individual characteristics of managers in the two sectors differed. The data implied that local government officers were committed to organisational objectives and dedicated to task achievement, but the low score for teamworkers suggested the high commitment to organisational tasks was not supplemented by a concern for interpersonal processes. In local government, the drive and enthusiasm and emphasis on task were exaggerated, while attention to idea generation and productive interpersonal relationships was less marked.[7]

Team roles among UK managers

Using Belbin's model, *Fisher et al.* undertook a study of the distribution of team roles among managers. Recently, many layers of management have been removed and the gap in people to lead and motivate has increasingly been filled by the creation of multitudes of teams. The participants of the study were 1,441 male and 355 female managers, all with some management experience. All had completed a personality questionnaire and were candidates short-listed for a range of management positions in both the private and public sectors. The study analysed data supplied by ASE/NFER Publishing Company and results were then compared with the Belbin model. The data broadly agreed with the Belbin model. The authors conclude that as much is still unknown about teams, it is reassuring that further support has been found for the popular Belbin team-role model. There are several unresolved problems with teamworking but these might lie more with practices in staff recruitment than in team theory.[8]

> ### *Critical reflection*
>
> 'Belbin's evolved team roles serve little practical value. Behaviour does not fit into neat categories and most people do not acknowledge allowable weaknesses. The two most important roles for effective teamwork are (i) a strong and decisive leader and (ii) the humorist to make people laugh and reduce tension.'
>
> *What are your views? How would you explain your role as a team member?*

PATTERNS OF COMMUNICATION

The level of interaction among members of a group or team is influenced by the structuring of channels of communication. Laboratory research by *Bavelas*[9] and subsequent studies by other researchers such as *Leavitt*[10] have resulted in the design of a series of communication networks. These networks were based on groups of five members engaged in a number of problem-solving tasks. Members were permitted to communicate with each other by written notes only and not everyone was always free to communicate with everyone else.

There are five main types of communication networks – wheel, circle, all-channel, Y and chains (*see* Figure 9.1).

■ The **wheel**, also sometimes known as the star, is the most **centralised network**. This network is most efficient for simple tasks. Problems are solved more quickly with fewer mistakes and with fewer information flows. However, as the problems become more complex and demands on the link person increase, effectiveness suffers. The link person

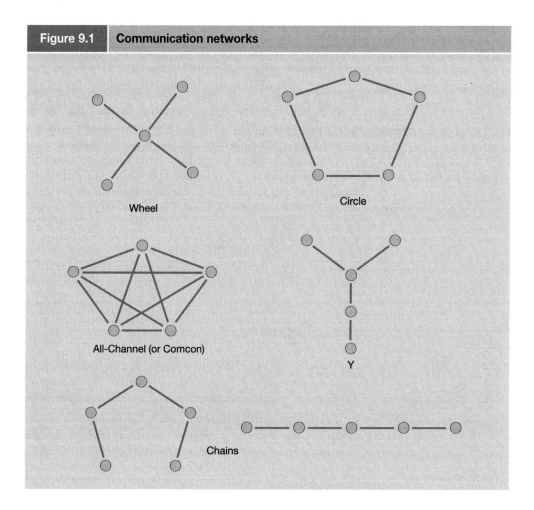

Figure 9.1 **Communication networks**

Wheel

Circle

All-Channel (or Comcon)

Y

Chains

is at the centre of the network and acts as the focus of activities and information flows and the co-ordinator of group tasks. The central person is perceived as leader of the group and experiences a high level of satisfaction. However, for members on the periphery, the wheel is the least satisfying network.

■ The **circle** is a more **decentralised network**. Overall it is less efficient. The group is un-organised, with low leadership predictability. Performance tends to be slow and erratic. However, the circle is quicker than the wheel in solving complex problems and also copes more efficiently with change or new tasks. The circle network is most satisfying for all the members. Decision-making is likely to involve some degree of participation.

■ The **all-channel (or comcon)** network is a decentralised network that involves full discussion and participation. This network appears to work best where a high level of interaction is required among all the members in order to solve complex problems. Leadership predictability is very low. There is a fairly high level of satisfaction for members. The all-channel network may not stand up well under pressure, in which case it will either disintegrate or re-form into a wheel network.

■ A **'Y'** or **chain** network might be appropriate for more simple problem-solving tasks, requiring little interaction among members. These networks are more centralised, with information flows along a predetermined channel. Leadership predictability is high to moderate. There is a low to moderate level of satisfaction for members.

The relationship between centralised and decentralised networks and performance of the group is outlined in Figure 9.2.

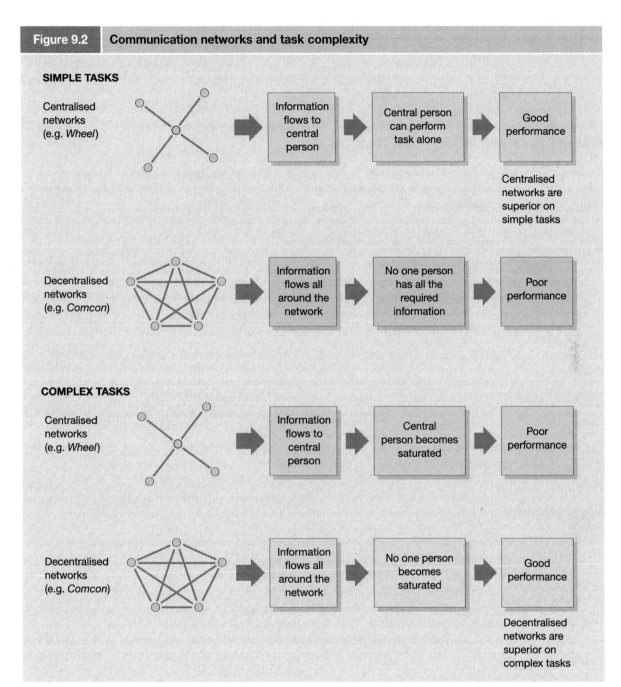

Figure 9.2	Communication networks and task complexity

Source: Greenberg, J. and Baron, R. A. *Behavior in Organizations*, sixth edition, Prentice Hall Inc. (1995), p. 306. Reproduced with permission from Pearson Education, Inc.

Implications for the manager

Despite the obvious artificiality and limitations of these communication network studies, they do have certain implications for the manager. Knowledge of the findings may be applied to influence the patterns of communication in meetings and committees. They also provide a reasonable representation of the situations that might apply in large organisations. It will be interesting for the manager to observe the patterns of communication adopted by different groups in different situations. The manager can also note how communication networks change over time and how they relate to the performance of the group.

No one network is likely to be effective for a range of given problems. The studies draw attention to the part of the manager's job that is to ensure the most appropriate communication network for the performance of a given task. Problems which require a high level of interaction among members of the group may not be handled efficiently if there are inadequate channels of communication or sharing of information. The choice of a particular communication network may involve trade-offs between the performance of the work group and the satisfaction of its members.

ANALYSIS OF INDIVIDUAL BEHAVIOUR

In order to understand and to influence the functioning and operation of a group or team, it is necessary to study patterns of interaction and the parts played by individual members. For example, in a more recent publication *Belbin* acknowledges:

> *Teamwork does not, of course, guarantee in itself good results. As in sport, there can be good teams and poor teams. And as in sport, it all depends on how the players play together.*[11]

It is necessary to balance the requirement for effective performance of the team with respect for the individuality of its members and to achieve the right mix. Not all skilled and capable individuals are necessarily good team players and it may sometimes be an advantage to have someone who will have a more sceptical attitude and be more open to change. For example, *Stanley* refers to the challenge of managing a high-performance team.

> *When assembling a high-performance team, you are gathering together energy-packed employees, who are a lot like thoroughbreds. Keep in mind, they have an innate drive to excel. Their thoughts run outside the mundane and familiar. With a flare for the unique, they are extraordinary and can generate new ideas that will keep the organisation ahead of the competition . . . Along with assigning each member appropriate tasks, the manager must monitor individual performance. By encouraging members to maximise their individual effort, the team will greatly increase the probability of success.*[12]

Two of the main methods of analysing the behaviour of individuals in group situations are **sociometry** and **interaction analysis**.

SOCIOMETRY

Originally developed by *Moreno* in 1953, **sociometry** is a method of indicating the feelings of acceptance or rejection among members of a group.[13] A sociogram is a diagrammatical illustration of the pattern of interpersonal relationships derived from sociometry. The sociogram depicts the choices, preferences, likes or dislikes and interactions between individual members. It can also be used to display the structure of the group and to record the observed frequency and/or duration of contacts among members.

The basis of sociometry, however, is usually 'buddy rating' or 'peer rating'. Each member is asked to nominate or to rate, privately, other members in terms of some given context or characteristic – for example, with whom they communicate, or how influential or how likeable they are. Questions may relate to either work or social activities. For example:

- Who would you most prefer or least prefer as a workmate?
- Who would make a good leader?
- With whom would you choose and not choose to go on holiday?

Positive and negative choices may be recorded for each person, although sometimes positive choices only are required. The choices may be limited to a given number or they may be unlimited. Sometimes individuals may be asked to rank their choices.

Sociograms

Members' choices could be shown in tabular form. For example, Table 9.2 shows first and second choices for a group of final-year degree students. Members were asked to indicate, in

Table 9.2 Example of a 'tabulated' sociogram (positive choices only)

Work-related problem			Personal problem	
Second choice	First choice		First choice	Second choice
		A		///
		B	/	//
///	/	C	//	/
/		D	//	
		E	/	
		F	/	//
	/	G	//	
/////	//	H	//	
		J	/	/
	//	K		
////	///////	L		//
	/	M	/	/
		N		//
/		O	/	
14	14		14	14

confidence, those whom they would most prefer to talk to about: (i) a major work-related problem, and (ii) a difficult personal problem. Positive choices only were requested.

An advantage of the diagrammatical illustration, however, is that the sociogram provides a visual description of the sociometric structure of a group. It can indicate cliques and sub-groups, compatibility, and members who are popular, isolated or who act as links. Figure 9.3 gives a simple illustration of an actual sociogram for a group of 15 members with single, positive choices only.

Figure 9.3 A simple illustration of a sociogram

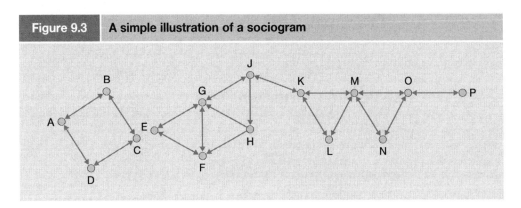

1 G and M are popular (the stars) and most often chosen by members.
2 M is the link between two overlapping cliques, KML and MNO.
3 H and P are unpopular (isolated) and chosen least by members.
4 JKMO is a chain.
5 ABCD is a sub-group and separated from the rest of the members.

It should be noted, however, that there are several methods of compiling and drawing sociograms, and a number of potential criticisms and limitations. Problems also arise over *how* to draw the sociogram and how to interpret the roles of individual members. In the experience of the author, less concern should be given to the concept of sociometry itself. It is better seen as a useful vehicle that, if handled sensitively, can serve to encourage meaningful discussions on patterns of social interactions, group behaviour and the perceptions of individual members towards each other.

Critical reflection

'All students should be encouraged in each year of their course to participate in a sociometry exercise with members of their class.'

Do you agree? What possible difficulties or opposition would you foresee and do you believe these outweigh the potential benefits?

INTERACTION ANALYSIS

The basic assumption behind **interaction analysis** is that behaviour in groups may be analysed from the viewpoint of its function. This approach has developed largely from the work of *Bales* on methods for the study of small groups. This aim is to provide ways of describing group process and indications of factors influencing the process.[14] In Bales' 'Interaction Process Analysis' every act of behaviour is categorised, as it occurs, under twelve headings. These differentiate between 'task' functions and 'socio-emotional' functions. The categories apply to both verbal interaction and non-verbal interaction.

A Socio-emotional: positive reactions
   1 **Shows solidarity**, raises others' status, gives help, reward.
   2 **Shows tension release**, jokes, laughs, shows satisfaction.
   3 **Agrees**, shows passive acceptance, understands, concurs, complies.

B Task: attempted answers
   4 **Gives suggestion**, direction, implying autonomy for others.
   5 **Gives opinion**, evaluation, analysis, expresses feeling, wish.
   6 **Gives orientation**, information, repeats, clarifies, confirms.

C Task: questions
   7 **Asks for orientation**, information, repetition, confirmation.
   8 **Asks for opinion**, evaluation, analysis, expression of feeling.
   9 **Asks for suggestion**, direction, possible ways of action.

D Socio-emotional: negative reactions
   10 **Disagrees**, shows passive rejection, formality, withholds help.
   11 **Shows tension**, asks for help, withdraws out of field.
   12 **Shows antagonism**, deflates others' status, defends or asserts self.

Task and maintenance functions

If the group is to be effective, then, whatever its structure or the pattern of interrelationships among members, there are two main sets of functions or processes that must be undertaken – **task functions** and **maintenance functions**.

- **Task functions** are directed towards problem-solving, the accomplishment of the tasks of the group and the achievement of its goals. Most of the task-oriented behaviour will be concerned with 'production' activities or the exchange and evaluation of ideas and information.
- **Maintenance functions** are concerned with the emotional life of the group and directed towards building and maintaining the group as an effective working unit. Most of the

maintenance-oriented behaviour will be concerned with relationships among members, giving encouragement and support, maintaining cohesiveness and the resolution of conflict.

Task and maintenance functions may be performed either by the group leader or by members. Ultimately it is the leader's responsibility to ensure that both sets of functions are carried out and the right balance is achieved between them. The appropriate combination of task-oriented behaviour and maintenance-oriented behaviour is essential to the success and continuity of the group.

In addition to these two types of behaviour, members of a group may say or do something in attempting to satisfy some personal need or goal. The display of behaviour in this way is termed **self-oriented behaviour**. This gives a classification of three main types of functional behaviour that can be exhibited by individual members of a group: **task-oriented**, **maintenance-oriented** and **self-oriented**.

Classification of member roles

A popular system for the classification of member roles in the study of group behaviour is that devised originally by *Benne and Sheats*.[15] The description of member roles performed in well-functioning groups is classified into three broad headings: **group task roles, group building and maintenance roles** and **individual roles**.

- **Group task roles**. These assume that the task of the group is to select, define and solve common problems. For example, initiator-contributor, opinion seeker, co-ordinator, evaluator, recorder. Any of the roles may be performed by the various members or the group leader.
- **Group building and maintenance roles**. The analysis of member functions is oriented towards activities which build group-centred attitudes or maintain group-centred behaviour. For example, encourager, gatekeeper, standard setter, group commentator. Contributions may involve a number of roles and members or the leader may perform each of these.
- **Individual roles**. These are directed towards the satisfaction of personal needs. Their purpose is not related either to group task or to the group functioning. For example, aggressor, blocker, dominator, help-seeker.

FRAMEWORKS OF BEHAVIOURAL ANALYSIS

Several frameworks have been designed for observers to categorise patterns of verbal and non-verbal behaviour of group or team members. Observers chart members' behaviour on specially designed forms. These forms may be used to focus on single individuals or to record the total interaction with no indication of individual behaviour. The system of categorisation may distinguish between different behaviours in terms of the functions they are performing. The completed observation forms can be used as a basis for discussion of individual or group performance in terms of the strengths/weaknesses of different functional behaviour.

Use of different frameworks

Different frameworks use a different number of categories for studying behaviour in groups. The interaction analysis method can become complex, especially if non-verbal behaviour is included. Many of the categories in different frameworks may at first sight appear to be very similar. It is important, therefore, to keep the framework simple and easy to understand and complete. The observer's personality, values and attitudes can influence the categorisation of behaviour. For these reasons it is preferable to use trained observers, and wherever possible and appropriate to use more than one observer for each group. The observers can then compare the level of consistency between their categorisations. Observation sheets can be designed to suit the particular requirements of the group situation and the nature of the activity involved. An example of a reasonably simple, ten-point observation sheet used by the author is given in Figure 9.4.

Completing the observation sheet

Where appropriate, it may be helpful to note the initial seating, or standing, arrangements of the group. This will help in the identification of group members. Depending on the nature of the activity involved, it might also be possible to indicate main channels of interaction among individuals – for example, to whom eye contact, hand movements or ideas and questions are most frequently directed. A note could also be made of changes in arrangements during, and at the end of, the activity. Headings on the observation sheet are not necessarily exclusive. For example, leadership could be included under 'taking initiative', or under 'performing group roles'. Similarly, the role of humorist could be included under 'performing group roles', but might also appropriately be included under the heading of 'harmonising'.

Observers will tend to use their own methods for completing the sheet: for example, a simple stroke or tick for each contribution and perhaps a thick stroke for a particularly significant contribution. Some observers might use some other distinguishing mark to indicate non-verbal behaviour such as body movements, smiles or eye contact. The most important point, however, is that the charting should not become too complex. The observer should feel happy with the framework and be capable of explaining the entries in a meaningful way. Where more than one observer is present there should be some degree of consistency between them.

BALANCE BETWEEN THE TEAM AND THE INDIVIDUAL

Groups and teams are an essential feature in the life of work organisations. Individuals on teams interact extensively with each other and with other teams in the organisation. Team-based management is used to improve communication, co-ordination and co-operation within the organisation.[16] For example, as *Green* maintains:

> *The generally perceived advantages of working in teams are the release of creativity and energy, much more interaction between people satisfying the need to belong . . . teamworking can improve efficiency by people planning activities together with cooperation and communication. Team members together should be able to identify many ways to improve work organisation; how information, ideas and outputs flow and how team-working can reduce costs and improve productivity.*[17]

We mentioned previously the need to balance effective team performance with respect for the individual members. Although everyone operates fundamentally as a loner at work, *James* draws attention to the need in most jobs for the eponymous teamworking.

> *Effective teams need equilibrium, no matter how uneasy. The perfect team will have balance, with each member aware of their role and happy to add that value to the task. The natural leaders for any given job will be in charge and their leadership will be cherished by mutual consent. Being a perfect team member means commitment to the task and overrides personal ambition and glory. Unfortunately this is rarely achieved in the workplace.*[18]

Successful organisations are good at building teams and exploiting teamwork. People need to be able to work in teams; they need to subordinate their own agenda to the wellbeing of the group. Further, organisations need to foster diversity, which entails respect for the individual and makes group decision making more creative.[19]

Figure 9.4	Observation sheet for behaviour in groups

Nature of group

Nature of activity

Date   Name of observer(s)

Initial arrangement of group

```
            C  D
         B          E
      A          F
```

Name of group members
(or reference letters)

	A	B	C	D	E	F
Taking initiative – e.g. attempted leadership, seeking suggestions, offering directions						
Brainstorming – e.g. offering ideas or suggestions, however valid						
Offering positive ideas – e.g. making helpful suggestions, attempting to problem-solve						
Drawing in others – e.g. encouraging contributions, seeking ideas and opinions						
Being responsive to others – e.g. giving encouragement and support, building on ideas						
Harmonising – e.g. acting as peacemaker, calming things down, compromising						
Challenging – e.g. seeking justification, showing disagreement in constructive way						
Being obstructive – e.g. criticising, putting others down, blocking contributions						
Clarifying/summarising – e.g. linking ideas, checking progress, clarifying objectives/proposals						
Performing group roles – e.g. spokesperson, recorder, time keeper, humorist						

Other comments

In order to help improve the performance of the organisation it is necessary to understand the nature of human relationships and what goes on when groups of people meet. Working in a group is likely to be both a psychologically rewarding, and a potentially demanding experience for the individual. Group performance and the satisfaction derived by individuals are influenced by the interactions among members of the group. As an example of this, Figure 9.5 gives an unsolicited commentary from five final-year business studies degree students after completing a group-based assignment.

Figure 9.5	Unsolicited commentary from students after completing a group-based assignment

WHAT WE FEEL WE HAVE LEARNED FROM WORKING IN A GROUP

1 'We learned that we had to listen to everybody's points of view and take these into consideration.'

2 'We found that we had to be prepared to make certain sacrifices and adopted a democratic decision process. However, if an individual felt very strongly about a specific point and persisted with a valid argument then this had to be included.'

3 'We often felt frustrated.'

4 'It was time-consuming and difficult to schedule meetings due to differences in timetables and preferences in working hours.'

5 'We learned that it is good to pool resources because this increased the overall standard of the piece of work. We feel this was only because we all set high personal standards and expected these from our fellow group members. We learned that it is possible to work in other less productive groups where individual levels of achievement may decrease.'

6 'We learned that it is better to work in a smaller and not a larger group, as there is a tendency for individual ideas to be diluted.'

7 'Groups formed on the basis of friendship alone are not as effective as groups formed with work as the major influence. The former tend to be unproductive.'

8 'We found that it was good to get positive response, encouragement and feedback from team members. Likewise, it was demotivating to receive a negative response.'

9 'We learned a lot about our individual personalities.'

10 'We benefited from sharing personal experiences from our industrial placements.'

11 'It is important to separate work and personal relationships.'

Critical reflection

'The nature of the hierarchical structure and inevitable role conflicts, power struggles, politics and personality clashes means that individuals will usually complete a task more quickly and effectively than a group or team.'

To what extent do you think this is fair comment? What has been your own experience?

INDIVIDUAL COMPARED WITH GROUP OR TEAM PERFORMANCE

It is, however, difficult to draw any firm conclusions from a comparison between individual and group or team performance. An example of this can be seen from a consideration of decision-making. Certain groups, such as committees, may be concerned more specifically with decision-making, but all groups must make some decisions. Group decision-making can be costly and time-consuming.

One particular feature of group versus individual performance is the concept of social loafing and the 'Ringelmann effect', which is the tendency for individuals to expend less effort when working as a member of a group than as an individual. A German psychologist, Ringelmann, compared the results of individual and group performance on a rope-pulling task. Workers were asked to pull as hard as they could on a rope, performing the task first individually and then with others in groups of varying size. A meter measured the strength of each pull. Although the total amount of force did increase with the size of the work group, the effort expended by each individual member decreased with the result that the total group effort was less than the expected sum of the individual contributions.[20] Replications of the Ringelmann effect have generally been supportive of the original findings.[21] (Recall the discussion in Chapter 8 on boat race crews and workplace teams.)

According to *Hall*, there is a danger of elevating teams into a 'silver bullet' – a magic solution to all business problems.

> *It is not that I don't think teams work. They clearly do and it would be difficult to run an organisation of any size if you couldn't create and manage a team . . . The truth is that teams are not always the right answer to a problem. Often a well-briefed and well-managed group of individuals will do a task fine . . . A further point is that some very skilled individuals are not good team players.*[22]

However, the general feeling appears to be that the collective power of a group outshines individual performance.[23] 'Even though individuals working on their own are capable of phenomenal ingenuity, working together as a team can produce astounding results and a better decision.'[24] *Guirdham* believes that 'Compared with individuals, groups can make objectively better decisions to which people feel more commitment, while teams can perform functions and carry out projects better and more efficiently. This can only happen, however, if the people have the special skills and abilities needed.'[25]

One might expect, therefore, a higher standard of decision-making to result from group discussion. However, on the one hand, there is the danger of compromise and decisions being made in line with the 'highest common view' and, on the other hand, there is the phenomenon of the so-called **risky-shift**.

The risky-shift phenomenon

This suggests that instead of the group taking fewer risks and making safer or more conservative decisions, the reverse is often the case. Pressures for conformity mean there is a tendency for groups to make more risky decisions than would individual members of the group on their own. Studies suggest that people working in groups generally advocate more risky alternatives than if they were making an individual decision on the same problem.[26] Presumably, this is because members do not feel the same sense of responsibility for group decisions or their outcomes. 'A decision which is everyone's is the responsibility of no one.'

Other explanations offered for the risky-shift phenomenon include:

1 People inclined to take risks are more influential in group discussions than more conservative people.
2 Risk-taking is regarded as a desirable cultural characteristic that is more likely to be expressed in a social situation such as group working.[27]

However, groups do appear to work well in the evaluation of ideas and to be more effective than individuals for problem-solving tasks requiring a range of knowledge and expertise. From a review of the research *Shaw* suggests that evidence supports the view that groups produce more solutions and better solutions to problems than do individuals.[28]

'Groupthink'

The effectiveness of group behaviour and performance can be adversely affected by the idea of 'groupthink'. From an examination of some well-known government policy-making groups, *Janis* concluded that decisions can be characterised by groupthink which he defines as 'a deterioration of mental efficiency, reality testing, and moral judgment that results from in-group pressures'.[29] Groupthink results in the propensity for the group to just drift along. It is a generalised feature and can be apparent in any organisational situation where groups are relied upon to make important decisions.

Janis identifies a number of specific symptoms of groupthink:

1 There is an illusion of invulnerability with excessive optimism and risk-taking.

2 The discounting or discrediting of negative feedback that contradicts group consensus results in rationalisation in order to explain away any disagreeable information.

3 An unquestioned belief in the inherent morality of the group leads members to be convinced of the logical correctness of what it is doing and to ignore ethical or moral consequences of decisions.

4 The group's desire to maintain consensus can lead to negative stereotyping of opponents or people outside the group, or to the acceptance of change.

5 There is pressure on individual members to conform and reach consensus so that minority or unpopular ideas may be suppressed.

6 Each member of the group may impose self-censorship in order to suppress their own objectives, or personal doubts or disagreements.

7 As a result of self-censorship, there is an illusion of unanimity with a lack of expressed dissent and a false sense of unity.

8 In the unlikely event of dissent or contrary information, this will give rise to the emergence of 'mind guards' who act as filters, guarding group leaders, deflecting opposition and applying pressure on deviants.

According to *Hambrick*,

Groupthink tends to occur when group members have very similar experiences and frame of references, particularly when they have relatively long tenures in the group. A company head who dislikes conflict or who punishes dissenters also creates the conditions for groupthink.[30]

Some commentators referred to groupthink as a feature of the perceived lack of decisive leadership and action associated with the economic depression in late 2008.

Three central criteria

Drawing on the work of Vroom and Yetton, discussed in Chapter 10, *Misselhorn* puts forward a framework for determining when to make a decision on your own and when to involve a group. Three central overall criteria are taken into account:

- the **competence** of the people to make the decision – this would include knowledge, experience, skill, access to information and their practical experience to make it work in practice;
- the **context** in which they are working – which would include the relationships among those involved as well as the physical conditions and culture of the organisation; and
- the **commitment** to the decision through the way it affects those involved, and the rewards and punishments they will experience.

The framework provides a set of criteria to help the leader/manager to make a systematic and rational choice. It also draws attention to low ratings where the leader/manager may need to take precautions when deciding whether to involve a group or leave it to an appropriate individual.[31]

BRAINSTORMING

A **brainstorming** approach (sometimes now referred to as '**thought showers**' or 'cloud bursting' in order not to offend people with disorders such as epilepsy) involves the group adopting a 'freewheeling' attitude and generating as many ideas as possible, the more wild or apparently far-fetched the better.[32] As an illustrative exercise a group may be asked to generate as many and varied possible uses as they can for, for example, a man or woman's leather belt. Brainstorming is based on encouraging members to suspend judgement, the assumption that creative thinking is achieved best by encouraging the natural inclinations of group members, and the rapid production and free association of ideas. The quantity of ideas will lead to quality of ideas.

There are a number of basic procedures for brainstorming:

- It is based on maximum freedom of expression with a totally relaxed and informal approach.
- The initial emphasis is on the quantity of ideas generated, not the quality of ideas.
- No individual ideas are criticised or rejected at this stage, however wild or fanciful they may appear.
- A group size of between six and ten members is recommended.
- Members are encouraged to elaborate or build on ideas expressed by others and to bounce suggestions off one another.
- There is no comment on or evaluation of any particular idea until all ideas have been generated.
- There is need for good reporting of all the ideas either in writing and/or by tape or video recording.

An interesting and popular exercise to help illustrate the suspension of initial perceived barriers and the encouragement of creative thinking is given in Figure 9.6. This exercise may also be used to compare individual and group/team-based performance. Your tutor will provide the (or least one) answer. There may be others that the author is unaware of!

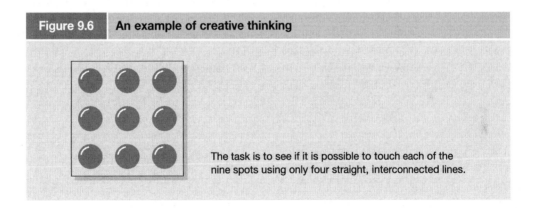

| Figure 9.6 | An example of creative thinking |

The task is to see if it is possible to touch each of the nine spots using only four straight, interconnected lines.

Effectiveness of brainstorming groups

One might reasonably expect that members of a brainstorming group would produce more creative problem-solving ideas than if the same members worked alone as individuals. Availability of time is an important factor. Over a longer period of time the group may produce more ideas through brainstorming than individuals could. Perhaps surprisingly, however, there appears to be doubt about the effectiveness of brainstorming groups over an individual working under the same conditions. Nevertheless, brainstorming still appears to have many advocates and is a popular activity for staff development programmes. Despite the rather negative view of nominal group brainstorming, we should recognise the importance of innovation for successful organisational performance.[33]

Aids to creativity

Any procedure which aids the process of creativity (discussed in Chapter 5) should be welcomed and there are a number of potential positive achievements in terms of related structural techniques for stimulating innovation. These include the Delphi technique and quality circles.

The **Delphi technique** is based on multiple, anonymous inputs from individual members of the group. Ideas and suggestions are recorded by a central manager and then recirculated to other members for their feedback. The central manager collates the responses and continues the circulation process again until consensus is reached. Although a time-consuming process, the Delphi technique helps to overcome the limitations of face-to-face brainstorming and symptoms of groupthink.

QUALITY CIRCLES

A **quality circle** is a group of people within an organisation who meet on a regular basis to identify, analyse and solve problems relating to quality, productivity or other aspects of day-to-day working arrangements using problem-solving techniques. Although quality circles actually originated in America they were exported to Japan and are more usually associated with their wide applications (since 1962) in Japanese manufacturing industries, as well as in some white-collar operations. Since the refinement of the quality circle process in Japan there has been increasing interest in their use in America and Britain as well as in many other countries. In America, quality circles appear to have been first implemented in 1974.[34]

The essential features of a quality circle group include the following:

- membership is voluntary;
- the group usually numbers between five and ten members;
- membership is normally drawn from people undertaking similar work or from the same work station;
- the group selects the problems to be tackled and the methods of operation;
- a leader can be chosen from within the group but is usually the immediate supervisor;
- the group members receive training in communication and problem-solving skills, quality control techniques and group processes;
- the group recommends solutions to management and, where possible, has authority to implement agreed solutions.

Potential limitations

There are a number of potential limitations on the effectiveness of quality circles:

- Any attempt at solving organisational problems cannot be considered as a single dimension. The promotion of quality circles needs to be approached in terms of possible effects on related sub-systems of the organisation, for example human resource management and industrial relations procedures.
- Quality circles can rely too heavily on intrinsic motivation and the assumption that involvement and recognition are sufficient rewards in themselves. This reflects a major difference between the operation of quality circles in the West and in Japan. Workers in Japan appear, for example, to accept that financial gains will go to the organisation.
- The greater involvement of members in problem-solving and decision-making may be resented by some groups, for example quality control departments, or by managers or trade union officials who may be suspicious of possible challenges to their traditional authority.

The application of quality circles does appear simple and straightforward, but early experience must be viewed in the context of Japanese culture and management systems. However, quality circles offer a number of potential benefits. They provide problem-solving at a more local level and the participation of employees in work-related decisions which concern them. Quality circles do work and have been used successfully by a number of

British organisations. There are some doubts, however, as to the extent to which the hopes for, or potential benefits of, quality circles are realised fully in organisations.[35]

GROUP DYNAMICS

Interest in the study of group process and behaviour has led to the development of group dynamics and a range of group training methods aimed at increasing group effectiveness through improving social interaction skills. A central feature of group dynamics is **sensitivity training**, in which members of a group direct attention to the understanding of their own behaviour and to perceiving themselves as others see them. The objectives are usually stated as:

- to increase sensitivity (the ability to perceive accurately how others react to oneself);
- diagnostic ability (the skill of assessing behavioural relationships between others and reasons for such behaviour); and
- behavioural flexibility or action skill (the ability to relate one's behaviour to the requirements of the situation).

T-groups

A usual method of sensitivity training (which is increasingly used as a generic term) is the T-group (training group), sometimes called laboratory training. A **T-group** has been defined as:

an approach to human relations training which, broadly speaking, provides participants with an opportunity to learn more about themselves and their impact on others, and in particular to learn how to function more effectively in face-to-face situations.[36]

The original form of a T-group is a small, leaderless, unstructured, face-to-face grouping. The group normally numbers between eight and twelve members who may be strangers to each other or who may come from the same organisation (a family group). A deliberate attempt is made to minimise any status differentials among members. There is no agenda or planned activities. Trainers are present to help guide the group, but do not usually take an active role or act as formal leader. The agenda becomes the group's own behaviour in attempting to cope with the lack of structure or planned activities. Training is intended to concentrate on process rather than content, that is on the feeling level of communication rather than the informational value of communication.

Faced with confusion and lack of direction, individuals will act in characteristic ways. With the guidance of the trainers these patterns of behaviour become the focus of attention for the group. Participants are encouraged to examine their self-concepts and to be more receptive to the feelings and behaviours of others. Feedback received by individuals from other members of the group is the main mechanism for learning. This feedback creates a feeling of anxiety and tension, and the individual's self-examination leads to consideration of new values, attitudes and behaviour. Typically, the group meets for a 1-to-2-hour session each day for up to a fortnight. The sessions are supported by related lectures, study groups, case studies and other exercises.

The Johari window

A simple framework for looking at self-insight, which is used frequently to help individuals in the T-group process, is the 'Johari window' (*see* Figure 9.7). This classifies behaviour in matrix form between what is known–unknown to self and what is known–unknown to others.[37] A central feature of the T-group is reduction of the individual's 'hidden' behaviour through self-disclosure and reduction of the 'blind' behaviour through feedback from others.

- **Hidden behaviour** is that which the individual wishes to conceal from, or not to communicate to, other group members. It is part of the private self. An important role of the

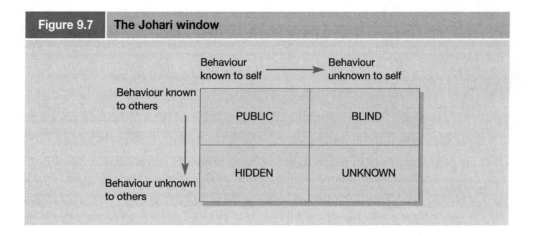

group is to establish whether members conceal too much, or too little, about themselves from other members.

■ **The blind area** (that is behaviour known to others but unknown to self) includes mannerisms, gestures and tone of voice and represents behaviour of the impact of which on others the individual is unaware. This is sometimes referred to as the 'bad breath' area.

Members must establish an atmosphere of openness and trust in order that hidden and blind behaviours are reduced and the public behaviour enhanced. (Recall also the comment in Chapter 4 on making public people's private attitudes.)

Value and effectiveness of T-groups

Reactions to the value and effectiveness of T-group training are very mixed. The experience can be disturbing and unpleasant, at least for some members. T-group training is difficult to evaluate objectively and there is still a main problem of the extent to which training is transferred 'back home' to practical work situations. However, a number of studies do suggest that participation as a member of a T-group does increase interpersonal skills, induce change and lead to open communications and more flexible behaviour. T-groups probably do result in a change of behaviour but it is not always clear whether such change is positive or related to improved organisational performance.[38]

T-groups now take a number of forms. Some place emphasis on the understanding of group processes, others place more emphasis on the development of the individual's self-awareness and feelings towards the behaviour of other people. They are now used frequently as a means of attempting to improve managerial development and organisational performance. The Blake and Mouton Managerial Grid® seminars, discussed in Chapter 12, can be seen as an applied, and refined, form of T-group. A number of training packages have been designed, often under the broad heading of interpersonal skills, which are less confrontational and less disturbing for participants.

Critical reflection

'Sensitivity training programmes are an unnecessary activity that have no practical value as a means of increasing the long-term standard of group performance, and for many people they are an embarrassing and demeaning experience.'

Under what circumstances can such programmes ever be justified? How do you feel about participating in such a programme?

SELF-MANAGED WORK GROUPS

An important development in work redesign and job enrichment is a form of work organisation based on self-managed work groups (or autonomous work groups). This involves a socio-technical approach with technological processes, production methods and the way in which work is carried out integrated with the social system of the organisation, including the informal group structure. Members of the group assume greater autonomy and responsibility for the effective performance of the work. With greater empowerment the belief is that members will feel more committed to the objectives and operations of the group.

Key features of the self-managed work group include the following:

- specific goals are set for the group but members decide the best means by which these goals are to be achieved;
- group members have greater freedom and choice and wider discretion over the planning, execution and control of their work;
- collectively members of the group have the necessary variety of expertise and skills to undertake the tasks of the group successfully;
- the level of external supervision is reduced and the role of supervisor becomes more one of giving advice and support to the group;
- feedback and evaluation are related to the performance of the group as a whole.

There is, however, a potential danger that a self-managed group is more likely to establish its own values and norms (discussed in Chapter 8) that may be at variance with those of the organisation.

Popularity and applications

Wilson points out that self-directed teams feature high in the list of most popular management tools in a study by the Institute of Management with Bain & Company. 'Once people are fully committed to teamworking and enthusiastic about getting on with it, training can be a rewarding experience for everyone involved and also great fun.'[39] However, despite the apparent potential advantages, to date self-managed teams appear to have only limited applications. For example, *Torrington, Hall and Taylor* suggest that teamwork has evolved from autonomous working groups and although it is still used as a means of empowering employees and facilitating their development, there is of late a more critical perspective. 'There remain many strong supporters of teamwork and many organisations are committed to this approach, although it is also criticised as management control by another means and has often failed to improve performance.'[40]

Autonomy and control

A strong supporter of the idea of the autonomous work group is *Waterman*. In order to build spirit, morale and commitment in any organisation Waterman believes that people should be in control of at least some part of their lives and that they should be given some influence over things that affect them. The quintessence of this belief is the self-managing team – groups of three to ten people who work without any direct supervision. Employees should be organised into teams that cut across old boundaries, trained and placed in jobs that challenge their abilities, given the information they need, informed of what they need to accomplish and then turned loose.[41]

ACAS also strongly supports autonomous work groups for both increased competitiveness and for the quality of working life.

The concept of autonomous teams may be misleading as teams will always be answerable to management and rely on the provision of resources and other support. Nevertheless, one of the best ways to ensure that teams continue to develop is to move towards self-regulation – an important way of monitoring the progress of teams is to assess the level of dependence on management. It is for management to encourage progress by helping the teams develop greater independence. Reorganising the workforce into teams is not easy but when successfully developed, teamworking has been shown to be a way of improving competitiveness and at the same time enhancing the quality of working life for employees.[42]

BUILDING SUCCESSFUL TEAMS

Whatever the debate about a comparison between individual and group or team performance, or self-managed groups, effective teamworking is of increasing importance in modern organisations. This demands that the manager must be aware of, and pay attention to, a number of interrelated factors, including:

- clarification of objectives and available resources;
- organisational processes and the clarification of roles;
- empowerment, decision-making and channels of communication;
- patterns of interaction, and attention to both task and maintenance functions;
- social processes and the informal organisation;
- management systems and style of leadership;
- training and development.

The effectiveness of the team will also be influenced by the tasks to be undertaken, the nature of technology and the organisational environment. Ultimately, however, the performance of the team will be determined very largely by the characteristics of its members. The nature of group personality means that what works well for one team may not work well for an apparently similar team in the organisation.

We know everyone is different. When selecting people for your team, the most important thing to look for is ones who are decent, honest, bright and capable. You will find that good people will naturally work together as a team, will interrelate well and will want each other to succeed. And while I'm on the subject of teams, don't send people off on those terrible outward-bound weekends. Have a party instead.[43]

As *Wilson* points out, although teamworking, like most management ideas, is very simple, nevertheless this simplicity conceals a great challenge.

The principles of teamworking may be easily understood, but the task of installing it can be quite daunting. Introducing teamworking is not a straightforward grafting job, the simple matter of adding a new idea to those already in place. It is about making a fundamental change in the way people work. Every teamworking application is different. Each organisation, department and individual group is faced with unique problems and in some situations it is more about getting rid of old ways of doing things than injecting new ones.[44]

A concept map of effective work groups is set out in Figure 9.8.

Skills for successful teamwork

The increasing need for collaboration and teamwork together with recognition for the individual has highlighted the need for attention to social skills and effectively relationships among people. If people are not working together they are essentially a collection of individuals. *Douglas* refers to the importance of helping people to master the so-called 'soft' skills:

Organisations in most sectors – and especially in ones that are particularly demanding from a scientific or technical point of view – are operating in environments where collaboration, teamwork, and an awareness of the commercial consequences and implications of technical research are as important as scientific and technical skills themselves. Personnel with scientific and technical skills significantly disproportionate to their 'people' skills – by which I primarily mean people management capabilities and the knowledge of how to work with maximum effectiveness as part of a team – are increasingly unlikely to be as much of an asset to their organisation as they ought to be.[45]

Figure 9.8 Concept map of effective work groups

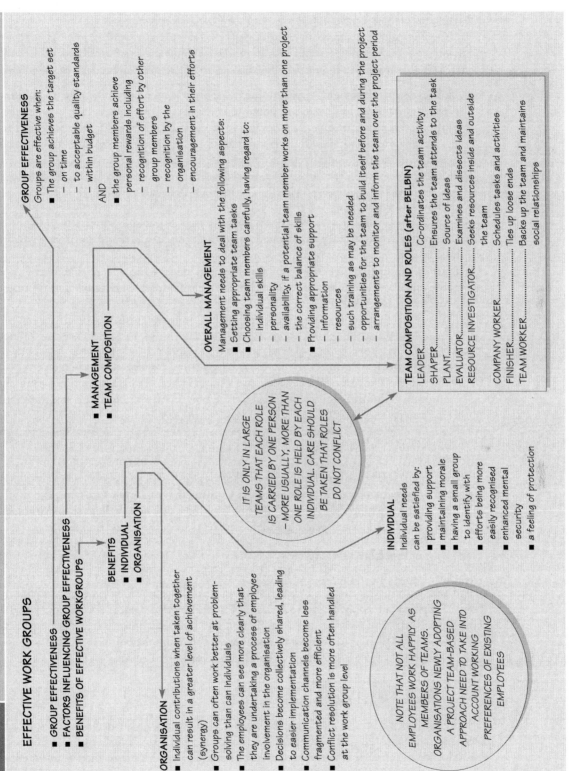

EFFECTIVE WORK GROUPS

- GROUP EFFECTIVENESS
- FACTORS INFLUENCING GROUP EFFECTIVENESS
- BENEFITS OF EFFECTIVE WORKGROUPS

BENEFITS
- INDIVIDUAL
- ORGANISATION

ORGANISATION
- Individual contributions when taken together can result in a greater level of achievement (synergy)
- Groups can often work better at problem-solving than can individuals
- The employees can see more clearly that they are undertaking a process of employee involvement in the organisation
- Decisions become collectively shared, leading to easier implementation
- Communication channels become less fragmented and more efficient
- Conflict resolution is more often handled at the work group level

NOTE THAT NOT ALL EMPLOYEES WORK HAPPILY AS MEMBERS OF TEAMS. ORGANISATIONS NEWLY ADOPTING A PROJECT TEAM-BASED APPROACH NEED TO TAKE INTO ACCOUNT WORKING PREFERENCES OF EXISTING EMPLOYEES

MANAGEMENT
TEAM COMPOSITION

IT IS ONLY IN LARGE TEAMS THAT EACH ROLE IS CARRIED BY ONE PERSON – MORE USUALLY, MORE THAN ONE ROLE IS HELD BY EACH INDIVIDUAL. CARE SHOULD BE TAKEN THAT ROLES DO NOT CONFLICT

GROUP EFFECTIVENESS

Groups are effective when:
- The group achieves the target set
  - on time
  - to acceptable quality standards
  - within budget
  AND
- the group members achieve personal rewards including
  - recognition of effort by other group members
  - recognition by the organisation
  - encouragement in their efforts

OVERALL MANAGEMENT

Management needs to deal with the following aspects:
- Setting appropriate team tasks
- Choosing team members carefully, having regard to:
  - individual skills
  - personality
  - availability, if a potential team member works on more than one project
  - the correct balance of skills
- Providing appropriate support
  - information
  - resources
  - such training as may be needed
  - opportunities for the team to build itself before and during the project
  - arrangements to monitor and inform the team over the project period

TEAM COMPOSITION AND ROLES (after BELBIN)
LEADER	Co-ordinates the team activity
SHAPER	Ensures the team attends to the task
PLANT	Source of ideas
EVALUATOR	Examines and dissects ideas
RESOURCE INVESTIGATOR	Seeks resources inside and outside the team
COMPANY WORKER	Schedules tasks and activities
FINISHER	Ties up loose ends
TEAM WORKER	Backs up the team and maintains social relationships

INDIVIDUAL

Individual needs can be satisfied by:
- providing support
- maintaining morale
- having a small group to identify with
- efforts being more easily recognised
- enhanced mental security
- a feeling of protection

However, Douglas points out that as we all interact with people to a greater or lesser extent in our everyday lives, there is a tendency to assume that people management skills are merely an extension of our natural abilities. In fact, people management skills are the more difficult and rare type of skill but to a large extent they can be learned.

Cloke and Goldsmith refer to the special skills required for successful teamwork and list ten skills team members can develop in order to build innovative self-managing teams. All of these skills are interrelated, mutually reinforcing and dependent upon each of the others.[46]

■ **Skill of self-management** – overcoming obstacles together and in the process building a sense of ownership, responsibility, commitment and efficiency within each team member.

■ **Skill of communication** – collaboratively developing their skills in becoming better listeners, commiserating with others, reframing communications so they can be heard, and communicating honestly about things that really matter.

■ **Skill of leadership** – creating opportunities for each member to serve as leader. Employees need to be skilled in linking, organising, co-ordinating, collaborating, planning, facilitating, coaching and mentoring.

■ **Skill of responsibility** – everyone is personally responsible not only for their own work but for the work of every other member of the team. Team members have to exercise responsibility in order to become self-managing.

■ **Skill of supportive diversity** – collaborative experiences allow team members to overcome prejudices and biases and not create winners and losers, reject outsiders or mistrust people who are different.

■ **Skills of feedback and evaluation** – essential to improving learning, team communication and the quality of products, processes and relationships. In a true team environment, self-critical perspectives are expected, welcomed, acknowledged and rewarded.

■ **Skill of strategic planning** – to identify challenges and opportunities collaboratively and influence the environment in which problems emerge. Strategic planning encourages employees to think long-term, be proactive and preventative and focus on solutions rather than problems.

■ **Skill of shaping successful meetings** – team meetings can be streamlined and made shorter, more satisfying and more productive, and result in expanded consensus.

■ **Skill of resolving conflicts** – encouraging team members to improve skills in problem-solving, collaborative negotiation, responding to difficult behaviour and conflict resolution.

■ **Skill of enjoyment** – most team members enjoy working together to accomplish difficult tasks. Their pleasure derives from meeting high performance challenges and producing results that benefit themselves and their teams, organisations and communities.

The role of emotional intelligence

Landale refers to the importance of emotional intelligence, discussed in Chapter 4, for effective team performance and to a research study by Yale University that found teams with high levels of EI outperformed teams with low levels of EI by a margin of two to one. However, high individual EI does not automatically translate into a high-EI team and an extra set of skills is needed such as inclusive and collaborative working, being open to new opportunities, adaptability to change, and direct and honest communications.[47]

The role of team leader

Building successful teams also requires effective leadership with an emphasis on trust, clear communications, full participation and self-management. 'The influence and usefulness of team leaders comes, not from their delivery of traditional supervisory and control methods, but from their ability to lead from the front and in training, coaching and counselling their team members to high standards of performance.'[48]

In her discussion of the 'democratic enterprise' (organisations which can flourish economically and can also be places of excitement and stimulation, fulfilment and tranquillity),

Gratton maintains that it is the leaders of the teams across the organisation who make the company vision a reality on a day-to-day basis. The team leaders are the creators of space in which choice and freedom can be exercised; they delineate the obligations and accountabilities contained within the business goals; they become role models for how members should behave; and they bring the philosophy of autonomy and personal development to realisation by the manner in which they act as mentors and coaches.[49]

According to *Powell*, if you want to see the efficacy of a leader and his or her leadership style, then you need to look no further than the team he or she leads.

> *A team rarely demonstrates more passion or behaves more positively than its leader. Similarly, cynical leaders produce, and therefore deserve, cynical teams. Innovative, creative and developmental leaders help to produce creative, innovative and developed followers. A team that is enthusiastic, energetic and innovative will have at its heart a leader who is correspondingly so.[50]*

Continuous process of improvement and innovation

The requirement for continual development and improvement is a necessary part of effective teamwork. However, as *Riches* points out,

> *Understandably, teams are pre-occupied with getting the job done. Few teams regularly take time out to reflect on how the team itself is working and what it needs to do to improve the way its modus operandi. Even fewer set measurable objectives for team functioning and/or get feedback from internal and external customers about the team's effectiveness.[51]*

The ACAS advisory booklet concludes that although self-regulation is necessary if the potential of teamworking is to be realised, teams will always need some degree of management direction. The task of management is to oversee the development of teams and provide the necessary support and training. Even when in place, teams will need constant monitoring and development. Teamworking is not a finite project but a process of continuous improvement and innovation.

> *The introduction of teamworking is a major step for an organisation to take. It is important that management, trade unions and employees ensure they know how teamworking will contribute to their business strategy and that it is likely to involve a long-term transformation . . . The early challenge and excitement of establishing teams may fade and it is easy for organisations to accept a level of performance which is short of optimum . . . In order to achieve high performance, teams require regular changes and challenges. These may include: changes to team personnel; new tasks; re-examining the contribution the team makes to the overall business aims; and ensuring that the team has regular dealings with other teams.[52]*

Critical reflection

'All this discussion about group membership and building successful teams is very interesting and sounds fine in the classroom. But it ignores the reality of the work environment for example with managing groups of workers in a restaurant kitchen, on a production assembly line, in a gay pub, or with professionals such as lecturers, doctors or lawyers.'

What are your views?

Cases

Top Gear

First aired in 1977 on BBC Midlands as an essentially factual programme about cars and road safety, *Top Gear* has been a familiar item on the BBC schedules since 1978 when it transferred to national TV. Originally hosted by the newsreader Angela Rippon amongst others, the show continued as a regular but uncontroversial series until 1988 when Jeremy Clarkson, a motoring journalist, joined the crew. This signalled a change of emphasis, and the show became famous for its macho, 'boy racer' enthusiasm for speed and excitement over informative content. It attracted a (predominantly) male audience, and thereafter the show's popularity has remained high, despite a slump in viewing figures when Clarkson left (temporarily as it turned out) in 1999. The 2008–9 season saw it once more achieving record viewing figures of between 7m and 7.5m, around 25 per cent of audience share. Since a major revamp of the show's format in 2001, it has morphed into a blend of car review, driving news and comment, liberally interspersed with stunts, challenges and unlikely races. These have become a centrepiece of the show; memorable items include the increasingly desperate attempts to 'kill' a Toyota Hilux, a drive across the desert in Botswana in locally bought used cars, and a race up (and back down) a mountain between an Audi and a speed climber; not to mention regular features involving caravan abuse.[53] The team's propensity for 'mucking about' gives the distinct impression that Richmal Crompton's William and the Outlaws have got older and become TV presenters. So, what makes the show tick? An important part of the appeal is certainly the blend of personalities in what is described on the show's microsite as 'the team with the best jobs in telly'.

What makes a team tick? Top Gear's Jezza, Captain Slow, the Hamster and the Stig blend of personalities make for the best jobs in telly.

Jezza

Jeremy Clarkson and *Top Gear* have become almost synonymous. His particular style of presentation coupled with outspoken, politically incorrect and often outrageous views boosted viewing figures, helping the show to exert a major influence over the choices of the car-buying public. His reviews can be ecstatic as well as wholly dismissive; he has been blamed in Luton for precipitating the closure of the Vauxhall plant in 2002 after a particularly bad review of the new Vectra.[54] Despite regular criticism from road safety campaigners, environmentalists, and public transport organisations together with a range of individual complaints from

Stonewall (the gay and lesbian pressure group), Headway (a brain injury charity) and the RNIB (when Clarkson insulted Gordon Brown) amongst others, Clarkson remains the main draw of the programme. Public opinion is divided as to whether he is clever and obnoxious or simply obnoxious – in either case he is self-assured, funny, occasionally bad-tempered, and never averse to a bit of cheating if it means he gets to win. He also knows a great deal about cars.

Captain Slow

James May was an established journalist when he joined the show briefly in 1999, returning to the new format of the programme in 2003. He appears slightly more 'posh', erudite and cultured (he is a musician) than avowed 'petrolheads' Clarkson and Hammond, and thus a butt of their jokes. He has been nicknamed 'Captain Slow' for his relatively careful driving style, combined with a preference for more sedate and classic vehicles over the racy, sporty machines favoured by the others. In the show's challenges, where the presenters are often required to adapt or alter a vehicle to serve some other purpose, he is careful, organised (he keeps tools clean and neatly arranged) and thoughtful. Where Clarkson and Hammond are likely to improvise or (particularly in Clarkson's case) go for the spectacular, May plans and pays attention to the minor details. In news pieces he is usually the one to show a fascination with technicalities and the 'boring' facts and figures.[55] He is not averse to practical jokes, but the one which got him sacked from Autocar Magazine in 1992 was perhaps more intellectual than some of the *Top Gear* capers; he devised an acrostic using the initial letters of a series of title texts in *Autocar*'s 'Road Test Year Book' to spell out a couple of fairly insulting sentences about the job. In addition to presenting *Top Gear*, May has been writing a regular motoring column for the *Telegraph* since 2003, has published a number of books, co-presented a series of programmes on wine, and made documentaries on various scientific subjects including the moon landings.

The Hamster

In 2002 Richard Hammond arrived from a job presenting *MotorWeek* on a satellite channel after a career in radio and public relations for the motor trade. Generally seen as the most likeable and good-humoured member of the team, his happy enthusiasm coupled with his size earned him the nickname 'Hamster'. He often finds himself between the abrasive Clarkson and the obsessive, sometimes tetchy, May, and seems to act as something of a buffer between the two. His popularity became evident when, on 20 September 2006, he had a catastrophic accident whilst test driving a jet-powered car for the series. Airlifted to Leeds General Infirmary, he was initially reported as having significant brain injury.[56] Fears that the Hamster would not recover, or would only recover slowly, were allayed when he left hospital a matter of weeks after the crash. He made a remarkably speedy return to the show in February 2007 to huge acclaim (the jokey handling of the crash by Clarkson and May was the incident which sparked the protest from Headway).[57] His status as the petrolhead with a heart of gold was affirmed when he adopted and restored the battered Opel Kadett (named Oliver) in which he had driven across Botswana for the 10th series.

The Stig

The show's 'tame racing driver' – the unidentified automaton in the white jumpsuit and helmet – is the subject of regular speculation and much press hype. The identity of the Stig is a closely guarded BBC secret. Over the years a number of racing and stunt drivers have been 'outed' as the man behind the visor; amid much publicity, Formula One driver Michael Schumacher was revealed as the Stig (or was he?) at the start of the 13th series. His contribution to the show

is to provide consistent, high-level technical and driving expertise for the speed trials of featured vehicles, and to tutor the 'star' who attempts a fast lap of the *Top Gear* track each week. He occasionally participates in challenges; memorably attempting to cross London by public transport in a race with a speedboat (Clarkson), a bicycle (Hammond) and a Mercedes (May).[58]

Under the bonnet

The executive producer of the show, Andy Wilman, is just as important a member of the team as the presenters. He is generally credited, along with Clarkson, with revising the show for the relaunch in 2001 and creating the formula which enabled it to climb back up the ratings. His contributions included the idea of the studio audience (the show is now shot in a hangar), the *Top Gear* race track and the features which make it accessible and entertaining even for those without an obsessive interest in cars. He clearly views the team spirit which prevails in the show as crucial to its success (in an interview with the *Observer* shortly after the crash he said he believed the show could not continue without Hammond) and admits that this wasn't an instant achievement:

> *It's taken us three, maybe four yours to get the show to this level of comfort. The presenters just muck about – it's obvious that they're at ease, even when they get niggly with each other.*[59]

He has also written about the continuing commitment and enthusiasm of the team:

> *I can assure you, though, that even if we do run out of talent, there's no cynicism in the Top Gear office. We go to work rubbing our hands, wondering what mischief can be made that day. So I'm afraid you're stuck with us for a while.*[60]

Some say . . .

Top Gear has both admirers and critics in large numbers. It is accused of political bias, the glorification of speed,[61] macho bigotry, political incorrectness and sexism. The only female petrolhead to have appeared on the show is Sabine Schmitz,[62] who beat Clarkson's fastest time round the Nürburgring in a Jaguar S-type by 47 seconds at her first attempt.[63] Yet one of Wilman's treasured moments was not on screen at all; it was when the team visited British troops in Afghanistan for three days before Christmas 2007.

> *For three days they shook hands, signed autographs and did their best to spread a bit of cheer to lads who wouldn't be with their families at Santa time, and the reaction of the soldiers was humbling.*[64]

Your tasks

1 Analyse the main team members using Belbin's team roles as a framework. Which roles do the members appear to fit? N.B. One person may have both a main role and a back-up role. Are there any significant components missing?

2 *Top Gear* is criticised for being all male and exhibiting 'laddish' behaviour. Do you think the BBC should add a woman to the team? Explain the reasoning for your answer.

3 To what extent do you think the team is susceptible to the 'groupthink' phenomenon? Suggest ways in which the production team could ensure that this does not damage the workings of the team.

4 Visit the *Top Gear* website and watch one of the longer pieces involving a challenge. Using the observation grid in Figure 9.4 or the classification of task roles, building and maintenance roles and individual roles, observe the team at work and report back on your findings. (The Botswana and Vietnamese trips are also available on DVD *Top Gear* – The Great Adventures vol. 2.)

The Botswana trip from series 10 can be accessed via the *Top Gear* website at http://www.topgear.com/uk/videos/botswana-1 and http://www.topgear.com/uk/videos/botswana-2.

The Vietnamese trip from series 12 can be accessed via the *Top Gear* website at http://www.topgear.com/uk/videos/vietnam-pt-1#/uk/videos-by-category?VideoCategory=TheBigFilms&Page=2 and http://www.topgear.com/uk/videos/vietnam-pt-2#/uk/videos-by-category?VideoCategory=TheBigFilms&Page=2.

The American trip from series 12 can be accessed via the *Top Gear* website at http://www.topgear.com/uk/videos/team-america-2-part-1; also http://www.topgear.com/uk/videos/team-america-2-part-2#/uk/videos-by-category?VideoCategory=TheBigFilms&Page=1 and http://www.topgear.com/uk/videos/team-america-2-part-3#/uk/videos-by-category?VideoCategory=TheBigFilms&Page=2.

Case study   Cisco Systems www.cisco.com

Cisco Systems is a company at the heart of the internet. It is a leading developer and supplier of the physical equipment and software that allow digital data to travel around the world over the internet, and also provides support services that enable companies to improve their use of the network. It was founded in 1984 by a group of scientists from Stanford University, and its engineers have focused on developing Internet Protocol (IP)-based networking technologies. The core areas of the business remain the supply of routing and switching equipment, but it is also working in areas such as home networking, network security and storage networking.

Courtesy of Cisco Systems, Inc. Unauthorised use not permitted

The company employs 34,000 staff working from 70 offices around the world, developing new systems and working with customers to implement and enhance their network infrastructure. Most projects are implemented by staff from several sites working as virtual teams, in the sense that they are responsible for a collective product but work in physically separate places.

The company created a team to co-ordinate the testing and release of a new version of Cisco's Element Management Framework (EMF), a highly complex piece of software that monitors the performance of large numbers of elements in a network. When the product was released a few months later, the members of the team were free to work on other projects. The team had eight members, drawn from four sites and three countries:

Name	Location	Role
Steve	Raleigh, North Carolina	Project co-ordinator
Richard	Cumbernauld, Scotland	Development manager
Graham	Cumbernauld, Scotland	Development engineer
Eddie	Cumbernauld, Scotland	Development engineer
Rai	Austin, Texas	Test engineer
Silvio	Austin, Texas	Test engineer
Jim	Raleigh, North Carolina	Network architect
Gunzal	Bangalore, India	Release support engineer

The role of the co-ordinator was to ensure the smooth operation of the team and to monitor actual progress against the challenging delivery schedule. The software was developed in Cumbernauld, by engineers writing the code and revising it as necessary after testing by the test engineers. They were responsible for rigorously testing all software and reporting all problems concisely and accurately to the development engineers.

The network architect has extensive knowledge of the network hardware that the software would manage, and supervised the development and testing of the software to ensure that it worked as efficiently as possible with the hardware. The release support engineer dealt with the logistics of software release, such as defining each version and ensuring that deliverables are available to the manufacturing departments at the appropriate times.

Each member worked full-time on the project, although they never met physically during its lifetime. All members took part in a weekly conference call, and also a daily call attended by the co-ordinator, development manager and a member of the test team. Communication throughout the team was mainly by electronic mail, together with instant messaging.

Source: Communication from members of the project team.

Case questions 17.1

- What challenges would you expect a team that never meets will face during its work?

- In what ways may it need to work differently from a conventional team?

Members of the project team commented on the way the team developed. A common issue was the problem of scheduling meetings:

> I've always found in virtual teams that when the team is first formed it isn't really getting any serious work done (unless we're under severe time pressure), it's about getting everyone together so they at least have some knowledge of the others in the team. (Steve)

Another member said:

> It was strange when we first started working together, because we didn't push on and get any testing or fixing done straight away. Steve was really pushing for us all to spend a few hours in conference calls getting to know each other and how we were all going to work together. We took our time to get into the actual work that was required. (Graham)

Other reflections included:

> I had a few discussions with Steve . . . he wanted us to spend most of our time in conference meetings with the rest of the team, while my engineers already had a good understanding of the work that was needed and just wanted to get on with it. But Steve is the team lead so we had to go along with his approach. (Richard)

> It's weird having to form such a close relationship with someone [when] you don't even know what they look like. But as we're using IM [Instant Messenger] just about every day you get used to it. I think you sometimes have to make an extra effort to talk directly to people, just to keep the relationship going. Sometimes it'd be easier for me to email Rai, but I phone him, just so we can have a bit of a chat. (Eddie)

> It means you have to be a bit more careful when it comes to communication. Most of the time you have to use email and IM to discuss issues, which means there can be misunderstandings if you're not careful. When you interact in person you use things like facial expression and hand gestures – none of these are available when emailing so you have to state your arguments more clearly. (Jim)

Source: Communication from members of the project team.

Case questions 17.4

- Relate these accounts to the stages of team development.
- What examples of forming, storming and norming does it contain?

CASE APPLICATION *2*

Making Order Out of Chaos

Imagine the scene. A FedEx 727 jet and a giant U.S. Air Force cargo jet at an impasse on the taxiway, another jet trying to reach a parking spot at the terminal, another headed for a runway, U.S. Navy and Canadian helicopters swarming overhead, a Bolivian DC-10 just landing, and a Boeing 757 carrying former President Bill Clinton just landing. What a nightmare! In the first few days after the devastating earthquake in Haiti, the airport in the capital city, Port-Au-Prince, was a chaotic free-for-all.[70] Aid planes were jostling for space on the single open runway and landing randomly. Then, the evening after the earthquake, a small team of U.S. Air Force special-operations troops whose job is to control air traffic set up to do what they've been trained to do. The airport's control tower was too badly damaged to be used. So, operating from a folding table on a patch of dirt, the team worked to safely bring in much-needed supply-laden cargo jets.

It didn't take long to establish a system. Haitian aviation officials, assisted by American and Canadian air traffic controllers, contacted planes 30 or 40 miles out and kept order as the aircraft headed toward Port-au-Prince. When the planes got within 10 or 20 miles, the Air Force team of controllers took over and guided the aircraft onto the lone runway. Despite the system, the team of controllers found themselves in conflict with arriving pilots and their governments. For instance, one argument arose with a French crew over who got to land first and stay parked the longest. Despite the challenges, the small team safely directed traffic in the crowded skies. Over the days and weeks, planes were able to take off and land every five minutes, bringing in 4 million pounds of supplies.

Discussion Questions

1. As this story illustrated, sometimes teams have to move quickly. How do you get a team up and running quickly?

2. In a crisis situation such as this, what role does a team leader need to play? Explain.

3. Using Exhibit 13-10, what characteristics of effective teams would this team need? Explain.

Review Questions and Tests

REVIEW AND DISCUSSION QUESTIONS

1 Discuss critically and with supporting practical examples the likely advantages and disadvantages of working in a small work group.

2 Contrast different types of communication networks. Give examples of a situation in which each type of network is likely to be most appropriate.

3 Assess the practical value to the manager of the analysis of individual behaviour. Explain how you would go about constructing a sociogram.

4 Distinguish between (a) group task roles, (b) group building and maintenance roles, and (c) individual roles. Give your own examples of each of these types of group member roles.

5 Suggest a framework for the analysis and categorisation of patterns of individual behaviour in group situations. What considerations need to be kept in mind when using such frameworks?

6 Explain what is meant by (a) 'groupthink', (b) the risky-shift phenomenon, and (c) brainstorming. Assess critically the likely standard of individual compared with group or team performance.

7 Explain the meaning and purpose of sensitivity training. Give your views on the relevance and practical value of group dynamics.

8 Detail fully the main factors to be considered in a review of effective teamworking.

Review questions

1 What are the potential benefits of teamwork to people and performance?

2 Katzenbach and Smith (1993) distinguish between working groups and real teams. Describe the differences, and suggest when each form is appropriate to a task.

3 W.L. Gore and Associates (see Part Case) is beginning to form more distant teams. What management issues are likely to arise in this form of team?

4 How many stages of development do teams go through? Use this model to compare two teams.

5 List the main categories of behaviour that can be identified in observing a group.

6 Compare the meaning of the terms 'task' and 'maintenance' roles.

7 Evaluate Belbin's model of team roles. Which three or four roles are of most importance in an effective team? What is your preferred role?

8 Give examples of the external factors that affect group performance. Compare the model with your experience as a group member.

9 What are the potential disadvantages of teams?

10 Summarise an idea from the chapter that adds to your understanding of the integrating themes.

Understanding Yourself

What's My Attitude Toward Working in Groups?

One thing is for certain about organizations these days: more and more work is being performed by teams. So, it's quite likely that you'll be part of a team at some point if you've not already been so.

Teams comprised of members who enjoy being part of a group can be quite effective. However, research has indicated that as little as one person with a negative attitude toward working in groups can hurt team performance. Why? Team members with negative attitudes can increase interpersonal conflict among group members, harming cohesiveness and team processes. Team morale and satisfaction are lowered, and performance ultimately declines.

INSTRUMENT Using the scale below, indicate the extent to which you agree or disagree with each of the following statements about your feelings toward working in groups or teams.

> **1** = Strongly disagree
>
> **2** = Disagree
>
> **3** = Neutral
>
> **4** = Agree
>
> **5** = Strongly agree

		1	2	3	4	5
1.	I don't miss group meetings or team practices.	1	2	3	4	5
2.	I enjoy being part of a group.	1	2	3	4	5
3.	I support my teammates or fellow group members.	1	2	3	4	5
4.	I feel I must respect the decisions made by my group.	1	2	3	4	5
5.	I am not good at working with a group.	1	2	3	4	5
6.	I prefer to do everything alone.	1	2	3	4	5
7.	I work best when I am alone.	1	2	3	4	5
8.	I keep to myself.	1	2	3	4	5
9.	I don't think it's important to socialize with others.	1	2	3	4	5

SCORING KEY To score the measure, first reverse-code items 5, 6, 7, 8, and 9 so that $1 = 5$, $2 = 4$, $3 = 3$, $4 = 2$, and $5 = 1$. Then, compute the sum of the nine items. Scores will range from 9 to 45.

ANALYSIS AND INTERPRETATION This measure assesses your attitude toward working in groups. Scores at or above 36 indicate that you enjoy working in groups and that you are a "team player." Scores at or below 18 indicate the opposite—that you prefer to work alone and do not enjoy being part of a team. Scores between 18 and 36 indicate no particularly strong feelings either way.

If you scored low on this measure and find yourself on a team at some point, try to see the benefits of teamwork. Not only is work shared among individuals, but teams also can facilitate feelings of inclusion and camaraderie among team members. Remember to be patient, however. Although teams often outperform individuals working by themselves (especially on complex tasks that require multiple skills and experience), they tend to take longer to reach decisions.

Source: L. R. Goldberg, J. A. Johnson, H. W. Eber, R. Hogan, M. C. Ashton, C. R. Cloninger, and H. G. Gough, "The International Personality Item Pool and the Future of Public-Domain Personality Measures," *Journal of Research in Personality* (40) (2006), 84–96.

SECTION 8:
LEADERSHIP

Chapter 14:
Styles of Management

THE MEANING OF LEADERSHIP

There are many ways of looking at **leadership** and many interpretations of its meaning. Leadership might be interpreted in simple terms, such as 'getting others to follow' or 'getting people to do things willingly', or interpreted more specifically, for example as 'the use of authority in decision-making'. It may be exercised as an attribute of position or because of personal knowledge or wisdom. Leadership might be based on a function of personality or it can be seen as a behavioural category. It may also be viewed in terms of the role of the leaders and their ability to achieve effective performance from others. Leadership can also be discussed in terms of a form of persuasion or power relationship.

From a comprehensive review of leadership theory and research, *Bass* concludes that: 'There are almost as many different definitions of leadership as there are persons who have attempted to define the concept.'[1] According to *Crainer* there are over 400 definitions of leadership and 'it is a veritable minefield of misunderstanding and difference through which theorists and practitioners must tread warily'.[2] It is difficult, therefore, to generalise about leadership, but essentially it is a **relationship through which one person influences the behaviour or actions of other people**. This means that the process of leadership cannot be separated from the activities of groups and effective teambuilding.

Changing nature of the work organisation

The changing nature of work organisations involves moving away from an emphasis on getting results by the close control of the workforce and towards an environment of coaching, support and empowerment. This places an ever growing importance on leadership. The leader–follower relationship is reciprocal and effective leadership is a two-way process that influences both individual and organisational performance. Leadership is related to motivation and interpersonal behaviour.[3] A major report from the Advanced Institute of Management Research refers to the dual role of leadership.

> *Leaders both motivate employees and design effective organisations. There are two broad conceptions of what leaders do – they motivate their followers and they design organisational contexts to enable their followers to function effectively.*[4]

Teamwork and inspiration

Leadership today is increasingly associated not with command and control but with the concept of teamwork, getting along with other people, inspiration and creating a vision with which others can identify. According to *Levine*, leaders need to focus on moving people and organisations forward by increasing the competency of staff and the co-operation of teams in order to improve the organisation. A leader's job is constantly to challenge the bureaucracy that smothers individual enthusiasm and the desire to contribute to an organisation. Leaders in the new millennium will create an environment that encourages the development of skills, learning and openness so that those on their team can participate in the deployment of financial and human resources.[5] A CBI report makes the point that 'Effective leaders, who can inspire their people to realise their personal and collective potential, are often the deciding factor between a company being good at what it does and achieving greatness.'[6]

STYLES OF LEADERSHIP

Attention to leadership as a behavioural category has drawn attention to the importance of leadership style. In the work situation it has become increasingly clear that managers can no longer rely solely on the use of their position in the hierarchical structure as a means of exercising the functions of leadership. In order to get the best results from subordinates the manager must also have regard for the need to encourage high morale, a spirit of involvement and co-operation, and a willingness to work. This gives rise to consideration of the style of leadership and provides another heading under which to analyse leadership behaviour.

Leadership style is the way in which the functions of leadership are carried out, the way in which the manager typically behaves towards members of the group.

The attention given to leadership style is based on the assumption that subordinates are more likely to work effectively for managers who adopt a certain style of leadership than for managers who adopt alternative styles. Attention to the manager's style of leadership has come about because of a greater understanding of the needs and expectations of people at work. It has also been influenced by such factors as:

■ increasing business competitiveness and recognition of efficient use of human resources;
■ changes in the value-system of society;
■ broader standards of education and training;
■ advances in scientific and technical knowledge;
■ changes in the nature of work organisation;
■ pressure for a greater social responsibility towards employees, for example through schemes of participation in decision-making and work/life balance; and
■ government legislation, for example in the areas of employment protection, and the influence of the European Union.

All of these factors have combined to create resistance against purely autocratic styles of leadership.

Broad framework of leadership style

There are many dimensions to leadership and many possible ways of describing leadership style, such as dictatorial, unitary, bureaucratic, benevolent, charismatic, consultative, participative and abdicatorial. With so many potential descriptions of leadership styles it is useful to have a broad framework in which to focus attention and study. The style of managerial leadership towards subordinate staff and the focus of power can therefore be considered within a simplified three-fold heading.

■ The **authoritarian (autocratic) style** is where the focus of power is with the manager and all interactions within the group move towards the manager. The manager alone exercises decision-making and authority for determining policy, procedures for achieving goals, work tasks and relationships, control of rewards or punishments.
■ The **democratic style** is where the focus of power is more with the group as a whole and there is greater interaction within the group. The leadership functions are shared with members of the group and the manager is more part of a team. The group members have a greater say in decision-making, determination of policy, implementation of systems and procedures.
■ A **laissez-faire (genuine) style** is where the manager observes that members of the group are working well on their own. The manager consciously makes a decision to pass the focus of power to members, to allow them freedom of action 'to do as they think best', and not to interfere; but is readily available if help is needed. There is often confusion over this style of leadership behaviour. The word 'genuine' is emphasised because this is to be contrasted with the manager who could not care, who deliberately keeps away from the trouble spots and does not want to get involved. The manager just lets members of the group get on with the work in hand. Members are left to face decisions that rightly belong with the manager. This is more a non-style of leadership or it could perhaps be labelled as abdication.

CONTINUUM OF LEADERSHIP BEHAVIOUR

One of the best-known works on leadership style is that by *Tannenbaum and Schmidt* (*see* Figure 10.4).[24] Originally written in 1958 and updated in 1973, their work suggests a continuum of possible leadership behaviour available to a manager and along which various styles of leadership may be placed. The continuum presents a range of action related to the degree of authority used by the manager and to the area of freedom available to non-managers in arriving at decisions. The Tannenbaum and Schmidt continuum can be related to McGregor's supposition of Theory X and Theory Y (discussed in Chapter 12). Boss-centred leadership is towards Theory X and subordinate-centred leadership is towards Theory Y.

Figure 10.4	Continuum of manager–non-manager behaviour

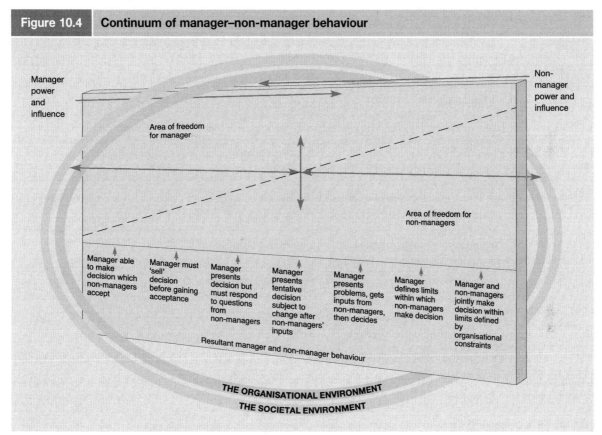

Four main styles of leadership

Moving along the continuum, the manager may be characterised according to the degree of control that is maintained. Neither extreme of the continuum is absolute as there is always some limitation on authority and on freedom. This approach can be seen as identifying four main styles of leadership by the manager: tells, sells, consults, joins.

■ **Tells**. The manager identifies a problem, makes a decision and announces this to subordinates, expecting them to implement it without an opportunity for participation.

■ **Sells**. The manager still makes a decision but recognises the possibility of some resistance from those faced with the decision and attempts to persuade subordinates to accept it.

- **Consults**. The manager identifies the problem but does not make a decision until the problem is presented to the group, and the manager has listened to the advice and solutions suggested by subordinates.
- **Joins**. The manager defines the problem and the limits within which the decision must be made and then passes to the group, with the manager as a member, the right to make decisions.

Three main forces

Tannenbaum and Schmidt suggest that there are three factors, or forces, of particular importance in deciding what types of leadership are practicable and desirable. These are: forces in the manager, forces in the subordinate and forces in the situation.

Forces in the manager. The manager's behaviour will be influenced by their personality, background, knowledge and experiences. These internal forces will include:

- value-systems
- confidence in subordinates
- leadership inclinations
- feelings of security in an uncertain situation.

Forces in the subordinate. Subordinates are influenced by many personality variables and their individual set of expectations about their relationship with the manager. Characteristics of the subordinate are:

- the strength of the need for independence
- readiness to assume responsibility for decision-making
- the degree of tolerance for ambiguity
- interest in the problem and feelings as to its importance
- understanding and identification with the goals of the organisation
- necessary knowledge and experience to deal with the problem
- the extent of learning to expect to share in decision-making.

The greater the positive response to these characteristics, the greater freedom of action can be allowed by the manager.

Forces in the situation. The manager's behaviour will be influenced by the general situation and environmental pressures. Characteristics in the situation include:

- type of organisation
- group effectiveness
- nature of the problem
- pressure of time.

Tannenbaum and Schmidt conclude that successful leaders are keenly aware of those forces which are most relevant to their behaviour at a particular time. They are able to behave appropriately in terms of their understanding of themselves, the individuals and the group, the organisation, and environmental influences. Successful managers are both perceptive and flexible. Forces lying outside the organisation are also included. Tannenbaum and Schmidt suggest a new continuum of patterns of leadership behaviour in which the total area of freedom shared between managers and non-managers is redefined constantly by interactions between them and the forces in the environment.

Critical reflection

'The Tannenbaum and Schmidt continuum is probably the single most important and relevant study of leadership. Successful managers clearly need to be both consistent in personality and behaviour, yet adaptable to the three forces that continually influence their leadership style and decision-making along the various points of the continuum.'

To what extent can you argue against this assertion? What do you think is the single most important study of leadership?

CONTINGENCY THEORIES OF LEADERSHIP

The continuum of leadership behaviour draws attention to forces in the situation as one of the main forces influencing the nature of managerial behaviour. The **situational approach** emphasises the situation as the dominant feature in considering the characteristics of effective leadership. There are, however, limitations to the situational approach. There are people who possess the appropriate knowledge and skills and appear to be the most suitable leaders in a given situation, but who do not emerge as effective leaders. Another limitation is that it does not explain fully the interpersonal behaviour or the different styles of leadership and their effect on members of the group. Finally, in the work organisation, it is not usually practicable to allow the situation continually to determine who should act as the leader.

Despite the limitations of the situational approach, situational factors are important in considering the characteristics of leadership. More recent studies focus on the interactions between the variables involved in a leadership situation and patterns of leadership behaviour, and provide another general approach to the study of leadership – contingency theory. Contingency theories are based on the belief that there is no single style of leadership appropriate to all situations. Major contingency models of leadership include:

- **Favourability of leadership situation** – Fiedler
- **Quality and acceptance of leader's decision** – Vroom and Yetton and Vroom and Jago
- **Path–goal theory** – House, and House and Dessler
- **Readiness level of followers** – Hersey and Blanchard.

FIEDLER'S CONTINGENCY MODEL

One of the first leader–situation models was developed by *Fiedler* in his contingency theory of leadership effectiveness.[25] Fiedler's contingency model was based on studies of a wide range of group situations and concentrated on the relationship between leadership and organisational performance. In order to measure the attitudes of the leader, Fiedler developed a 'least preferred co-worker' (LPC) scale. This measures the rating given by leaders about the person with whom they could work least well. The questionnaire contains up to 20 items. Examples of items in the LPC scale are pleasant/unpleasant, friendly/unfriendly, helpful/frustrating, distant/close, co-operative/unco-operative, boring/interesting, self-assured/hesitant, open/guarded.

Each item is given a single ranking of between one and eight points, with eight points indicating the most favourable rating. For example:

Pleasant	:	:	:	:	:	:	:	Unpleasant
	8	7	6	5	4	3	2	1

The LPC score is the sum of the numerical ratings on all the items for the 'least preferred co-worker'. The original interpretation of the LPC scale was that the leader with a high LPC score derived most satisfaction from interpersonal relationships and, when relationships with subordinates need to be improved, is motivated to act in a supportive, considerate manner. The leader with a low LPC score derived most satisfaction from performance of the task and achieving objectives. Establishing good relationships with subordinates is a secondary motivation. It was thought that high LPC scores would be associated with effective performance by the group. However, the interpretation of LPC has changed a number of times and there is still uncertainty about its actual meaning.

Favourability of leadership situation

Fiedler suggests that leadership behaviour is dependent upon the favourability of the leadership situation. There are three major variables which determine the favourability of the situation and which affect the leader's role and influence:

- **Leader–member relations** – the degree to which the leader is trusted and liked by group members, and their willingness to follow the leader's guidance.
- **The task structure** – the degree to which the task is clearly defined for the group and the extent to which it can be carried out by detailed instructions or standard procedures.
- **Position power** – the power of the leader by virtue of position in the organisation, and the degree to which the leader can exercise authority to influence (for example) rewards and punishments, or promotions and demotions.

| Figure 10.5 | Correlations between leader's LPC scores and group effectiveness |

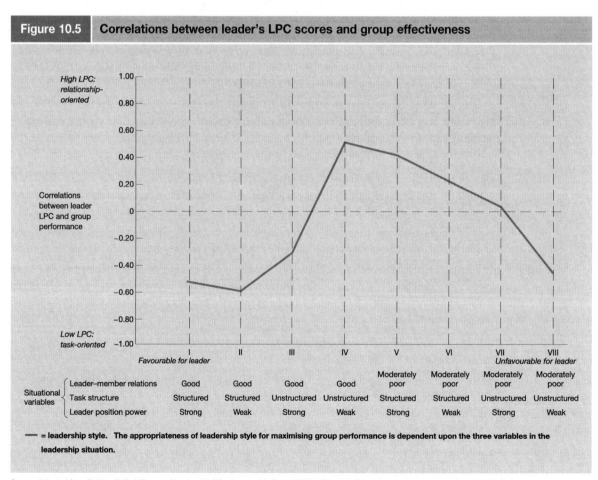

Situational variables	I	II	III	IV	V	VI	VII	VIII
Leader–member relations	Good	Good	Good	Good	Moderately poor	Moderately poor	Moderately poor	Moderately poor
Task structure	Structured	Structured	Unstructured	Unstructured	Structured	Structured	Unstructured	Unstructured
Leader position power	Strong	Weak	Strong	Weak	Strong	Weak	Strong	Weak

—— = leadership style. **The appropriateness of leadership style for maximising group performance is dependent upon the three variables in the leadership situation.**

Source: Adapted from Fiedler, F. E. *A Theory of Leadership Effectiveness*, McGraw-Hill (1967), p. 146. Reproduced with permission from Fred E. Fiedler.

From these three variables, Fiedler constructed eight combinations of group–task situations through which to relate leadership style (*see* Figure 10.5).

When the situation is

- **very favourable** (good leader–member relations, structured task, strong position power), or
- **very unfavourable** (poor leader–member relations, unstructured task, weak position power),
- then a **task-oriented leader** (low LPC score) with a directive, controlling style will be more effective.

When the situation is

- **moderately favourable** and the variables are mixed, then the leader with an interpersonal relationship orientation (high LPC score) and a **participative approach** will be more effective.

Fiedler is suggesting, therefore, that leadership style will vary as the favourability of the leadership situation varies.

Organisational variables

Fiedler's work has been subject to much debate and criticism but it does provide a further dimension to the study of leadership.[26] It brings into consideration the organisational variables that affect leadership effectiveness and suggests that in given situations a task-oriented, or structured, style of leadership is most appropriate. The 'best' styles of leadership will be dependent upon the variable factors in the leadership situation.

Fiedler argues that leadership effectiveness may be improved by changing the leadership situation. Position power, task structure and leader–member relations can be changed to make the situation more compatible with the characteristics of the leader. Leaders with a low LPC score could be placed in a leadership situation that is very favourable or very unfavourable. Leaders with a high LPC score could be placed in a leadership situation that is of moderate favourability.

VROOM AND YETTON CONTINGENCY MODEL

Another contingency model of leadership is provided by *Vroom and Yetton*.[27] They base their analysis on two main aspects of a leader's decision: its quality and its acceptance.

- **Decision quality**, or rationality, is the effect that the decision has on group performance.
- **Decision acceptance** refers to the motivation and commitment of group members in implementing the decision.

A third consideration is

- the amount of **time required** to make the decision.

The Vroom and Yetton model suggests five main management decision styles:

- **Autocratic**
  A.I: Leader solves the problem or makes the decision alone using information available at the time.
  A.II: Leader obtains information from subordinates but then decides on solution alone.

- **Consultative**
  C.I: The problem is shared with relevant subordinates, individually. The leader then makes the decision that may or may not reflect the influence of subordinates.
  C.II: The problem is shared with subordinates as a group. The leader then makes the decision that may or may not reflect the influence of subordinates.

- **Group**
  - **G.II:** The problem is shared with subordinates as a group. The leader acts as chairperson rather than an advocate. Together the leader and subordinates generate and evaluate alternatives and attempt to reach group consensus on a solution.

Decision rules

Vroom and Yetton suggest seven decision rules to help the manager discover the most appropriate leadership style in a given situation. The first three rules protect the **quality of decisions**.

1 Is there a quality requirement such that one solution is likely to be more rational than another?
2 Is there sufficient information to make a high-quality decision?
3 Is the problem structured?

The last four rules protect the **acceptance of decisions**.

4 Is acceptance of the decision by subordinates critical to effective implementation?
5 If you were to make the decision yourself, is it reasonably certain that it would be accepted by subordinates?
6 Do subordinates share the organisational goals to be obtained in solving the problem?
7 Is conflict among subordinates likely in preferred solutions?

These rules indicate decision styles that the manager should **avoid** in a given situation and indicate the use of others. Decision tree charts can be produced to help in the application of the rules and to relate the situation to the appropriate leadership style.

THE VROOM AND JAGO REVISED DECISION MODEL

In a revised version of the original model, *Vroom and Jago* retain the five main decision-making styles but incorporate a larger number – 12 – of contingency variables.[28] The new model specifies that any of the five decision styles may be effective in given situations. The contingency variables relate to:

- quality requirement;
- commitment requirement;
- leader information;
- problem structure;
- commitment probability;
- goal congruence;
- subordinate conflict;
- subordinate information;
- time constraint;
- geographical dispersion;
- motivation time; and
- motivation development.

Unlike the Vroom and Yetton model that requires a definite yes/no answer, ten of these situational variables are answered on a five-point scale. For example, to the question 'How important is subordinate commitment to the decision?', the manager selects one of the following responses: no importance; low importance; average importance; high importance; critical importance.

Use of decision trees

Vroom and Jago developed four decision trees relating to a generic type of managerial problem:

- an individual-level problem with time constraints;
- an individual-level problem in which the manager wishes to develop an employee's decision-making ability;
- a group-level problem in which the manager wishes to develop employees' decision-making abilities; and
- a time-driven group problem.

The manager selects one of the trees and moves along the branches by answering the questions at each decision point. This leads to one of the five described decision-making styles.

PATH–GOAL THEORY

A third contingency model of leadership is the **path–goal theory**, the main work on which has been undertaken by *House*,[29] and by *House and Dessler*.[30] The model is based on the belief that the individual's motivation is dependent upon expectations that increased effort to achieve an improved level of performance will be successful, and expectations that improved performance will be instrumental in obtaining positive rewards and avoiding negative outcomes. This is the 'expectancy' theory of motivation, which was discussed in Chapter 7.

Main types of leadership behaviour

The path–goal theory of leadership suggests that the performance of subordinates is affected by the extent to which the manager satisfies their expectations. Path–goal theory holds that subordinates will see leadership behaviour as a motivating influence to the extent that it means:

- satisfaction of their needs is dependent upon effective performance; and
- the necessary direction, guidance, training and support, which would otherwise be lacking, is provided.

House identifies four main types of leadership behaviour:

- **Directive leadership** involves letting subordinates know exactly what is expected of them and giving specific directions. Subordinates are expected to follow rules and regulations. This type of behaviour is similar to 'initiating structure' in the Ohio State Leadership Studies.
- **Supportive leadership** involves a friendly and approachable manner and displaying concern for the needs and welfare of subordinates. This type of behaviour is similar to 'consideration' in the Ohio State Leadership Studies.
- **Participative leadership** involves consulting with subordinates and the evaluation of their opinions and suggestions before the manager makes the decision.
- **Achievement-oriented leadership** involves setting challenging goals for subordinates, seeking improvement in their performance and showing confidence in subordinates' ability to perform well.

Path–goal theory suggests that the different types of behaviour can be practised by the same person at different times in varying situations. By using one of the four styles of leadership behaviour the manager attempts to influence subordinates' perceptions and motivation, and smooth the path to their goals (*see* Figure 10.6).

Two main situational factors

Leadership behaviour is determined by two main situational factors: the personal characteristics of subordinates and the nature of the task.

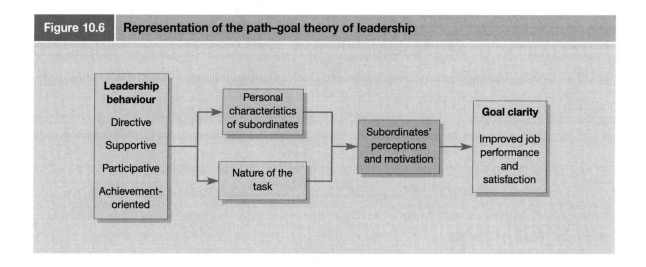

Figure 10.6 Representation of the path–goal theory of leadership

■ **The personal characteristics of subordinates** determine how they will react to the manager's behaviour and the extent to which they see such behaviour as an immediate or potential source of need satisfaction.
■ **The nature of the task** relates to the extent that it is routine and structured or non-routine and unstructured.

For example, when a task is highly structured, the goals readily apparent and subordinates are confident, then attempts to further explain the job or to give directions are likely to be viewed as unacceptable behaviour. However, when a task is highly unstructured, the nature of the goals is not clear and subordinates lack experience, then a more directive style of leadership behaviour is likely to be welcomed by subordinates. Effective leadership behaviour is based, therefore, on both the willingness of the manager to help subordinates and the needs of subordinates for help. Leadership behaviour will be motivational to the extent that it provides necessary direction, guidance and support, helps clarify path–goal relationships and removes any obstacles which hinder attainment of goals.

READINESS OF THE FOLLOWERS OR GROUP

A major variable in the style of leadership adopted by the manager is the nature of subordinate staff. This view is developed by *Hersey and Blanchard* who present a form of situational leadership based on the 'readiness' level of the people the leader is attempting to influence. Readiness is the extent to which followers have the ability and willingness to accomplish a specific task. It is not a personal characteristic of the individual but how ready the individual is to perform a particular task.[31]

Readiness (R) is divided into a continuum of four levels: R1 (low), R2 and R3 (moderate) and R4 (high).

■ **R1 – low follower readiness** – refers to followers who are both *unable and unwilling* and who lack commitment and motivation; or who are *unable and insecure*.
■ **R2 – low to moderate follower readiness** – refers to followers who are *unable but willing* and who lack ability but are motivated to make an effort; or who are *unable but confident*.
■ **R3 – moderate to high follower readiness** – refers to followers who are *able but unwilling*, and who have the ability to perform but are unwilling to apply their ability; or who are *able but insecure*.
■ **R4 – high follower readiness** – refers to followers who are both *able and willing* and who have the **ability** and commitment to perform; or who are *able and confident*.

Task behaviour and relationship behaviour

For each of the four levels of maturity, the appropriate style of leadership is a combination of task behaviour and relationship behaviour.

- **Task behaviour** is the extent to which the leader provides directions for the actions of followers, sets goals for them and defines their roles and how to undertake them.
- **Relationship behaviour** is the extent to which the leader engages in two-way communication with followers, listens to them and provides support and encouragement.

From the combination of task behaviour and relationship behaviour derive four leadership styles (S): telling (S1), selling (S2), participating (S3) and delegating (S4). The appropriate leadership style corresponds with the readiness of the followers (*see* Figure 10.7).

- **S1 – telling** – emphasises high amounts of guidance (task behaviour) but limited supportive (relationship) behaviour. This style is most appropriate for *low follower readiness* (R1).
- **S2 – selling** – emphasises high amounts of both directive (task) and relationship behaviours. This style is most appropriate for *low to moderate follower readiness* (R2).

Figure 10.7	Situational Leadership® model

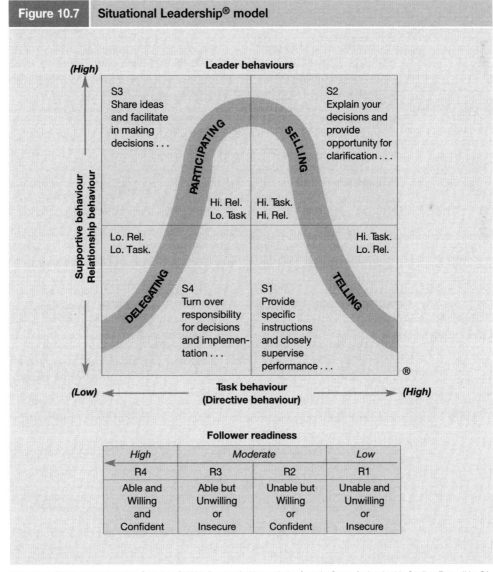

- S3 – **participating** – emphasises a high amount of two-way communication and supportive (relationship) behaviour but low amounts of guidance (task behaviour). This style is most appropriate for *moderate to high follower readiness* (R3).
- S4 – **delegating** – emphasises little direction or support with low levels of both task and relationship behaviours. This style is most appropriate for *high follower readiness* (R4).

Development of subordinates

Hersey and Blanchard suggest that the key to using situational leadership is that any leader behaviour may be more or less effective according to the readiness of the person the leader is attempting to influence. The model draws attention to the importance of developing the ability, confidence and commitment of subordinates. The manager should help subordinates to develop in readiness to the extent that they are able and willing to go. This development should take place by adjusting leadership behaviour through the four styles of telling, selling, participating and delegating.

TRANSFORMATIONAL LEADERSHIP

Increasing business competitiveness and the need for the most effective use of human resources has resulted in writers on management focusing attention on how leaders revitalise or transform organisations. Based on the work of writers such as *Burns* this has given rise to a distinction between two fundamental forms of leadership: transactional or transformational.[32]

- **Transactional leadership** is based on legitimate authority within the bureaucratic structure of the organisation. The emphasis is on the clarification of goals and objectives, work task and outcomes, and organisational rewards and punishments. Transactional leadership appeals to the self-interest of followers. It is based on a relationship of mutual dependence and an exchange process of 'I will give you this, if you do that.'
- **Transformational leadership**, by contrast, is a process of engendering higher levels of motivation and commitment among followers. The emphasis is on generating a vision for the organisation and the leader's ability to appeal to higher ideals and values of followers, and creating a feeling of justice, loyalty and trust. In the organisational sense, transformational leadership is about transforming the performance or fortunes of a business.

Components of transformational leadership

According to *Bass*, the transformational leader motivates followers to do more than originally expected and the extent of transformation is measured in terms of the leader's effects on followers. Applying the ideas of Burns to organisational management, Bass proposed a theory of transformational leadership that argues that the leader transforms and motivates followers by:

1 generating greater awareness of the importance of the purpose of the organisation and task outcomes;
2 inducing them to transcend their own self-interests for the sake of the organisation or team; and
3 activating their higher-level needs.[33]

Transformational leadership is comprised of four basic components:

- **idealised influence** – the charisma of the leader, and the respect and admiration of the followers;
- **inspirational motivation** – the behaviour of the leader which provides meaning and challenge to the work of the followers;

- **intellectual stimulation** – leaders who solicit new and novel approaches for the performance of work and creative problem solutions from followers; and
- **individualised consideration** – leaders who listen and give special concern to the growth and developmental needs of the followers.[34]

Yukl provides a set of guidelines for transformational leadership:

- **Articulate a clear and appealing vision** of what the organisation could accomplish or become to help people understand the purpose, objectives and priorities of the organisation, and to help guide the actions and decisions of members.
- **Explain how the vision can be attained** and establish a clear link between the vision and a credible conventional yet straightforward strategy for attaining it.
- **Act confident and optimistic** about likely success, demonstrate self-confidence and conviction, and emphasise positive aspects of the vision rather than the obstacles and dangers.
- **Express confidence in followers** and their ability to carry out the strategy for accomplishing the vision, especially when the task is difficult or dangerous, or when members lack confidence in themselves.
- **Use dramatic, symbolic actions to emphasise key values** and demonstrate leadership behaviour through dramatic, highly visible actions including risking personal loss, self-sacrifice or acting unconventionally.
- **Lead by example** by recognising actions speak louder than words, through exemplary behaviour in day-to-day interactions with subordinates and by demonstrating consistency in daily behaviour.[35]

INSPIRATIONAL OR VISIONARY LEADERSHIP

Many writers see transformational leadership as the same thing as charismatic, visionary or inspirational leadership. *Kreitner et al.* refer to charismatic leadership as transforming employees to pursue organisational goals over self-interests:

> *Charismatic leaders transform followers by creating changes in their goals, values, needs, beliefs, and aspirations. They accomplish this transformation by appealing to followers' self-concepts – namely, their values and personal identity.*[36]

Writers such as Burns and Bass identified leaders by their actions and the impact those actions have on other people.

Successful transformational leaders are usually identified in terms of providing a strong vision and sense of mission, arousing strong emotions in followers and a sense of identification with the leader. As mentioned at the start of this chapter, leadership today is increasingly associated with the concept of creating a vision with which others can identify, getting along with other people and the concept of inspiration. This might be considered as part of transformational leadership or arguably it has given rise to a new approach to leadership – that of **inspirational** or **visionary leadership**. Inspirational leadership is not concerned so much with the theory of leadership but more with the skills of motivating and inspiring people.

The importance of vision

Effective transformational leaders are those who inspire people and create a vision for the organisation and its future direction. According to *Whitehead*:

> *The big word now associated with leadership is vision. The ability to see the bigger picture. To take the long-term view. What the ultimate objectives of the organisation are and how people can work together to achieve them . . . Perhaps the most important attribute is that a good leader inspires people by creating a climate where it is OK for people to make mistakes and learn from them, rather than what happened in the past which was to blame and punish them. Leading from this position, they gain a higher level of commitment from their people than mere compliance.*[37]

Kahan sees visionary leadership as transformative. It involves greatness, penetrating the ordinary, and requires total involvement. Among the qualities visionary leaders cultivate are imagination, engagement, tangible results and penetrating self-reflection. They engage society with its competitive, divergent viewpoints. Visionary leadership is ultimately about increasing performance but also with the rewards of tangible results to your membership and deep personal satisfaction.[38]

> *Leadership is not about the leader, it is about how he or she builds the confidence of everyone else. Leaders are responsible for both the big structures that serve as the cornerstone of confidence, and for the human touches that shape a positive emotional climate to inspire and motivate people . . . Leaders deliver confidence by espousing high standards in their messages, exemplifying these standards in the conduct they model and establishing formal mechanisms to provide a structure for acting on those standards.*[39]

Critical reflection

'Charisma and the ability truly to inspire and move loyal followers in the desired direction is one of the most controversial and elusive leadership qualities.'

Do you believe charismatic leadership brings about improved individual and organisational performance? Can you relate personal experience(s) of charismatic leadership that has truly inspired? Do you possess charisma?

Personal qualities or charisma

Leadership may be based on the personal qualities, or charisma, of the leader and the manner in which influence is exercised. The concept of charismatic or inspirational leadership is not new and has been applied in the organisational context by writers such as Max Weber (1864–1920).[40] The importance of charisma for effective leadership today is emphasised by *Conger*, who also believes that many of the traits that make a successful leader can be taught, including charisma.

> *Now the big question is whether you are born with charisma or whether you can develop it. I believe you can develop elements of it. For example, you can take courses to improve your speaking skills. You can learn to stage events that send powerful messages. You can learn to think more critically about the status quo and its shortcomings. You can do more on a daily basis to motivate your team. What you simply cannot learn is how to be passionate about what you do. You have to discover that for yourself, and passion is a big part of what drives a charismatic leader. It is also what motivates and inspires those who work for the charismatic leader.*[41]

Is charisma enough?

However, the extent to which charismatic or inspirational leadership helps bring about improvement in organisational performance is open to much debate. *Conger* also draws attention to the danger that the leader's vision, dynamism and inspirational nature are highly attractive to followers, which leads to a natural dependence. Staff see this extraordinary figure as a model to be emulated and the leader's abilities become the yardstick by which they measure their own performance. This is a potential source of leadership derailment. Dependence makes the followers more susceptible to deception.[42]

Dearlove draws attention to the increasing focus on leaders as real people managing in a consensus-seeking manner. 'While traditional views of leadership tend eventually to concentrate on vision and charisma, the message now seems to be that charisma is no longer enough to carry leaders through.'[43] *Bloomfield* also refers to the cult of the individual, supposedly charismatic leader and the danger that this leads businesses into deep water far more often than the application of rational leadership. Too often the charismatic leader, aided and abetted by the language of current management fashion, attempts to 'inspire', to delight with their vision and to produce a mission statement of where the business might be – at the expense of real substance.[44]

Adair argues that to be a truly inspirational leader one must understand the spirit within. All people have the potential for greatness. The inspirational leader connects with the led, appreciates the capabilities of others and through trust will unlock the powers in others. Adair refers to 'the inspired moment' – a recognition and seizure of a brief window of opportunity that can act as a powerful catalyst that inspires both the leader and the led.[45]

Need for visionary leadership

Many writers are calling for leaders at all levels with vision and who can inspire with passion and emotion, as well as deliver bottom-line results. For example, during the American presidential election of 2008 there was considerable debate over the comparative appeal between the experience of Hillary Clinton and the charisma of Barack Obama.

In her discussion of the creation of the democratic enterprise (organisations that can flourish economically and can also be places of excitement and stimulation, fulfilment and tranquillity), *Gratton* maintains that it is the creation of a shared purpose and the role of the leadership team that are most vital. The role of the leader as visionary is fundamental to creating the broad philosophical context of democracy and as the architect of shared purpose.[46]

Referring to the work of Goffee and Jones, *Witzel* suggests: 'Leadership is one of the most vital and yet elusive ingredients in modern business. Leaders provide vision, direction, inspiration, give the business a sense of purpose and at the same time act as a moral compass.'[47] *Goffee and Jones* point out that the need for visionary leadership is becoming increasingly important. Traditional business hierarchies gave managers and workers a sense of their own position and what was expected of them. Now, as these hierarchies break down, it is leaders themselves who must fill the void, helping subordinates to understand their place and purpose. Personal leadership is beginning to replace organisational structure.[48]

> *What sets great leaders apart is their ability to engage those around them in a shared vision of the future. By making the right decisions, they demonstrate their commitment to turning that vision into reality; and by doing so successfully, they instil in others the confidence to trust in their leadership.*
>
> Sir Bryan Nicholson[49]

The inspirational gap

According to a survey by the Chartered Management Institute, the power to inspire is rated highest among desirable leadership qualities. A detailed survey of almost 1,500 practising managers in a broad cross-section of organisations found that the key characteristic that leaders should ideally possess, inspiration, was identified by 55 per cent of managers. However, most leaders appeared to lack this characteristic, with only 11 per cent of respondents saying they experienced this in reality.[50]

The survey from the Chartered Management Institute highlighted a significant 'inspirational gap' in leadership across UK organisations. The Department of Trade and Industry undertook a research project to explore how to start closing this critical leadership inspiration gap.[51] 'It is now accepted that for the UK to maintain its competitiveness there is a growing need for companies to adopt strategies that will enable a greater level of innovation and the provision of higher value and services.' The report is based on a study of 568 followers at different management levels working in a wide variety of organisations. It confirms that today's workforce is more diverse, informed and sophisticated than ever before. Ultimately people are still looking for something different and better in organisational leadership.

Key conclusions of the report include:

■ For the past 30 years there have been increasing amounts of data to suggest that leadership has a lot more to do with inspiration and vision than with straightforward technical competence. Leadership is now recognised as a transferable skill, and it can be developed by continued learning and development throughout a person's career.

■ Managers demand visionary leaders who win not only results but also the trust and respect of their teams. It is the relationship between people that results in action.

■ In order to keep followers motivated and committed in an era of unrelenting change, leaders must be able to create organisation cultures that foster not only performance but also a sense of pride and fun.

A summary of leadership and management is set out in the concept map in Figure 10.8.

LEADERSHIP AND INNOVATION

A 2005 report by the Advanced Institute of Management Research in co-operation with the Chartered Management Institute draws attention to the impact of leadership on innovation.[52] The report refers to the dual role of leaders, first as motivators, inspiring people to transcend the ordinary, and second as architects, designing an organisational environment that enables employees to be innovative. 'The impact of leadership on innovation goes well beyond the motivating effect of the inspirational or charismatic leader. Leaders also affect innovation through organisational design and must create appropriate organisational environments to suit the different innovation processes.' The primary challenges for organisational leaders in promoting innovation are to:

■ recognise and develop appropriate leadership for the different stages of the innovation process; and

■ create organisational contexts that support complete innovation processes of different degrees of novelty.

Conceptual framework

The report distinguishes between leaders who primarily motivate through transformational actions – a 'motivational' perspective – and those who take a more transactional approach and emphasise the co-ordination of organisational tasks – a 'structuralist' perspective. In order to address the question of how leadership affects innovation within organisations, the report proposes a conceptual framework that reflects the complex interaction among leadership, the organisational context and innovation (Figure 10.9).

There is, however, a need for being mindful that leadership:

■ can manifest itself at all levels in the organisation, not just the top;

■ need not be concentrated in the person of a single leader but may act through distributed leadership systems; and

■ sets the organisational context for followers' activities both through motivation and the administrative co-ordination of systems that support innovation.

Figure 10.8   Concept map of leadership and management

LEADERSHIP AND MANAGEMENT

MANAGERS have to ensure their subordinates collectively or separately reach their goals

- MANAGEMENT
- LEADERSHIP

Leadership by function
Leadership by personality

LEADERSHIP
– the ability to ensure subordinates perform their tasks and duties up to the standards required, by inspiration or inducement

Leaders cannot achieve the goals by themselves Subordinates require direction to obtain the goals

Therefore co-operation or coercion required
– Leaders are those individuals who are perceived most frequently to perform those roles and functions which initiate or control behaviour of others towards the achievement of group goals or sub goals (Gibb)

THE ESSENTIALS OF LEADERSHIP
– Social skills
– Ability to communicate
– Flexibility/judgement as to which management style to adopt

ACTION-CENTRED LEADERSHIP (ADAIR)

INDIVIDUAL NEEDS
– Concern for the individual
■ fairness and consistency in disciplinary matters
■ help with training, career prospects with . . .
preparation for retirement
recognition of performance
■ good or adequate with . . .
commendation or helpful criticism
– Job enrichment
– Giving status

Group Needs
Task Needs
Individual Needs

GROUP NEEDS
Defence of the group needs
– laterally and vertically
– Building up teamwork, recognising informal groups
Protection of interests which may lead to disruption e.g. relocation to another site; uneven work loads; accomodation; pay differentials

TASK NEEDS
Task definition
Planning
Allocating work and resources
Controlling quality, pace of work
Monitoring
Amending the plans
Co-ordinating with other groups
Obtaining resources required

No single trait or group of characteristics has been isolated which sets off the leader from members of groups (Jenkins)

Charisma ⟷ Technocrat

FOUR VARIABLES
1 Characteristics/traits of the leader
2 Attitudes of the followers
3 Organisation purpose, technology, ethos, values, structure
4 Social economic and political milieu (McGregor) between countries between cultures

MANAGERS have the authority to direct work and behaviour
LEADERS have influence through example, persuading, motivating, teaching

■ Group tasks usually complex
■ Organisations require stability not continuous change in leader

■ Situational Theory Leadership is specific to the situation under investigation, i.e. a leader emerges in response to the problem or challenge

■ Personnel with highly technical skills possessing wide sapiential (knowledge) gives authority/ leadership

Leadership may be situationally governed
– arising due to a set of circumstances
Some managers are more suitable to operate in one set of situations than others

LEADERSHIP TRAITS
■ Intelligence
■ Self-confidence
■ Initiative taking
■ Empathy
■ Self-awareness
■ Objectivity (human relationships)

Use of authority by manager / Area of freedom by subordinate

tell	sell	consult	share	delegate	abdicate
1	2	3	4	5	6	7

1 Tell them
2 Tell them and sell it to them
3 Tell them and talk about it
4 Tentative decision and talk
5 Problem – talk and manager decides
6 Manager gives limits; all discuss, group decides
7 Manager gives limits; group discusses and decides

■ Organisational leadership
■ Personal leadership . . . . contribution by the individual in the post showing – charisma/energy/vision

Authoritarian ⟷ Democratic

KINDS OF LEADERSHIP
Formal
– appointed in the hierarchy by the management
Informal
– exercises influence but is not in formal position; can initiate or block actions; can be in conflict with the formal leader; can set the group norms

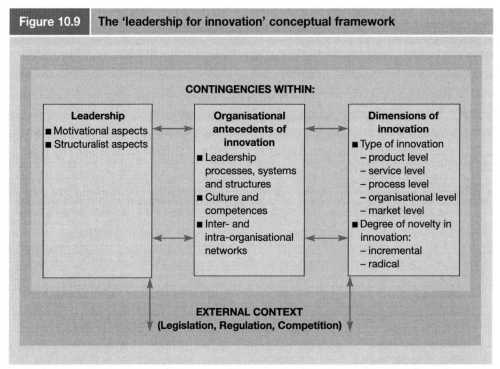

| Figure 10.9 | The 'leadership for innovation' conceptual framework |

Source: From Munshi, N. *et al.* *Leading for Innovation: The Impact of Leadership on Innovation*, Advanced Institute of Management Research (AIM) (2005), Figure 5, p. 18. Reproduced with thanks to AIM fellows and scholars: A. Munshi, A. Oke, P. Puranam, M. Stafylarakis, S. Towells, K. Moeslein and A. Neely.

THE LEADERSHIP RELATIONSHIP

Whatever the perceived approach to leadership, the most important point is the nature of the leadership relationship and the manner in which the leader influences the behaviour and actions of other people. Leadership is a dynamic form of behaviour and there are a number of variables that affect the leadership relationship. For example, *Bass* reviews leadership influence in terms of persuasion, a power relation, an instrument of goal achievement, an emerging effect of interaction and the initiation of structure.[53] Four major variables are identified by *McGregor* as:

- the characteristics of the leader;
- the attitude, needs and other personal characteristics of the followers;
- the nature of the organisation, such as its purpose, its structure, and the tasks to be performed; and
- the social, economic and political environment.

McGregor concludes that 'leadership is not a property of the individual, but a complex relationship among these variables'.[54]

According to *Kouzes and Posner*, 'credibility is the foundation of leadership'. From extensive research in over 30 countries and response to the question of what people 'look for and admire in a leader, in a person whose direction they would willingly follow', people have consistently replied that they want

leaders who exemplify four qualities: they want them to be honest, forward-looking, inspiring and competent. In our research our respondents strongly agree that they want leaders with integrity and trustworthiness, with vision and a sense of direction, with enthusiasm and passion, and with expertise and a track record for getting things done.[55]

Fullan refers to the importance of relationship building as a basic component of the change process and effective leadership: 'Leaders must be consummate relationship builders with diverse people and groups – especially with people different from themselves. Effective leaders constantly foster purposeful interaction and problem solving, and are wary of easy consensus.'[56]

Power and leadership influence

Within an organisation, leadership influence will be dependent upon the type of power that the leader can exercise over the followers. The exercise of power is a social process which helps to explain how different people can influence the behaviour/actions of others. Five main sources of power upon which the influence of the leader is based have been identified by *French and Raven* as reward power, coercive power, legitimate power, referent power and expert power.[57] We shall consider these in terms of the manager (as a leader) and subordinate relationship.

- **Reward power** is based on the subordinate's *perception* that the leader has the ability and resources to obtain rewards for those who comply with directives; for example, pay, promotion, praise, recognition, increased responsibilities, allocation and arrangement of work, granting of privileges.
- **Coercive power** is based on fear and the subordinate's *perception* that the leader has the ability to punish or to bring about undesirable outcomes for those who do not comply with directives; for example, withholding pay rises, promotion or privileges; allocation of undesirable duties or responsibilities; withdrawal of friendship or support; formal reprimands or possibly dismissal. This is in effect the opposite of reward power.
- **Legitimate power** is based on the subordinate's *perception* that the leader has a right to exercise influence because of the leader's role or position in the organisation. Legitimate power is based on authority, for example that of managers and supervisors within the hierarchical structure of an organisation. Legitimate power is therefore 'position' power because it is based on the role of the leader in the organisation, and not on the nature of the personal relationship with others.
- **Referent power** is based on the subordinate's *identification* with the leader. The leader exercises influence because of perceived attractiveness, personal characteristics, reputation or what is called 'charisma'. For example, a particular manager may not be in a position to reward or punish certain subordinates, but may still exercise power over the subordinates because the manager commands their respect or esteem.
- **Expert power** is based on the subordinate's *perception* of the leader as someone who is competent and who has some special knowledge or expertise in a given area. Expert power is based on credibility and clear evidence of knowledge or expertise; for example, the expert knowledge of 'functional' specialists such as the human resources manager, management accountant or systems analyst. The expert power is usually limited to narrow, well-defined areas or specialisms.

Subordinates' perception of influence

It is important to note that these sources of power are based on the subordinates' perception of the influence of the leader, whether it is real or not. For example, if a leader has the ability to control rewards and punishments but subordinates do not believe this, then in effect the leader has no reward or coercive power. Similarly, if subordinates in a line department believe a manager in a (different) staff department has executive authority over them then even if, *de facto*, that manager has no such authority there is still a perceived legitimate power.

French and Raven point out that the five sources of power are interrelated and the use of one type of power (for example, coercive) may affect the ability to use another type of power (for example, referent). Furthermore, the same person may exercise different types of power, in particular circumstances and at different times.

Other sources of power

Finlay suggests that in addition to the five sources of power identified by French and Raven can be added:

- **personal power**, supported and trusted by their colleagues and subordinates; and
- **connection power**, which results from personal and professional access to key people and information.[58]

Yukl suggests that a further relevant source of power is **control over information**.[59]

> *You have to look at leadership through the eyes of the followers and you have to live the message. What I have learned is that people become motivated when you guide them to the source of their own power and when you make heroes out of employees who personify what you want to see in the organisation.*
>
> Anita Roddick[60]

Power, responsibility and wisdom

Lloyd suggests that the way we think about leadership is a contributory factor to the leadership crisis. Leadership has traditionally been associated with those who have power and there is a need to re-examine the core relationship between power and responsibility. Rather than gaining and keeping power for ourselves, more emphasis should be given to unifying consideration of the two concepts together with greater attention to the subject of wisdom.

> *The new agenda moves us from that narrow focus to a much broader concept of leadership that is more concerned with how power is used, i.e. in whose interest power is used. This explicitly recognises that the use of power is deeply values driven . . . We need to give much greater attention to the values agenda by exploring wisdom, then seeing that emphasis reflected as wise leadership.*[61]

Critical reflection

'Despite the vast amount of writing on the subject by both academics and practising managers, it is extremely difficult to give a precise and agreed meaning of leadership. Nor is there agreement on one best model or style of leadership, or how leadership potential can best be developed.'

Do you find this confusing and a hindrance to your studies? What do you believe are the essential and distinctive characteristics that make for an effective leader?

NO ONE BEST FORM OF LEADERSHIP

We have seen that there are many alternative forms and styles of managerial leadership. Within an organisation different individuals may fulfil the functions of leadership and there are many different styles of leadership. A potential danger with the contingency approach is that the manager may appear to lack consistency in leadership style. However, although subordinates may reasonably expect some degree of consistency from the manager in approaching the same type of problem with the same style, this is not to say that different types of problems should be approached in the same manner. Subordinates would ordinarily expect a different style of managerial leadership according to the contingencies of the situation.

The right leader for the right situation

A good manager will clearly recognise that different styles of leadership are called for in different situations. As an obvious and (hopefully) extreme example, emergency situations such as a major fire in a building demand an assertive, directive style of action. As *Rajan* also points out: 'Of course, different leadership styles are needed to cope with different situations: for example, the autocratic style makes sense when an organisation is in deep trouble and needs to achieve a rapid turn-around. That style would be counter-productive when the organisation is in a growth situation.'[76] And *Stern* maintains that although in more carefree times business gurus exalted leaders who admitted to frailty, this is not so any more. The task of sustaining growth in a sluggish market calls for driven, leather-skinned bosses. Instead of touchy-feely management the quality of 'mental toughness' is needed to help elite performers to prevail.[77]

Different types of leadership may also be most appropriate at different stages in the development of a business organisation. Leadership can also vary between public and private sectors and depend upon the size of the organisation. A primary challenge for organisational leaders in promoting innovation is:

> *Recognise and develop appropriate leadership for the different stages of the innovation process. How leaders are selected, supported, evaluated, motivated and developed is likely to differ depending upon the stage of the innovation process they are responsible for. For instance, transformational leadership skills may be more useful in early-stage innovation activity, such as R & D and product development, but transactional leadership skills are also essential to the smooth functioning of commercialisation.*[78]

LEADERS OF THE FUTURE

Gratton points out that while we are part of organisations shaped by technology that created the patents, ideas and innovations that brought success, the past will not bring sustainable competitive advantage for the future. To do this we have to build the potential of people in our organisations, the knowledge they bring and their commitment and enthusiasm. Building human potential demands a new agenda, a new set of challenges for leaders and a redefined set of managerial capabilities. This new agenda creates a set of expectations of the leaders. Gratton sets out four expectations as the message for leaders.

- **Expectation 1: dream collectively** – create a time and a process for you and your colleagues to dream about the future; create enthusiasm and excitement and a vision for the future; view the present as a pathway to the future; allow people to work independently but within the frame of the general direction; and work to identify and co-ordinate the major themes for action.
- **Expectation 2: balance the short term with the longer term** – think in the past, the present and the future; be aware of the human scale of change and create plans of action that reflect human time scales and a capacity in human potential; build a vision for the future that engages people and allows them to understand their future role.
- **Expectation 3: build an organisation that values people** – treat people with respect and have their ideas taken seriously and allow them to believe they can make a difference; be aware of the need to create communication channels with employees; demonstrate a commitment to people; treat people with politeness, respect and dignity and create a strong role model for others to follow.
- **Expectation 4: understand the reality of the organisation** – create a deep, shared understanding of the current state of the business, and examine the metaphor of the organisation; put the building of a highly committed workforce at the centre of strategy; build a model of your organisation around high levels of trust, commitment and inspiration; develop an understanding of process fairness and justice, and understand employees' perceptions of integrity, consistency and pride.[79]

New skills and competencies

Bennis hails the arrival of new leadership and suggests that 'the leaders of the future will have to cast off the heavy burden of command and control, hierarchically based leadership'. Leaders will have to learn an entirely new set of skills and four competencies will determine the success of new leadership.

1 **The new leader understands and practises the power of appreciation** – as a generalisation most organisations are woefully neglectful of bestowing acknowledgement or appreciation, yet it is one of the most powerful motivators, especially for knowledge workers.
2 **The new leader keeps reminding people of what is important** – organisations drift into entropy and bureaucratisation of imagination when they forget what's important. Reminding people of what is important can give meaning and value to work, and collective focused energy.
3 **The new leader generates and sustains trust** – the terms of the new social contract of work have changed and no one can depend on lifelong loyalty or commitment to any organisation. Trust has powerful connotations and the ingredients are a combination of competencies, constancy, caring, fairness, candour and, most of all, authenticity.
4 **The new leader and the led are intimate allies** – new leadership is all about great leaders being made by great groups and by organisations that create the social architecture of respect and dignity, and great leadership brings that about. Without each other, the leader and the led are culturally impoverished.

> *The post-bureaucratic organization requires a new kind of alliance between leaders and the led. Today's organizations are evolving into federations, networks, clusters, cross-functional teams, temporary systems, ad hoc task forces, lattices, modules, matrices – almost anything but pyramids with their obsolete top–down leadership. The new leader will encourage healthy dissent and value those followers courageous enough to say no. It will go to the leader who exults in cultural differences and knows that diversity is the best hope for long-term survival and success. This does not mark the end of leadership. Rather the need for a new, far more subtle and indirect form of influence for leaders to be effective.*[80]

In his discussion on the future of management, *Hamel* argues the point that in any constitutional democracy success does not depend upon brilliant leadership. If democracies are more resilient than large companies it is not because they are better led. In a democracy, the pace of change depends only tangentially on the vision and moral courage of those in power. 'The real challenge, then, isn't to hire or grow great leaders, but to build companies that can thrive with less-than-perfect leaders.'[81]

Critical reflection

'There is much commentary on the need for less hierarchical structures and for a changed culture of leadership based on skills and competencies throughout the organisation as a whole.'

But how realistic is this? What does such a changed culture actually entail and how can leadership potential best be developed? And what do you see as the future of leadership?

Chapter 15:
Trait Theories of Leadership

Trait Theories of Leadership

Traits
Enduring and distinguishing personal characteristics that may be inherited, learned, or developed.

Trait theories
Models that attempt to explain leadership effectiveness by articulation of physical, psychological, and social characteristics, as well as abilities, knowledge, and expertise.

Traits are enduring and distinguishing personal characteristics that may be inherited, learned, or developed. Traits include psychological characteristics such as optimism, pessimism, self-confidence, and sociability, as well as physical characteristics such as energy and stamina. A person's traits also include things like intelligence, maturity, and integrity.

In the early 1900s, leadership **trait theories** were prominent. Trait theories are models that attempt to explain leadership effectiveness by articulation of physical, psychological, and social characteristics, as well as abilities, knowledge, and expertise. In many cases, early theorists focused on studying people thought to be excellent leaders, so this method came to be called the "Great Man Approach." Many of these studies in fact focused only on men, and in many cases the studies paid an inordinate amount of attention to characteristics such as height, "bearing" (e.g., military posture), and neatness.[63] These studies were seriously flawed, and subsequent research did not support a relationship between these traits and leadership success.[64] Another inaccurate assumption in many of these theories was that all traits—physical and psychological alike—were immutable. In fact, some of what these researchers considered traits can and do change over time.

Trait theories operate implicitly and powerfully when it comes to what people believe about leadership. Unfortunately, much of what people believe about leadership traits is based on unfounded research, folklore, or even cultural stereotypes. For example, ask three people what they believe to be a good leader's most important characteristics. You are likely to get a wide range of responses, only some of which may be relevant to leadership. Also, it is highly unlikely that all three people will agree about which traits are most important—what one person feels are the five most important qualities of a leader may be another person's bottom five, and researchers might say none of them are important! For these reasons, it is important to understand what implicit trait models you may have developed and to compare these with what research suggests.

Despite the fact that a good deal of the research on traits has been flawed, several categories of traits or characteristics do seem to be somewhat related to leadership. Numerous studies have been conducted over the years, and the results of these studies are presented in ■Exhibit 2.10. These traits and characteristics can be shown in six categories: personality, physical characteristics, intelligence and ability, social background, work-related characteristics, and social characteristics.[65]

Some of the characteristics in Exhibit 2.10 are actually traits, whereas others are more correctly described as knowledge, competencies, or expertise. Although each of these characteristics affects leadership, rarely do good leaders possess all of the traits listed in the exhibit. Moreover, some people who possess many of these characteristics are not effective leaders at all. This is because traits or characteristics alone are not sufficient to explain a person's effectiveness as a leader. Because of this, in the mid-1960s, researchers began to turn their focus toward how leaders *behaved* rather than what qualities they seemed to possess.

■Exhibit **2.10**

Leadership Traits Identified in Research[66]					
Personality	Physical Characteristics	Intelligence and Ability	Social Background	Work-Related Characteristics	Social Characteristics

Emotional intelligence
Emotional control/
  stability
Empathy
Integrity/honesty
Conscientiousness
Self-monitoring
Flexibility/
  adaptability
Open to experience
Comfortable with
  uncertainty/chaos
Divergent thinking
Assertive/
  aggressive
Extroverted
Enthusiastic
Confident
	Age
	Energetic
	Appearance/
	  grooming
		Cognitive ability
		Intelligence
		Knowledge
		Creativity
		Comprehension
		  skills
		Oral and written
		  communication
		  skills
			Education
			Social status
			Mobility
				Achievement drive
				Responsibility/
				  power drive
				Motivation to lead
				Vision
				Stewardship
				Task/performance
				  orientation
				Entrepreneurial
				Explicit/tacit
				  knowledge of
				  the business
				Competence
				  expertise
				Administrative
				  expertise
					Ability to
					  influence and
					  persuade
					Ability to inspire
					Charisma
					Empowerment
					  of others
					Ability to
					  delegate
					Administrative
					  expertise
					Trust/credibility
					Diplomatic
					Shows
					  appreciation
					Desires to serve
					  others
					Team oriented

Behavior Models and Approaches to Leadership

The behavioral approach to studying and understanding leadership effectiveness goes beyond personal characteristics and traits. It looks at the actual behaviors leaders engaged in when guiding and influencing others. These models drew on disciplines such as sociology, psychology, and anthropology, and they examined human interaction in an organizational environment.

Ohio State Studies: Consideration and Initiating Structure

Toward the middle of the twentieth century, researchers at Ohio State University surveyed leaders and found two major dimensions of behaviors associated with leadership: consideration and initiating structure.[67] **Consideration** refers to people-oriented behaviors such as respect, openness to employees' ideas, and concern for employees' well-being. Leaders who emphasize consideration would likely create trusting, supportive, and amiable environments marked by open communication and teamwork.

Initiating structure includes behaviors related to task and goal orientation, such as giving clear directions, monitoring employees' performance, and planning and setting work schedules and deadlines. Leaders who emphasize structure are likely to emphasize efficiency and effectiveness and to support employees by identifying what needs to be done in order for them to succeed at the job or task. The Ohio State studies started a trend that focused on which style was the "best."[68]

University of Michigan Studies: Production- and Employee-Oriented Behavior

Around the same time the Ohio State studies were under way, researchers at the University of Michigan began studying the behavior of effective supervisors.[69] They identified two dimensions of behavior. The first dimension, *production-oriented behavior*, focuses on efficiency, costs, adhering to schedules, and meeting deadlines. These super-

Consideration
People-oriented behaviors such as respect, openness to employees' ideas and concern for employees' well-being.

Initiating structure
Behaviors related to task and goal orientation, such as giving clear directions, monitoring employees' performance, and planning and setting work schedules and deadlines.

visors focused their energies on job tasks and work procedures and regarded employees as a means to the end of achieving work goals.

Supervisors who favored production-oriented behavior tended to be less effective than those favoring *employee-oriented behavior*. Supervisors who favored the employee-oriented behavior approach were supportive of employees, emphasized relationships, and focused on engaging employees through setting and assisting in the attainment of high-performance goals. The study concluded that employees preferred employee-oriented behavior and would perform better when supervisors embraced it.

Leadership Grid

Researchers Robert Blake and Jane Mouton of the University of Texas built on the University of Michigan and Ohio studies.[70] In 1964, they proposed that managerial behaviors could be plotted along horizontal and vertical axes measuring concern for people and concern for production, and then could be grouped into management or leadership styles. Now called the *Leadership Grid*, this model is still in use today, and it has been periodically updated.[71] Five of the leadership styles are well known and are presented in ▤Exhibit 2.11. As you can see, behavioral emphasis on people is measured on

▤Exhibit **2.11**

The leadership grid presents five leadership styles.

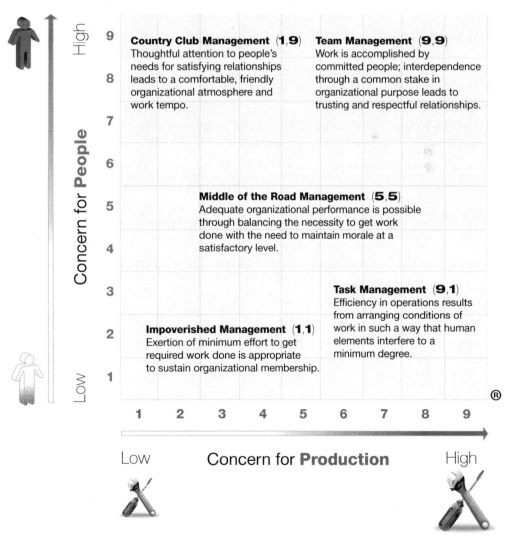

Country Club Management (**1**,**9**)
Thoughtful attention to people's needs for satisfying relationships leads to a comfortable, friendly organizational atmosphere and work tempo.

Team Management (**9**,**9**)
Work is accomplished by committed people; interdependence through a common stake in organizational purpose leads to trusting and respectful relationships.

Middle of the Road Management (**5**,**5**)
Adequate organizational performance is possible through balancing the necessity to get work done with the need to maintain morale at a satisfactory level.

Task Management (**9**,**1**)
Efficiency in operations results from arranging conditions of work in such a way that human elements interfere to a minimum degree.

Impoverished Management (**1**,**1**)
Exertion of minimum effort to get required work done is appropriate to sustain organizational membership.

Concern for People

Low   **Concern for Production**   High

the vertical axis, and the focus on production is shown on the horizontal axis. Although the model indicates the positive attributes of each style, the research team contended that the team management style worked best.[72]

Contingency Approaches to Leadership

Contingency approaches to leadership
Models and theories of leadership that take into account leader behavior and various aspects of the organizational situation and/or characteristics of followers.

Contingency approaches to leadership are based on the perspective that when it comes to leadership and management, one size does not fit all. These models and theories of leadership take into account leader behavior *and* various aspects of the organizational situation and/or characteristics of followers. In other words, different situations call for different approaches. For example, leading a small team of people in an entrepreneurial start-up will call for a different approach than leading a large division of a multinational company. In the start-up, you will rely heavily on interpersonal communication, strong personal relationships, and inspiring people by painting a picture of the future. In a large division, you can't possibly have personal relationships with everyone, so you will need to rely on reaching people in other ways—via webinars, speeches, e-mail, and the like. You will also need to rely on organizational processes and culture to guide people's behavior. Contingency models state that many different variables come into play, and that each situation is unique and requires its own approach. In the next four sections, we will look at several contingency approaches to leadership.

Fiedler's Contingency Theory

Fiedler's contingency theory
Theory stating that leadership effectiveness is dependent on the characteristics of the leader and the characteristics of the situation.

Relationship-oriented leaders
Leaders who emphasize good relationships and being liked by employees.

Task-oriented leaders
Leaders who focus on accomplishments and seek to ensure that employees perform well on the job.

Fiedler's contingency theory, developed by Fred Fiedler in 1967, states that leadership effectiveness is dependent on the characteristics of the leader and the characteristics of the situation.[73] Fiedler proposed that *leader style* is either task oriented or relationship oriented. **Relationship-oriented leaders** emphasize good relationships and being liked by employees. **Task-oriented leaders** focus on accomplishments and seek to ensure that employees perform well on the job. The theory also states that changing one's leadership style is difficult. Effectiveness, therefore, is dependent on matching a leader's style to the situation.[74]

Situational Leadership Theory

Situational leadership theory
Contingency model that links leader style with followers' readiness for tasks.

Situational leadership theory links leader style with followers' readiness for tasks. This model, developed by Paul Hersey and Ken Blanchard, focuses on followers' readiness to do their jobs and leaders' responsibility to notice this and adapt accordingly.[75] The term *readiness* refers to the extent to which employees are capable, confident, and willing to complete an assigned task or perform well on the job. These factors enable a leader to determine how much guidance and direction employees need.

The model suggests that when leaders attend to these factors, they can then vary their level of attention to task and relationship behaviors and choose one of four styles to employ. The four leadership styles identified by Hersey and Blanchard are listed here:

- *Telling style:* Appropriate when followers are unable, unwilling, or insecure—they need clear direction, close supervision, and guidance
- *Selling style:* Appropriate when employees are unable to complete tasks, but they are willing and/or confident
- *Participating style:* Can be used when employees are able, but unwilling or insecure
- *Delegating style:* Can be used when employees are able, willing, or confident

The situational theory is somewhat appealing in that it focuses on *followers* and their competencies and capabilities, or their progress from immaturity to maturity. Leaders who can accurately diagnose followers' readiness are more likely to match their leadership behavior to employee needs. That said, the model assumes that leaders can accurately read followers' readiness. Unfortunately, that is not always the case. You may have had an experience in which a leader didn't match his or her style to your level of readiness. Maybe you worked on a team, for example, where the leader gave far too many instructions and treated you as if you didn't know what you were doing. This, by the way, is a common mistake for new managers. They think they have to direct everything, and they ignore the fact that they need to adjust their behavior to people and situations.

Path-Goal Theory

Path-goal theory
A contingency approach to leadership stating that the leader is responsible for motivating employees to attain goals.

Path-goal theory states that a leader is responsible for motivating employees to attain goals.[76] The path-goal theory is based on the expectancy theory of motivation, covered in Chapter 3. In this model, effective leaders boost employee motivation (and presumably effectiveness) by illuminating the path toward organizational and personal goals and linking rewards to goal attainment. Leaders must ensure that the path to the goal is free of obstacles, that goals are meaningful, and that rewards are valued. Path-goal theory supports the notion that leaders can change their behaviors and styles.[77] According to this theory, leaders can choose to behave in four different ways, depending on employees' goal-related needs and expectations, as shown in ■Exhibit 2.12.

■Exhibit **2.12**

Path-goal theory: Choose a style that helps people reach their goals.

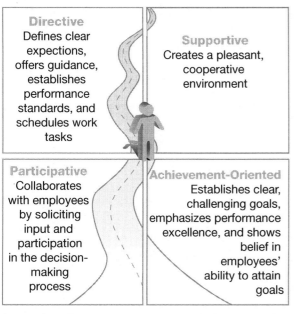

Directive
Defines clear expectations, offers guidance, establishes performance standards, and schedules work tasks

Supportive
Creates a pleasant, cooperative environment

Participative
Collaborates with employees by soliciting input and participation in the decision-making process

Achievement-Oriented
Establishes clear, challenging goals, emphasizes performance excellence, and shows belief in employees' ability to attain goals

Source: House, Robert J., and T. R. Mitchell. 1986. Path-goal theory of leadership. In *Decision making: An organizational behavior approach*, ed. J. M. Pennings. Princeton, NJ: Markus Wiener Publishers.

Leader Substitutes Model

The **leader substitutes model** states that certain characteristics of people or of the situation can make direct leadership unnecessary.[78] For example, when employees are knowledgeable, well trained, and highly motivated, people often don't need close supervision. They will self-regulate to get the job done.

This theory is quite useful, because it challenges the traditional idea that people *have* to be managed and led, and that if they are not, they will avoid work entirely or not work to their full potential. The notion that people need to be cajoled, told, and controlled, colors many of the early theories of management and leadership. Today, most people assume that others are willing and capable. This, then, leads to the possibility of "substituting" personalized leadership with clear goals and a compelling vision, along with an empowering, resonant culture.

Leader substitutes model
A contingency model of leadership that states that certain characteristics of people or of the situation can make direct leadership unnecessary.

Contingency approaches to leadership are quite popular today, and many variations and models are used in organizations. For a student of management, probably the most useful lesson is that it is important to attend to one's own leadership behavior as well as the situation, employees' abilities, confidence, self-efficacy, and motivation. Understanding these dimensions can be quite helpful in determining how to influence, engage, and support people.

The Study of Leadership Continues

As you can see from this discussion of common theories and models that seek to explain leadership, there is tremendous interest in this topic. This interest makes sense: If we can better understand how to guide, direct, and influence people, organizations will be more effective and probably more enjoyable places to work. Each of the theories you have studied in this section has a kernel of wisdom. To utilize the theories, however, you need to discern what aspects of the research apply to work and organizations today. This means you need to be an educated consumer of knowledge—carefully evaluating the models that you hold implicitly and explicitly. You also need to be able to discern which models are operating in the minds of others and in organizations. Very often, these models are not overt or explicit—they are embedded in organizational culture and systems. It can be difficult to identify which model or models are operating. If you do, however, you will be in a much better position to understand what drives behavior in an organization.

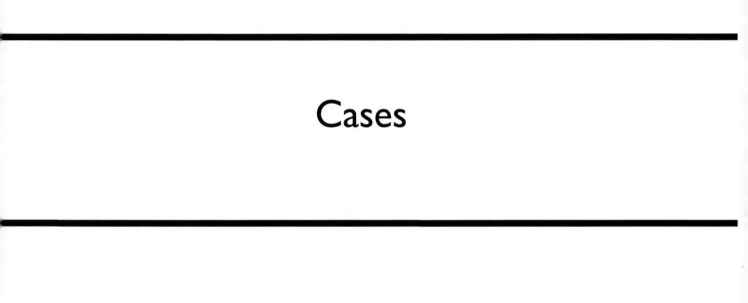

Cases

MANAGEMENT IN THE NEWS

Managing the mood is crucial

Stefan Stern

'Moaning is not a management task,' Rupert Stadler, chief executive of the German carmaker Audi, told this newspaper this month. 'We can all join in the moaning, or we can make a virtue out of the plight. I am rather doing the latter.' Mr Stadler is choosing to accentuate the positive. After all, who wants to be led by a pessimist? Jeffrey Immelt, chief executive of

General Electric, keeps his darker thoughts to himself while maintaining a public breeziness. As he told the Harvard Business School conference last October: 'You can't sit there in front of over 300,000 people and say: "I don't know what to do!" You have to say: "We're gonna nail this one, and here's why!"'

Management in the news – continued

Leaders have to be resilient. At the moment the bad news is coming not in single spies, but in battalions. Tough trading conditions test character as much as business acumen. Your physical and emotional response to these challenges is just as important as the decisions you actually take, because employees are more sensitive to mood than leaders often realise. And moods are contagious. Research carried out at New York University and the University of Michigan found that in 70 different teams, people working together in meetings ended up sharing moods – whether good or bad – within two hours. And bad moods spread faster than good ones. In their 2001 Harvard Business Review article 'Primal Leadership', Daniel Goleman, Richard Boyatzis and Annie McKie argued that one of the key duties of leadership is to manage your emotions with care. 'Moods that start at the top tend to move the fastest because everyone watches the boss,' they wrote. 'They take their emotional cues from him. Even when the boss isn't highly visible his attitude affects the mood of his direct reports, and a domino effect ripples throughout the company.'

Leaders risk reverting to earlier, less skilful versions of themselves under pressure. They can slip into a default mode of frantic busyness, which to colleagues may look a lot like panic. They can find themselves instinctively adopting a crude command and control management style, even though they know this might not be the best way to deal with an intelligent, questioning (but anxious) workforce. Instead leaders should be trying to create a greater sense of safety. There are four things they can do to achieve this.

- First, they must take prompt and considered action in the face of any crisis.
- Second, leaders need to communicate honestly and consistently.
- Third, leaders have to make an emotional connection with the workforce. This is not a time to be remote or aloof. That will only add to the sense of uncertainty.
- Lastly, leaders need to inspire. A 'call to arms' can work if it follows on from the sort of confidence-boosting measures described above. But it will fall flat if the leader has failed to make a strong connection with his colleagues, and they are too fearful to be able to buy into it.

So yes, the way leaders behave matters. Temperament and character can help stop a bad situation from getting worse. But markets are tough, and recovery seems a long way off. Mr Stadler is going to need all his optimism.

Source: Stern, S. 'Managing the Mood Is Crucial', *Financial Times*, 23 March 2009. Copyright © 2009 The Financial Times Limited, reproduced with permission.

Discussion questions

1 What does this article tell us about the qualities or traits needed to be a good leader?

2 Analyse the article using Hersey and Blanchard's situational leadership model. Which of the four 'situations' is described? What skills would you add to those suggested in the article to enable managers to lead effectively in these circumstances?

CASE STUDY

Being Apple: Steve Jobs

Steve Jobs is currently CEO of Apple and one of the world's best-known business leaders. The many biographies of Jobs on the internet[82] agree on the basic details. He was born in 1955 in California. In 1976, he and Steve Wozniak founded the Apple Computer Company. The next year saw the launch of the company's second computer – the Apple II – whose success established Apple as one of the main brands in the fledgling personal computer (PC) industry. Apple went public in 1980 and by 1983 Jobs was looking for an experienced corporate manager to oversee the company's continuing expansion; he hired John Sculley from Pepsi Cola. In 1984, Apple launched the Macintosh,[83] whose innovative design was surely one of the key steps forward in the development of today's user-friendly PCs.

In 1985, Jobs fell out with the Apple board and with Sculley and resigned from the company. He went on to found the computer company NeXT, whose workstation products were seen as innovative and influential, but which were too expensive for mass market success. By the early 1990s, NeXT was concentrating on software rather than hardware, and Apple was experiencing significant financial problems as the PC market started to mature. In 1996, Apple bought NeXT and installed Jobs as interim CEO in 1997. Jobs was back and set about some radical surgery to improve Apple's profitability. The technology that arrived with the NeXT purchase allowed a new operating system to be developed and Jobs was closely associated with the development and launch of the brightly-coloured and inspirational iMac in 1998.

The 'i' prefix was adopted by Apple for a series of further innovations as its renaissance under Jobs continued, including the launch in 2001 of the spectacularly successful iPod music player and the iTunes service to support it. This success has provided the company with a whole new set of strategic options in music and entertainment. Then came the the iPhone in 2007 and the Macbook Air, produced from an A4 envelope at its launch in 2008.[84] Steve Jobs, however, is not someone to concentrate his efforts on just a single industry. In 1986, he bought a computer graphics operation from Lucasfilm and renamed it Pixar, which became one of the leading players in computer animation. In partnership with Disney it produced a stream of immensely successful animation movies from *Toy Story* (1995) to the surprising, multi-award-winning box-office hit *Wall-e* (2008) whose character Eve owes

Source: Kimberly White/Reuters

Where would they be without him? Apple's way of doing business has been strongly influenced by its charismatic founder Steve Jobs.

more than a little to Apple design principles. In 2006, Disney and Pixar merged, leaving Jobs as a significant shareholder in Disney and a member of the Disney board.

Cool entrepreneurship

At one level, Steve Jobs can be seen as one of the group of successful young men who made the information revolution happen over the last three decades. These new entrepreneurs didn't fit the traditional model of the buttoned-down businessman – they weren't always academically successful (like Michael Dell, Jobs dropped out of college), they dressed casually and thought unconventionally. While they may differ greatly in leadership style and manner, they share a dedicated, driven, even obsessive approach to work coupled to a strong vision of the change they want to create. There has always, however, been something distinctive about the Apple way of doing things, resulting in the fierce loyalty that often inspires Apple users. As one commentator put it:

> Lodged in the DNA of Silicon Valley, there is a rebel gene known as Apple Computer. Most of the other ingredients are the generally uniform, inoffensive elements you would expect to find in the soul of an engineer . . . The Apple gene comes from an altogether different place. Its essence is one part design flair, two parts marketing hype. It carries elements of risk-taking and inventiveness. It is closely intertwined with the technical drive that pervades Silicon Valley and is the source of occasional startling originality, yet the technology is always subservient to

something else. If Apple's genetic make-up stands apart, it owes much to Steve Jobs.[85]

Evidence that Apple is centred on the personality of its leader is plentiful. Jobs supplies the inspiration and vision and is the company's face. When there is a key new product to launch, it is usually the CEO who reveals it to the world, having been personally involved in whatever it took to bring the product into being. As a recent report observed, his keynote speeches at Apple conferences are 'more like rock concerts than corporate events',[86] with Jobs centre stage.

What is it about Steve Jobs' leadership that commands such attention? He values pure creativity very highly, but in the thousands of words written about him on the internet, adjectives such as 'tolerant' or 'easygoing' do not feature very often. The words 'passionate, charming, inspirational, abrasive'[87] are much more representative, with many expressing much stronger views. Jobs seems to be someone who sets himself very high standards and then demands the same of everyone around him. This can lead to disappointment, frustration, anger and – on occasion – harsh treatment of those who are seen as having let him and the company down. Jobs provided an insight into this mentality in an interview in 1995 with the Smithsonian Institution:[88]

I always considered part of my job was to keep the quality level of people in the organizations I work with very high. That's what I consider one of the few things I actually can contribute individually . . . to instil in the organization the goal of only having 'A' players. . . . the difference between the worst taxi cab driver and the best taxi cab driver to get you crosstown Manhattan might be two to one. The best one will get you there in fifteen minutes, the worst one will get you there in a half an hour. . . . In the field that I'm in the difference between the best person and the worst person is about a hundred to one or more. The difference between a good software person and a great software person is fifty to one. . . . Therefore, I have found, not just in software, but in everything I've done it really pays to go after the best people in the world. It's painful when you have some people who are not the best people in the world and you have to get rid of them; but I found that my job has sometimes exactly been that: to get rid of some people who didn't measure up and I've always tried to do it in a humane way. But nonetheless it has to be done and it is never fun.

Although Jobs became and remained wealthy over most of his career, his motivation seems not to centre on money. His annual salary as Apple's CEO is famously set at $1. What drives him is innovation: he is the man who wants 'to put a ding in the universe'.[89] This means not purely technical innovation, but the ability to imagine products that are revolutionary in their impact on everyday life. Design and marketing have been integral to the Apple appeal, resulting in some truly transformative (and very successful) products like the Macintosh and the iPod, but also many that did not really connect commercially. This demanding agenda has had its costs, both for the company and for Jobs personally. Business strategy commentators sometimes observe that the real money is to be made by changing the way a business works, not by pure innovation.

Technical innovation will earn you lots of adoring fans (think Apple). Business-model innovation will earn you lots of money (think Dell) . . . If your cool new thing doesn't generate enough money to cover costs and make a profit, it isn't innovation. It's art.[90]

If wealth is the scorecard, then Steve Jobs, who is at 178 on the 2009 Forbes list of the world's richest people, doesn't come close to Bill Gates at number one or Michael Dell at 25.[91] The overall impression though is that this is not the point for Jobs; changing the world is more important than building the biggest pile of money.

The succession problem

The comparison with Bill Gates leads to another issue that often crops up for organisations that are dominated by a strong and charismatic leader: that of succession. A recent business news article[92] pointed out that Microsoft had recently gone to some lengths to plan for Bill Gates' gradual retirement from the company. Gates' role had been split into two, with a successor lined up within the company for each part. The pre-announced two-year transition was intended to reassure the markets about the future for a post-Gates Microsoft. At Apple, things weren't so clear. In August 2004, Jobs underwent surgery for a rare form of pancreatic cancer. He survived and was back at work after just one month; and amidst much speculation he took a further six months of medical leave in 2009. His brush with mortality caused many to wonder about Apple's prospects without him, although Jobs himself seems sanguine;

Remembering that I'll be dead soon is the most important tool I've ever encountered to help me make the big choices in life.[93]

Nevertheless, this remains an important question for the company. A quote from venture capitalist Michael Moritz sums up Jobs' importance to Apple:

Steve is an utterly remarkable man – one of the most interesting, original and creative businessmen of the last 50 years. His achievements at both Apple and Pixar over the last ten years put paid to the doubters who say that no individual can change the course of a company or industry – let alone two companies or industries.[94]

Apple has never done things in a conventional way and it may be that asking about succession planning is missing the point about the way the organisation is run. As a leader, Steve Jobs' charismatic and demanding presence has pervaded Apple and made it what it is today. The question must now be faced: is it impossible to replace the magic of Steve Jobs, or is he 'awesome, but not the entire company'?[95]

Your tasks

1 How and to what extent does Steve Jobs' career illuminate the difference between management and leadership?

2 How can Steve Jobs' leadership style be analysed? To what extent does the evidence so far conform to the Burns model of transformational leadership?

3 Jobs' career has been in two industries that are characterised by rapid market change, fast technological development and considerable turbulence. Critically examine the extent to which these situational factors bear upon the leadership style that Jobs has shown over the years.

Review Questions and Tests

REVIEW AND DISCUSSION QUESTIONS

1 Explain clearly what you understand by the meaning of leadership. How would you distinguish leadership from management?

2 Distinguish between different approaches to the study of leadership and discuss critically what you see as the relevance today of each of these approaches.

3 Using the Tannenbaum and Schmidt continuum, identify, with reasons, your preferred style of leadership. Give an example of a situation in which you might need to adopt an alternative style of leadership.

4 What do you understand by leader–situation models of leadership? Assess the practical value to the manager of: (i) Fiedler's contingency model of leadership effectiveness; and (ii) Hersey and Blanchard's readiness of the followers or group situational model.

5 Discuss the main sources of power and leadership influence. Give a practical example of each of these main sources of power and influence within your own organisation.

6 Explain clearly the nature and main features of transformational leadership. Give your own examples of people you would regard as transformational leaders. Discuss critically the relevance of personality and charisma for effective leadership.

7 If you were a consultant on leadership, what areas of needs would you include in designing a leadership development programme for managers in a large work organisation? Justify your ideas.

8 Discuss the main situational variables that are likely to influence the most appropriate form of managerial leadership behaviour. Detail three work situations in which a different style of leadership is likely to be most effective.

SECTION 9:
MOTIVATION

Chapter 16:
Motivation Theories and Management

THE MEANING OF MOTIVATION

The study of motivation is concerned, basically, with why people behave in a certain way. The basic underlying question is 'Why do people do what they do?' In general terms, motivation can be described as the direction and persistence of action. It is concerned with why people choose a particular course of action in preference to others, and why they continue with a chosen action, often over a long period and in the face of difficulties and problems.[1]

From a review of motivation theory, *Mitchell* identifies four common characteristics which underlie the definition of motivation:[2]

- **Motivation is typified as an individual phenomenon.** Every person is unique and all the major theories of motivation allow for this uniqueness to be demonstrated in one way or another.
- **Motivation is described, usually, as intentional.** Motivation is assumed to be under the worker's control, and behaviours that are influenced by motivation, such as effort expended, are seen as choices of action.
- **Motivation is multifaceted.** The two factors of greatest importance are: (i) what gets people activated (arousal); and (ii) the force of an individual to engage in desired behaviour (direction or choice of behaviour).
- **The purpose of motivational theories is to predict behaviour.** Motivation is not the behaviour itself and it is not performance. Motivation concerns action and the internal and external forces which influence a person's choice of action.

On the basis of these characteristics, Mitchell defines motivation as 'the degree to which an individual wants and chooses to engage in certain specified behaviours'.

A fuller definition is given by the Chartered Management Institute:

Motivation is the creation of stimuli, incentives and working environments that enable people to perform to the best of their ability. The heart of motivation is to give people what they really want most from work. In return managers should expect more in the form of productivity, quality and service.[3]

Underlying concept of motivation

The underlying concept of motivation is some driving force within individuals by which they attempt to achieve some goal in order to fulfil some need or expectation. This concept gives rise to the basic motivational model, which is illustrated in Figure 7.1. People's behaviour is

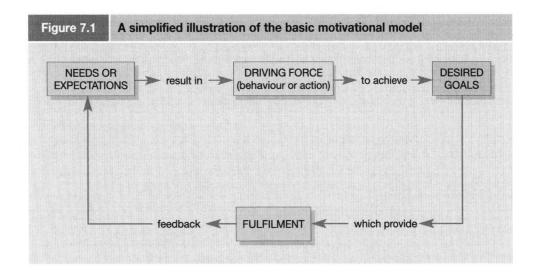

Figure 7.1   A simplified illustration of the basic motivational model

determined by what motivates them. Their performance is a product of both ability level and motivation.

Performance = function (ability × motivation)

Kreitner et al. suggest that although motivation is a necessary contributor for job performance, it is not the only one. Along with ability, motivation is also a combination of level of skill, knowledge about how to complete the task, feelings and emotions, and facilitating and inhibiting conditions not under the individual's control.[4] However, what is clearly evident is that if the manager is to improve the work of the organisation, attention must be given to the level of motivation of its members. The manager must also encourage staff to direct their efforts (their driving force) towards the successful attainment of the goals and objectives of the organisation.

NEEDS AND EXPECTATIONS AT WORK

But what is this driving force and what is it that people really want from work? What are people's needs and expectations and how do they influence behaviour and performance at work? Motivation is a complex subject, it is a very personal thing, and it is influenced by many variables. *Farren* reminds us of the 12 human needs that have been around since the beginning of recorded history: family, health and well-being, work/career, economic, learning, home/shelter, social relationships, spirituality, community, leisure, mobility, and environment/safety. 'Work and private life in the new millennium will continue to revolve around the 12 human needs.'[5]

The various needs and expectations at work can be categorised in a number of ways – for example the simple divisions into physiological and social motives or into extrinsic and intrinsic motivation.

- **Extrinsic motivation** is related to 'tangible' rewards such as salary and fringe benefits, security, promotion, contract of service, the work environment and conditions of work. Such tangible rewards are often determined at the organisational level and may be largely outside the control of individual managers.
- **Intrinsic motivation** is related to 'psychological' rewards such as the opportunity to use one's ability, a sense of challenge and achievement, receiving appreciation, positive recognition and being treated in a caring and considerate manner. The psychological rewards are those that can usually be determined by the actions and behaviour of individual managers.[6]

Higher set of motivational needs

According to *Kets de Vries*, the best-performing companies possess a set of values that creates the right conditions for high performance; he questions whether in such best companies there is something more going on that touches upon a deeper layer of human functioning, causing people to make an extra effort. The emphasis is on widening choice that enables people to choose more freely, instead of being led by forces of which they are unaware; and it is a motivational needs system on which such choice is based. Kets de Vries suggests that in addition to the motivation needs system for physiological needs, sensual and enjoyment needs, and the need to respond to threatening situations, companies that get the best out of their people are characterised by a system based on a higher set of motivational needs:

- **attachment/affiliation** – concerning the need for engagement and sharing, a feeling of community and a sense of belonging to the company; and
- **exploration/assertion** – concerning the ability to play and work, a sense of fun and enjoyment, the need for self-assertion and the ability to choose.[7]

Figure 7.2	Needs and expectations of people at work

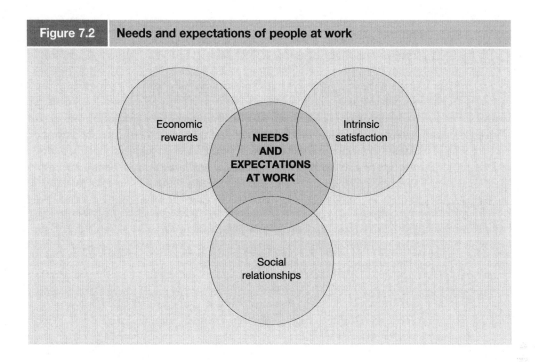

A three-fold classification

Given the complex and variable nature of needs and expectations, the following is a simplistic but useful, broad three-fold classification as a starting point for reviewing the motivation to work (*see* Figure 7.2):

■ **Economic rewards** – such as pay, fringe benefits, pension rights, material goods and security. This is an **instrumental** orientation to work and concerned with 'other things'.
■ **Intrinsic satisfaction** – derived from the nature of the work itself, interest in the job, and personal growth and development. This is a **personal** orientation to work and concerned with 'oneself'.
■ **Social relationships** – such as friendships, group working and the desire for affiliation, status and dependency. This is a **relational** orientation to work and concerned with 'other people'.

A person's motivation, job satisfaction and work performance will be determined by the comparative strength of these sets of needs and expectations and the extent to which they are fulfilled. For example, some people may make a deliberate choice to forgo intrinsic satisfaction and social relationships (particularly in the short term or in the earlier years of their working life) in return for high economic rewards. Other people are happy to accept comparatively lower economic rewards in favour of a job that has high intrinsic satisfaction and/or social relationships. Social relationships would appear to be an important feature for many people, especially, for example, for those working in the hospitality industry where interactions with other people and the importance of supportive working relationships and good teamwork can be strong motivators at work.[8]

MONEY AS A MOTIVATOR

Earlier writers, such as F. W. Taylor, believed in economic needs motivation. Workers would be motivated by obtaining the highest possible wages through working in the most efficient and productive way. Performance was limited by physiological fatigue. For Taylor, motivation was a comparatively simple issue – what the workers wanted from their employers more than anything else was high wages. This approach is the **rational–economic concept of motivation**. The ideas of F. W. Taylor and his 'rational–economic needs' concept of motivation (discussed in Chapter 2) and subsequent approaches to motivation at work have fuelled the continuing debate about financial rewards as a motivator and their influence on productivity.

Where there is little pleasure in the work itself or the job offers little opportunity for career advancement, personal challenge or growth, many people may appear to be motivated primarily, if not exclusively, by money. Weaver suggests that for many hourly workers in the hospitality industry, such as dishwashing, waiting or housekeeping staff, the work does not change much among different companies and there is little attachment to a particular company. For such staff, *Weaver* proposes a 'Theory M' programme of motivation based on direct cash rewards for above-average performance. A percentage base is calculated from the average performance of workers on the staff.[9] Yet we frequently see pronouncements from prominent business figures that motivation is about much more than money.

> *Work is about letting people know they are important, their hard work and efforts matter, and they're doing a good job. And this kind of recognition, in fact, can sometimes be more important than money.*
>
> Gary Kusin, CEO, FedEx Kinko's[10]

The short answer appears to be that for the vast majority of people, money is clearly important and a motivator at work **but** to what extent and **how** important depends upon their personal circumstances and the other satisfactions they derive from work. The bottom line is surely the extent to which money motivates people to work **well** and to the best of their abilities. Although pay may still make people tick, there are now a number of other important influences on motivation. For many people, the feeling of being recognised and valued appears more important than money in motivating them to stay in a particular job. (See the discussion of Herzberg's two-factor theory of motivation later in this chapter.)

BROADER INTRINSIC MOTIVATION

Popular press reports appear to indicate that many people are increasingly motivated by broader concerns such as their work/life balance (discussed in Chapter 3), opportunities for flexible working, career advancement and personal development and growth, and a feeling of identification with the values of the organisation. The motivation to work is also influenced by the changing nature of the work environment and the concept of the 'psychological contract', which was discussed in Chapter 1.

> *If your staff do something good, tell them. And then tell them again. And again. Keep it up. Put it in writing. Send them a memo – something they can keep. Put it in the company newsletter. Add a note to their file. Whatever, but make it widely known they did good. This is a quick and cheap method of praising and motivating your team and it lets everyone know you are monitoring, praising, motivating.[11]*

As *Grayson and Hodges* point out, historically loyalty was bought and employers offered gradual progression up the hierarchy, a decent salary and job security in return for a hard day's work. 'Increasingly, motivation is based on values rather than purely on financial reward.'[12]

However, according to *Gratton* finding intrinsically motivating tasks is not easy.

Finding tasks and experiences that are intrinsically motivating sounds relatively straightforward but in fact it requires a heightened awareness of who we are. Without this emotional self-awareness we have no capacity to judge whether the tasks available to us could be intrinsically motivating . . . Finding intrinsically motivating tasks also requires the companies of which we are members to communicate the tasks available and to encourage volunteering.[13]

Waller refers to the importance today of identity and that work inevitably plays a key role on shaping identity. Waller questions how much of ourselves do we put into our job. He points out that not long ago, a job was something you did to put bread on the table but nowadays (global financial situation apart) people in a cushy job with a decent salary, paid holiday, pension, health care and a well-stocked sandwich trolley will jack it all in, saying 'It's not really me'. If people are getting absorbed by their work-life, they expect their job to help them to discover and develop themselves.[14]

Critical reflection

'It's all very well talking about a contented workforce, praise and recognition but at times of high unemployment, rapid change or uncertainty a secure job, increased training and steady income are the true motivators. In the real world money is the most potent need and strongest motivator.'

Can you argue convincingly against this contention?

FRUSTRATION-INDUCED BEHAVIOUR

What happens if a person's motivational driving force is blocked and they are unable to satisfy their needs and expectations, and what is the likely effect on their work performance? There are two possible sets of outcomes: constructive behaviour or frustration (*see* Figure 7.3).

Constructive behaviour

Constructive behaviour is a positive reaction to the blockage of a desired goal and can take two main forms: problem-solving or restructuring.

Figure 7.3	A basic model of frustration

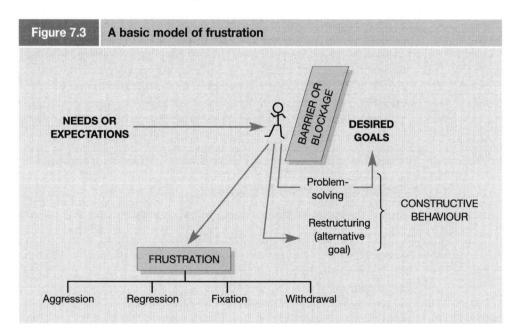

- **Problem-solving** is the removal of the barrier – for example finding an alternative means of undertaking a task, repairing a damaged machine or bypassing an unco-operative superior.
- **Restructuring**, or compromise, is the substitution of an alternative goal, although such a goal may be of a lower or different order – for example taking an additional part-time job because of failure to be promoted to a higher grade, or reassessing the work/life balance.

Note: Even if a person engages in constructive behaviour in response to a barrier or blockage, it could be said that the person was 'frustrated', if only mildly or in the short term, in an attempt to satisfy a desired goal. However, the term 'frustration' is usually interpreted as applying to **negative responses** to a barrier or blockage which prevents satisfaction of a desired goal.

Frustration (negative responses)

Frustration is a negative response to the blockage of a desired goal and results in a defensive form of behaviour. There are many possible reactions to frustration caused by the failure to achieve a desired goal. These can be summarised under four broad headings: aggression, regression, fixation and withdrawal.[15] However, these categories are not mutually exclusive. Most forms of frustration-induced behaviour at work are a combination of aggression, regression and fixation.

Aggression is a physical or verbal attack on some person or object, for example striking a supervisor, rage or abusive language, destruction of equipment or documents, or malicious gossip about a superior. This form of behaviour may be directed against the person or object that is perceived as the source of frustration, that is the actual barrier or blocking agent. However, where such a direct attack cannot be made, because, for example, the source of frustration is not clear or not specific, or where the source is feared, as with a powerful superior, aggression may be displaced towards some other person or object.

With **displaced aggression** the person may find an easier, safer person or object as a scapegoat for the outlet of frustration – for example picking arguments with colleagues, being short-tempered with subordinates, shouting at the cleaners or kicking the waste-paper bin. A more constructive form of displaced aggression is working off frustrated feelings through demanding physical work or sport, or perhaps by shouting/cursing when alone or in the company of an understanding colleague.

Regression is reverting to a childish or more primitive form of behaviour – for example sulking, crying, tantrums or kicking a broken machine or piece of equipment.

Fixation is persisting in a form of behaviour which has no adaptive value and continuing to repeat actions which have no positive results – for example the inability to accept change or new ideas, repeatedly trying a door that is clearly locked or a machine which clearly will not work, or insisting on applying for promotion even though not qualified for the job.

Withdrawal is apathy, giving up or resignation – for example arriving at work late and leaving early, sickness and absenteeism, refusal to accept responsibility, avoiding decision-making, passing work over to colleagues or leaving the job altogether.

Factors influencing frustration

Among the factors which determine an individual's reaction to frustration are the:

- level and potency of need (*see*, for example, Maslow's theory of motivation, discussed below);
- degree of attachment to the desired goal;
- strength of motivation;
- perceived nature of the barrier or blocking agent; and
- personality characteristics of the individual.

It is important that managers attempt to reduce potential frustration, for example through:

- effective recruitment, selection and socialisation;
- training and development;
- job design and work organisation;
- equitable HRM policies;
- recognition and rewards;
- effective communications;
- participative styles of management;
- attempting to understand the individual's perception of the situation.

Proper attention to motivation and to the needs and expectations of people at work will help overcome boredom and frustration-induced behaviour.

THEORIES OF MOTIVATION

There are many competing theories that attempt to explain the nature of motivation. These theories may all be at least partially true and help to explain the behaviour of certain people at certain times. The issue of motivation is often most acute for younger people starting on their career, for people at mid-career positions or for those who find limited opportunities for promotion or further advancement. For employers there may be difficulties in motivating staff both in the longer term and in the short run. It is because of the complexity of motivation and the fact that there is no ready-made solution or single answer to what motivates people to work well that the different theories are important to the manager. They show there are many motives that influence people's behaviour and performance. Collectively, the different theories provide a framework within which to direct attention to the problem of how best to motivate staff to work willingly and effectively.

Criticisms and reservations

It is important to emphasise, however, that these various theories are not conclusive. They all have their critics (this is particularly true of the content theories of motivation) or have been subject to alternative findings that purport to contradict original ideas. Many of these theories were not intended initially to have the significance that some writers have subsequently placed upon them. It is always easy to quote an example that appears to contradict any generalised observation on what motivates people to work. Despite these reservations the different theories provide a basis for study and discussion, and for review of the most effective motivational style (*see* Figure 7.4).

> *You don't motivate individuals. You provide them with an environment to be self-motivated. It is a personal decision, but it's management's job to provide the right environment.*
>
> Kathy Schofield, Director of Human Resources, HFC Bank[16]

The manager, therefore, must judge the relevance of these different theories, how best to draw upon them, and how they might effectively be applied in particular work situations. The manager should be aware of at least the main theories of motivation.

Content theories and process theories

The usual approach to the study of motivation is through an understanding of internal cognitive processes – that is, what people feel and how they think. This understanding should help the manager to predict likely behaviour of staff in given situations. These different cognitive theories of motivation are usually divided into two contrasting approaches: content theories and process theories.

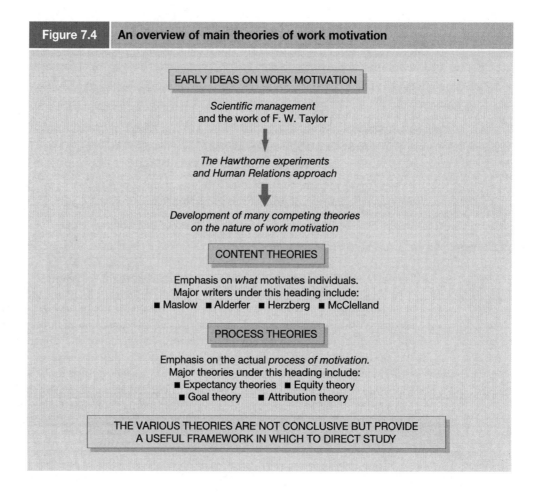

Figure 7.4	An overview of main theories of work motivation

EARLY IDEAS ON WORK MOTIVATION

Scientific management
and the work of F. W. Taylor

The Hawthorne experiments
and Human Relations approach

Development of many competing theories
on the nature of work motivation

CONTENT THEORIES

Emphasis on *what* motivates individuals.
Major writers under this heading include:
■ Maslow ■ Alderfer ■ Herzberg ■ McClelland

PROCESS THEORIES

Emphasis on the actual *process of motivation*.
Major theories under this heading include:
■ Expectancy theories ■ Equity theory
■ Goal theory ■ Attribution theory

THE VARIOUS THEORIES ARE NOT CONCLUSIVE BUT PROVIDE
A USEFUL FRAMEWORK IN WHICH TO DIRECT STUDY

■ **Content theories** attempt to explain those specific things that actually motivate the individual at work. These theories are concerned with identifying people's needs and their relative strengths, and the goals they pursue in order to satisfy these needs. Content theories place emphasis on the nature of needs and **what motivates**.

■ **Process theories** attempt to identify the relationship among the dynamic variables that make up motivation. These theories are concerned more with how behaviour is initiated, directed and sustained. Process theories place emphasis on the **actual process of motivation**. These theories are discussed later in this chapter.

CONTENT THEORIES OF MOTIVATION

Major content theories of motivation include:

■ Maslow's hierarchy of needs model;
■ Alderfer's modified need hierarchy model;
■ Herzberg's two-factor theory;
■ McClelland's achievement motivation theory.

MASLOW'S HIERARCHY OF NEEDS THEORY

A useful starting point is the work of *Maslow* and his theory of individual development and motivation, published originally in 1943.[17] Maslow's basic proposition is that people are

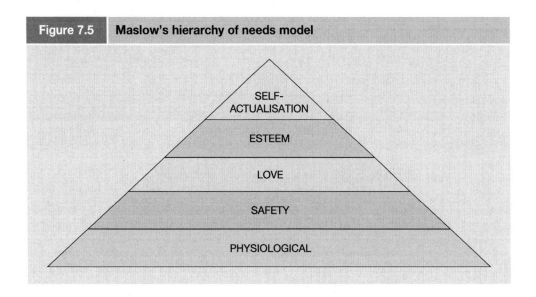

Figure 7.5 | **Maslow's hierarchy of needs model**

wanting beings, they always want more, and what they want depends on what they already have. He suggests that human needs are arranged in a series of levels, a hierarchy of importance.

Maslow identified eight innate needs, including the need to know and understand, aesthetic needs and the need for transcendence. However, the hierarchy is usually shown as ranging through five main levels, from, at the lowest level, physiological needs, through safety needs, love needs and esteem needs, to the need for self-actualisation at the highest level. The **hierarchy of needs** may be shown as a series of steps but is usually displayed in the form of a pyramid (*see* Figure 7.5). This is an appropriate form of illustration as it implies a thinning out of needs as people progress up the hierarchy.

- **Physiological needs**. These include homeostasis (the body's automatic efforts to retain normal functioning) such as satisfaction of hunger and thirst, the need for oxygen and to maintain temperature regulation. Also sleep, sensory pleasures, activity, maternal behaviour and, arguably, sexual desire.
- **Safety needs**. These include safety and security, freedom from pain or threat of physical attack, protection from danger or deprivation, the need for predictability and orderliness.
- **Love needs** (often referred to as social needs). These include affection, sense of belonging, social activities, friendships, and both the giving and receiving of love.
- **Esteem needs** (sometimes referred to as ego needs). These include both self-respect and the esteem of others. Self-respect involves the desire for confidence, strength, independence and freedom, and achievement. Esteem of others involves reputation or prestige, status, recognition, attention and appreciation.
- **Self-actualisation needs**. This is the development and realisation of one's full potential. Maslow sees this as 'What humans can be, they must be' or 'becoming everything that one is capable of becoming'. Self-actualisation needs are not necessarily a creative urge and may take many forms which vary widely from one individual to another.

Once a lower need has been satisfied, it no longer acts as a strong motivator. The needs of the next higher level in the hierarchy demand satisfaction and become the motivating influence. Only unsatisfied needs motivate a person. Thus Maslow asserts that *'a satisfied need is no longer a motivator'*.

Not necessarily a fixed order

Although Maslow suggests that most people have these basic needs in about the order indicated, he also makes it clear that the hierarchy is not necessarily a fixed order. There will be a number of exceptions to the order indicated. For some people there will be a reversal of the hierarchy, for example:

- Self-esteem may seem to be more important than love to some people. This is the most common reversal of the hierarchy. It is often based on the belief that the person most loved is strong, confident or inspires respect. People seeking love try to put on a show of aggressive, confident behaviour. They are not really seeking self-esteem as an end in itself but for the sake of love needs.
- For some innately creative people the drive for creativity and self-actualisation may arise despite lack of satisfaction of more basic needs.
- Higher-level needs may be lost in some people who will continue to be satisfied at lower levels only: for example, a person who has experienced chronic unemployment.
- Some people who have been deprived of love in early childhood may experience the permanent loss of love needs.
- A need which has continued to be satisfied over a long period of time may be undervalued. For example, people who have never suffered from chronic hunger may tend to under-estimate its effects, and regard food as rather an unimportant thing. Where people are dominated by a higher-level need this may assume greater importance than more basic needs.
- People with high ideals or values may become martyrs and give up everything else for the sake of their beliefs.

Maslow claims that the hierarchy is relatively universal among different cultures, but he recognises that there are differences in an individual's motivational content in a particular culture.

Degrees of satisfaction

Maslow points out that a false impression may be given that a need must be satisfied fully before a subsequent need arises. **He suggests that a more realistic description is in terms of decreasing percentages of satisfaction along levels of the hierarchy.** For example, arbitrary figures for the average person may be: satisfied 85 per cent in physiological needs; 70 per cent in safety needs; 50 per cent in love needs; 40 per cent in esteem needs; and 10 per cent in self-actualisation needs. There is a gradual emergence of a higher-level need as lower-level needs become more satisfied. The relative importance of these needs changes during the psychological development of the individual. Maslow subsequently modified his views by noting that satisfaction of self-actualisation needs by growth-motivated individuals can actually enhance these needs rather than reduce them. Furthermore, he accepted that some higher-level needs may still emerge after long deprivation of lower-level needs rather than only after their satisfaction.

Evaluation of Maslow's theory

Based on Maslow's theory, once lower-level needs have been satisfied (say at the physiological and safety levels), giving more of the same does not provide motivation. Individuals advance up the hierarchy as each lower-level need becomes satisfied. Therefore, to provide motivation for a change in behaviour, the manager must direct attention to the next higher level of needs (in this case, love or social needs) that seek satisfaction.

Applications to the work situation

There are a number of problems in relating Maslow's theory to the work situation. These include the following:

- People do not necessarily satisfy their needs, especially higher-level needs, just through the work situation; they satisfy them through other areas of their life as well. Therefore the manager would need to have a complete understanding of people's private and social lives, not just their behaviour at work.

- There is doubt about the time that elapses between the satisfaction of a lower-level need and the emergence of a higher-level need.
- Individual differences mean that people place different values on the same need. For example, some people prefer what they might see as the comparative safety of working in a bureaucratic organisation to a more highly paid and higher status position, but with less job security, in a different organisation.
- Some rewards or outcomes at work satisfy more than one need. Higher salary or promotion, for example, can be applied to all levels of the hierarchy.
- Even for people within the same level of the hierarchy, the motivating factors will not be the same. There are many different ways in which people may seek satisfaction of, for example, their esteem needs.
- Maslow viewed satisfaction as the main motivational outcome of behaviour. But job satisfaction does not necessarily lead to improved work performance.

A useful basis for evaluation

Although Maslow did not originally intend that the need hierarchy should necessarily be applied to the work situation, it remains popular as a theory of motivation at work. Despite criticisms and doubts about its limitations, the theory has had a significant impact on management approaches to motivation and the design of organisations to meet individual needs. It is a convenient framework for viewing the different needs and expectations that people have, where they are in the hierarchy, and the different motivators that might be applied to people at different levels. The work of Maslow has drawn attention to a number of motivators and stimulated study and research. The need hierarchy model provides a useful base for the evaluation of motivation at work. For example, *Steers and Porter* suggest a list of general rewards and organisational factors used to satisfy different needs (*see* Table 7.1).[18]

Saunders contends that despite the time that has elapsed, Maslow's theory remains watertight.

> *When prehistoric man first took shelter in a cave and lit a fire, he was satisfying his lowest – physiological and safety needs. When a Buddhist achieves a state of nirvana, she is satisfying the fifth and highest – self-actualisation . . . The cave these days might be a three-bedroom semi with garden and*

Table 7.1	Applying Maslow's need hierarchy	
Needs levels	**General rewards**	**Organisational factors**
1 Physiological	Food, water, sex, sleep	**a** Pay
		b Pleasant working conditions
		c Cafeteria
2 Safety	Safety, security, stability, protection	**a** Safe working conditions
		b Company benefits
		c Job security
3 Social	Love, affection, belongingness	**a** Cohesive work group
		b Friendly supervision
		c Professional associations
4 Esteem	Self-esteem, self-respect, prestige, status	**a** Social recognition
		b Job title
		c High-status job
		d Feedback from the job itself
5 Self-actualisation	Growth, advancement, creativity	**a** Challenging job
		b Opportunities for creativity
		c Achievement in work
		d Advancement in the organisation

Source: Steers, R. M. and Porter, L. W. *Motivation and Work Behaviour*, fifth edition, McGraw-Hill (1991), p. 35. Reproduced with permission from the McGraw-Hill Companies.

off-street parking, but the fact remains that once we've got enough to feed, clothe and house our families money is a low-level motivator for most people. The dash for cash is soon replaced by the desire for recognition, status and ultimately (although Maslow reckoned that a lot of us never get this far) the need to express yourself through your work.[19]

> ## Critical reflection
>
> 'John Adair points out that presenting Maslow's hierarchy as a pyramid model gives the impression that the greatest needs are in the lower levels. Adair suggests that the pyramid should be inverted as physiological needs, for example, are limited but there are fewer limitations the further up you go.'[20]
>
> *How would you best explain and present Maslow's hierarchy of human needs?*

ALDERFER'S MODIFIED NEED HIERARCHY MODEL

A modified need hierarchy model has been presented by *Alderfer*.[21] This model condenses Maslow's five levels of need into only three levels based on the core needs of existence, relatedness and growth (ERG theory) (*see* Table 7.2 on p. 267).

- **Existence needs** are concerned with sustaining human existence and survival and cover physiological and safety needs of a material nature.
- **Relatedness needs** are concerned with relationships to the social environment and cover love or belonging, affiliation and meaningful interpersonal relationships of a safety or esteem nature.
- **Growth needs** are concerned with the development of potential and cover self-esteem and self-actualisation.

A continuum of needs

Like Maslow, Alderfer suggests that individuals progress through the hierarchy from existence needs to relatedness needs to growth needs as the lower-level needs become satisfied. However, Alderfer suggests these needs are more a continuum than hierarchical levels. More than one need may be activated at the same time. Individuals may also progress down the hierarchy. There is a frustration–regression process. For example, if an individual is continually frustrated in attempting to satisfy growth needs, relatedness needs may reassume most importance. The lower-level needs become the main focus of the individual's efforts.

Alderfer proposed a number of basic propositions relating to the three need relationships. Some of these propositions followed Maslow's theory, some were the reverse of the theory. A number of studies were undertaken to test these propositions across different samples of people in different types of organisations. Results from the studies were mixed. For example, the proposition that the less existence needs are satisfied the more they will be desired received constant support from all six samples. However, the proposition that satisfaction of existence needs activates desire for relatedness needs was not supported in any of the six samples.

Satisfaction of needs

Unlike Maslow's theory, the results of Alderfer's work suggest that lower-level needs do not have to be satisfied before a higher-level need emerges as a motivating influence. The results, however, do support the idea that lower-level needs decrease in strength as they become satisfied. ERG theory states that an individual is motivated to satisfy one or more basic sets of needs. Therefore if a person's needs at a particular level are blocked, attention should be focused on the satisfaction of needs at the other levels. For example, if a subordinate's growth needs are blocked because the job does not allow sufficient opportunity for personal development, the manager should attempt to provide greater opportunities for the subordinate to satisfy existence and relatedness needs.

HERZBERG'S TWO-FACTOR THEORY

Herzberg's original study consisted of interviews with 203 accountants and engineers, chosen because of their growing importance in the business world, from different industries in the Pittsburgh area of America.[22] He used the critical incident method. Subjects were asked to relate times when they felt exceptionally good or exceptionally bad about their present job or any previous job. They were asked to give reasons and a description of the sequence of events giving rise to that feeling. Responses to the interviews were generally consistent and revealed that there were two different sets of factors affecting motivation and work. **This led to the two-factor theory of motivation and job satisfaction.**

Hygiene and motivating factors

One set of factors are those which, if absent, cause dissatisfaction. These factors are related to job context, they are concerned with job environment and extrinsic to the job itself. These factors are the '**hygiene**' or '**maintenance**' **factors** ('hygiene' being used as analogous to the medical term meaning preventive and environmental). They serve to prevent dissatisfaction. The other set of factors are those that, if present, serve to motivate the individual to superior effort and performance. These factors are related to job content of the work itself. They are the '**motivators**' or **growth factors**. The strength of these factors will affect feelings of satisfaction or no satisfaction, but not dissatisfaction. **The opposite of dissatisfaction is not satisfaction but, simply, no dissatisfaction** (*see* Figure 7.6).

The hygiene factors can be related roughly to Maslow's lower-level needs and the motivators to Maslow's higher-level needs (*see* Table 7.2). To motivate workers to give of their best, the manager must give proper attention to the motivators or growth factors. Herzberg emphasises that hygiene factors are not a 'second-class citizen system'. They are as important as the motivators, but for different reasons. Hygiene factors are necessary to avoid unpleasantness at work and to deny unfair treatment. 'Management should never deny people proper treatment at work.' The motivators relate to what people are allowed to do and the quality of human experience at work. They are the variables which actually motivate people. The work of Herzberg indicates that it is more likely good performance leads to job satisfaction rather than the reverse.

Evaluation of Herzberg's work

Herzberg's theory is, however, a source of frequent debate. There have been many other studies to test the theory. The conclusions have been mixed. Some studies provide support for the theory. However, it has also been attacked by a number of writers. There are two common general criticisms of Herzberg's theory. One is that the theory has only limited application to 'manual' workers. The other is that the theory is 'methodologically bound'.

It is often claimed that the theory applies least to people with largely unskilled jobs or whose work is uninteresting, repetitive and monotonous, and limited in scope. Yet these are the people who often present management with the biggest problem of motivation. Some workers do not seem greatly interested in the job content of their work or with the motivators or growth factors.

A second, general criticism concerns methodology. It is claimed that the critical incident method, and the description of events giving rise to good or bad feelings, influences the

| Figure 7.6 | Representation of Herzberg's two-factor theory |

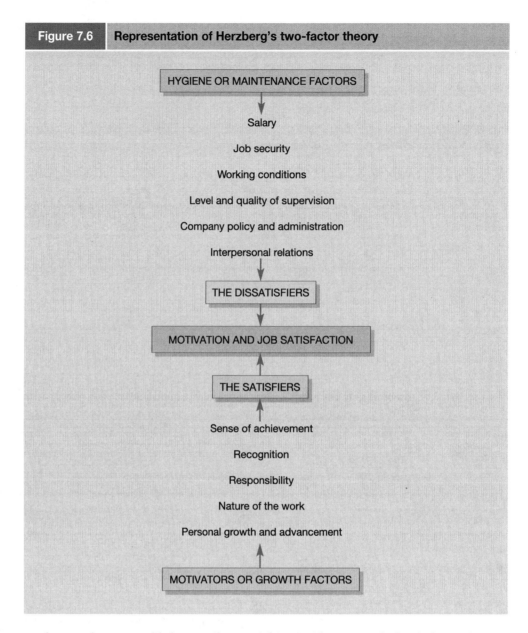

results. People are more likely to attribute satisfying incidents at work, that is the motivators, as a favourable reflection on their own performance. The dissatisfying incidents, that is, the hygiene factors, are more likely to be attributed to external influences and the efforts of other people. Descriptions from the respondents had to be interpreted by the interviewers. This gives rise to the difficulty of distinguishing clearly between the different dimensions and to the risk of possible interviewer bias.

Despite such criticisms, there is still evidence of support for the continuing relevance of the theory. According to *Crainer and Dearlove*:

> *Herzberg's work has had a considerable effect on the rewards and remuneration packages offered by corporations. Increasingly, there is a trend towards 'cafeteria' benefits in which people can choose from a range of options. In effect, they can select the elements they recognise as providing their own motivation to work. Similarly, the current emphasis on self-development, career management and self-managed learning can be seen as having evolved from Herzberg's insights.*[23]

Whatever the validity of the two-factor theory, much of the criticism is with the benefit of hindsight, and Herzberg did at least attempt an empirical approach to the study of motivation

Table 7.2	Linking Maslow's, Alderfer's and Herzberg's theories of motivation	
Maslow's hierarchy of needs	**Alderfer's ERG theory**	**Herzberg's two-factor theory**
PHYSIOLOGICAL	EXISTENCE	HYGIENE FACTORS
SAFETY		
LOVE	RELATEDNESS	
ESTEEM	GROWTH	MOTIVATORS
SELF-ACTUALISATION		

at work and job satisfaction. Furthermore, his work has drawn attention to the importance of job design in the 'quality of work life'.

McCLELLAND'S ACHIEVEMENT MOTIVATION THEORY

McClelland's work originated from investigations into the relationship between hunger needs and the extent to which imagery of food dominated thought processes. From subsequent research McClelland identified four main arousal-based, and socially developed, motives:

- the **Achievement** motive;
- the **Power** motive;
- the **Affiliative** motive;
- the **Avoidance** motive.[24]

The first three motives correspond, roughly, to Maslow's self-actualisation, esteem and love needs. The relative intensity of these motives varies between individuals. It also tends to vary between different occupations. Managers appear to be higher in achievement motivation than in affiliation motivation. McClelland saw the achievement need (n-Ach) as the most critical for the country's economic growth and success. The need to achieve is linked to entrepreneurial spirit and the development of available resources.

Use of projective tests

Research studies by McClelland use a series of projective 'tests' – Thematic Apperception Tests (TATs) – to gauge an individual's motivation. For example, individuals are shown a number of pictures in which some activity is depicted. Respondents are asked to look briefly (10–15 seconds) at the pictures and then to describe what they think is happening, what the people in the picture are thinking and what events have led to the situation depicted.[25] An example of a picture used in a projective test is given in Assignment 2 at the end of this chapter. The descriptions are used as a basis for analysing the strength of the individual's motives.

People with high achievement needs

Despite the apparent subjective nature of the judgements, research studies tend to support the validity of TAT as an indicator of the need for achievement.[26] McClelland has, over years of empirical research, identified four characteristics of people with a strong achievement need (n-Ach): a preference for moderate task difficulty, a preference for personal responsibility for performance, the need for feedback, and innovativeness.

- They prefer **moderate task difficulty** and goals as an achievement incentive. This provides the best opportunity of proving they can do better. If the task is too difficult or too risky, it would reduce the chances of success and of gaining need satisfaction. If the course of action is too easy or too safe, there is little challenge in accomplishing the task and little satisfaction from success.
- They prefer **personal responsibility for performance**. They like to attain success through the focus of their own abilities and efforts rather than by teamwork or chance factors outside their control. Personal satisfaction is derived from the accomplishment of the task and recognition need not come from other people.
- They have the need for **clear and unambiguous feedback** on how well they are performing. A knowledge of results within a reasonable time is necessary for self-evaluation. Feedback enables them to determine success or failure in the accomplishment of their goals and to derive satisfaction from their activities.
- They are **more innovative**. As they always seek moderately challenging tasks they tend always to be moving on to something a little more challenging. In seeking short cuts they are more likely to cheat. There is a constant search for variety and for information to find new ways of doing things. They are more restless and avoid routine and also tend to travel more.

Characteristics of achievement motivation

The extent of achievement motivation varies between individuals. Some people rate very highly in achievement motivation. They are challenged by opportunities and work hard to achieve a goal. Money is not an incentive but may serve as a means of giving feedback on performance. High achievers seem unlikely to remain long with an organisation that does not pay them well for good performance. Money may seem to be important to high achievers, but they value it more as symbolising successful task performance and goal achievement.

McClelland's research has attempted to understand the characteristics of high achievers. He suggests that n-Ach is not hereditary but results from environmental influences and he has investigated the possibility of training people to develop a greater motivation to achieve.[27]

McClelland suggests four steps in attempting to develop achievement drive:

- Striving to attain feedback on performance. Reinforcement of success serves to strengthen the desire to attain higher performance.
- Developing models of achievement by seeking to emulate people who have performed well.
- Attempting to modify their self-image and to see themselves as needing challenges and success.
- Controlling day-dreaming and thinking about themselves in more positive terms.

McClelland was concerned with economic growth in underdeveloped countries. He has designed training programmes intended to increase the achievement motivation and entrepreneurial activity of managers.

McClelland and Burnham has also suggested that as effective managers need to be successful leaders and to influence other people, they should possess a high need for power.[28] However, the effective manager also scores high on inhibition. Power is directed more towards the organisation and concern for group goals and is exercised on behalf of other people. This is 'socialised' power. It is distinguished from 'personalised' power that is characterised by satisfaction from exercising dominance over other people, and personal aggrandisement.

PROCESS THEORIES OF MOTIVATION

Process theories, or extrinsic theories, attempt to identify the relationships among the dynamic variables that make up motivation and the actions required to influence behaviour and actions. They provide a further contribution to our understanding of the complex nature of work motivation. Many of the process theories cannot be linked to a single writer, but major approaches and leading writers under this heading include:

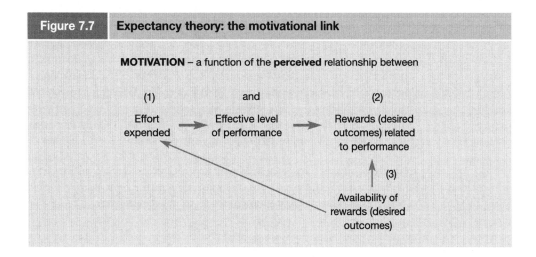

Figure 7.7   **Expectancy theory: the motivational link**

- expectancy-based models – Vroom, and Porter and Lawler;
- equity theory – Adams;
- goal theory – Locke;
- attribution theory – Heider and Kelley (discussed in Chapter 6).

Expectancy theories of motivation

The underlying basis of **expectancy theory** is that people are influenced by the expected results of their actions. Motivation is a function of the relationship between:

1 effort expended and perceived level of performance; and
2 the expectation that rewards (desired outcomes) will be related to performance.

There must also be:

3 the expectation that rewards (desired outcomes) are available.

These relationships determine the strength of the 'motivational link' (*see* Figure 7.7).

Performance therefore depends upon the perceived expectation regarding effort expended and achieving the desired outcome. For example, the desire for promotion will result in high performance only if the person believes there is a strong expectation that this will lead to promotion. If, however, the person believes promotion to be based solely on age and length of service, there is no motivation to achieve high performance. A person's behaviour reflects a conscious choice between the comparative evaluation of alternative behaviours. **The choice of behaviour is based on the expectancy of the most favourable consequences.**

Expectancy theory is a generic theory of motivation and cannot be linked to a single individual writer. There are a number of versions and some of the models are rather complex. More recent approaches to expectancy theory have been associated with the work of Vroom and of Porter and Lawler.

VROOM'S EXPECTANCY THEORY

Vroom was the first person to propose an expectancy theory aimed specifically at work motivation.[29] His model is based on three key variables: **valence, instrumentality** and **expectancy** (VIE theory or expectancy/valence theory). The theory is founded on the idea that people prefer certain outcomes from their behaviour over others. They anticipate feelings of satisfaction should the preferred outcome be achieved.

Valence

The feeling about specific outcomes is termed **valence. This is the attractiveness of, or preference for, a particular outcome to the individual.** Vroom distinguishes valence from value. A person may desire an object but then gain little satisfaction from obtaining it. Alternatively, a person may strive to avoid an object but find, subsequently, that it provides satisfaction. **Valence is the anticipated satisfaction from an outcome.** This may differ substantially from value, which is the actual satisfaction provided by an outcome.

The valences of certain outcomes may be derived in their own right, but more usually they are derived from the other outcomes to which they are expected to lead. An obvious example is money. Some people may see money as having an intrinsic worth and derive satisfaction from the actual accumulation of wealth. Most people, however, see money in terms of the many satisfying outcomes to which it can lead.

Instrumentality

The valence of outcomes derives, therefore, from their instrumentality. This leads to a distinction between first-level outcomes and second-level outcomes.

- **The first-level outcomes are performance-related.** They refer to the quantity of output or to the comparative level of performance. Some people may seek to perform well 'for its own sake' and without thought to expected consequences of their actions. Usually, however, performance outcomes acquire valence because of the expectation that they will lead to other outcomes as an anticipated source of satisfaction – second-level outcomes.
- **The second-level outcomes are need-related.** They are derived through achievement of first-level outcomes – that is, through achieving high performance. Many need-related outcomes are dependent upon actual performance rather than effort expended. People generally receive rewards for what they have achieved rather than for effort alone or through trying hard.

On the basis of Vroom's expectancy theory it is possible to depict a general model of behaviour (*see* Figure 7.8).

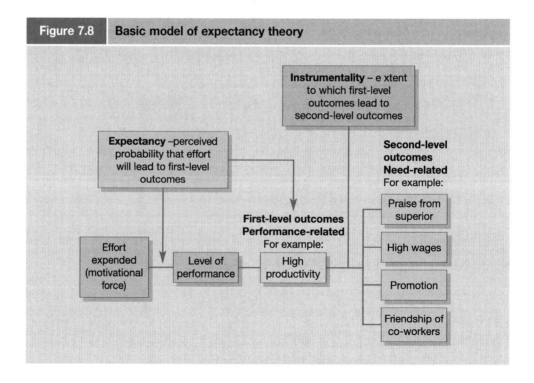

| Figure 7.8 | Basic model of expectancy theory |

Expectancy

When a person chooses between alternative behaviours which have uncertain outcomes, the choice is affected not only by the preference for a particular outcome but also by the probability that such an outcome will be achieved. People develop a **perception** of the degree of probability that the choice of a particular action will actually lead to the desired outcome. This is **expectancy**. It is the relationship between a chosen course of action and its predicted outcome. Expectancy relates effort expended to the achievement of first-level outcomes. Its value ranges between 0, indicating zero probability that an action will be followed by the outcome, and 1, indicating certainty that an action will result in the outcome.

Motivational force

The combination of valence and expectancy determines the person's motivation for a given form of behaviour. This is the **motivational force**. The force of an action is unaffected by outcomes which have no valence or by outcomes that are regarded as unlikely to result from a course of action. Expressed as an equation, motivation (M) is the sum of the products of the valences of all outcomes (V), times the strength of expectancies that action will result in achieving these outcomes (E). Therefore, if either, or both, valence or expectancy is zero, then motivation is zero. The choice between alternative behaviours is indicated by the highest attractiveness score.

$$M = \sum^{n} E \cdot V$$

There are likely to be a number of outcomes expected for a given action. Therefore, the measure of $E \cdot V$ is summed across the total number of possible outcomes to arrive at a single figure indicating the attractiveness for the contemplated choice of behaviour.

THE PORTER AND LAWLER EXPECTANCY MODEL

Vroom's expectancy/valence theory has been developed by *Porter and Lawler*.[30] Their model goes beyond motivational force and considers performance as a whole. They point out that effort expended (motivational force) does not lead directly to performance. It is mediated by individual abilities and traits, and by the person's role perceptions. They also introduce rewards as an intervening variable. Porter and Lawler see motivation, satisfaction and performance as separate variables and attempt to explain the complex relationships among them. Their model recognises that job satisfaction is more dependent upon performance, than performance is upon satisfaction.

Explanation of relationships

These relationships are expressed diagrammatically (*see* Figure 7.9) rather than mathematically. In contrast to the human relations approach which tended to assume that job satisfaction leads to improved performance, Porter and Lawler suggest that satisfaction is an effect rather than a cause of performance. It is performance that leads to job satisfaction.

- **Value of reward** (Box 1) is similar to valence in Vroom's model. People desire various outcomes (rewards) which they hope to achieve from work. The value placed on a reward depends on the strength of its desirability.
- **Perceived effort–reward probability** (Box 2) is similar to expectancy. It refers to a person's expectation that certain outcomes (rewards) are dependent upon a given amount of effort.
- **Effort** (Box 3) is how hard the person tries, the amount of energy a person exerts on a given activity. It does not relate to how successful a person is in carrying out an activity. The amount of energy exerted is dependent upon the interaction of the input variables of value of reward and perception of the effort–reward relationship.

| Figure 7.9 | The Porter and Lawler motivation model |

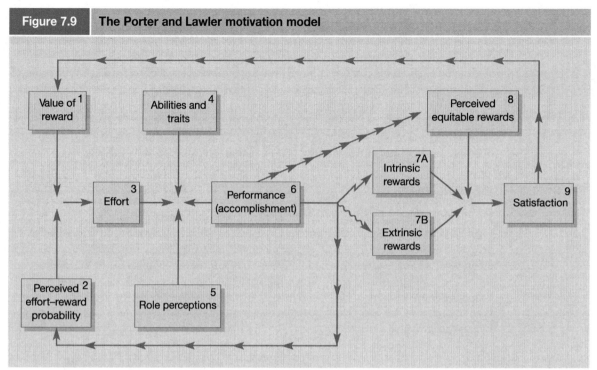

Source: From Porter, L. W. and Lawler, E. E. *Managerial Attitudes and Performance* (1968), p. 165. Copyright © 1968 Richard D. Irwin Inc. Reproduced with permission from the McGraw-Hill Companies.

■ **Abilities and traits** (Box 4). Porter and Lawler suggest that effort does not lead directly to performance but is influenced by individual characteristics. Factors such as intelligence, skills, knowledge, training and personality affect the ability to perform a given activity.

■ **Role perceptions** (Box 5) refer to the way in which individuals view their work and the role they should adopt. This influences the type of effort exerted. Role perceptions will influence the direction and level of action which is believed to be necessary for effective performance.

■ **Performance** (Box 6) depends not only on the amount of effort exerted but also on the intervening influences of the person's abilities and traits, and their role perceptions. If the person lacks the right ability or personality, or has an inaccurate role perception of what is required, then the exertion of a large amount of energy may still result in a low level of performance or task accomplishment.

■ **Rewards** (Boxes 7A and 7B) are desirable outcomes. Intrinsic rewards derive from the individuals themselves and include a sense of achievement, a feeling of responsibility and recognition (for example Herzberg's motivators). Extrinsic rewards derive from the organisation and the actions of others and include salary, working conditions and supervision (for example Herzberg's hygiene factors). The relationship between performance and intrinsic rewards is shown as a jagged line. This is because the extent of the relationship depends upon the nature of the job. If the design of the job permits variety and challenge, so that people feel able to reward themselves for good performance, there is a direct relationship. Where job design does not involve variety and challenge, there is no direct relationship between good performance and intrinsic rewards. The wavy line between performance and extrinsic rewards indicates that such rewards do not often provide a direct link to performance.

■ **Perceived equitable rewards** (Box 8). This is the level of rewards people feel they should fairly receive for a given standard of performance. Most people have an implicit perception about the level of rewards they should receive commensurate with the requirements and demands of the job, and the contribution expected of them. Self-rating of performance links directly with the perceived equitable reward variable. Higher levels of self-rated performance are associated with higher levels of expected equitable rewards. The heavily arrowed line indicates a relationship from the self-rated part of performance to perceived equitable rewards.

■ **Satisfaction** (Box 9). This is not the same as motivation. It is an attitude, an individual's internal state. Satisfaction is determined by both actual rewards received and perceived level of rewards from the organisation for a given standard of performance. If perceived equitable rewards are greater than actual rewards received, the person experiences dissatisfaction. The experience of satisfaction derives from actual rewards that meet or exceed the perceived equitable rewards.

LAWLER'S REVISED EXPECTANCY MODEL

Following the original Porter and Lawler model, further work was undertaken by *Lawler* (*see* Figure 7.10).[31] He suggests that in deciding on the attractiveness of alternative behaviours, there are two types of expectancies to be considered: effort–performance expectancies (E → P) and performance–outcome expectancies (P → O).

The **first expectancy (E → P)** is the person's perception of the probability that a given amount of effort will result in achieving an intended level of performance. It is measured on a scale between 0 and 1. The closer the perceived relationship between effort and performance, the higher the E → P expectancy score.

The **second expectancy (P → O)** is the person's perception of the probability that a given level of performance will actually lead to particular need-related outcomes. This is measured also on a scale between 0 and 1. The closer the perceived relationship between performance and outcome, the higher the P → O expectancy score.

Motivational force to perform

The multiplicative combination of the two types of expectancies, E → P and the sum of the products P → O, determines expectancy. The motivational force to perform (effort

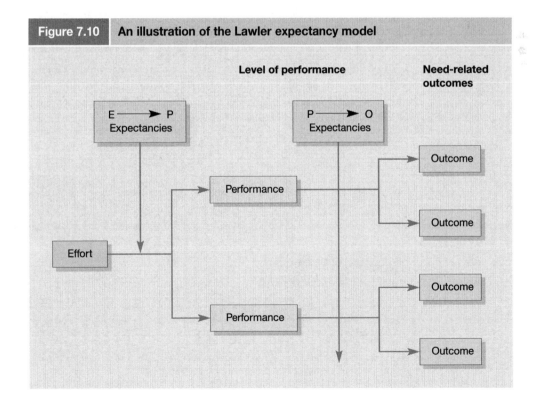

Figure 7.10   An illustration of the Lawler expectancy model

expended) is determined by multiplying E → P and P → O by the strength of outcome valence (V).

$$E(\text{Effort}) = (E \to P) \times \sum [(P \to O)V]$$

The distinction between the two types of expectancies arises because they are determined by different conditions. E → P expectancy is determined in part by the person's ability and self-confidence, past experience and the difficulty of the task. P → O expectancy is determined by the attractiveness of the outcomes and the belief about who controls the outcomes, the person him/herself or other people.

IMPLICATIONS FOR MANAGERS OF EXPECTANCY THEORIES

There are a number of versions of expectancy theory. The main elements tend to be very similar, however, and this suggests the development of a generally accepted approach. Expectancy models are not always easy to understand, or to apply. There are many variables which affect behaviour at work. A problem can arise in attempting to include a large number of variables or in identifying those variables which are most appropriate in particular situations.

Expectancy theory does, however, draw attention to the complexities of work motivation. It provides further information in helping to explain the nature of behaviour and motivation in the work situation, and helps to identify problems in performance. Expectancy theory indicates that managers should give attention to a number of factors, including the following:

- Use rewards appropriate in terms of individual performance. Outcomes with high valence should be used as an incentive for improved performance.
- Attempt to establish clear relationships between effort–performance and rewards, as perceived by the individual.
- Establish clear procedures for the evaluation of individual levels of performance.
- Pay attention to intervening variables such as abilities and traits, role perceptions, organisational procedures and support facilities, which, although not necessarily direct motivational factors, may still affect performance.
- Minimise undesirable outcomes which may be perceived to result from a high level of performance, such as industrial accidents or sanctions from co-workers, or to result despite a high level of performance, such as short-time working or layoffs.

Porter and Lawler also emphasise that the expectancy model is just a model and that expectancy theory applies only to behaviours which are under the voluntary control of the individual. The two general types of choices over which individuals have voluntary control of work performance in organisations are:

1 the amount of effort and energy expended; and
2 the manner in which they go about performing their work.

> *There is always a choice about the way you do your work, even if there is not a choice about the work itself. You always have a choice about the attitude you bring to the job.*
>
> World famous Pike Place Fish Market, Seattle[32]

Critical reflection

'Expectancy theories of motivation appear to make sense in the classroom and form the basis of an interesting academic debate, but it is unlikely the practising manager will be impressed or take much notice.'

What do you think? How would you explain the potential benefits of expectancy theory to a sceptical manager?

EQUITY THEORY OF MOTIVATION

One of the major variables of satisfaction in the Porter and Lawler expectancy model is perceived equitable rewards. This leads to consideration of another process theory of motivation – **equity theory**. Applied to the work situation, equity theory is usually associated with the work of *Adams*.[33]

Equity theory focuses on people's feelings of how fairly they have been treated in comparison with the treatment received by others. It is based on exchange theory. Social relationships involve an exchange process. For example, a person may expect promotion as an outcome of a high level of contribution (input) in helping to achieve an important organisational objective. People also compare their own position with that of others. They determine the perceived equity of their own position. Their feelings about the equity of the exchange are affected by the treatment they receive when compared with what happens to other people. Most exchanges involve a number of inputs and outcomes. According to equity theory, people place a weighting on these various inputs and outcomes according to how they perceive their importance. When there is an unequal comparison of ratios the person experiences a sense of **inequity**.

Behaviour as a consequence of inequity

A feeling of inequity causes tension, which is an unpleasant experience. The presence of inequity therefore motivates the person to remove or to reduce the level of tension and the perceived inequity. The magnitude of perceived inequity determines the level of tension. The level of tension created determines the strength of motivation. Adams identifies six broad types of possible behaviour as consequences of inequity (*see* Figure 7.11):

- **Changes to inputs**. A person may increase or decrease the level of their inputs, for example through the amount or quality of work, absenteeism, or working additional hours without pay.

Figure 7.11 | **An illustration of Adams's equity theory of motivation**

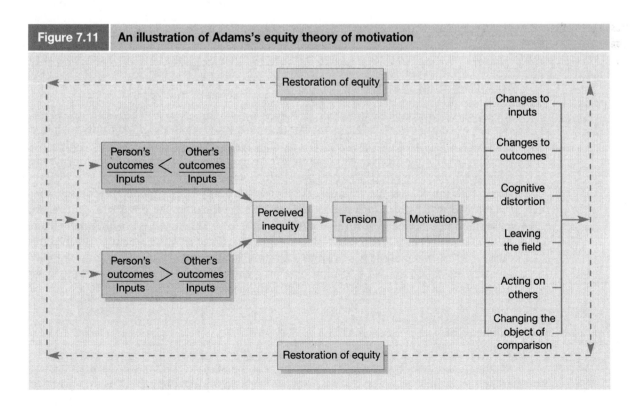

- **Changes to outcomes**. A person may attempt to change outcomes such as pay, working conditions, status and recognition, without changes to inputs.
- **Cognitive distortion of inputs and outcomes**. In contrast to actual changes, people may distort, cognitively, their inputs or outcomes to achieve the same results. Adams suggests that although it is difficult for people to distort facts about themselves, it is possible, within limits, to distort the utility of those facts: for example, the belief about how hard they are really working, the relevance of a particular qualification, or what they can or cannot obtain with a given level of pay.
- **Leaving the field**. A person may try to find a new situation with a more favourable balance, for example by absenteeism, request for a transfer, resigning from a job or from the organisation altogether.
- **Acting on others**. A person may attempt to bring about changes in others, for example to lower their inputs or accept greater outcomes. Or the person may cognitively distort the inputs and outcomes of others. Alternatively, a person may try to force others to leave the field.
- **Changing the object of comparison**. This involves changing the reference group with whom comparison is made. For example, where another person with a previously similar outcome–input ratio receives greater outcomes without any apparent increase in contribution, that other person may be perceived as now belonging to a different level in the organisation structure. The comparison need not necessarily be made with people who have the same inputs and outcomes. The important thing is a similar ratio of outcomes to inputs.

Under the control of the manager

The manager may seek to remove or reduce tension and perceived inequity among staff by influencing these types of behaviour – for example by attempting to change a person's inputs or encouraging a different object of comparison. People measure and compare their total inputs and outcomes so, for example, a working parent may prefer greater flexibility in working hours in return for lower monetary rewards. However, there are likely to be only two courses of action under the direct control of the manager. Outcomes can be changed by, for example, increased pay, additional perks or improved working conditions, or by instigating a person leaving the field through transfer, resignation or, as an extreme measure, dismissal. It is important to remember that equity theory is about the perceived ratio of inputs to outputs and these perceptions may not reflect the reality of the situation.

The ultimatum game

The **ultimatum game** is an economic behavioural game that can arguably be related to the concept of equity theory.[34] Two participants, A and B, are given the opportunity to split a given sum of money between them. The game is played anonymously and once only. One person (A) has to decide to make a one-time, take it or leave it, offer to B (ultimatum). If the other person (B) agrees to the division, both A and B keep their share of the money. However, if the offer is rejected neither person receives anything. Experiments indicate that if A offers around 50% of the money then B will accept the offer. But if A offers a noticeably lesser amount than 50%, B will typically refuse the offer in which case neither participant receives anything. One might expect B to accept because even a lesser amount, whatever the offer, is better than nothing. Can you see how this might be related to perceptions of equity theory? Viewers of the ITV1 television quiz programme *Divided*, in which contestants have to agree how to divide a cash prize, may see a similarity with the ultimatum game.

GOAL THEORY

Another theory usually considered under the heading of motivation to work is **goal theory**, or the theory of goal-setting (*see* Figure 7.12). This theory is based mainly on the work of

Figure 7.12	An illustration of Locke's theory of goal-setting

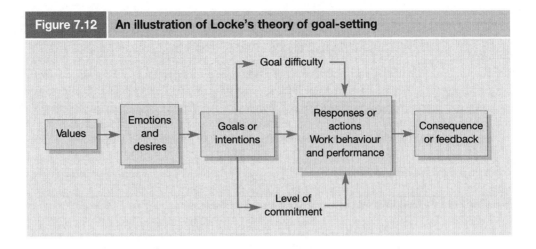

Locke.[35] The basic premise of goal theory is that people's goals or intentions play an important part in determining behaviour. Locke accepts the importance of perceived value, as indicated in expectancy theories of motivation, and suggests that these values give rise to the experience of emotions and desires. People strive to achieve goals in order to satisfy their emotions and desires. Goals guide people's responses and actions. Goals direct work behaviour and performance and lead to certain consequences or feedback. *Locke* subsequently pointed out that 'goal-setting is more appropriately viewed as a motivational technique rather than as a formal theory of motivation'.[36]

Goal-setting and performance

The combination of goal difficulty and the extent of the person's commitment to achieving the goal regulates the level of effort expended. People with specific quantitative goals, such as a defined level of performance or a given deadline for completion of a task, will perform better than people with no set goal or only a vague goal such as 'do the best you can'. People who have difficult goals will perform better than people with easier goals.

Gratton refers to 'stretch goals' which are ambitious, highly targeted opportunities for breakthrough improvements in performance. These goals should stem from critical success indicators and come from deep discussions within the company, and from collaboration within and across task forces, and lead to the development of activities and tactics to achieve the goals.[37] People lacking positive motivation at work may also help gain improved results and a better sense of achievement by setting themselves specific goals and identifying tasks directly related to their work and measurable targets of time and performance.

Practical implications for the manager

Goal theory has a number of practical implications for the manager:

■ Individuals lacking in motivation often do not have clear goals. Specific performance goals should systematically be identified and set in order to direct behaviour and maintain motivation.

■ Goals should be set at a challenging but realistic level. Difficult goals lead to higher performance. However, if goals are set at too high a level or are regarded as impossible to achieve, this can lead to stress and performance will suffer, especially over a longer period.

■ Complete, accurate and timely feedback and knowledge of results is usually associated with high performance. Feedback provides a means of checking progress on goal attainment and forms the basis for any revision of goals.

■ Goals can be determined either by a superior or by individuals themselves. Goals set by other people are more likely to be accepted when there is participation. Employee participation in the setting of goals may lead to higher performance.

Much of the theory of goal-setting can be related to the system of management by objectives (discussed in Chapter 12). MBO is often viewed as an application of goal-setting, although it was devised originally before the development of goal-setting theory. However it is viewed, the theory of goal-setting provides a useful approach to work motivation and performance. And *Hannagan* goes so far as to suggest: 'At present goal-setting is one of the most influential theories of work motivation applicable to all cultures.'[38]

ATTRIBUTION THEORY

A more recent approach to the study of motivation is attribution theory. Attribution is the process by which people interpret the perceived causes of behaviour. This was discussed in Chapter 6.

RELEVANCE TODAY FOR THE MANAGER

Given that most major theories of motivation date back many years it is inevitable that questions will be raised about their relevance today. *Reis and Pena* question whether motivating people to work in the 21st century with theories conceived during the past hundred years is likely to be feasible. They conclude that the core message is that managers should reconsider the outdated motivational patterns utilised to maintain role performance in organisations and adopt a fresh motivation formula for the 21st century based on friendship, work and respect.[39]

However, we have seen from the discussions above that there still appears to be general support for the theories – and, perhaps ironically, particularly for the early theories of Maslow, Herzberg and McClelland. A Chartered Management Institute checklist maintains that these theories are still valid today. 'A basic understanding of their main principles will provide the background for building a climate of honesty, openness and trust.'[40] From a 12-year study of the use of management concepts in technical organisations, *Flores and Utley* found the work of Maslow and McGregor the most popular motivational theories and also refer to the relationship between Maslow and Herzberg and the successful implementation of quality systems.[41]

Whatever the relevance of the different theories of motivation, to what extent do individuals have control over their own level of motivation or how much is dependent upon the leadership they encounter? *Adair* reassesses the theories of Maslow and Herzberg in terms of action-centred leadership, which is discussed in Chapter 10. Adair also argues that the extent to which you can motivate anyone else is limited and refers to the fifty-fifty rule of motivation, that is:

Fifty percent of motivation comes from within a person and 50% from his or her environment, especially from the leadership encountered there. The fifty-fifty rule in motivation does not claim to identify the different proportions in the equation exactly. It is more like a rough and ready rule of thumb. In effect it says no more than a substantial part of motivation lies with a person while a substantial part lies, so to speak, outside and beyond control.[42]

ORGANISATIONAL BEHAVIOUR MODIFICATION

Another possible approach to motivation is that of **organisational behaviour modification (OBMod)**. This is the application of learning principles to influence organisational behaviour. In particular it can be seen as a form of Skinner's operant conditioning, or reinforcement theory, discussed in Chapter 5. Reinforcement is a feature of the behaviourism approach and shaped by environmental influences. The reward for a particular form of behaviour is likely to result in the reinforcement of that behaviour. A negative outcome or lack of acknowledgement for the behaviour is likely to mean that the behaviour will stop. *Luthans and Kreitner* suggest that OBMod 'represents a merging of behavioral learning theory on the one hand and organizational behavior theory on the other'.[43]

According to Luthans and Kreitner, a major premise of OBMod is that positive consequence management is much more effective than negative consequence management. Organisations that encourage the members to learn and undertake desired behaviours and not to undertake undesired behaviours follow five main steps:

1 **Identify** the observable, objective and measurable behaviours relevant to the desired organisational performance.
2 **Measure** the frequency with which those behaviours actually occur under normal conditions. Provide baseline performance data as a point of reference to compare with changes in step 5.
3 **Determine** the antecedents of the behaviours, the reinforcements to encourage patterns of behaviour and the consequences that follow from those behaviours.
4 **Develop** an intervention strategy for change in order to strengthen desirable behaviours and weaken undesirable behaviours, through the use of operant conditioning and reinforcement theory including punishment if necessary.
5 **Measure and evaluate** systematically (using the same measure as in step 2) the extent to which the frequency of desired behaviours and undesired behaviours have changed, and improvements in organisational performance.

Applications of OBMod

To what extent can OBMod be applied effectively to improve motivation and performance in work organisations? OBMod works best for behaviours that are specific, objective and countable. There have been a number of studies in the United States that indicate positive results in behaviours that improved performance in reducing errors, attendance and punctuality, health and safety and customer service.[44] In a study of a Russian textile factory, following the OBMod approach, workers were subjected to two forms of intervention – extrinsic rewards and social rewards. The extrinsic rewards provided valued American products, such as clothing, music tapes and hard-to-get foods, for improved performance. Social rewards such as attention, recognition and praise from supervisors were for performing specified actions such as checking looms, undertaking repairs and helping others. Both the extrinsic and social interventions led to highly significant increases in performance. This contrasted with a previous participative job design approach that involved asking workers for ideas for improving performance and enriching their jobs that did not work. The researchers suggest cultural issues and the workers' past experiences may explain the failure of the participative intervention strategy, and that the OBMod approach has wider application.[45]

Although there appear to be a number of supporters in America, in the UK it is a controversial concept. Critics claim that OBMod is not an accepted theory of motivation and that there are too many individual differences for people to be treated as subjects of operant conditioning. OBMod is concerned only with shaping. There is the added criticism of a 'Big Brother' approach with excessive management manipulation and control over employees, more in line with scientific management (recall the discussion in Chapter 2). This in turn could also have the added disadvantage of discouraging individual initiative and adaptability to change circumstances. Workers subject to OBMod programmes may tend to ignore those aspects of voluntary behaviours, such as social support or assistance to colleagues, that are not subject to direct reward and reinforcement.

THE MOTIVATION OF KNOWLEDGE WORKERS

Recent advantages in telecommunications and in scientific and technological knowledge have led to greater emphasis on the knowledge and expertise of staff and the importance of creativity. *Tampoe* suggests that at the core of the new industrial trend are the 'knowledge workers' – those employees who apply their theoretical and practical understanding of a specific area of knowledge to produce outcomes of a commercial, social or personal value. The performance of knowledge workers should be judged on both the cleverness of ideas and the utility and commercial value of their applied knowledge. Creativity is necessary and needs to be encouraged but should be bounded by commercial realism. This presents management with a new challenge of how to motivate the knowledge workers.[46]

Tampoe suggests that the personal motivation of knowledge workers is based on the value they place on the rewards they expect to earn at work. In addition to the individual's own motivation, the performance of knowledge workers is dependent upon four key characteristics (*see* Figure 7.13):

- task competence;
- peer and management support;
- task and role clarity; and
- corporate awareness.

The challenge to management is to ensure the effectiveness of the four key variables and to recognise the need for staff to supervise and manage themselves and the wider rewards expected by knowledge workers.

A climate of creativity

Lucas draws attention to skills shortages as one of the biggest challenges facing employers in the new millennium. In order to attract and keep talented individuals, the so-called knowledge workers, organisations cannot rely simply on a pay rise or cash bonus but have to be more creative about the way they structure remuneration packages. Individual performance-related pay is still the most widely used reward strategy, but attention is also given to employee share ownership, competence-related pay and team reward – and also to non-cash incentives such as gift vouchers. However, Lucas points out that employees, especially high flyers, rank challenging and interesting work and freedom higher on their motivational list than money

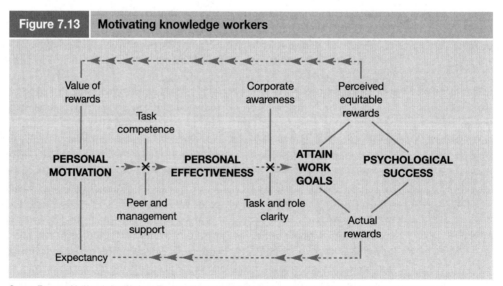

| Figure 7.13 | Motivating knowledge workers |

Source: Tampoe, M. 'Knowledge Workers: The New Management Challenge', *Professional Manager*, Institute of Management, November 1994, p. 13. Reproduced with permission from Chartered Management Institute.

and performance-related pay. 'Research suggests that most organisations haven't recognised the need to identify and tap into their employees' personal motivators.'[47]

A report from the Chartered Institute of Personnel and Development draws attention to the management of knowledge workers, highlighting the importance of autonomy, challenging work and sharing in the creation of organisational values. With the development of new technology it is important to motivate employees to capture, share and transfer knowledge.[48]

Whitmore suggests that in order to create a climate for creativity among employees, recognition must be given to the importance of two human needs that rise above all others and exist independent of race, creed and culture – the need for self-belief and the development of emotional intelligence; and the ever-present need that every human being has for a sense of meaning and purpose in their lives.

> *Self-belief and meaningful work are the fundamental bedrocks that underlie business performance. Of course, pay and conditions are important too, but we know that. It is these two others that are barely recognised . . . but business leaders ignore them at their peril.*[49]

CROSS-CULTURAL DIMENSIONS OF MOTIVATION

Whatever the popularity of different theories of motivation, doubts are raised about their universality on the ground that they have not adequately addressed the factor of culture.[50] Are theories of motivation universally applicable or are there meaningful differences in motivation at work, or in life more generally, in different societies? Many readers may feel able to recognise perceived variations in extrinsic, intrinsic and relational aspects of motivation as a result of experience of foreign cultures. Do similarities in workplace attitudes and behaviour outweigh differences? A number of writers have questioned whether motivational theories and models originating in one culture are amenable to transference to other parts of the world. *Francesco and Gold* devote a substantial proportion of a discussion of motivation to examining the extent to which American motivation theories are applicable outside the United States.

When discussing Maslow's contribution to this topic and, in particular, the concept of a hierarchy of needs, Francesco and Gold suggest: 'In an international context the circumstances and values of a particular culture can influence the ordering and importance of needs. The values of individualism and collectivism can make the hierarchy more or less relevant.'[51] In evaluating McClelland's work, Francesco and Gold question whether the meaning of an underlying concept, in this case achievement, can even be understood worldwide in the sense it was intended: 'Another concern with Learning Needs Theory is that the concept of achievement is difficult, if not impossible, to translate into languages other than English.'[52] A study of motivation and job satisfaction among hotel workers in Brazil found that a number of Herzberg's hygiene and motivating factors did not affect job satisfaction or dissatisfaction. A main cause of this difference appeared to be the influence of organisational culture.[53]

It has already been suggested that one criticism of content theories of motivation centres on its relative applicability in different circumstances, and the suggestion that there may be variations across cultures falls within this line of reasoning. However, perhaps less obviously, process theories of motivation have also been criticised for being culture-bound. As they focus on process rather than content, such theories may appear to be more applicable in diverse cultural contexts. Nonetheless it has been suggested that process theories of motivation contain certain inbuilt assumptions that are themselves culturally derived.

Adler reminds us that expectancy models of motivation assume that individuals believe that they can, to some extent, control their environment and influence their fate. If, as in the cases of more fatalistic cultures such as China, people do not have the same sense of internal attribution, the expectancy model may have less force and therefore less applicability. When Adams's equity theory is applied across the world, differences in interpretation have been recorded.[54] *Chen* suggests that while individualistic cultures place a high regard on equity, collectivist cultures value equality more than equity. Again we see here the possibility that while a theory of motivation may be essentially valid in principle, it is legitimate to think about the ways in which national culture can intervene in terms of its interpretation in different societies.[55]

> ### Critical reflection
>
> 'Motivation and job satisfaction are very subjective and affected by many variables including cultural influences, unknown domestic situations and personal relationships outside of work. Generalised management models cannot meet all individual circumstances and are therefore a complete waste of your study time.'
>
> *To what extent do you agree?*

JOB SATISFACTION

The meaning and nature of job satisfaction

Attempting to understand the nature of job satisfaction and its effects on work performance is not easy. Job satisfaction is a complex and multifaceted concept, which can mean different things to different people. It is usually linked with motivation, but the nature of this relationship is not clear. Satisfaction is not the same as motivation. **Job satisfaction** is more of an attitude, an internal state. It could, for example, be associated with a personal feeling of achievement, either quantitative or qualitative.

It is often suggested that job satisfaction is necessary in order to achieve a high level of motivation and performance. However, although the level of job satisfaction may well affect strength of motivation, this is not always the case. The relationship between job satisfaction and performance is an issue of continuing debate and controversy. One view, associated with the early human relations approach, is that satisfaction leads to performance. An alternative view is that performance leads to satisfaction. *Reeves* draws attention to the relationship between accomplishment at work and the need to 'work harder'.

> *All this busy-ness and stress is creating more heat than light. It is a sign not of work being too hard but too shallow. Human nature is driven by a desire to accomplish things, and so the fewer opportunities for accomplishment a job contains, the more likely we are to fill the void by tearing around in a frenzy in an effort to persuade ourselves and others that our work has a purpose, that it is important.*[56]

Dimensions of job satisfaction

There is some doubt whether job satisfaction consists of a single dimension or a number of separate dimensions. Some workers may be satisfied with certain aspects of their work and dissatisfied with other aspects. Job satisfaction is itself a complex concept and difficult to measure objectively. The level of job satisfaction is affected by a wide range of variables relating to individual, social, cultural, organisational and environmental factors.

- **Individual factors** include personality, education and qualifications, intelligence and abilities, age, marital status, orientation to work.
- **Social factors** include relationships with co-workers, group working and norms, opportunities for interaction, informal organisation.
- **Cultural factors** include underlying attitudes, beliefs and values.

- **Organisational factors** include nature and size, formal structure, HR policies and procedures, employee relations, nature of the work, technology and work organisation, supervision and styles of leadership, management systems, working conditions.
- **Environmental factors** include economic, social, technical and governmental influences.

These different factors all affect the job satisfaction of certain individuals in a given set of circumstances but not necessarily in others. For example in times of economic depression and fears of high unemployment, job security is likely to be the prominent concern for many members of staff. According to the FreshMinds survey discussed in Chapter 3, when it comes to job satisfaction it pays to be older. Apparently 100 per cent of older boomers (born between 1946 and 1963) are satisfied with their job, but only 66 per cent of Generation Y (typified by travel first, then a career) feel the same way. And Generation Y want more at work such as gym membership and sabbaticals.[57]

A survey by the Chartered Management Institute found that organisational culture and values emerged as very strong motivational drivers, and a manager's relationship with their line manager had a powerful impact on job satisfaction and related measures.[58]

Five contractual areas

Mumford examines job satisfaction in two ways:

1 in terms of the fit between what the organisation requires and what the employee is seeking; and
2 in terms of the fit between what the employee is seeking and what they are actually receiving.

On the basis of various schools of thought on job satisfaction, Mumford identifies five contractual areas by which this organisational/employee relationship can be examined: the knowledge contract, the psychological contract, the efficiency/reward contract, the ethical contract and the task structure contract (*see* Table 7.3).[59]

Table 7.3	Five contractual areas relating to job satisfaction	
	The firm	**The employee**
The knowledge contract	Needs a certain level of skill and knowledge in its employees if it is to function efficiently	Wishes the skills and knowledge they bring with them to be used and developed
The psychological contract	Needs employees who are motivated to look after its interests	Seeks to further interests private to self, e.g. to secure: achievement, recognition, responsibility, status
The efficiency/rewards contract	Needs to implement generalised output, quality standards and reward systems	Seeks a personal, equitable effort–reward bargain and controls, including supervisory ones, which are perceived as acceptable
The ethical (social value) contract	Needs employees who will accept the firm's ethos and values	Seeks to work for an employer whose values do not contravene their own
The task structure contract	Needs employees who will accept technical and other constraints which produce task specificity or task differentiation	Seeks a set of tasks which meets their requirements for task differentiation, e.g. which incorporate variety, interests, targets, feedback, task identity and autonomy

Source: Mumford, E. 'Job Satisfaction: A Method of Analysis', *Personnel Review*, vol. 20, no. 3, p. 14, 1991. Copyright © Emerald Group Publishing Limited. All Rights Reserved. Reproduced with permission.

The work environment

An increasingly important issue affecting job satisfaction and efficiency is the nature of the work environment and workplace facilities. *Handy* argues that an inspired workplace will result in inspired workers and draws attention to the importance for work performance of the atmosphere, quality and style of buildings and offices.[60]

A 2003 study by the Chartered Management Institute reports on UK managers' attitudes to and experiences of their physical working environment. The study was undertaken among a random sample of 4,000 managers across all levels and sectors and size of organisation. Topics addressed included hours worked, commuting and travel, flexible working, the existing and preferred layout of offices and the use of new technologies. Concerns were expressed about the need for more quiet areas, under-equipped meeting rooms, lack of adequate meeting space, and their offices not making a good impression on clients and visitors. Nearly half of those surveyed would relinquish one week's annual leave for a better office, and sizeable numbers would forgo £1,000 in salary or private medical insurance for a significantly upgraded workspace. And even if the role, salary and benefits were no better, 45 per cent would contemplate changing companies in return for an improved work environment.[61]

> *More than any other element, fun is the secret of Virgin's success. I am aware that the idea of business being fun and creative goes right against the grain of convention, and it's certainly not how they teach it at some of those business schools, where business means hard grind and lots of 'discounted cash flows' and 'net present values' . . . For us, our employees matter most. It just seems common sense to me that, if you start off with a happy, well motivated workforce, you're much more likely to have happy customers. And in due course the resulting profits will make your shareholders happy.*
>
> Richard Branson[62]

According to *De Vita*, well-being at work pays because employees who are happy and healthy take fewer days off sick, are more productive and more likely to stay with their organisation. The starting point to supporting and promoting well-being in the workplace has to be good people management and effective work organisation. Good line management is the most important of the characteristics of a high-quality workplace that has high levels of commitment and low absence rates.[63]

Flexible working arrangements

An increasingly significant aspect of motivation and job satisfaction is flexible working. According to CIPD, 'This relates to an organisation's working arrangements in terms of working time, working location and the pattern of working.'[64] Moves towards greater flexibility may afford opportunities for employees to have more freedom and control over their working arrangements and have noticeable effects on their job satisfaction and performance. Flexible working arrangements are discussed in Chapter 15.

Broader approaches

Broader approaches to job satisfaction aim to give the person improved empowerment and job enrichment through greater autonomy and authority over the planning, execution and control of their work. It focuses attention on intrinsic satisfaction. Job enrichment increases the complexity of the work. It should provide the person with a more meaningful and challenging job and offer greater opportunities for psychological growth.

The main methods of achieving job enrichment include the following:

- permitting workers greater freedom and control over the scheduling and pacing of their work as opposed to machine pacing;

- allowing workers to undertake a full task cycle, build or assemble a complete product or component, or deliver a complete service;
- providing workers with tasks or jobs which challenge their abilities and make fuller use of their training, expertise and skills;
- giving workers greater freedom to work in self-managing teams with greater responsibility for monitoring their own performance and the minimum of direct supervision; and
- providing workers with the opportunity to have greater direct contact with clients, consumers or users of the product or service.

In an organisation, empowerment means that each staff member is responsible for creating that organisation's culture. There aren't many motivating forces more potent than giving your staff an opportunity to exercise and express their idealism.

Anita Roddick[65]

ALIENATION AT WORK

One main approach to job satisfaction is in terms of frustration and alienation at work. Job satisfaction can be seen as the obverse of frustration at work (discussed earlier in this chapter). **Alienation** refers to the detachment of the person from their work role. The concept of alienation at work is associated originally with the views of *Marx*.[66] He saw the division of labour in pursuit of profit, and exploitation by employers, as a denial of the workers' need for self-expression. Workers become estranged from the product of their work. Work no longer provided a satisfying experience in itself, but represented a means of satisfying other external demands. The concept of alienation has been extended by *Blauner*.[67] He describes alienation in terms of four dimensions: powerlessness, meaninglessness, isolation and self-estrangement.

- **Powerlessness** denotes the workers' lack of control over management policy, immediate work processes, or conditions of employment.
- **Meaninglessness** stems from standardisation and division of labour. It denotes the inability to see the purpose of work done or to identify with the total production process or finished product.
- **Isolation** is not belonging to an integrated work group or to the social work organisation and not being guided by group norms of behaviour.
- **Self-estrangement** is the failure to see work as an end in itself or as a central life issue. Workers experience a depersonalised detachment and work is seen solely as a means to an end.

In recent years attention to job satisfaction has also become more closely associated with broader approaches to improved job design and work organisation, and the quality of working life movement, and with stress and the work/life balance (discussed in Chapter 3).

A concept map of job satisfaction is set out in Figure 7.14.

A COMPREHENSIVE MODEL OF JOB ENRICHMENT

Attempts to improve intrinsic motivation must not only include considerations of job characteristics but also take account of individual differences and attributes, and people's orientation to work. A popular and comprehensive model of job enrichment has been developed by *Hackman and Oldham* (*see* Figure 7.15).[68] The model views job enrichment

Figure 7.14 Concept map of job satisfaction

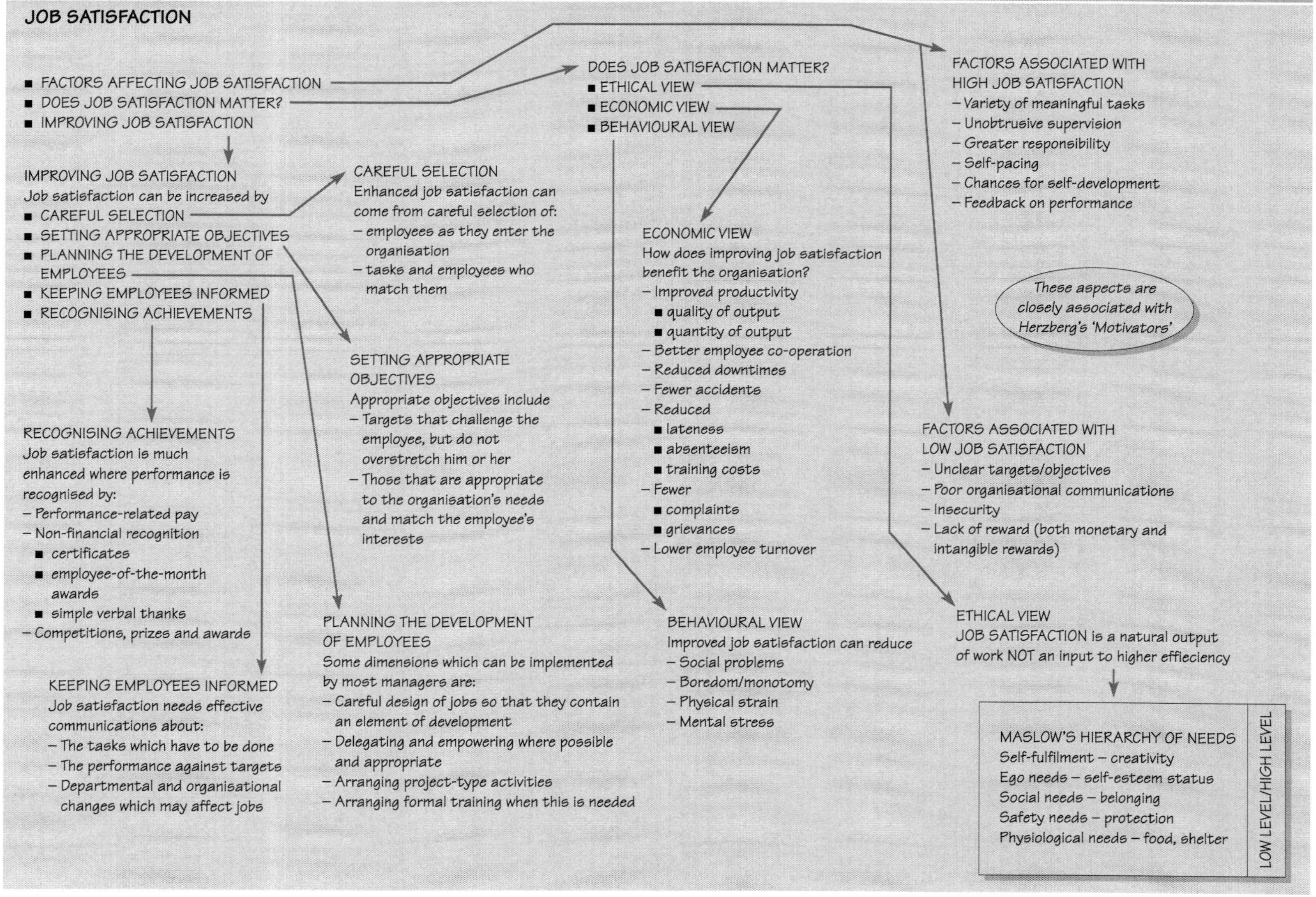
JOB SATISFACTION
■ FACTORS AFFECTING JOB SATISFACTION
■ DOES JOB SATISFACTION MATTER?
■ IMPROVING JOB SATISFACTION
IMPROVING JOB SATISFACTION
Job satisfaction can be increased by
■ CAREFUL SELECTION
■ SETTING APPROPRIATE OBJECTIVES
■ PLANNING THE DEVELOPMENT OF EMPLOYEES
■ KEEPING EMPLOYEES INFORMED
■ RECOGNISING ACHIEVEMENTS
CAREFUL SELECTION
Enhanced job satisfaction can come from careful selection of:
– employees as they enter the organisation
– tasks and employees who match them
SETTING APPROPRIATE OBJECTIVES
Appropriate objectives include
– Targets that challenge the employee, but do not overstretch him or her
– Those that are appropriate to the organisation's needs and match the employee's interests
RECOGNISING ACHIEVEMENTS
Job satisfaction is much enhanced where performance is recognised by:
– Performance-related pay
– Non-financial recognition
■ certificates
■ employee-of-the-month awards
■ simple verbal thanks
– Competitions, prizes and awards
KEEPING EMPLOYEES INFORMED
Job satisfaction needs effective communications about:
– The tasks which have to be done
– The performance against targets
– Departmental and organisational changes which may affect jobs
PLANNING THE DEVELOPMENT OF EMPLOYEES
Some dimensions which can be implemented by most managers are:
– Careful design of jobs so that they contain an element of development
– Delegating and empowering where possible and appropriate
– Arranging project-type activities
– Arranging formal training when this is needed
DOES JOB SATISFACTION MATTER?
■ ETHICAL VIEW
■ ECONOMIC VIEW
■ BEHAVIOURAL VIEW
ECONOMIC VIEW
How does improving job satisfaction benefit the organisation?
– Improved productivity
■ quality of output
■ quantity of output
– Better employee co-operation
– Reduced downtimes
– Fewer accidents
– Reduced
■ lateness
■ absenteeism
■ training costs
– Fewer
■ complaints
■ grievances
– Lower employee turnover
BEHAVIOURAL VIEW
Improved job satisfaction can reduce
– Social problems
– Boredom/monotomy
– Physical strain
– Mental stress
FACTORS ASSOCIATED WITH HIGH JOB SATISFACTION
– Variety of meaningful tasks
– Unobtrusive supervision
– Greater responsibility
– Self-pacing
– Chances for self-development
– Feedback on performance
These aspects are closely associated with Herzberg's 'Motivators'
FACTORS ASSOCIATED WITH LOW JOB SATISFACTION
– Unclear targets/objectives
– Poor organisational communications
– Insecurity
– Lack of reward (both monetary and intangible rewards)
ETHICAL VIEW
JOB SATISFACTION is a natural output of work NOT an input to higher effieciency
MASLOW'S HIERARCHY OF NEEDS
Self-fulfilment – creativity
Ego needs – self-esteem status
Social needs – belonging
Safety needs – protection
Physiological needs – food, shelter
LOW LEVEL/HIGH LEVEL

Source: Copyright © 2008 The Virtual Learning Materials Workshop. Reproduced with permission.

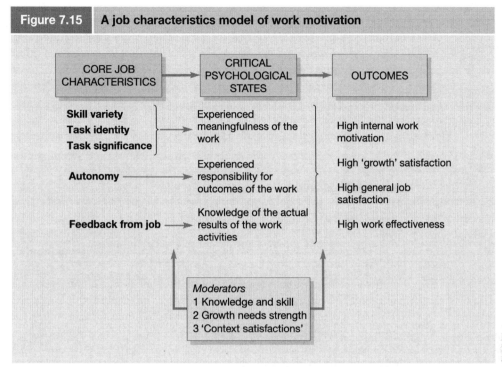

| Figure 7.15 | A job characteristics model of work motivation |

Source: Hackman, J. R. and Oldham, G. R. *Work Redesign*, Addison-Wesley Publishing Company, Inc. (1980), Figure 4.6, p. 90. Reproduced with permission from Pearson Education, Inc.

in terms of increasing five core job dimensions: skill variety, task identity, task significance, autonomy and feedback. These core job characteristics create three psychological states:

■ experienced meaningfulness of the work;
■ experienced responsibility for the outcomes of the work; and
■ knowledge of the actual results of the work activities.

Five core dimensions

The five core job dimensions can be summarised as follows:

■ **skill variety** – the extent to which a job entails different activities and involves a range of skills and talents;
■ **task identity** – the extent to which a job involves completion of a whole piece of work with a visible outcome;
■ **task significance** – the extent to which a job has a meaningful impact on other people, either inside or outside the organisation;
■ **autonomy** – the extent to which a job provides freedom, independence and discretion in planning the work and determining how to undertake it;
■ **feedback** – the extent to which work activities result in direct and clear information on the effectiveness of job performance.

An example of a job with little enrichment could be that of a production assembly line worker or a kitchen porter, where all five core characteristics are likely to score low. An example of an enriched job could be that of a parish priest who draws upon a wide range of social skills and talents, who can usually identify with the whole task and whose job has clear and important meaning and significance. There is a very high level of autonomy and likely to be direct and clear feedback.

Motivating potential score

From these five core job dimensions, Hackman and Oldham have developed an equation which gives a single index of a person's job profile. By answering a questionnaire – the Job Diagnostic Survey (JDS) – and by giving a score (between 1 and 7) to each job dimension, the person can calculate an overall measure of job enrichment, called the motivating potential score (MPS).

Examples of questions from the JDS are:

- How much variety is there in your job?
- To what extent does your job involve doing a whole and identifiable piece of work?
- In general, how significant or important is your job?
- How much autonomy is there in your job?
- To what extent does doing the job itself provide you with information about your work performance?

$$\text{MPS} = \frac{\{\text{Skill variety} + \text{Task identity} + \text{Task significance}\}}{3} \times \text{Autonomy} \times \text{Feedback}$$

The first three job dimensions of skill variety, task identity and task significance are averaged, since it is the combination of these dimensions which contributes to experienced meaningfulness of work. The remaining two job dimensions, autonomy and feedback, stand on their own. Since scores for skill variety, task identity and task significance are additive, this means that the absence of one dimension can be partially offset by the presence of the other dimensions. However, if either autonomy or feedback is absent then, because of the multiplicative relationship, the MPS would be zero. The job would offer no potential to motivate the person.

Empirical support for the model

Empirical support for the model is mixed. From their studies, Hackman and Oldham claim that people with enriched jobs and high score levels on the Job Diagnostic Survey experienced more satisfaction and internal motivation. The core job dimensions of skill variety, task identity and task significance combined to predict the level of experienced meaningfulness of the work. The core dimensions of autonomy and feedback did not relate so clearly to experienced responsibility and knowledge of results. Some of the other dimensions were as good, or better, in predicting these psychological conditions. In general, however, the results of their studies showed that jobs that scored high on the core dimensions were associated with high levels of personal and work outcomes.

Luthans et al. report on evidence from a number of studies of American workers that the job design approach leads to improvement in motivation and performance, but also that the approach did not work in the Russian factory study discussed earlier in this chapter.[69]

In a study of a sample of six hotels (with between 35 and 65 bedrooms) in Great Yarmouth, *Lee-Ross* undertook an examination of the reliability of the JDS among seasonal workers. From an analysis of 163 questionnaires, Lee-Ross concludes that in general, reliability scores were compatible with those of Hackman and Oldham. The JDS appears to hold just as well for hotel workers as for workers in other industries.[70]

Based on integrating Hackman and Oldham's job characteristics model with Maslow's hierarchy of needs, *Roe et al.* propose a general model of work motivation, tested with Bulgarian, Hungarian and Dutch workers. The model indicates that situational characteristics lead to critical psychological factors, inducing two main motivational factors – **job involvement** and **organisational commitment** – which in turn lead to two proximal outcomes of work motivation – **effort** and **job satisfaction** – which affect **performance, stress** and **tendency to leave the organisation**. Although there were some differences that draw attention to cultural variables, there was also a large degree of similarity in results across the three countries.[71]

CONTEXTUAL FACTORS IN JOB DESIGN

The different methods of job design are not necessarily separate approaches. They are inter-related and there is some overlapping among them. For example, goal-setting is sometimes viewed as another approach to job design. Goal-setting involves building goals, feedback and incentives into the structure of the job. In addition, there are many other associated (contextual) factors which affect job design, including, for example: organisational culture, structure, systems of management and style of leadership, trade unions, HR policies and procedures, communications, group norms, ergonomics, the management of change, and the working environment.

The potential benefits of improved job design are unlikely to be realised if attention is focused on the content of jobs alone. Of equal, if not more, importance is the process by which redesign is carried out. This has led to recognition of the importance of management style and, increasingly, of organisation culture.[72] Central to improving the quality of working life is a participative, open style of management involving employees in decisions that affect them, including the design or choice of technology. Management should attempt to develop a relationship of trust among all members and sections of the organisation and a meaningful partnership approach with trade unions.

Theories of work motivation and job satisfaction have influenced management systems and styles of leadership, and developments in HR policies and procedures. The human resource management function is centred on people's needs while working in an organisation and ways in which their work promotes or frustrates the fulfilment of these needs.[73] The practice of modern human resource management is directed towards providing conditions under which people work willingly and effectively, and contribute to the success of the organisation. This involves concern for employee motivation and job satisfaction.

Critical reflection

'Individuals have a variety of changing, and often conflicting, needs and expectations which they attempt to satisfy in a number of ways at different times.'

What are the most powerful influences on your own work motivation and job satisfaction? How do you think these will change in five years' time?

Cases

Top marks for the best employee awards

FT

Rhymer Rigby

Employee of the month (or the week, or the year) awards have a bad image. They are popularly associated with low-paid, low-status service sector jobs – a dollop of worthless recognition on top of an already low-value package. Implemented properly, they can be a valuable form of recognition that motivates staff, especially in today's reward-constrained climate. Handled wrongly, however, they can backfire and foster cynicism.

Stephen Carella, a team leader at Kwik-Fit Financial Services, an insurance intermediary, was its Employee of the Year 2008. 'It was a goal I'd set myself at the start of the year,' he explains. Once he had won six employee of the month awards, he knew he was in with a good chance. He adds: 'It's a great incentive and what really motivated me is the recognition you get. It's a fantastic thing to put on your CV.' Mr Carella was presented with his award at a dinner for 100 of the company's top performers and their partners at Edinburgh's Balmoral Hotel. He also received a cash prize of £10,000. 'It was,' he says, 'the best night of my life.'

The scheme, explains Brendan Devine, KFFS group managing director, has been running for four years and is part of a complex structure of recognition. Each department has an employee of the month award, which accords privileges such as free food in the staff bistro, gym membership and parking. From these are drawn quarterly qualifiers who could make it on to a shortlist for employee of the year. 'It's part of an overall strategy to identify who top performers are,' says Mr Devine, adding that at the dinner, the 34 departmental winners of the annual title also receive awards and £1,000. 'In a way, the recognition is the most important part though – [the] reward goes beyond your pay packet.'

Ben Williams, a corporate psychologist, says such schemes can be valuable but cautions that they must be implemented properly. He says: 'By and large they're a good thing and encourage beliefs and behaviours the company might want to promote such as high sales or great customer care. In industries where people move round, they can encourage them to stay.' However, he says: 'You need to avoid a celebrity-like cult of the individual. Teams need to be considered together. If everyone's a high performer, it can be divisive to only reward the single highest performer.'

There is also the vexed question of recognition versus material reward. The key is getting the underlying corporate culture right. If it is wrong, says Williams, 'recipients can be made to look obsequious sycophants,

Source: iStockphoto

Employee award schemes can be a valuable form of recognising the contributions of employees but if handled badly can backfire and foster cynicism. How can employers strike the right balance in both deciding what to do and what to avoid?

like swots at school'. Still, no matter what you do, there will always be groups that are damning about such recognition: 'That's one of the reasons to give cash rewards – you get buy-in from the cynical brigade.'

But for all the organisations that take these considerations on board, there are still plenty that do not. 'I was the best-performing employee of the quarter,' says one salesman at another company, 'and I went up on stage and was given a £20 M&S voucher – which makes you feel a bit like a monkey performing for bananas.' He spent his voucher on strawberries and a few months later he won employee of the year. Soon after he left the company.

Source: Rigby, R. 'Top Marks for the Best Employee Award', *Financial Times*, 11 May 2009. Copyright © 2009 The Financial Times Limited, reproduced with permission.

Discussion questions

1 What evidence is there in the article that employee award schemes can help meet the needs and expectations of people at work outlined in Figure 7.2?

2 Explain which two motivation theories you think are most useful for a manager who is planning an employee award scheme both to decide what to include in the scheme and what to avoid.

CASE STUDY

Don't get mad, get on-line!

In 2005 the word 'blog', meaning an on-line journal or web log which is regularly updated by the author, entered the Oxford English Dictionary for the first time. Figures collected by internet monitoring organisations suggest that by the time the word made it into the dictionary there were about 30 million blogs in existence, and the numbers were increasing at the rate of about 70,000 per day.[74] Add to this the emergence of social networking and communication sites such as Facebook and Twitter and there has never been such a wide range of possible ways to launch personal thoughts into a waiting cyberworld. Not all are about work, but the fact that life in the office or workplace is a significant part of many people's lives means that many blogs, posts and tweets include references to work, bosses, colleagues and customers alongside other normal daily experiences, opinions about news events and so on. A number of blogs are specifically about work, and these are the ones which tend to hit the headlines, usually when an employee gets into trouble for airing their opinions about the organisation they work for in the blogosphere.

Why do individuals blog about work? At one level, blogging is no different from gossip. Many bloggers expect to have small audiences, possibly of like-minded people who have similar experiences to discuss; the content of blogs may be much like the discussions with colleagues that are routinely held in the round the water cooler or coffee machine, or with friends in a pub or bar after work. Most blogs include opportunities for email and on-line discussion, and so become a lively mix of intimate diary items and chatroom-style comments. For some authors the aim is to give an insight into their working life, perhaps discussing a type of job which many people know about but few really understand. In the UK, at least one chief police constable and a number of ambulance service workers are known to blog primarily about their work.[75] However, many see it as a way of letting off steam about aspects of their work which enrage them, be it the organisation, their individual managers, their annoying colleagues or – as often – the absurd behaviour of members of the general public and customers in particular.[76] This can make blogging a particularly risky activity, at least if the blogger wishes to keep their job.

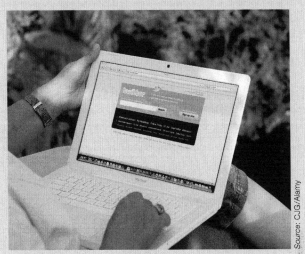

Is it acceptable to blog, post or tweet about your company? Social networking and communication sites provide a wide range of ways to share personal thoughts in a public venue resulting in organisational responses that can range from accepting to creative to hostile.

Careless blogging can get you dooced

In 2004 Ellen Simonetti hit the headlines[77] when she was sacked by her employer, the American Delta Airlines, essentially for identifying them as the company about which she was blogging on her 'Queen of the Sky' website. The offence which got her sacked was not the blog itself, but the fact that by posting photographs of herself draped across the seats of an aircraft in her uniform (pictures which were described by the company as 'inappropriate') she identified the organisation itself, and therefore was considered to have brought it into disrepute. In January 2005, in a similar British case, Joe Gordon, an employee of Waterstone's bookshop in Edinburgh of 11 years' standing, was dismissed for gross misconduct[78] after 'bringing the company into disrepute' by complaining about his 'evil boss' at the fictionalised but nevertheless sufficiently recognisable bookstore 'Bastardones' in his blog 'The Wolamaloo Gazette'.[79]

The term 'doocing' has since been used to describe the phenomenon of being sacked for blogging, a fate which also befell Catherine Sanderson or 'La Petite Anglaise' who was dismissed from the Parisian branch of British accounting firm Dixon Wilson in July 2006

of British accounting firm Dixon Wilson in July 2006 for committing the 'real and serious' offence of blogging mischievously but anonymously about her boss and colleagues.[80] As with Simonetti, it was when she posted photographs of herself on the site that the company decided that she, and therefore it, could be identified, and that it had to act against its employee. Market Sentinel offers an internet monitoring service (much like that of a press agency) to companies who want to know what is being posted about them, and be alerted to potential threats posed to their brand image in cyberspace. This too can result in disciplinary action as 13 cabin crew at Virgin Atlantic discovered to their cost when they were dismissed for posting derogatory comments about Virgin customers on Facebook.[81]

Learning to love bloggers

Not every organisation has reacted with hostility to bloggers. The chief constable and the ambulance workers mentioned above are at least tolerated and at best supported by their employers (the chief constable's blog is hosted by the North Wales Police website). The same was also true for Robert Scoble, at Microsoft, whose blog (Scobleizer) not only turned him into a cyber-celebrity, but also acted to help humanise the previously monolithic corporate face of the company.[82] Other organisations have actively embraced blog culture, and sought to use it to their advantage, mainly to aid recruitment. Dell, the US computer giant, has also created its own blog (Direct2Dell) as a means of engaging with customer criticism. An increasing number of organisations have recognised the impossibility of controlling employees' private blogs, but have offered guidance and codes of practice for their workforce as a means of setting out company policy and thereby setting boundaries of acceptable behaviour. IBM, for example has developed a set of eleven guidelines for its staff, some of which are summarised below:[83]

- Know and follow IBM's Business Conduct Guidelines.
- IBMers are personally responsible for their posts.
- You must make it clear that you are speaking for yourself and not on behalf of IBM.
- Respect copyright, fair use and financial disclosure laws.
- Don't provide IBM's or another's confidential or other proprietary information.
- Don't use ethnic slurs, personal insults, obscenity etc.; and show proper consideration for others' privacy and topics that may be considered objectionable or inflammatory such as politics and religion.
- Don't pick fights, be the first to correct your own mistakes and don't alter previous posts without indicating that you have done so.
- Try to add value. Provide worthwhile information and perspective.

A great many organisations have seized the opportunity to communicate with staff, customers, members and others via website-based blogs.

Organisational consequences: possibilities and challenges

IBM's approach, the development of guidelines for employees, is increasingly being seen as the way forward for organisations which are concerned about blogging. It prevents them from appearing heavy-handed, avoids the adverse publicity that can sometimes be stirred up by a sacking, and might also preclude legal challenges, for instance on the grounds of unfair dismissal, or as an attempt to curtail freedom of speech. Simonetti, Gordon and Sanderson all challenged their dismissals using employment tribunals or their equivalents, opening the question of the validity of dismissal for blogging. The existence of company guidelines which have clearly been breached by a blogger is likely to support an employer's case for dismissal.

The UK Chartered Institute of Personnel and Development considers that there are occasions when blogging might be easily identifiable as a disciplinary offence but would not necessarily support a dismissal; for instance, the abuse of company equipment and time by workers 'blogging or tweeting on the job' might not be deemed to warrant dismissal by an employment tribunal unless the post additionally caused harm to the organisation's reputation and interests.[84] On the other hand, disclosure of confidential information might well breach company data protection policies; and dismissal for libellous or defamatory comments might stand up to the test of a tribunal. The spectre of cyber-bullying is another concern, since social networking sites like Facebook have the potential for defamatory and libellous comments and even illicit recordings to be posted for circulation to a specified group. Similarly, it seems possible that if employees are using blogs to air their work grievances rather than using the more normal (and in the UK statutorily required) grievance procedures, then they might well be risking fair dismissal. However, it is also worth considering how far disgruntled employees' blogs indicate that organisational grievance procedures or other employee feedback mechanisms (such as attitude surveys) are not operating very successfully and that important information about employee morale and job dissatisfaction is being overlooked.

Finally it might also be necessary to consider how far blogs are acceptable as a form of whistleblowing, and whether employees who use blogs in this way would be protected by relevant legislation such as the Public Interest Disclosure Act (PIDA) of 1998 in the UK. The PIDA extends protection to whistleblowers, but normally on the basis that they have already exhausted internal organisational methods of raising their concerns before going public. Here again, blogs might be of enormous value to senior managers within an organisation whose ability to monitor the reality of working life in relation to aims regarding (for example) employee morale or issues of corporate social responsibility is limited.

The last word should perhaps go to an anonymous blogger who reported to *Personnel Today* magazine:

Blogging – with its potential audience of millions, is an easy way to exercise my creativity and make my views heard. I'm dissatisfied with my job and unhappy with the way recent restructuring and management decisions have led to low morale, although I do not have an 'evil boss' like the Waterstone's employee. Most of my work-related moans on my blog are minor, everyday niggles about annoying colleagues or the dull nature of my employment, but I am not afraid to occasionally pull out the big guns over issues I feel passionately about.[85]

Your tasks

1 Using a basic model of expectancy theory such as that in Figure 7.8 or one of goal-setting theory such as Locke's (Figure 7.12) assess the various motivational forces which might be operating when employees blog about their employer.

2 It seems that for some people, blogging about work can be viewed as a form of frustration-induced behaviour. Critically review the process of blogging as a method of expressing job dissatisfaction. How do you think managers should respond to cases of work-related blogging by frustrated employees?

3 Organisational responses to employee blogs or Facebook posts outlined in the case might be categorised as either hostile (sack and sue); accepting (control and monitor); or creative (encourage and use). For each of these approaches, identify some basic guidelines for handling cases such as those of Simonetti, Gordon and Sanderson, bearing in mind the motivational effects that your proposals might have on both bloggers and other employees.

Case study   The Eden Project www.edenproject.com

The Eden Project is one of the most visited attractions in Europe: over 10 million people have visited it since it opened in 2001. Tim Smit (who had earlier been responsible for re-opening the Lost Gardens of Heligan to the public, which have become the most visited gardens in Britain) co-founded the project, which developed from his Heligan experience. This had convinced him that people (even those who did not initially like gardens) could be attracted by anecdotes – accessible stories about what they were looking at. He also noticed that people felt very positive about being in well-made, abundant gardens.

This led him to develop the idea of creating a place that looked good, was technically sophisticated, and which was dedicated to explaining how all life on Earth depends on plants. More than that, it could become:

> a place where you started to think about your connection with nature, and whether you might want to get closer to nature again and whether some lessons of life might not be buried in there.

From this initial vision, Eden has, within only nine years, become one of the 50 most recognised brands, alongside established businesses such as Nokia and Pepsi-Cola; has generated over £90 million in revenues for other businesses in Cornwall; and employs some 500 staff.

The first task in turning the idea into reality was to persuade people to invest in the project – which was to cost about £76 million to build. Smit approached one of the leading architects of the time, who, after consulting with his colleagues, agreed to work on the project: Smit says:

> So for the next 18 months we had possibly the best design team in the world working for us for nothing. I think the reason Eden came into being was that we formed an enormous gang. There was a bunch of people that were really interested in the idea and we would meet in motorway service stations and in pubs and in people's houses and this just grew as people heard about it. People started leaving their jobs because

Eden Project

> they became so obsessed with it. And it suddenly had an inevitability, when we realised we were saying 'when' not 'if' . . . and the dice rolled unbelievably well for us.

> The environment became a big thing, plants are good, people can imagine the Crystal Palace and this is bigger than the Crystal Palace. We said we wanted the biggest in the world, to contain a full-size rainforest, we don't just want some namby-pamby greenhouse. I said we wanted to build a global must-see like the Guggenheim. The tourism people thought we might get 500,000 visitors in the first year: we actually had 1.8 million.

> And in the middle of all that there was a huge fund-raising effort to raise the money for what we called the eighth wonder of the world.

Source: Interview with Tim Smit; Eden Project website.

Case questions 15.1

Creating Eden has depended on motivating people.

- Which groups of people have featured in the case so far?
- What has Tim Smit wanted these people to do for the Eden Project?
- What clues are there about what motivates them to give their support?

Gaynor Coley is managing director at the Eden Project, and her financial background was crucial in raising the money which the project needed.

I left a safe, pensionable university job to join Eden in early 1997, having met this crew who had no money in the bank, but who were going to build the eighth wonder of the world in a derelict Cornish clay pit. I spent the next three years raising the money: a really exciting period, using all those skills you learn in the City about having a robust business plan, together with skills you may use in fringe theatre, which are about how to get something off the ground when nothing exists. The art of persuasion was putting Tim in front of the right people so he could really get them behind the purpose, but then following that up with the real mechanics of what the business needs which is a robust plan and a bank and a set of stakeholders who are prepared to come with you.

One thing that's really important about this project is teamwork – we had a horticultural director who was superb, we had an education director who could persuade anybody that education really is the route to a better world.

To get the finance we had to identify people with a similar purpose to us. So the Millennium Commission wanted to put really landmark architecture into the landscape and it was obvious that there was nothing else in the south west that would meet this brief. The South West Regional Development Agency was there to generate economic activity, well-paid jobs, and a reason for people to come to the south west. So they had a different agenda, and part of our task there was also to say, 'well, we will fulfil that agenda'. So it was research around what agendas a portfolio of stakeholders had, understanding them and actually making a pitch relevant to that particular stakeholder.

Source: Interview with Gaynor Coley.

Case questions 15.2

- What motivational skills has the managing director demonstrated in raising the funds that Eden required?
- How transferable do you think they would be to other management situations?

Tim Smit on the reasons for Eden:

Of course we have to give people a good day out, a cup of tea they enjoy and all that. But I think we have actually struck a vein which has got deeper and more important to us as a society, which is people are not just looking for leisure: what many are looking for is a purpose in their lives, and I think the combination of a great day out, with something meaningful, learning about your environment, learning about your relationship with nature, was a killer proposition. That's why I think we get the numbers we do.

The mission of Eden has changed and developed over the years, but I think there's a seed of an idea that's never gone away and that is about how important it is for us as human beings to understand our relationship with nature. We aren't independent of it: we are dependent on it and part of it. So we give visitors a narrative which is about 'let's protect the habitat of the plants we rely on: coffee, tea, sugar, the things we use in out everyday life'. It's about understanding humans' place in nature, understanding that human ingenuity is going to be the thing that provides really good solutions to challenges as well as to some of the poor behaviour.

We think about how we operate, how we do business, and we believe that what you do is really, really important. So the authenticity of the welcome that you get when you come here, the authenticity of how we treat our suppliers, is what I think lies behind the strength of the Eden brand.

Source: Interview with Tim Smit.

Case questions 15.3

- What human needs is Eden seeking to satisfy?
- How attractive do you think you would find Eden if you worked there, and for what reasons?

Tim Smit on work at Eden:

To work at Eden you've got to be interested in a lot of stuff. You've got to be prepared to catch people when they fall, because people are trying stuff all the time, and you've got to be prepared for the unexpected because part of the way we work is almost deliberately create chaos by doing more stuff than we've possibly got time to do, which means more junior members have more chance to become leaders because the senior ones can't do it all.

One of the things I think is very special about Eden is that the letters after your name don't make any difference. It's what you can do . . . Sure the Finance Director's got to be an accountant and all that sort of stuff, but in the wider scheme of things, to be an Eden person you've got to be optimistic and smiley and damned hard working.

Gayle Conley adds:

We try not to be prescriptive about defining talent and we try to encourage people to take individual responsibility for their own career path here as much as we can help them to a career path

Jess Ratty speaks about her work:

I began at Eden as a waitress when I was 16 years old with no qualifications: I'm now 24 and the Press Officer. So I've worked in about eight departments and worked my way up through the company. I think Eden's been a fantastic opportunity for me – the ethos and the way you don't have to have a degree – you know they'll give people a chance . . . after working as a waitress I moved to the Stewards team where I learnt a lot about dealing with people. I worked

in plant sales, learning a lot about different plants, which was great to learn at 18. Then I worked in retail, the product side of things, and was then picked up by the design team . . . . and after a few more jobs one of the managers said 'do you want to go for the job of communications assistant?' And I thought, 'people actually believe in me, they want me to do a job they think I'll be good at'!

Sources: Interviews with staff members.

Case questions 15.4

- Consider how the company has helped to generate positive attitudes with this member of staff.
- Analyse these accounts using Herzberg's theory – which of his 'motivating factors' do staff refer to?

Review Questions and Tests

REVIEW AND DISCUSSION QUESTIONS

1 Explain what you understand by the underlying concept of motivation. Summarise the main needs and expectations to be taken into account in considering the motivation of people at work.

2 What do you understand by frustration-induced behaviour? Give a practical example, preferably from your work experience, of each of the main forms of this behaviour.

3 Critically assess the practical value of Maslow's hierarchy of needs model to improving the motivation of people at work. Give examples of the extent to which the theory could meaningfully be applied to staff in your own organisation.

4 Debate critically the validity of the contention that the motivation for staff to work well depends on more than a high salary and good working conditions.

5 Explain your understanding of expectancy-based theories of motivation. Use a simple diagram to help explain an expectancy theory of your choice. What implications do expectancy theories of motivation have for the manager?

6 Give detailed practical examples of situations in which each of the following theories of motivation might be appropriate: (i) achievement motivation; (ii) equity theory; (iii) goal theory.

7 What exactly do you understand by job satisfaction? What are the main dimensions of job satisfaction? Give specific examples of causes of both job satisfaction and job dissatisfaction that you have experienced.

8 Evaluate critically the relationship between motivation, job satisfaction and effective work performance. Give reasons in support of your views.

Review and discussion questions

1 *What are the practical implications of need theories?*

2 *How might you use expectancy theory to influence performance?*

3 *How would you apply goal setting to guarantee high performance?*

4 *How would you identify and use antecedents and consequents to motivate people to perform?*

5 *How should job redesign be approached to ensure that it motivates people to perform?*

Review questions

1 Outline the basic assumptions of McGregor's Theory X and Theory Y.

2 Describe the psychological contract. What are you expecting: (a) from an employer in your career; and (b) from an employer who provides you with part-time work while you are studying?

3 Which three things are pinpointed when using behaviour modification?

4 How does Maslow's theory of human needs relate to the ideas of Frederick Taylor?

5 How does Alderfer's theory differ from Maslow's? What research lay behind the two theories?

6 How did you score on the McClelland test? How did your scores compare with those of others?

7 Explain the difference between Herzberg's hygiene and motivating factors.

8 Explain the difference between $E \rightarrow P$ and $P \rightarrow O$ in expectancy theory.

9 What are the five job design elements that may affect a person's satisfaction with their work?

10 Give an example of an implementing concept associated with each element.

11 Summarise an idea from the chapter that adds to your understanding of the integrating themes.

SECTION 10:
HUMAN RESOURCE MANAGEMENT

Chapter 17:
Human Resource Management

A Manager's Dilemma

It's probably one of the hardest things a manager may have to do.[1] Telling an employee that he or she is being laid off. And some 8 million Americans who have been laid off since the economic recession began in early 2008 have been given that news by someone. In smaller businesses, it's especially difficult because it's often more personal and employees are more like family. In delivering that news, managers may fear that employees will get highly emotional or angry, although those reactions don't happen often. Such reactions are more likely when workers have no notice that layoffs are coming. That's when the situation can become especially raw as those being laid off respond with expressions of shock and disbelief and sometimes crying.

At Ram Tool, a small family-owned manufacturing company in Grafton, Wisconsin, the task fell to Shelly Polum, the company's vice president of administration. After the nine-member management team met to consider which employees would be laid off, Shelly had to inform four workers that they were being let go. "When it was over, trying to maintain her composure, she rushed back to her office and shut the door quickly. Then she sank to the floor and burst into tears." How could this process be made less stressful?

What Would You Do?

With the organization's structure in place, managers have to find people to fill the jobs that have been created or to remove people from jobs if business circumstances require. That's where human resource management (HRM) comes in. It's an important task that involves having the right number of the right people in the right place at the right time. In this chapter, we'll look at the process managers use to do just that. In addition, we'll look at some contemporary HRM issues facing managers.

A major HRM challenge for managers is ensuring that their company has a high-quality workforce. Getting and keeping competent and talented employees is critical to the success of every organization, whether an organization is just starting or has been in business for years. If an organization doesn't take its HRM responsibilities seriously, performance may suffer. Therefore, part of every manager's job when organizing is human resource management. All managers engage in some HRM activities such as interviewing job candidates, orienting new employees, and evaluating their employees' work performance, even if there is a separate HRM department.

LEARNING OUTCOME **12.1**
Explain the importance of the human resource management process and the external influences that might affect that process.

The Human Resource Management Process

"At L'Oreal, success starts with people. Our people are our most precious asset. Respect for people, their ideas and differences, is the only path to our sustainable long-term growth."[2] Many organizations profess that their people are their most important asset and acknowledge the important role that employees play in organizational success. However, why is HRM important and what external factors influence the HRM process?

Why Is HRM Important?

HRM is important for three reasons. First, it can be a significant source of competitive advantage as various studies have concluded.[3] And that's true for organizations around the world, not just U.S. firms. The Human Capital Index, a comprehensive study of more than 2,000 global firms, concluded that people-oriented HR gives an organization an edge by creating superior shareholder value.[4]

Second, HRM is an important part of organizational strategies. Achieving competitive success through people means managers must change how they think about their employees and how they view the work relationship. They must work with people and treat them as partners, not just as costs to be minimized or avoided. That's what people-oriented organizations such as Southwest Airlines and W. L. Gore do.

Finally, the way organizations treat their people has been found to significantly impact organizational performance.[5] For instance, one study reported that improving work practices could increase market value by as much as 30 percent.[6] Another study that tracked average annual shareholder returns of companies on *Fortune's* list of 100 Best Companies to Work For found that these companies significantly beat the S&P 500 over 10-year, 5-year, 3-year, and 1-year periods.[7] Work practices that lead to both high individual and high organizational performance are known as **high-performance work practices**. (See some examples in Exhibit 12-1.) The common thread among these practices seems to be a commitment to involving employees; improving the knowledge, skills, and abilities of an organization's employees; increasing their motivation; reducing loafing on the job; and enhancing the retention of quality employees while encouraging low performers to leave.

Even if an organization doesn't use high-performance work practices, other specific HRM activities must be completed in order to ensure that the organization has qualified people to perform the work that needs to be done—activities that comprise the HRM process. Exhibit 12-2 shows the eight activities in this process. The first three activities ensure that competent employees are identified and selected; the next two involve providing employees with up-to-date knowledge and skills; and the final three ensure that the organization retains competent and high-performing employees. Before we discuss those specific activities, we need to look at external factors that affect the HRM process.

External Factors That Affect the HRM Process

The administrative assistant job opening paying $13 an hour at a Burns Harbor, Indiana, truck driver training school for C. R. England, a nationwide trucking company, was posted on a Friday afternoon.[8] By the time the company's head of corporate recruiting arrived at work on Monday morning, there were about 300 applications in the company's e-mail inbox. And an inch-and-a-half stack of résumés was piled up by the now out-of-paper fax machine. Out of those 500 plus applicants, one person, who had lost her job

---

EXHIBIT 12-1

High-Performance Work Practices

- Self-managed teams
- Decentralized decision making
- Training programs to develop knowledge, skills, and abilities
- Flexible job assignments
- Open communication
- Performance-based compensation
- Staffing based on person–job and person–organization fit
- Extensive employee involvement
- Giving employees more control over decision making
- Increasing employee access to information

Sources: C. H. Chuang and H. Liao, "Strategic Human Resource Management in Service Context: Taking Care of Business by Taking Care of Employees and Customers," *Personnel Psychology,* Spring 2010, pp. 153–196; M. Subramony, "A Meta-Analytic Investigation of the Relationship Between HRM Bundles and Firm Performance," *Human Resource Management,* September–October 2009, pp. 745–768; M. M. Butts et al., "Individual Reactions to High Involvement Work Practices: Investigating the Role of Empowerment and Perceived Organizational Support," *Journal of Occupational Health Psychology,* April 2009, pp. 122–136; and W. R. Evans and W. D. Davis, "High-Performance Work Systems and Organizational Performance: The Mediating Role of Internal Social Structure," *Journal of Management,* October 2005, p. 760.

---

high-performance work practices
Work practices that lead to both high individual and high organizational performance

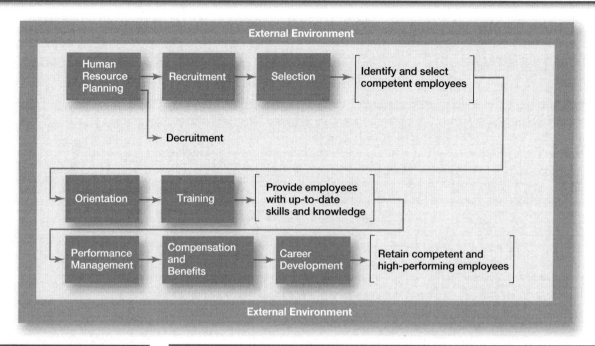

EXHIBIT 12-2

HRM Process

four months earlier, impressed the hiring manager so much that the job was hers, leaving the remaining 499 plus people, including a former IBM analyst with 18 years' experience, a former director of human resources, and someone with a master's degree and 12 years' experience at accounting firm Deloitte & Touche, still searching for a job. This is not a unique example. The economic slowdown has made filling a job opening an almost mind-boggling exercise.

Such is the new reality facing HRM. The entire HRM process is influenced by the external environment. Those factors most directly influencing it include the economy, employee labor unions, governmental laws and regulations, and demographic trends.

THE ECONOMY'S EFFECT ON HRM. The global economic downturn has left what many experts believe to be an enduring mark on HRM practices worldwide. For instance, in Japan, workers used to count on two things: a job for life and a decent pension. Now, lifetime employment is long gone and corporate pension plans are crumbling.[9] In European Union member countries, it's anticipated that the jobless rate will continue to increase, with Spain being hit hardest.[10] And in Thailand, employees in the automotive industry dealt with reduced work hours, which affected their pay and their skill upgrades.[11] In the United States, labor economists say that although jobs may be coming back slowly, they aren't the same ones that employees were used to. Many of these jobs are temporary or contract positions, rather than full-time jobs with benefits. And many of the more than 8.4 million jobs lost during the recession aren't coming back at all, but may be replaced by other types of work in growing industries.[12] All of these changes have affected employers and workers. A Global Workforce Study survey by global professional services company Towers Watson confirmed that the recession has "fundamentally altered the way U.S. employees view their work and leaders. . . . U.S. workers have dramatically lowered their career and retirement expectations for the foreseeable future."[13] Such findings have profound implications for how an organization manages its human resources.

EMPLOYEE LABOR UNIONS. A planned series of three five-day work stoppages by Unite, the union representing British Airways cabin crews, had the potential for a serious negative effect on Europe's third-largest airline in an industry already struggling from the prolonged economic downturn.[14] If negotiations between management and the union didn't resolve the disputes over work practices, then employees vowed to hit the airline with more strikes during the busy summer period. Then, in China, strikes at Honda and Toyota factories highlighted that country's struggle with income inequality, rising inflation, and soaring property prices. Factory workers, who had been "pushed to work 12-hour days, six days a week on monotonous low-wage assembly line tasks, are pushing back."[15] Work stoppages, labor disputes, and negotiations between management and labor are just a few of the challenges organizations and managers face when their workforce is unionized.

A **labor union** is an organization that represents workers and seeks to protect their interests through collective bargaining. In unionized organizations, many HRM decisions are dictated by collective bargaining agreements, which usually define things such as recruitment sources; criteria for hiring, promotions, and layoffs; training eligibility; and disciplinary practices. Due to information availability, it's difficult to pin down how unionized global workforces are. Current estimates are that about 12.3 percent of the U.S. workforce is unionized.[16] But the percentage of unionized workers tends to be higher in other countries except in France, where some 9.6 percent of workers are unionized. For instance, in Japan, some 19.6 percent of the labor force belongs to a union; in Germany, 27 percent; in Denmark, 75 percent; in Australia, 27.4 percent; in Canada, 30.4 percent; and in Mexico, 19 percent.[17] One union membership trend we're seeing, especially in the more industrialized countries, is that the rate in private enterprise is declining while that in the public sector (which includes teachers, police officers, firefighters, and government workers) is climbing. Although labor unions can affect an organization's HRM practices, the most significant environmental constraint is governmental laws, especially in North America.

LEGAL ENVIRONMENT OF HRM. $250 million. That's the amount a New York City jury awarded in punitive damages to plaintiffs who claim drug company Novartis AG discriminated against women.[18] Billions of dollars. That's the staggering amount that Walmart stores could potentially be liable for in a class-action sex discrimination suit.[19] As you can see, an organization's HRM practices are governed by a country's laws. (See Exhibit 12-3 for some of the important U.S. laws that affect the HRM process.) For example, decisions regarding who will be hired or which employees will be chosen for a training program or what an employee's compensation will be must be made without regard to race, sex, religion, age, color, national origin, or disability. Exceptions can occur only in special circumstances. For instance, a community fire department can deny employment to a firefighter applicant who is confined to a wheelchair; but if that same individual is applying for a desk job, such as a dispatcher, the disability cannot be used as a reason to deny employment. The issues, however, are rarely that clear-cut. For example, employment laws protect most employees whose religious beliefs require a specific style of dress—robes, long shirts, long hair, and the like. However, if the specific style of dress may be hazardous or unsafe in the work setting (such as when operating machinery), a company could refuse to hire a person who won't adopt a safer dress code.

As you can see, a number of important laws and regulations affect what you can and cannot do legally as a manager. Because workplace lawsuits are increasingly targeting supervisors, as well as their organizations, managers must know what they can and cannot do by law.[20] Trying to balance the "shoulds and should-nots" of many laws often falls within the realm of **affirmative action**. Many U.S. organizations have affirmative action programs to ensure that decisions and practices enhance the employment, upgrading, and retention of members from protected groups such as minorities and females. That is, an organization refrains from discrimination and actively seeks to enhance the status of members from protected groups. However, U.S. managers are not completely free to choose whom they hire, promote, or fire, or free to treat employees any way they want. Although laws have helped reduce employment discrimination and unfair work practices, they have, at the same time, reduced managers' discretion over HRM decisions.

labor union
An organization that represents workers and seeks to protect their interests through collective bargaining

affirmative action
Organizational programs that enhance the status of members of protected groups

Laws		
Law or Ruling	**Year**	**Description**
Equal Employment Opportunity and Discrimination		
Equal Pay Act	1963	Prohibits pay differences for equal work based on gender
Civil Rights Act, Title VII	1964 (amended in 1972)	Prohibits discrimination based on race, color, religion, national origin, or gender.
Age Discrimination in Employment Act	1967 (amended in 1978)	Prohibits discrimination against employees 40 years and older
Vocational Rehabilitation Act	1973	Prohibits discrimination on the basis of physical or mental disabilities
Americans with Disabilities Act	1990	Prohibits discrimination against individuals who have disabilities or chronic illnesses; also requires reasonable accommodations for these individuals
Compensation/Benefits		
Worker Adjustment and Retraining Notification Act	1990	Requires employers with more than 100 employees to provide 60 days' notice before a mass layoff or facility closing
Family and Medical Leave Act	1993	Gives employees in organizations with 50 or more employees up to 12 weeks of unpaid leave each year for family or medical reasons
Health Insurance Portability and Accountability Act	1996	Permits portability of employees' insurance from one employer to another
Lilly Ledbetter Fair Pay Act	2009	Changes the statute of limitations on pay discrimination to 180 days from each paycheck
Health/Safety		
Occupational Safety and Health Act (OSHA)	1970	Establishes mandatory and health standards in organizations
Privacy Act	1974	Gives employees the legal right to examine personnel files and letters of reference
Consolidated Omnibus Reconciliation Act (COBRA)	1985	Requires continued health coverage following termination (paid by employee)

EXHIBIT 12-3

Major HRM Laws

We do want to mention three current U.S. laws—one has been signed by the president and the other two are still being debated in Congress—that each have the potential to affect future HRM practices. The first of these, the Patient Protection and Affordable Care Act (commonly called the Health Care Reform Act), was signed into law in March 2010.[21] Employers are beginning to sort through the requirements of the law and the deadlines for compliance. For instance, one employer disclosure requirement says that by 2012, all employers must disclose the value of the benefits they provided in 2011 for each employee's health insurance coverage on the employees' annual Form W-2s. Other parts of the law include compliance deadlines for additional specific information that must be disclosed or provided and protections for employees who provide information or testimony about possible employer violations of Title 1 of the law.[22] Another proposed law—the Work–Life Balance Award Act—is still being debated. This particular piece of legislation would highlight the importance of workplace flexibility issues.[23] The other proposed law stalled in Congressional debates—the Employee Free Choice Act—would amend the National Labor Relations Act and make it easier for workers to form a union.[24]

What about HRM laws globally? It's important that managers in other countries be familiar with the specific laws that apply there. Let's take a look at some of the federal legislation in countries such as Canada, Mexico, Australia, and Germany.

Canadian laws pertaining to HRM practices closely parallel those in the United States. The Canadian Human Rights Act prohibits discrimination on the basis of race, religion, age, marital status, sex, physical or mental disability, or national origin. This act governs practices throughout the country. Canada's HRM environment, however, is somewhat different from that in the United States in that it involves more decentralization of lawmaking to the provincial level. For example, discrimination on the basis of language is not prohibited anywhere in Canada except in Quebec.

In Mexico, employees are more likely to be unionized than they are in the United States. Labor matters in Mexico are governed by the Mexican Federal Labor Law. One hiring law states that an employer has 28 days to evaluate a new employee's work performance. After that period, the employee is granted job security and termination is quite difficult and expensive. Those who violate the Mexican Federal Labor Law are subject to severe penalties, including criminal action that can result in steep fines and even jail sentences for employers who fail to pay, for example, the minimum wage.

Australia's discrimination laws were not enacted until the 1980s, and generally apply to discrimination and affirmative action for women. Yet, gender opportunities for women in Australia appear to lag behind those in the United States. In Australia, however, a significant proportion of the workforce is unionized. The higher percentage of unionized workers has placed increased importance on industrial relations specialists in Australia, and reduced the control of line managers over workplace labor issues. In 1997, Australia overhauled its labor and industrial relations laws with the objective of increasing productivity and reducing union power. The Workplace Relations Bill gives employers greater flexibility to negotiate directly with employees on pay, hours, and benefits. It also simplifies federal regulation of labor–management relations.

Our final example, Germany, is similar to most Western European countries when it comes to HRM practices. Legislation requires companies to practice representative participation, in which the goal is to redistribute power within the organization, putting labor on a more equal footing with the interests of management and stockholders. The two most common forms of representative participation are work councils and board representatives. **Work councils** link employees with management. They are groups of nominated or elected employees who must be consulted when management makes decisions involving personnel. **Board representatives** are employees who sit on a company's board of directors and represent the interests of the firm's employees.

DEMOGRAPHIC TRENDS. Back in 2007, the head of BMW's 2,500-employee power train plant in Dingolfing, Lower Bavaria, was worried about the potential inevitable future decline in productivity due to an aging workforce.[26] That's when company executives decided to redesign its factory for older workers. With input from employees, they implemented physical changes to the workplace—for instance, new wooden floors to reduce joint strain and special chairs for sitting down or relaxing for short periods—that would reduce wear and tear on workers' bodies. As this example shows, demographic trends are impacting HRM practices, worldwide and in the United States.

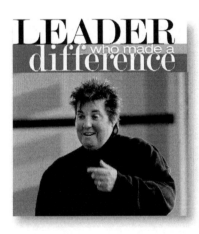

Lisa Brummel, a successful Microsoft product development manager with no HR experience, was named HR chief in 2005. Her mandate: improve the mood around here.[25] Lisa, who had always been a strong people leader, stepped up to do just that and looked for ways that the company could reshape HR at Microsoft. With any HR issue that arose, Lisa used her people skills to find a solution. For instance, one thing she did was to introduce innovative office designs that allowed employees to reconfigure their workspaces for the task they were working on. The customized workspaces included options such as sliding doors, movable walls, and features that made the space seem more like an urban loft than an office. When beginning a workspace redesign, "employees are first divided into four worker types: providers (the godfathers of work groups), travelers (the types who work anywhere but work), concentrators (head-down, always-at-work types), and orchestrators (the company's natural diplomats)." Based on their "type," employees then pick the kind of workspace that works best for them. By allowing their creative, quirky, and talented people freedom to design their workspaces, the company was able to give them some control over their chaotic and often hectic environment.

---

work councils
Groups of nominated or elected employees who must be consulted when management makes decisions involving personnel

board representatives
Employees who sit on a company's board of directors and represent the interests of the firm's employees

Much of the change in the U.S. workforce over the last 50 years can be attributed to federal legislation enacted in the 1960s that prohibited employment discrimination. With these laws, avenues opened up for minority and female job applicants. These two groups dramatically changed the workplace in the latter half of the twentieth century. Women, in particular, have changed the composition of the workforce as they now hold some 49.1 percent of jobs. And that percentage may increase as some 82 percent of jobs lost during the economic crisis were ones held by men. Why the disproportion? Because women tend to be employed in education and health care industries, which are less sensitive to economic ups and downs.[27] If this trend continues, women are set to become the majority group in the workforce.

Workforce trends in the first half of the twenty-first century will be notable for three reasons: (1) changes in racial and ethnic composition, (2) an aging baby boom generation, and (3) an expanding cohort of Gen Y workers. By 2050, Hispanics will grow from today's 13 percent of the workforce to 24 percent; blacks will increase from 12 percent to 14 percent, and Asians will increase from 5 percent to 11 percent. Meanwhile, the labor force is aging. The 55-and-older age group, which currently makes up 13 percent of the workforce, will increase to 20 percent by 2014. However, labor force analysts who had predicted a mass exodus of baby boomers into retirement have pulled back somewhat on those forecasts, especially since many baby boomers lost significant personal financial resources as the economy and stock market floundered. Many baby boomers are postponing retirement until they can better afford it. Another group that's having a significant impact on today's workforce is Gen Y, a population group that includes individuals born from about 1978 to 1994. Gen Y has been the fastest-growing segment of the workforce—increasing from 14 percent to over 24 percent. With Gen Y now in the workforce, analysts point to the four generations that are working side-by-side in the workplace[28]:

▶ The oldest, most experienced workers (those born before 1946) make up 6 percent of the workforce.
▶ The baby boomers (those born between 1946 and 1964) make up 41.5 percent of the workforce.
▶ Gen Xers (those born 1965 to 1977) make up almost 29 percent of the workforce.
▶ Gen Yers (those born 1978 to 1994) make up almost 24 percent of the workforce.

These and other demographic trends are important because of the impact they're having on current and future HRM practices.

Let's Get Real

HRM responsibilities I have include:
- Promote the company's safety program.
- Oversee the hiring process.
- Oversee and assist in the execution of the plant's affirmative action plan.
- Ensure compliance with state and federal laws and regulations.
- Develop and conduct employee training to minimize skill gaps.
- Address employee concerns and resolve complaints.
- Implement ideas that will allow the HR department become a better strategic partner within the organization.

LEARNING OUTCOME 12.2
Discuss the tasks associated with identifying and selecting competent employees.

Identifying and Selecting Competent Employees

Is a job in the insurance industry on your list of jobs you'll apply for after graduation? Unfortunately for the insurance industry, it's not for many college graduates. Like many other nonglamorous industries including transportation, utilities, and manufacturing, the insurance industry is not "particularly attractive to the so-called 'millennials'—people who turned 21 in 2000 or later." In all these industries, the number of skilled jobs is already starting to overtake the number of qualified people available to fill them.[29]

Every organization needs people to do whatever work is necessary for doing what the organization is in business to do. How do they get those people? And more importantly, what can they do to ensure they get competent, talented people? This first phase of the HRM process involves three tasks: human resource planning, recruitment and decruitment, and selection.

Human Resource Planning

Human resource planning is the process by which managers ensure that they have the right number and kinds of capable people in the right places and at the right times. Through planning, organizations avoid sudden people shortages and surpluses.[30] HR planning entails two steps: (1) assessing current human resources, and (2) meeting future HR needs.

CURRENT ASSESSMENT.   Managers begin HR planning by inventorying current employees. This inventory usually includes information on employees such as name, education, training, prior employment, languages spoken, special capabilities, and specialized skills. Sophisticated databases make getting and keeping this information quite easy. For example, Stephanie Cox, Schlumberger's director of personnel for North and South America, uses a company planning program called PeopleMatch to help pinpoint managerial talent. Suppose that she needs a manager for Brazil. She types in the qualifications: someone who can relocate, speak Portuguese, and is a "high potential" employee. Within a minute, 31 names of possible candidates pop up.[31] That's what good HR planning should do—help managers identify the people they need.

An important part of a current assessment is *job analysis*, an assessment that defines a job and the behaviors necessary to perform it. For instance, what are the duties of a level 3 accountant who works for Kodak? What minimal knowledge, skills, and abilities are necessary to adequately perform this job? How do these requirements compare with those for a level 2 accountant or for an accounting manager? Information for a job analysis is gathered by directly observing individuals on the job, interviewing employees individually or in a group, having employees complete a questionnaire or record daily activities in a diary, or having job "experts" (usually managers) identify a job's specific characteristics.

Using this information from the job analysis, managers develop or revise job descriptions and job specifications. A *job description* is a written statement describing a job—typically job content, environment, and conditions of employment. A *job specification* states the minimum qualifications that a person must possess to successfully perform a given job. It identifies the knowledge, skills, and attitudes needed to do the job effectively. Both the job description and job specification are important documents when managers begin recruiting and selecting.

MEETING FUTURE HR NEEDS.   Future HR needs are determined by the organization's mission, goals, and strategies. Demand for employees results from demand for the organization's products or services. For instance, Corning's expansion into developing countries was slowed by the lack of qualified employees. To continue its growth strategy, it had to plan how to find those qualified employees.[32]

After assessing both current capabilities and future needs, managers can estimate areas in which the organization will be understaffed or overstaffed. Then they're ready to proceed to the next step in the HRM process.

Let's Get Real

2

Best ways to find the best job candidates are *networking with local community organizations and also being descriptive about the job requirements and qualifications in a job ad.*

Recruitment and Decruitment

Competition for talent by India's two largest technology outsourcing companies has led to an all-out recruiting war. In the United States, the tech sector is also in a hiring push pitting start-up companies against giants such as Google and Intel in the hunt for employees.[33]

If employee vacancies exist, managers should use the information gathered through job analysis to guide them in *recruitment*—that is, locating, identifying, and attracting capable applicants.[34] On the other hand, if HR planning shows a surplus of employees, managers may want to reduce the organization's workforce through *decruitment*.[35]

---

human resource planning
Ensuring that the organization has the right number and kinds of capable people in the right places and at the right times

job analysis
An assessment that defines jobs and the behaviors necessary to perform them

job description
A written statement that describes a job

job specification
A written statement of the minimum qualifications that a person must possess to perform a given job successfully

recruitment
Locating, identifying, and attracting capable applicants

decruitment
Reducing an organization's workforce

EXHIBIT **12-4**

Recruiting Sources

Source	Advantages	Disadvantages
Internet	Reaches large numbers of people; can get immediate feedback	Generates many unqualified candidates
Employee referrals	Knowledge about the organization provided by current employee; can generate strong candidates because a good referral reflects on the recommender	May not increase the diversity and mix of employees
Company Web site	Wide distribution; can be targeted to specific groups	Generates many unqualified candidates
College recruiting	Large centralized body of candidates	Limited to entry-level positions
Professional recruiting organizations	Good knowledge of industry challenges and requirements	Little commitment to specific organization

RECRUITMENT. Some organizations have interesting approaches to finding employees. For instance, Microsoft launched a new Web site that integrated 103 country sites into one career-related site. There, potential applicants find employee blogs on everything from interview tips to whether a failed start-up on a résumé hurts in applying for a job at the company.[36] Even though Google receives 3,000 applications a day and can afford to be picky about whom it hires, it still needs qualified computer science and engineering candidates. One fun thing the company does is Google Games, a day devoted to student team competitions on the company's campus.[37] Accounting firm Deloitte & Touche created its Deloitte Film Festival to get employee team-produced films about "life" at Deloitte to use in college recruiting.[38] Exhibit 12-4 explains different recruitment sources managers can use to find potential job candidates.[39]

Although online recruiting is popular and allows organizations to identify applicants cheaply and quickly, applicant quality may not be as good as other sources. Research has found that employee referrals generally produce the best candidates.[40] Why? Because current employees know both the job and the person being recommended, they tend to refer applicants who are well qualified. Also, current employees often feel their reputation is at stake and refer others only when they're confident that the person will not make them look bad.

DECRUITMENT. The other approach to controlling labor supply is decruitment, which is not a pleasant task for any manager. Decruitment options are shown in Exhibit 12-5. Although employees can be fired, other choices may be better. However, no matter how you do it, it's never easy to reduce an organization's workforce.

EXHIBIT **12-5**

Decruitment Options

Option	Description
Firing	Permanent involuntary termination
Layoffs	Temporary involuntary termination; may last only a few days or extend to years
Attrition	Not filling openings created by voluntary resignations or normal retirements
Transfers	Moving employees either laterally or downward; usually does not reduce costs but can reduce intraorganizational supply–demand imbalances
Reduced workweeks	Having employees work fewer hours per week, share jobs, or perform their jobs on a part-time basis
Early retirements	Providing incentives to older and more senior employees for retiring before their normal retirement date
Job sharing	Having employees share one full-time position

Selection

Once you have a pool of candidates, the next step in the HRM process is **selection**, screening job applicants to determine who is best qualified for the job. Managers need to "select" carefully since hiring errors can have significant implications. For instance, a driver at Fresh Direct, an online grocer that delivers food to masses of apartment-dwelling New Yorkers, was charged with, and later pled guilty to, stalking and harassing female customers.[41] At T-Mobile, lousy customer service led to its last-place ranking in the J.D. Power's customer-satisfaction survey. The first step in a total overhaul of the customer service area was revamping the company's hiring practices to increase the odds of hiring employees who would be good at customer service.[42]

WHAT IS SELECTION?   Selection involves predicting which applicants will be successful if hired. For example, in hiring for a sales position, the selection process should predict which applicants will generate a high volume of sales. As shown in Exhibit 12-6, any selection decision can result in four possible outcomes—two correct and two errors.

A decision is correct when the applicant was predicted to be successful and proved to be successful on the job, or when the applicant was predicted to be unsuccessful and was not hired. In the first instance, we have successfully accepted; in the second, we have successfully rejected.

Problems arise when errors are made in rejecting candidates who would have performed successfully on the job (reject errors) or accepting those who ultimately perform poorly (accept errors). These problems can be significant. Given today's HR laws and regulations, reject errors can cost more than the additional screening needed to find acceptable candidates. Why? Because they can expose the organization to discrimination charges, especially if applicants from protected groups are disproportionately rejected. For instance, two written firefighter exams used by the New York City Fire Department were found to have had a disparate impact on black and Hispanic candidates.[43] On the other hand, the costs of accept errors include the cost of training the employee, the profits lost because of the employee's incompetence, the cost of severance, and the subsequent costs of further recruiting and screening. The major emphasis of any selection activity should be reducing the probability of reject errors or accept errors while increasing the probability of making correct decisions. Managers do this by using selection procedures that are both valid and reliable.

Selection Decision Outcomes

selection
Screening job applicants to ensure that the most appropriate candidates are hired

VALIDITY AND RELIABILITY.   A valid selection device is characterized by a proven relationship between the selection device and some relevant criterion. Federal employment laws prohibit managers from using a test score to select employees unless clear evidence shows that, once on the job, individuals with high scores on this test outperform individuals with low test scores. The burden is on managers to support that any selection device they use to differentiate applicants is validly related to job performance.

A reliable selection device indicates that it measures the same thing consistently. On a test that's reliable, any single individual's score should remain fairly consistent over time, assuming that the characteristics being measured are also stable. No selection device can be effective if it's not reliable. Using such a device would be like weighing yourself every day on an erratic scale. If the scale is unreliable—randomly fluctuating, say 5 to 10 pounds every time you step on it—the results don't mean much.

A growing number of companies are adopting a new measure of recruitment effectiveness called "quality of fill."[44] This measure looks at the contributions of good hires versus those of hires who have failed to live up to their potential. Five key factors are considered in defining this quality measure: employee retention, performance evaluations, number of first-year hires who make it into high-potential training programs, number of employees who are promoted, and what surveys of new hires indicate. Such measures help an organization assess whether its selection process is working well.

TYPES OF SELECTION TOOLS.   The best-known selection tools include application forms, written and performance-simulation tests, interviews, background investigations, and in some cases, physical exams. Exhibit 12-7 lists the strengths and weaknesses of each.[45] Because many selection tools have limited value for making selection decisions, managers should use ones that effectively predict performance for a given job.

EXHIBIT 12-7

Selection Tools

Application Forms
- Almost universally used
- Most useful for gathering information
- Can predict job performance but not easy to create one that does

Written Tests
- Must be job related
- Include intelligence, aptitude, ability, personality, and interest tests
- Are popular (e.g., personality tests; aptitude tests)
- Relatively good predictor for supervisory positions

Performance-Simulation Tests
- Use actual job behaviors
- Work sampling—test applicants on tasks associated with that job; appropriate for routine or standardized work
- Assessment center—simulate jobs; appropriate for evaluating managerial potential

Interviews
- Almost universally used
- Must know what can and cannot be asked
- Can be useful for managerial positions

Background Investigations
- Used for verifying application data—valuable source of information
- Used for verifying reference checks—not a valuable source of information

Physical Examinations
- Are for jobs that have certain physical requirements
- Mostly used for insurance purposes

REALISTIC JOB PREVIEWS.   One thing managers need to carefully watch is how they portray the organization and the work that an applicant will be doing. If they tell applicants only the good aspects, they're likely to have a workforce that's dissatisfied and prone to high turnover.[46] Negative things can happen when the information an applicant receives is excessively inflated. First, mismatched applicants probably won't withdraw from the selection process. Second, inflated information builds unrealistic expectations so new employees may quickly become dissatisfied and leave the organization. Third, new hires become disillusioned and less committed to the organization when they face the unexpected harsh realities of the job. In addition, these individuals may feel that they were misled during the hiring process and then become problem employees.

To increase employee job satisfaction and reduce turnover, managers should consider a **realistic job preview (RJP)**, which is one that includes both positive and negative information about the job and the company. For instance, in addition to the positive comments typically expressed during an interview, the job applicant might be told that there are limited opportunities to talk to coworkers during work hours, that promotional advancement is unlikely, or that work hours are erratic and they may have to work weekends. Research indicates that applicants who receive an RJP have more realistic expectations about the jobs they'll be performing and are better able to cope with the frustrating elements than are applicants who receive only inflated information.

Providing Employees with Needed Skills and Knowledge

12.3

LEARNING OUTCOME
Explain the different types of orientation and training.

As one of the nation's busiest airports, Miami International Airport served nearly 34 million passengers in 2009. But Miami International is doing something that no other airport has done. It's "trying to persuade disparate groups of employees to think and act as ambassadors for regional tourism. Airport workers in all jobs are learning the importance of finding solutions to the myriad issues that beset travelers on their way to and from Miami." Accomplishing that means that all employees who work on airport grounds are required to master customer service through a series of tourism training efforts. The required training is tied to renewal of airport ID badges, providing a critical incentive for employees to participate.[47]

If we've done our recruiting and selecting properly, we should have hired competent individuals who can perform successfully on the job. But successful performance requires more than possessing certain skills. New hires must be acclimated to the organization's culture and be trained and given the knowledge to do the job in a manner consistent with the organization's goals. Current employees, like those at Miami International Airport, may have to complete training programs to improve or update their skills. For these acclimation and skill improvement tasks, HRM uses orientation and training.

Orientation

Did you participate in some type of organized "introduction to college life" when you started school? If so, you may have been told about your school's rules and the procedures for activities such as applying for financial aid, cashing a check, or registering for classes; and you were probably introduced to some of the college administrators. A person starting a new job needs the same type of introduction to his or her job and the organization. This introduction is called **orientation**.

There are two types of orientation. *Work unit orientation* familiarizes the employee with the goals of the work unit, clarifies how his or her job contributes to the unit's

realistic job preview (RJP)
A preview of a job that provides both positive and negative information about the job and the company

orientation
Introducing a new employee to his or her job and the organization

goals, and includes an introduction to his or her new coworkers. *Organization orientation* informs the new employee about the company's goals, history, philosophy, procedures and rules. It should also include relevant HR policies and maybe even a tour of the facilities.

Many organizations have formal orientation programs, while others use a more informal approach in which the manager assigns the new employee to a senior member of the work group who introduces the new hire to immediate coworkers and shows him or her where important things are located. And then there are intense orientation programs like that at Randstad USA, a staffing company based in Atlanta. The company's 16-week program covers everything from the company's culture to on-the-job training. The executive in charge of curriculum development says, "It's a very defined process. It's not just about what new hires have to learn and do, but also about what managers have to do."[48] And managers do have an obligation to effectively and efficiently integrate any new employee into the organization. They should openly discuss mutual obligations of the organization and the employee.[49] It's in the best interests of both the organization and the new employee to get the person up and running in the job as soon as possible. Successful orientation results in an outsider-insider transition that makes the new employee feel comfortable and fairly well adjusted, lowers the likelihood of poor work performance, and reduces the probability of a surprise resignation only a week or two into the job.

by the numbers[50]

36 percent of managers who contact references are most interested in a description of past job duties.

69 percent of employees say they've been asked to do things at work for which they have not received any training.

30 percent of students say that a company's market success was a preferred attribute.

60 percent of employers now offer wellness benefits.

31 percent of HR leaders say that the most important employee characteristic is fitting in with the organization's culture.

40 percent of employees say that their most appealing career model is working for two to three organizations throughout their career.

59 percent of HR recruiters said that the most neglected grooming for job interviews was fingernails.

75 percent of recruiters say that a chronological format is most preferred for a résumé.

Employee Training

On the whole, planes don't cause airline accidents, people do. Most collisions, crashes, and other airline mishaps—nearly three-quarters of them—result from errors by the pilot or air traffic controller, or from inadequate maintenance. Weather and structural failures typically account for the remaining accidents.[51] We cite these statistics to illustrate the importance of training in the airline industry. Such maintenance and human errors could be prevented or significantly reduced by better employee training, as shown by the amazing "landing" of US Airways Flight 1549 in the Hudson River in January 2009 with no loss of life. Pilot Captain Chesley Sullenberger attributed the positive outcome to the extensive and intensive training that all pilots and flight crews undergo.[52] At management and technology consulting firm BearingPoint, the ethics and compliance training program became a series of fictional films modeled after *The Office*, even with a "Michael Scott-esque leader."[53] The film episodes were an immediate sensation in the company with comments like, "This is the best training I've ever had" or "I think that episode was based on my team." The new episodes became so popular that employees started tracking them down on the company's staging server, which is pretty amazing considering these training videos covered issues that most employees find boring even though it's critical information. Everything that employees at Ruth's Chris Steak House restaurants need to know can be found on sets of $4 \times 8\frac{1}{2}$-inch cards. Whether it's a recipe for caramelized banana cream pie or how to acknowledge customers, it's on the cards. And since the cards for all jobs are readily available, employees know the behaviors and skills it takes to get promoted. It's a unique approach to employee training, but it seems to work. Since the card system was implemented, employee turnover has decreased, something that's not easy to accomplish in the restaurant industry.[54]

Employee training is an important HRM activity. As job demands change, employee skills have to change. It's been estimated that U.S. business firms spend more than $52.2 billion annually on formal employee training, an amount that has declined during the economic downturn.[55] Managers, of course, are responsible for deciding what type of training employees need, when they need it, and what form that training should take.

TYPES OF TRAINING. Exhibit 12-8 describes the major types of training that organizations provide. Some of the most popular types include profession/industry-specific training, management/supervisory skills, mandatory/compliance information (such as sexual

Type	Includes
General	Communication skills, computer systems application and programming, customer service, executive development, management skills and development, personal growth, sales, supervisory skills, and technological skills and knowledge
Specific	Basic life/work skills, creativity, customer education, diversity/cultural awareness, remedial writing, managing change, leadership, product knowledge, public speaking/presentation skills, safety, ethics, sexual harassment, team building, wellness, and others

Source: Based on "2005 Industry Report—Types of Training." *Training*, December 2005, p. 22.

EXHIBIT 12-8

Types of Training

harassment, safety, etc.), and customer service training. For many organizations, employee interpersonal skills training—communication, conflict resolution, team building, customer service, and so forth—is a high priority. For example, the director of training and development for Vancouver-based Boston Pizza International said, "Our people know the Boston Pizza concept; they have all the hard skills. It's the soft skills they lack."[56] So the company launched Boston Pizza College, a training program that uses hands-on, scenario-based learning about many interpersonal skills topics. For Canon, Inc., it's the repair personnel's technical skills that are important.[57] As part of their training, repair people play a video game based on the familiar kids' board game Operation in which "lights flashed and buzzers sounded if copier parts were dragged and dropped poorly." The company found that comprehension levels were 5 to 8 percent higher than when traditional training manuals were used.

TRAINING METHODS.   Although employee training can be done in traditional ways, many organizations are relying more on technology-based training methods because of their accessibility, cost, and ability to deliver information. Exhibit 12-9 provides a description of the various traditional and technology-based training methods that managers might use. Of all these training methods, experts believe that organizations will increasingly rely on e-learning applications to deliver important information and to develop employees' skills.

On-the-job—Employees learn how to do tasks simply by performing them, usually after an initial introduction to the task.

Job rotation—Employees work at different jobs in a particular area, getting exposure to a variety of tasks.

Mentoring and coaching—Employees work with an experienced worker who provides information, support, and encouragement; also called apprenticeships in certain industries.

Experiential exercises—Employees participate in role playing, simulations, or other face-to-face types of training.

Workbooks/manuals—Employees refer to training workbooks and manuals for information.

Classroom lectures—Employees attend lectures designed to convey specific information.

Technology-Based Training Methods

CD-ROM/DVD/videotapes/audiotapes/podcasts—Employees listen to or watch selected media that convey information or demonstrate certain techniques.

Videoconferencing/teleconferencing/satellite TV—Employees listen to or participate as information is conveyed or techniques demonstrated.

E-learning—Internet-based learning where employees participate in multimedia simulations or other interactive modules.

EXHIBIT 12-9

Traditional Training Methods

12.4 Retaining Competent, High-Performing Employees

At Procter & Gamble, mid-year employee evaluations were used to adjust work goals to reflect more accurately what could be achieved in such a challenging economic environment. The company has directed managers to focus on employees' achievements rather than just to point out areas that need improvement. P&G's director of human resources said that, "Particularly in this economy, people are living in the survival zone. Setting attainable targets was important to keeping up morale."[58]

Once an organization has invested significant dollars in recruiting, selecting, orienting, and training employees, it wants to keep them, especially the competent, high-performing ones! Two HRM activities that play a role in this area are managing employee performance and developing an appropriate compensation and benefits program.

Employee Performance Management

Managers need to know whether their employees are performing their jobs efficiently and effectively. That's what a **performance management system** does—establishes performance standards that are used to evaluate employee performance. How do managers evaluate employees' performance? That's where the different performance appraisal methods come in.

PERFORMANCE APPRAISAL METHODS.   More than 70 percent of managers admit they have trouble giving a critical performance review to an underachieving employee.[59] It's particularly challenging when managers and employees alike sense that they're not beneficial.[60] Although appraising someone's performance is never easy, especially with employees who aren't doing their jobs well, managers can be better at it by using any of the seven different performance appraisal methods. A description of each of these methods, including advantages and disadvantages, is shown in Exhibit 12-10.

Compensation and Benefits

Executives at Discovery Communications Inc. had an employee morale problem on their hands. Many of the company's top performers were making the same salaries as the poorer performers and the company's compensation program didn't allow for giving raises to people who stayed in the same position. The only way for managers to reward the top performers was to give them a bonus or promote them to another position. Executives were discovering that not only was that unfair, it was counterproductive. So they overhauled the program.[61]

Most of us expect to receive appropriate compensation from our employer. Developing an effective and appropriate compensation system is an important part of the HRM process.[62] It can help attract and retain competent and talented individuals who help the organization accomplish its mission and goals. In addition, an organization's compensation system has been shown to have an impact on its strategic performance.[63]

Managers must develop a compensation system that reflects the changing nature of work and the workplace in order to keep people motivated. Organizational compensation can include many different types of rewards and benefits such as base wages and salaries, wage and salary add-ons, incentive payments, and other benefits and services. Some organizations offer employees some unusual, but popular, benefits. For instance, at Qualcomm, employees can receive surfing lessons, kayaking tours, and baseball game tickets. Employees at CHG Healthcare Services enjoy an on-site fitness center, fresh fruit baskets every morning, and an annual wellness fair. And at J. M. Smucker, new hires get a gift basket sent to their homes and all employees enjoy softball games and bowling nights.[64]

EXHIBIT **12-10**
Performance Appraisal Methods

Written Essay

Evaluator writes a description of employee's strengths and weaknesses, past performance, and potential; provides suggestions for improvement.

+ Simple to use

− May be better measure of evaluator's writing ability than of employee's actual performance

Critical Incident

Evaluator focuses on critical behaviors that separate effective and ineffective performance.

+ Rich examples, behaviorally based

− Time-consuming, lacks quantification

Graphic Rating Scale

Popular method that lists a set of performance factors and an incremental scale; evaluator goes down the list and rates employee on each factor.

+ Provides quantitative data; not time-consuming

− Doesn't provide in-depth information on job behavior

BARS (Behaviorally Anchored Rating Scale)

Popular approach that combines elements from critical incident and graphic rating scale; evaluator uses a rating scale, but items are examples of actual job behaviors.

+ Focuses on specific and measurable job behaviors

− Time-consuming; difficult to develop

Multiperson Comparison

Employees are rated in comparison to others in work group.

+ Compares employees with one another

− Difficult with large number of employees; legal concerns

MBO

Employees are evaluated on how well they accomplish specific goals.

+ Focuses on goals; results oriented

− Time-consuming

360-Degree Appraisal

Utilizes feedback from supervisors, employees, and coworkers.

+ Thorough

− Time-consuming

How do managers determine who gets paid what? Several factors influence the compensation and benefit packages that different employees receive. Exhibit 12-11 summarizes these factors, which are job-based and business- or industry-based. Many organizations, however, are using alternative approaches to determining compensation: skill-based pay and variable pay.

Skill-based pay systems reward employees for the job skills and competencies they can demonstrate. Under this type of pay system, an employee's job title doesn't define his or her pay category, skills do.[65] Research shows that these types of pay systems tend to be more successful in manufacturing organizations than in service organizations and organizations pursuing technical innovations.[66] On the other hand, many organizations use variable pay systems, in which an individual's compensation is contingent on

performance management system
Establishes performance standards that are used to evaluate employee performance

skill-based pay
A pay system that rewards employees for the job skills they can demonstrate

variable pay
A pay system in which an individual's compensation is contingent on performance

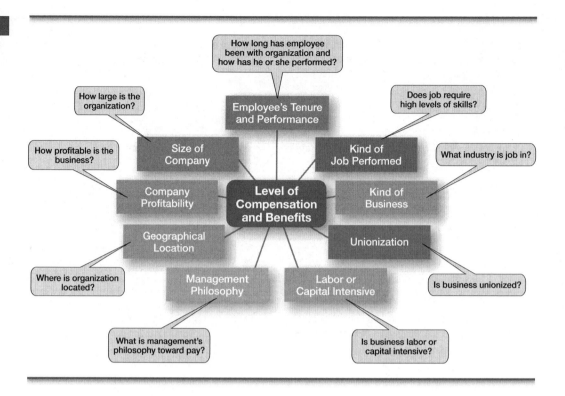

performance—90 percent of U.S. organizations use some type of variable pay plans, and 81 percent of Canadian and Taiwanese organizations do.[67] In Chapter 16, we'll discuss variable pay systems further as they relate to employee motivation.

Although many factors influence the design of an organization's compensation system, flexibility is a key consideration. The traditional approach to paying people reflected a more stable time when an employee's pay was largely determined by seniority and job level. Given the dynamic environments that many organizations face, the trend is to make pay systems more flexible and to reduce the number of pay levels. However, whatever approach managers use, they must establish a fair, equitable, and motivating compensation system that allows the organization to recruit and keep a talented and productive workforce.

LEARNING OUTCOME
Discuss contemporary issues in managing human resources.

12.5

Contemporary Issues in Managing Human Resources

We'll conclude this chapter by looking at some contemporary HR issues facing today's managers. These concerns include managing downsizing, sexual harassment, work–life balance, and controlling HR costs.

Managing Downsizing

"Before 1981, the word 'layoff' in the sense of permanent separation from a job with no prospects for recall, was so uncommon that the U.S. Bureau of Labor Statistics didn't even keep track of such cuts."[68] How things have changed!

Downsizing (or layoffs) is the planned elimination of jobs in an organization. When an organization has too many employees—which can happen when it's faced with an economic recession, declining market share, too aggressive growth, or poorly managed operations—one option for improving profits is to eliminate some of those excess workers. During the most current economic recession, many well-known companies downsized—including, among others, Boeing, Volkswagen, McDonald's, Dell, General Motors, Unisys, Siemens, Merck, Honeywell, and eBay. Now, some HR experts are suggesting that a "cost" associated with mass layoffs is the damage they can cause to long-term growth prospects.[69]

EXHIBIT 12-12

Tips for Managing Downsizing

- Communicate openly and honestly:
  - Inform those being let go as soon as possible.
  - Tell surviving employees the new goals and expectations.
  - Explain impact of layoffs.
- Follow any laws regulating severance pay or benefits.
- Provide support/counseling for surviving (remaining) employees.
- Reassign roles according to individuals' talents and backgrounds.
- Focus on boosting morale:
  - Offer individualized reassurance.
  - Continue to communicate, especially one-on-one.
  - Remain involved and available.
- Have a plan for the empty office spaces/cubicles so it isn't so depressing for surviving employees.

How can managers best manage a downsized workplace? Disruptions in the workplace and in employees' personal lives should be expected. Stress, frustration, anxiety, and anger are typical reactions of both individuals being laid off and the job survivors. Exhibit 12-12 lists some ways that managers can lessen the trauma both for the employees being laid off and for the survivors.[70]

Managing Sexual Harassment

A Kentucky appeals court said that McDonald's Corporation is liable in the sexual assault case of an employee detained by supervisors who were following the instructions of a prank caller pretending to be a police officer. The ruling said that McDonald's knew of 30 hoax telephone calls made to its restaurants from 1994 to 2004, including several calls to Kentucky restaurants in which the caller persuaded managers and employees to conduct strip searches and sexual assaults.[71]

Sexual harassment is a serious issue in both public and private sector organizations. During 2009 (the latest data available), almost 12,700 complaints were filed with the Equal Employment Opportunity Commission (EEOC). Although most complaints are filed by women, the percentage of charges filed by males reached an all-time high of 16 percent.[72] The costs of sexual harassment are high. Almost all *Fortune* 500 companies in the United States have had complaints lodged by employees, and at least a third have been sued.[73] Settlements typically average over $15 million.[74] In addition, it's estimated that sexual harassment costs a "typical *Fortune* 500 company $6.7 million per year in absenteeism, low productivity, and turnover."[75]

Sexual harassment isn't a problem just in the United States. It's a global issue. For instance, data collected by the European Commission found that 30 to 50 percent of female employees in European Union countries had experienced some form of sexual harassment.[76] And sexual harassment charges have been filed against employers in other countries such as Japan, Australia, New Zealand, and Mexico.[77]

Even though discussions of sexual harassment cases often focus on the large awards granted by a court, there are other concerns for employers. It creates an unpleasant, oftentimes hostile, work environment and undermines workers' ability to perform their job.

So what is **sexual harassment**? It's defined as any unwanted action or activity of a sexual nature that explicitly or implicitly affects an individual's employment, performance, or work environment. And as we indicated earlier, it can occur between members of the opposite sex or of the same sex.

---

downsizing
The planned elimination of jobs in an organization

sexual harassment
Any unwanted action or activity of a sexual nature that explicitly or implicitly affects an individual's employment, performance, or work environment

Many problems associated with sexual harassment involve determining exactly what constitutes this illegal behavior. The EEOC defines sexual harassment this way: "Unwelcome sexual advances, requests for sexual favors, and other verbal or physical conduct of a sexual nature constitute sexual harassment when this conduct explicitly or implicitly affects an individual's employment, unreasonably interferes with an individual's work performance, or creates an intimidating, hostile or offensive work environment."[78] For many organizations, it's the offensive or hostile environment issue that is problematic. Managers must be aware of what constitutes such an environment. Another thing that managers must understand is that the victim doesn't necessarily have to be the person harassed but could be anyone affected by the offensive conduct.[79] The key is being attuned to what makes fellow employees uncomfortable—and if we don't know, we should ask![80]

What can an organization do to protect itself against sexual harassment claims?[81] The courts want to know two things: First, did the organization know about, or should it have known about, the alleged behavior? And secondly, what did managers do to stop it? With the number and dollar amounts of the awards against organizations increasing, it's vital that all employees be educated on sexual harassment matters. In addition, organizations need to ensure that no retaliatory actions—such as cutting back hours, assigning back-to-back work shifts without a rest break, etc.—are taken against a person who has filed harassment charges, especially in light of a U.S. Supreme Court ruling that broadened what retaliation is.[82] One final area of interest we want to discuss in terms of sexual harassment is workplace romances.

WORKPLACE ROMANCES. If you're employed, have you ever dated someone at work? If not, have you ever been attracted to someone in your workplace and thought about pursuing a relationship? Such situations are more common than you might think—40 percent of employees surveyed by the *Wall Street Journal* said that they have had an office romance.[83] And another survey found that 43 percent of single men and 28 percent of single women said they would be open to dating a coworker.[84] The environment in today's organizations with mixed-gender work teams and long work hours has likely contributed to this situation. "People realize they're going to be at work such long hours, it's almost inevitable that this takes place," said one survey director.[85] And some 67 percent of employees feel there's no need to hide their office relationships.[86]

But workplace romances can potentially become big problems for organizations.[87] In addition to the potential conflicts and retaliation between coworkers who decide to stop dating or to end a romantic relationship, more serious problems stem from the potential for sexual harassment accusations, especially when it's between supervisor and subordinate. The standard used by judicial courts has been that workplace sexual conduct is prohibited sexual harassment *if* it is unwelcome. If it's welcome, it still may be inappropriate, but usually is not unlawful. However, a new ruling by the California Supreme Court concerning specifically a supervisor–subordinate relationship that got out of hand is worth noting. That ruling said the "completely consensual workplace romances can create a hostile work environment for others in the workplace."[88]

What should managers do about workplace romances? Over the last decade, companies have become more flexible about workplace romances. People spend so much time at the office that coworker romances are almost inevitable.[89] However, it's important to educate employees about the potential for sexual harassment. And because the potential liability is more serious when it comes to supervisor–subordinate relationships, a more proactive approach is needed in terms of discouraging such relationships and perhaps even requiring supervisors to report any such relationships to the HR department. At some point, the organization may even want to consider banning such relationships, although an outright ban may be difficult to put into practice.

Managing Work–Life Balance

In 2009, Verizon employees contacted VZ-LIFE, the company's employee assistance program, more than 1,100 times a month by phone and logged more than 35,000 visits a month to the Web site. This program provides resources on parenting and childcare, adult care, health and wellness, moving and relocation, and much more.[90]

Smart managers recognize that employees don't leave their families and personal lives behind when they come to work. Although managers can't be sympathetic with every detail of an employee's family life, organizations are becoming more attuned to the fact that employees have sick children, elderly parents who need special care, and other family issues that may require special arrangements. In response, many organizations are offering **family-friendly benefits**, which accommodate employees' needs for work–family life balance. They've introduced programs such as on-site child care, summer day camps, flextime, job sharing, time off for school functions, telecommuting, and part-time employment. Work–family life conflicts are as relevant to male workers with children and women without children as they are for female employees with children. Heavy workloads and increased travel demands have made it hard for many employees to satisfactorily juggle both work and personal responsibilities. A *Fortune* survey found that 84 percent of male executives surveyed said that "they'd like job options that let them realize their professional aspirations while having more time for things outside work."[91] Also, 87 percent of these executives believed that any company that restructured top-level management jobs in ways that would both increase productivity and make more time available for life outside the office would have a competitive advantage in attracting talented employees. Younger employees, particularly, put a higher priority on family and a lower priority on jobs and are looking for organizations that give them more work flexibility.[92]

Serving as a showpiece of its family support program, Pacific Gas and Electric developed its own child care center at its corporate headquarters in downtown San Francisco. Accommodating 75 children, the center was designed to respond to the developmental needs of each age group served. It includes classrooms and play areas inside the building as well as a large outdoor playground shown in this photo. In addition to on-site child care, PG&E helps career-committed parents balance work and family by offering flexible working arrangements.

Today's progressive workplaces must accommodate the varied needs of a diverse workforce. How? By providing a wide range of scheduling options and benefits that allow employees more flexibility at work and to better balance or integrate their work and personal lives. Despite these organizational efforts, work–family life programs certainly have room for improvement. One survey showed that over 31 percent of college-educated male workers spend 50 or more hours a week at work (up from 22 percent in 1980) and that about 40 percent of American adults get less than seven hours of sleep on weekdays (up from 34 percent in 2001).[93] What about women? Another survey showed that the percentage of American women working 40 hours or more per week had increased. By the way, this same survey showed that the percentage of European women working 40 hours or more had actually declined.[94] Other workplace surveys still show high levels of employee stress stemming from work–family life conflicts. And large groups of women and minority workers remain unemployed or underemployed because of family responsibilities and bias in the workplace.[95] So what can managers do?

FUTURE VISION   The Working World in 2020

Technology and globalization have played major roles in blurring the lines between work and leisure time. It's increasingly expected that today's professional worker be available 24/7. So employees regularly check their e-mail before going to bed, take calls from the boss during dinner, participate in global conference calls at 6 A.M., and read tweets from colleagues on weekends.

The 24/7 work life eventually undermines real social relationships. Face-to-face interactions with family and friends suffer and people are likely to feel stressed out and emotionally empty. In response, employees are likely to demand real and virtual barriers that can separate their work and personal lives. For instance, you'll set up separate accounts, Web sites, and networks for work and friends. Employers will find that employees balk at work demands that are outside defined work hours. In order to get and keep good employees, organizations will need to restructure work communications so as to confine them to more traditional hours.

family-friendly benefits
Benefits that accommodate employees' needs for work–life balance

Research on work–family life balance has shown positive outcomes when individuals are able to combine work and family roles.[96] As one study participant noted, "I think being a mother and having patience and watching someone else grow has made me a better manager. I am better able to be patient with other people and let them grow and develop in a way that is good for them."[97] In addition, individuals who have family-friendly workplace support appear to be more satisfied on the job.[98] This finding seems to strengthen the notion that organizations benefit by creating a workplace in which employee work–family life balance is possible. And the benefits are financial as well. Research has shown a significant, positive relationship between work–family life initiatives and an organization's stock price.[99] However, managers need to understand that people do differ in their preferences for work–family life scheduling options and benefits.[100] Some prefer organizational initiatives that better *segment* work from their personal lives. Others prefer programs that facilitate *integration*. For instance, flextime schedules segment because they allow employees to schedule work hours that are less likely to conflict with personal responsibilities. On the other hand, on-site child care integrates the boundaries between work and family responsibilities. People who prefer segmentation are more likely to be satisfied and committed to their jobs when offered options such as flextime, job sharing, and part-time hours. People who prefer integration are more likely to respond positively to options such as on-site child care, gym facilities, and company-sponsored family picnics.

Controlling HR Costs

According to a report by the Conference Board, a nonprofit research group, obesity alone costs U.S. companies as much as $47 billion annually.[101] HR costs are skyrocketing, especially employee health care and employee pensions. Organizations are looking for ways to control these costs.

EMPLOYEE HEALTH CARE COSTS. Employees at Paychex who undergo a confidential health screening and risk assessment, and for those who smoke who agree to enroll in a smoking cessation program, can get free annual physicals, colonoscopies, and 100 percent coverage of preventive care as well as lower deductibles and costs. At Black and Decker Corporation, employees and dependents who certify in an honor system that they have been tobacco-free for at least six months pay $75 less per month for their medical and dental coverage. At Amerigas Propane, employees were given an ultimatum: get their medical checkups or lose their health insurance.[102]

All these examples illustrate how companies are trying to control skyrocketing employee health care costs. Since 2002, health care costs have risen an average of 15 percent a year and are expected to double by the year 2016 from the $2.2 trillion spent in 2007.[103] And smokers cost companies even more—about 25 percent more for health care than nonsmokers do.[104] However, the biggest health care cost for companies is obesity and its related costs arising from medical expenditures and absenteeism.[105] A study of manufacturing organizations found that presenteeism, which is defined as employees not performing at full capacity, was 1.8 percent higher for workers with moderate to severe obesity than for all other employees.[106] The reason for the lost productivity is likely the result of reduced mobility because of body size or pain problems such as arthritis. Is it any wonder that organizations are looking for ways to control their health care costs? How? First, many organizations are providing opportunities for employees to lead healthy lifestyles. From financial incentives to company-sponsored health and wellness programs, the goal is to limit rising health care costs. About 41 percent of companies use some type of positive incentives aimed at encouraging healthy behavior, up from 34 percent in 1996.[107] Another recent study indicated that nearly 90 percent of companies surveyed planned to aggressively promote healthy lifestyles to their employees during the next three to five years.[108] Many are starting sooner: Google, Yamaha Corporation of America, Caterpillar, and others are putting health food in company break rooms, cafeterias, and vending machines; providing deliveries of fresh organic fruit; and putting "calorie taxes" on fatty foods.[109] In the case of smokers, however, some companies have taken a more aggressive stance by increasing the amount smokers pay for health insurance or by firing them if they refuse to stop smoking.

EMPLOYEE PENSION PLAN COSTS.   The other area where organizations are looking to control costs is employee pension plans. Corporate pensions have been around since the nineteenth century.[110] But the days when companies could afford to give employees a broad-based pension that provided them a guaranteed retirement income have changed. Pension commitments have become such an enormous burden that companies can no longer afford them. In fact, the corporate pension system has been described as "fundamentally broken."[111] Many companies no longer provide pensions. Even IBM, which closed its pension plan to new hires in December 2004, told employees that their pension benefits would be frozen.[112] Obviously, the pension issue is one that directly affects HR decisions. On the one hand, organizations want to attract talented, capable employees by offering them desirable benefits such as pensions. But on the other hand, organizations have to balance offering benefits with the costs of providing such benefits.

Let's Get Real:

My Response *to A Manager's Dilemma, page 340*

What Would You Do?

The first thing Shelly must accept is that the decision of a layoff is not a personal attack against a specific person or a group of people, but a business decision that had to be made. A key to making this process less stressful is preparing for the conversation about to take place. A few suggestions that I would have for Shelly:

- Reach out to other companies to understand their hiring needs and help the employees being laid off with the job transitioning process.

- If Ram Tool offers an Employee Assistance Program (EAP), contact them so they can prepare some assistance for Shelly and the affected employees.

- Emphasize to the affected employees that it was not a personal attack but a necessary business decision.

- Try to not get emotionally attached to the employees regardless of the personal relationship; Shelly must learn to separate business decisions from personal relationships.

If Shelly can help the affected employees in the transition process to the best of her abilities, the laid-off employees may cope with the news a little better and understand that opportunities will come if they stay positive. Many great leaders have been laid off at some point or another, and it is what they did during those difficult times that made them a better and stronger leader.

Jose Quirarte
HR Manager
D&W Fine Pack, LLC
Fort Calhoun, NE

Chapter 18:

Employee Relations

EMPLOYEE RELATIONS

→ Ch. 9

This concerns how the relationship between employees and the organisation is managed (see Chapter 9). It includes relationships with trade unions, the management of workplace conflict, consultation processes and employee involvement and participation. Employee engagement can be viewed as the alignment of employees with the organisation's goals – this is also affected by how employee relations is managed.

Relations with trade unions and the management of workplace conflict will also be discussed in relation to employment legislation later in this chapter.

Trade unions

The period since 1978 has seen a decline in the level of union membership (Machin, 2000). The Employment Relations Act 1999 lays out a procedure for unionised employees' request for union recognition by an employer.

The culture, management style and organisational philosophy of an organisation will affect its view of unions – some organisations embrace unionisation whereas others resist it as strongly as possible.

Examples described in Gennard and Judge (2005) highlight the difference in tone between two types of organisations. For an organisation with a policy of not recognising unions for any employees or groups of employees, this arises from management policy, which is not to recognise a collective arrangement. In another organisation where there is no or low union membership the lack of union recognition may be because the employees have not chosen to join a union. The focus towards any potential unionisation appears quite different, although this cannot be confirmed until a situation occurs where unionised employees request union recognition.

The European Works Councils

The European Works Council (EWC) directive requires that an EWC be established in EU companies with at least 1000 employees and at least 150 employees in each of at least two member states. The directives give the EWC the right to meet with central management once a year. The directive also defines the areas requiring information or consultation as:

- the structure, economic and financial situation of the business;
- developments in production and sales;
- the employment situation;
- investment trends;
- substantial changes concerning the introduction of new working methods, production processes, transfers of production, mergers, cutbacks or closures.

Employee involvement and participation

Employee involvement concentrates on the employee as an individual. Its focus is on developing a workforce that is committed to the organisation. The strategy is the *management* of staff rather than the control of staff.

Organisation programmes to encourage employee involvement include upward and downward communication, the active development of team working, quality circles and total quality working along with financial schemes to directly involve the employee with the increased profitability of the organisation such as share owner-ship schemes, profit-related pay and profit sharing, and representative participation.

Research conducted by Pecci *et al.* (2005) found that

> *'management's systematic sharing on performance targets relating from various aspects of the organisation can help to enhance employee commitment, and this in turn has a positive impact on labour productivity.'*

Employee participation centres on the involvement of employees with manage-ment in decision-making systems. The organisation relates to employees as a group communicating through staff representatives. This allows staff to feel part of the decision-making process. This may take the form of a staff–management joint con-sultation committee, worker representation on the company board, a trade union body or, in multinational organisations, the European Works Council.

Organisations that have systems for employee involvement and participation treat their employees as stakeholders in the organisation – in the same way that organisations see other stakeholders such as owners, customers, suppliers and the public. The culture of these organisations tends towards developing a partnership between the organisation and its employees.

Potential advantages of employee involvement and participation programmes for organisations are given in Gennard and Judge (2005).

- Employees are better informed about their work tasks.
- Employees are given increased intrinsic rewards from their work.
- Employees enjoy increase job satisfaction.
- Employee motivation is enhanced to achieve new goals.
- Mutual trust and commitment are increased.
- Labour turnover is reduced.

By empowering employees, the need for complex control systems is reduced which results in improved efficiency.

Employee engagement

Employee engagement describes a high level of commitment that can be developed between an organisation and its employees. It has been defined as:

> *'a positive attitude held by the employee towards the organisation and its values. An engaged employee is aware of business context, and works with colleagues to improve performance within the job for the benefit of the organisation. The organisation must work to develop and nurture engagement, which requires a two-way relationship between employer and employee.'*   (Robinson *et al.*, 2004)

Employee engagement is more than job satisfaction – it describes the involvement that can be developed between an employee's values and commitment to the organisation's goals.

The term 'organisational citizenship' (CIPD, 2007) describes this combination of commitment to the organisation and its values plus a willingness to help out colleagues.

Three dimensions of engagement are outlined in the CIPD (2007) report as:

- **emotional engagement** – to be emotionally involved in your work;
- **cognitive engagement** – focusing very hard at work;
- **physical engagement** – willingness to go the extra mile for your employer.

The successful development of employee engagement depends on how employees are managed, which means that the partnership between HR managers and line managers on managing employees and employee relations with the organisation are vital to achieving employee engagement.

In the annual report of the '100 Best Companies to Work For' sponsored by the *Sunday Times* (Brandon and Leonard, 2007) a link is made between employee retention and employee engagement. The report includes results from their research concerning where managers should focus to develop employee engagement:

- get employees on board and excited about the company and where it is going;
- keep them informed about the firm's progress and future plans;
- make sure you praise staff and give them feedback to acknowledge the level of their contribution;
- create a team atmosphere and make them feel valued, so they feel they can make a difference;
- give staff opportunities to grow and to develop with clearly defined targets and a distinct career path.

For the organisation there are a range of advantages of employee engagement – the staff promote the organisation as an employer of choice, show higher retention rates and engaged employees deliver improved business performance (CIPD, 2007).

THE FOUR Cs MODEL OF HUMAN RESOURCES MANAGEMENT

The four Cs model – commitment, competence, congruence and cost-effectiveness – was developed by researchers at the Harvard Business School as a means of investigating HRM issues in a wider environmental context than the mundane and instrumental tasks of recruitment and selection, training, appraisal, maintenance of employee records and so on (Beer *et al.*, 1985). According to the Harvard model, HRM policies need to derive from a critical analysis of:

- the demands of the various stakeholders in a business;
- a number of 'situational factors'.

Stakeholder theory

This asserts that since organisations are owned and operated by differing interest groups (stakeholders), management's main task is to balance the returns to various group interests (see Chapters 3 and 4). Examples of stakeholders are shareholders, different categories of employee, customers/users of the product, creditors (including banks), unions and (possibly) local or national government. Managers therefore need to be politicians and diplomats. They must establish good relations with each group, develop persuasive skills, create alliances, represent one faction to others, etc.

Stakeholder theory implies the recognition that each interest group possesses certain basic rights. Thus, for example, management should consider workers' interests as well as those of shareholders when making important decisions.

Stakeholders may or may not hold formal authority, although many will have invested something in the organisation whether this be work, finance or other resources. Accordingly, every investing stakeholder will expect a reward from the enterprise and normally will wish to influence how this is determined. Management must:

→ Chs 3 & 4

- identify the stakeholders in the organisation;
- determine the minimum return each stakeholder is willing to accept;
- seek to influence stakeholders' perceptions of the organisation – for example by persuading shareholders that a high dividend is not in a company's best long-term interest or convincing workers that a high wage settlement is not possible during the current year;
- identify key individuals in specific stakeholder groups and establish good relations with them.

Some stakeholders are simply groups or individuals who are affected by the organisation's activities, or who seek to represent certain 'constituencies' which cannot represent themselves, for example animals, the environment or overseas workers. Sometimes these have little influence and managers have to make moral judgements as to the responses they make to them. However, such groups can sometimes form powerful coalitions, excite the interest of the press or unsettle the organisation's staff – to the extreme detriment of the organisation!

Situational factors

These include the state of the labour market, the calibre and motivation of employees, management style (which itself depends in part on the culture of the local community), the technologies used in production and the nature of working methods (e.g. whether specialisation and the division of labour are required). Labour market situations are crucial to the analysis. The labour market comprises all the people seeking work and all the companies, government bodies and other organisations that require employees. Labour markets operate at regional, industry sector, national and (increasingly) international levels. There are submarkets for various categories of occupation, skill, educational background and other employee characteristics, and for different types of task.

Further situational factors that might be relevant are:

- the form of ownership of the organisation – and hence to whom management is accountable;
- the influence of trade unions and employers' associations;
- the laws and business practices of the society in which the organisation operates;
- the competitive environment;
- senior management's ability to coordinate and control.

Stakeholder expectations and situational factors need to be taken into account when formulating human resources strategies, and will affect HRM policies concerning such matters as remuneration systems, degree of supervision of workers, use of labour-intensive rather than capital-intensive methods, etc. An increase in the intensity of business competition may cause a firm to improve labour productivity, discard employees, restructure administrative systems and so on. A change in the age structure of the population can lead an organisation to hire more women. Rising educational standards may make it appropriate to redesign jobs in order to give workers more autonomy.

Outcomes to human resources management

According to the Harvard researchers, the effectiveness of the outcomes to human resources management should be evaluated under four headings: commitment, competence, congruence and cost-effectiveness.

- **Commitment** concerns employees' loyalty to the organisation, personal motivation and liking for their work. The degree of employee commitment may be assessed through attitude surveys, labour turnover and absenteeism statistics, and through interviews with workers who quit their jobs.

- **Competence** relates to employees' skills and abilities, training requirements and potential for higher-level work. These may be estimated through employee appraisal systems and the preparation of skills inventories (see p. 338). HRM policies should be designed to attract, retain and motivate competent workers.

- **Congruence** means that management and workers share the same vision of the organisation's goals and work together to attain them. In a well-managed organisation employees at all levels of authority will share common perspectives about the factors that determine its prosperity and future prospects. Such perspectives concern the guiding principles that govern the organisation's work – how things should be done, when, by whom and how enthusiastically.

  To some extent these perceptions may be created by management via its internal communications, style of leadership, organisation system and working methods but they can only be sustained and brought to bear on day-to-day operations by the organisation's workers. Staff should *feel* they possess a common objective. They need to experience a sense of affinity with the organisation and *want* to pursue a common cause. Congruence is evident in the absence of grievances and conflicts within the organisation, and in harmonious industrial relations.

- **Cost-effectiveness** concerns operational efficiency. Human resources should be used to the best advantage and in the most productive ways. Outputs must be maximised at the lowest input cost and the organisation must be quick to respond to market opportunities and environmental change.

Problems with the four Cs approach

The Harvard model suggests that human resources policies should seek to increase the level of each of the four Cs. For example, commitment may be enhanced through improving the flow of management–worker communication, while competence can be increased through extra training. Problems with the four Cs approach are:

- how *exactly* to measure these variables;

- possible conflicts between cost-effectiveness and congruence – especially if the drive for the former generates low wages;

- the huge variety of variables potentially relevant to any given HRM situation – often it is impossible to distinguish the key factors defining the true character of a particular state of affairs;

- the fact that sometimes a technology or set of working conditions makes it virtually impossible to increase the levels of some of the Cs – certain jobs are inevitably dirty, boring and repetitive, yet they still have to be done.

THE MANAGEMENT OF HUMAN RESOURCES

The modern approach to the management of human resources is to emphasise cooperation rather than conflict and to integrate HRM policies into the overall corporate strategies of the organisation. This requires senior management to:

- recognise the critical importance of harmonious relations with the workforce;
- relate HRM to the attainment of increased competitiveness, improved product quality and better customer care.

Well-constructed human resources policies are essential for the well-being of the firm and all efforts must be made to minimise the potential for conflicts between management and workers.

Strategic human resources management

The development of human resources management as a strategic function – strategic human resources management (SHRM) – brings the function into line with the other strategic functions of the business – finance and marketing. It acknowledges the contribution of the skills and knowledge of employees to continuing business competitiveness, together with the planning for future human resources needs.

Linking human resources management to the organisation's strategy is the basis of SHRM, so that human resources management underpins the business goals and vision of the organisation. To achieve this, HRM needs to be aligned horizontally so the major components (reward, resourcing, development, retention and employee relations) are aligned to achieve the organisation's strategy. The HR function must also be vertically integrated into the overall strategic plan.

The balanced scorecard

The **balanced scorecard** aims to link business areas of the organisation to its business strategy. Key measures are tracked and monitored. These measures have a direct link to the business strategy and are visible and applicable.

The key measures of the business in the main strategic areas are determined using cause-and-effect maps. Financial measures are seen as a major area in determining effective performance, but not as the sole area. Financial measures are important to shareholders but, unlike other areas of the business, they are short-term indicators. The balanced scorecard includes the monitoring of desirable long-term outcomes and performance drivers together with these short-term measures. They are used for setting targets. Having the same areas of measurement for all levels of the organisation, all employees can see how the objectives are linked to the organisation's goals.

The performance drivers selected for the balanced scorecard will be specific to the organisation and linked to customers, stakeholders, internal business processes and financial measures. This ensures that key business stakeholders – investors, customers and employees – are recognised.

The use of the balanced scorecard provides a system that helps to measure the effect of human resources management on the organisation's competitive success.

Role of the personnel department

In most, but not all, organisations human resources management is the responsibility of the personnel department. The personnel officer is often a generalist, since the variety of issues typically dealt with in a personnel department is so diverse that no one person can master all aspects of the job. Such a personnel manager requires a working, rather than a detailed, knowledge of:

- the organisation, its products and the industry or sector in which it operates;
- production methods and organisational structure;
- pension schemes, wage and bonus arrangements;
- law relating to employment;
- the fundamentals of management theory and practice.

The mundane tasks of writing copy for job advertisements, organising training courses, keeping personnel records, operating wages systems, looking after health and safety at work arrangements, etc. are known collectively as the 'service function' of the personnel role. Other major personnel management functions are:

- The **control function**, comprising:
  - analysis of key operational indices in the personnel field – labour turnover, wage costs, absenteeism and so on;
  - monitoring labour performance (staff appraisal, for example);
  - recommending appropriate remedial action to line managers.
- The **advisory function**, whereby the personnel department offers expert advice on personnel policies and procedures:
  - which employees are ready for promotion;
  - who should attend a certain training course;
  - how a grievance procedure should be operated;
  - interpretation of contracts of employment, health and safety regulations, etc.

Evaluating the effectiveness of a personnel department

Effective personnel management should feed through into improved organisational performance, higher productivity among employees, better customer service and hence increased long-term sales (Burn, 1996). Measuring the value of the short-run activities of a personnel department, however, can be problematic. Specific difficulties attached to the evaluation of the personnel function are that:

- since organisations operate in widely disparate commercial environments, wide differences in labour turnover, absenteeism, etc. are to be expected among firms engaged in similar lines of work;
- personnel management is such a wide-ranging activity that it may not be appropriate to select just a handful of variables for appraisal.

Quantitative indices of a personnel department's work may be available in relation to:

■ unit labour costs compared to those in competing companies;

■ staff turnover;

■ absenteeism rates;

■ incidence of invocation of grievance procedures;

■ the proportion of the personnel department's staff that obtain professional qualifications;

■ number of days lost through strikes;

■ how long it takes to recruit a new employee;

■ successes achieved in the implementation of equal opportunities policies.

Subjective criteria include employee motivation, team spirit and willingness to accept change; the extent to which proposals emerging from the personnel department are accepted by senior management; the quality of relationships with trade unions; the calibre of job applicants responding to job advertisements; the usefulness of documents drafted by the department (job descriptions and person specifications, for example); and so on. Staff from other parts of the firm may be questioned in order to ascertain how they rate the personnel department in terms of such matters as:

■ how promptly it responds to requests for information or advice;

■ the quality of advice given by personnel department staff;

■ politeness and approachability of the department's members;

■ individual knowledge of technical personnel matters;

■ the department's overall contributions to the work of other sections.

Senior management may evaluate a personnel department's contributions on the basis of its ability to handle satisfactorily sensitive human relations problems arising from downsizing, organisational restructuring and the implementation of change. Also the personnel/human resources officer will be expected to make meaningful contributions to top management team decisions and to assist with strategic issues such as the formulation of mission statements, the determination of corporate culture, the facilitation of technological change and so on.

Decentralisation and devolution

Many personnel and HRM functions can be undertaken by managers in local units rather than through a central personnel department. Note that the individuals completing such duties in subsidiaries, divisions, etc. might *themselves* be personnel specialists rather than general line managers, although in practice this is rare because of the duplication of effort involved. The main problem with devolution of personnel and/or HRM work to non-specialist line managers is that they may be neither competent nor interested in personnel or HRM issues and may not be motivated to complete HRM duties properly, so that critically important personnel tasks are neglected. Bad HRM decisions lead to a poor corporate image, higher long-term costs and loss of output due to industrial conflict. Also line managers may focus all their attention on immediate and pressing personnel problems at the expense of long-term HRM planning, and it can result in HRM considerations not influencing strategic management decisions.

Effective devolution requires:

- the provision of backup services in relation to technical problems arising from contracts of employment, legal aspects of redundancy and dismissal, union recognition, etc. – an outside consultancy might assume this role;
- acceptance by everyone that line managers' workloads will have to increase following their assuming personnel responsibilities;
- the training of line managers in HRM techniques and concepts.

EUROPEAN UNION INFLUENCES

Following the UK general election of 1997 the incoming government announced its policy of positive engagement with the European Union and, in particular, that the UK would accept the European Social Charter. The latter originated during the 1987 Belgian presidency of the EU's Council of Ministers. It was put forward as a suggested device for ensuring that basic employment rights would not be eroded following the intense business competition expected to occur in consequence of the completion of the single internal market. Further objectives were to encourage EU governments to harmonise national employment laws and practices and to confirm the EU's commitment to an active social policy. The Social Charter was intended as a grand gesture towards the EU's labour force representing an unequivocal statement that *people* matter as well as business competition and that the interests of employees are just as important as those of firms.

The first draft of the Charter was published by the European Commission in May 1989 with the intention that each member state would implement its requirements at the national (rather than EU) level. Action would not be taken by the EU (via directives, regulations, etc.), provided the Charter's basic objectives could be effectively attained by member states or bodies within them.

Contents of the Social Charter

The basic rights to be established by the Charter were as follows:

- **Fair remuneration** – this would involve the specification of rules for establishing a fair wage.
- **Health, protection and safety at the workplace.**
- **Access to vocational training throughout a person's working life, including the right to retraining.**
- **Freedom of association and collective bargaining** – to belong or not belong to a trade union and for unions to have the right to bargain with employing firms.
- **Integration into working life of disabled people** – the provision of training for the disabled, accessibility to work premises, availability of special transport and explicit consideration of disabled people during the ergonomic design of equipment.
- **Information, consultation and worker participation in company decision making** – especially in enterprises that operate in more than one EU country.

- **Freedom of occupation, residence and movement of workers** – including equal treatment with regard to local taxes and social security entitlements.

- **Improvement in living and working conditions** – this embraces equality of treatment for part-time and temporary workers, controls on night working and requirements for weekly rest periods and paid holidays.

- **Social protection** – including adequate unemployment and other social security benefits.

- **Equal treatment of men and women.**

- **Protection of young people** – with a minimum working age of 15 years (16 for full-time employment) and a ban on night work for those under 18.

- **Reasonable living standards for senior citizens** – with a specified minimum income underwritten by the state.

There has recently been a wave of laws and regulations in the UK in the spirit of some of these basic objectives and, at time of writing, there are a good deal more in the pipeline. One effect of this may be to raise the profile of HR managers within organisations as employers seek to ensure that they keep within the new laws and regulations (many of which came into force very quickly, despite being quite complicated).

Some of the more recent acts and statutory instruments that organisations have been affected by are:

- Data Protection Act 1998
- Employment Relations Act 1999
- Public Interest Disclosure Act 1998
- Working Time Regulations 1998 and 1999
- Maternity and Parental Leave, etc. Regulations 1999
- National Minimum Wage Act 1999
- Part-time Workers (Prevention of Less Favourable Treatment) Regulations 2000
- The Regulation of Investigatory Powers Act 2000
- Fixed-Term Employees (Prevention of Less Favourable Treatment) Regulations 2002
- Employment Act 2002

The Human Rights Act 1998

This statute came into force in October 2000. It incorporates the provisions of the European Convention on Human Rights into UK law. Its articles include the right to respect for private and family life, and the right to freedom of expression. Courts and tribunals must now interpret law in a way that is compatible with the Convention. If this does not prove possible, UK law takes precedence. In fact, the British have been able to enforce their rights under the Convention since 1951, but only in the appropriate European court in Strasbourg.

Work–life balance

During the 1990s a culture of long hours and 'presentism' (being seen to be staying late at work) developed until it became the norm, and this trend has continued in recent years. This has resulted in an increasing tension between an employee's family commitments and work responsibilities. These changes have important considerations for the development of HR policies. Pressures pushing for improving changes in the work–life balance include compensation payments for stress caused by work pressures, an increase in the proportion of women returning to work following maternity leave, employees' expectation of work, the need to care for elderly adults and single-parent families. Flexible working patterns were initially highlighted to give firms a flexible workforce to meet changing customer requirements in Atkinson's flexible firm model (Atkinson, 1984). Political pressure from changes in European and UK law is also causing changes in the view of work–life balance. The best work–life balance depends on the individual's needs and it changes with the various life stages.

Government backing for improved work–life balance for families

The government launched an improved ACAS helpline service in January 2003. It is designed to give help and guidance on family-friendly employment rights for both employers and parents. New employment measures became law on 6 April 2003 giving parents with children under six years or disabled children under 18 years the right to request to work flexibly, and to have that request considered seriously.

Although there is no right to flexible working, a refusal may result in a claim of indirect sex discrimination, so that the employer would have to show an objective reason for justifying full-time working as a requirement and the refusal to permit part-time working (Willey, 2003). Maternity leave has been increased to 26 weeks paid and 26 weeks unpaid. Paternity leave has been set at two weeks' paid leave to be taken within eight weeks of the birth. Adoption leave has been set to mirror the provision of maternity leave and pay as closely as possible.

SUMMARY

- Human resources are an organisation's most important asset and the effective management of human resources is a key determinant of an organisation's success. All managers who control others are necessarily involved in human resources management and thus require at least a rudimentary understanding of what the subject is about – its problems, possibilities and prospects, and how it relates to the organisation's strategy and management overall.

- Human resources are much more difficult to manage than material resources, partly because conflict often occurs between the employer's and employees' wishes and partly because, to an increasing extent, employees try to share in making decisions about their working environment. Management must recognise workers' aspirations and harness and develop their innate abilities for the good of the organisation. Employees will not submit passively to manipulation or dictatorial control by management but more and more expect and demand some influence in the way they are employed. Research in the behavioural sciences shows that an appropriate response by management will benefit the organisation.

- HRM is much more than the application within an organisation of a set of management techniques. It is concerned with the wider implications of the management of change and not just with the effects of change on working practices. It seeks proactively to encourage flexible attitudes and the acceptance of new methods.

Cases

CASE APPLICATION **1**
Thinking Outside the Box

I t's the world's largest package delivery company with the instantly recognizable brown trucks.[114] Every day United Parcel Service (UPS) transports some 15 million packages and documents throughout the United States and to more than 200 countries and territories. Delivering those packages efficiently is what it gets paid to do, and that massive effort wouldn't be possible without its 99,000-plus drivers. UPS recognizes that it has an HR challenge: hiring and training some 25,000 drivers over the next five years to replace retiring Baby Boomers. But the company has a plan in place that combines its tested business model of uniformity and efficiency (for instance, drivers are trained to hold their keys on a pinky finger so they don't waste time fumbling in their pockets for the keys) with a new approach to driver training.

Replacing its traditional classroom training for drivers, UPS now prepares applicants for the rigorous task of delivering packages and documents efficiently by using videogames, a "slip and fall" simulator, and an obstacle course around a mock village.

UPS's traditional classroom driver training obviously wasn't working as some 30 percent of its driver candidates didn't make it. The company was convinced that the twenty-somethings—the bulk of its driver recruits—responded best to high-tech instruction instead of books and lectures. Now, trainees use videogames, a "slip and fall simulator which combines a greased floor with slippery shoes," and an obstacle course around a mock village.

At a UPS training center outside of Washington, D.C., applicants for a driver's job, which pays an average of $74,000 annually, spend one week practicing and training to be a driver. They move from one station to the next practicing the company's "340 Methods," which are techniques developed by industrial engineers "to save seconds and improve safety in every task from lifting and loading boxes to selecting a package from a shelf in the truck." Applicants play a videogame where they're in the driver's seat and must identify obstacles. From computer simulations, they move to "Clarksville," a mock village with miniature houses and faux businesses. There, they drive a real truck and "must successfully execute five deliveries in 19 minutes." And, in the interest of safety and efficiency, trainees learn to carefully walk on ice with the slip and fall simulator.

How are the new training methods working? So far, so good. Of the 1,629 trainees who have completed it, "only 10 percent have failed the training program, which takes a total of six weeks overall including 30 days of driving a truck in the real world."

Discussion Questions

1. What external factors were affecting UPS's HR practices? How did UPS respond to these trends?

2. Why is efficiency and safety so important to UPS? What role do the company's industrial engineers play in how employees do their work?

3. What changes did the company make to its driver training program? What do you think of these changes?

4. What advantages and drawbacks do you see to this training approach for (a) the trainee and (b) the company?

CASE APPLICATION 2
Social Connections

400 million users served. That's the traffic milestone achieved by Facebook in early 2010. One of those users is Big Four accounting firm Ernst & Young (E&Y), which has had a Facebook page since the summer of 2006.[115] According to the company's Recruiting Director, E&Y uses its Facebook page to reach out to potential new employees. "Our goal was to find a medium Generation Y commonly goes to, so we could communicate with them in a way that's relevant to their day-to-day activities." The company also hoped to promote its brand and culture and show students (future employees) what E&Y was all about and what it would be like to work there.

A quick look at E&Y's Facebook page confirms that the focus is on what the company most values including the learning and development resources available to its employees, its commitment to social responsibility, its focus on inclusiveness, and its internships. Videos show interns and workers in the workplace describing their experiences with the company. The company's 46,000 plus "fans" can use the company's message board to write questions and comments. And those questions and comments aren't ignored. A response is given quickly in an attempt to create an interactive relationship with students. Again, the purpose is to serve as a recruitment tool for future talent. And Facebook isn't the only social media E&Y is using. Company interns Tweet about their experiences—what their first day was like, work experiences, and experiences with E&Y community events.

The practice of using social networking sites to source applicants isn't without its critics. One law firm partner said, "Social networking sites are problematic because the population is limited and highly selective. I anticipate more race and age claims over the next couple of years, and a significant portion will be from sourcing through social networking sites. . . . We'll see lawsuits." Then, there's the possibility that a company using social media to recruit also could use that same method to check out candidate's personal pages. E&Y has promised not to look at candidates' personal pages.

Discussion Questions

1. What are advantages and drawbacks of using social media in the recruiting process for (a) an applicant and (b) a company?

2. Is the use of social media in recruiting applicants a way to hire smarter or a lawsuit waiting to happen? Explain your position.

3. Go to Facebook and check out Ernst & Young's page. What's your impression? Is it an attractive recruiting tool? Why or why not?

CASE APPLICATION

HRM IN THE HONG KONG POLICE FORCE

Believing that "people are the greatest asset" of the organization, the Hong Kong Police Force spends considerable resources and effort to acquire and develop their police officers. It adopts sophisticated human resources management (HRM) practices, in order to win the war for talent against the private employers.

Acquisition of the right people begins with the recruitment and selection of the entry-level posts, mostly the police constables and police inspectors. The human resources branch, under the personnel wing, is actively engaged in publicizing the recruitment program using various media sources, including schools and universities. In 2004, it commenced an internship program—the police mentorship program (PMP)—to attract interested university undergraduate students through an eight-week summer job attachment and a close mentor-mentee relationship. The PMP participants usually have a higher success rate in securing full-time posts upon graduation than those achieved through other recruitment channels.

Nevertheless, the selection process of the police officers is rigorous. Various core competencies like communication, judgment, confidence, and leadership are identified. For example, candidates for the police inspectors' posts have to pass a written examination (which includes English and Chinese language proficiency tests, an aptitude test, and the Basic Law test). In 2010, a psychometric test will be introduced to assess candidates' personalities. An extended interview (or assessment center) that requires group discussion, presentation, and management and leadership exercises is also conducted to gauge competencies such as communication, judgment, confidence, leadership, staff, and resource management. Then, a panel interview, physical fitness test, as well as an integrity check and a medical examination are organized. But since the work is more demanding, police officers are paid a little higher than civil servants in other departments.

The Police College is responsible for training and developing the new recruits. Its Foundation Training Centre organizes stringent recruit training programs with a strong foundation of police knowledge and skills. They include law and procedures, practical exercises, police tactics, weaponry, parade, first aid, and public order. The vision, common purpose, and values of the force are also laid out. In addition, the Professional Development Learning Centre of the Police College organizes a variety of development training for the junior police officers, inspectors, and superintendents upon their reaching a specified number of years of service or promotion. Overseas development opportunities may also be provided.

Upon graduating from the Police College, the police officers are assigned to a specific unit or formation for a few years. Then, they regularly rotate through posts in different units or districts. Such rotation is believed to benefit the individual officers and the organization. The officers can gain a wider experience in policing, administrative and human resource issues, and so on, and thus have a better career development. They build more relationships, develop greater confidence in the job, and gain a holistic view of the force. The police organization achieves better coordination, succession planning, and suffers less from corruption in the local communities. As a result, a learning culture is developed that constitutes an important part of the Hong Kong Police Force's strategic human resource management framework.

Discussion Questions

1. Identify the environmental forces that affect the current development of various HRM activities in the Hong Kong Police Force.
2. What are the advantages or disadvantages of the police mentoring program for the force and the prospective candidates?
3. Evaluate the reliability and validity of one of the written tests used in the selection of the police officers.
4. The Hong Kong Police Force successfully nurtures a learning culture in the organization. Identify various training and development activities that help to shape the culture.

Sources: Based on interviews with the police officers; Hong Kong Police Force Web site. http://www.police.gov.hk; and Allan Y. Jiao, *The Police in Hong Kong: A Contemporary View* (Lanham: University Press of America, 2007).

Don't get fooled again – you're not too old for the job

How would you expect a distinguished 61-year-old man to behave? With restraint, perhaps, a certain decorum and calm? What you would probably not expect him to do is adopt a heroic, macho pose while windmilling his right arm through the air to the delight of the crowd standing in front of him.

But that was the image that confronted me on late-night television just over a week ago. The arm in question belonged, of course, to Pete Townshend, lead guitarist of The Who, and the crowd were the lucky few who had gathered in London's Roundhouse to enjoy the highlight of the BBC's recent 'Electric Proms' concerts.

The Who still perform their 1965 hit 'My Generation', written by Mr Townshend, which contains the famously defiant line, 'Hope I die before I get old' – a goal that, sadly, two of the original band members managed to achieve. The lead singer who delivers this line – with as much conviction as he did 40 years ago – is 62-year-old Roger Daltrey.

It is not only actuaries and pensions advisers who have had their expectations confounded by increased longevity. All of us are having to reassess our views on age.

For managers who may have begun their career with a clear idea about what the future held for them and knew precisely, given their age, where they stood in the corporate hierarchy, things have changed quite dramatically. Fiftysomethings face the prospect of being managed by people young enough (and perhaps disrespectful enough) to be their children. But in other organisations, ambitious thirtysomethings may find their progress blocked by a tier of older, underperforming bosses who are clinging on for fear of being pushed out before their pension has grown to an acceptable level.

Businesses need to get much smarter about age, and fast. The demographics insist on it. And it is no use expecting government to sort out these problems for you. In any case, legislation has, so far, not proved terribly effective in bringing about what you might call cultural re-education in this area.

The US's Age Discrimination in Employment Act dates back to 1967, offering some protection to workers over the age of 40. The European age equality directive will be in force throughout the European Union only by the end of this year but its text was agreed in 2000 and it has been firmly on the agenda since that time.

In spite of all this law-making, traditional attitudes (and prejudices) about people's age and what it tells you about them are solidly in place. Research published last month by the Cranfield School of Management confirmed that age discrimination remains widespread, among UK employers at least. Preparation for, and compliance with, the new laws has done little to alter the view that, for example, younger workers are less reliable than their more seasoned colleagues, take more sick days and display less loyalty while older workers struggle with IT and new ways of working and are generally much more resistant to change.

Review Questions and Tests

Understanding Yourself

How Much Do I Know About HRM?

This scale measures how much you know about human resource management. Although it assesses your knowledge of some key findings within the HRM field, there are many other important things to know.

INSTRUMENT   Below are a number of statements about research findings in human resource management. For each statement, indicate whether you think it is true or false.

> **0** = False
>
> **1** = True

1. Most managers give employees lower performance appraisals than they objectively deserve.   **0   1**
2. Poor performers are generally more realistic about their performance than good performers are.   **0   1**
3. Despite the popularity of drug testing, there is no clear evidence that applicants who score positive on drug tests are any less reliable or less productive employees.   **0   1**
4. Most people over-evaluate how well they perform on the job.   **0   1**
5. The most important determinant of how much training employees actually use on their jobs is how much they learned during training.   **0   1**
6. The most valid employment interviews are designed around each candidate's unique background.   **0   1**
7. Although there are "integrity tests" that try to predict whether someone will steal, be absent, or otherwise take advantage of an employer, they don't work well in practice because so many people lie on them.   **0   1**
8. On average, conscientiousness is a better predictor of job performance than is intelligence.   **0   1**
9. Most employees prefer to be paid on the basis of individual performance rather than on team or organizational performance.   **0   1**
10. There is a positive relationship between the proportion of managers receiving organizationally based pay incentives and company profitability.   **0   1**

SCORING KEY   To score the measure, compare your answers to the correct answers, which are as follows: (1) False, (2) False, (3) False, (4) True, (5) False, (6) False, (7) False, (8) False, (9) True, and (10) True. Matches should be counted as one. Compute the number of correct responses. Scores will range from zero (all responses incorrect) to 10 (all responses correct).

ANALYSIS AND INTERPRETATION   If you didn't achieve a high score, don't worry just yet. These questions were given to nearly 1,000 HR professionals in a variety of organizations. These professionals had an average of 14 years of work experience in HRM. How did they do? On some of the questions (such as, "Most managers give employees lower performance appraisals than they objectively deserve"), the vast majority gave the correct answer (which is false, by the way). On other questions, however, a much smaller percentage gave the correct answer. For example, for the statement: "On average, conscientiousness is a better predictor of job performance than is intelligence," only 18 percent of the HR professionals gave the correct response (false)!

Why the discrepancies? There are several reasons. It could be that practicing HR professionals are unaware of research findings, either because they don't have time to read academic journals (or textbooks), or because the journals are so technically complex that it's difficult to extract the main findings. It also could be that practicing professionals are aware of the research findings but choose not to utilize them because of factors such as political reasons, organizational inertia, or aversion to risk. In any event, closing the gap between research and practice is likely to be beneficial, as research has indicated that organizations that implement effective HRM practices perform better than those that don't.

Source: Based on S. L. Rynes, A. E. Colbert, and K. G. Brown, "HR Professionals' Beliefs About Effective Human Resource Practices: Correspondence Between Research and Practice," *Human Resource Management* (Summer, 2002), pp. 149–74.

SECTION 11:
OPERATIONS, QUALITY AND
PRODUCTION METHODS

Chapter 19:

What is Operations Management?

INTRODUCTION

The structure of the chapter reflects the theoretical basis around which it is built – that of operations being transformation processes where input resources are transformed into outputs. Following consideration of the past history and present organisational context of the process, future trends and means of classification are discussed. The role of the operations manager is also considered. Current and developing ways of measuring output are presented within the context of wider changes affecting operations. Finally the relationship between operations and the customer is analysed and some comment made on the implications of globalisation and multinational management on the operations manager. Five case studies are included to support and develop the key points raised in this chapter.

OPERATIONS MANAGEMENT AS A TRANSFORMATION PROCESS

Any organisation, whether it be a manufacturer, retailer, educational establishment, hospital or even government agency, exists to satisfy the needs of its customers or consumers – those who are the recipients of what is produced or the services carried out by the organisation (see Figure 14.1).

So within the context of an organisation what are 'operations'? An operation may be defined as

'a process, method or series of acts especially of a practical nature.'

In general, operations simply harness resources in order to produce something or to provide a service – they are part of every kind of organised activity within the

Figure 14.1 **The closed loop of customer satisfaction**

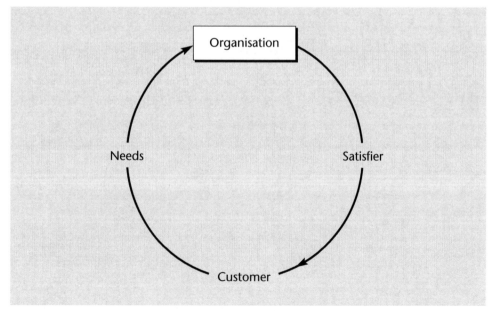

Source: K Lockyer, J Oakland and A Muhlemann (1992) *Production and Operations Management* (6th edition), Pearson Education Limited.

organisation. It is argued by some authors that operations management is an integral part of any managerial role (see Exhibit 14.1).

More specifically, operations can refer to a department or functional area within an organisation where certain resources are transformed into products or services by adding value to them. 'Operations managers' therefore have to manage this process in some way.

There are several definitions of operations management which highlight the key features. Schroeder (1993) defines the key terms as:

> *'Operations managers are responsible for producing the supply of goods or services in organisations. Operations managers make decisions regarding the operations function and the transformation systems used. Operations management is the study of decision making in the operations function.'*

Harris (1989) uses a simpler definition which highlights all the key features of the task:

> *'operations management is the management of a system which provides goods or services to or for a customer, and involves the design, planning and control of the system.'*

Denzler (2000) defines operations management by 'what it does':

> *'Operations management is the business function that manages that part of a business that transforms raw materials and human inputs into goods and services of higher value.'*

Slack *et al.* (2006) discuss operations management in terms of process:

> *'operations and process management is the activity of managing the resources and processes that produce products and services.'*

Many authors view operations management as a transformation process, and this helps to highlight some of the key features of the task (see Figure 14.2).

Exhibit 14.1 Operations

- **A manufacturing company conducts operations in a mill, a foundry or a factory.**

- **Banks operate from offices and branches.**

- **Restaurant operations take place on chopping blocks, serving tables and takeaway counters.**

- **Builders operate in offices where proposals are prepared and on construction sites.**

- **University operations take place in lecture theatres, research laboratories, seminar rooms and on the sports field.**

Source: Adapted from R J Schonberger and E M Knod (1994) *Operations Management: Continuous Improvement* (5th edition), Burr Ridge, IL: Richard D Irwin. Reprinted with permission from R D Irwin Inc.

Figure 14.2 **The transformation process**

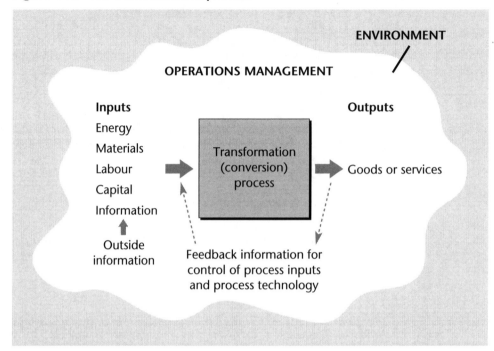

Examples of various operations classified in this way are shown in Table 14.1.
Slack *et al.* (2004) discuss the importance of operations management in terms of reducing the costs of producing products and services by increasing process efficiency, increasing revenue through good customer satisfaction and service quality, and by using innovation to reduce the need for investment in physical resources.

Table 14.1 **Examples of operations classified as transformation processes**

OPERATION	INPUTS	OUTPUTS
Bank	Cashiers, staff, computer equipment, facilities, energy	Financial services (loans, deposits)
Restaurant	Cooks, waiting staff, food, equipment, facilities, energy	Meals, entertainment, satisfied customers
Hospital	Doctors, nurses, staff, equipment, facilities, energy	Health services, healthy patients
University	Staff, equipment, facilities, energy, knowledge	Educated students, research
Airline	Planes, facilities, pilots, flight attendants, engineers, labour, energy	Transportation from one area to another

Source: Developed from R G Schroeder (1993) *Operations Management* (4th edition), © Copyright The McGraw-Hill Companies, Inc. 1993.

As part of the transformation process (see Figure 14.2) it is useful to make a distinction between transformed and transforming resources – those which are treated or transformed in a certain way and those which act upon the transformed resources (see Exhibit 14.2).

Exhibit 14.2 **Transformed and transforming resources**

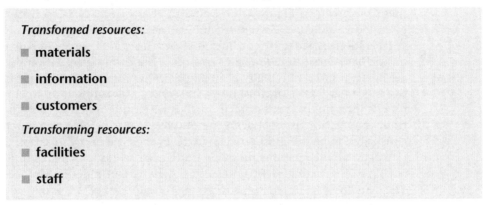

Transformed resources:

■ **materials**

■ **information**

■ **customers**

Transforming resources:

■ **facilities**

■ **staff**

Source: Adapted from N Slack, S Chambers, C Harland, A Harrison and R Johnston (2004) *Operations Management* (4th edition), Harlow: FT Prentice Hall.

One of the transformed resources is usually dominant in an operation – a bank deals with materials and customers but is primarily concerned with processing information. Manufacturing is primarily concerned with processing material but information is also very important. Classification of operations according to their predominant transformed resource is shown in Table 14.2.

Table 14.2 **Operations classified according to primary transformed resource**

PREDOMINANTLY MATERIALS PROCESSORS	PREDOMINANTLY INFORMATION PROCESSORS	PREDOMINANTLY CUSTOMER PROCESSORS
All manufacturers	Accountants	Hairdressers
Retail operations	Market research companies	Hotels
Warehouses	University research units	Hospitals
Postal service	Telecommunications companies	Theatres

Source: Adapted from N Slack, S Chambers, C Harland, A Harrison and R Johnston (2004) *Operations Management* (4th edition), Harlow: FT Prentice Hall.

In terms of the transforming resources, facilities may be high or low tech but are still important for any type of organisation. Staff will have various degrees of skill depending on the operation but reliability will be important in all cases. The role of staff in service operations is relatively more important than manufacturing because of the greater labour intensity of the transformation process.

THE CONTEXT OF THE TRANSFORMATION PROCESS: OPERATIONS STRATEGY

The interface between the transformation process and the environment is particularly important – both the environment within the organisation and the external environment must be considered. The relationship of operations to the environment is shown in Figure 14.3. Some of the aspects of these interfaces will be discussed in more detail when the role of the customer in operations is described.

Operations is generally considered to be a functional area – like marketing, etc. – rather than a basic discipline area of study – like economics, sociology, systems concepts, etc. It has traditionally been emphasised more in manufacturing because it is the major part of the organisation – in services, marketing is often considered to be more important. In terms of relationships with other functions within the organisation, the relationship between the marketing and operations functions is often considered to be the most crucial whatever the type of organisation. Lockyer *et al.* (1992) detail the relationship by defining a 'closed loop' which summarises all the key tasks involved in identifying and satisfying consumer needs (see Figure 14.4). The marketing role therefore covers stages (i) and (v) of this loop – identifying and forecasting, and distribution.

Figure 14.3 The relationship of operations to the environment

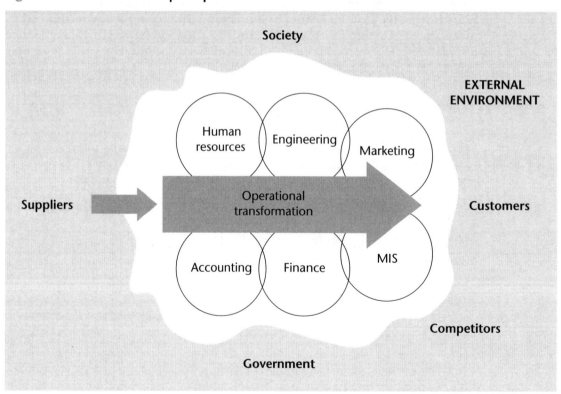

Source: R G Schroeder (1993) *Operations Management* (4th edition), Copyright © The McGraw-Hill Companies Inc.

Figure 14.4 **From customer to customer – a closed loop**

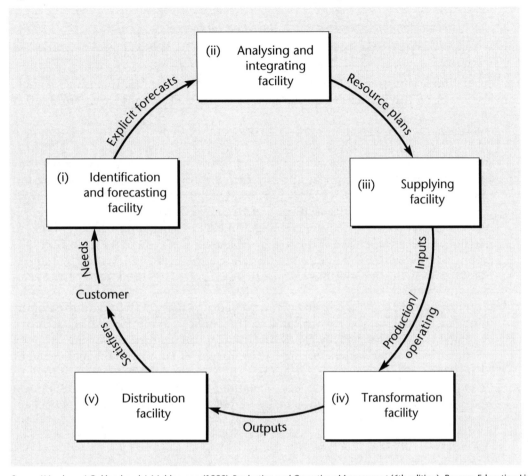

Source: K Lockyer, J Oakland and A Muhlemann (1992) *Production and Operations Management* (6th edition), Pearson Education Limited.

However, this approach may be criticised by those who believe that operations can offer competitive advantage to an organisation (e.g. Wheelwright and Hayes, 1985) and that customers and operations should be working more closely together. Other authors (Hill, 1993) believe that marketing strategy actually drives operations strategy following from the premise that customer requirements should drive the operations function. This is very much in line with the recent popularity of total quality approaches, which are identified by an increasing emphasis on putting the customer first, although this may be expressed in different ways (see Chapter 3).

→ Ch. 3

There has been a great deal of progress in the past five years in terms of developing the concept of operations strategy. This has arisen from the widespread adoption of the view that operations can offer competitive advantage to an organisation, be it manufacturing or service. One of the leading texts in the area (Slack and Lewis, 2002) defines operations strategy as

'the total pattern of decisions which shape the long-term capabilities of any type of operation and their contribution to overall strategy, through the reconciliation of market requirements with operations resources.'

It argues strongly that the approach is applicable to both manufacturing and service organisations. It is concerned with the

'total transformation process that is the whole business.'

Slack and Lewis's model of operations strategy does not dictate the form of the operations function but proposes that giving consideration to the resources of the operation is consistent with the resource-based view of the firm that is increasingly well regarded and acts as a counterbalance to the traditionally dominant market perspective.

Another way of considering the role of operations within an organisation is to use the 'value chain' concept proposed by Porter (1985). A **value chain** is defined as the collection of activities used to design, produce, market, deliver and support its product. Customers, suppliers and the firm are broken down into discrete but related activities, with the value chain showing how value is created by the firm for its customers. Porter argues that competitive advantage is then gained when the value created exceeds the cost of creating it. 'Value' is what customers are willing to pay for and is created within the firm by the activities shown in Figure 14.5 This approach links with the definition of operations management proposed by Denzler (2000) who identifies adding value as the main activity carried out by the operations function.

It can be seen that operations is considered a primary activity and the importance of its role will be shown later in the chapter. While 'logistics' is shown separately by Porter it actually forms part of the broad definition of operations used within this chapter which includes the concept of supply chain management (Lamming, 1996). Cousins *et al.* (2007) discuss the need for organisations to manage their own internal processes (operations management) while maintaining a focus on obtaining and managing the best inputs for the organisation (supply chain

Figure 14.5 The firm chain value

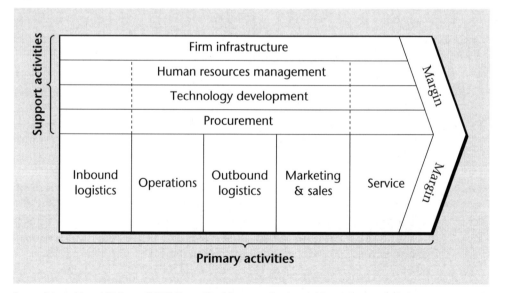

Source: Adapted from M E Porter (1985) *Competitive Advantage: Creating and Sustaining Superior Performance*, New York: Free Press, a division of Simon & Schuster. Copyright © 1985, 1998 by M E Porter.

management). Typical functions that might be included in such a broad definition of operations management include:

- purchasing
- production
- logistics
- maintenance
- goods receiving
- dispatch.

THE TRANSFORMATION PROCESS

Past history

In one sense operations management has existed as long as people have made things, although it was not recognised as such. Attention to 'production management' has been greatest in the past 200 years, and attention to operations management as a discipline only during the last 20 years or so. Operations management developed as a discipline because people realised that many different organisations were experiencing similar problems and whether they were service, manufacturing or public sector organisations did not make a significant difference.

It is not possible to give a strict chronological account of the way in which the area has developed but there are a number of major theoretical and practical contributions which have affected it (see Exhibit 14.3). Fuller accounts can be found in Fogarty *et al.* (1989) and Evans (1997) (see also Chapter 1).

→ Ch. 1

Division of labour

→ Ch. 9

George (1968) argues that the concept of division of labour (see Chapter 9) can be traced back to the ancient Greeks (Plato's *The Republic*), where it was recognised that specialisation of labour on a single task can result in greater productivity and efficiency than assigning a number of tasks to one worker. This was also discussed by

Exhibit 14.3 **Major contributions to the theoretical development of operations management**

- **The division of labour – Adam Smith and Charles Babbage**
- **Standardisation of parts**
- **The Industrial Revolution**
- **The scientific study of work – Frederick Taylor**
- **Human relations – the Hawthorne experiments**
- **Decision modelling**
- **Technology**

→ Ch. 20 Adam Smith, author of the classic *The Wealth of Nations* (1776), who noted that output is increased by specialisation of labour (see Chapter 20). Workers become increasingly expert at one task, there is an avoidance of lost time due to changing to other jobs, and tools and machines can be added to improve efficiency. Charles Babbage (1832) noted that specialisation of labour makes it possible to pay wages only for the specific skills required. Division of labour is now being reviewed because of its effect on worker morale, turnover, job boredom and performance but it has been the foundation of many operations management techniques and methods of organising production systems.

Standardisation of parts

Manufacturing parts so that they are as interchangeable as possible is now commonplace in our society – for example, light bulbs of different wattage and shape but all with the same fitting. This was not, however, the case in the past and designing parts in this way is one of the major features of operations management which enabled increasing efficiency and specialisation of labour.

The Industrial Revolution

The Industrial Revolution took place during the late 1700s and early 1800s and was the time when machine power was substituted for human power. It was made possible by inventions such as the steam engine (invented by James Watt in 1764) and electricity. The demand for manufactured goods generated by the First World War (1914–18) aided the development of 'mass production' where very large quantities of goods were made using relatively high levels of automation. Society now appears to have shifted to a post-industrial period where manufacturing is not the primary source of income for many countries and services form the basis of the economy.

Scientific study of work

This method determines the best method of working using scientific principles – observing present work methods, developing an improved method through scientific measurement and analysis, training workers in the new method and continuing feedback and management of the work process. Taylor (1911) was the originator of these ideas and they gained widespread acceptance, although they have been criticised for being misapplied and used by management simply to 'speed up' workers without giving full consideration to their total range of needs. The scientific method is now seen by many as a means of exploiting workers and in opposition to newer methods of working which seek to take human needs into account.

Human relations

Motivation and the human element in the design of work are vital and were highlighted by the Hawthorne experiments which indicated that worker motivation – along with the physical and technical environment – is crucial in improving pro- → Ch. 12 ductivity (see Chapter 12). The proponents of scientific management were forced as a result of these experiments to moderate their methods, which had placed an overemphasis on the technical elements of work design, and the concept of job enrichment was developed (Hackman *et al.*, 1975).

Decision models

Many of the traditional texts on production management concentrate almost entirely on the use of mathematical models to represent a production system in order to find optimal solutions within certain constraints. Examples of these models include the economic order quantity model used for inventory management and linear programming. Such models are still an important part of operations management but their limitations are now more clearly acknowledged, particularly in terms of their disregard for the human elements of operations and the limited range of assumptions on which many of the models had to be based in order to make them workable.

Technology

The application of computer technology has revolutionised operations management with computers being used for many planning and controlling tasks such as inventory management, production scheduling, costing and managing projects. Computers have been used for a number of years within the manufacturing process itself and this is still an important application. The advent of information technology in particular, where computer technology is used to store and process information, has been of particular significance within operations (Underwood, 1994). The Internet has enabled many organisations to increase the visibility of their supply processes (Cousins *et al.*, 2007) as it allows customers to select and purchase products via the web (for example, books and CDs) and to create bespoke service packages (for example, holidays) (Johnston and Clark, 2005).

PRESENT ORGANISATIONAL CONTEXT

Operations management plays an important role in any type of organisation, but different emphasis is placed on operations in manufacturing and service organisations. The differences and similarities between these types of organisation are important for operations managers since they need to understand clearly the nature of the organisation in which they are working and the relative importance of various aspects of operations management.

Operations can be classified in various ways. One useful classification is from Wild (1989), who identifies four different types.

- **Manufacture** – where the physical output differs from the input: there is a change in the **form** utility of resources; *making something* – examples include car manufacture, food manufacture.
- **Transport** – where the customer, or something belonging to the customer, is moved without any change in physical resources: there is a change in **place** utility; *moving something or someone* – examples include trains, distribution companies.
- **Supply** – where the ownership of goods is changed without a change in form: there is a change in **possession** utility; *providing some physical goods* – examples include retailing, petrol stations.
- **Service** – where the customer, or something belonging to the customer, is treated in some way: there is a change in **state** utility; *something happens to someone or something* – examples include dentists, the fire service.

It is not, however, always appropriate to assign an organisation solely to one category – most organisations have aspects of all of the above to varying degrees – but it is usual to be able to assign a primary category to an organisation and this will have implications for operations management.

It can be useful to distinguish between organisations according to the degree to which their transformation processes produce goods, i.e. tangible entities, or services, i.e. intangible entities. Goods are physical in nature and can be stored, transformed and transported. A service is produced and consumed more or less simultaneously but cannot be stored or transported (see Exhibit 14.4).

It can be argued that it is not appropriate to distinguish at all between manufacturing and service, but that there is simply a continuum of organisations with some having more emphasis on goods than others. However, most academics still maintain the distinction for the purposes of analysis and the UK government continues to issue economic statistics based on these classifications.

Even within service organisations there are difficulties of classification and the operations management implications vary. Schmenner (1986) has proposed the classification in Table 14.3 which is widely accepted. Degree of labour intensity refers to the ratio of capital to labour.

Schmenner goes on to discuss the implications of this classification for managerial roles and the points he makes are summarised in Table 14.4.

The major characteristics of services and their implications for operations management can be summarised as follows:

- intangible output
- variable, non-standard output
- a service is perishable
- high customer contact
- customer participation
- cannot be mass-produced
- high personal judgement used by employees
- labour intensity
- decentralised facilities, near to the customer
- demand varies greatly over a short period.

Exhibit 14.4 **Goods or services**

Primarily goods producers:
- mines, chemical factories, oil refineries, farms, with little or no customer contact and not offering services as part of their marketing package.

Mixed production organisations:
- most manufacturing companies, insurance companies and fast food outlets. All offer both goods and services. Manufacturing organisations often sell warranties and provide repair and after-sales service.

Primarily service producers:
- dentists, management consultants, banks, educational institutions. Any tangible goods provided in connection with the service is incidental.

Table 14.3 **The service process matrix**

		DEGREE OF CONSUMER/SERVICE INTERACTION AND CUSTOMISATION	
		LOW	HIGH
DEGREE OF LABOUR INTENSITY	HIGH	**Mass service** e.g. retailing, banking, education	**Professional service** e.g. doctors, lawyers, accountants
	LOW	**Service factory** e.g. airlines, truck transportation, hotels, leisure resorts	**Service shop** e.g. hospitals, repair services

Table 14.4 **Challenges for managers in service organisations**

CLASSIFICATION	CHALLENGES
Low labour intensity	Capital expenditure Technology development Managing demand to avoid peaks and promote off-peaks Scheduling service delivery
High labour intensity	Hiring staff Training staff Developing and controlling methods of working Scheduling workers Controlling a large number of dispersed locations Managing growth
Low interaction/customisation	Marketing Attention to physical surroundings Managing a rigid organisation structure
High interaction/customisation	Managing cost increases Maintaining quality Dealing with customer participation in the process Managing the advancement of staff Managing a flat organisation Gaining employee loyalty

Intangible output

This describes the uniqueness of services more than any other aspect. Services are not a 'thing' that is produced but an activity that is experienced in some way, either by the customer directly or as a process carried out on possessions of the customer. The physical output from the process, therefore, does not exist in a tangible state and customer satisfaction is based on both the *process* (the service experience) and the *outcome* (the end result). There is often no clear boundary between process and outcome (Johnston and Clark, 2005) – for example, customers in a restaurant buy both the meal and they way it is served. Therefore service operations managers must manage the service process and the service outcome simultaneously.

Variable, non-standard output

The extent of this will depend on the exact type of service provided, as shown by Schmenner (1986), and in particular the degree of labour intensity, which makes quality control difficult. Quality is difficult to predict both for the organisation and the customer, and the reputation of the organisation is an important factor. Quality of service depends to a large extent, however, on the expectations of the consumer. With this in mind service operations, such as telephone call centres, use standard questions and processes when dealing with customer queries in an attempt to standardise the output of the customer service experience and manage customer expectation.

A service is perishable

A service is consumed instantly, for example using a hotel room or an airline seat, and cannot be stored, although consumers may enjoy the *benefit* for a long while afterwards – for example, a heart transplant.

This has a major impact on capacity planning, which is a key aspect of operations management. Periods of slack demand cannot be used to build stock to meet high demand in other periods, so capacity has to be varied. The large numbers of checkouts in supermarkets, not all of which are used at slack times, is an example of this. It is, however, expensive to build in extra capacity which may only be used at certain times, and it is not possible to hire employees at very short notice to cope with extra demand so they may have to appear as a fixed overhead rather than being varied with demand. In an attempt to make use of the available capacity, service organisations offer price incentives to encourage customers to move to less busy times. For example, train companies offer discounts for off-peak travel and restaurants offer cheaper 'early evening menus' from 5 to 7 pm.

High customer contact

Although this varies with the nature of the service (Schmenner, 1986), in general service organisations have a higher degree of customer contact than manufacturers – nevertheless this is changing even for manufacturing organisations. The customer may not be physically in contact with the provider, especially where technology is used, for example a telephone enquiry line, but in any case employee interaction is critical. In some cases organisations move 'messy' parts of the service process to places where they cannot be seen by the customer – sometimes referred to as back-room operations. This then allows the organisation to focus more on employee/customer interaction at the crucial point. Other organisations are proud to show all the parts of the operation to the customer – for example, McDonald's restaurants where all the kitchen operations are deliberately made visible, or Subway where the customer is part of the sandwich-making process.

Customer participation

The extent of customer participation depends on the type of service, and there may be a formal or informal relationship between the organisation and customer. It is a crucial factor in determination of quality and timeliness. Service operations need to guide the customer through the process using clear cues and visual management. For example, restaurants need to give clear cues as to whether it is self-service or has a table service to prevent customer confusion, frustration and ultimately dissatisfaction.

Cannot be mass-produced

This does not apply within the service factory quadrant of Schmenner's matrix and considerable benefits have been gained by service organisations applying mass-production principles to providing a service. For example, telephone call centres use technology to ask callers to select options on their keypad so that the service operation can quickly filter and meet the requirements of the high volume of customers. It is perhaps in this quadrant that operations management has had the greatest impact on service organisations. However, the customised nature of many services, such as medical treatment and legal advice, makes these types of service organisation very difficult to manage effectively.

High personal judgement used by employees

This is particularly marked in professional services – for example, lawyers and doctors who have a reputation for being the most difficult to manage. It applies to services which cannot be mass-produced and are often relatively labour intensive.

Labour intensity

This has implications for productivity (the ratio of output to input resources). Service organisations nearly always have lower overall productivity than manufacturing organisations. Where service organisations have substituted equipment for people (e.g. automatic cash dispensers in banks instead of going to the counter to obtain cash) or reorganised processes (e.g. self-service buffets rather than waiter service), there have been productivity improvements. People and equipment are not, however, always in opposition and may complement each other.

Decentralised facilities near to the customer

This is especially important where physical contact with the customer is involved and service location is critical to revenue for many organisations. It is not possible to ship services, because they have to be produced at the point of customer contact. In order to minimise variation between large numbers of locations there is a trend towards uniformity – many high streets look the same now – where all branches appear to be very similar and common procedures are used, with central common training.

Demand varies greatly over a short period

Relative to manufacturing organisations demand varies more often in service companies, with more of a random pattern (e.g. emergency services), and stocks cannot be made to help out. Some organisations try to alter demand (e.g. cheap off-peak offers), manage supply by building flexibility into operations (e.g. more checkouts open at busy times) or in some cases by ignoring variations (accepting that there will be longer queues at lunchtime). This third option is becoming less easy to justify as consumers are offered more choice and appear to be becoming more particular about service quality. The USA is an example of a society where service quality is now a crucial determinant of market position.

CURRENT INFLUENCES

Production management was important when the Western world was an 'industrial society', but the rise of service organisations and the decline of manufacturing have caused some people to question the relevance of operations. However, there are a number of reasons why operations management is considered to be increasingly important rather than in decline.

The resurgence of interest in operations during the 1980s was fuelled by the decline in the international competitiveness of Western industry, whose markets were taken over by foreign products and competition. The rate of productivity growth was also falling behind other countries, especially those in the Far East, and this was seen as being the province (and the fault) of the operations function. Whatever the 'solution' may be to the economic problems of the West (if, indeed, there is a single solution), increased investment, more research and development and changes in the approaches used to manage people all have to be put into action by operations managers and therefore affect the operations function.

Many of the fashionable ideas in management – total quality management (TQM), supply chain management (SCM), 'lean' thinking, business process re-engineering (BPR) and six sigma – not only affect but are centred around the operations function and focus on the process. Part of the appeal of such management techniques is the data-driven evidence-based approach to analysing processes. Many have also realised that focusing on, and improving, operations can increase efficiency (therefore reducing costs) as well as providing improved quality and service (which improves revenue). Slack and Lewis (2002) are clear that

'"operations" is not always "operational" – operations management has an important strategic dimension.'

Some have not only seen operations as the key to future economic prosperity but also as a means of securing competitive advantage (Wheelwright and Hayes, 1985). It is clear that weak operations will affect the competitive position of the organisation, and as operations has become more closely linked to other parts of the organisation so its role in competitive positioning has become more important. At one time a good product, superior marketing or a technology which was difficult to imitate could make up for weak operations management. The role of operations is, however, different now:

'Superior operations management blends with superior design, marketing, accounting, supplier relations, human resource management and business strategy as an essential component of success. Weak operations management, on the other hand, tends to coincide with many other management weaknesses.' (Schonberger and Knod, 1994)

Current influences on operations include:

- customer-directed operations
- continuous improvement and quality
- lean and agile production
- integration with other functions
- globalisation of operations
- risk
- business ethics, corporate responsibility and the environment.

Customer-directed operations imply that operations have an external orientation so that they are well placed to meet customer requirements. However, customers may be internal as well as external to the organisation – 'customer' can mean the next process as well as the final end user of the product or recipient of the service. The trend towards subcontracting and outsourcing of services has made it more difficult for organisations to control their external suppliers and contractors. However, the related growth of interest in supply chain management (Christopher, 1998) is a response to this influence and is becoming increasingly important. Strategic supplier selection is now seen by many as key to supporting an organisation's long-term objectives (Cousins *et al.*, 2007).

Continuous improvement and quality are influences that have increased in importance, not only as a result of increased emphasis on customer relationships but also because of the influence of Japanese manufacturers in the West (see Ishikawa, 1985). Many have described the changes in emphasis in Western organisations as a 'quality revolution' (Evans, 1997) and there is no doubt that a focus on quality is now a prerequisite for effective competitiveness in most markets. Although it originally started in the manufacturing sector, service quality is now a major focus for all organisations as it is often how customers differentiate between similar products and services. This is evidenced by the inclusion in this book of a whole chapter on quality management (see Chapter 7) which details its influence and highlights the strategic importance of quality management.

→ Ch. 7

Lean and agile production are influences that have become important as

> *'the goals of low cost and high productivity became "givens".'*   (Evans, 1997)

Lean production emphasises the reduction of waste and effective utilisation of resources in all aspects of the manufacturing process and utilises cross-functional teams, multiskilled workers, integration of supplier relationships and communications and flexible automation. Agile production focuses on the ability of the manufacturing process to respond quickly to changes in demand, in terms of volume and specification, and utilises lean production techniques to achieve this agility. Although the original applications were in manufacturing the concepts are also becoming accepted in service organisations, especially those where customer 'flow' is particularly important, for example hospitals, hotels and banks.

Integration with other functions is to some extent a result of some of the influences already described. However, it has also developed from the recent emphasis on business process improvement (Harrington, 1991) and business process re-engineering (Hammer and Champy, 1993). Counter to this influence is the increasing trend to decentralisation, although this can be alleviated to some extent by improvements in communications technology leading to 'virtual' organisations. Improved integration can enable reductions in total cycle time and facilitate a quicker response to customers thus improving customer service.

Globalisation of operations is inevitable as organisations compete internationally – many organisations describe themselves as competing in a global marketplace. However, the implications of such globalisation for operations has not always been simple, particularly where global companies are formed by mergers between organisations with very different operating procedures and organisational cultures (see Chapter 19). The characteristics of 'world class' manufacturers are well described by Schonberger (1996).

→ Ch. 19

Risk of technology failure, supplier failure and natural and man-made disasters can affect all operations. A focus on processes to prevent failures occurring, to minimise their effects and to continually improve is a key role for today's operations manager. Slack *et al.* (2006) use the terms *risk* and *resilience*:

> *'Risk is the potential for unwanted negative consequences from some event. Resilience is the ability to prevent, withstand and recover from those events.'*

Continuous improvement and quality techniques can be used to understand where risk or failure might occur and to improve and implement processes to prevent further occurrence.

→ Chs 17 & 18

Business ethics, corporate responsibility and the environment are key to all organisational functions including operations management (see Chapters 17 and 18). Recent legislation on emissions and the disposal of products at the end of their useful life has led to manufacturers being responsible for reducing waste and recycling, reusing or remanufacturing the products they produce. This has implications for product design and manufacture – two key operations management functions. A large number of computer hardware manufacturers provide a free recycling service for their customers. This service must be designed into the operations process.

Within the organisation it is argued that operations has an important role and, although this may be hotly debated by other functional areas, the argument proposed by Slack (1983) and developed subsequently by him and other authors, is based on facts rather than emotion. The case can be developed as follows.

Operations...

- concerns the management of most of the people within the organisation, either production workers or service personnel, and often represents 70–80 per cent of the total workforce;
- has responsibility for the effective use of the organisation's assets, both fixed assets and inventory (current assets), and therefore for the management of most of the organisation's funds;
- is responsible for most of the organisation's expenditure and has the largest budget allocation of any one function;
- is a pervasive activity (i.e. interacts with everything else);
- is the area in the organisation where many social and technological changes are taking place.

The role of an operations manager can be illustrated by the following two case studies which give accounts of what an operations manager does.

Cases

Case study   Zara

Amancio Ortega Gaona began working as a delivery boy for a shirt-maker when he was 13 years old. He later managed a tailor's shop where he made nightshirts and pyjamas. In 1963, when still in his 20s, he started 'Confecciones GOA' in La Coruña to manufacture women's pyjamas (and later lingerie products), initially for sale directly to garment wholesalers. In 1975, however, when a German customer cancelled a large order, the firm opened its first Zara retail shop in La Coruña, Spain. The original intent was simply to have an outlet for cancelled orders, but this experience taught Ortega the importance of the 'marriage' between the operations of production and retailing. This was a lesson that guided the evolution of the company from then on. As Mr Miguel Diaz, a senior marketing executive reiterated in 2001:

Copyright © Inditex

> **It is critical for us to have five fingers touching the factory and the other five touching the customer.**

The company had six stores by 1979 and established retail operations in all the major Spanish cities during the 1980s. In 1988 the first international Zara store opened in Porto, Portugal, followed shortly by New York City in 1989 and Paris in 1990. But the real 'step-up' in foreign expansion took place during the 1990s when Zara entered Europe, the Americas and Asia.

Zara is now present across the world, with a network of over 1,500 stores. Its international presence shows that national frontiers are no impediment to sharing a single fashion culture. Zara claims to move with society, dressing the ideas, trends and tastes that society itself creates. It is claimed that Zara needs only two weeks to develop a product and get it into stores, in comparison with the industry average of nearly six months. Zara has a large design team and the design process is closely linked to the public. Information travels from the stores to the design teams, transmitting the demands and concerns of the market. The vertical integration of activities – design, production, logistics and sales in the company's own stores – means that Zara is flexible and fast in adapting to the market. Its model is characterised by continuous product renovation. Zara pays special attention to the design of its stores, its shop windows and interior decor, and locates them in the best sites of major shopping districts.

Source: Author's own, based on www.zara.com

Case question 18.1

Good operations management is based on process consistency.

- What do you think are the major managerial challenges in setting up an operations system to serve a fast-moving and fickle market such as fashion?

Review Questions and Tests

REVIEW AND DISCUSSION QUESTIONS

1. What is operations management?

2. Do you think that manufacturing or service organizations have the greater need for operations management? Explain.

3. What is a value chain and what is value chain management? What is the goal of value chain management? What are the benefits of value chain management?

4. What is required for successful value chain management? What obstacles exist to successful value chain management?

5. How could you use value chain management in your everyday life?

6. How does technology play a role in manufacturing?

7. What are ISO 9000 and Six Sigma?

8. Describe lean management and explain why it's important.

9. How might operations management apply to other managerial functions besides control?

10. Which is more critical to success in organizations: continuous improvement or quality control? Support your position.

Chapter 20:
Quality

WHAT IS 'QUALITY'?

> *'In today's competitive environment, ignoring the quality issue is tantamount to corporate suicide.'*
> (President of Hewlett-Packard, *Fortune*, October 1985)

In business and management terms there is an attempt to focus on a measurable concept of quality by concentrating on 'fitness for purpose'. A specification is supplied by the customer and the quality of the product is measured by how closely it conforms to this specification. It is based on the customer's perception of quality. In these terms quality can be defined as

> *'continually meeting agreed customer needs'* or *'what it takes to satisfy the customer'*, or simply *'fitness for purpose'.*

This last phrase has become a cliché, normally in the form of 'fit for purpose' and often without any clear idea of exactly what it means. In quality terms it means the closeness of the match between a product or service and the needs of the customer. In more general terms, quality is an elusive concept and the usual dictionary definition does not help to make it less so: 'That which makes a thing what it is, its attributes, its characteristics'. The 'quality' of a person may be measured by certain characteristics such as honesty and courage.

This approach involves values and judgements, while a statement such as 'the quality of a strawberry plant is that it bears strawberries' is value and judgement free – it is a statement of what the plant is. However, the fruit from different plants will be compared in size, colour and flavour and then may be graded into strawberries of different 'quality' in the more limited commercial sense of how well it satisfies customers and how well it sells. Supermarkets want their suppliers to provide strawberries, apples, potatoes and so on which conform to a particular size and appearance, while outlets such as farmers' markets concentrate more on taste, flavour and providing local produce.

In Helene Giroux's article on management fashions (2006), she charts the development of definitions and ideas about quality from

> *'if quality is perceived as merely meeting technical specifications ... only mediocre results will be achieved'*
> (Hoerschemeyer, 1989)

to

> *'quality means internal and external customer satisfaction.'* (Juran and Gryna, 1993)

> *'Currently, definitions such as "delighting the customer" and "satisfaction" are tossed about. The fact that these definitions are not measurable or expandable and are impossible to communicate has not changed many minds.'* (Crosby, 1997)

Earlier Crosby argued that manufacturing-based definitions have been misunderstood:

> *'Many writers have taken my definition of conformance to requirements, and twisted it as "conformance to specification". This creates a narrow, highly technical , manufacturing-orientated consideration.'* (Crosby, 1996).

A comprehensive definition is provided by Galgano (1994):

> *'Quality, therefore, includes the following: competitiveness; deliver; cost; morale; productivity; profit; product quality; quantity or volume; performance; service; safety; concern for the environment; the stockholders interest.'*

Quality can be seen as an attribute of a product or service which ensures that it is attractive in the eyes of the customer. It is a relative property rather than an absolute one, in that a given product or service will be attractive to customers if it fulfils their expectations more fully than any other product or service under consideration. It means delivering the right product or service that is fit for the purposes required by the customer, at the right price, and at the right time and place. A company that produces and delivers a beautiful-looking car to a customer will not be considered to produce quality goods if the car does not work well. Whatever the costs involved, the materials used or the care taken in manufacture, the quality of the car will be considered poor if it is unreliable. A lawnmower that does not cut the lawn effectively is of no use to the customer whatever its price or however firmly the manufacturer describes it as a 'quality' or 'excellent' product.

WHY IS THE MANAGEMENT OF QUALITY IMPORTANT?

The management of quality is important because of the need to focus on the customer and because meeting customer needs is the foundation of any successful organisation (see Chapter 3). Products and services have to be of a quality to meet customer requirements, as the quality of a product or service may be the distinguishing factor between the offerings of competing companies from which the consumer has to choose. Two products may serve the same purpose but if they sell for the same price and one is well designed and constructed from high-standard materials and the other is not then consumer demand is likely to be for the well-made product. This is even more likely to be the case if this product is more reliable and the company offers good after-sales service. If two restaurants in the same street charge similar prices for meals, but one provides slapdash service and the other looks after its customers, it is the one that provides a good service which is likely to be more successful.

→ Ch. 3

'You get what you pay for' is a saying which suggests that the more you pay the better the quality of a product or service. Of course, this does not always follow but in consumer surveys there may be a distinction between the best product on offer in terms of quality and the best in relation to a balance between quality and price, or what may be called 'value for money'. The very highest quality may be expensive to achieve in relation to the material costs in the use of the very best materials and labour costs because of the time involved in ensuring high quality. However, whatever the costs and the price, the quality has to be sufficient to meet the requirements of enough customers to make the sale of the product or service successful.

In organisational terms a lack of quality is likely to be a waste of resources through scrapped materials and wasted time as well as through rejection by consumers. Market research can help to identify what customers want (see Chapter 8), their purchasing behaviour and the requirements that organisations need to meet if they are to be successful. Quality-improvement programmes in organisations combine product improvement, the closer matching of customer needs, and process improvement. They not only result in a focus on quality matters but they can also create a demand for ever-higher standards, therefore making quality improvement an ongoing process.

→ Ch. 8

The idea of managing the quality of products and services is important if not new, it can be traced through history (Juran, 1995).

'Many of the core principles and techniques of modern quality management were developed in the 1930s and 1940s and have been in use in the USA ever since – although maybe not as extensively as they could or should have been.' (Giroux, 2006)

The American Society for Quality Control was founded in 1946 and brought together quality practitioners. The interest in quality management increased rapidly in the 1980s as a result of American trade deficits and recession while Japan's exports were soaring and the Japanese economy booming. These differences between the two economies suggested that if American industry adopted the quality approach of the Japanese then it could prosper.

FOCUS ON THE CUSTOMER

If it is accepted that high quality is a measure of excellence taken from the customer's point of view then, although producers may grade their goods in terms of quality, whether the producers' view of the grading is upheld will depend on customer perception. If customers like their strawberries to be large, firm, red and sweet then fruit with those characteristics will be considered to be of the highest quality, and the producer of smaller, paler strawberries may not be able to convince customers of the high quality of their output, however sweet they may taste.

The focus on the customer means that quality is conceptualised in terms of the customer's perceptions. The organisation's objective is to identify customer requirements so that both the customer's and the organisation's needs are met. It is also the intention to meet these requirements first time and thus avoid the cost of sorting out problems. The process involves:

■ **research**

■ **specification and planning**

■ **delivery**

■ **review.**

→ Chs 5 & 6

This process focuses on the customer at key points and returns constantly to research (see Chapters 5 and 6) into changing customer needs (see Figure 7.1). When customer needs are identified, planning can take place into exactly what has to be delivered. The specifications and standards are determined so that priorities can be established to ensure that the product or service delivered is what the customer needs and that it meets customer perceptions. Although costs and price play an important part in this, most customers will pay what is necessary in order to receive what, in their view, is good quality. This in turn will generate profits as customers demand this product or service above others.

A customer can be defined as anyone who receives a product or service. This approach has been extended by many companies beyond the satisfaction of the external consumer in order to include the internal customer as well. One department in an organisation receives products or services from another department and passes these on to a third group. On an assembly line a commodity is passed along the line from one individual or team to another, each dependent on the other for the receipt of the commodity at the correct quality at the correct time, and aiming to pass it on with the correct added value and, again, on time.

The concept of the internal customer means that each process is viewed as a product so that evaluation takes place at once by the immediate customer or by the

Figure 7.1 **Focus on the customer**

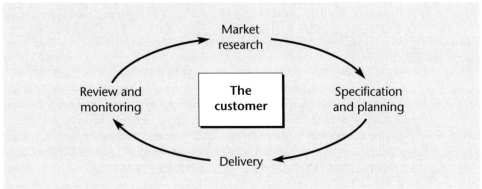

processor. This system will help to eliminate waste and reduce costs, while the overall objective will remain the satisfaction of the external customer. The product or service will be 'right first time' so that errors will be prevented through the need to satisfy the internal customer at each stage rather than through a final inspection.

TOTAL QUALITY MANAGEMENT

As companies have made a conscious effort to 'focus on the customer', total quality management (TQM) and other methods have been introduced to implement this. Total quality management is known by other names such as total quality improvement (TQI) or total quality control (TQC), or as strategic quality management (SQM), or simply as total quality (see Chapters 10 and 14).

→ Chs 10 & 14

It is possible to identify differences between total quality management and titles such as strategic quality management. How important these are remains a matter of opinion. Total quality management is often described as a 'value-based' approach to quality management; it may be seen as a goal which an organisation aims to achieve, or the idea of *total* quality may be considered unattainable. On the other hand strategic quality management can be described as both systematic and value based. It can be seen to suggest that the reason for improving quality is that it will have maximum strategic impact on the future of the organisation. Strategic quality management is designed as a practical and pragmatic framework in which the drive towards quality improvement can be sustained while not making claims on *total* quality. A counterargument to this is to consider the word 'total', in the context of total quality management, to mean that every part of an organisation is involved.

The approach can be recognised, whatever its title, by its objectives. Total (or strategic) quality management can be defined as:

'an intensive, long-term effort to transform all parts of the organisation in order to produce the best product and service possible to meet customer needs.'

In some Japanese companies there is no such thing as total or strategic quality management – it is simply the way they operate and it does not need a title, although it could be described as 'right first time', in order to make sure that it happens (see Chapter 19). The management at the Toyota plant in Japan has stated that:

→ Ch. 19

'We estimate it will take you twenty years to be where we are now, and by that time we will have progressed further. We have moved from quality philosophy to measuring defects on an acceptable quality level basis to reducing our defect rate to below five to six parts per billion. Our last product recall was 1969 when we first started introducing what you know as Total Quality Management.' (Atkinson, 1990)

Total quality management can be seen as a metaphor for the process and management of change, designed to realign the culture and working practices of an organisation for the pursuit of continued quality improvement. Initially the concept of quality tended to be considered in terms of narrow and specific techniques, such as quality circles (see p. 210) or statistical process (or quality) control (see pp. 219–222). The concept has developed into a pervasive one (see p. 221, the Taguchi method), touching every aspect of the organisation including suppliers and customers.

It can be argued that there have been phases in the evolution of TQM, starting with the idea that processes such as 'quality control', 'quality assurance' and 'statistical quality control' are all aspects of TQM that have to be managed. This phase may concentrate on methods and systems and lead on to the application of the concept of quality to people and the view that the management implications of quality are all-pervasive. This concentration on people may lead to the view that quality is about satisfying the customer and may move beyond the idea of providing what the customer thinks they want on to the idea of satisfying the latent needs of customers, providing them with goods and services and quality they had not fully realised they wanted.

In an organisation that practises total quality management, quality becomes the standard operating procedure and part of the culture (see p. 192 for a description of benchmarking). It is not simply a programme or project, but a way of life. It is proved by the quality of materials purchased from suppliers, the approach to defect control on the production line, the appearance of the building, the way problems are solved for customers, the way employees are organised and the organisation's
→ Ch. 10 internal communication system (see Chapter 10 for an analysis of organisational communication and TQM). This approach is founded on the premise that quality depends on individual effort and attitude. It is a rigorous, highly disciplined and skilled process which may challenge present practice and depends on a training programme throughout the organisation. Total quality management is predicated on a commitment to customer interests, needs, requirements and expectations, and on the commitment of everyone to the constant improvement of the quality of everything that the organisation does and provides for its customers (see pp. 220, 493 and 688 for a description of 'just-in-time' techniques).

TQM is a strategic approach within an organisation which can provide an 'umbrella' under which a number of quality initiatives can be managed (see Figure 7.2). These are all part of a quality culture. The philosophy that supported this culture and the practical application of it originated through the ideas of Dr W Edwards Deming (1982, 1986), an American who provided the intellectual and practical drive behind Japan's post-war reconstruction. He encouraged Japanese companies to introduce total quality, and in particular to involve and consult with customers in an attempt to bring about continuous improvement of the product. Juran (1992) worked with Deming and concentrated on people-based management. He argued that, in a normal situation, the general attitude to maintaining and perpetuating current standards or levels of performance was good enough. He insisted that present performance in any function, at any level, can and should be improved

Figure 7.2 **Total quality**

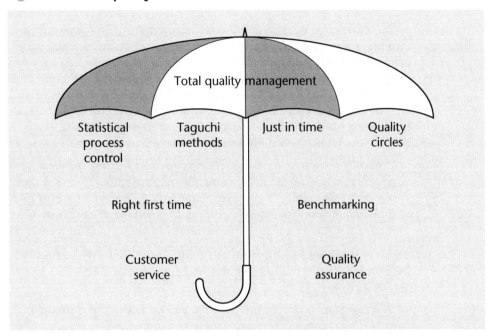

and that to achieve this improvement an organisation begins with identifying the internal obstacles that prevent people from doing the best they can and then eliminates them.

Philip Crosby (1978) has been another important influence on total quality, again with a focus on the people responsible for improving quality. Peters and Waterman expanded on these approaches in their book *In Search of Excellence* (1982). They found that many of the foremost 'excellent' companies were equally obsessed by quality and punctuality. They describe how the Caterpillar Tractor Company offers customers a 48-hour guaranteed parts delivery service anywhere in the world. If this guarantee is not met then the customer receives the part free. An article in *Fortune* magazine is quoted as stating:

> *'The company's operating principles are excellence of quality, reliability of performance, and loyalty in dealer relationships. Caterpillar has zealously pursued the goal of building a better, more efficient crawler tractor than anybody else in the world.'*
>
> (Peters and Waterman, 1982)

Another company highlighted by Peters and Waterman is McDonald's, whose theme is 'Quality, Service, Cleanliness and Value'. Founder Ray Kroc says, 'If I had a brick for every time I've repeated the phrase QSCV, I think I'd probably be able to bridge the Atlantic Ocean with them.' Quality is the priority because that is what McDonald's wants customers to enjoy every time they visit a McDonald's restaurant. All establishments are regularly monitored for QSCV and the results are linked to the manager's pay, while consistent failure to meet the McDonald's standards can lead to managers being sacked or the termination of the franchise. QSCV is applied not only to customer service but to all aspects of the business. The best ingredients are used in the food and cleanliness is insisted on. Peters and Waterman quote a former griddle tender as saying *'there was never an idle moment, whenever there was a slack time in the store, we were cleaning something.'*

The computer company Hewlett-Packard has the same approach to quality. Routine systems in the company are made to reinforce the quality objectives. These are built into the management-by-objectives programme so that everyone receives the latest quality information as well as data on orders, sales and profits. There is a 'quality web' throughout the company, appropriately called the LACE (lab awareness of customer environment) programme, in which Hewlett-Packard customers make presentations to company engineers about their own needs and their reactions to the products and services they receive.

'A Quality focus is ubiquitous in Hewlett-Packard because the employees don't seem to be able to separate it from anything else they are doing. If you ask them about personnel, they talk quality. If you ask them about field sales, they talk quality. If you ask them about management-by-objectives, they talk about quality-by-objectives.'

(Peters and Waterman, 1982)

Peters and Waterman found that quality and reliability were preferred by many leading companies to innovation or being first in the field. Hewlett-Packard is quoted again:

'The company is seldom first into the market with its new products. The company's marketing strategy is normally that of a counterpuncher. A competitor's new product comes on the market and Hewlett-Packard engineers, when making service calls on Hewlett-Packard equipment, ask the customers what they like or dislike about the new product, what features the customers would like to have ... and pretty soon the Hewlett-Packard salesmen are calling on customers again with a new product that answers their needs and wants. The result: happy and loyal customers.'

In these examples, and during the period of development of quality as the top priority for an organisation, it is apparent that total quality management involves the creation of an appropriate company culture – a climate based on 'never being satisfied' with the current quality of product and service in meeting customers' identified needs, requirements, interests and expectations. This search for opportunities for improvements can be referred to as total quality improvement. Not being satisfied with current inputs, processes, practices and outcomes encourages a system to be established covering research, analysis of needs, measurement of results and consideration of efficiency and effectiveness in order to improve what is produced and how it is produced.

Benchmarking is a process whereby a business compares its operations with those of similar organisations and, if it is able to, the best of its competitors. Companies have always benchmarked themselves with other companies in an informal way, although it is relatively recently that a formal and rigorous process has been introduced. The objective is to create and sustain excellence. The usual method is to select a business process to improve and to select a project team with the person responsible for the process in the business as team leader. The team develops a set of key process measures to compare with other companies' processes.

Comparisons are then made with companies within the same corporation, competitors and the best companies in other industries. Although some processes cannot easily be compared across industries, areas such as customer service can. It is then a question of obtaining collaboration from the target companies and investigating their processes. Whereas some of this investigation can be carried out at a 'distance' through documents and looking at delivery systems, benchmarking really requires visits to the target company – without them it is likely to be of little value. The investigation should reveal gaps between the company's processes and best practices. The team then develops an action plan to implement the improved process. It is at this stage that having the person responsible for the process as team leader, or as a member of the team, can prove a critical success factor for implementation.

The main areas to be benchmarked are usually those processes known to be inefficient or where there is some evidence that competitors or companies in other industries have better processes. The main advantages of benchmarking are the overcoming of a natural disbelief in the feasibility of improvements, making sure that improvement targets are high enough and helping to create a learning and outward-looking culture in the company.

In Figure 7.3 a competitive edge is achieved by encouraging the best possible utilisation of resources by a highly adaptable workforce in order to achieve corporate quality objectives. Competitive advantage is achieved and maintained within a framework of efficiency and effectiveness and acceptance of a process of continuous improvement. TQM as a 'metaphor for the management of change' is a process for encouraging the attitude that change is the usual situation, because through this comes quality improvement and success.

The keys to total quality management can be summarised as:

- **measuring quality;**
- **incorporating quality objectives into strategic planning;**
- **obtaining the commitment of top management;**
- **forming teams in a structure of participative management;**
- **using resources efficiently and effectively;**

Figure 7.3 **Total quality improvement**

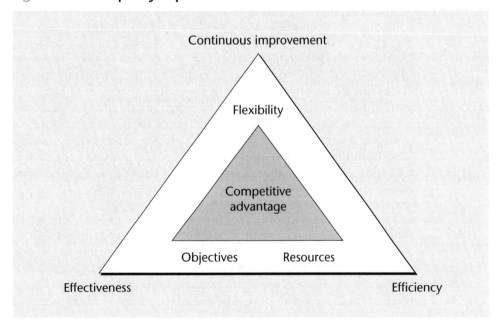

- **including suppliers and customers in quality improvement;**
- **building skills through training** (see pp. 354–7);
- **developing an attitude which welcomes change.**

This is perhaps summed up in Japanese management by *kaizen*, which is a continuous striving for perfection and, in quality terms, constant and continuous improvement. This includes all aspects of the organisation, such as staff training and development, product improvement, production and output improvement and attention to administration. At its best, this results in the output of high volumes of high-quality products supported by adaption and innovation.

IMPLICATIONS FOR MANAGEMENT

Total quality management impinges on every function in an organisation and will include marketing, product design, human resource development, financial resourcing, sites and buildings and estates management and so on. The cultural change required in most organisations in order to introduce and maintain TQM has to be led by senior managers. They need to be aware of and understand the principles and practices of total quality and be prepared to support it at every level. Particularly important is the need to ensure monitoring, measurement and evaluation of progress in all functions against identified and, if possible, quantified needs and specifications. Managers can use this evaluation in order to plan developments in TQM, as well as measuring the extent to which quality has been improved. The process can be applied inside an organisation as well as outside it in the sense that everyone has a 'customer' and is a 'customer' inside the organisation, relying on others' work and service and passing on work and service to others. Factual evidence can be obtained by monitoring progress against agreed objectives and this can inform the plans of each team in meeting its particular targets or objectives, which will in turn depend on other teams or individuals providing support in the form of high-quality goods or services.

TQM is implemented at the top of an organisation first because it is at this level that change can be initiated. Top managers require skills to enable them to change the way they work, so they can practise and promote quality management and then help others to acquire the necessary techniques and understanding.

The introduction of TQM through the whole organisation is a long-term strategy requiring a variety of approaches. For most organisations it is about the management of change and involves all aspects of human resources management, including leadership, problem solving, coaching, counselling, communication and team building. Training will be required at all levels, usually starting with those with a coordinating, supervisory or management role, but also concentrating on teams. Although TQM encourages consideration of factual information it also encourages 'people-based' management.

This style of management is participative, designed to enable people at every level to share in management decisions and in responsibility for them. This means in one way or another devolving decision making to the closest possible point to where the effects of the decisions are felt. Decision making may be delegated to an individual or a team. People are encouraged to identify and 'own' problems and their solutions, rather than passing them up or around the organisation. Teamwork becomes essential at an early stage if problems are to be identified and addressed and not hidden away. This approach focuses on corporate goals and teams identify with problems of specific relevance to their functions.

Teams need to know how their work relates to corporate goals and objectives so that they can understand the direction in which they are moving and can look for improvement opportunities. They need to have a clear idea of the resources at their disposal in order to achieve their particular objectives. It is then possible for the team to decide which members will carry out particular tasks, the methods to be employed, materials and equipment to use, and how and when to work. All of this puts great pressure on teamwork and on the team's responsibility for their own results (see Figure 7.4).

In the 1970s the Saab motor company broke away from the assembly-line system customarily used in car manufacturing and organised its workforce into teams working around each car. Teams could decide to rotate jobs and introduce other flexibilities into the way they worked so long as they achieved their target output at the requisite cost and quality levels.

Black & Decker adopted a total quality plan in 1980 to include every aspect of the business. A 'People Plan' was formed in order to 'free the people for their fullest contribution to business success'. To implement total quality the company formed 'quality circles' and after four years there were 35 successful circles in operation. In 1984 this development was reviewed and was considered to require rejuvenation. A new total customer service initiative was introduced which encompassed quality circles while focusing on 'excellence in everything we do'.

The Ciba Corning company also believes in total quality as a complete way of life affecting attitudes and commitments, 'a framework for bringing out the best in all employees'. The four principles underlying its approach are:

Figure 7.4 **Introducing total quality management**

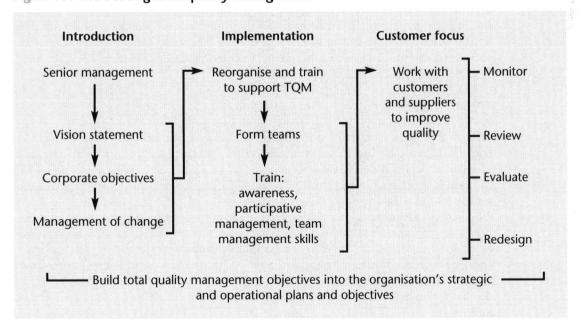

- **meeting the requirements of customers**
- **error-free work**
- **managing by preventing errors rather than inspecting for error**
- **measuring by cost of quality.**

These principles are delivered through a ten-point action plan which includes commitment from the top, communication, education and involvement for all employees. One approach to obtaining this involvement is the organisation of quality circles.

TEAM PROBLEM-SOLVING AND QUALITY CIRCLES

→ Ch. 9

Team problem-solving has been a major workplace innovation aimed at improving the variety and reliability of products and services (see Chapter 9). Issue handling in large organisations is an interactive process, because the issues are complex they require a range of informational inputs and they have widespread repercussions, while implementation is difficult. Using a group of people in order to solve these problems has the advantage that the group has more information and knowledge than a single individual and implementation is easier if the implementers are involved in the issue discussions. The problem with group discussions is that it can take longer to reach conclusions than an individual and the result may be a compromise rather than a clear-cut decision.

Teams are popular in organisations because they can develop an *esprit de corps*, because team members expect and demand that every member contributes to the team's objectives in one way or another. The team can make use of the different experience, skills and capabilities of its members, and at the same time the team approach facilitates cooperation and improves morale by increasing job satisfaction. While traditional teams were formed on a homogeneous functional basis, such as accounting teams and marketing teams, organisations have increased the use of multifunctional teams drawn from across the organisation. 'Project' teams comprise a wide range of people from different functional areas who can all contribute to the success of the project. When they work well teams can perform at a higher level than the same individuals working alone.

Teams are composed of individuals and have a formal or an informal structure. The increased popularity of team formation has made them the subject of study, particularly in relation to team dynamics, the way individuals interact and the influences of team leadership and structure. One approach to analysing the work of teams developed by Tuckman and Jensen (1977, summarised in Cartwright, 2002) is in terms of 'forming, storming, norming and performing' to which can be added 'dorming, reforming and adjourning'. These awkward terms are an attempt to summarise the processes through which the 'typical' team may pass, that is the 'life' of a team. The first meeting of a team can be crucial in establishing the way it works, how team members will interact, who will provide leadership and who might waste everybody's time. The 'forming' stage may involve team members introducing themselves to each other, establishing the team objective and the expertise contained within the team and its 'culture'.

The 'storming' stage represents the period during which the team experiences and settles conflicts so that progress can be made. Individuals will have their own agendas, they may jockey for position and they may take part in inappropriate behaviour. Either these conflicts are resolved or the team may be ineffective and break up. However, the storming stage can result in mutual respect being developed and greater openness established, so that the 'norming' stage is reached where working methods, rules and norms are agreed within the team. This may include a process for conflict resolution and allow the team to make progress towards its objectives. This can lead to 'performing' with the focus on achieving the team aims and goals. A 'dorming' team has reached a comfort point when it reaches a plateau and its performance stops improving, while a team which is disrupted may go through a 'reforming' stage where it experiences some of the earlier stages before it is fully operational. Finally, unless the team is formed more or less permanently, there will be an 'adjourning' stage where the team is disbanded because it has achieved its objectives, even if team members have established a bond which they want to perpetuate.

Belbin (1981) developed ideas about the role of individuals in teams. He argued that individuals had two roles – the first was a functional one related to particular competence and skills, while the other was more individual and personal, concerned with creativity, or attention to detail or sociability. Belbin identified eight team roles – a further role was added later:

- **coordinator**
- **plant**
- **shaper**
- **monitor–evaluator**
- **implementer**
- **resource investigator**
- **team worker**
- **completer–finisher**
- **(specialist)**.

The 'coordinator' or chairman is the individual who presides over the team and coordinates its efforts to meet its objectives. This is a person with the ability to focus on objectives and to understand and harness the skills and abilities of the team members. The plant is the team's source of original ideas, suggestions and proposals and may be 'planted' in a team to help to inspire it. The plant may be so full of ideas that the team's objectives are forgotten and the coordinator has to refocus the team. The 'shaper' is challenging, argumentative and impatient, while at the same time helping to shape the team's efforts and move it towards its objectives. The 'monitor–evaluator' is the analyst of the team assessing and evaluating the team's progress and acting as a critic rather than originating new ideas.

The 'implementer' is the team's organiser, turning decisions into manageable tasks. This individual will be the one who produces organisation charts and schedules and likes to have structure and order in the team's work. The 'resource investigator' is the team's communicator and will have lively, although sometimes short-lived enthusiasms, which may require focus, like the plant. The 'team worker' promotes unity and harmony in the team and provides loyalty and support, but may lack ideas and decisiveness. The 'completer–finisher' is concerned with detail and checking that everything has been done and nothing overlooked. This member provides a sense of urgency to meet deadlines, although may become bogged down in detail. The 'specialist' is a team role that has been added since Belbin's original work because there are times when teams need specialist input. A balanced team will include this cast of characters and while the clear absence of one of them can weaken the team, the presence of too many of one type can unbalance it. After all a team has been described (Katzenbach and Smith, 1993) as

> *'a small number of people with complementary skills who are committed to a common purpose, performance goals and working approach for which they hold themselves mutually accountable.'*

One of the characteristics of total quality management has been the use of teams because TQM is process improvement and employee participation is an essential element of this. TQM involves encouraging employees to share ideas and act on what they suggest. One application of this approach has been the use of quality circles.

A quality circle can be described as

> *'a group who meet regularly, with management approval, to identify and solve their own work-related problems and implement their solutions to these problems.'*

Small groups of employees, usually from the same workplace and under the same supervisor, volunteer to meet to identify problems and find solutions. They look at the problems that occur in their work area and that affect their own job. The group itself applies the solutions if it has the authority, otherwise management is presented with recommendations and decides on implementation.

Membership of quality circles is usually voluntary with a welcome for anyone who wishes to join and no official pressure for anyone to become a member. If the circle is successful, active and enthusiastic then it is expected that people will want to join. The supervisor of a work area will usually lead the circle. His or her role is to encourage volunteers to establish a group which he or she will chair because of previous experience and training in organising and running quality circles. The supervisor guides the circle in order to help it develop into a cohesive team and to focus on solving problems and improving quality. The circle will usually consist of between six and twelve members – large enough to generate a variety of ideas; small enough for everybody to be involved and have their say. If there are too many volunteers then either membership can be rotated or subgroups can be formed to consider particular tasks.

Management has to follow a 'hands-off' policy up to the point of implementation of a decision. Success depends on the members of a quality circle being assured that it 'belongs to them' and has not been formed by management. Management can be supportive and may suggest topics for consideration by the circle, but if it is any more heavy handed the role of members will be restricted. The most important consideration for management is to ensure that actions do follow any ideas or decisions reached by a quality circle, or to provide good reasons for not following up such ideas or decisions.

Quality circles were originally an American idea but were first practised on a wide scale in Japan. In order to compete with other industrial nations, Japanese industry realised in the late 1940s and 1950s that old ideas of management had to be discarded and that the initiative and skills of everybody on the workforce had to be harnessed. Emphasis was placed on training at shopfloor level and every effort was made to pass as much responsibility as possible to supervisors and operators. There was a particular emphasis on identifying quality problems at all levels and in all areas of companies.

In the late 1950s and through the 1960s Japanese companies introduced quality circles extensively, so that by 1980 it was estimated that there were over a million quality circles with ten million workers involved. It is significant that the literal translation of the Japanese term for quality circles is:

The gathering of the wisdom of the people.

The concept of the quality circle coincides with the culture of Japanese companies and builds on loyalty to the company. The 'family company' approach of duty to the company by employees allied with responsibility by the company for the welfare of its employees is well developed, while there is also a well-nurtured culture of it being in everyone's interest for the company to succeed, combined with peer pressure to encourage the success of a voluntary approach. Professor Ishikawa has suggested (1984) that quality circles act as a 'focus of perception' to identify personal pride and self-esteem with corporate achievement (see Chapter 14).

→ Ch. 14

Quality circles have been used across the world to draw on the expertise and knowledge of workers on the shopfloor in order to improve quality. They have been adapted by such companies as General Motors, Honeywell & Lockheed in the USA, and by Philips, Ford, Rolls-Royce and Marks & Spencer in the UK.

In many British companies, however, the culture has not been conducive to the development of quality circles. Where there is a strongly defended hierarchical structure, or sections and departments based on specialised expertise, the view that ideas from the shopfloor should be given priority is difficult to foster. At the same time the attitude that it is up to 'them' to solve problems may be strong at an operational level. Management/union dissension in the past has certainly discouraged the effective development of this kind of initiative.

It is clear that successful quality circles are not concerned with grumbles or complaints or irrelevant discussion of non-related subjects such as pay, personality conflicts or other grievances. The stress is on solving problems and producing action plans. For this approach to be understood and to be successful, the culture of the company has to be one which encourages participative management. If the culture has bred suspicion and secrecy, then grumbles and complaints may be at the top of the agenda. Quality circles are encouraged to discuss practicalities and not theories, so that positive results are produced rather than simply argument. One approach is to list problem areas and then to establish priorities and seek solutions by drawing on the skill and knowledge of the group. When problems are beyond solution by the group, specialists may be asked to join the circle for a number of meetings, or a sub-group may be established to investigate the problem in more detail.

Where the members of the quality circle have the power to make a decision they will carry it out, while on matters where they do not have authority they will make a presentation to the managers involved in the proposed change (see Figure 7.5). This may be a technical problem to do with the operation of machinery or equipment, it may be a staffing problem to do with skills or working times, it may be a question of the supply of materials, the purchase of spare parts, or it may be to do with costs and finance. The managers must then decide to take action or explain in detail the reasons for not taking action at this time. Managers also have to make sure that people do not identify too strongly with their particular circle when total quality has to be identified with the aims and objectives of the organisation as a whole. At the same time, some problems need to be solved on the spot rather than waiting for a quality circle meeting to sort them out.

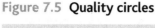

Figure 7.5 **Quality circles**

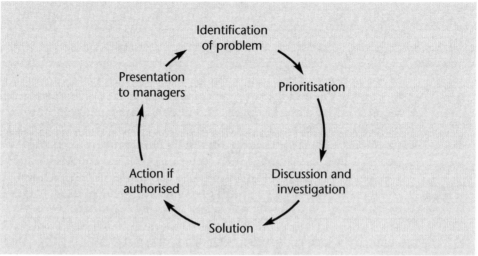

An enterprising quality circle will, of course, anticipate as many problems as possible and solve them.

ITT has provided an example of a solution discovered by a quality circle:

> *'It was standard practice to completely remove capacitors from the metal handling equipment to check for correct nominal capacitance. After this operation the capacitors were discarded. By purchasing hand held capacitance meters it is possible to take the equipment to the work and simply applying one terminal lead, measure the nominal capacitance while the remaining terminal lead is retained on the handling strip. This enables the capacitor to continue with the batch through the finishing operations. This change will result in a saving of more than $10,000 when it is fully implemented.'*   (ITT *Circle News*, March 1981)

Managers play an important part in the success of quality circles. There has to be a commitment to the system throughout the organisation and one or two unsympathetic managers can ruin the whole process. Managers have to allow time and money for circle meetings and for preliminary training. They must be ready to attend presentations, to listen with an open mind to the proposals and to decide on their value on merit. Unions need also to be involved in the process so that their representatives understand what is happening. Unions will usually be supportive of the process because it involves the workforce more closely in the organisation and has the objective of improving job satisfaction. After all, quality circles have been described as 'a structured way of making management listen' by the Industrial Society.

FOCUS ON TOTAL QUALITY

Whether it is quality circles or another method of providing a focus on quality, the pursuit of total quality must be led from the front, by the chief executive, otherwise it may be considered as an afterthought. Deming (1982) put this another way:

'There is so much talk about involvement of employees, quality of work life, communications and other poetic words. What is needed is involvement of management: get the management involved. Employees will become involved, the quality of life will improve, once management takes on the job of restoring dignity to the hourly worker.'

Combined with competitive pressures and the higher priority given to human resource management, the focus on quality encouraged reorganisation in many companies in the 1980s and 1990s. These developments have been away from the single, giant pyramid structures consisting of many different layers of management and grades of operative towards flatter structures often based on a total quality concept. Whole functions and levels have been eliminated in order to produce an organisation which is more flexible and speedier in response to market needs.

Waterman (1988) cites the Dana Company in the USA which in the mid-1970s had 14 layers of management between the chief executive and the staff floor. By the mid-1980s these layers had been reduced to five:

'At the extreme the company has one plant in Nebraska that employs 120 people – the organisation structure there is simple: 120 people, one plant manager, nothing in between.'

The key to this approach is often greater delegation. Many areas of decision making and accountability have been pushed down the organisation to be nearer the point where the decision takes effect. Senior management will adopt a more strategic role, setting broad objectives as a framework to ensure that all units are functioning effectively and working towards the corporate goals. The operational units are the closest group to their markets and they know best the requirements of the consumer. It is impossible for this level of delegation to work unless the practice and beliefs of management adapt to the new circumstances. There is a decline in supervision throughout the organisation as employees take on greater responsibility. The role of the manager is to initiate new ideas and policies, to facilitate the work of the operational units and to monitor their progress.

In order to introduce this level of involvement there has to be a clear recognition that the purpose of this strategy is to increase mutual understanding and to improve the individual's contribution. This is a policy of openness, of encouraging individual creativity and initiative in the interests of the organisation.

In order to achieve this level of delegation it is necessary to:

- make certain that individuals understand what is expected from them in terms of their time at work;
- set the limits of delegation so that everyone knows the extent of their responsibility;
- train individuals so that they understand the aims and objectives of the delegated system and are technically able to cope with it;
- communicate the corporate business goals effectively so that everyone understands how these relate to them;
- enable a reverse flow of information to take place, from the shopfloor upwards, so that each manager knows the attitudes and aspirations of each person reporting to them.

At the same time as this focus on the individual there has to be a clear understanding of teamwork. In the introduction of total quality, teams are not the same as quality circles. The quality-circle approach is based on voluntary groups of employees considering particular tasks. Total quality management teams include everybody working in a particular area or function or in a cross-functional role. Individuals cannot opt out of this team or of meetings to consider the working of the group, or fail to take responsibility for their work. The team will be responsible for making sure that everybody contributes to its success and for discussing and implementing ways in which the whole team can improve performance. These teams may coincide with quality circles or the latter may form a separate system for considering quality – an alternative, perhaps task-oriented group. The usual process is for the functional team itself to become a type of quality circle on its own.

This process of delegating decision and responsibility to teams at the 'salt face' or 'firing line' is again not quite the same as a process popular in the 1980s known as 'team briefing'. These are meetings held at regular intervals when leaders bring their teams together to communicate what is happening at the workplace. In the team briefing system the priority is to achieve understanding of what people need to know because it affects their job – it is a systematic way of telling all employees about progress, policy, decisions, performance and future plans. It is not necessarily consultative and is not usually a method of encouraging two-way communication. Team briefing is a useful method of communication for management but it should not be confused with the purposes behind setting up teams in a TQM system.

The same is true of consultative committees, which are structured meetings of management and employee representatives, with the purpose of discussing management matters of common interest. They are a way of seeking the views of employees before management decisions are finally made or before they are implemented. They may be used whenever decisions affect employees, but they are not about negotiation on such matters as pay which requires once again a separate format of meetings. Consultative committees can play an important part in, for example, the management of change and can be a way of informing discussion on quality teams when managers are considering the initiation of new policies.

The Confederation of British Industry in *The Will to Win* (1980) stated that 'the system of giving the line employee more responsibility increases his/her job satisfaction and involvement'. In contrast the division of labour and scientific management, or 'Taylorism', have encouraged the analysis of work into constituent activities and given particular tasks to individual workers. The close definition of the worker's specialist role has meant that, at its extreme, workers respond by living up to the limited expectations of them by carrying out the tasks they have been given and no more or less.

Some organisations may have been paternalistic in their approach by not treating employees as adults – at the same time other organisations do not regard their employees as the prime source of their prosperity. With a limited view of their job, employees substitute habit for understanding and every change can, in Drucker's view (1968), represent to the employee 'a challenge of the incomprehensible and ... threatens his psychological security'. Drucker attacks scientific management for confusing analysis with action, for divorcing planning from doing. The successful companies 'hire a whole man or woman' and realise that 'with every pair of hands a mind comes free'. Ignoring the ideas of employees is epitomised by a General Motors' car worker in the USA whom Drucker (1968) quotes as saying:

'I guess I got laid off because I made poor quality cars. In 16 years not once was I ever asked for a suggestion as to how to do my job better. Not once.'

In response to this many successful companies have introduced suggestion schemes. In the USA, IBM has said that its suggestion plan yielded ideas from 30,000 employees during 1985 which resulted in savings of more than $125 million. The company was happy to pay the employees $18 million in cash awards for these suggestions. While these schemes can be very effective, they have to fit into the overall company policy because it may be difficult to run financial inducements for ideas alongside voluntary consultation and a delegated team approach. If the company ethos encourages everybody to think in terms of constant improvement and enables people to communicate ideas, a suggestion box may not be necessary (see Figure 7.6).

Strategies designed to maximise the potential and actual contribution of every employee have to give considerable emphasis to communication and involvement policies. The move away from an organisation based on command and authority from the top, with limited and routine tasks at the bottom, has created a re-evaluation of the way companies communicate internally. It is no longer a question of ensuring that instructions are passed to the relevant people and then monitoring what happens. Communication is now seen as a means of improving understanding, of securing involvement through a free flow of information in order to create cohesion and mutual commitment on the part of all members of the organisation.

Managers rely on the capabilities of those carrying out the various tasks allotted to them. Managers have to ensure effective teamwork and cooperation and are responsible for coordinating, planning and monitoring to make sure that more flexible and less authoritarian structures nevertheless meet their objectives. This requires the listening skills of a facilitator able to anticipate and solve problems, to treat individuals sympathetically and with respect, and to identify the relative strengths and weaknesses of everyone involved.

Managers need to communicate the corporate business goals effectively to every team or group so that they are understood in sufficient depth and are related to the team and the individuals in it. This understanding must also include an appreciation of the external influences on the organisation, such as the nature of the competition, the impact of new technologies, the influence of government policy

Figure 7.6 **Focus on quality**

and the importance of markets and customers. Managers have to assess the level of understanding of these matters by teams and individuals. Surveys, meetings and discussions can help to do this and many organisations have found the most effective means of 'upward' communication to be a system of appraisal and performance → Chs 4 & 6 review (see Chapters 4 and 6).

MEASURING QUALITY

The measurement of quality should not be thought of as a single and simple process, although in fact it can be if the one measurement that is used is profit. A simple indicator such as profit growth, market share or the return on capital invested can be used to judge how well a quality management system has worked and these certainly should be among the measures used. The problem is that taken on their own they do not indicate how they were achieved and, if successful, how they can be maintained. For this an analysis of the organisation is required with measurement taken at various levels.

At a strategic level, for example, in order to decide whether or not a performance management system has helped to put quality management into effect, it may be sensible to seek the answers to a number of questions:

- Is there a strategic plan supported by senior managers which establishes the organisation's direction?
- Is there a well-defined structure to support and develop a quality approach by managers, including a performance management system?
- Are skills and techniques for quality improvement part of the training for managers and supervisors?
- Are employees held accountable for on-the-job performance (see pp. 294–8 and 358–361)?

At the same time, there has to be a decision about what is to be evaluated. This can be achieved by a clear statement of overall objectives, plus objectives for every unit and team as well as individuals. At the operational level this will mean detailed production or service targets. At a more strategic level managers may prefer non-routine activities and those of short duration – they may prefer to be problem solvers rather than planners (see Table 7.1). This tendency can be offset by a participative process for establishing objectives and forms of evaluation so that managers can see the importance of longer-term objectives in establishing the context for detailed targets.

A manager needs to be both a problem solver and a planner and to be able to communicate the importance of medium and long-term objectives to employees at all levels so as to support the attainment of objectives and targets and measure performance against these.

In *Thriving on Chaos* (1987) Tom Peters identifies 12 attributes of a quality system, which in themselves represent a checklist against which an organisation's management can assess the stage it has reached in the development of such a system:

- management is obsessed with quality;
- the company has a guiding system or ideology;
- quality is measured;
- quality is rewarded;

Table 7.1 **Planners and problem solvers**

PROBLEM SOLVERS	PLANNERS
Short-duration activities	Advance planning
Non-routine tasks	Agreed systems
Emphasis on decisive action	Systems and schedules
Informal interaction	Formal, regular sessions
Effectiveness through authority	Roles of coach and counsellor
Low priority given to personnel task	Human resource management

- everyone is trained in techniques for assessing quality;
- there is a shift of managerial philosophy from adversarial to cooperative;
- it is recognised that there is no such thing as an insignificant improvement;
- there is constant stimulation to improve quality;
- there is a structure within the company dedicated to quality improvement;
- everybody is involved in quality management, including suppliers, distributors and customers;
- it is understood that costs decline as quality increases;
- it is recognised that quality is relative and improvement is never-ending.

QUALITY CONTROL AND QUALITY ASSURANCE

One of the 12 items on Peters' checklist suggests that quality improvement is never-ending. It is a relative value compared with the competition as perceived through the customer's eyes. It is an elusive concept because customer perception is itself difficult to predict. Peters argues that if you own a car in which some major part goes wrong, you may have a better view of its quality than if a number of small things go wrong. If the carburettor stops working or the gear box collapses you take the car to the garage and have the component repaired or replaced. If the service is efficient and problems do not recur then you can forget about the problem.

If the radio crackles, the door squeaks, the window sticks and there are a number of other small problems then they may not, even cumulatively, be worth the trouble of taking the car to the garage until the next service. Meanwhile they remain a constant reminder of the poor quality of the car. All these problems can be seen as a problem of quality control, which can be defined as being:

concerned with checking for errors during and after the process of manufacture.

Quality control often occurs at the end of the manufacturing process as a check to see if the commodity works. If it does not it is rejected and either scrapped or reworked. The problem with this approach is that there is heavy dependence on inspectors. This is expensive and obviously it is much better to identify the error at an earlier stage. Statistical process control (SPC) is a method of monitoring the conformity of a product to agreed specifications. By sampling units of the product, deviations from these specifications can be identified and adjustments made during the production process (see p. 688).

Modern control techniques are based on the idea of an 'error-free' or 'zero-defect' approach, or 'doing it right first time'. This concept arises because of the costs involved in correcting errors and the fact that the costs are usually greater the later they are identified. Under the TQM approach the team is made responsible for quality control, for reducing wastage and for ensuring that adjustments are made as soon as they are identified.

At a strategic level, quality can be built into the planning of the product or service. Juran and Deming worked extensively with the Japanese to enhance product quality through statistical methods. The first stage is to ensure that the product conforms to design specifications. The next stage is the use of SQC (statistical quality control) or process-control procedures in order to monitor quality during the production of the commodity or rendering of the service. Work teams or quality circles can decide and be delegated the power to decide how to reduce errors and 'do it right first time', while management has to support this process at every stage.

The Ford Motor Company introduced a slogan in the 1980s, 'At Ford, Quality is Job One.' A programme of quality control was introduced along with a new policy of participative management. The emphasis on achieving quotas was changed so that the quality of the product came first. Employee groups were made an important element in the quality control process rather than relying on a separate team of inspectors. Ford's President, Donald Peterson, stated his commitment to quality:

'The principles by which we will live and die, is that once we can do something well, we have to figure out how to do it even better.'

(Quoted by Stoner and Freeman, 1989)

A concept which builds on quality control is the 'just-in-time' (JIT) principle. This is concerned with improving production efficiency and reducing waste. It is a technique for minimising storage through careful planning and purchasing to meet the exact requirements of the customer, internal or external, and this is only possible if the product does in fact meet agreed specifications and suppliers cooperate fully.

It is at the strategic management level that decisions are made about total quality management and systems of quality control. The strategic approach includes:

- analysis of current position;
- choice of an appropriate starting point;
- implementation of policy, deciding what will be done, how, by whom and by when.

Quality assurance (QA) provides a framework for quality control and quality improvement. Quality assurance supports teams of employees with systems, resources and discretion appropriate to their unique contribution to the organisation to keep them in tune with progress of quality management and improvement. This aspect of management can help teams:

- understand quality characteristics;
- be realistic about the standards to be attained;
- undertake quality control through a measurement process, interpret the results and make or propose changes.

This process may be supported by a number of techniques such as QUEST (quality in every single task). This is the idea that everybody in an organisation is a 'customer' and 'supplier' and receives products and services from colleagues within the organisation.

The idea of service within the organisation enables each individual or group to undertake a QUEST analysis:

- Who are my customers?
- What do they demand from me?
- In what way do I meet these demands?
- How can I improve my service?

And

- Who are my suppliers?
- What service do I demand of them?
- In what way do they meet these demands?
- How can they improve their service?

KRA (key result areas) is a technique aimed at focusing on realistic outcomes for each team or individual. This may be by:

- identifying a range of quality characteristics for the team which are consistent with the company's strategy;
- agreeing realistic standards for each of these quality characteristics;
- devising a system which can be measured and monitored.

The Taguchi method is based on the ideas of Dr Genichi Taguchi (1986) who developed his approach to improving quality engineering at a low cost. It helps to quantify the loss due to lack of quality of a performance characteristic, with the objective of identifying the real cause of a problem. It concentrates on the design of products, reducing variation of performance against the target specification. The Taguchi method depends on a management culture committed to TQM and it has, therefore, developed most successfully in Japan and the USA.

The concentration on customer specification has produced approaches such as the British Standard 5750 registration mark and its international counterpart ISO 9000. These do not establish a level of excellence for a product or service but they do provide:

a way of describing the capability of a system to produce goods or services to a specification.

Customers and potential customers should not expect BS 5750 to make a product the best available, and the registration mark is not a necessary prerequisite to total quality management. Quality is as much about 'doing the right thing' as 'doing things right', while BS 5750 is about 'doing things right'. It arises from the need in quality assurance to supply evidence to other organisations about a particular organisation's effectiveness.

These other organisations may be other companies being supplied with the product or service, government agencies, consumer organisations or any other group which perceives, rightly or wrongly, that the possession of BS 5750 or ISO 9000 is a kitemark of effectiveness, efficiency or quality. The UK has been the leader in this process of certification since a Government White Paper in 1982 required BS 5750 registration for nationalised industries and for public sector procurement generally.

BS 5750 places great emphasis on written evidence, documented systems and procedures. It is based on the status quo rather than on continual improvement, which is the main goal of TQM. The British Standard is a procedural system for companies to follow in order to set up and document an organisation's operational systems. The approach is designed to control each step in a process so that products or services match the specification. This type of process originally developed in industries where safety was a critical factor, such as aerospace, nuclear power and defence. This background is what has provided its particular approach – a very careful, closely audited step-by-step control for procedures. The procedures are established to meet a particular specification and then audited to ensure that they are being adhered to in detail. In the 1960s and 1970s the Ministry of Defence and the Central Electricity Board used their inspectors to visit potential suppliers to check that they could produce goods uniformly.

This is still the most important type of use for BS 5750, although some large companies (such as Ford and Marks & Spencer) 'inspect' potential suppliers and set their own operational and product quality standards which suppliers must meet. Some firms conduct their own auditing system in order to standardise procedures. None of these approaches should be confused with TQM.

INVESTING IN PEOPLE

For many organisations, people represent their largest cost – often 70 or 80 per cent of the total. In the UK an initiative which recognises this fact and has the goal of attaining quality in organisations has been 'Investors in People' (IIP). This rests on the premise that companies which have developed, or are developing, an awareness of quality acknowledge that people are the real key to achieving improvements. In a 'quality' culture people take ownership of their work and responsibility for the quality of their work. This arises from 'gap analysis', such as the gap identified by the Confederation of British Industry:

> *'The crucial importance of people to business success is now almost universally recognised by companies. But there is a huge gap between recognising this, and knowing exactly what to do about it.'*   (Department of Employment, 1990c)

IIP is concerned with the contribution people can make to business success. By learning from the actions of those organisations which are already developing and using their people successfully, other organisations can adopt, and benefit from, an 'investing in people' approach.

IIP arose from the 1988 UK Government White Paper *Employment for the 1990s* which launched a partnership between business and government. The National Training Task Force was established and the Training and Enterprise Councils (TECs) and Local Enterprise Councils (in Scotland) were launched. A major priority of this initiative was to raise employer commitment to training by listening to businesses' ideas and needs, and looking at the people factors which made one organisation more successful than another.

Organisations' own agendas are centred around:

■ **productivity**

■ **quality**

■ **focus on the customer**

■ **flexibility.**

These priorities have given rise to operational and management practices such as TQM, and include customer care programmes, 'just-in-time' manufacturing and workplace teams. In all these practices people are understood to be the key to achieving total quality, and there is an emphasis on teams and seeing colleagues as internal customers, while being genuinely motivated to develop existing skills, develop new ones, accept the devolution of responsibility, make the best use of current or new resources and, if required, acquire new managerial skills.

The IIP approach aims to help organisations to improve performance through a planned approach to:

■ **setting and communicating business goals;**

■ **developing people to meet these goals;**

so that:

■ **what people can do and are motivated to do;**

■ **matches what the organisation needs them to do.**

This can be seen diagrammatically in Figure 7.7.

The objective is to encourage organisations to think consistently of their people as an investment and not a cost and act in a way which reflects this perspective. Organisations need to recognise people as a valuable business resource that can be used to create, protect or waste assets; that there are investment costs as well as benefits in this process; that the benefits will be greater than the costs; and that organisations will only benefit fully from investing in people if they start with clearly defined objectives and actions.

The actions required to improve quality through the IIP approach can be summarised in a form based on the UK IIP programme:

Figure 7.7 **Investing in people**

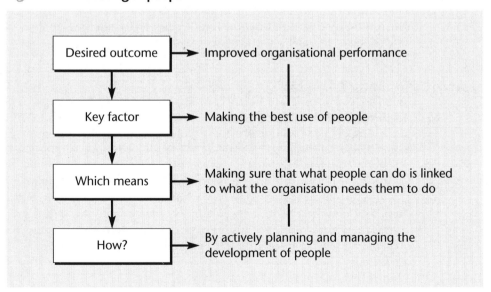

- Every employer should have a written but flexible plan which sets out business goals and targets, considers how employees will contribute to achieving the plan and specifies how development needs in particular will be assessed and met.

- Management should develop and communicate to all employees a vision of where the organisation is going and the contribution employees will make to its success, involving employee representatives as appropriate.

- The resources for training and developing employees should be clearly identified in the business plan.

- Managers should be responsible for regularly agreeing training and development needs with each employee in the context of business objectives, setting targets and standards linked, where appropriate, to the achievement of National Vocational Qualifications (or relevant units) and, in Scotland, Scottish Vocational Qualifications.

- Action should focus on the training needs of all new recruits and continually developing and improving the skills of existing employees.

- All employees should be encouraged to contribute to identifying and meeting their own job-related development needs.

- The investment, the competence and commitment of employees and the use made of skills learned should be reviewed at all levels against business goals and targets.

- The effectiveness of training and development should be reviewed at the top level and lead to renewed commitment and target setting.

In 1999 the UK Government introduced a White Paper called *Learning to Succeed*, which heralded another change in vocational education and training by establishing a Learning and Skills Council in 2001 to replace the previous funding arrangement and the Training and Enterprise Councils. The objective of the new skills body was to 'drive forward improvements in standards and bring together coherence and response' (HMSO, 1999) by putting the whole of vocational training under the Council so that the standards of skills and the lifelong learning required by the country in the twenty-first century could be achieved. Whatever the result of government initiatives may be, and whatever the techniques that may be applied, the importance of the contribution of people to organisational success remains a crucial factor in quality management strategy.

MANAGERS AND THE LAW

Managers need to understand the law as it relates to the operation of their organisations. The civil law is concerned with the rights of people, while the criminal law is concerned with the area of conduct that society will not tolerate. The basis of law in the UK is common law, that is the succession of decisions made by judges over the centuries. It is founded on precedents and not on Acts of Parliament and is based on the concept of reasonableness – what a reasonable person would conclude. So that, for example, a reasonable person would conclude that murder is unacceptable and is therefore an offence under common law. In consumer law, reasonableness plays a part when considering the legal rights of a customer, while a contract is any agreement enforceable by law between two or more consenting parties which obliges them to undertake certain acts.

Statute laws are those made by the Government and in the UK they have been passed by Parliament and signed by the Monarch. Every country has its own legal system and wherever an issue occurs then the legal system of that country, or a wider body such as the European Union, will generally apply. Depending on their role, managers will need to have some understanding of areas such as contract law, consumer law, employment law, health and safety at work and competition legislation in the countries in which they operate. When introducing a total quality management system particularly, as it affects consumers and employees, managers will need to make sure that any processes or procedures and the design of products comply with the relevant laws and regulations. Managers need to keep up to date with legislation that affects their business, it is part of the environment (see Chapter 8) in which their organisation operates.

→ Ch. 8

CONCLUSION

Improving productivity and effectiveness means not only raising the quantity of output per unit, it also involves improving quality. A key to understanding the importance of quality management is the conviction that costs decline as quality increases. The opposite point of view is well rehearsed in all sorts of organisations and situations. A frequent approach centres on the point of view that 'of course we could improve the quality if we had more money and resources', and on the idea that 'you get what you pay for', based on the premise that the more you pay the better the quality.

There is, of course, some truth in these ideas and they may in fact describe the position very accurately in some situations. On the other hand, very often this is not the case. The increase in Japanese car sales in the 1980s and 1990s was based on producing cars which are 'fit for the purpose' – they are designed to fulfil customer requirements, they are reliable and they are relatively cheap. Their success has been based on providing what people want at a price they can afford. At the extreme it can be argued that a Rolls-Royce is a very carefully made car, which is reliable and of very high 'quality' or excellence, but its price puts it out of the reach of most people so that its quality will be compared with other 'handmade' cars and not with family saloons. Volvo has based the success of its cars on such factors as safety, reliability and longevity rather than price because it believes that these are the qualities that potential customers want. In fact, the important feature of its cars is that they are different and it is the difference in quality which the company relies on for its sales and profit.

If a company concentrates mainly on price, as for example cars produced by organisations in some eastern European countries, then there is a chance the relatively cheap car may not sell well because it does not have other qualities which customers require. The essential point is to produce goods which customers want at a price they can afford in a particular market, and the key to producing goods at a competitive price and with good quality is high productivity. The difference between the productivity of car manufacturers in Britain is considerable, with the most productive British workers employed by Japanese companies able to produce twice as many cars a year as the least productive British workers employed by British/American companies.

Differences between companies in terms of productivity arise as a result of greater investment in new equipment and technology, but as important as this are differences in management. The emphasis on quality, focusing of people's jobs, participative management, gaining the cooperation of unions, encouraging teamwork, setting clearly understood performance targets – these are all part of the difference. The lack of these aspects of management encourages expensive situations such as the rejection of products at the point of inspection, or eventually by the customer, the waste of materials, unnecessary expense on troubleshooters, wasteful hold-ups on supply lines and the maintenance of large and costly inventories to replace rejected products or parts. At the same time, if too much energy is expended on fighting internal battles within the organisation, either between management and unions or between different sections and departments, there is a dissipation of the effort required to fight the real external competition. The competitive edge is achieved by creating a positive and productive internal organisation while focusing on beating external competitors.

A 'quality first', 'right first time' approach means that customers are satisfied and stocks of spare parts and replacements can be kept to a minimum. If performance targets are the responsibility of the individual and team and the internal customer approach is prevalent then there is little need for inspection of the end product, supervision can be reduced to a minimum and a comparatively flat hierarchy can manage the company. All of this will save costs.

The TQM approach is based on the idea that managers are sure of their objectives within a broad vision, and for everybody in the organisation to have both a clear focus on their aims and goals and an understanding of the context in which they are working, as well as taking responsibility for work over which they have control. Accountability then becomes a question of peer pressure for most people within the 'internal customer' framework. Quality improvement within an organisation structured in this way is not delegated or subcontracted, it is a responsibility that everyone actively shares.

Management has a responsibility for leading this approach by providing the structural framework and by presenting an example of hard, productive and effective work. The Japanese suggest that management is a way of life which is a progression towards self-enlightenment. They perceive the human skills of imagination, personality, leadership and creativity as just as important as management skills, so that managers are engaged in creating a vision or mission to motivate the workforce. Quality management is concerned with how managers see themselves, what standards they set for themselves and how they motivate others. Out of this analysis should arise the appropriate structure for the organisation.

TQM is a business management philosophy which recognises that customer needs and business goals are inseparable. It pervades an organisation's culture, inspires commitment and encourages communication in all directions, based on work teams and quality systems which utilise resources effectively (see Figure 7.8). At its best, TQM can release a dynamic factor within an organisation which encourages success and profitability.

Figure 7.8 **Total quality management**

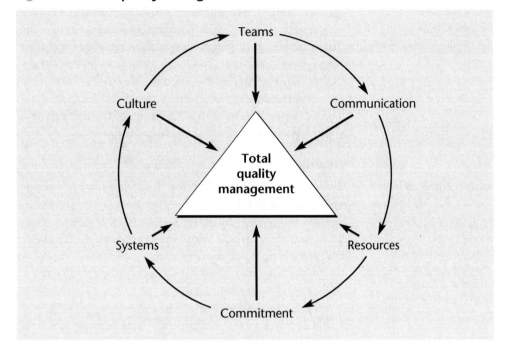

Quality Control

Operations management is the transformation of inputs—materials, labor, and ideas—into outputs, such as products or services. A number of approaches are used to design and measure operations management processes while controlling for quality. These include quality initiatives such as business process reengineering, Total Quality Management, Six Sigma, and Lean Management. Each of these approaches is described in the following sections, followed by a discussion of ISO 9000 and 14000—well-known management systems for ensuring quality and adhering to environmental standards. The section concludes with a discussion of the Baldrige Award, an honor bestowed on companies in recognition of outstanding quality.

Business Process Reengineering

Business process reengineering (BPR) is a management approach that utilizes available technology and management science to redesign business processes, products, and systems to increase efficiency and focus attention on customer needs. According to Thomas Davenport and James Short, two leaders in the field, reengineering is a process that starts from scratch. Rather than simply modifying the design of existing processes, the goal is to redesign from the ground up, even if the result is a radical reconceptualization of the organization.[45]

Scholars Michael Hammer and James Champy argue that BPR is "the fundamental rethinking and radical redesign of business processes to achieve dramatic improvements in critical, contemporary measures of performance, such as cost, quality, service and speed."[46] Whereas Taylor's scientific management approach sought to divorce decision making from labor by pushing decisions up the organizational hierarchy, Hammer and Champy point out "Workers themselves now do that portion of a job that, formerly, managers produced."[47] BPR includes the customer as well: It is a process that is customer-centric, not technology-centric.[48]

The twentieth century was dominated by the notion of a mass market, and the response was mass production for an abstract mass customer. In contrast, in BPR, the notion of "*the* customer" is replaced by "*this* customer," resulting in a refocus on individual customer needs.[49] Information technology is often at the center of the redesign, with the intended outcome being creation of added value for the customer.

Davenport and Short suggest that BPR be incorporated into an organization by way of a five-step approach.[50] The first step in BPR is to define the business vision and objectives. The second step is to identify which business processes need to be reengineered and which changes will make the biggest impact. The third step is to understand what is and what isn't working. The fourth step is to determine which IT systems and functions should influence the business process reengineering. The last step is to design the new process and build a pilot project or prototype based on the new design.

While other approaches such as Total Quality Management (discussed next) offer incremental improvements, BPR seeks improvements through a fundamental rethinking and redesign of business. Describing the goal of BPR, Thomas Davenport notes, "Today firms must seek not fractional, but multiplicative levels of improvement—10X rather than 10%."[51]

Although critics have pointed out that BPR has ultimately led to downsizing and a more stifling workplace environment, the approach was quickly adopted by many companies in the early 1990s. In fact, it is estimated that by 1993, more than 80% of large companies in North America had adopted BPR.[52] It's important to note that if BPR is not performed rigorously, the results can have a strong negative impact on the business, especially for small- and medium-sized enterprises, which are more fragile than large, stable organizations. Research suggests that for such businesses, owners and managers can facilitate success by demonstrating knowledge of and support for the BPR process.[53]

Total Quality Management

Total Quality Management (TQM)
A quality control philosophy that supports the elimination of deficiencies and removes variation in output quality through employee involvement in decision making, continuous improvement in processes, and a strong focus on the customer.

Kaizen is a Japanese philosophy that underlies the model known as Total Quality Management. **Total Quality Management (TQM)** is a quality control philosophy that supports the elimination of deficiencies and removes variation in output quality through employee involvement in decision making, continuous improvement in processes, and a strong focus on the customer. TQM revolves around the idea that, rather than wiping a slate clean, life and organizations should be incrementally and constantly improved. The central principles of this approach are described in ◼Exhibit 12.15.

◼Exhibit **12.15**

Fundamental Principles of TQM[54]

1. *Kaizen:* A focus on continuous process improvement, often through incremental changes. Kaizen involves the following five elements that facilitate the elimination of waste:[55]
   - Teamwork
   - Personal discipline
   - Improved morale
   - Quality circles (employee groups that seek solutions for quality problems)
   - Suggestions for improvement.
2. *Atarimae hinshitsu:* The idea that "things" will work according to their function and purpose (e.g., a pen will write).
3. *Kansei:* The idea that understanding the way people use products leads to the improvement of these products.
4. *Miryokuteki hinshitsu:* The idea that manufactured products should have an aesthetic quality.

TQM has been widely used in manufacturing industries, as well as in call centers and technical fields such as aerospace. It is important to note, however, that TQM is not just used in big manufacturing companies. In fact, Rafidah Mohamad Noor, an assistant director of AKEPT, describes in the following *Perspectives* feature the principles of employee participation in problem solving can be used in any organization with great results.

AKEPT is a higher education leadership academy created under the Ministry of Education in Malaysia in 2008. AKEPT's mission is to revitalize and improve higher education in Malaysia. The agency's goal is inspiring: It wants to prepare the country's higher education system to better serve the needs of students and faculty from all over Asia. As Rafidah Mohamad Noor put it:

We want AKEPT to be truly successful, so we are always looking for ways to move us forward. We have an important mission at AKEPT, and we have big challenges. When you think about the kinds of changes that will be needed to reach our goal, and what we need to do in a very short time, it is clear that we will have to focus on innovation and enhancing the quality of our work.

Rafidah Mohamad Noor, Assistant Director, AKEPT

We are faced with new challenges and new activities every day, and we are constantly reminded that things will be different, and we need to be able to adapt and change to improve how we work. We are always focusing on how we can improve ourselves and AKEPT. One of the ways we want to do this is to be sure everyone's opinion can be heard, no matter what role they have in our institution. When everyone's voice is heard, they can have discussions, spot problems, capture ideas, and find solutions.

Source: Personal interview conducted with Rafidah Mohamad Noor by Annie McKee, 2009.

Six Sigma

Six Sigma
A management strategy that employs quality management methods in a specific sequence to either reduce costs or increase profits.

Originally developed by Motorola in an effort to eliminate defects in their manufacturing processes, **Six Sigma** is a management strategy that employs quality management methods in a specific sequence to either reduce costs or increase profits. It has evolved into a business management strategy that is used to improve a wide array of manufacturing and business processes.[56] People trained in Six Sigma are placed into a hierarchical infrastructure with "Champions" at the top. After "Champions," the descending levels of expertise are termed as follows: Master Black Belts, Black Belts, Green Belts, and Yellow Belts.[57]

Companies such as GE, Boeing, Caterpillar, and Raytheon have implemented Six Sigma. It is worth noting that these companies are among the largest in the world. Large companies have the expansive financial resources required for implementation of Six Sigma, whereas smaller companies may not. Training one person to attain Yellow Belt status, for example, can cost more than $1,000.[58] In larger organizations, hundreds if not thousands of employees receive Six Sigma training, making it a significant investment of time and money.

The goal of Six Sigma is to limit defects through a process of incremental adjustments and attention to even the smallest details of the manufacturing process. Two common uses of the Six Sigma method are for process improvement and for new product or service development. These two situations require different approaches, as seen in ■Exhibits 12.16 and ■12.17.

The results of Six Sigma implementation have been mixed. GE, for example, boasts of a $10 billion gain through cost reduction and/or increased profits over the initial five-year period following implementation.[59] 3M, however, found that the implementation of Six Sigma

■Exhibit **12.16**

Six Sigma for Process Improvement: Define, Measure, Analyze, Improve, and Control

- *Define* high-level project goals and the current process.
- *Measure* key aspects of the current process and collect relevant data.
- *Analyze* the data to verify cause-and-effect relationships.
- *Improve* or optimize the process based on data analysis.
- *Control* to ensure that any deviations from the target are corrected before they result in defects.

■Exhibit **12.17**

Six Sigma for New Product and Service Development: Define, Measure, Analyze, Design, and Verify

- *Define* design goals that are consistent with customer demands and the enterprise strategy.
- *Measure* and identify *CTQs* (characteristics that are *Critical To Quality*), product capabilities, production process capability, and risks.
- *Analyze* to develop and design alternatives, create a high-level design, and evaluate design capability to select the best design.
- *Design* details, optimize the design, and plan for design verification.
- *Verify* the design, set up pilot runs, implement the production process, and hand it over to the process owners.[60]

dampened creativity and innovation.[61] This conflict between innovation and the efficiency improvements from Six Sigma has been explored by author Stephen Ruffa, who points to data that show the Six Sigma program did little to help Ford Motor Company.[62] Despite widespread critiques, Six Sigma initiatives are still widely pursued by companies today.

Lean Management

Lean Management
A management approach that organizes manufacturing and logistics to maximize efficiency and eliminate waste by reducing variation in every process.

Lean Management is a management approach that organizes manufacturing and logistics to maximize efficiency and eliminate waste by reducing variation in every process. Although the term "Lean Management" has appeared sporadically in various contexts in Europe since the 1980s, it was popularized in a 1990 book on Japanese lean production systems.[63] Currently, one of the best-known lean production methodologies is the Toyota Production System, which relies on the following Lean Management goals to eliminate waste and maximize efficiency:[64]

1. *Improve quality:* To be competitive, a company must have a quality product that exceeds customers' expectations.
2. *Eliminate waste:* There are several different types of waste, including overproduction, downtime, defects, and rework. All such waste must be eliminated to stay "lean" and profitable.
3. *Reduce time:* Time from the beginning of the manufacturing process to the end must be reduced in order to stay competitive.
4. *Reduce total costs:* Any extra costs, such as those that come from keeping an unnecessary inventory of parts or finished projects, hinder a company's profitability and should be reduced.

Lean management, and indeed all lean systems, improves efficiency primarily by reducing wasted time, space, effort, materials, and so forth. This can be done, for instance, by identifying and removing redundancies.[65] Although many Lean Management principles are common sense and can result in greater efficiency, when taken to the extreme and/or when efficiency trumps effectiveness and quality, results can be catastrophic. There have been occasions in companies such as Toyota, where despite control processes like Lean Management, product quality has been compromised significantly. Therefore, when processes like Lean Management are employed, it is important to ensure that processes are not so "lean" that they can't adapt or that human errors become more likely.[66]

ISO 9000 and 14000

The ISO 9000 and 14000 families of management system standards are some of the best known in the world, and they have been implemented by more than 1 million organizations in approximately 175 countries.[67] The ISO (International Organization for Standardization) is an international standards-setting body composed of national-level representatives. ISO 9000 and 14000 address quality management and environmental management, respectively. While widely used in the automotive and industrial sectors, the standards are not specific to any one industry.[68] In fact, the ISO strongly encourages small- and medium-sized enterprises across all industries to consider adoption of these standards, particularly ISO 14000, so that they can reap the economic benefits they offer.[69]

The ISO 9000 standards are auditable international standards that have guided quality control since 1987, when they were first published.[70] Revised repeatedly since then, the standards are rooted in eight quality management principles that are designed to enable companies to exceed the quality requirements of their customers and enhance customer satisfaction while at the same time meeting regulatory requirements.[71] These principles include focusing on the customer, providing leadership, involving people, utilizing a process approach, employing a systems approach to management, striving for continual improvement, implementing a factual approach to decision making, and developing mutually beneficial supplier relationships.[72]

In support of these eight principles, ISO 9000 requires that any company using the system produce documentation in support of quality management, such as a quality manuals and procedural instructions.[73] Companies can also seek independent certification, or registration, of their quality management system that recognizes successful maintenance of standard requirements. This certification is not required of companies that implement ISO 9000, but it is often beneficial in terms of marketing and securing customers that require certification.[74]

ISO 14000 was developed in 1992.[75] The goal of this set of standards is to encourage environmental responsibility within the business community by helping companies reduce their environmental impact and increase their long-term sustainability.[76] The key points of ISO 14000 are identifying the ways in which companies impact the environment, improving environmental product labeling, promoting company life cycle analyses, and evaluating environmental performance on an ongoing basis.[77] Ultimately, this will lead companies to get more out of their inputs and develop positive relationships with their stakeholders.[78] Companies may pursue ISO 14000 certification via an independent audit in much the same manner that they seek ISO 9000 certification. This certification signals that the company is going above and beyond minimum government regulations regarding waste disposal and pollution control.[79]

ISO 9000 and ISO 14000 standards are not intended to dictate specific quality or environmental practices. Rather, they are designed to provide a framework and a systematic approach to evaluating processes.[80] Both systems take time and money to implement, but both lead to improved profits by way of more effective management; moreover, they also enable companies to be more ethically responsible to their customers and the environment.[81] Perhaps that is why so many companies worldwide have adopted these standards as part of their day-to-day operations.

Baldrige Award

The need for quality assurance and improvement in industry is not solely a concern of the private sector; it is a governmental concern as well, as evidenced by the Malcolm Baldrige National Quality Award. This award was established by U.S. Public Law 100-107 in 1987, and it was first awarded in 1988. It is named for Malcolm Baldrige, U.S. Secretary of Commerce from 1981 through 1987.[82] During his tenure as secretary, Baldrige espoused the idea that long-term economic improvement in the United States was closely tied to quality management, and he put these concepts into practice within the Commerce Department. Under his leadership, the department's budget and administrative overhead were drastically reduced, and its effectiveness and efficiency greatly improved.[83]

The Baldrige award is presented each year by the president of the United States to manufacturing and service businesses, educational institutions, health care enterprises, and nonprofit organizations of all sizes. Companies apply for the award themselves and are judged on their performance in seven specific areas: leadership; strategic planning; customer and market focus; measurement, analysis, and knowledge management; workforce focus; process management; and results. Award winners typically exercise good citizenship and public responsibility as well as superior relationships with customers and employees. In addition, they exhibit outstanding production and delivery processes that are aligned with organizational objectives.[84] Far from simply recognizing exceptional companies, however, the Baldrige criteria have become a "way of organizational life" for many businesses that have introduced them into their daily operating standards.

When applied to business operations as a whole, the Baldrige principles assist organizations in focusing on strategy-driven performance, and they promote organizational sustainability.[85] To that end, Baldrige Award winners are asked to share their performance strategies with others in order to perpetuate a culture of excellence in industry.[86] It is this culture of excellence that helps keep U.S. companies vital to the world economy and keeps the Malcolm Baldrige National Quality Award relevant in our ever-changing business climate.

Most Popular » Discussion Questions

1. Have you ever worked for—or been served by—an organization in which the customer really was the center of all decisions? How was this organization different from others you have experienced?
2. Imagine that your school or workplace plans to implement TQM, Six Sigma, or Lean Management. What changes might you see in how resources are used? In how people are managed?

Cases

CASE STUDY

British Aerospace

The Airbus Division is part of British Aerospace commercial division which handles work arising from the company's 20 per cent stake in Airbus Industries. Approximately two-thirds of the Airbus Division's payroll of 9000 is engaged in producing Airbus wingsets, while the other activities include a maintenance contract for the US Air Force.

Quality assurance has been developed in the Airbus Division over the last 22 years. Quality managers have progressively been introduced to replace inspectors, whose numbers have gradually fallen. A different philosophy of product quality has accompanied this change. Formerly, the aim was to produce 'engineering excellence' but now the goal is 'excellent engineering', a concept requiring a broader view of an item's function and with a higher priority for costs and the complexities of production. Essentially, the need is for excellent engineering at an affordable cost.

This has led to fresh approaches to all activities from design onwards. Statistical quality control methods still have some applications, but not as many as in mass-production flowline operations. Training has been a high priority from apprentices through to management. Stress is placed on topics such as customer orientation, the awareness of suppliers and what constitutes an affordable cost. There is an approved list of suppliers, with inspections every two years. This has been found to work well with large suppliers but not so well with smaller suppliers, and those with a proven record of high quality have come to be valued.

It has been found that growth at British Aerospace has enhanced quality rather than caused a decline in it. This has been put down to the scale of investment, the long production lines with increased volume and the concentration on quality as the top priority. Where amendments are made to production, a rule has been introduced that quality has to stay constant or improve. As a result, the larger the production lines, the more changes are made and the greater the number of quality improvements. This has been reinforced by the introduction of a total quality programme.

Case Study: GNY Building Materials

GNY Building Materials is a multi-location ready mix concrete, sand and gravel supplier. It employs over 350 staff and is currently faced with the twin problems of escalating costs and failing customer service. After an important board meeting it was decided to create a new business culture, a culture which valued quality, customer service and continuous improvement. A business consultant was commissioned to perform a TQM readiness assessment, organise a Quality Steering Committee, train the management and hourly employees in TQM and support the work of the departmentally based Quality Teams and the cross functional Corrective Action Teams.

When the consultant began work it was apparent that the company did not have a history of participative management and reacted slowly to opportunities. Initial interviews confirmed that management was viewed sceptically. Poor internal communication led to employees feeling fear and resentment. Also, the business faced increasingly aggressive competition. A major objective for implementing TQM was to eliminate the waste in delivery and improve the reliability of delivery. The chairman made it plain that the savings from improvements would fund the culture he needed to foster in order to implement TQM.

Implementing TQM

There was a number of steps involved in implementing TQM at the business.

STEP 1 Perform a TQM readiness assessment. Over a five day period all of the senior management team and several hourly employees were interviewed. This highlighted several areas for targeted customer service improvement and cost reduction. TQM training was developed and initial Corrective Action Teams (CATs) were formed.

STEP 2 Communicate the vision to every single employee in the company. The chairman told each employee his vision for the business.

STEP 3 Organise the steering committee and train the management team. Training was further developed in the six TQM training sessions.

By incorporating their culture, credibility was improved. In addition, training improved the application of TQM ideas and broke down barriers to change. Four groups of twenty employees were then trained. The consultant trained in-house trainers to continue the training of employees. A second, but equally important, task continued parallel to the training. The Corrective Action Team (CAT) used the TQM process to improve the customer service levels and eliminate waste in trucking. It used each of the five critical areas in TQM to generate the needed changes in their trucking operations. These were considered to be the following.

- Customer Focus
- Waste Elimination
- Teamwork
- Continuous Improvement
- Problem Solving

Over three months the business generated cost reduction initiatives worth £600,000 and implemented over £300,000 of cost savings. This major victory by hourly and first line management demonstrated the effectiveness of TQM. GNY Building Materials realised a 25:1 payback on its investment in Total Quality Management. Their premier service reputation was restored and it became the preferred supplier to many contractors. According to the chairman, the company has become much more flexible and responsive. Improvements to the bottom line confirm this.

(a) **What is a TQM readiness assessment? (4 marks)**
(b) **Why did GNY Building Materials introduce TQM? (6 marks)**
(c) **How important was training in the implementation of TQM at GNY Building Materials? (8 marks)**
(d) **Examine the likely costs incurred by GNY Building Materials when implementing TQM. (10 marks)**
(e) **Evaluate the benefits to GNY Building Materials of introducing TQM. (16 marks)**

CASE APPLICATION 2

Lean Manufacturing in China

China is known today as the world's largest manufacturing hub. Chinese manufacturers, however, have started to diversify and are planning to be more than just a low-cost production plant for international brands. They are working on enhancing their capabilities to expand their involvement in a wider range of value chain activities such as product design and process planning. To this end, Chinese manufacturers are working to transform their production bases from traditional low-cost, labor-intensive operations to more flexible, value-based lean manufacturing systems. Over the last 10 years, Chinese factories have been trying to move from traditional forms of assembly line production to lean manufacturing, modular teams, and cell-based layout production centers. Lean manufacturing in particular encourages waste elimination, high performance, continuous improvement, just-in-time delivery, and ultimately more efficient and profitable production.

The Pegasus plant, a 13,000-employee sports shoe factory in northern Guangdong Province, is one of China's largest manufacturers that has utilized lean system ideas and techniques. It was established in 2003, to produce sports shoes for Nike, a leading international sportswear brand. The plant is among the second generation of foreign-invested enterprises in southern China that have moved inland from the southeast coast to benefit from cheaper land, services, and manpower. Since it has moved to its new location from another facility in the city of Guangzhou province, the plant and its processes have been designed on lean manufacturing principles.

The transition toward lean manufacturing could not be rushed. For example, small teams in cellular layouts could not easily be adapted to a factory with such large-scale operations and thousands of workers. Plant management had to be trained to understand the main concepts of lean principles and to facilitate its implementation. In traditional production, the factory was divided into process-based departments or production areas, each generating a single or a group of components of the final product. The semifinished items moved (and were stored) between departments for more processes until they reached the final assembly area. The Pegasus plant employed lean manufacturing techniques that tried to restructure this production process. Instead of large, single-process departments, lean manufacturing established small production "cells" or teams of workers who complete the whole product—for instance shoes. Each cell is responsible for extensive operations including cutting raw materials, sewing, gluing, assembling, inspection, and packaging.

A key element of efficient lean manufacturing systems is the increased role of workers, who are "empowered" to participate in decision making. The lean system has also resulted in a significant increase in labor productivity. When the plant started, a new product would have a 90-day lead time (the time from when an order is placed by a brand to when the finished product is delivered to the market). Today, the factory has an average 60-day lead time, while some styles have even shorter lead times—one week. It has also considerably reduced its work-in-progress inventories (components of the finished shoes). The factory has implemented just-in-time delivery of materials and parts, thus significantly reducing delays or overstocks. Overall, productivity has increased, quality has improved, the factory can produce more styles and change between these styles more quickly, and profits have also increased.[63]

Discussion Questions

1. What are the key elements of the lean manufacturing systems the Chinese manufacturers implemented?
2. Discuss how lean manufacturing helped the shoe factory to eliminate waste.
3. How could the changes in the factory layout enhance the factory's productivity?

Review Questions and Tests

Review questions

1 Review some consumer goods such as mobile phones, cars and kitchen appliances. Identify the service elements attached to the purchase of these products.

2 Discuss why variation in the inputs to the transformation process is a bad thing. Which of the five inputs is likely to be subject to most variation and which to least?

3 Why is control over quality at source so important?

4 How does service quality differ from manufacturing quality?

5 Why is delivery reliability more important than delivery speed?

6 Describe and discuss the importance of the demand/supply balance.

7 Discuss why it is impossible to have a single production system that is equally efficient at all volumes of throughput.

8 Describe the differences between product, process and cell layouts.

9 Discuss the concepts of order winners and order qualifiers.

10 Summarise an idea from the chapter that adds to your understanding of the integrating themes.

Chapter 21:
Production Methods

81 Types of production

Deciding how to produce

A business must decide on the most suitable method to manufacture its goods or to provide services. It is likely that products which are different will be produced differently. For example, a plastic drinks bottle may be produced using automated machinery, but a wrist watch may be assembled by hand. Products that are similar can also be produced in different ways. The Ford Motor Company and Morgan Cars both produce cars, but different processes are used. Ford builds cars using a production line and semi-skilled labour, but Morgan cars are hand built by skilled workers. There are three important decisions that businesses must make when choosing how to produce. These are shown in Figure 1, along with the factors which influence these decisions. In the diagram it is assumed that the firm has already decided 'what' to produce. When deciding how to produce, the objective of the firm will be to minimise the cost per unit of output, i.e. PRODUCTIVE EFFICIENCY.

What production method will be used? Production is sometimes divided into one of three methods. JOB PRODUCTION is where one job is completed at a time before moving on to another. An example might be a costume made for a television play set in the nineteenth century. BATCH PRODUCTION involves dividing the work into a number of different operations. An example would be bread production, where each batch goes through several different baking stages before it is completed. FLOW PRODUCTION involves work being completed continuously without stopping. The production of cars on a production line might be one example.

Some industries may combine different methods of production. For example, a large brewery may produce 'batches' of beer, but then send them to a bottling line for packaging, where flow production is used. Such combinations are particularly common in the food industry.

What factors of production will be used? Businesses are often faced with a wide choice between alternative production factors. For example, a builder planning to construct a new house must decide what building materials to buy, which tools to use, which sub-contractors to employ and whether to hire any extra labour. The builder will be faced with a choice in all of these cases. If he decides to hire a labourer, there may be hundreds or even thousands of people to choose from in the area.

How will the factors of production be combined? A third production decision concerns the way in which the available production factors should be combined. For example, should an assembly plant invest in a highly automated assembly operation, or employ a large semi-skilled labour force to undertake the work?

This unit focuses on the types of production a business might choose from.

Job production

Job production involves the production of a single product at a time. It is used when orders for products are small, such as 'one-offs'. Production is organised so that one 'job' is completed at a time. There is a wide variety of goods and services which are produced or provided using this method of production. Small-scale examples include the baking of a child's birthday cake, a dentist's treatment session or the construction of an extension to a house. On a large scale, examples could include the building of a ship, the construction of the Channel Tunnel or the manufacture of specialised machinery. Job production is found in both manufacturing and the service industries. Because the numbers of units produced is small, the production process tends to be labour intensive. The workforce is usually made up of skilled craftsmen or specialists and the possibility of using labour-saving machinery is limited. Many businesses adopt this method of production when they are 'starting up'. The advantages and disadvantages of job production are shown in Table 1.

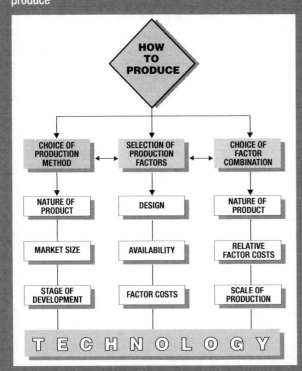

Figure 1: Factors which affect the decision about how to produce

Table 1: Advantages and disadvantages of job production

Advantages

- Firms can produce unique or 'one-off' orders according to customer needs. For example, a wedding dress may be designed and produced for the individual taste of a client. It is also possible to change the specifications of a job at the last minute, even if the work has actually begun.
- Workers are more likely to be motivated. The tasks employees carry out often require a variety of skills, knowledge and expertise. Their work will be more demanding and interesting. They will also see the end result of their efforts and be able to take pride in their work. Jobs may be carried out by a team of workers aiming to achieve the same objectives. This should help raise the level of job satisfaction.
- The organisation of job production is fairly simple. Because only one job is done at a time, co-ordination, communication, supervision and inspection can take place regularly. Also, it is easier to identify and deal with problems, such as a defective damp proof course in a house or a poorly cooked meal in a restaurant.

Disadvantages

- Labour costs will be high because production tends to be labour intensive. The workforce is likely to be skilled and more versatile. Such employees will be more expensive. The amount of time each employee spends on a particular job will also be long.
- Because there is a variety of work, subject to many specifications, the business would need a wide range of tools, machines and equipment. This can prove expensive. Also, it may not be possible to achieve economies of scale because only one 'job' is produced at a time.
- Lead times can be lengthy. When building a house, the business has to incur costs which cannot be recovered until the house is sold. Sometimes the sale of a house can take a long time.
- Selling costs may also be high. This is likely if the product is highly complex and technical. The sales team will need to be well qualified, able to cope with questions and deal with problems concerning sales and installation. Some firms employ agencies to help reduce their selling costs.
- Once the demand for a firm's product rises, job production may become costly. Firms may prefer to use a method more suited to producing larger quantities. This is not always the case. Even if demand is high, each customer may require a unique order. In addition, many firms believe that the 'personal touch' they can offer in job production is important. As a result, they may choose not to change to other production methods. Other production methods require some degree of product standardisation. This may result in more efficient production, but a loss of 'individuality'.

Table 2: Operations involved in the production of a batch of bread

1.	Blend ingredients in a mixing container until a dough is formed.
2.	Knead the dough for a period of time.
3.	Leave the dough to rise for a period of time.
4.	Divide the dough into suitable units (loaves) for baking.
5.	Bake the loaves.
6.	Allow loaves to cool.

Batch production

Batch production may be used when demand for a firm's product or service is regular rather than a 'one off'. An example might be a furniture factory, where a batch of armchairs is made to a particular design. Production is divided into a number of operations. A particular operation is carried out on all products in a batch. The batch then moves to the next operation. A baker uses batch production when baking bread. The operations in the baking process are broken down in Table 2.

These operations would be performed on every batch of bread. There is some standardisation because each loaf in the batch will be the same. However, it may be possible to vary each batch. The ingredients could be changed to produce brown bread or the style of baking tin could be changed for different shaped loaves.

A great number of products are produced using this method, particularly in manufacturing, such as the production of components and food processing. For example, in a canning plant, a firm may can several different batches of soup, each batch being a different recipe. Products can be produced in very large or very small batches, depending on the level of demand. Larger production runs tend to lower the **unit** or **average cost** of production. New technology is increasingly being introduced to make batch production more efficient. The advantages and disadvantages of batch production are shown in Table 3.

Flow production

Most people will have some idea of flow production from pictures of motor car factories. Production is organised so that different operations can be carried out, one after the other, in a continuous sequence. Vehicles move from one operation to the next, often on a conveyer belt. The main features of flow production are:

- the production of large quantities;
- a simplified or standardised product;
- a semi-skilled workforce, specialising in one operation only;
- large amounts of machinery and equipment;
- large stocks of raw materials and components.

Table 3: Advantages and disadvantges of batch production

Advantages

- Even though larger quantities are produced than in job production, there is still flexibility. Each batch can be changed to meet customers' wishes. It is particularly suitable for a wide range of similar products. The settings on machines can be changed according to specifications, such as different clothes sizes.
- Employees can concentrate on one operation rather than on the whole task. This reduces the need for costly, skilled employees.
- Less variety of machinery would be needed than in job production because the products are standardised. Also, it is possible to use more standardised machinery.
- It often results in stocks of partly finished goods which have to be stored. This means firms can respond more quickly to an urgent order by processing a batch quickly through the final stages of production.

Disadvantages

- Careful planning and co-ordination are needed, or machines and workers may be idle, waiting for a whole batch to finish its previous operation. There is often a need to clean and adjust machinery before the next batch can be produced. This can mean delays. In brewing, one day of the week is used to clean equipment before the next batch begins.
- Some machinery may have to be more complex to compensate for the lower skill levels required from the labour force. This may lead to higher costs.
- The workforce may be less motivated, since they have to repeat operations on every single unit in the batch. In addition, they are unlikely to be involved with production from start to finish.
- If batches are small then unit costs will remain relatively high.
- Money will be tied up in work-in-progress, since an order cannot be dispatched until the whole batch has been finished.

Question 1.

Alex Stone is a chartered accountant. He runs a small business from an office in Kidderminster producing final accounts for sole traders, partnerships and small private limited companies. He has a client base of around 110 businesses and employs a secretary and a young trainee accountant. In addition to preparing accounts He offers other services such as:

- completing tax returns;
- taxation planning;
- advice on the financial management of businesses;
- advice on investment;
- auditing.

(a) Use this case as an example to explain what is meant by job production.

(b) Explain why job production might help to motivate Alex and his trainee.

Flow production is used in the manufacture of products as varied as newspapers, food and cement. It is sometimes called **mass production**, as it tends to be used for the production of large numbers of standard products, such as cars or breakfast cereals. Certain types of flow production are known as **continual flow production**, because products such as clothing material pass continually through a series of processes. **Repetitive flow production** is the manufacture of large numbers of the same product, such as plastic toy parts or metal cans.

The advantages and disadvantages of flow production are shown in Table 4. In the 1990s flow production processes were changed in an attempt to solve some of the problems. Japanese manufacturers setting up businesses in the UK introduced methods to improve efficiency. Just-in-time manufacturing, for example, helped to reduce the cost of holding stocks. Some vehicle manufacturers attempted to introduce an element of job production into flow processes by **customising** products for clients. For example, a range of different cars was produced on the same production line. Cars in the same model range differed in colour, engine size, trim and interior design.

Process production

PROCESS PRODUCTION is a form of flow production which is used in the oil or chemical industry. Materials pass through a plant where a series of processes are carried out in order to change the product. An example might be the refining of crude oil into petrol.

Flow production relies on the use of computers. Computers send instructions to machines, control production speeds and conditions, and monitor quality. They allow large numbers of products to be produced continuously to exact standards or control continuous production, which requires many processes.

Table 4: Advantages and disadvantages of flow production

Advantages
- Unit costs are reduced as firms gain from economies of scale.
- In many industries the process is highly automated. Production is controlled by computers. Many of the operations are performed by robots and other types of machinery. Once the production line is set up and running, products can flow off the end non stop for lengthy periods of time. This can reduce the need for labour, as only machine supervisors are needed.
- The need to stockpile finished goods is reduced. The production line can respond to short-term changes in demand. For example, if demand falls the line can be shut down for a period of time. If it rises then the line can be opened.

Disadvantages
- The set--up costs are very high. An enormous investment in plant and equipment is needed. Firms must therefore be confident that demand for the product is sufficient over a period of time to make the investment pay.
- The product will be standardised. It is not possible to offer a wide product range and meet different customers' needs. However, modern machinery is becoming more flexible and is beginning to overcome this problem.
- For a number of reasons, worker motivation can be a serious problem. Most of the manual operations required on the production line will be repetitive and boring. Factories with production lines tend to be very noisy. Each worker will only be involved in a very small part of the job cycle. As a result of these problems worker morale may be low and labour turnover and absenteeism high.
- Breakdowns can prove costly. The whole production system is interdependent. If one part of the supply or production line fails the whole system may break down.

Choice of production method

The method of production chosen might depend on a number of factors.

The nature of the product Many products require a specific method of production. For example, in the construction industry, projects such as bridges, roads, office blocks and sewers must be produced using job production. Cereal farming involves batch production. A plot of land undergoes several processes before it 'produces' a crop.

The size of the market Fast-moving consumer goods like soap, confectionery and canned drinks are normally produced using flow production because the market is so big. When the market is small, flow production techniques are not cost effective.

The stage of development a business has reached When firms are first set up, they often produce small levels of output and employ job or batch production methods. As they grow and enjoy higher sales levels, they may switch to flow production.

Technology The current state of technology will affect all decisions concerning how to produce. As technology advances, new materials and machinery become available. Changes in technology often result in firms adopting new methods of production. For example, the development of computers and robotic welders has radically changed the way in which cars are manufactured. Also, car manufacturers are now able to produce different models on the same production line at the same time.

Question 2.

Uniform+ was established in 1997 and has become a leading supplier of workwear, leisurewear and promotional clothing to businesses and organisations across the UK. In 2006, the company moved to a purpose-built freehold head office and factory in Cannock. Uniform+ supplies over 12,000 garments a week to more than 5,500 customers. The company has an excellent reputation in the industry because of their:
- commitment to offering a wide choice of quality clothing at unbeatable prices;
- dedication to providing excellent customer service and value for money;
- fast turnaround and flexibilty to meet customers' needs;
- unique free logo and delivery service.

Like most companies in the clothes industry, Uniform+ uses batch production. The company can meet a wide range of different orders due the flexibility of its machinery and its multi-skilled workforce.

(a) Use the clothes industry as an example to explain what is meant by batch production.
(b) Why is batch production common in the clothes industry?
(c) How do you think Uniform+ has overcome some of the typical problems associated with batch production?

Cases

Case Study: *Nacional*

Nacional is a major breakfast cereal manufacturer in Portugal and forms part of the grain milling Amorim-Lage Group. The popularity of breakfast cereals has grown in Portugal in recent years and one of Nacional's main production facilities was in need of a major update and expansion using new technology and new ideas. Early in 2004, Nacional carried out a major refit and expansion plan that was completed by mid-September. The investment in the new facility was estimated at 11.2 million euros.

Nacional's main product was cornflakes but since the expansion the facility has been able to manufacture a variety of extruded breakfast cereal products for marketing under its own brand names and also for supermarket own-brand labels. The adoption of extrusion techniques (drawing a dough mixture through a shape to produce a continuous strand with an identical cross section which can be cut into shapes such as stars or squares for example) in processing breakfast cereal at the Nacional plant has widened the production possibilities because a variety of grains can now be used. This has allowed the blending of different grains into unique cereal pieces. Extrusion has also made production more efficient by combining several processing steps into a single, continuous flow.

PV Baker has supplied and installed a complete processing plant for Nacional. It incorporates the entire production process, from compounding and mixing the recipe 'dough' through extrusion and cooking to drying and coating the final extruded product shapes. The new facility can make a variety of different products, including corn-balls, coco-balls, choco curls, golden squares, stars and rings, as well as co-extruded filled pillow shapes. All of these extruded shapes, except the pillows, will be coated with a honey, sugar or glucose based glaze.

Most of the products are cut into individual pieces by a die as they leave the extruder. A key design feature of the facility is the ability to change over rapidly between products in response to market demand, including those products involving different raw materials and syrup. For example, to create filled pillow products, which cannot be cut at the die, a mobile crimping unit is wheeled in and out of the line.

Source: adapted from www.foodprocessing-technology.com

(a) State four processes used in the production of breakfast cereals at Nacional. (4 marks)

(b) Explain how Nacional is using both batch production and flow production methods in its factory. (10 marks)

(c) When upgrading its production facilities, what role did technology play at Nacional? (6 marks)

(d) To what extent do you think the 11.2 million euro investment will benefit Nacional? (20 marks)

Review Questions and Tests

KNOWLEDGE

1. What are the three main decisions which have to be made regarding the method of production?
2. Under what circumstances might a business become more capital intensive?
3. State three types of products which may be manufactured using job production.
4. Describe the advantages and disadvantages of job production.
5. State three products that are generally manufactured using batch production.
6. Describe the advantages and disadvantages of batch production.
7. Describe four features of flow production.

Chapter 22:
Just-in-Time Management

95 | Lean production

What is lean production?

LEAN PRODUCTION is an approach to production developed in Japan. Toyota, the Japanese car manufacturer, was the first company to adopt this approach. Its aim is to reduce the quantity of resources used up in production. Lean producers use less of everything, including factory space, materials, stocks, suppliers, labour, capital and time. As a result, lean production raises productivity and reduces costs. The number of defective products is reduced, lead times are cut and reliability improves. Lean producers are also able to design new products more quickly and can offer customers a wider range of products to choose from. Lean production involves using a range of practices designed to reduce waste and to improve productivity and quality.

Kaizen (continuous improvement)

KAIZEN is perhaps the most important concept in Japanese management. It means continuous improvement. Every aspect of life, including social life, working life and home life, is constantly improved. Everyone in the business is involved. Kaizen is said to be an 'umbrella concept'. A wide range of different production techniques and working practices must be carried out for it to be effective. Figure 1 shows examples of the techniques, principles and practices. They should result in ongoing improvements. This approach argues that a day should not pass without some kind of improvement being made

somewhere in the business.

There is a number of features of Kaizen which affect a business.

Continuous improvement Kaizen has been the main difference between the Japanese and the Western approaches to management in the past. The attempts of Western businesses to improve efficiency and quality have tended to be 'one-offs'. In Figure 2 the solid line illustrates the Western approach. Productivity remains the same for long periods of time, then suddenly rises. The increase is followed by another period of stability, before another rise. Increases in productivity may result from new working practices or new technology. The dotted line shows the Japanese approach. Improvements are continuous. They result from changes in production techniques which are introduced gradually.

Eliminating waste The elimination of waste (called muda in Japan) in business practices is an important part of Kaizen. Waste is any activity which raises costs without adding value to a product. Examples may be:

*   time wasted while staff wait around before starting tasks, such as waiting for materials to arrive;
*   time wasted when workers move unnecessarily in the workplace, such as walking to a central point in the factory to get tools;
*   the irregular use of a machine, such as a machine which is only used once a month for a special order;
*   excessive demands upon machines or workers, such as staff working overtime seven days a week which causes them to be tired and work poorly.

Firms that adopt the Kaizen approach train and reward

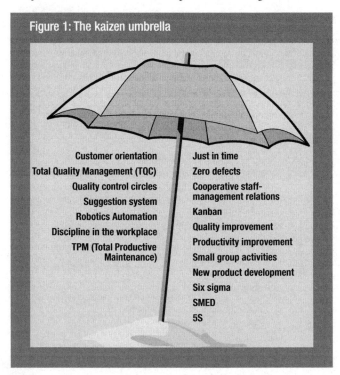

Figure 1: The kaizen umbrella

Customer orientation
Total Quality Management (TQC)
Quality control circles
Suggestion system
Robotics Automation
Discipline in the workplace
TPM (Total Productive Maintenance)

Just in time
Zero defects
Cooperative staff-management relations
Kanban
Quality improvement
Productivity improvement
Small group activities
New product development
Six sigma
SMED
5S

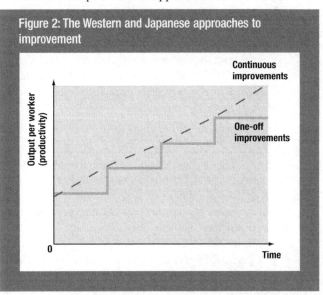

Figure 2: The Western and Japanese approaches to improvement

Output per worker (productivity)

Continuous improvements

One-off improvements

0   Time

workers to continually search for waste and to suggest how it might be eliminated.

Implementing continuous improvement It is often difficult for workers in a business to look for continuous improvement all the time. Japanese businesses tried to solve this problem by introducing the PDCA (Plan, Do, Check, Action) cycle. It is a series of activities that lead to improvement.

- Plan. Businesses must identify where improvement is needed. Data must be gathered and used to develop a plan which will result in improvement.
- Do. Once the plan has been finalised it must be carried out. The plan is likely to be implemented by workers, on the production line perhaps.
- Check. The next stage in the cycle is to check whether or not there has been an improvement. This task may be carried out by inspectors.
- Action. If the plan has been successful, it must be introduced in all parts of the business.

Just-in-time manufacturing

JUST-IN-TIME (JIT) MANUFACTURING is an important part of lean production and the kaizen approach. It was developed in the Japanese shipbuilding industry in the 1950s and 1960s. The industry recognised that a great deal of money was tied up in stocks. Traditionally, one month's supply of steel was held by a shipyard. However, as the industry became more competitive, shipbuilders insisted that steel suppliers deliver orders 'just-in-time', i.e. a few hours or less before the steel was needed. This reduced the need for high levels of working capital and improved the financial performance of the business. JIT was extended to every stage of production. For example, raw materials were delivered JIT to be made into parts, parts were delivered JIT to be made into goods and goods were produced and delivered JIT to be sold.

JIT was introduced in other Japanese industries, such as the car industry, and then spread to other parts of the world, such as the USA and Europe. JCB has used JIT in its Rochester plant. When JCB excavators are manufactured, every machine on the production line has already been sold. Supplies of components, such as engines from Perkins, and raw materials, such as steel plate, arrive on the day they are needed. JIT manufacturing requires high levels of organisational skills and reliable suppliers.

Table 1 shows the advantages and disadvantages of JIT manufacturing.

The 'Kanban' system

KANBAN is a Japanese term which means signboards or cards. The Kanban system is a method used to control the transfer of materials between different stages of production. The kanban might be a solid plastic marker or coloured ping-pong ball. They might be used to:

- inform employees in the previous stage of production that a particular part must be taken from stocks and sent to a

specific destination (conveyance kanbans);
- tell employees involved in a particular operation that they can begin production and add their output to stock (production kanbans);
- instruct external suppliers to send parts to a destination (vendor kanbans).

Kanbans are used to trigger the movement or production of resources. Used properly, they will be the only means of authorising movement. Kanbans are an important part of JIT manufacturing as they prevent the build-up of stock or parts in a factory.

Time-based management

TIME-BASED MANAGEMENT involves reducing the amount of time businesses take to carry out certain tasks, such as launching new products or cutting lead times in production. Time-based management is a feature of lean production because it involves eliminating a type of waste, i.e. time. Time in business is a valuable resource. Productivity can be improved if tasks are carried out more quickly. Time-based management has a number of effects on a business.

Table 1: Advantages and disadvantages of JIT manufacturing

Advantages

- It improves cash flow since money is not tied up in stocks.
- The system reduces waste, obsolete and damaged stock.
- More factory space is made available for productive use.
- The costs of stockholding are reduced significantly.
- Links with and the control of suppliers are improved.
- The supplier base is reduced significantly.
- More scope for integration within the factory's computer system.
- The motivation of workers is improved. They are given more responsibility and encouraged to work in teams.

Disadvantages

- A lot of faith is placed in the reliability and flexibility of suppliers.
- Increased ordering and administration costs.
- Advantages of bulk buying may be lost.
- Vulnerable to a break in supply and machinery breakdowns.
- Difficult to cope with sharp increases in demand.
- Possible loss of reputation if customers are let down by late deliveries.

Focus on customer needs Customers are given a wide range of products to choose from, i.e. different models with different specifications. The same model car can be produced according to different specifications, such as different colours, engine sizes and trims. Manufacturers can achieve this by reducing the length of production runs. Shorter production runs will also allow a firm to cut customer lead times, so customers are not kept waiting.

Use other lean production methods Examples include:
- just-in-time manufacturing;
- simultaneous engineering
- Single Minute Exchange of Dies (SMED);
- flexible manufacturing.

These methods prevent delays on production lines, reduce stock levels and improve scheduling. This means employees are not waiting around for work to arrive.

Machines must be versatile They must be able to produce a variety of products and be adjusted to a range of settings. Settings must be changed quickly and easily to deal with shorter production runs.

Speed up the design process They do this by carrying out a number of design tasks simultaneously. The traditional approach to design is to carry out one task after another. However, time can be saved if design tasks can be completed at the same time. This is called SIMULTANEOUS ENGINEERING. It is a project management approach, not a method of production. Such an approach needs co-ordination and communication between each design team. This approach to speeding up the design process has been called LEAN DESIGN.

Mass producers argue that economies of scale will only be achieved and costs cut if products are standardised and production runs are long. Producing a variety of different models will lead to shorter production runs and higher average costs. Time-based management challenges this view. It may be possible to produce smaller quantities, because costs can be reduced by time savings.

There may be certain advantages for a business using a time-based management system.

- Customers will benefit. A wider range of products will be available and there will be faster delivery times. This might result in higher sales levels for the firm.
- Lean design will result in shorter lead times. This means that resources will be used more effectively and product development will be faster. This will give the business a competitive edge in the market.
- Other lean production techniques will increase efficiency, the quality of products will be improved and waste will be minimised.
- The time spent on a range of production tasks is reduced. This helps to improve productivity and reduce unit costs. As a result manufacturers may offer their products at lower prices or enjoy higher profit margins.

However, it could be argued that some costs might rise as a

result of using time-based management. The versatile machinery which this method requires may be more expensive. Staff may also need to be trained in a wider range of skills and tasks to cope with the flexibility in production. Shorter production runs may result in the loss of some economies of scale.

Flexible manufacturing One of the reasons why flow production techniques tend to lead to lower average costs than batch production or job production is because time is not lost changing tools or other equipment to make a new product. For example, a chocolate manufacturer could easily lose a day or two days' production when changing from production of one chocolate bar to another using batch production techniques. Machines have to be completely cleaned to prevent contamination and tooling within the machines has to be changed.

FLEXIBLE MANUFACTURING aims to reduce or even

Question 1.

New Balance Athletic Shoes (UK) Ltd is a US owned company producing a range of high performance athletic shoes. The business has been manufacturing in the UK since 1982 and moved to its current site in Flimby, near Workington, in 1991. New Balance had developed a five year strategic business plan to increase turnover from £70 million to £250 million. In order to achieve this, the manufacturing plant would have to triple the output of the one million pairs of shoes produced in 2005. Land was acquired adjacent to the current site to build another factory unit and the management team was looking for new ways to increase capacity and productivity.

The company employed a consultant to run a series of team workshops with process workers to introduce the basic principles of lean manufacturing. These teams were then challenged to analyse their current process, which led to the development of a new cellular layout requiring 35 per cent less space and only four operatives instead of five. The total work content was balanced between the four operatives to create product flow around the cell. Once the cell footprint had been agreed, a new future state 'ideal' factory layout was developed to convert freed up space into additional cells. The switch to lean production generated a number of benefits for the company.

- Output increased from 10 to 14 pairs of shoes per person per hour.
- Cell teams reduced from five to four people.
- Thirty five per cent reduction in space taken up by manufacturing cell.
- New cells created.
- £1.5 million positive cost variance compared to 2005 manufacturing costs.
- £1.5 million cost avoidance, as there was no longer any requirement to build an additional factory.

Source: adapted from www.mas.dti.gov.uk.

(a) Using this case as an example, explain what is meant by cell production.
(b) Explain why cell production lends itself well to teamworking.
(c) How did the introduction of cell production benefit New Balance Athletic Shoes Ltd?

eliminate changeover time from one product to another so that it becomes as cheap to produce 10 units of one item, 8 of another, and 12 of a third as it is to produce 30 units of the same item. On a car production line, the ideal is for every car produced to be unique. It might be the same model with different specifications. Or it might be two or more models being made at the same time. Flexible manufacturing is achieved by using equipment which can be changed from one use to another use very quickly and ideally instantaneously. It also means that workers must be flexible too, having the skills to deal with different products. Flexible manufacturing requires the back-up of other lean production techniques. For example, on a vehicle production line, if there are 14 different sets of doors

fitted during a shift, each a different colour, then there must be just-in-time production techniques used to deliver those doors to that work station at the right time. Otherwise flexible manufacturing would require huge levels of stocks. Similarly, every worker must be responsible for the quality of work done.

Just-in-time production Just-in-time (JIT) manufacturing can be seen as another example of time-based management. JIT cuts the amount of time that stocks are held by a business. In a car manufacturing company, for example, car seats may have been held on average 10 days at the factory in the 1970s before being assembled inside a car. Today, the average stock time held may be three hours because seats are being delivered three times a day to the car plant.

Empowerment

Empowerment involves giving employees the power to make decisions in a business. The aim of empowerment is to give employees more control over their own work conditions. Workers in the past have tended to follow the instructions of managers. They were rarely required to think, make decisions, solve problems or work creatively. There was often conflict between management and workers, and little co-operation and team-spirit.

In recent years many businesses have learned that efficiency will improve if workers are given the opportunity to involve themselves in decision making. Workers will be better motivated and the business may gain from the creativity of its workers. Workers may also be more flexible and adaptable. For example, a worker may speak directly to a customer about changes in an order. For empowerment to be successful, managers must have faith in their workforce. They must also trust them and work in partnership without conflict.

Empowerment is not without difficulties. Some workers may not be able to make their own decisions and training may be required to teach them such skills. Managers may resent giving up authority. Some staff may even abuse their power to make decisions.

Teamworking

A growing number of businesses are introducing teamworking into their organisations. This involves dividing the workforce into fairly small groups. Each team will focus on a particular area of production and team members will have the same common aims. Teamworking probably works best in businesses that do not have a hierarchical structure and which have an organisational culture which supports group work. Effective teamworking requires co-operation between workers and management, training for staff and decision making responsibility for workers.

Both the business and its employees might benefit from teamwork. Workers should develop relationships with colleagues and a 'team spirit' which may improve motivation and productivity. Flexibility might improve. For example, team

---

Question 2.

Jenx Ltd is one of the UK's longest established companies designing innovative, therapeutic and development products for children with spinal problems. The company was founded in 1982 and is still run by a Paediatric Physiotherapist and her husband. The company sells its products to over twenty countries worldwide and is committed to a continuous process of review and improvement to offer children the best products available.

After attending a lean training workshop in 2005, Mr Jenkins learned about lean production and the importance of developing an improvement plan. He could see where this could potentially help his business to improve, develop and grow. The key objective from the outset was to involve employees in an improvement programme that allowed them to learn how to make and sustain their own improvements. A team was formed in the machine shop and they were taught the fundamentals of lean manufacturing. This set the foundations for implementing a 5S improvement programme in the machine shop. It was felt that this would help to create a better working environment, improve productivity and provide the best way forward for a programme of change.

As a result of the 15 day 5S Improvement Project, the company has achieved the following.

- Noticeable change in employee commitment and contribution to business improvement.
- Gross value added has increased by £60,000, and productivity by 15 per cent, as a result of the creation of manufacturing cells.
- Distance travelled to manufacture products has reduced from 80 metres to 5 metres (93 per cent).
- Manufacturing finishing cells have been developed and lead times have reduced (60 per cent).
- Stock and WIP (work in progress) has reduced.
- Investment in a new extraction system and sawing equipment has been made.
- Work flow and space utilisation has improved by 20 per cent

Source: adapted from www.mas.dti.gov.uk.

(a) Which lean production method may have been used to reduce stock and WIP?
(b) What is meant by 5S?
(c) How did the implementation of 5S help Jenx Ltd?

members might be more willing to cover for an absent colleague. Teams might plan their own work schedules, share out tasks, choose their methods of work and solve their own problems. This should lead to quicker decision making and the generation of more ideas. It is also suggested that communication and labour relations may improve as a result of teamworking. However, there may be conflict between team members and managers may resent the responsibility delegated to teams. Teamwork also results to some extent in a loss of specialisation among workers, which is often found in flow or mass production techniques.

Cellular manufacturing

Flow production involves mass producing a standard product on a production line. The product undergoes a series of operations in sequence on a continuous basis until a finished product rolls off the 'end of the line'.

CELLULAR MANUFACTURING or CELL PRODUCTION adopts a different approach and involves dividing the workplace into 'cells'. Each cell occupies an area on the factory floor and focuses on the production of a 'product family'. A 'product family' is a group of products which requires a sequence of similar operations. For example, the metal body part of a machine might require the operations cut, punch, fold, spot weld, dispatch. This could all be carried out in one cell. Inside a cell, machines are grouped together and a team of workers sees the production of a good from start to finish.

Take the example of a furniture manufacturer making parts for a kitchen range in a cell. The raw material, such as wood, would be brought into the cell. Tasks such as turning on a lathe or shaping by routing would be carried out at workstations. The part would then be assembled and passed on to stock. The cell may also be responsible for tasks such as designing, schedule planning, maintenance and problem solving, as well as the manufacturing tasks which are shared by the team.

The advantages of cellular manufacturing include:
* floor space is released because cells use less space than a linear production line;
* product flexibility is improved;
* lead times are cut;
* movement of resources and handling time is reduced;
* there is less work-in-progress;
* teamworking is encouraged;
* there may be a safer working environment and more efficient maintenance.

Benchmarking

BEST PRACTICE BENCHMARKING (BPB) is a technique used by some businesses to help them discover the 'best' methods of production available and then adopt them. BPB involves:
* finding out what makes the difference, in the customer's eyes, between an ordinary supplier and an excellent supplier;
* setting standards for business operations based on the best

practice that can be found;
* finding out how these best companies meet those standards;
* applying both competitors' standards and their own to meet the new standards and, if possible, to exceed them.

Figure 3 illustrates the five main steps in BPB. The first step is to **identify** exactly what the company intends to benchmark. Benchmarks that are important for customer satisfaction might include consistency of product, correct invoices, shorter delivery times, shorter lead times and improved after-sales service. For example, Motorola, the communications company, has benchmarked the yield and product characteristics of a range of its activities including its assembly, warehousing and purchasing performance.

The second step involves **choosing a company** to set the benchmark against. This may be done by asking customers who they feel is the best in the field. Business analysts, journalists, stockbrokers or industrialists may also be used. Rank Xerox and Centreparc, the leisure group, have used other parts of their own organisations which have developed a reputation for excellence.

In the third step, information can be **gathered** from a number of sources, such as magazines, newspapers, trade association reports, specialist databases, customers and suppliers. Companies in the same industry often share information. An example may be businesses supplying local markets, such as garden centres. The benefits of this are that the worst performers can get advice from the best and perhaps visit their premises.

The **analysis** of information is best done with quantitative techniques. For example, a firm might compare numerical data relating to delivery times.

The final stage involves **using** the information. Once

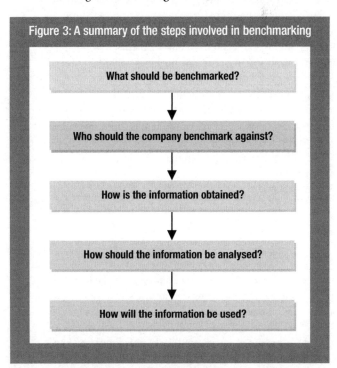

Figure 3: A summary of the steps involved in benchmarking

What should be benchmarked?

Who should the company benchmark against?

How is the information obtained?

How should the information be analysed?

How will the information be used?

standards have been found and set, they must be communicated throughout the business. Improvements must be funded, introduced and monitored. Once a company becomes the best in the field others will begin to benchmark against them. This means the company must continue to benchmark its own process.

Six Sigma

Six Sigma is a Japanese method developed by Motorola. It takes its name from the Greek letter 'sigma' used in statistics to indicate standard deviation. It is a statistical approach designed to eliminate defects in processes. A process must not produce more than 3.4 defects per million. A Six Sigma defect is defined as anything that fails to match customer specifications. Six Sigma involves collecting data on performance in processes and then evaluating it. Businesses can reduce variations in performance by using one of two Six Sigma approaches. DMAIC (define, measure, analyse, improve, control) is an improvement system for existing processes that result in too many defects. DMADV (define, measure, analyse, design, verify) is an improvement system used to develop new processes.

Single Minute Exchange of Dies (SMED)

Many manufacturers are under pressure to offer a wider variety of products. This has resulted in companies having to reduce the size of the batches they produce. So it is important to reduce changeover or set-up time. Bottling industries can spend more than 20 per cent of production time on changeovers, for example. Single Minute Exchange of Dies (SMED) is an approach to reduce output and quality losses due to changeovers. It was developed in Japan by Shigeo Shingo and has allowed companies to reduce changeover times from hours to minutes. He developed a method to analyse the changeover process, enabling workers to find out for themselves why the changeover took so long, and how this time could be reduced. There are four key steps in SMED.

- Suppress useless operations and convert IS operations (those which must be done while the machine is stopped) into ES operations (those which can be done when the machine is running).
- Simplify fittings and tightenings.
- Work together.
- Suppress adjustments and trials.

SMED has often resulted in workers approaching changeovers with a 'pit-stop mentality'.

5S (Sort, Set, Shine, Standardise and Sustain)

5S is a Japanese approach to housekeeping in the factory. It is a method of organising, cleaning, developing and sustaining a productive work environment. What does 5S stand for?

- **Sort.** This is about getting rid of the clutter in the factory. Only items such as necessary work tools should be in the factory environment. All other items, such as excess

inventory, should be removed.
- **Set in order.** The work area should be organised so that it is easy to find what is needed.
- **Shine.** This is to do with keeping the work area clean. Make it 'shine'.
- **Standardise.** Once the most effective cleaning and sorting methods have been established, they should be used as standards for the whole factory.
- **Sustain.** Mechanisms should be implemented to ensure that the standards achieved are recognised by everyone and used in the future.

This approach has helped businesses to improve efficiency because the work environment is less cluttered and more organised.

KEYTERMS

Best practice benchmarking – imitating the standards of an established leader in quality and attempting to better them.

Cellular manufacturing or cell production – involves producing a 'family of products' in a small self-contained unit (a cell) within a factory.

Flexible manufacturing – a system designed to allow a number of products and product variants to be produced using the same resources over a short space of time.

Just-in-time manufacturing – a production technique which is highly responsive to customer orders and uses very little stock holding.

Kanban – a card which acts as a signal to move or provide resources in a factory.

Kaizen – a Japanese term which means continuous improvement.

Lean design – keeping the resources and time used in the design process to a minimum.

Lean production – an approach to operations management aimed at reducing the quantity of resources used up in production.

Simultaneous engineering – an approach to project management where some, or all of the tasks involved in a project, are carried out at the same time.

Time-based-management – involves setting strict time limits in which tasks must be completed.

Cases

Case Study: FTL Company Ltd

Family-owned FTL Company Ltd manufactures stainless steel hose assemblies in various types and sizes for a number of industry sectors. The utilities market is the largest share of the business; supported by automotive tuners for power assisted steering applications, payphone handsets, stainless steel metallic hoses and associated pipework. The management team at FTL operates with continuous improvement in mind, and have always encouraged employee involvement in the development of new processes. The company has so far achieved ISO9001:2000 quality standard and is currently working towards BS EN ISO14001.

The company has implemented kaizen principles to reduce costs and improve output. FTL had been successful in winning new contracts which required an increase in production of 50 per cent to support the continued company growth. The company also had an underlying need to reduce waste and improve productivity to respond to competitive pressures and offset recent energy cost increases. FTL therefore decided to bring all of its production in house – a vital step for the company if it was to continue to grow and remain competitive, fighting off competition from India, Turkey and China.

To begin the programme of work, a presentation was delivered to the entire workforce explaining, in simple terms, the need for change. The principles of 'lean' were introduced along with the need for 'total employee involvement'. A kaizen project team was formed comprising operators from the multi-spindle auto-production area, engineers and supervisors. The team was invited to discuss the current method of manufacturing for turned parts and to identify any areas of concern. The major problem area they highlighted was in set-up and changeover times. As a result SMED training was given to the team leading to a full analysis of the process using video footage. Opportunities for improvement were identified, which resulted in a reduction from 27 minutes per shift to 9.5 minutes per shift in set up for turning and grinding.

The team then explored potential improvements in the machine tooling layout and the tooling technology that was being used. A number of improvements were made which extended tool change frequencies further and reduced cycle times from 12 seconds per part to 10 seconds per part. A quality plan was also developed and introduced to ensure that defects were checked for as they happened. The operators were fully trained to carry out the checks independently, giving them greater control of their working environment.

The kaizen team was trained to monitor the machines' ongoing performance and react to any output. Their training also covered how to deliver these results via a Power Point Presentation to management on a monthly basis.

As a result of a 10 day manufacturing efficiency project, FTL has achieved the following.

- 30 new jobs created.
- 65 per cent reduction in set-up times using SMED analysis.
- An additional £72,000 in Gross Value Added.
- 60 per cent increase in people productivity.
- Kaizen activities highlighted a 75 per cent reduction in rework.
- Customer demand is being satisfied from 100 per cent in-house production.
- No loss of customers to low cost labour economies of China, Turkey and India despite increasing competition.
- A quality plan introduced which checks for defects as they happen.
- A self managed Kaizen team has been established to monitor and improve production.
- Staff morale has improved as the multifunctional team has driven improvement - all ideas have been listened to and actions deployed as a team.

Source: adapted from www.mas.dti.gov.uk.

(a) (i) What prompted FTL Ltd to introduce kaizen principles? (4 marks)
    (ii) Explain what is meant by kaizen. (6 marks)
(b) Explain the purpose of introducing SMED at FTL. (8 marks)
(c) How important was training when introducing kaizen principles at FTL? (8 marks)
(d) What evidence is there in the case to suggest that FTL is committed to quality? (8 marks)
(e) To what extent has FTL benefited from the introduction of lean production? (16 marks)

Review Questions and Tests

KNOWLEDGE

1. What are the aims of lean production?
2. What is meant by the Kaizen umbrella?
3. Explain the purpose of the PDCA cycle.
4. Describe four advantages of JIT manufacturing.
5. What is the purpose of the Kanban system?
6. Describe the three principles of time-based manufacturing.
7. What are the advantages of time-based manufacturing?
8. Give two advantages and two disadvantages of empowerment.
9. Why is teamworking a growing trend in businesses?
10. Describe how cellular manufacturing works.

Index

ABB 150–1
Adams, John Stacey 507–8, 514
AddictingGames 118
agency theory 191
AKEPT 636
Alderfer, Clayton 496–7
Amazon.com 100
American Idol 119
American Standard Cos 124
Apple 123, 476–8
Argyris, Chris 12–13, 19
AT & T 103–4
automation 364

Bang & Olufsen 318
Barnard, Chester 23
BCG matrix 124–5
Beckman Coulter Inc 123
Belbin, Meredith 392, 403–5, 617
benchmarking
best practice 663–4
Bertalanffy, Ludwig von 19
Bethlehem Steel Corporation 7
Black and Decker 615
Blauner, R. 21
blogging 525–7
Bloomberg L.P. 98
Boeing 96
Bosch 177–8
Boulding, Kenneth 19–20
Bowey, A. M. 24
BMW 541
Brech, Edward 6
British Aerospace 642
British Army 51
Brundtland Report 199
bureaucracy 11–12
    costs of 12–13
    evaluation of 13–15
Burns, Ursula 124
Business Charter for Sustainable Development 202–3
business model 119–200
BYD 119

capabilities 122, 147
Carrier-Carlyle Compressor Facility 101
C. Dean Metropoulos & Company 118

change management *see* organisational change
Chouinard, Yvon 260
Ciba Corning 615–16
Cisco 270, 340, 431–2
Clegg, Stewart R. 26
CLP Power, Hong Kong 382
Coca-Cola 333–4
Combined Code 193
competences 45, 146
competitive strategies 137
    choosing 127–8
competitive advantage 125–7
    cost leadership strategy 127
    definition 125
    differentiation strategy 128
    five forces model 127, 145, 181–3
    focus strategy 128
    functional strategies 128
competitor intelligence 106
concentration 123
construction industry, UK 111
context
    choice 62
    determinism 62
    external 61
    historical 61
    interaction 63
    internal 60
corporate governance 66–7, 159, 191–2, 243
corporate philanthropy 273–4
corporate strategies 147
corporate mission 150
    definition 122–3
    and EU environmental policy 203–7
    growth 123–4
    management of 124–5
    renewal 124
    stability 124
    strategic direction 150–3
    and sustainable development 200–3, 600
cost leadership 153–4
Coventry Building Society 196
customer relationship management 229–31
customer satisfaction 221
customers 221

DavyMarkham 46

Dell Computers 36–7, 104
demands 223–4
Disney 164
diversification 124
division of labour 591–2
dynamic capabilities 147

Ebay 123
economies of scale 153–4
Eden Project 528–30
ego strength 263
emotional intelligence components 72
employees
compensation/benefits 550–2
empowerment 662
   health care costs 556
   involvement and participation 561–3
   pension plan costs 557
   performance management 550
   role demands 370
   stress 369–72
   teamworking 662–3
   trade unions 538–9, 561
   Type A and B personalities 370
   volunteering 274
   see also human resources management; job satisfaction
Encana 98
entrepreneur 44, 50
environmental scanning 106–7
ESPN.com 130–1
ethical behaviour 261–2
   codes of ethics 268–9
   corporate philanthropy 273
   determinants of ethical and unethical
   behaviour 262–5
   employee volunteering 274
   encouraging 267–71
   ethics training 270
   international context 265–7
   management of bad ethical behaviour 271–4
   moral grey areas 279
   protective mechanisms 271
   social audits 271
   social entrepreneurism 272–2
   see also social responsibility
ethical cultures 338–40
ethical leadership 269, 272
ethnography 335–6
experience curve 154
Express Engineering 58
E&Y 575

Facebook 118, 121, 595
Fayol, Henri 6, 49
Fiedler, Fred 447–9, 470

five forces model 127, 145, 181–3
Ford Motor Company 10, 257, 626
Foreign Corrupt Practices Act 266
Fox, Alan 23–4
fraud 215
Friedman, Milton 256
FTL company 666
functional principle 6

General Motors 380, 622
GlaxoSmithKline 157, 371
Global Compact 266–7
GNY Building Materials 643
goals 97
   management by objectives (MBO) 101–2
   steps in goal setting 102–3
   traditional goal setting 100–1
   types of 98–100
Google 373
groups 391
   bank wiring room experiment 393
   definition 391–2
   effective work groups concept map 423
   formal 395
   informal 395–7
   informal social relations 393
   norms 393–5
   see also teams
Guest, R. H. 21

Handy, Charles 179–80
Hanger Insertion Programme 10–11
Hawthorne experiments 15–17
Herzberg, Frederick 19, 497–9, 513
Hewlett-Packard 612
hierarchy 12
Hiscox 229
HMRC 316
HMV 136, 165–6, 185
Hong Kong police force 576
horizontal integration 123–4, 152–3
human resource management 179, 592
   age issues 577
   appraisal methods 551
   Australian law 541
   balanced scorecard 566
   Canadian law 540–1
   compensation and benefits 550–2
   decentralisation and devolution 568–9
   decruitment 544
   demographic trends 541–2
   downsizing 552–3
   economy's effect on 538
   employee health care costs 556
   employee involvement and participation 561–3

employee pension plan costs 557
employee performance management 550–2
evaluation 567–8
European Union influences 569–71
European Works Council 561
external factors that affect 537–42
four Cs model 563–5
future of 555
German law 541
high performance work practices 537
importance of 536–7
and innovation 377
Investing in People 628–30
law as it affects 539–40
Mexican law 541
orientation 547–8
personnel department 567
planning 542–3
recruitment 543–4
role of 567
selection 545–7
sexual harassment 553–4
situational factors 564
stakeholder theory 563–4
strategic human resources management 566
trade unions 538–9, 561
training 548–9
US law 540
work–life balance 554–6, 570–1
workplace romances 554
see also employees
Human Rights Act 1998 570
Hyundai 104–5

IBM 623
IDEO 295–6
Ikea 140
impersonality 12
innovation 373–4
creativity vs innovation 374
cultural variables 376–7
human resource variables 377
structural variables 374–6
intangible output 595–6
intangible resources 45
internationalisation 67, 159, 193, 244
IPCC 192–3
Iris 193–4

Jago, Arthur G. 450–1
J.C. Penney Company 130
job satisfaction
alienation at work 517
broader approaches to 517–18
concept map of 518

dimensions of 514–15
employee awards 524
factors in job design 521
5 contractual areas relating to 515
5 core job dimensions 519–20
job characteristics model of work
motivation 519
job enrichment 517–18
jobs 302–3
meaning of 514
work environment 516
see also motivation
Jobs, Steve 476–8
Johnson & Johnson 338, 339

kaizen 635, 659
Kellogg 126
Kmart 118–19
Korean Airlines 367–8

Lady Gaga 162
Lawler, Edward 503–6
leadership 70–1, 72, 443, 475
achievement leadership 451
authoritarian style 444
charisma 456–7
concept map for leadership and
management 459
and culture 346
democratic style 444
directive leadership 451
ethical 269, 272
future 463–4
influence 460–2
and innovation 458–60
inspirational gap 457–8
laissez-faire 444
meaning of 443
participative leadership 451
power 461–2
readiness of followers 452
situational leadership model 453, 470–1
strategic 129–30
styles 444–5
supportive leadership 451
Tannenbaum and Schmidt continuum 445–6
task and relationship behaviour 453–4
transformational 454–5
visionary 455–8
leadership, theories of contingency approach 447, 470
leadership substitutes model 471
situational 470–1
leadership, trait theories of
Fiedler's contingency model 447–9, 470
leadership grid 469–70

Ohio State studies 468
    path-goal theory 451–2, 471
    University of Michigan studies 468–9
    Vroom and Jago revised decision model 450–1
    Vroom and Yetton contingency model 449–50
lean management 637, 644
lean production 644, 659
    best practice benchmarking 663–4
    cellular manufacturing 663
    5S 664
    flexible manufacturing 661–2
    kaizen 659
    'kanban system' 660
    simultaneous engineering 661
    Single Minute Exchange of Dies (SMED) 664
    Six Sigma 664
    time-based management 660–1
Lehman Brothers 277–8
Levinson model of career evolution 74–5
Levitt, Theodore 234
Lewin, Kurt 361
Life is good company 85
Lindblom, Charles E. 141
Live Nation 123–4
Locke, Edwin A. 508–10
locus of control 263
Longwall coal-mining study 20
L'Oreal 123

Maersk 155
management careers 73–6
management development 76–9
management and law 630–1
management by objectives (MBO) 101–2
management and organisational behaviour theory 4–5,
    25, 27–31
    action theory 24
    bureaucracy 11–15
    classicalapproach 5–7, 31
    concept map of management theory 22
    contingency approach 21, 31
    cultural context of theories 28
    decision-making approach 21, 23
    human relations approach 15–18, 23, 31
    neo-human relations 18–19
    pluralistic approach 24
    postmodernism 26–7, 31
    scientific management 7–10, 29
    social action approach 23, 31, 622
    socio-technical system 20
    structuralism approach 15
    systems approach 19–21, 23, 31
    technology approach 20, 23
    unitary/pluralistic approach 24
management role 44–7, 69–71
    board of directors 51–2
    context-shaping 60–3
    critical thinking 63–4
    decisional role 54–6
    definition 48
    direct operation 50–1
    disseminator role 54
    as a distinct role 48–9
    disturbance-handler role 54
    entrepreneurial role 54
    first-line managers 51
    functional managers 50
    general managers 49–50
    influence of 52
    informational role 53–4
    interpersonal role 54
    leader role 54
    liaison role 54
    line managers 50
    management hierarchies 50–2, 69–71
    Mintzberg's 10 roles of management 53–6
    monitor role 53–4
    negotiator role 55
    networking 56
    project managers 50
    staff managers 50
    resource-allocator role 55
    supervisors 51
    tasks, influencing through 57–60
    as a universal human activity 48
management skills 71–2
Manchester United 220, 227, 242–3, 247–8
marketing management
    B2B 222
    customer-centred organisation 234
    customer relationship management 229–32
    definition 221–2
    governance and control 243–4
    influences on buying behaviour 223–4
    internationalisation244
    market segmentation 227–9
    marketing environment 226–7
    marketing information systems 224–5
    marketing intelligence 225
    marketing mix 236–40
    marketing orientation 232–40
    needs, wants and demands 222
    offering 229
    online communities 231–2
    product lifecycle 240–3
    sustainable performance 243
    trend identification 226–7
    in voluntary sector 222
Marks and Spencer 201, 628
Maslow, Abraham 18, 492–6, 513

matrix organisation 9
Mayo, Elton 15
McClelland, David 499–500, 513
McDonalds 98, 553, 611
McGregor, Douglas 19
Microsoft 541
middle management 35
Mintzberg, Henry 53–6, 139–41
mission statement 121, 150
Mooney, James 6
moral development 262–3
motivation
    Adams' equity theory of motivation 507–8, 514
    Alderfer's modified need hierarchy model 496–7
    attribution theory 510
    constructive behaviour 490
    content theories of 492–500
    cross-cultural dimensions of 513–14
    definition 485–6
    expectancy theory 501–6
    extrinsic 486
    frustration 490–1
    Herzberg's 2-factor theory 497–9, 513
    higher needs 486
    intrinsic 486, 488–9
    job satisfaction 514–21
    of knowledge workers 512–13
    Lawler's revised expectancy model 505–6
    Locke's goal theory 508–10
    Maslow's hierarchy of needs theory 492–6, 513
    McClelland's achievement motivation theory 499–500, 513
    money as motivator 487–8
    motivation to work 487
    motivational force 503
    needs and expectations 486–7
    negative responses 490–1
    organisational behaviour modification (OBMod) 510–11
    Porter and Lawler expectancy model 503–5
    process theories of 500–10
    reinforcement 511
    Thematic Apperception Tests (TATs) 499–500
    ultimatum game 508
    underlying concept of 485–6
    Vroom's expectancy theory 501–3
    see also job satisfaction
Motorola 145, 636–7. 664
Motown Records 100

Nacionale 654
NASA 360
National Heart Foundation 121
needs 223
Network Rail 58

New Balance Athletic Shoes 661
Nike 98
Nokia 174, 211–14
norms 328–9

Office Depot 120
oil companies' strategic planning study 142–3
operations management 584, 634
    closed loop of 584, 588, 589
    customer-directed operations 598–9
    development of 591–3
    globalisation 599
    influences on 598–600
    lean and agile production 599
    risk 599–600
    service organisations 594–7
    strategy 588–91
    as a transformation process 584–8
    types of 593–7
    value chain 590
organisation change 360–1
    calm waters metaphor 361
    change agent 363
    changing structure 363–4
    changing technology 364
    employee stress 369–72
    innovation 373–7
organisation development/change 364–5, 367–8
    resistance to change 366–7
    successful change 372–3
    3-step change process 361
    white water rapids metaphor 362
organisation culture 175–7, 327, 343
    appreciative enquiry 336
    attitudes 3238
    bet-your-company culture 345
    competing values framework 178–9
    components of 177
    control culture 348
    cultural web 347–8
    culture change 351
    customer service cultures 337–8
    diversity cultures 338
    ethical cultures 338–40
    ethnography 335–6
    folkways 329
    influences on development of 346–7
    innovative cultures 337
    language 334–5
    managerial tools 350
    mores 329
    multiple cultures 180–1
    myths and heroes 332
    national and international 351–2
    norms 328–9

and organisational performance 350
and performance 181, 350
person culture 180, 344
power culture 179, 344
process culture 345
role culture 179, 344
quality of working life culture 328
sacred symbols 333–4
Schein's levels of culture 330–1, 343
in short-life organisations 350
socialisation 332
sustainability 340–1
taboos 332–3
task culture 179, 344
tough-guy, macho culture 345
whole person support 341–2
and work ethic 349
work-hard/play-hard culture 345
organisation design 287
organisation environment 174–5
  competitive environment 175
  corporate governance 66–7, 191–2
  environmental management 195–8
  external environment 175
  and European environmental principles 203–7
  governance and control 193
  internal environment 174–5
  perceptions of 188–90
  PESTEL analysis 184–8
  price mechanism to alleviate pollution 197–8
  and stakeholders 190
  sustainable development 198–203
  sustainable performance 192–3
  see also organisation culture
organisation structure
  accountability 289
  authority in 288
  centralised decision making 290
  company size 305
  cross-functional teams 295
  customer departmentalisation 298
  decentralised decision making 290
  definition 286–7
  departmentlisation 296
  differentiation culture 180
  divisional structures 296–7, 314
  environmental uncertainty 304–5
  flat structures 295–6
  fragmentation culture 180
  functional departmentalisation 297, 309–11
  geographic departmentalisation 298
  geography 305–6
  hierarchy in 180–1, 287–8
  hybrid structure 299–300
  integration culture 180

matrix structure 298–9, 311–12
networked structure 300–1
organisational chart 291–3, 308–9
process departmentalisation 297–8
product departmentalisation 297
responsibility 289
span of control 289
span of leadership 289–90
and strategy 303
tall vertical structures 294–5
technology 305
virtual organisation 301
work structure 302–3
organisations 45

Pacific Gas and Electric 555
PepsiCo 106
PESTEL analysis
  economic factors 185
  environmental factors 187
  legal factors 187–8
  political factors 184–5
  socio-cultural factors 185–6
  technological factors 186–7
Peter principle 70
Peters, Tom 611–12, 621, 624–5
Pfizer 87, 317
Pitney Bowes 375
place 240
planning
  approaches to 104
  commitment concept 103
  contemporary issues in 104–5
  contingency factors in 103–4
  definition 96
  directional plans 99–100
  in dynamic environments 105–6
  environmental scanning 106–7
  goals 97–103
  long-term plans 99
  means-ends chain 101
  operational plans 99
  reasons for 97
  short-term plans 99
  single-use plan 100
  specific plans 99
  standing plans 100
  strategic plans 99
  success of 97
Port of Rotterdam 381
Porter, M. E. 126–7, 128, 145, 147, 155, 181, 590
Porter, Lyman 503–5
price 237–8
principle of co-ordination 6
Procter and Gamble 102, 132, 152

product 236–7
   lifecycle 240–3
production
   batch 650
   choosing method of 649, 652
   empowerment 662
   flow 650–1
   JIT manufacturing 660, 662
   job 649–50
   lean 659
   process 651–2
   teamworking 662–3
   waste elimination 659–60
promotion 69–70, 238–89
public sector organisations 14

quality management 631–4
   Baldrige Award 638–9
   benchmarking 612–13
   BS5750 627–8
   business process reengineering (BPR) 634–5
   consultative committees 622
   customer focus 608–9
   definition 606–7
   delegation 621–2
   focus on 620–4
   importance of 607–8
   Investing in People 628–30
   ISO 9000 and 14000 637–8
   lean management 637, 644
   measuring 624–5
quality assurance 626–7
quality control 625, 634–9
quality circles 616, 618–20
QUEST analysis 627
   Six Sigma 636–7, 664
   statistical process control (SPC) 625–6
   suggestion schemes 623
   Taguchi method 627
   team problem-solving 616–18
   total quality management (TQM) 609–14, 632, 633, 635–6
   TQM implications for management 614–16

Reiley, A. C. 6
renewal strategies 124
retrenchment strategies 124
Ryanair 44, 83–4

Saab 615
Sayles, L. R. 21
scalar principle 6
Schein, Edgar
   levels of culture 330–1, 343
Schmidt, Warren 445

Schwab, Charles 118
silos 295
Simon, Herbert 23
Sixth Environmental Programme 204–7
social entrepreneurism 272–3
social responsibility 257
   arguments for and against 258–9
   determinants of ethical/non-ethical behaviour 262–5
   green management evaluation 261
   green management and sustainability 259–61
   internal ethics 265–7
   managers and ethical behaviour 261–2
   obligation 256
social responsiveness 257
socially responsible investing funds 259
socioeconomic view 257
   see also ethical behaviour
sociograms 408–10
Spartan Motors 130
specialisation 12
stakeholder theory 563–4
stakeholders 52
Starbucks 376
Star Cars 319–20
Stewart, Rosemary 12, 52
strategic business units 125
strategic management
   at business unit level 153–6
   context 137–8
   at corporate level 150–3
   current issues 128–33
   customer service 131–2
   definition 118–19, 137
   development of 142–4
   differentiation strategy 154
   e-business 131
   emergent strategies 140
   external analysis 144–6
   first movers 132–3
   five forces model 127, 145, 181–3
   flexibility 130
   focus strategy 155
   functional level strategy 156–7
   governance and control 159, 192–3
   importance of 119–20
   innovation strategies 132–3
   internal analysis 146–7
   internal development 156
   internationalisation 159, 193–4
   joint developments and alliances 156–7
   leadership 129–30
   learning 139–41
   merger and acquisition 156
   planning 138–9

political perspective 141
process 120–3, 137
revisions 157–8
strategy loop 144
and structure 303–4
sustainable performance 158–9, 192–3
SWOT analysis 122, 125, 149
value chain analysis 147–8
workshops 143–4
see also competitive strategies; corporate strategies
stress, employee
   causes 369–70
   definition 369
   reducing 371–2
   symptoms 370–1
sustainable development 198–203
sustainable performance 65–6, 243
Swatch 237
SWOT analysis 122, 125, 149
Sykes Enterprises 98
system of rules 12

Tannenbaum, Robert 445
tangible resources 45
Tata 376
Taylor, F. W. 7–10, 592
teams 443, 662–3
   autonomous 421–2
   Belbin's team roles 403–5, 617
   brainstorming 416–17
   communication categories 402
   communication networks 405–8
   continual development 425
   criteria for group or individual decisions 416
   definition 391–3
   Delphi technique 418
   development 398–400
   effective meetings 401
   emotional intelligence 424
   frameworks of behavioural analysis 411–12, 413
   'groupthink' 415–16
   individual behaviour analysis 408
   interaction analysis 403, 410–11
   interactions among members 403
   Johari window 419–20
   observation 401
   performance 394
   problem-solving 616–18
   processes 400–2
   quality circles 418–19, 618–20
   Ringelmann effect 414–15
   risky-shift phenomenon 415
   role classification 411
   self-managed work groups 421–2
   sensitivity training 419
   sociograms 409

   sociometry 408–10
   successful 422–5
   team-individual balance 412, 414–16
   team leader role 424–5
   T-groups 419–20
      virtual team lifecycle 399
      virtuoso 395
      see also groups
Tesco Clubcard 225
threshold capabilities 147
Timberland 264
TOMS 256, 274
Top Gear 428–9
total quality management (TQM) *see* quality
      management
Toyota Motor Corporation 106, 354–6, 609–10, 659
trade unions 538–9, 561
Trader Joe's 131
transaction 229

UN Global Compact, Ten Principles of 266
Unilever 235, 340–1
unique resources 146
unrelated diversification 153
UPS 257, 260, 372, 574
Urwick, Lyndall 6
USPS 120

valence 502
value 45
value chain 590
value chain analysis 147–8
values 327–8, 331
values-based management 264
Verizon 554
vertical integration 123, 153
Virgin Group 249–51
Vroom, Victor 449–51, 501–3
VT Group 185

Waitrose 195
Walker, C. R. 21
Walmart 118–19, 120, 126, 127, 128, 183, 257, 278
wants 223
Waterman, Robert 611–12, 621
Watertown Arsenal 8
Watson, Tony 26, 49
Weber, M. 11–12, 15
Wipro 105
World Food Program 96

Yahoo! Inc 374
Yetton, Phillip 449–50

Zara 602